ALL-IN-1 User's Guide

ALL-IN-1™

ALL-IN-1

User's Guide

Patrick S. Murray

Digital Press

Boston Oxford Melbourne Singapore Toronto Munich New Delhi Tokyo

Digital Press™ is an imprint of Butterworth–Heinemann, Publisher for Digital Equipment Corporation.

Recognizing the importance of preserving what has been written, Butterworth–Heinemann prints its books on acid-free paper whenever possible.

Library of Congress Cataloging-in-Publication Data
Murray, Patrick S.
ALL-IN-1 user's guide / Patrick S. Murray.
p. cm.
Includes bibliographical references and index.
ISBN 1-55558-138-2
1. DEC computers—Programming. 2. ALL-IN-1. 3. Office practice —Automation. I. Title.
QA76.8.D43M87 1995
651.8'5349--dc20 95-11926
CIP

British Library Cataloguing-in-Publication Data
A catalogue record for this book is available from the British Library.

The publisher offers discounts on bulk orders of this book. For information, please write:

Manager of Special Sales, Digital Press
Butterworth–Heinemann
313 Washington Street
Newton, MA 02158-1626

Order Number: EY-S797E-DP

10 9 8 7 6 5 4 3 2 1

Printed in the United States of America

Contents

PART III WORD AND DOCUMENT PROCESSING 161

New Features

Preface

During the past two decades, computer technology has "invaded" everywhere. You probably purchased your first hand-held calculator sometime during the early seventies, cleared desk space for a terminal when a midsize system was installed in the early eighties, and perhaps replaced the terminal with a desktop personal computer (PC) in the early nineties. Even if you've resisted purchasing a home computer, you can't deny the fact that it would make certain tasks much easier. When you purchased that hand-held calculator twenty years ago, did you imagine that today you can purchase groceries with the help of a home computer or that the same calculator would cost a fraction of the price of a bag of groceries?

Our knowledge of computers has had to grow along with these technological advances. This presents a problem. New computer equipment is constantly being introduced into the workplace. We understand the enormous amount of time that can be saved when we become proficient with the equipment, and we know that we'll benefit in the long run from using it, but who has the time to learn how to use new computer equipment and programs, let alone become fully proficient?

PURPOSE

I had two reasons for writing this book. First, I wanted to provide a reference that describes in simple terms how to use the valuable tools in ALL-IN-1, and I wanted this manual to be comprehensive. For many sites, providing every ALL-IN-1 user with copies of the *ALL-IN-1 User's Reference* and the *WPS-PLUS User's Reference* or *WordPerfect for VAX/VMS Reference* is just not viable. This manual combines important material from all of these manuals.

Second, I wanted to provide some "inside" information on how to use ALL-IN-1 efficiently. You'll find question-and-answer (Q&A) columns, lists of do's and don'ts, and hints scattered throughout the book. Exercises are provided that show you some shortcuts while teaching you the basics.

AUDIENCE

This book is targeted toward all business professionals who need to improve their ALL-IN-1 skills. For readers with no ALL-IN-1 experience, there are introductions to each major component of ALL-IN-1, followed by chapters titled "Getting Started with . . ." These chapters are written so as to teach you quickly the essentials of working with a particular feature. For example, Chapter 6, "Getting Started with

Electronic Messaging," provides step-by-step instructions for creating, sending, and reading memos.

For readers with some ALL-IN-1 experience, there are chapters titled "Becoming More Proficient with . . ." and "Advanced . . ." These chapters describe more advanced topics for a particular subsystem.

ORGANIZATION

This book has eight parts, each of which covers a different component of ALL-IN-1. The first part contains four chapters on the fundamentals of working with ALL-IN-1. Electronic Messaging and Word and Document Processing are the two most popular components; these are discussed next. The remaining parts of the book cover the File Cabinet, Time Management, Group Conferencing, Desk Management, and Communications.

Each part contains an introduction describing the component. Here you'll find an overview explaining the concepts of the component, plus the Q&A column and lists of do's and don'ts. The first chapter that follows teaches you basic procedures. The remaining chapters in each part cover more advanced topics that help you work more efficiently or perform specialized operations.

Exercises are included in each chapter to reinforce the material. It's a good idea to perform these exercises as you read through each chapter.

HOW TO READ THIS BOOK

This book is not intended to be read from cover to cover. It is better to read this book in stages. Start with the basics of ALL-IN-1, and learn additional components as time permits. Here are some suggestions for reading:

- Start with the fundamentals. Chapters 2 through 5 cover the basic procedures used throughout ALL-IN-1. The rest of the book assumes that you know this material. If you're a beginner, cover this material before continuing on to work with a particular component, such as Electronic Messaging. Shortcuts and helpful features are described in these chapters.

- As you begin working with a new subsystem (such as Electronic Messaging, Word and Document Processing, or Group Conferencing), read through the introduction to get the basic concepts. Review the Q&A section and the list of do's and don'ts. Don't worry if some material doesn't apply; it probably will at a later date.

- After reading the introduction to a subsystem, read the "Getting Started" chapter and perform the exercises. Review the topics in the remaining chapters to get a feel for some of the component's advanced features. Return to these chapters as the need arises.

- Much of the material in this book is reference, which means that you should refer to it only when necessary. Tables describing menu options and screen contents don't make for easy reading, so skim this material at first. Also, skim the step-by-step procedures to get a feel for the information required, but don't bother with the descriptions of each step. (The left side of each procedure shows you the necessary keystrokes.) Refer back to the details when you perform the procedure.

- It helps if you have a terminal available to try procedures as you read. Don't worry about destroying the computer! Also, it's very difficult to erase information.
- By all means, perform the exercises! The exercises are intended to show you the most important techniques of working with ALL-IN-1. Often, you'll get as much out of performing the exercises as you'll get from reading the preceding text.

CONVENTIONS USED IN THIS BOOK

Procedures in this book use the following conventions to denote information that you must enter or that the system displays.

[RETURN]	Capitalized words enclosed in brackets refer to the names of keys on your keyboard. For example, [RETURN] indicates that you should press the return key. The name enclosed in brackets might not match the name appearing on any key. In this case, the actual key names are often enclosed in parentheses afterward. For example, [EXIT] (F10 or Keypad-0) indicates that you should press either the F10 key or the 0 key on your numeric keypad.
Folder: **NEW [RETURN]**	Plain type indicates information that the system displays. Bold type indicates information that you must enter. In this example, the system displays the prompt "Folder:" and you must respond by typing "NEW" and pressing the return key.
Y [RETURN] ***line-number* [SELECT]**	Regular bold type specifies the exact information that you must enter or the key that you must press. Italicized bold type in lowercase describes the information to enter, but you must determine the exact information to type. For example, in the first line, you would type the character "Y," then press the return key. In the second line, you would type a line number, such as "11," then press the return key.

OTHER RELATED BOOKS

Further information on topics discussed in this book can be found in the following manuals:

ALL-IN-1 User's Reference

ALL-IN-1 WPS-PLUS User's Reference

WordPerfect for VAX/VMS

ALL-IN-1 Application Programming: Reference Volumes 1 and 2

ALL-IN-1 Application Programming: Guide

ALL-IN-1 Manager's Guide

ALL-IN-1 Mail Management Guide

Working with WPS-PLUS by Charlotte Temple and Dolores Cordeiro (Digital Press)

ALL-IN-1: A Technical Odyssey by Tony Redmond (Digital Press)

ALL-IN-1: Managing and Programming in Version 3.0 by Tony Redmond (Digital Press)

ALL-IN-1: Integrating Applications in Version 3.0 by John Rhoton (Digital Press)

ACKNOWLEDGMENTS

Many people contributed to the development of this book. Many of the hints were provided by "expert" users, including Barbara Baker of Codar Technology, Donna Lancy of Kaiser-Permanente, Linda Arms of the Colorado Department of Transportation, and Sharon Heath and the rest of the staff at the Washington State Legislative Service Center.

A group of technical experts reviewed preliminary drafts of this book and contributed valuable ideas and information. I am grateful to all of these individuals for their assistance and to Jan Svendsen and Colleen Martin of Digital Equipment Corporation for helping me access the resources I needed to prepare this book. Last but not least, special thanks to the editors of Digital Press for their advice and encouragement during the many months it took to develop this book.

ALL-IN-1 User's Guide

Introduction

CHAPTER 1

My first experience with ALL-IN-1 occurred in 1983. As a system manager, it was my responsibility to install version 1.1 of ALL-IN-1 and to look after its implementation. I remember thinking at the time that the name ALL-IN-1 was rather grand, along the lines of "All things to all people."

During the past 12 years, I've worked with ALL-IN-1 in various capacities: as a system manager, programmer, trainer, and, of course, user. I've seen the product grow tremendously in the past decade. Improvements are added almost every year. The original version contained only Electronic Messaging and Word Processing. Since then, Time Management, Desk Management, Communications, and Group Conferencing features have been added.

The number of people using ALL-IN-1 has also grown tremendously. Originally distributed only in the United States, ALL-IN-1 is now used by over six million subscribers worldwide and has been translated into 18 different languages.

Indeed, ALL-IN-1 seems to be living up to its name!

1.1 WHAT IS ALL-IN-1?

ALL-IN-1 is an extensive software product (computer program) that runs on Digital's computer systems. ALL-IN-1 provides a number of tools to help individuals work more efficiently in an office environment. These tools are packaged within a single menu environment, hence the name ALL-IN-1: *all* applications integrated with*in one* menu system.

The concept of integrated applications is important. ALL-IN-1's menu environment provides easy access to applications like electronic mail and calendar management. Because the applications are integrated, you can easily move information from one application to another. For example, you can create a travel itinerary with ALL-IN-1's Time Management, then quickly send the itinerary to another employee with the Electronic Messaging application. You can use Electronic Messaging to send a draft of a document to a co-worker who will add the finishing touches with Word and Document Processing.

There are a number of products within the ALL-IN-1 family:

- ALL-IN-1 Integrated Office System (IOS)
- ALL-IN-1 Services for DECwindows

- ALL-IN-1 DESKtop for DOS, ALL-IN-1 Mobilizer, and ALL-IN-1 DESKtop for Macintosh
- TeamLinks

ALL-IN-1 IOS provides services to a large number of office workers who share resources on a centralized host computer system. Workers access ALL-IN-1 through video terminals (VTs) connected to the host computer.

ALL-IN-1 Services for DECwindows allows office workers with VAX workstations to access ALL-IN-1 IOS in a Windows environment.

ALL-IN-1 DESKtop and ALL-IN-1 Mobilizer are software programs that run on a personal computer and provide services to a single office worker. Personal computers within an office are typically linked by communications lines to a host computer system. This link, with ALL-IN-1 IOS running on the host computer, enables co-workers to transfer mail messages to one another.

TeamLinks is Digital's most recently developed product for the desktop. TeamLinks runs on a personal computer under Microsoft Windows™ version 3.1. TeamLinks integrates powerful PC applications like Microsoft Word, Microsoft Excel, and WordPerfect for Windows with DEC MAILworks, the ALL-IN-1 IOS File Cabinet, and other services provided by host systems in the network.

An advantage of having ALL-IN-1 DESKtop or TeamLinks on a personal computer is that you can prepare memos and edit files even without continuous access to the host system. When the host system is down, for example, you can continue to work productively.

This book deals primarily with ALL-IN-1 IOS.

1.2 ALL-IN-1 SUBSYSTEMS

Electronic Messaging is one component of ALL-IN-1. It allows you to send and receive memos. Time Management is another component. It helps you maintain a calendar of appointments. Each component is called a *subsystem*. Following is a brief description of the primary subsystems of ALL-IN-1. Each subsystem is preceded by the menu selection that takes you directly to the subsystem menu. Subsystems are often referred to by these two- or three-character acronyms.

EM	Electronic Messaging	Electronic Messaging allows you to communicate with other employees. You create messages with the editor of your choice and send the messages to one or more co-workers. ALL-IN-1 typically notifies you of incoming messages, regardless of which subsystem you're currently using. Electronic Messaging menu options allow you to read, print, and forward incoming messages.

WP	Word and Document Processing	Word and Document Processing allows you to create, edit, and print documents. Documents are automatically filed in a personal File Cabinet or, if you prefer, in a File Cabinet shared with other users. Several different editing programs are available for creating and modifying documents. You can choose whichever editor or word processor best suits your needs. There are spell-checking and writing aids for proofing your documents before printing. Numerous options are available for the high-quality output of your finished documents.
TM	Time Management	Time Management helps you schedule time more efficiently by maintaining a detailed calendar of important appointments, meetings, and action items. You can display your calendar whenever you work with ALL-IN-1, or you can print a copy of your calendar for trips away from the office. Reminders recorded in your calendar are automatically displayed on your screen when you enter ALL-IN-1.
GPC	Group Conferencing	Group Conferencing allows individuals to share ideas about important topics. A group conference is essentially an electronic bulletin board. Participants state their views by preparing notes. Group Conferencing organizes these notes by topic and stores them in a central location, making them available to all participants in the conference. Participants can review the discussion by simply reading any or all of the notes. Group Conferencing is an ideal communications tool, especially for a group of people who find it difficult to be in the same place at the same time.
DM	Desk Management	Desk Management provides access to two features of ALL-IN-1: the Desktop Calcu-

lator and Directories. The Desktop Calculator provides the capabilities of a pocket calculator. The Directories feature helps you maintain and access lists of information, including the corporate phone directory, your personal phone directory, and a directory of ALL-IN-1 users.

COM	Communications	The Communications subsystem allows you to connect to remote computer systems, transfer documents between systems, and communicate interactively with other users.

1.2.1 Utility Subsystems

Additional ALL-IN-1 subsystems provide tools to help you work more efficiently with the primary subsystems. The following are brief descriptions of the utility subsystems.

US	User Setup	User Setup allows you to tailor your ALL-IN-1 working environment to suit your needs. User Setup controls a variety of ALL-IN-1 features. For example, you can select the editor (EDT, WPS-PLUS, etc.) that you will use to prepare mail messages and documents. ALL-IN-1 remembers options set in User Setup, even when you log off the system. Therefore, you access User Setup only when you want to change your ALL-IN-1 environment.
FC	File Cabinet Maintenance	File Cabinet Maintenance helps you manage your personal File Cabinet. The tasks that you can perform with File Cabinet Maintenance include archiving a document to off-line storage, cross-referencing a document in two or more folders, deleting obsolete documents, and reorganizing the File Cabinet index for efficiency.
GS	Group Services	Group Services helps you create and manage lists of users who share documents or send messages to one another.

JS	Job Services	Job Services allows you to manage your print and batch jobs. For example, you can stop a print job once printing has begun.
TR	Training	Training provides computer-based instruction to help you learn more about a particular subsystem or feature of ALL-IN-1.
IM	Information Management	Information Management provides access to the Calculations, Communications, Directories, or Group Conferencing subsystems. In addition, Information Management provides access to VAX VTX (VideoTeXt system) and DATATRIEVE if you have these optional software products installed on your system.
AD	Application Development	Application Development provides tools for building new applications within the ALL-IN-1 menu environment. These include Forms Development, Programming Functions, and Customization Management.

1.3 ALL-IN-1 CUSTOMIZATION

ALL-IN-1's greatest advantage is that if you don't like it, you can change it.[1] ALL-IN-1 provides tools for changing features to better suit your organization's needs. These "customization" tools also document changes made to the system.

Application Development provides access to the tools for customizing ALL-IN-1. Application Development also allows your organization to develop new custom applications to supplement ALL-IN-1's capabilities.

1. Actually, programmers within your organization can change it. Privileges are required to customize features of ALL-IN-1. These privileges are not granted to most users because the customization process is somewhat complicated and requires programming expertise. This process is not discussed in this book. Refer to *ALL-IN-1 Application Programmers Reference Manual* in Digital's documentation for further details.

NOTE: If your site has customized ALL-IN-1, some features may not work as described in this manual or as described in Digital's documentation set for ALL-IN-1. Before proceeding, it is recommended that you contact your system administrator to find out which features have been changed and how these features differ from the standard version of ALL-IN-1 described in this book.

The following two subsystems are provided solely for incorporating your organization's applications into the ALL-IN-1 menu system. Blank menu screens for these subsystems are provided with the standard version of ALL-IN-1. Programmers at your site must modify these menus to list the available applications. For example, one organization might list accounting applications under Business Applications, while another might list engineering applications there.

BA	Business Applications	This subsystem provides access to corporate applications.
PS	Profession Specific	This subsystem provides access to applications used by specific departments or work groups.

1.4 VERSION DIFFERENCES

This book describes version 3.1 of ALL-IN-1. Certain features described in this book might not be available or might function differently than described if you're working with an earlier version of ALL-IN-1.

You'll find that most of the material in this book applies, however, if you're working with version 2.3, 2.4, or 3.0 of ALL-IN-1. If you're working with a version prior to 2.3, you'll find a significant number of differences between the descriptions in this book and your system.

ALL-IN-1 Fundamentals

PART I

This part of the manual teaches you the fundamentals of working with ALL-IN-1. In the following chapters, you'll learn how to get into ALL-IN-1, find your way around the menu system, select options, and perform tasks. Once you learn these fundamentals, you'll find it easy to master any function in ALL-IN-1. This part contains four chapters: "Getting Started," "Working with ALL-IN-1 Forms," "Reading and Printing in ALL-IN-1," and "ALL-IN-1 Utilities: User Setup, Interrupt Menu, and Scratch Pad."

Chapter 2, "Getting Started," provides an orientation to ALL-IN-1. This chapter begins by explaining how to get in and out of ALL-IN-1. If you've been using ALL-IN-1 for a while, you might skip this log-in procedure and move on to the next topic: an overview of function keys and video forms. Following the discussion of forms is a summary of the basic steps for accomplishing work in ALL-IN-1. The last two topics in "Getting Started" show you how to access help information and computer-based instruction in ALL-IN-1.

Chapter 3, "Working with ALL-IN-1 Forms," describes the basics of working with video forms in ALL-IN-1. Even if you have experience with ALL-IN-1, it might help to review this section for hints. The first topic in this chapter describes how to work with menus, including how to move through the menu system, select items to work with, and enter menu options. The second topic describes how to work with data-entry forms, including how to move around in a form and enter data. The last topic in this chapter shows you how to work with index forms; this skill is very important for working productively with ALL-IN-1.

Chapter 4, "Reading and Printing in ALL-IN-1," shows you how to access the information you enter. The first topic in this chapter shows you how to read items, including how to scan forward through documents and search for text. The second topic covers how to print an item, including how to specify options like the destination printer, the number of copies, and the page orientation (portrait or landscape). The end of this chapter discusses Job Services, the subsystem that manages print and batch jobs. Here you can find out how to stop a print job.

The final chapter in this part, "ALL-IN-1 Utilities," describes time-saving tools that help you work more efficiently. The first topic describes how to set up and control your ALL-IN-1 environment with User Setup. The second topic is the Interrupt menu, which allows you to interrupt your work and take care of another task. The last topic is the Scratch Pad, which enables you to save a copy of your screen's contents.

FUNDAMENTALS Q&A

Following is a list of common questions about the material covered in the next four chapters.

Q *ALL-IN-1 is so extensive. I find that there are too many choices and that it is too confusing. How do I begin to learn my way around?*

A ALL-IN-1 might certainly seem overwhelming to a newcomer. Longtime users of the product have been overwhelmed just by the enhancements! Here are some tips on how to begin learning your way around:

- Although there are numerous menus, there are only four major functions (subsystems) in ALL-IN-1 (Electronic Messaging, Word and Document Processing, Time Management, and Group Conferencing) plus a few minor subsystems (Communications, the Desktop Calculator, and Directories). All other menus are provided to support these functions. So you really need to learn fewer menus and selections than you might think.
- Learn one subsystem at a time. Begin with the basic options of the subsystem: how to create, edit, delete, read, and print an item. Most people choose Electronic Messaging as their first subsystem. It's one of the most important subsystems and one of the easiest to learn.
- Start by learning the basics. A good way to do this is by reading discussions under each topic in the next four chapters, but skim through the procedures. You can refer back to these later when you need to perform a specific task. By all means, though, perform the exercises! They illustrate important concepts and techniques.

Q *How do I get into ALL-IN-1?*

A System managers often set up accounts to start ALL-IN-1 automatically when the user logs in. If this is not the case, you must enter your username and password to log into the system, then enter the command "ALLIN1" in response to the system command prompt (usually "$"). Section 2.2, "Getting into ALL-IN-1," discusses this in greater detail.

Q *How do I move around in ALL-IN-1?*

A The easiest way to move around is to type the selection for the subsystem you want to work with next ("EM" for Electronic Messaging, "WP" for Word and Document Processing, "TM" for Time Management, and "GPC" for Group Conferencing). Then select the option for the task you want to perform: Create (C), Edit (E), Print (P), etc. You can save time by entering both at the same time; for example, type "EM C" to move to Electronic Messaging and create a memo. See Section 3.1.2, "Moving through the Menu System," for more information.

Q *Where is the GOLD key?*

A On DEC keyboards, the GOLD key is labeled PF1. On some DEC keyboards, it is actually painted gold. If you have a non-DEC keyboard, the GOLD key is usually labeled either "NUM LOCK" or "F1." An easy test is to press [NUM LOCK] or [F1], then press "\" (backslash key). If you see the date displayed at the bottom of the screen, you've discovered the GOLD key.

If you're running a terminal-emulations program on a personal computer and you can't find the GOLD key, check the documentation for the program or contact the manufacturer of the emulations program to find out where the various ALL-IN-1 function keys are located.

Q *How do I clear a message from my screen?*

A Press and hold the control key (marked "CTRL"), then press either "W" or "R." This refreshes, or repaints, your screen to clear any messages, such as the notification of new mail. You can try this at any time without affecting your work.

Q *How do I change my password?*

A Change your password from the User Setup menu. From any menu, type "US CP" and press [RETURN]. Then enter your existing password and the new password twice. Section 5.1.1, "Changing your VMS Password," describes the steps in detail.

Q *Can I read my mail without getting out of my document?*

A Yes. Press [GOLD] I to display the Interrupt menu, then select Read New Mail Messages (RN). See Section 5.2, "The Interrupt Menu," for further details.

Q *What is the Scratch Pad? How do I use it?*

A The Scratch Pad is an area for saving the contents of your screen. You can "dump" information on your screen to the Scratch Pad at any time by pressing [GOLD] P. You can edit, read, print, and delete the contents of the Scratch Pad from the Scratch Pad menu. The Scratch Pad menu is displayed when you press [GOLD] *. There are a number of reasons to use the Scratch Pad, including these:

- To record error messages displayed on your screen.
- To print a hard copy of important information displayed on your screen—for example, a list of documents displayed in an index or a keyboard-layout diagram showing the location of function keys.

Chapter 5 contains more information about the Scratch Pad.

Q *How do I delete a group of mail messages? How do I print multiple documents?*

A You can delete multiple messages or print multiple documents from an index. Move to either the Electronic Messaging menu or the Word and Document Processing menu, and enter "I" followed by a folder name—for example, "I READ." This is a quick way to create a list of items. Type the line numbers of all of the messages or documents you want to manage, and press [SELECT]. Then enter "XD" to delete or "XP" to print all selected items.

Section 3.3.6, "Working with Multiple Items in an Index," shows you how to select and manipulate a group of items (messages or documents). You can also refer to the chapters on Electronic Messaging and Word and Document Processing for detailed instructions.

Q *Can I skip forward to a specific page when reading a document? Can I search for specific text when reading a document?*

A You can perform both functions in versions 3.0 and 3.1 of ALL-IN-1. To move to a specific page when reading a document, press [GOLD] T to move to the beginning of the document. Then type the page number (less one), and press [GOLD] [DOWN ARROW]. This advances the document by the number of pages you enter.

To locate a string of text while reading a document, type the text string and press [FIND] (or [GOLD] Comma). Press [GOLD] [FIND] (or [GOLD] Period) to find the next occurrence of the string. Refer to Section 4.1.1, "Reading a Document," for further details.

Q *How do I know when my document's finished printing?*

A Type "US SWC" to display the Set Working Conditions form. Press [TAB] to advance to the Print Completion field, type "Y," and press [RETURN]. ALL-IN-1 will now notify you whenever your print jobs finish. Section 5.1.4, "Setting Working Conditions," tells you more about how to control your environment with Set Working Conditions.

Q *How do I stop a document from printing?*

A When you select the Print option, the name of the document is submitted to programs that run in the background and handle printing. This allows you to continue working on other projects while the document is printing. Job Services allows you to communicate with these programs and prevent your document from printing or abort your job if it is currently printing.

To stop a print job, type "JS IP" from any menu, and press [RETURN]. ALL-IN-1 displays an index of your current print jobs. Type the line number of the job you want to stop, followed by a space and the letter "D" and press [RETURN]. For example, "2 D [RETURN]" deletes the second job. ALL-IN-1 deletes the entry from the list of document names waiting to be printed or stops outputting the document if it is currently being printed. Refer to Section 4.3, "Print and Batch Job Services," for further information.

Q *How do I print a document sideways?*

A If you're preparing documents with WPS-PLUS or WordPerfect, a common method for printing the document sideways (that is, landscape mode) is to place printer control information at the top of the document. This must be done while editing the document, as described in Chapter 10. Refer to the topic "Landscape Mode" in Appendix B for specific instructions on how to insert print control information for landscape mode.

Some sites set up printers to allow users to select landscape mode when printing a document. This allows users to print documents sideways, regardless of the editor used to prepare the document. ALL-IN-1 displays the Printing Document form when you select the Print option (P). The second field of this form, Print Style, is typically where you would select landscape print mode. Press [ERASE LINE] (F13 or LF) to clear this field, then press [FIND] (or [GOLD] L) to display possible choices. Select one that provides landscape printing.

Some advanced printers, such as DEC's LPS20, also allow you to choose landscape mode when printing the document by selecting a specific print option. Press [GOLD] E when the Printing Document form is displayed, then press [NEXT SCREEN] and [TAB] to advance to the Page Orientation field, and enter "LANDSCAPE." Press [RETURN] to complete the Print Settings form.

See Section 4.2, "Printing in ALL-IN-1," for additional details. Note, however, that methods to print in landscape mode vary from one site to another. Contact your system administrator for assistance if none of the above solutions works for you.

FUNDAMENTALS DOs AND DON'Ts

Here are some suggestions to help you form good habits when working in ALL-IN-1:

Do

- Do exit ALL-IN-1 and log off when you don't need to work with the system for a period of time. This frees up computing resources for other users.
- Do change your password regularly—at least every 60 to 90 days—to ensure security.
- Do enter all of the menu selections at once to move to a different menu and select a task. For example, to read all of your new mail quickly, type "EM II ALL XR" and press [RETURN]. This method of entering multiple options, called *stacking selections*, can reduce the amount of time you spend moving from one menu to another. See Section 3.1.2, "Moving through the Menu System," for further details.
- Do make use of the [FIND] (or [GOLD] L) key to list possible entries for a field on a form.
- Do explore working with indexes. You'll find the index to be a user-friendly tool for listing and working with multiple items. Read Section 3.3, "Managing Multiple Items with Index Forms," and perform the exercise at the end of the chapter to get the feel of working with an index.

Don't

- Don't move back to the main menu when you want to work in a different subsystem. Simply enter the selection for the subsystem from any menu ("EM" for Electronic Messaging, "WP" for Word and Document Processing, etc.).
- Don't tie up the printer with a large document if you can afford to wait until off-hours. Press [GOLD] E when the Printing Document form is displayed, press [TAB] to advance forward to the Release Time field, and enter a time of 12:00 (noon) or 17:00 (5 P.M.).

Getting Started

CHAPTER 2

This chapter, which teaches you how to begin working with ALL-IN-1, is the place to start if you have no experience with ALL-IN-1. However, you can probably skim or even skip this chapter if you've already worked a little with ALL-IN-1.

The first two topics cover very basic material for beginners. Most readers can skip these topics, except those who've never logged in or are unfamiliar with the computer equipment. The last four topics cover fundamental concepts of working with ALL-IN-1. You should cover this material because the rest of the book assumes that you know these concepts.

The following topics are discussed in this chapter:

- What you must have before you can access ALL-IN-1, including your account setup and necessary equipment.
- How to get into ALL-IN-1 and how to get out of ALL-IN-1.
- An overview of your keyboard, including the purpose of various function keys. You might want to copy the keyboard templates in this section and keep them near your terminal while you learn ALL-IN-1.
- A description of the different types of video forms you'll see in ALL-IN-1.
- An overview of the four basic steps for accomplishing work in ALL-IN-1. Understanding this basic procedure helps you work with any menu.
- How to access the help information and computer-based training available in ALL-IN-1.

2.1 BEFORE YOU GET STARTED

There's a little business to take care of before you can start working with ALL-IN-1. Your account and ALL-IN-1 environment must be established. Most of this work is performed by someone else, though. Work with your system manager, ALL-IN-1 administrator, or perhaps your supervisor to meet these prerequisites.

- A VMS ACCOUNT ON THE ALL-IN-1 HOST SYSTEM

  Your system manager must create a VMS[1] account for you on the ALL-IN-1 host system by entering information into an *authorization* file. This information includes

1. *VMS* is an acronym for Virtual Memory System, the operating system software that manages work on most VAX computers.

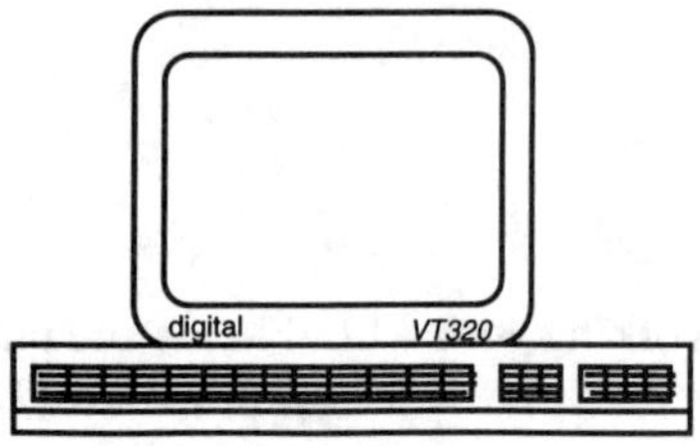

DEC VT Terminal and Keyboard

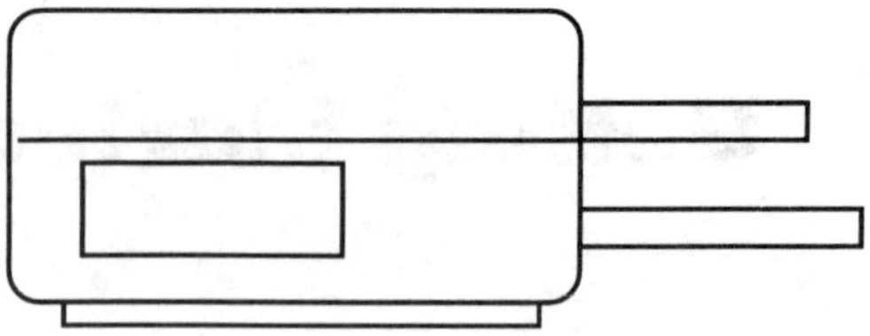

DEC Laser Printer

Figure 2.1 ALL-IN-1 workstation

your full name, department, and, most important, the *username* and *password* that you must enter when logging into the system.

- AN ALL-IN-1 ACCOUNT ON THE HOST SYSTEM

  Your ALL-IN-1 administrator or system manager must create an ALL-IN-1 account for you by entering information into a file called the *ALL-IN-1 Profile.* This information includes your ALL-IN-1 username, which is typically the same as your VMS username, and other information that controls your ALL-IN-1 working environment. The profile is always checked when you start ALL-IN-1 to make sure that you're an authorized user.

- ACCESS TO AN ALL-IN-1 WORKSTATION

  Your workstation includes the following components (Figure 2.1):

  - Video display screen, or CRT, where information is displayed.
  - Keyboard, which resembles a typewriter keyboard but includes function keys and a numeric keypad.
  - Printer for outputting hard copy.

This workstation may be either a video display terminal connected to the host system or a personal computer with a communications line to the ALL-IN-1 host. The VT series of terminals manufactured by Digital Equipment Corporation and VT-compatible terminals are common workstations.

2.2 GETTING INTO ALL-IN-1

Getting into ALL-IN-1 takes a few short steps, which are detailed below for those who are new to ALL-IN-1. If you already know how to get into ALL-IN-1, skip forward to the discussion of the ALL-IN-1 keyboard. It is recommended that you ask your system manager, ALL-IN-1 administrator, or an experienced user for assistance the first time you get into ALL-IN-1.

1. POWER ON YOUR WORKSTATION.

   Make sure your workstation is plugged in and powered on. If you are using a modem to connect to the ALL-IN-1 host, make sure that your modem is plugged in, powered on, and properly connected to your workstation. If you have a local printer, also ensure that your printer is plugged in and powered on.

2. CONNECT TO THE ALL-IN-1 HOST SYSTEM.

   The next step varies, depending on how your workstation is connected to the host system. There are three typical ways of connecting a workstation.

   - Simply press [RETURN] if you have a communications line that runs from the back of your workstation directly to the host.
   - Type "CONNECT," followed by the host system service name, and press [RETURN] if you have a communications line that runs from the back of the workstation to a nearby *terminal server*, which is then connected by network line to one or more host computers.
   - Enter the commands necessary to dial the appropriate telephone number if you have a communications line that runs from the back of the workstation to a modem through which you "dial into" a host system.

   Contact your system manager for assistance if you're not sure how your workstation is connected to the host.

3. LOG INTO VMS.

   Supply a valid username and password to log into your VMS account.

Username: ***username* [RETURN]**	a. Type your username and press [RETURN].
Password: ***password* [RETURN]**	b. Type your password and then press [RETURN]. Note that for security, your password is *not* echoed.

4. LOG INTO ALL-IN-1.

   System managers often set up VMS accounts to start ALL-IN-1 automatically when you log into the host system. If this is the case, you will see a menu shortly after logging in. Skip the following if your account is set up to start ALL-IN-1 automatically on log-in.

   If you see the VMS command prompt (usually "$") after logging in, then enter the ALLIN1 command to start ALL-IN-1:

ALLIN1[RETURN]	Type "ALLIN1" and press [RETURN].

The system manager also may set up your ALL-IN-1 account so that you have to enter an ALL-IN-1 username, password, or both. Perform the following steps if this is the case:

Enter your username:
***username* [RETURN]**

a. Type your ALL-IN-1 username and press [RETURN].

You can bypass this prompt by including your ALL-IN-1 username with the ALLIN1 command:

$ ALLIN1/USER=*username*

Password: ***password* [RETURN]**

b. If you see the password prompt, type your ALL-IN-1 password and press [RETURN].

2.3 GETTING OUT OF ALL-IN-1

Whenever you don't intend to use ALL-IN-1 for a period of time, you should exit ALL-IN-1 and log off the host system. This frees up computing resources so that other users on the system can work more efficiently.

Perform the following steps to get out of ALL-IN-1:

EX[RETURN]

a. At any menu, type "EX" and press [RETURN].

$ LOG[RETURN]

b. If you see the VMS command prompt, type LOG (the LOGOUT command, abbreviated) and press [RETURN]. If you need to access other features of VMS, enter the appropriate commands instead of logging off the system.

c. If you won't be using your workstation for a long period of time, power off your workstation (including the modem and local printer if you have these pieces of equipment).

2.4 ALL-IN-1 KEYBOARD

Your workstation keyboard allows you to enter information. A typical keyboard consists of the following components, shown in Figure 2.2:

- A main keyboard, containing all of the keys of a standard typewriter, that allows you to enter text, numbers, and punctuation characters.
- A numeric keypad that allows you to enter numbers rapidly.
- Function keys that allow you to perform special operations in ALL-IN-1, such as displaying the next screen of menu selections or displaying help information.

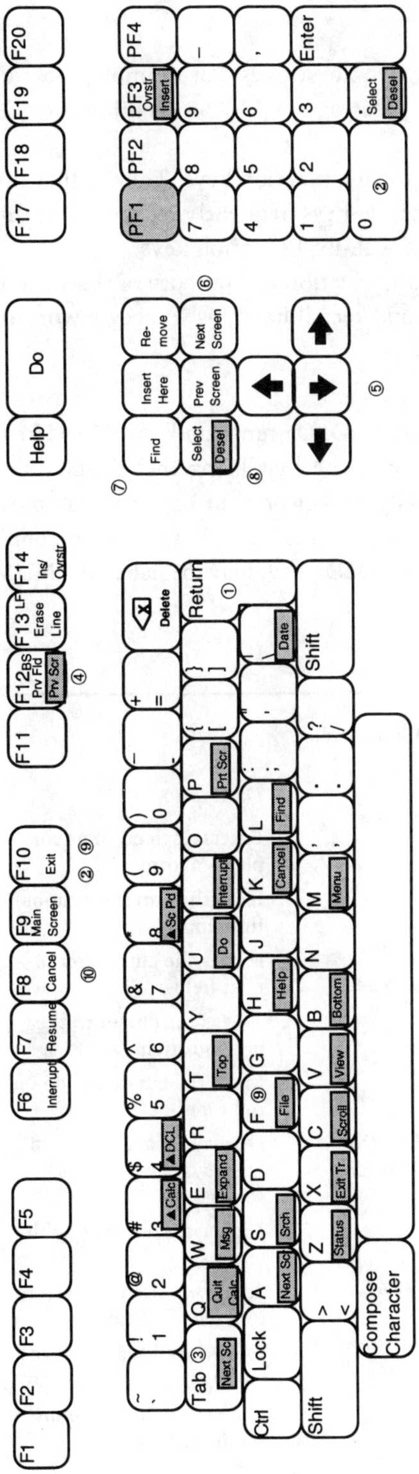

Figure 2.2 ALL-IN-1 function keys on LR201 keyboard (VT200-series)

2.4.1 ALL-IN-1 Function Keys

Function keys perform operations with one or two keystrokes. For example, pressing the [HELP] key displays help information, and pressing the [ERASE LINE] (F13 or LF) key erases the current field of information.

It's impossible to work in ALL-IN-1 without using function keys. They're that important! Table 2.1 summarizes a handful of function keys frequently referred to in this manual. Appendix A contains a complete list of ALL-IN-1 function keys.

Review Figure 2.2 to become familiar with the location and purpose of the various function keys. It's a good idea to copy this page and keep it handy as you begin working with ALL-IN-1.

Two keys deserve special attention:

[GOLD] Many of the function keys are "GOLD" function keys. These keys require two separate keystrokes, the first being the [GOLD] key. Take a second to locate the [GOLD] key on your keyboard. On most DEC or DEC-compatible keyboards, it is labeled "PF1." If you don't have a DEC keyboard, the [GOLD] key may be labeled "NUM LOCK" or "F1."

Table 2.1 Frequently used ALL-IN-1 function keys (LK201 keyboard)

Function key	*Label*	*Alternate*	*Description*
① [RETURN]	Return		Enters a selection or completes a form
② [EXIT]	F10	Keypad-0	Exits the current form or function
③ [TAB]	Tab		Moves the cursor to the next field
④ [BACKSPACE]	F12	[CTRL]+H	Moves the cursor to the previous field
⑤ ARROW KEYS			Move the cursor up, down, right, or left
⑥ [NEXT SCREEN] [PREV SCREEN]	Next Screen Prev Screen	[GOLD] [TAB], [GOLD]A [GOLD] [BACKSPACE]	Displays the next screen Displays the previous screen
⑦ [FIND]	Find	[GOLD]L	Displays a list of possible entries
⑧ [SELECT]	Select	Keypad-Period	Selects an item (or selects text when editing)
⑨ [EXIT]	F10	[GOLD]F	Exits the editor and saves changes
⑩ [CANCEL]	F8	[GOLD]K	Exits the editor without saving changes

NOTE: When you see a key sequence like "[GOLD] M" in this book, remember to enter two separate keystrokes; press the [GOLD] (PF1) key and release it, then press the second key listed (in this case the "M").

[CTRL] The control [CTRL] key is on the left side of your main keyboard. This key is pressed and held along with a second key to perform a function, much like using the [SHIFT] key. Here are some examples:

[CTRL] + R
[CTRL] + W Both [CTRL] + R and [CTRL] + W refresh, or repaint, the screen. This is handy when you want to clear broadcast messages.

[CTRL] + S Suspends output and effectively "freezes" your screen.

[CTRL] + Q Resumes output and "unfreezes" your screen.

2.4.2 Exercise: Displaying the Current Date and Time

This exercise shows you how to enter a GOLD function and CTRL function to display the current date and time, then repaint the screen.

**[GOLD] ** a. From any menu, press the [GOLD] (PF1) key and release it. Then press the backslash key (\) and release it. ALL-IN-1 displays the current date and time at the bottom of your terminal screen.

[CTRL] + R b. Press and hold the [CTRL] key, then press R. Your screen is refreshed, and the date and time are erased.

2.5 INTRODUCTION TO ALL-IN-1 FORMS

ALL-IN-1 communicates with you by accepting input and displaying output on *video forms*. A video form is much like a paper form. Both contain text that describes the information to enter and blank fields where you enter the requested information. Blank fields on a video form are called *data-entry fields*.

There are different types of video forms in ALL-IN-1. Three common types are the menu form, data-entry form, and the index form, which are described briefly in this section.

A basic four-step procedure for accomplishing work in ALL-IN-1 is discussed right after this overview of forms. There are also standard procedures for working with each type of form. These procedures are discussed in Chapter 3. Once you learn these basics, you'll find it easy to work with any subsystem in ALL-IN-1.

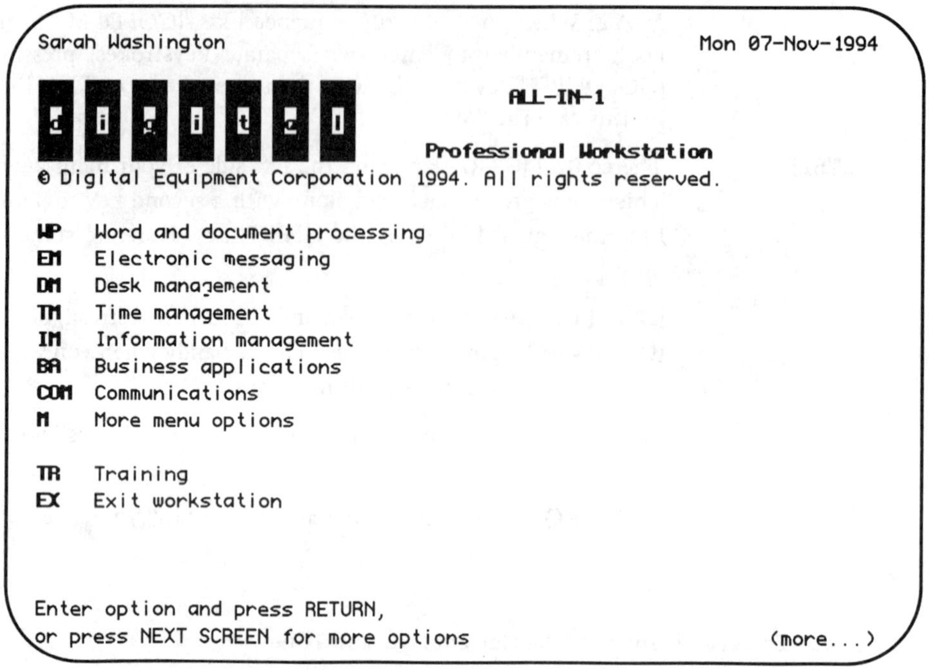

Figure 2.3 The ALL-IN-1 menu form

2.5.1 Menu Form

The ALL-IN-1 menu form (Figure 2.3) serves the same purpose as a menu at a restaurant. It lists selections. Typically, the only information you enter on a menu will be a selection from the list. When you enter a menu selection, ALL-IN-1 takes action, either displaying another menu, called a *submenu*, or performing a specific task. Often, the task requires you to enter further information, typically by filling out a data-entry form.

2.5.2 Data-Entry Form

At times, you'll enter information on a data-entry form (Figure 2.4). This is just like filling out such forms as an employment application or a tax return. Data-entry forms are a convenient way to enter information because you see exactly which pieces of information must be entered and exactly how many characters are allowed.

2.5.3 Index Form

Index forms (Figure 2.5) list items, such as your daily appointments. Index forms are an important productivity tool because they allow you to manage multiple items with a single operation. For example, you can easily select and print the appointments shown in the figure when working from an index.

```
                    Set Working Conditions

Status:
Main screen: MAIN                              Edit style: WPSPLUS
Mail menu:   EMC                         Mail destination: ALL-IN-1

Notification of:

  New mail:        Y    Print completion: Y    Batch completion:    Y
  Display Tasks:   Y    Count Tasks:      Y    Send mail receipts:  Y

Initial TM form: TMMENU                    12 hour clock: Y

Working week:

  First day:   2     Start hour: 08:00am     Meal hour: Start: 12:00pm
  No. of days: 5     End hour:   05:00pm                  End: 01:00pm

  Advanced calendar day position: 2
  Calendar time increment (in minutes): 00015

Press RETURN to complete or press NEXT SCREEN for more details
                                                              (more...)
```

Figure 2.4 The ALL-IN-1 data-entry form

```
               Events at a Glance: Tuesday      08-Nov-1994
(Selections: 0  )      (Meetings waiting: 0  )      (New messages: 0  )
Events for: WASHINGTONS

  No. Type Start   End     Purpose

> 1    A  08:00am 09:00am Eye Doctor's appointment
  2    A  10:30am 11:30am Meet with clients from Westbrook Technology
  3    A  12:00pm 01:30pm Department lunch at the Broker
  4    A  02:30pm 03:00pm Conference call: New York sales

Move to item and enter option (press GOLD MENU to see options,
or HELP for more information)
```

Figure 2.5 The ALL-IN-1 index form

You can work with items from an index just as you would work with items at a menu. As you advance, you'll find that index forms provide two important advantages when compared with menus:

- You can see the list of items with which you're working.
- You can manage multiple items with a single menu selection.

2.6 BASIC PROCEDURE FOR ACCOMPLISHING WORK IN ALL-IN-1

There are four basic steps for accomplishing almost any task in ALL-IN-1:

1. LOCATE THE MENU THAT LISTS THE DESIRED TASK.

   Selections in ALL-IN-1 are listed on a series of menus and submenus. You must first move to the menu for the subsystem you want to work with (Electronic Messaging, Word and Document Processing, etc.) before choosing a task. Section 3.1.2, "Moving through the Menu System," shows you how to do this efficiently.

2. SELECT AN ITEM WITH WHICH TO WORK.

   Your next step might be choosing a selection like Read, Edit, Delete, or Print. These menu selections manipulate the current item identified in the highlighted *current item block*. This is typically the message, document, or event that you worked with the last time you were at the menu. If the current item isn't the one you want to work with, you must first select the desired item. Section 3.1.3, "Selecting an Item at a Menu," shows you how to do this.

3. ENTER A MENU SELECTION TO PERFORM THE TASK.

   You can enter a menu option to perform a task once you've selected an item. Enter an option from the menu, and press [RETURN]. Selections are displayed on the menu next to descriptions. In some cases, multiple screens are required to display all the selections, and you might want to press [NEXT SCREEN] to display additional selections.

4. ENTER ANY INFORMATION REQUIRED FOR THE TASK.

   Completing a task often requires you to enter further information by filling out a data-entry form. For example, when you select the Print option, you have to enter the name of the printer you want to use and the number of copies you want printed. The task is performed, and the menu is redisplayed for you to select another option.

Following is an exercise that takes you through these four basic steps. These steps are described in greater detail in Chapter 3.

2.6.1 Exercise: Four Basic Steps for Accomplishing Work

In this exercise, you create an appointment in your electronic calendar in the Time Management subsystem. Before proceeding, make sure you are at a menu in ALL-IN-1.

1. Move to the Time Management menu.

TM[RETURN]	a. From any menu, type "TM" and press [RETURN].
EV[RETURN]	b. Type "EV" and press [RETURN].

2. Create an event in your calendar.

C[RETURN]	a. Type "C" and press [RETURN]. ALL-IN-1 displays the data-entry form shown in Figure 2.6.
[TAB]4:30pm	b. Leave the Date field alone. Press [TAB] and type "4:30pm" in the Start Time field.
[TAB]5:00pm	c. Press [TAB] and type "5:00pm" in the End Time field.
[TAB]Staff Meeting	d. Press [TAB] and enter the text in the Purpose field.
[RETURN]	e. Press [RETURN] to complete the data-entry form and return to the menu.

3. Select the event you just created. (Even though this event is the current item, try the Select option to see how it works.)

SEL[RETURN]	a. Type "SEL" and press [RETURN]. ALL-IN-1 displays another data-entry form.
[TAB]4:30pm	b. Press [TAB] and type "4:30pm" in the Start Time field.
[RETURN]	c. Press [RETURN] to complete the data-entry form and return to the menu.

```
                                 Create Event

Scheduler:   WASHINGTON

Date:        08-Nov-1994        Start Time: 04:30pm     End Time: 05:00pm
Purpose:     Staff Meeting_____________________________________________
Confidential? (Y/N)        N
Invite Attendees? (Y/N)    N
Location (if attendees):   ______________________________

Enter information and press RETURN
```

Figure 2.6 The Create Event form

4. Your event now appears as the current item. Display the event with the Read option.

R[RETURN]	a. Type "R" and press [RETURN]. ALL-IN-1 displays the event.
[RETURN]	b. Press [RETURN] to clear the event and return to the menu.

2.7 ALL-IN-1 HELP

ALL-IN-1 provides extensive Help information that you can access from *anywhere* in ALL-IN-1 by pressing [HELP] (or [GOLD] H). Help information is displayed in a Help window. Figure 2.7 shows the Help window displayed for the Read New Mail option on the Electronic Messaging menu.

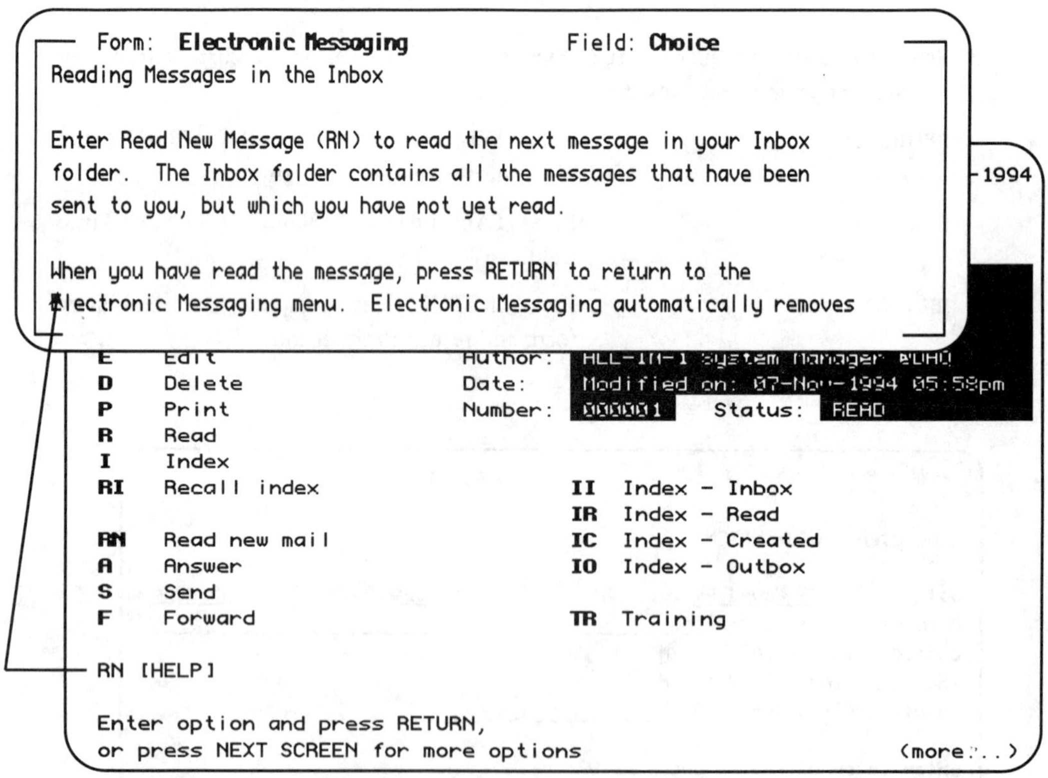

Figure 2.7 ALL-IN-1 Help at a menu

Perform the following steps to access Help information from anywhere in ALL-IN-1:

[HELP]

a. Press the [HELP] key (or [GOLD] H). ALL-IN-1 clears a portion of the screen and displays instructional text in a Help window. The following prompt appears at the bottom of your screen:

```
Press RETURN to continue or EXIT to exit
```

[RETURN]...

b. Press [RETURN] to advance through the Help text, or exit Help at any point by pressing [EXIT] (F10 or Keypad-0). As you press [RETURN], ALL-IN-1 scrolls through the Help text until the following prompt is displayed:

```
For a list of related topics, press RETURN;
press EXIT to exit
```

[RETURN]

c. Press [RETURN] again, and ALL-IN-1 displays a list of additional topics similar to the list shown in Figure 2.8. At the bottom of your screen is the following prompt:

```
Enter number from list and press RETURN;
just press RETURN for more topics
```

***line-number*[RETURN]**

d. Type the line number corresponding to the topic you're interested in and press [RETURN].

Repeat steps c and d as often as you like to display additional topics. ALL-IN-1 marks topics you've already read by placing an asterisk next to the line number.

```
Form:  Electronic Messaging                 Field: Choice

Help is available on the following topics:

  1* Electronic Messaging
  2       Answering a Message
  3       Attaching a Document
  4       Sending an Automatic Reply
  5       Attaching a Document
```

Figure 2.8 Additional Help topics

[EXIT] e. Press [EXIT] (F10 or Keypad-0) to exit the Help function when you're finished.

2.7.1 Getting Help Information at a Menu

General information describing the purpose of the current menu is displayed when you press [HELP] (or [GOLD] H). This is useful if you find yourself in unfamiliar territory and want to know what purpose the menu serves. Additional Help information describes the purpose of each menu option.

Follow these steps to display a description of a menu option:

***menu-option*[HELP]** a. Enter the menu selection and press [HELP] *before* pressing [RETURN]. For example, to display help for the Create option, type C and press [HELP].

[RETURN]... b. Press [RETURN] to see additional help.

[EXIT] c. Press [EXIT] (F10 or Keypad-0) when you're finished reading the help text.

2.7.2 Getting Help at a Data-Entry Form

Descriptions of the fields on data-entry forms are provided to help you complete forms in ALL-IN-1. These descriptions, as shown in Figure 2.9, are useful when you can't figure out what is required by reading the labels on the form.

Follow these steps to display Help information for a particular field on a data-entry form:

[TAB]...
[BACKSPACE]... a. Move your cursor to the specific field by pressing [TAB] to move forward or [BACKSPACE] (F12) to move backward.

[HELP] b. Press [HELP] when you reach the desired field.

[RETURN]... c. Press [RETURN] to see additional help.

[EXIT] d. Press [EXIT] (F10 or Keypad-0) when you're finished reading the Help text.

ALL-IN-1 also provides a handy "lookup" feature to display possible entries for certain fields. In these fields, you can press [FIND] to list the possible entries. A common example involves sending an electronic mail message. When addressing the memo, you must enter the names of individuals. At the point where you enter these names, you can press [FIND] to display names of all individuals with ALL-IN-1 accounts. Refer to Section 3.2.2, "Using [FIND] to Complete a Field," for details of using [FIND] to list possible entries.

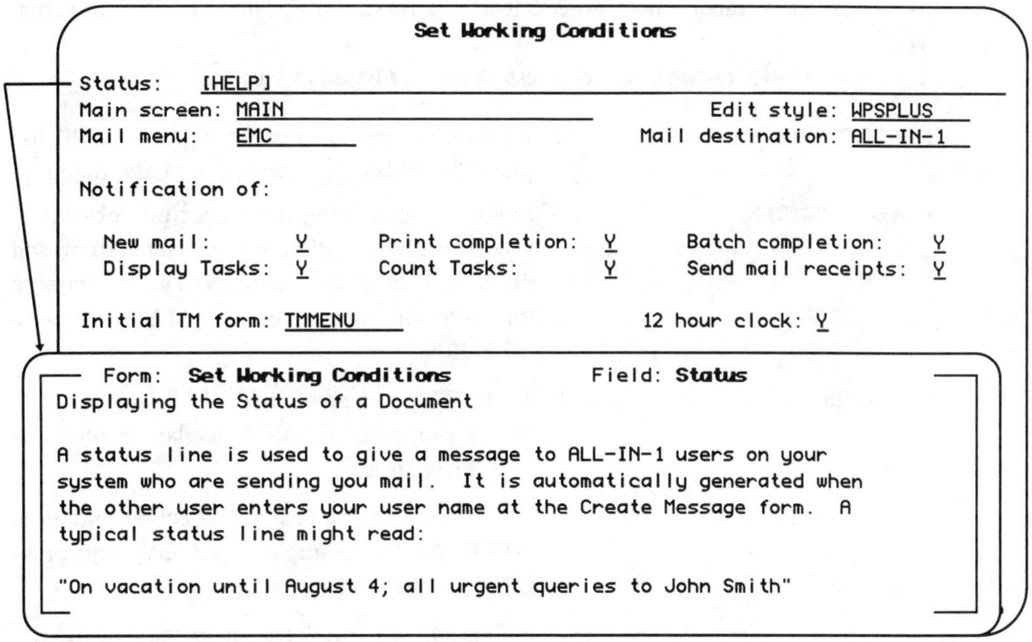

Figure 2.9 ALL-IN-1 Help for a data-entry form

2.8 COMPUTER-BASED INSTRUCTION

Self-paced training is available throughout ALL-IN-1 to show you how to use a particular subsystem. This training is structured to teach you the concepts and procedures for the subsystem *before* you begin working with it. In ALL-IN-1, this self-paced training is known as *Computer-Based Instruction* (CBI).

No prior experience is necessary to take Computer-Based Instruction. CBIs display pictures and text to help you learn more about a subsystem. You progress through a course at your own pace by pressing [RETURN] and entering information. You can press [GOLD] X at any time to leave the training course and return to the Training menu.

When you start a training course, ALL-IN-1 tells you how far you've progressed through the course. At the bottom of the screen, you see two numbers separated by a slash (/)—for example, "3/11." The first number indicates the current page; the second number indicates the total number of pages in the course. (In some cases, a particular "page" can actually contain multiple screens; for example, page 5 can contain screens 5a, 5b, and 5c. Therefore, the total number of pages can sometimes be misleading.)

The Training (TR) option, available on most menus, starts Computer-Based Instruction. The CBI then guides you through the steps necessary to work in the subsystem. Actual menus and screens are often displayed along with instructions telling you what to do next. It is important to note that during the training, you *will* perform actual work.

Perform the following steps to access Computer-Based Instruction:

MAIN[RETURN]	a. If you want general training, type "MAIN" and press [RETURN] to move to the MAIN menu.
subsystem**[RETURN]**	If you want training for a specific subsystem, type the menu option for the subsystem and press [RETURN]. For example, to access training for Electronic Messaging, type "EM" and press [RETURN].
TR[RETURN]	b. Type "TR" and press [RETURN] to select the Training option. ALL-IN-1 displays a menu of training courses.
training-option**[RETURN]**	c. Type the option for a particular course and press [RETURN]. For example, type "OV" and press [RETURN] to get an overview.
	d. Follow the instructions presented during the training.
[GOLD] X	e. Press [GOLD] (PF1), then type "X" to exit the course and return to the Training menu if you do not want to complete the course.
[EXIT]	f. Press [EXIT] (F10 or Keypad-0) to return to the previous menu.

Working with ALL-IN-1 Forms

CHAPTER 3

ALL-IN-1 communicates with you by accepting input and displaying output on video forms. In the last chapter, you learned about three basic types of forms: the menu form, data-entry form, and index form. This chapter teaches you more about working with menu, data-entry, and index forms, including how to perform the following tasks:

- How to move efficiently through the menu system, select an item to work with, and select an option to perform a task.
- How to move around in a data-entry form and enter information to complete the form.
- How to list and work with multiple items from an index form.

3.1 WORKING WITH ALL-IN-1 MENUS

ALL-IN-1 is a menu-driven system, as opposed to a command-driven environment like PC DOS or the command level of VMS. In the command environment, you're responsible for remembering commands. In the menu environment, however, you don't have to remember commands or know how one command is related to another. All operations are listed on menus and are grouped by function.

The ALL-IN-1 menu form serves the same purpose as a menu at a restaurant. It lists your possible choices (*options*). There are far too many options in ALL-IN-1 to fit on a single menu screen. Therefore, menu options are listed on a number of screens. This is similar to having separate pages for appetizers and entrées in a restaurant menu. Often, a menu option in ALL-IN-1 simply displays another menu (a *submenu*).

Refer to the example of the Electronic Messaging subsystem shown in Figure 3.1, and note the following components of a menu form:

① Information display fields	ALL-IN-1 displays the following information at the top of most menus: username, job title, and day and date.
② Menu title	The menu title identifies the subsystem (Electronic Messaging, Word and Document Processing, etc.).

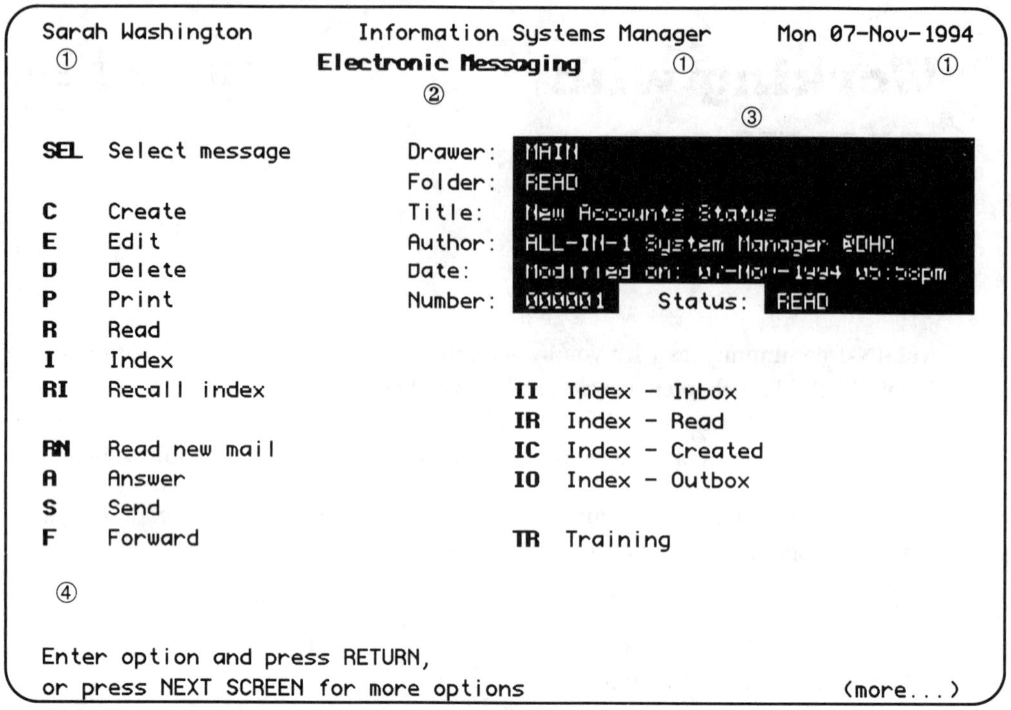

Figure 3.1 Electronic Messaging menu

③ Current item block	The current item block contains information about the current item. Standard menu options (Read, Edit, etc.) manipulate the current item.
④ Choice field	The choice field is the blank line where you enter your menu option.

3.1.1 Menu Function Keys

The function keys active at a menu perform such operations as displaying the previous screen or the next screen of options. Table 3.1 contains a list of menu function keys. Figure 3.2 illustrates some of the function keys used to move through the menu screens.

3.1.2 Moving through the Menu System

There are two ways to move through the ALL-IN-1 menu system and perform tasks. Briefly, these are the methods:

- Enter the option to move directly to a subsystem menu. Review the selections, and enter an option to display a submenu or perform a task. This method is the best for new ALL-IN-1 users who are unfamiliar with the menus.

Table 3.1 Menu function keys

Press the Following Key(s)	*To Perform This Action*
[EXIT] (F10 or Keypad-0)	Return to the previous menu screen.
[MAIN SCREEN] (F9)	Return to the main menu setting (VT-series terminals). Refer to Section 5.1.4, "Setting Working Conditions," to learn how to select a different menu as your main menu setting.
[NEXT SCREEN] (or [GOLD] A)	Display the next series of menu options for the current menu.
[PREV SCREEN] (or [GOLD] [BACKSPACE])	Display the previous series of menu options for the current menu.
[DOWN ARROW]	Update the current item block by selecting the next item. For example, pressing [DOWN ARROW] in the Electronic Messaging menu selects (and makes current) the next message in the current folder.
[UP ARROW]	Update the current item block by selecting the first item. For example, pressing [UP ARROW] in the Electronic Messaging menu selects (and makes current) the first message in the current folder.

- Enter a string of options to move directly to a menu and execute a task. This method is the best way to move around the menu system once you have become familiar with the options.

Method 1: Moving through Menus by Selecting Options

You do *not* have to return to the main menu before moving to a different subsystem. You can move directly from one subsystem to another by entering an option listed in Table 3.2. These are called *global options* because they can be entered from any menu, even though they aren't listed. You will find a more complete list of global options in Appendix A. Your site may customize ALL-IN-1 to add or remove global options.

The next step is rather intuitive. Once you reach the menu for the desired subsystem, review the options and enter a selection to display a submenu or execute a task. If the menu contains the word "(more...)" in the lower right-hand corner, there are more menu options. Press [NEXT SCREEN] (or [GOLD] A) to display additional options.

Method 2: Moving through Menus by Stacking Options

This method is more efficient because you move directly to the task you want to perform without having to look at intervening menu screens. You do this by entering all of the necessary options at one time. This technique, called *stacking options*, has two simple rules:

- The list must contain all of the options necessary to reach and select the desired task.
- The options must be separated by spaces.

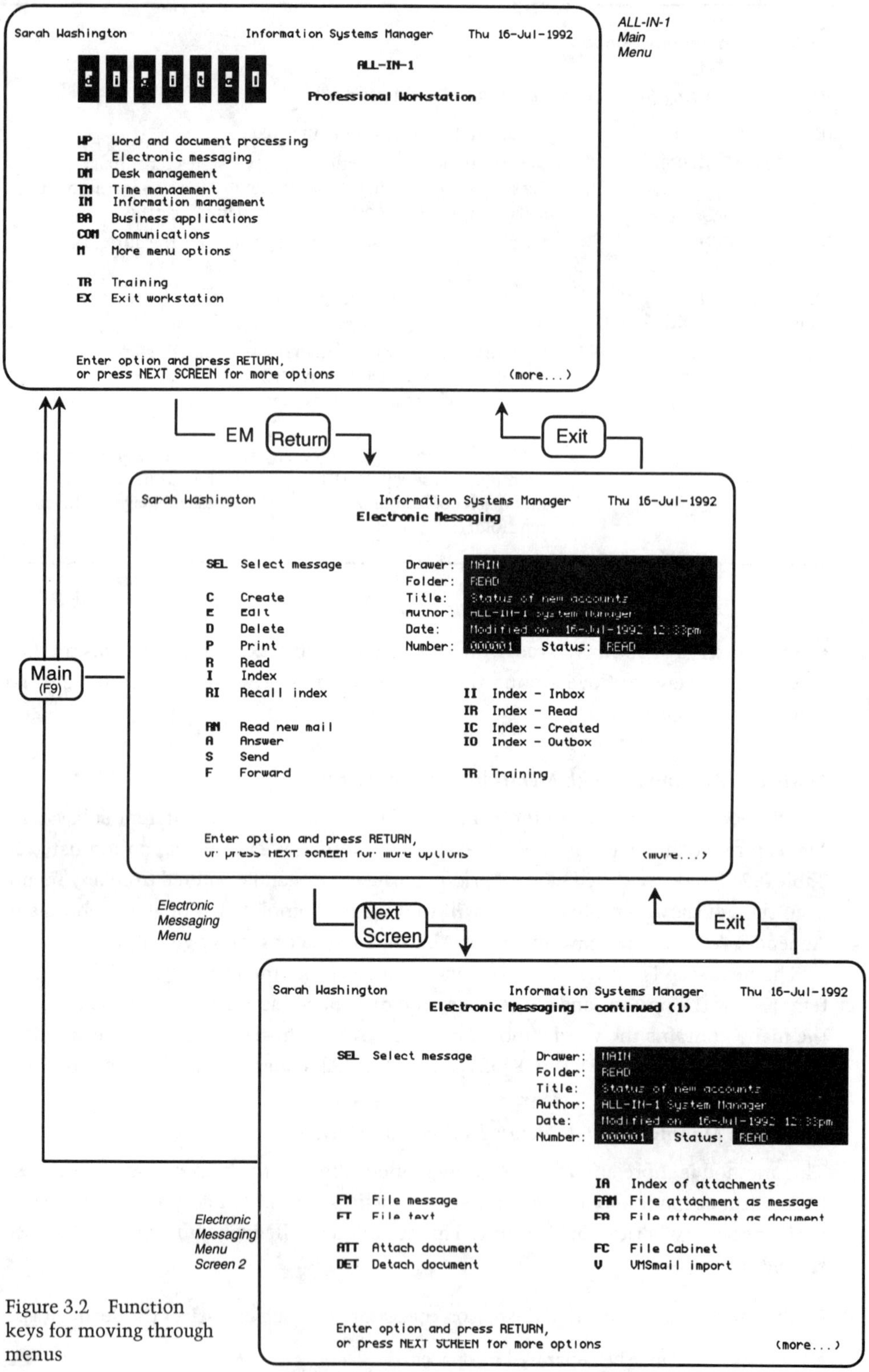

Figure 3.2 Function keys for moving through menus

Table 3.2 Subsystem menu options

Enter the Following Option	*To Move to This Menu*
COM	Communications
DC	Desktop Calculator
DL	Distribution Lists
DM	Desk Management
DT	Document Transfer
EM	Electronic Messaging
EX	Exit Workstation
FC	File Cabinet Maintenance
GPC	Group Conferencing
GS	Group Services
JS	Job Services
MAIN	Main menu
NI	Nickname Management
SP	Scratch Pad
TM	Time Management
US	User Setup
WP	Word and Document Processing

Therefore, to stack menu options, follow these steps:

[EXIT]... — a. Continue to press [EXIT] (F10 or Keypad-0) to return to any previous menu.

***option option option*...[RETURN]** — b. Enter all of the options necessary to access the desired function, starting with the global option for the subsystem (see Table 3.2). Remember to type a space between each option.

You can also sometimes add information after the last menu option to identify a specific item or group of items. The Select option in both Electronic Messaging and Word and Document Processing, for example, accepts a folder name. Enter "SEL OUTBOX" and press [RETURN] to select the message at the top of your Outbox folder without having to complete a form.

Here are some useful examples:

EM SEL READ — Moves to the Electronic Messaging menu and selects the last message you read. (See the next section, "Selecting an Item at a Menu.")

WP I LETTERS — Moves to the Word and Document Processing menu and creates an index of documents in the Letters folder.

EM II ALL XR	Moves to the Electronic Messaging menu and lists and reads all new mail messages. (This is a great feature for people who get a lot of mail.)
TM EV I	Moves to the Events menu and creates an index of events.

Stacking options obviously requires that you be familiar with the menus and menu options. You'll be surprised at how fast you learn the menus, particularly those you work with every day. So, the next time you enter options, save time and try to think ahead.

3.1.3 Selecting an Item at a Menu

Many menu options act on the current item shown in the highlighted block in the upper right-hand corner of the menu. For example, Figure 3.1 shows the Electronic Messaging menu with the current message dated November 7, 1994. Before entering options like Read, Edit, Delete, and so on, make sure that you select the item with which you want to work.

There are two basic methods for selecting a single item:

- Enter the Select option (SEL), then fill out a form to select a specific item. You can bypass the form in many instances by adding information after "SEL." For example, "SEL *folder*" selects the document at the top of the specified folder.
- Select items by pressing your up or down arrow key. (However, not every menu supports the use of the arrow keys to select items.)

You might find it efficient to use a combination of both methods. For example, quickly select the message at the top of your Read folder by entering "SEL READ" at the Electronic Messaging menu. This is the last message you read. Then press [DOWN ARROW] to select other messages in this folder. The most recent messages are filed at the top of this folder. One word of caution, if you go past the message or document you want to work with, you have to press [UP ARROW] to go back to the top of the folder.

A better example of where it makes sense to enter information after "SEL" is when you're working with attachments to messages. Suppose you're reading a message with an attached document. You file the attachment by entering "FA," then enter "Procedures" in the Folder field. You can then quickly move to Word and Document Processing and select this document by entering "WP SEL PROCEDURES" because the filed document is at the top of the Procedures folder.

Both methods for selecting an item are described in the following sections. Note that these methods apply to selecting items at a menu. You can also select and work with items from an index. Refer to Section 3.3, "Managing Multiple Items with Index Forms," for details.

Method 1: Selecting an Item with the Select Option

Perform the following steps to select a new item with the Select option (SEL):

[SELECT] — a. Press [SELECT] (or type SEL and press [RETURN]). ALL-IN-1 displays a data-entry form.

Hint: You can often bypass the form by entering the format "SEL *item*."

data **[TAB]...** — b. Enter information for the item you wish to select and press [RETURN]. When completing the fields, press [TAB] to move to the next field, or press [BACKSPACE] (F12) to move to the previous field.

Hint: Are you having difficulty remembering items previously entered? Press the [FIND] key (or [GOLD] L) to list possible entries for the current field. Refer to Section 3.2.2, "Using [FIND] to Complete a Field," for further information.

[RETURN] — c. Press [RETURN] when you complete the necessary fields of information.

Table 3.3 summarizes the function keys that help you complete the Select form. You can quickly select an item at a menu without having to fill out a form. Simply enter information after "SEL," as described in Table 3.4.

Method 2: Selecting an Item with the Arrow Keys

Most menus let you select an item with your arrow keys, as described in Table 3.5 on page 37. Arrow keys provide a quick way to scroll down through a list of items. For example, pressing the down arrow in Word and Document Processing causes ALL-IN-1 to select the next document in the current folder.

Table 3.3 Function keys for completing a Select form

Press the Following Key(s)	*To Perform This Action*
[RETURN]	Select the item and return to the menu.
[EXIT] (F10 or Keypad-0)	Return to the menu *without* selecting the item.
[TAB]	Move to the next field in the form.
[BACKSPACE] (F12)	Move to the previous field.
[ERASE LINE] (F13, LF or [CTRL]+J)	Erase the contents of the current field.
[FIND] (or [GOLD] L)	Display a list of possible entries for the current field.

Table 3.4 Selecting an item with "SEL *item*"

Subsystem	*Abbr.*	*SEL Format*	*Example*	*Description*
Directories	DIR	N/S		
Distribution Lists	DL	SEL *dist-list*	SEL @MGMT	Selects the specified list.
Document Transfer	DT	SEL *folder*	SEL OUTBOX	Selects the document at the top of the specified folder.
	DT	SDR *drawer*	SDR FINANCE	Selects the specified drawer.
Drawer Management	FC DRM	SEL *drawer*	SEL FINANCE	Selects the specified drawer.
Electronic Messaging	EM	SEL *folder*	SEL READ	Selects the document at the top of the specified folder.
	EM	SDR *drawer*	SDR ADAMS	Selects the specified drawer.
File Cabinet	FC	SEL *folder*	SEL BUDGET	Selects the document at the top of the specified folder.
	FC	SDR *drawer*	SDR FINANCE	Selects the specified drawer.
Group Conferencing	GPC	SEL *note-number*	SEL 1.2	Selects the specified note.
Group Services	GS	SEL *group*	SEL EXEC	Selects the specified group.
Time Management	TM	N/S		
Word and Document Processing	WP	SEL *folder*	SEL BUDGET	Selects the document at the top of the specified folder.
	WP	SDR *drawer*	SDR FINANCE	Selects the specified drawer.

N/S = not supported.

3.1.4 Exercise: Creating and Selecting an Item

The following exercise illustrates the two methods for selecting an item. In this exercise, you create and select with Time Management.

1. Move to the Time Management Events menu.

TM EV [RETURN]	From any menu, type "TM EV" and press [RETURN] to display the Events menu.

2. Create two events in your calendar.

C[RETURN]	a. Type "C" and press [RETURN]. ALL-IN-1 displays the data-entry form shown in Figure 3.3.
[TAB]	b. Leave the Date field alone. Press [TAB] to move to the next field.
4:30pm[TAB]	c. Type "4:30pm" in the Start Time field and press [TAB].
4:45pm[TAB]	d. Type "4:45pm" in the End Time field and press [TAB].
Go to bank	e. Enter text in the Purpose field.

Table 3.5 Selecting with arrow keys

Press the Following Key(s)	*To Perform This Action*
Electronic Messaging File Cabinet Word and Document Processing	
[UP ARROW]	Select the first document in the current folder.
[DOWN ARROW]	Select the next document in the current folder.
[GOLD] [UP ARROW]	Select the first document in the first folder.
[GOLD] [DOWN ARROW]	Select the first document in the next folder.
Directories Distribution Lists Group Services Nicknames	
[UP ARROW]	Select the first item in the list (first directory entry, first distribution list, first group, or first nickname).
[DOWN ARROW]	Select the next item in the list.
Group Conferencing	
[UP ARROW]	Select the first note under the current topic.
[DOWN ARROW]	Select the next note under the current topic.
[GOLD] [UP ARROW]	Select the first topic in the conference.
[GOLD] [DOWN ARROW]	Select the first note under the next topic.
Time Management	
[GOLD] [RIGHT ARROW]	Set the calendar date back one day and select the first event or task on the resulting date.
[GOLD] [LEFT ARROW]	Set the calendar date forward one day and select the first event or task on the resulting date.
[GOLD] [UP ARROW]	Set the calendar date back one week and select the first event or task on the resulting date.
[GOLD] [DOWN ARROW]	Set the calendar date forward one week and select the first 'event or task on the resulting date.

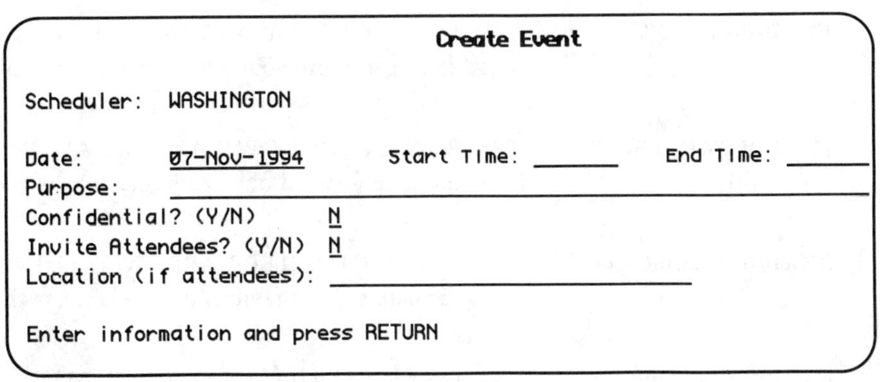
Create Event

Scheduler: WASHINGTON

Date: 07-Nov-1994 Start Time: ______ End Time: ______
Purpose: ________________________________
Confidential? (Y/N) N
Invite Attendees? (Y/N) N
Location (if attendees): ____________________

Enter information and press RETURN

Figure 3.3 Create Event form

[RETURN] f. Press [RETURN] to complete the data-entry form and return to the menu.

C[RETURN] g. Type "C" and press [RETURN].

[TAB] h. Press [TAB] to move to the next field.

5:00pm[TAB] i. Type "5:00pm" in the Start Time field and press [TAB].

6:00pm[TAB] j. Type "6:00pm" in the End Time field and press [TAB].

Dentist's appointment k. Enter text in the Purpose field.

[RETURN] l. Press [RETURN] to complete the data-entry form and return to the menu.

3. Select an event with the Select option.

SEL[RETURN] a. Type "SEL" and press [RETURN]. ALL-IN-1 displays a data-entry form.

[ERASE LINE] b. Press [ERASE LINE] (F13 or LF) to clear the contents of the Date field.

[FIND] c. Press [FIND] (or [GOLD] L) to display a list of events.

***line-number*[RETURN]** d. Type the line number of the event you wish to select and press [RETURN]. The selection list is cleared, and the data-entry form appears with the Date and Time fields completed for the selected event.

[RETURN] e. Press [RETURN] again. Note that the current item block is filled in with the specified event.

4. Select events with the arrow keys.

[GOLD] [UP ARROW] a. Press [GOLD] [UP ARROW]. ALL-IN-1 sets the date to the previous week and selects the first event for the resulting day (if one exists).

[GOLD] [DOWN ARROW] b. Press [GOLD] [DOWN ARROW]. ALL-IN-1 sets the date forward one week and selects the first event.

[GOLD] [LEFT ARROW] c. Press [GOLD] [LEFT ARROW]. ALL-IN-1 sets the date to the previous day and selects the first event (if one exists).

[GOLD] [RIGHT ARROW] d. Press [GOLD] [RIGHT ARROW]. ALL-IN-1 sets the date forward one day and selects the first event.

Table 3.6 Standard menu options

Enter This Option	*To Perform the Following Action*
C (Create)	Create a new item (document, message, appointment, etc.). After selecting this option: • Enter details for the new item. In some cases, you may also enter text (creating a document or message, for example).
D (Delete)	Delete an item. After selecting this option: • Enter "Y" (yes) or "N" (no) to confirm whether to delete the item. Note that this prompt doesn't appear if you've turned off this mechanism with Set Working Conditions.
E (Edit)	Modify the item. After selecting this option: • Change the details for the new item or in some cases edit text (document or message, for example).
I (Index)	Display an index or list of items. After selecting this option: • Enter information to select items for the index. • Select the items with which you want to work. • Enter menu options to manage the selected items.
P (Print)	Send a copy of the current item to a printer. After selecting this option: • Enter information for printing, including the name of the printer and the number of copies.
R (Read)	Display the current item on your screen. After selecting this option: • Press [RETURN], [NEXT SCREEN], or [PREV SCREEN] and other function keys to display additional pages.
SEL (Select)	Select an item with which to work. After selecting this option: • Enter information specifying the item with which you want to work.

3.1.5 Working with Standard Menu Options

Most menus in ALL-IN-1 contain the seven standard menu options listed in Table 3.6. These options perform such basic operations as creating, editing, reading, deleting, or printing an item. The word *item* here refers to a single piece of work, such as a document in Word and Document Processing, a message in Electronic Messaging, or an event in Time Management.

The steps to complete any standard option are amazingly similar, regardless of which subsystem you're using. For example, the Delete option works pretty much the same way in Word and Document Processing as it does in Electronic Messaging and Time Management. Once you learn how to use standard options in one subsystem, you will find it very easy to learn a new subsystem.

3.2 WORKING WITH DATA-ENTRY FORMS

ALL-IN-1 is primarily a tool for storing and managing information. You will frequently enter information in ALL-IN-1 by filling out a form. In some instances, you'll enter information as free-form text (a *document*). Entering information by filling out forms is discussed here; entering free-form text is discussed later in the chapters on Word and Document Processing.

Figure 3.4 shows an example of a data-entry form. Data-entry forms simplify the task of entering information. The data-entry form shows what information to enter and exactly how many characters to enter in each field. ALL-IN-1 often checks data as it is entered and immediately notifies you if it's invalid.

Refer to the sample form shown in Figure 3.4, and note the key components of a data-entry form:

① Form title — The form title identifies the purpose of the information entered on the form.

② Labels — Labels clearly specify the information to enter in the adjacent data field.

③ Data fields — The blank field next to the label "Status:" is a data field. A data field can be either *enterable* (you can move your cursor to the field and enter data) or *display only* (you will not be able to move your cursor to the field or alter its contents).

```
                          ① Set Working Conditions
 ②
Status:            ③  ____________________________________________
Main screen: MAIN                               Edit style: WPSPLUS
Mail menu:   EMC                          Mail destination: ALL-IN-1

Notification of:

  New mail:       Y    Print completion:  Y     Batch completion:    Y
  Display Tasks:  Y    Count Tasks:       Y     Send mail receipts:  Y

Initial TM form: TMMENU                     12 hour clock: Y

Working week:

  First day:   2     Start hour: 08:00am       Meal hour: Start: 12:00pm
  No. of days: 5     End hour:   05:00pm                    End: 01:00pm

  Advanced calendar day position: 2
  Calendar time increment (in minutes): 00015

Enter information and press RETURN, or press NEXT SCREEN for more   (more..)
```

Figure 3.4 Sample data-entry form

3.2.1 Completing a Data-Entry Form

The procedure for completing a data-entry form is fairly obvious:

data	a. Enter data for the current field (the flashing cursor identifies the current field).
[TAB]	b. Press [TAB] to move to the next field.
	c. Repeat steps a and b until you have completed all fields on the screen.
[NEXT SCREEN]	d. If "(more...)" appears in the lower right-hand corner of the screen, there is at least one more screen of fields. Press [NEXT SCREEN] (or [GOLD] [TAB]) to move to the next screen of data fields.
	e. Repeat steps a through d until you have completed all fields on all screens.
[RETURN]	f. After completing all fields on the data-entry form, press [RETURN].
[RETURN] or [EXIT]	g. Press [RETURN] again if the information is complete, or press [EXIT] (F10 or Keypad-0) to make changes to any field.

The function keys active at a data-entry form perform such operations as moving to the next field, moving to the previous field, and clearing a field, as described in Table 3.7.

Table 3.7 Data-entry form function keys

Press the Following Key(s)	*To Perform This Action*
[RETURN]	Save any new or modified data and return to the menu.
[EXIT] (F10 or Keypad-0)	Return to the menu *without* saving new or modified data.
[FIND] (or [GOLD] L)	List possible entries for the current field.
[HELP] (or [GOLD] H)	Display information describing the current field.
[TAB]	Move to the next data field.
[BACKSPACE] (F12)	Move to the previous data field.
[DOWN ARROW]	Move to the next line of data fields.
[UP ARROW]	Move to the previous line of data fields.

(continued)

Table 3.7 Data-entry form function keys *(continued)*

[ERASE LINE] (F13 or LF)	Erase the contents of the current data field.
[PF3]	Change to overstrike mode for the current field.
[GOLD] [PF3]	Change to insert mode for the current field.
[INSERT/OVERSTRIKE] (F14)	Toggle between insert and overstrike mode for the current field.
[NEXT SCREEN] (or [GOLD] [TAB])	Display the next screen of data fields for the current form.
[PREV SCREEN] (or [GOLD] [BACKSPACE])	Display the previous screen of data fields for the current form.
[GOLD] T (or [GOLD] [UP ARROW])	Move to the first field on the current form.
[GOLD] B (or [GOLD] [DOWN ARROW])	Move to the last field on the current form.

3.2.2 Using [FIND] to Complete a Field

ALL-IN-1 provides a time-saving "lookup" feature to assist you in completing a data-entry form. Certain data fields allow you to list possible entries for the field by pressing [FIND]. If you've typed any letters in the field, the list contains all matching entries—that is, entries that begin with the characters you've entered. Figure 3.5 shows an example. If you type "E" and press [FIND] while completing the Edit Style field on the Set Working Conditions form, you will see the list displayed in Figure 3.5. Lists are always similar to the one shown: possible entries, each preceded by a line number. To select an entry, simply type the corresponding line number, and press [RETURN].

The lookup feature is used often, simply because people have trouble remembering folder names, titles, and so on. Keep in mind the phrase, "When in doubt, press [FIND]." The worst that can happen is that ALL-IN-1 will display a message that the Find capability isn't supported by the current field.

Follow these steps to use ALL-IN-1's lookup feature when completing a data-entry form:

1. Move the cursor to the target field.

[TAB]... or **[BACKSPACE]...**	Press [TAB] or [BACKSPACE] (F12) as many times as necessary to move the cursor to the desired field.

2. Clear the field to list all entries, or enter a search string.

[ERASE LINE]	Press [ERASE LINE] (F13 or LF) to clear the field if it contains any information. If you want to list only entries that start with or contain certain characters, type the characters for which you want to search. For example, to find all entries beginning with the letter *W*, type "W".

```
Please select one of the following entries:

1  EDT
2  EVE
3  EVE_EDT
4  EVE_WPS

Press RETURN to continue, or line number you want to select, or EXIT
```

```
Status: ____________________________________________________________
Main screen: MAIN                               Edit style: E [FIND]
Mail menu:   EMC                          Mail destination: ALL-IN-1

Notification of:

  New mail:       Y     Print completion:  Y     Batch completion:    Y
  Display Tasks:  Y     Count Tasks:       Y     Send mail receipts:  Y

Initial TM form: TMMENU                      12 hour clock: Y

Working week:

  First day:    2     Start hour: 08:00am      Meal hour: Start: 12:00pm
  No. of days:  5     End hour:   05:00pm                   End: 01:00pm

  Advanced calendar day position: 2
  Calendar time increment (in minutes): 00015

Press RETURN to complete or press NEXT SCREEN for more details
                                                              (more...)
```

Figure 3.5 Sample data-entry form and selection list

3. Press [FIND] ([GOLD] L) or [GOLD] S to list possible entries for the field, then select an entry.

[FIND] — a. Press [FIND] (or [GOLD] L) to display all entries that *begin* with characters already entered in the field (all possible entries if the field is blank).

[GOLD] S — Press [GOLD] S to display all entries that *contain* the characters already entered in the field. This function key, known as GOLD EMBEDDED SEARCH, requires authorization from the system administrator because it uses more computing resources to accomplish a search.

Notes: If there is only one entry that matches the characters you've entered, ALL-IN-1 completes the field with the matching entry and does not display a list.

The following message indicates that the look-up feature is not available for the current field. In this case, try pressing [HELP] (or [GOLD] H) to display information about the field.

```
You cannot use FIND or GOLD EMBEDDED SEARCH
here.
```

***line-number*[RETURN]**

b. Type the line number corresponding to the entry you wish to select, and press [RETURN].

3.2.3 Exercise: Completing a Data-Entry Form

The following exercise illustrates the steps for completing a data-entry form. This example is based on the Set Working Conditions form, which controls many attributes of your ALL-IN-1 environment. This form is described in Section 5.1, "Controlling Your Environment with User Setup."

1. Move to the Set Working Conditions form.

   US SWC [RETURN]

   From any menu, type "US SWC" and press [RETURN] to display the Set Working Conditions form.

2. The next series of steps illustrates how the [FIND] key lists possible entries for a field.

   IMPORTANT: Jot down the contents of the Edit Style field (on the second line). The following exercise alters this field and then instructs you to enter the original contents.

   [DOWN ARROW]

   a. Press [DOWN ARROW] to move to the Main Screen field. Note that you can use the [UP ARROW] and [DOWN ARROW] keys to quickly move through the lines of a data-entry form.

   [TAB] [ERASE LINE]

   b. Press [TAB] to move to the Edit Style field, then press [ERASE LINE] (F13 or LF) to clear the contents of the field.

   [FIND]

   c. Press [FIND] (or [GOLD] L) to display a list of possible entries for the Edit Style field.

   ***line-number*[RETURN]**

   d. Type the line number corresponding to your original Edit Style and press [RETURN]. For example, if your Edit Style was originally EDT and the corresponding line number is 2, type "2" and press [RETURN].

3. The next series of steps illustrates what happens when you enter an invalid entry in a field checked by ALL-IN-1.

IMPORTANT: Jot down the contents of the Edit Style field (on the second line). The following exercise alters this field and then instructs you to reset it to its original contents.

[ERASE LINE]	a. With your cursor in the Edit Style field, press [ERASE LINE] (F13 or LF) to clear the field.

XXX[TAB]	b. Type "XXX" and press [TAB]. Because this is an invalid value for Edit Style, ALL-IN-1 displays this message:
	`That entry was not recognized`
	`(Press HELP for Help)`

[HELP]	c. Press [HELP] (or [GOLD] H). ALL-IN-1 displays Help information at the bottom of your screen.
[EXIT]	d. Read the Help information, and press [EXIT] (F10 or Keypad-0).
original-edit-style	e. Type the original contents of the Edit Style field. For example, type "EDT" if your Edit Style was originally EDT.

4. The next series of steps illustrates the keys that move through the data-entry form.

[BACKSPACE] **[BACKSPACE]** **[BACKSPACE]** **[BACKSPACE]**	a. Press [BACKSPACE] (F12) four times to confirm that this key moves to previous fields. ALL-IN-1 displays the following message when you attempt to move before the first field. `You cannot use PREV FIELD at this point`
[NEXT SCREEN]	b. Press [NEXT SCREEN] (or [GOLD] [TAB]) to display the next screen of fields in the data-entry form. You can now move your cursor forward and change any field on this screen.
[PREV SCREEN]	c. Press [PREV SCREEN] (or [GOLD] [BACKSPACE]) to display the original screen.

5. Finally, complete the data-entry form.

[RETURN] **[RETURN]**	Press [RETURN] twice to complete the form and return to the menu.

3.3 MANAGING MULTIPLE ITEMS WITH INDEX FORMS

Index forms are an important productivity tool, perhaps the most important in ALL-IN-1. The principle behind the index is simple: First create a list of items, then work from the list. You've probably used this method in the past to organize your work.

Whenever you have a lot of things to do, it always helps to make a list of tasks before you proceed. This is equally true when working in ALL-IN-1.

Figure 3.6 shows an example of an index: the Events at a Glance index provided by Time Management. You can work with items from an index just as you would work with items at a menu. Just enter a menu option at the bottom of the index. Menu options are listed on another screen, the Index menu (displayed with [GOLD] M).

Working with an index form provides the following benefits when compared with the menu:

- You can easily create a list of items for review (a list of documents, messages, appointments, etc.). The list of appointments shown in Figure 3.6 is a good example.
- It is easier to select and manage a single item when working from an index. See Section 3.3.5, "Working with a Single Item in an Index."
- Working with an index enables you to select and work with multiple items. Section 3.3.6, "Working with Multiple Items in an Index," shows you how to do this.

An index is actually a multipart form. The three different forms (see page 48) that make up an index are shown in Figure 3.7.

```
                 Events at a Glance: Tuesday      08-Nov-1994
(Selections: 0  )         (Meetings waiting: 0  )         (New messages: 0  )
Events for: WASHINGTON
--------------------------------------------------------------------------------
  No. Type Start   End     Purpose
--------------------------------------------------------------------------------
> 1     A  08:00am 09:00am Eye Doctor's appointment
  2     A  10:30am 11:30am Meet with clients from Westbrook Technology
  3     A  12:00pm 01:30pm Department lunch at the Broker
  4     A  02:30pm 03:00pm Conference call: New York sales

--------------------------------------------------------------------------------
Move to item and enter option (press GOLD MENU to see options,
or HELP for more information)
```

Figure 3.6 Events at a Glance index form

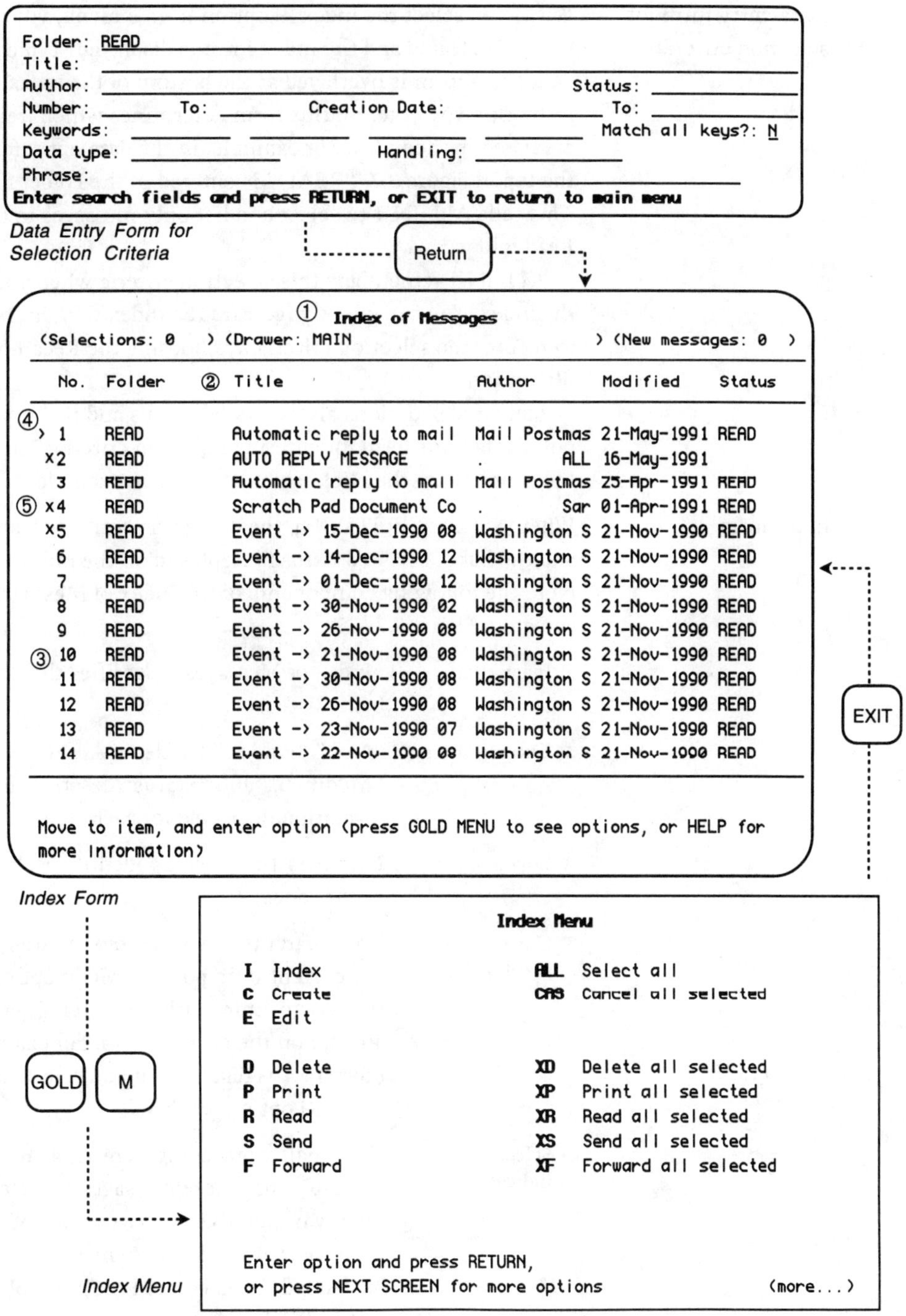

Figure 3.7 Index of messages

Data-entry form for selection criteria	When you select the index (I) option from a menu, your screen is cleared and the index form is displayed. Typically, a data-entry form is overlayed at the bottom of the index. Information you enter on this form determines which items are listed in the index. For example, in the data-entry form at the top of Figure 3.7, "READ" is entered in the Folder field. This tells ALL-IN-1 to select and list only messages in the Read folder. ALL-IN-1 remembers this selection criteria when you exit the index. You can quickly recreate the index *without* having to reenter the selection criteria by choosing the Recall Index (RI) option. Some index options always list all items and therefore do not display this form for entering selection criteria. The Index option on the Nicknames menu is an example.
Index form	When you press [RETURN], the data-entry form is cleared, and the list of selected items is displayed on the index form. Note the following components of the Index of Messages shown in Figure 3.7:

① Index title	"Index of Messages" identifies the items being listed.
② Column titles	"No.," "Folder," "Title," "Author," "Modified," and "Status" describe the information displayed for each item.
③ Line numbers	Numbers 1 through 14 identify each item in the index.
④ Current item pointer	The greater than sign (>) next to item 1 is the current item pointer. Menu options that do not start with the letter *X* generally act on the current item. For example, message 1 is displayed if you select the Read (R) option.
⑤ Selected item indicator	The small *x* preceding items 2, 4, and 5 indicates that these messages are selected for any option that manages multiple items. For example, these messages would be deleted if you entered the Multiple Delete (XD) option.

Index menu	The last part of the index is the Index menu, which lists options that you can enter from an index. This form is "hidden" behind the index of items, but you can display it by

pressing [GOLD] M. Once you learn the options listed on the menu, you rarely need to display the menu because you can enter menu options at the bottom of the index.

3.3.1 Working with an Index

In summary, there are four basic steps for working with an index. The sections that follow describe each of these steps in detail.

1. Create the index of items.
2. Select or deselect items in the index.
3. Choose menu options to manage the selected items.
4. Exit the index when finished.

3.3.2 Creating an Index of Items

This section describes how to create an index, or list, of items with which to work. The following procedure works for most index options, although there are some index options that work in a slightly different manner.

To create and display an index of items:

***subsystem*[RETURN]**

a. From any menu, type the option for the subsystem (WP for Word and Document Processing, EM for Electronic Messaging, etc.), then press [RETURN]. Remember, you can stack options, so why not add a space followed by "I" and skip step b? For example, enter "WP I" and press [RETURN].

I[RETURN]

b. Type "I" and press [RETURN] to create an index. ALL-IN-1 displays the index with a data-entry form at the bottom.

Hint: When creating an index from the Word and Document Processing, Electronic Messaging, or File Cabinet maintenance menus, you can add a folder name after the "I" to quickly build an index for the folder. For example, "I READ" creates an index of documents in your Read folder.

***data*[TAB]...**

c. Enter information to select items for the index. Remember that any item selected for the index must match the information you enter. Refer to Section 3.2.1, "Completing a Data-Entry Form," for details.

Leave all fields blank to create an index of *all* items (documents, messages, appointments, etc.).

[RETURN]

d. Press [RETURN] to create the index. ALL-IN-1 clears the data-entry form and displays the index of selected items.

[NEXT SCREEN]

e. Display any additional pages of the index by pressing [NEXT SCREEN] (or [GOLD] [TAB]).

You are now ready to select items and enter menu options to manage items. Note that after you have finished working with this index of items and return to the menu, you can quickly recreate this index without having to reenter selection criteria by choosing the Recall Index (RI) option. This option always redisplays the *last* index you created.

3.3.3 Index Form Function Keys

The function keys active at an index perform such operations as moving the current item pointer (>) and displaying the Index menu. Review the list of keys in Table 3.8 to become familiar with the various functions they perform. It helps to try the keys while reviewing the list.

Table 3.8 Index form function keys

Press the Following Key(s)	*To Perform This Action*
[DOWN ARROW]	Move the current item pointer (>) down one line.
[UP ARROW]	Move the current item pointer (>) up one line.
[NEXT SCREEN] (or [GOLD] [TAB])	Display the next screen of items.
[PREV SCREEN] (or [GOLD] [BACKSPACE])	Display the previous screen of items.
[GOLD] B	Move the current item pointer to the last item in the index.
[GOLD] T	Move the current item pointer to the first item in the index.
[SELECT] (or Keypad-Period)	Select the item next to the current item pointer (>). A small *x* appears next to the selected item.
[GOLD] [SELECT] (or [GOLD] Keypad-Period)	Deselect the item next to the current item pointer (>) and remove the *x*.
[GOLD] F	Return from the index to the subsystem menu and place the current item in the menu's current item block.
[GOLD] M	Display the Index menu.
[GOLD] V	Display the current item or information about the current item. Often the same as entering the Read option.
[EXIT] (F10 or Keypad-0)	Return from the menu to the index.

3.3.4 Displaying the Index Menu

You work with items appearing in the index by entering menu options at the bottom of the index form. The menu can be displayed at any time with [GOLD] M. Most of the options on the subsystem menu that manage the current item also appear on the Index menu. There are also options on the Index menu to manage multiple items.

Note that you don't have to display the Index menu to enter an option. If you know the option, simply type it at the bottom of the index, and press [RETURN].

Perform the following steps to display the Index menu and select an option:

[GOLD] M	a. Press [GOLD] (PF1), then type "M" to display the menu.
[NEXT SCREEN]...	b. Display any additional pages of the Index menu by pressing [NEXT SCREEN] (or [GOLD] [TAB]).
***option*[RETURN]**	c. Enter an option and press [RETURN]. The option is executed. When complete, the index of items is redisplayed.

3.3.5 Working with a Single Item in an Index

You can select and work with a single item in an index just as you would work with an item at a menu. You have two advantages when working from an index:

- You see the list of items you're working with. As you create, edit, and delete items, the list of items in the index changes to reflect your work. For example, if you deleted the current item (item 1) in the index shown in Figure 3.7, the folder name would be changed to Wastebasket.
- It is easier to select an item from an index. For example, to select the third message shown in Figure 3.7, simply type "3" and press [RETURN]. The current item pointer (>) then moves to line 3.

Perform the following steps to select and work with a single item in an index.

***line-number*[RETURN]**	a. Move the current item pointer (>) to the item you want to select. Type the line number and press [RETURN] (or press [DOWN ARROW] or [UP ARROW] to move the pointer). Press [NEXT SCREEN] (or [GOLD] [TAB]) to see any additional pages of items. *Hint:* Save time by combining steps a and b. Type the line number followed by a space and the menu option. For example, type "2 R" and press [RETURN] to read item 2.

menu-option[RETURN]

b. Type a menu option and press [RETURN] to manage the current item. For example, type "E" and press [RETURN] to edit the item.

Press [GOLD] M to display the Index menu if you don't remember the options. Options that manage a single item are generally listed on the left side of the Index menu.

c. Enter whatever information is required for the menu option.

3.3.6 Working with Multiple Items in an Index

The greatest advantage to working with an index, as compared to working with a menu, is that you can easily manage multiple items. Simply select all desired items, then enter one of the menu options that manages "all selected" items.

The easiest way to select items is to type the corresponding line numbers, then press [SELECT]. A small *x* appears next to the selected items. For example, in Figure 3.7, you can see that items 2, 4 , and 5 are selected. If you make a mistake in selecting items, simply type the line numbers of the items you want to deselect, and press [GOLD] [SELECT].

Note that the item next to the current item pointer is *not* one of the selected items. Only the items marked with an *x* are selected. You can work with the current item by entering a menu option such as Read, however, without affecting the selection process. This is handy if you want to review an item before selecting it.

To select or deselect multiple items in an index, perform these steps:

line,line-line,...[SELECT]

a. Type the line numbers, separated by commas, and press [SELECT]. You can also specify a range of items by entering the lower line number and higher line number, separated by a hyphen. Examples are shown in Table 3.9. ALL-IN-1 places an *x* next to selected items.

line,line-line,...[GOLD][SELECT]

To deselect items, type the line numbers or range of line numbers, separated by commas, then press [GOLD] [SELECT] (or [GOLD] Keypad-Period).

[NEXT SCREEN]

b. Press [NEXT SCREEN] (or [GOLD] [TAB]) to see any additional pages of items, and repeat the selection process.

To select or deselect all items on the index, follow these steps:

ALL[RETURN]

a. Type ALL and press [RETURN]. ALL-IN-1 places an *x* next to every item.

Table 3.9 Examples of selecting items in an index

Enter the Following	*To Perform This Action*
3 [SELECT]	Select item 3.
3 [RETURN] [SELECT]	Move the cursor to line 3 and select the item.
3 [GOLD] [SELECT]	Deselect item 3.
4,7,9-13 [SELECT]	Select items 4, 7, 9, 10, 11, 12, and 13.
9-11 [GOLD] [SELECT]	Deselect items 9, 10, and 11.
ALL [RETURN]	Select all items in the index.
CAS [RETURN]	Deselect all selected items.

CAS[RETURN]

b. To deselect *all* selected items, type "CAS" and press [RETURN].

After selecting items, enter a menu option to manage all selected items. These are menu options that begin with the letter *X* (XR to read all selected items, XP to print all selected items, etc.). The names of these options begin with an *X* because you are managing all items marked with an *x*. If you don't remember the menu options, press [GOLD] M to display the menu.

NOTE: Items are processed in the order selected. For example, item 5 is printed before item 3 if you type 5, 3, press [SELECT], and choose the Print All Selected (XP) option.

3.3.7 Exercise: Working with an Index of Events

In this exercise, you'll schedule four appointments in your calendar to create the following daily schedule. You will work with the Events at a Glance index in the Time Management subsystem. Events at a Glance is extremely useful because it lists appointments and meetings for a single day.

Sample daily schedule

Date	*Start*	*End*	*Description*
(today)	8:00 A.M.	9:00 A.M.	Eye doctor's appointment
(today)	10:30 A.M.	11:30 A.M.	Meet with clients from Westbrook Technology
(today)	12:00 P.M.	1:30 P.M.	Department lunch at the Broker
(today)	2:30 P.M.	3:00 P.M.	Conference call: New York sales

Perform the steps on the next page to schedule these events in your calendar.

1. Move to the Events at a Glance index in Time Management.

   TM EG[RETURN] — From any menu, type "TM EG" and press [RETURN] to move to the Events at a Glance index.

2. Set the calendar date to today's date.

   SD[RETURN] — a. Type "SD" and press [RETURN].

   Set Date: **TODAY[RETURN]** — b. Enter "TODAY" (or simply the abbreviation "TOD") and press [RETURN].

3. Create the first event in your calendar.

   C[RETURN] — a. Type "C" and press [RETURN]. ALL-IN-1 displays the Create Event form shown in Figure 3.8.

   [TAB]08:00am[TAB]... — b. Enter the details of the first event. Press [TAB] after completing a field to move to the next field.

   [RETURN] — c. Press [RETURN] to complete the Create Event form and schedule the event in your calendar. ALL-IN-1 displays the new appointment in the index.

4. Create the remaining appointments in the sample daily schedule. Repeat the procedure in step 3 for all three remaining events. The resulting display will look like the Events at a Glance index shown in Figure 2.5 in Chapter 2.

5. Edit the first appointment to change the start time to 8:15 A.M.

   1[RETURN] — a. Type "1" and press [RETURN] to make sure that the current item pointer (>) is next to the first event.

   E[RETURN] — b. Type "E" and press [RETURN] to edit the first appointment. ALL-IN-1 displays the first event.

```
                              Create Event

Scheduler:  WASHINGTON

Date:       08-Nov-1994      Start Time: 08:00am    End Time: 09:00am
Purpose:    Eye Doctor's Appointment
Confidential? (Y/N)      N
Invite Attendees? (Y/N)  N
Location (if attendees): ____________________

Enter information and press RETURN
```

Figure 3.8 Create Event form

Date: **[TAB]**	c. Press [TAB] to move to the Start Time field.
Start Time: **08:15am**	d. Type "08:15am" to change the time.
[RETURN]	e. Press [RETURN] to complete the form and change the appointment in your calendar. The change is reflected in the Events at a Glance index.

6. Select and display several appointments.

1,2,4[SELECT]	a. Type line numbers "1,2,4" and then press [SELECT]. An *x* appears next to each selected appointment.
XR[RETURN]	b. Type "XR" and press [RETURN] to display all selected events.
[RETURN] **[RETURN]** **[RETURN]**	c. Press [RETURN] three times to view the appointments in full.
CAS[RETURN]	d. Type "CAS" and press [RETURN] to cancel all selections. The small *x* is removed from each item.

7. Select all appointments, display the Index menu, and then delete all selected appointments.

ALL[RETURN]	a. Type "ALL" and press [RETURN] to select all items. An *x* appears next to every item.
[GOLD] M	b. Press [GOLD] (PF1), then type "M" to display the menu.
XD[RETURN]	c. Type "XD" and press [RETURN] to delete the appointments.
Y[RETURN]	d. Type "Y" and press [RETURN] when ALL-IN-1 asks you to confirm whether you want to delete these events. The change is reflected in the Events at a Glance index.
[EXIT SCREEN]	e. Press [EXIT SCREEN] (F10 or Keypad-0) to return to the menu.

Reading and Printing in ALL-IN-1

CHAPTER 4

In Chapter 3, you learned how to enter information by filling out a form. In upcoming chapters, you'll learn how to enter text information with one of the various ALL-IN-1 editors. ALL-IN-1 stores and organizes this information so you can display or print it on demand.

The Read (R) and Print (P) options appear on most menus in ALL-IN-1. These options allow you to display information on your terminal or send it to the printer. Learning how these options work is fundamental to accessing information in ALL-IN-1.

In this chapter, you'll learn how to

- Display information on your terminal, including how to scan back and forth while reading documents and how to search for specific strings of text.
- Send information to your printer to make hard copies.
- Manage print jobs with Job Services.

4.1 READING IN ALL-IN-1

The Read (R) option is one of the seven standard options that appear on almost every menu in ALL-IN-1. This option displays the current item on your terminal screen, the current item being the current message in Electronic Messaging, the current document in Word and Document Processing, the current event in Time Management (Events), and so on.

The Read option has many features, including these:

- Items (messages, documents, events, etc.) are displayed one screen at a time. ALL-IN-1 waits for you to enter [RETURN] before displaying the next screen. This gives you all the time you need to read information.
- You can copy the current screen to your Scratch Pad at any time while reading information.
- When reading a message or document, you can scan back and forth to view the information. You can also move multiple lines, screens, or pages either forward or backward and search for text in either direction.

- When reading a message or document, you can enter menu options to perform operations like printing and refiling.

To read an item in ALL-IN-1, perform the following steps:

1. If the current item is not the one you want to display, select the correct item. (Sections 3.1.3, 3.3.5, and 3.3.6 describe these steps in greater detail.)

   When working with a menu:

[SELECT]	a. Press [SELECT] (or type "SEL" and press [RETURN]). ALL-IN-1 displays a data-entry form.
...[RETURN]	b. Enter information to specify the item you want to display, and press [RETURN].

   When working with an index:

***line* [RETURN]**	Type the line number of the single item you want to display, and press [RETURN]. The current item pointer (>) will be positioned next to the item.
***line,line-line,...* [SELECT]**	Or type the line numbers or range of line numbers of all items you want to display and press [SELECT]. An *x* is placed next to all selected items.

2. Choose the Read option.

R [RETURN]	a. Type "R" and press [RETURN] (or type "XR" to read all selected items in an index). ALL-IN-1 displays the item or items.
[RETURN]...	b. Continue to press [RETURN] to see additional screens of information. ALL-IN-1 returns to the menu after the last screen.

4.1.1 Reading a Document

The Read (R) option on the Electronic Messaging and Word and Document Processing menus displays the current message or document. A number of additional features are available when reading text that you don't have when reading screen-oriented items, such as events. These include the ability to scan back and forth between pages and to enter menu options to manage the current document.

4.1.1.1 Read Document Function Keys

Table 4.1 lists the function keys that are active when you're reading a document. These keys perform special operations, such as skipping back and forth through pages of text. In the table, certain function keys are preceded by the letter *n*. These function keys accept a number that indicates how far you want to move through the text. For example, you can type "3" and press [GOLD] [DOWN ARROW] to move three pages forward in the current document. You can omit the number to move just one line, screen, page, and so on.

Table 4.1 Function keys for reading documents

Press the Following Key(s)	*To Perform This Action While Reading a Document*
n [DOWN ARROW]	Move down one or more lines in the text.
n [UP ARROW]	Move up one or more lines in the text.
n [NEXT SCREEN] (or *n* [GOLD] A)	Move forward one or more screens in the text.
n [PREV SCREEN] (or *n* [GOLD] [BKSP])	Move backward one or more screens in the text.
n [GOLD] [DOWN ARROW]	Move forward one or more pages.
n [GOLD] [UP ARROW]	Move backward one or more pages.
n [GOLD] [LEFT ARROW]	Shift the text eight or more columns to the left (useful for wide documents).
n [GOLD] [RIGHT ARROW]	Shift the text eight or more columns to the right.
text [FIND]	Locate the next occurrence of the specified string of text. If you omit the text and simply press [FIND], ALL-IN-1 displays a form on which you can enter the text.
[GOLD] [FIND] (or [GOLD] Period)	Continue searching for the next occurrence of the string.
[GOLD] B	Move to the bottom of the document.
[GOLD] T	Move to the top of the document.
[RETURN]	Display the next screen or return to the menu.
[EXIT] (F10 or Keypad-0)	Quit reading the current document and return to the menu.
[GOLD] C	Start continuous forward scrolling of the document.
[GOLD] E	Toggle between 80 and 132 columns shown in the display (useful for reading wide documents).
[GOLD] K	Quit reading the current new mail message and leave the message in your INBOX folder.
[GOLD] M	Display a menu of options you can enter while reading a document. (Table 4.2 describes these options.)
[GOLD] P	Copy the current screen to the Scratch Pad.
[GOLD] V	Redisplay the current message and display or suppress (toggle) the full distribution list.
[GOLD] Z	Display or clear document status information.

4.1.1.2 *Read Menu Options*

You can enter any of the options listed in Table 4.2 when reading a message or document. You can display this list of options with [GOLD] M, but you don't need to display the menu to enter an option. Simply type the option in response to the following prompt, and press [RETURN]:

```
Press RETURN to continue, GOLD MENU for options or EXIT to cancel option [RETURN]
```

Don't expect all of the selections listed in the table to appear on the Read menu. Certain options pertain to reading messages, and others pertain to reading documents.

Table 4.2 Read menu options

Enter This Read Menu Option	*To Perform the Following Action*
A (Answer)	Create a response to the current message.
CD (Convert Document)	Create a copy of the current document and convert the format.
CNS (Create Nickname for Sender)	Create a nickname for the sender of the current message.
CTS (Continue Text Search)	Locate the next occurrence of the search string.
D (Delete)	Place the current document in the Wastebasket.
DLM (Create Distribution List from Message)	Create a distribution list from the list of addressees in the current message.
E (Edit)	Edit the current document.
F (Forward)	Forward current message or document to another user.
FA (File Attachment)	File an attachment to the current document as a separate document.
FAM (File Attachment as Message)	File an attachment to the current document as a message with the status of "read."
FM (File Message)	Cross-file the current message and its attachments in a second folder.
FT (File Text)	File text of the current message as a separate document.
LM (Move to Left Margin)	Shift the document to display the left margin.
LU (Leave Message Unread)	Shift the document to display the right margin.
RM (Move to Right Margin)	Clear current message and leave it in the Inbox with an unread status. Applies only to new mail messages.
MCD (Make Copy of Document)	Make a copy of the current document.
MH (Modify Message Header)	Modify the list of addressees, the subject, the message priority, or the read/delivery receipt requests for the current created message.
N (Read Next Selected Document)	Display the next selected document.
NA (Read from Next Attachment)	Display the next attachment.
NDL (View Message without Distribution List)	Redisplay message, suppress names of addressees.
VDL (View Message with Distribution List)	Redisplay message including all addressees.

Table 4.2 *(continued)*

Enter This Read Menu Option	*To Perform the Following Action*
PA (Read Previous Attachment)	Redisplay the previous attachment.
NS (Narrow Screen)	Redisplay the document in 80-column format.
NSC (Read Next Screenful)	Display next screen of text.
PSC (Read Previous Screenful)	Display previous screen of text.
WS (Wide Screen)	Redisplay the document in 132-column format.
P (Print)	Print the current document.
RFD (Refile Document)	Refile the current document in another folder.
S (Send)	Send the current document to another user with Electronic Messaging.
SH (Show Document Header)	Display document status information.
TS (Text Search)	Search for a specific string of text in the document.
U (Update Index Information)	Update the current document's drawer, folder, title, keywords, author, or handling (format).
XFD (Cross-file Document)	Cross-file the current document in a second folder.

```
                          Text Search

 Search string:

 ______________________________________________________________

 Search direction: FORWARD

 Enter information and press RETURN
```

Figure 4.1 Text Search form for reading a document

4.1.1.3 Searching for Text While Reading a Document

ALL-IN-1 allows you to search for text when reading a message or document. This comes in handy when you're reading large documents and want to skip forward to a particular section within the document.

Perform the following steps to search for text while reading a document:

[FIND]

a. Press [FIND] (or [GOLD] Comma), or type "TS" and press [RETURN]. ALL-IN-1 displays the Text Search form shown in Figure 4.1.

   Hint: It's quicker if you type the text at the bottom of the screen first, then press [FIND]. You skip the form by doing this, but you cannot specify the direction.

text [RETURN] — b. To search for text in the current direction, type the text and press [RETURN].

text [TAB]
direction [RETURN] — c. To search in the reverse direction, type the text, press [TAB], change the direction by typing "FORWARD" or "REVERSE," and press [RETURN].

To find the next occurrence of the text string, do the following:

[GOLD] [FIND] — Press [GOLD] [FIND] (or [GOLD] Period). ALL-IN-1 locates and highlights the next occurrence of the string in the current direction. If the string is not found, ALL-IN-1 asks if you want to search in the reverse direction.

4.1.2 Exercise: Reading a Document

The following exercise shows you some of the features provided for reading documents. You begin by creating a new document and then retrieving text from a file shipped with version 3.0 of ALL-IN-1. This produces a relatively lengthy document to use for practice. It describes WPS-PLUS version 4 enhancements. (If you are a WPS-PLUS user, it might be worthwhile to read this document more thoroughly.) Although creating this document is not pertinent to learning how to read a document, it is useful in learning how to import external files into your File Cabinet.

1. First move to the Word and Document Processing menu.

   WP [RETURN] — Type "WP" and press [RETURN]. ALL-IN-1 displays the Word and Document Processing menu.

2. Create a new document by retrieving the library document V4_DEMO.WPL.

   C [RETURN] — a. Type "C" and press [RETURN]. ALL-IN-1 displays the Creating New Document form shown in Figure 4.2.

   [GOLD] T — b. Press [GOLD] T to move to the top of this form.

   Drawer: **MAIN [TAB]**
   Folder: **TEST [TAB]**
   Title: **WPS+ V4 [RETURN]** — c. Enter the drawer name "MAIN," folder name "TEST," and document name "WPS+ V4." Press [TAB] between fields, and press [RETURN] after the title. ALL-IN-1 invokes the editor.

   [GOLD] G — d. When the edit screen appears, press [GOLD] G to retrieve a document. ALL-IN-1 displays the Get Document menu.

```
                         Creating New Document

Drawer:   MAIN

Folder:

Title:

Keywords:

        Enter information and press RETURN,
        or press NEXT SCREEN for more fields                    (more...)
```

Figure 4.2 Creating New Document form

VMS [RETURN]

e. Type "VMS" and press [RETURN] to indicate that you want to retrieve a document from the VMS file system. ALL-IN-1 prompts you for the VMS file specification.

VMS file name:
WPL$LIB:V4_DEMO.WPL [RETURN]

f. Type the file name "WPL$LIB:V4_DEMO.WPL" and press [RETURN]. ALL-IN-1 retrieves the file. An error will be displayed when this file is not available. If this occurs, you might try selecting one of your existing documents or messages and making the appropriate substitutions in step 3 of this exercise.

[GOLD] F

g. Press [GOLD] F to exit the editor and file the document.

3. Read the document, and try various function keys to scan through the text.

R [RETURN]

a. Type "R" and press [RETURN]. ALL-IN-1 displays the first page of the document.

[RETURN]

b. Press [RETURN] to advance to the next screen of text. You should see the screen shown in Figure 4.3 if your editor is set to WPS-PLUS. If you have a different editor selected, you might see a different area of the document.

[NEXT SCREEN]

c. Press [NEXT SCREEN] to advance to the next screen of text.

[PREV SCREEN]

d. Press [PREV SCREEN] to go back one screen.

60 [DOWN ARROW]

e. Type "60" and press [DOWN ARROW] to move 60 lines forward in the document.

```
                         New Features

                       of WPS-PLUS V4.0

                         for ALL-IN-1

----------------------------------- NEW PAGE -----------------------------------



              New Features of WPS-PLUS V4.0 for ALL-IN-1

This document summarizes the new, improved, and enhanced features contained
in WPS-PLUS V4.0 for ALL-IN-1.  It was created using WPS-PLUS V4.0!!

(1) MULTIPLE DOCUMENT EDITING

    Users can now edit up to 10 documents simultaneously, with various means
    of switching the edit session from one document to another.  These
    documents can be created, edited, and filed individually, and CUT and
    PASTE operations can be performed between open documents.

Press RETURN to continue, GOLD MENU for options or EXIT to cancel
```

Figure 4.3 Reading a document

3 [GOLD] [DOWN ARROW]	f. Type "3" and press [GOLD] [DOWN ARROW] to move three pages forward in the document.
[GOLD] T	g. Press [GOLD] T to move to the top of the document.
multi [FIND]	h. Type "multi" and press [FIND] (or [GOLD] Comma) to locate this string of text.
[GOLD] [FIND]	i. Press [GOLD] [FIND] (or [GOLD] Period) to find the next occurrence of the string.

4. Display the Read menu, and enter an option.

[GOLD] M	a. Press [GOLD] M. ALL-IN-1 displays the Read menu, shown in Figure 4.4.
SH [RETURN]	b. Type "SH" and press [RETURN] to display document status information.
[EXIT]	c. Press [EXIT] (F10 or Keypad-0) to return to the document.
[EXIT]	d. Press [EXIT] again to exit the Read option and return to the menu.

```
                              Read Menu

  E   Edit                          FAM  File attachment as message
  D   Delete                        FA   File attachment as document
  P   Print                         NA   Read from next attachment
  S   Send                          PA   Read previous attachment
  F   Forward

  CD  Convert document              RFD  Refile document
  SH  Show document header          XFD  Cross-file document
                                    MCD  Make copy of document
                                    U    Update index information




  Enter option and press RETURN,
  or press NEXT SCREEN for more options                    (more...)
```

Figure 4.4 Read menu

4.2 PRINTING IN ALL-IN-1

The Print (P) option is another option that appears on most menus in ALL-IN-1. Print sends the current item (message, document, event, etc.) to a printer to produce a hard copy. Technically speaking, your document is sent as a single print *job* to a queue of documents waiting to be formatted, then printed. Most of this technical stuff is transparent to you. You simply select the Print option, and your document comes out on the printer sooner or later. The mechanics of printing are discussed further in Section 4.3, "Print and Batch Job Services," to help you understand what happens in those situations when your document does not print.

The Print option offers these features:

- You can select a different print destination with each print operation. Print destinations include any system printer set up properly by your system manager, a local printer attached to your terminal, or the terminal screen itself. In addition, the Print option enables you to send the output to a document in your ALL-IN-1 File Cabinet or a VMS file.
- You can specify a series of printing options, including the number of copies to produce, the time of day to print the document, whether to print a cover page, and whether to issue a notification upon print completion.
- Once you've set your printer destination and printing options, ALL-IN-1 remembers these settings for the next print operation.

Additional options available for printing documents prepared with WPS-PLUS are discussed in Section 10.1.9, "Printing WPS-PLUS Documents." When printing WPS-PLUS documents, you can further control such formatting characteristics as pagination, page margins, and footnote placement.

There are four basic steps to printing any item in ALL-IN-1:

1. Move to the subsystem menu or index for the item you wish to print.
2. Select the item you wish to print.
3. Select the Print (P) option.
4. Modify print settings on the Printing Document form (if necessary), and press [RETURN] to print the document.

It takes just a few seconds to execute these steps, but don't run immediately to the printer to grab your printout. Some time is required to print your document, even with the fastest printers. It is also possible that someone else might be using the printer.

It is recommended that you set the Print Completion Notification flag to "Y" with Set Working Conditions in User Setup (US SWC) to deal with any delay in printing. Setting this option causes the system to send you a message when your document is almost finished printing. You can then go to the printer to retrieve your document. By the way, if the print notification message rearranges text on your screen, press [CTRL] W to repaint the screen and clear the message.

Following are the detailed steps for printing an item in ALL-IN-1:

1. If the current item is not the one you want to print, select the correct item. (Sections 3.1.3, 3.3.5, and 3.3.6 describe these steps in greater detail.)

   When working with a menu:

[SELECT]	a. Press [SELECT] (or type "SEL" and press [RETURN]). ALL-IN-1 displays a data-entry form.
...[RETURN]	b. Enter information to specify the item you want to print, and press [RETURN].

   When working with an index:

line-number **[RETURN]**	Type the line number of the single item you want to print, and press [RETURN]. The current item pointer (>) is positioned next to the item.
line,line-line,... **[SELECT]**	Or type the line numbers or range of line numbers of all items you want to print, and press [SELECT]. An *x* is placed next to all selected items.

```
                          Printing Document

Document destination: SYS$PRINT_____

Print style:          ______________________________

Number of copies:     1_

Enter information and press RETURN,
or GOLD EXPAND to change printing settings
or NEXT SCREEN to change WPS-PLUS formatting settings        (more...)
```

Figure 4.5 Printing Document form

2. Choose the Print option.

P [RETURN]

a. Type "P" and press [RETURN] (or type "XP" to print all selected items in an index). ALL-IN-1 displays the Printing Document form, shown in Figure 4.5.

[RETURN]

b. If the printer name shown in the Document Destination field and the number of copies are correct, press [RETURN] to print. ALL-IN-1 redisplays the menu and prints your document. If you want to change the document destination, the number of copies, or other print settings, proceed to step 3.

3. Perform the following steps to change print document options. (Look ahead to Table 4.3 for a description of these options.)

Document destination:

***printer* [TAB]**

a. You can send your printout to a different printer by changing the Document Destination field. If you know your document destination, type the name, press [TAB], and proceed to step 3b.

[ERASE LINE] [FIND]
***line-number* [RETURN]**
[TAB]

If you do not know printer names, press [ERASE LINE] (F13 or LF) to clear the field, and press [FIND] (or [GOLD] L) to display a list of printer names. To select a printer, type the corresponding line number and press [RETURN]. The selected printer name appears in the Document Destination field. Press [TAB] to move to the Print Style field.

Print style: ***format-style* [TAB]**

b. The Print Style field is automatically filled in when you select a document destination. In general, you should use the default value. You can select a different Print Style to alter the formatting of your document. If you don't know style names, press [ERASE LINE] (F13 or LF), then press [FIND] (or [GOLD] L) to display and select from a list of styles. Press [TAB] to move to the next field.

Number of copies: ***number***

c. Change the number of copies to print more than one copy.

[RETURN]

d. To print with the current print settings, press [RETURN]. ALL-IN-1 redisplays the menu and prints your document.

[GOLD] E

If you want to change the print settings, press [GOLD] E to display the Print Settings form, and proceed to step 4.

[NEXT SCREEN]

If you want to change the printing options for a WPS-PLUS document, press [NEXT SCREEN] (or [GOLD] A). Refer to Section 10.1.9, "Printing WPS-PLUS Documents," in Chapter 10 for further details.

4. Complete the Print Settings form to change print settings. The first screen of this form is shown in Figure 4.6.

a. Modify the parameters on the first screen of the Print Settings form. Refer to Section 3.2.1, "Completing a Data-Entry Form," for details on how to move around and enter information. (Look ahead to Table 4.4 for a description of the purpose of each field.)

[NEXT SCREEN]

b. Press [NEXT SCREEN] (or [GOLD] [TAB]) to move to the second screen of the form. Modify these print settings as necessary.

[RETURN]
[RETURN]

c. Press [RETURN] twice when you've finished modifying the print settings. ALL-IN-1 redisplays the menu and prints your document.

[EXIT]

Press [EXIT] (F10 or Keypad-0) to exit this form without changing the print settings.

```
                              Print Settings

Print Style:                LP11
Description:                Digital LP11 ANSI format
Printer Device:             LP11
Final Form:                 LP11
Destination Type:

Burst page          (Y/N):  N
Flag page           (Y/N):  N
Trailer page        (Y/N):  N
Form feed           (Y/N):  N
Notify user         (Y/N):  N
Headers             (Y/N):  N
Distribution list   (Y/N):  Y

Number of copies:           1
Print priority:             100
Job Name:                   TEST_DOCUMENT
Hold Job            (Y/N):  N
Release time:

Press RETURN to complete, or press NEXT SCREEN for more fields    (more...)
```

Figure 4.6 Print Settings form

Once you've completed the Printing Document form and the Print Settings form, ALL-IN-1 formats your document for printing and submits the formatted output to a queue of documents waiting to be printed. You can monitor the activity of the queue with the Job Services subsystem.

4.2.1 Print Document Options

Table 4.3 on the next page lists the values that you specify when printing an item in ALL-IN-1. These fields appear on the Printing Document form, which is displayed immediately after you select the Print (P) or Multiple Print (XP) option.

4.2.2 Print Settings

You can change the print settings shown on page 71 in Table 4.4 with [GOLD] E at the time you print a document, or beforehand with the Set Default Printer Settings (PO) option on the User Defined Print Styles menu in User Setup. Note that you do not have to complete every one of the following fields of information to print your document. The default values are suitable for printing almost any document. Also, depending on the printer setup, you might not be able to access each setting described in the table.

Table 4.3 Print Document options

<table>
<tr><th>Print Option</th><th>Description</th></tr>
<tr><td>Document Destination[a]</td><td>This option refers to the name of the printer where you want to send your document. "SYS$PRINT" is a typical example that specifies the system line printer. Document destinations (printer names) vary greatly from one site to another. Generally, though, system managers establish a list of meaningful names that include the location and printer type: ACCTG_LN03R or COMPUTER_ROOM_LP32, for example.
You can also specify one of the following special names as a document destination:
<table>
<tr><td>TERMINAL</td><td>Sends the output to your terminal screen. This is extremely useful if you want to preview a document to check page breaks or multicolumn formatting before printing.</td></tr>
<tr><td>DOCUMENT</td><td>Outputs a formatted copy of the document to another document in your File Cabinet. This new formatted copy of the document can then be transferred to a co-worker, who can print or read the document, but not edit it. (See Section 4.2.3, "Formatting a Document," for more information.)</td></tr>
<tr><td>FILE</td><td>Creates a copy of the document, fully formatted, in a VMS file. This file can then be transferred to and printed on a system without ALL-IN-1's formatting capabilities.</td></tr>
<tr><td>PORT</td><td>Sends the output to a printer attached to your terminal or PC.</td></tr>
</table></td></tr>
<tr><td>Print Style[a]</td><td>This option determines the formatting of your document. This field is filled in automatically with the default value that best suits the printer's capabilities. You can, however, select a different style to perform special formatting if your site supports it. You can also define your own print styles with User Setup and then specify the name of your own print style here.</td></tr>
<tr><td>Number of Copies</td><td>For the number of copies to print, enter a value from 1 to 255.</td></tr>
</table>

[a] ALL-IN-1's lookup feature can be used in this field. Press [ERASE LINE] (F13 or LF) to clear the field, then press [FIND] (or [GOLD] L) to display a list of possible entries. Refer to Section 3.2.2, "Using [FIND] to Complete a Field," for further information on the lookup feature.

Some printers, such as DEC's PrinterServer 40 Plus LPS40, have advanced printing capabilities that you can select with the Print Settings form. You can specify the additional print settings listed in Table 4.5 when you choose this type of printer as your document destination.

Table 4.4 Print settings

Print Setting	*Description*
First Screen:	
Burst Page, Flag Page, Trailer Page, Form Feed	All of these parameters can be set to "Y" or "N" to indicate whether you want extra pages. Burst and flag pages are cover pages, a trailer is a page printed after your job, and form feed gives you an extra blank page before your document. In general, selecting these options wastes paper. Most laser printers issue a cover page by default. It is recommended that you set all of these flags to "N" unless you have problems separating your printout from those of other users.
Notify User	This setting indicates whether you want to be notified when printing is complete. The default is set with Set Working Conditions in User Setup. You can override the default here by entering "Y" or "N". ("Y" is recommended.)
Headers	This setting determines whether a header is printed at the top of each page. Enter "Y" or "N." (Headers are undesirable for most formal documents.)
Distribution List	This setting indicates whether or not you want to print the entire list of names in a distribution list, and applies to messages only. The default is set with Set Working Conditions in User Setup. You can override the default here by entering "Y" or "N" ("N" is recommended).
Number of Copies	Enter a value from 1 to 255 to specify the number of copies to print.
Print Priority	The print priority determines the order of entries in the print queue. Enter a value from 0 to 255. Typically, you must have special privileges to specify a print priority higher than everyone else.
Job Name	This setting refers to the name that appears on the cover page and in the Index of Jobs in Job Services. This defaults to the document name, which is sufficient in most cases.
Hold Job	Indicates whether you want the job to be held permanently on the print queue. Set this parameter to "N". If you enter "Y", you must later release the job with the Release Job (RJ) option on the Job Services index menu.
Release Time	This setting allows you to select the future date, time of day, or both when you want the document printed. If blank, the document prints immediately. This parameter is handy when you want to start printing a large document during off-hours. Enter a date/time in the format "dd-mmm-yyyy:hh:mm" or just "hh:mm"—for example, 21-SEP-1992:07:00A, 06:00P, or 18:00. Hold Job should be set to "N" if you specify a Release Time.
Second Screen:	
Combine XP Jobs	Enter "Y" when printing multiple documents with the XP option to tell ALL-IN-1 to print all selected documents together as a single job. If you enter "N," your documents are printed as separate jobs and might be interspersed with other users' output.
Maximum XP Jobs	Enter a value from 1 to 100 to tell the system the maximum number of documents to print together when Combine XP Jobs is set to "Y." If you're printing a large number of documents, you might enter a value of 10 or so to prevent your work from tying up the printer.

(continued)

Table 4.4 Print settings *(continued)*

Print Setting	*Description*
Passall	Sometimes, the system does not send special characters to a printer if it's possible that they might cause the printer to "go haywire." This action can suppress certain formatting triggered by these special characters. Set this parameter to "Y" in these instances.
Double Space	Enter "Y" to print your document double-spaced. Enter "N" for single spacing.
Lowercase	Enter "Y" to indicate that your document should be printed using both uppercase and lowercase characters. Enter "N" to print in all uppercase.
Restart	Enter "Y" to retain your job for a restart if a problem occurs with the system or the printer. Enter "N" if you prefer to reprint the document manually if a problem occurs.
First Page, Last Page	Enter the range of page numbers that you want printed. Leave these fields blank to print the entire document.
Print Form	This setting refers to the name or number of the form on which you want your document printed. A form is a group of characteristics (height, width, page orientation, etc.) that control formatting of your document. Contact your system manager for the names of the forms used at your site.
Note Text	This setting permits you to print a text message on the cover page of your document. This field is useful if you're printing a document for someone else.
Operator Text	This setting refers to a text message sent to the computer operator before your document is printed. A typical message might be to warn the operator that you need a special form loaded on the printer.
File setup, Characteristics	File setups and characteristics are special instructions that can be sent out before your document to tell the printer to perform a special print operation. For example, a file setup might instruct the printer to print the text sideways (landscape mode). These instructions are stored in a system table prepared by the system manager. Each instruction is given a unique name that you can enter here. Contact your system manager for the names of file setup modules and characteristics.

Table 4.5 Advanced print settings

Print Setting	*Description*
Number Up	Some printers can print multiple pages of text in a reduced size on a single sheet of paper. Enter a value from 1 to 100, indicating the number of pages per sheet (2 and 4 are recommended values).
Data Type[a]	Indicate the type of information being sent to the printer. PostScript is a common value; it specifies that the document contains PostScript format (fonts, graphics, etc.).
Input Tray[a]	Indicate the tray from which paper is pulled. Examples are top, bottom, etc.

Table 4.5 Advanced print settings *(continued)*

Print Setting	*Description*
Output Tray[a]	Some printers have multiple trays for output. Enter the name of the tray where you want your document placed after printing.
Page Orientation[a]	Enter "PORTRAIT" or "LANDSCAPE" to indicate that you want your document printed normally (letter format) or sideways.
Layup Definition	Enter the name of an external file that contains layup definition commands to control many of the characteristics listed on this page.
Fonts Used[a]	Enter the names of software fonts that must be loaded before your document is printed.
Sides[a]	Indicate whether you want your document printed on one side of the paper (simplex) or on both sides of the paper (duplex).
Keep Messages	Enter "Y" if you want print error messages kept in a file. Enter "N" to send the messages to your screen only.
Print Messages	Enter "Y" if you want error messages printed on a cover sheet.
Page Size[a]	Select the relative dimensions of the page for your printout (letter, legal, ledger, etc.) when printing multiple pages per sheet (see Number Up).
Sheet Size[a]	Select the paper size for your document (letter, legal, etc.).
Lower Page Limit, Upper Page Limit	Enter the numbers of the first and last pages of your document that you want printed. Leave these fields blank to print the entire document.
Sheet Count	Enter the number of copies you want made of each page. Copies are printed one after another and must be collated by hand.

[a] ALL-IN-1's lookup feature can be used in this field. Press [ERASE LINE] (F13 or LF) to clear the field, then press [FIND] (or [GOLD] L) to display a list of possible entries. Refer to Section 3.2.2, "Using [FIND] to Complete a Field," for further information on the lookup feature.

4.2.3 Formatting a Document

Formatting is the process of converting your document from what you see within the editor to what you see on the final, printed sheet of paper. Formatting is essentially the "typesetting" of your document. The final product of the formatting process is a file containing all of the text in the document, plus instructions to the printer explaining how to highlight and arrange text on the page: sort of a "camera-ready" version of your document that can be sent directly to the printer.

The capabilities of the printer are considered during formatting. For example, if the target printer does not support boldface, instructions might be placed in the output file to tell the printer to overpunch characters instead. Output formatted for a specific printer, therefore, cannot be sent to an entirely different type of printer.

Formatting occurs whenever you print a document. It occurs either in the foreground (while you wait) or in the background. The formatted output is then sent to the printer. This can be a time-consuming process, especially if you've included a lot of advanced formatting in your document.

The Format Document option allows you to perform the format process without printing the document. Output is then placed in a new document created in your File

Cabinet. This document cannot be edited, but it can be printed or transferred to another user. There are several reasons for formatting a document without printing:

- You can transfer the formatted output document to another system that does not have ALL-IN-1's formatting capabilities.
- You can transfer the formatted output document to another user who can print, but not modify, the document.
- You can print the formatted document repeatedly without having to wait for the formatting process to finish.

To format the current document without printing, move to either the Word and Document Processing menu or the Electronic Messaging menu, select the document, type "FMD," and press [RETURN]. ALL-IN-1 displays the Document Formatting form. Enter the type of printer you want the document formatted for, and press [RETURN]. If you're not sure what to enter, press [FIND] (or [GOLD] L) to display a list of available printer types. ALL-IN-1 displays the Creating Formatted Document form. Complete the form by changing the drawer and folder (if necessary) and entering a title for the document. Add something to the title, such as "(Formatted)," to indicate that this is a formatted copy of the original. Then press [RETURN].

If the document you're formatting is a WPS-PLUS document, ALL-IN-1 asks if you want to change WPS-PLUS formatting settings (pagination settings, footnote settings, etc.). Respond with "Y" if you want to change these settings. Section 10.1.9, "Printing WPS-PLUS Documents," describes this procedure in detail.

ALL-IN-1 formats the document, then displays a message that formatting is complete. You can then print the output document (without having to wait for formatting) or send the output document to another user with the Send (S) option.

4.2.4 User-Defined Print Styles

You can select numerous options when printing documents. In an effort to simplify the process of setting printing options, ALL-IN-1 allows you to define and save a group of print settings under a name of your own choosing. You can then enter this name as a Print Style when printing a document. This means that you fill out the Print Settings form once for each document type—not each and every time you are ready to print a document.

The User Defined Print Styles (UPS) option on the User Setup menu allows you to create and maintain user-defined print styles. You can also modify your default print settings with the PO option.

Perform the following steps to access the User Defined Print Styles menu:

US UPS [RETURN]	a. Type "US UPS" and press [RETURN]. ALL-IN-1 displays the User Defined Print Styles menu.
***option* [RETURN]**	b. Select one of the following options to create or maintain an existing print style:

SEL	Selects an existing print style.
C	Creates a new user-defined print style.
E	Modifies the current print style.
D	Deletes the current print style.
P	Prints the current print style.
R	Displays the current print style.
I	Lists existing print styles.
PO	Modifies your default print settings.

Select the Create option to create a brand-new print style. ALL-IN-1 prompts for the name of your new print style and for the name of an existing print style to be used as a template. Enter a new name that includes something unique, such as your initials. To enter the existing print style, it's easiest to press [FIND] (or [GOLD] L) to display a selection list of existing styles. You will then be asked to complete a Print Settings form, as described in Section 4.2, "Printing in ALL-IN-1." Refer back to Tables 4.4 and 4.5 for a description of print settings.

Once you have created a new print style, you can specify this name in the Print Style field of the Printing Document form the next time you print a document.

4.3 PRINT AND BATCH JOB SERVICES

ALL-IN-1 takes advantage of the operating system's queuing mechanism to avoid conflicts when a number of people share a printer. When you print, your document is placed in a *queue* (waiting line) of documents lined up to be sent to the printer. It is analogous to giving a bag to a ticket agent when you check in for a flight. Your document is placed on a list of documents for a specific printer, just as your bag is placed on a conveyor belt to be loaded onto a specific plane. Documents move "up" on the printer queue until they reach the top and are then printed, just as bags move forward on the conveyor belt until they are loaded onto a plane.

Why is it important to understand the details of print queues? It is important because you can control what happens to your document once it's been submitted for printing, even though you can't control what happens to your bag once you give it to the ticket agent. Remember, though, that print queues run a lot faster than conveyor belts. You sometimes have to act fast to prevent a large document from printing once it has been submitted.

Figure 4.7 illustrates a print queue. Each document waiting to be printed constitutes a separate *entry* in the queue. Entries in the queue are processed one at a time by background jobs that send documents in the queue to the printer. When you print a document, a copy of the document is added as a new entry (entry 109) at the end of the queue. When the current entry (entry 106) completes printing, the background jobs remove the entry from the queue and commence printing the next entry (entry 107). Eventually, your entry reaches the front of the the queue and is printed.

In addition to print queues, there are two other types of queues: server queues and batch queues. A server queue is a list of files waiting to be processed for a variety of

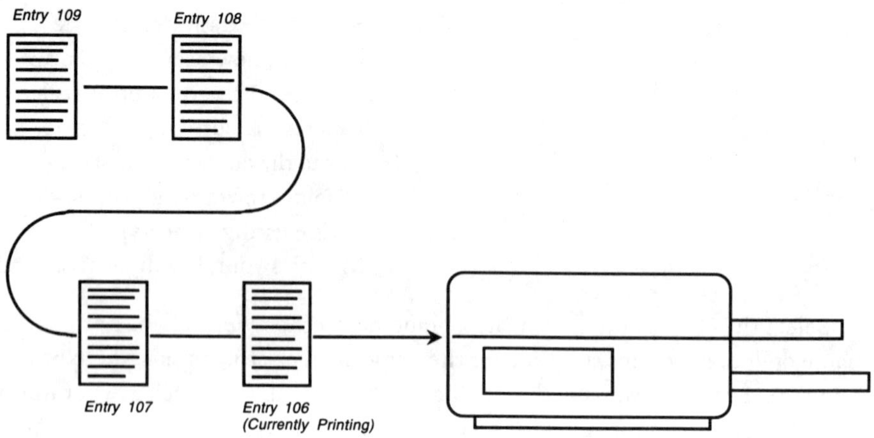

Figure 4.7 Printer queue

reasons. A good example is document formatting. Your system manager can set up printing so that formatting is done in the background. Documents are then automatically sent to a server queue for formatting before printing, and users don't have to wait for formatting to be completed when they print documents. A batch queue is a list of programs waiting to be run in the background. Many ALL-IN-1 system housekeeping procedures are run in batch; the Janitor is a good example. As a user of ALL-IN-1, you probably won't work very much with batch queues.

Job Services allows you to monitor the queue and, to some extent, control the printing after having submitted the document. For example, you can remove your document from the queue to stop it from printing. This would be analogous to removing your bag from the conveyor belt if you decided you didn't want to travel.

4.3.1 Accessing Job Services

Job Services allows you to manage your print jobs waiting in a queue. You can perform such operations as moving the job to another printer, changing the time of printing, or simply stopping the print job. Remember that this discussion applies only to jobs waiting in a queue. Jobs that have finished printing are removed from the queue and cannot be managed with Job Services.

Options on the Job Services menu create an index of pending jobs, similar to the index shown in Figure 4.8. Each line in this index represents a separate job waiting to be printed. You can select one or more jobs appearing in the index and manage these jobs by entering one of the menu options listed in Table 4.6 on page 79. Section 3.3.6, "Working with Multiple Items in an Index," shows you how to select and manage items in an index.

```
                              Index of Jobs
(Selections: 0  )                                        (New messages: 0  )
--------------------------------------------------------------------------------
  No.   Job              Queue          Submitted              Job status
--------------------------------------------------------------------------------
> 1     WPS_V4           OA$FORMATTER   11-Nov-1994 03:42pm    Holding
  2     OPERATOR_PROCED  OA$FORMATTER   11-Nov-1994 03:43pm    Timed release









--------------------------------------------------------------------------------

Move to item and enter option (press GOLD MENU to see options, or HELP for
more information)
```

Figure 4.8 Index of Jobs

Perform the following steps to access the Job Services menu and work with jobs waiting in a queue:

1. Move to the Job Services menu form.

   JS [RETURN] — From any menu, type "JS" and press [RETURN] to display the Job Services menu.

2. Select an option on the Job Services menu.

   ***menu-option* [RETURN]** — Type one of the following options from the Job Services menu and press [RETURN]. For example, type "IP" and press [RETURN] in order to list your print jobs.

I	Creates an index of print and/or batch jobs meeting certain selection criteria.
UI	Creates a new index with the same criteria entered the last time you selected the Index (I) option.

IAJ	Creates an index of print and batch jobs.
IP	Creates an index of pending print jobs.
IB	Creates an index of pending batch jobs.
IS	Creates an index of pending format jobs.

ALL-IN-1 displays a list of jobs waiting in queue or displays a message indicating that you have no pending jobs.

3. Select and manage a job.

***line-number* [RETURN]**

a. Type the line number of the job you want to manage and press [RETURN]. The current item pointer (>)moves to this line.

***menu-option* [RETURN]**

b. Type a menu option and press [RETURN]. For example, type "D" and press [RETURN] to delete the entry (and prevent or stop printing). Table 4.6 describes the menu options.

c. Enter any information required for the selected menu option. The index of jobs is redisplayed to reflect any changes you've made.

[EXIT]

d. Press [EXIT] (F10 or Keypad-0) to return to the Job Services menu.

Table 4.6 describes the menu options on the Job Services index menu. These menu options can be entered after you've built an index of pending jobs with any option from the Job Services menu. Options that manage the current item are listed under the column heading "Option." Options that manage multiple items are listed under "Xoption." These options require you to first select multiple jobs.

Table 4.6 Job Services index menu options

Option	*Xoption*	*Action*
ALL (Select All)		Selects all jobs appearing in the index.
CAS (Cancel All)		Deselects all selected jobs.
UI (Update Index)		Creates a new list of your print and/or batch jobs waiting in a queue with the same selection criteria entered the last time you used the Index (I) option.
E (Edit)	XE	Modifies the settings for the current job or selected jobs, including printer destination, release time, types of cover pages, and notification flag. XE allows you to make different changes to each job.
GE (Global Edit)		Modifies all selected jobs. The same changes are made to all jobs, so the selected jobs must be of the same type (print or batch).
D (Delete)	XD	Removes the current job or all selected jobs from the queue—in other words, stops them from printing (or executing).
R (Read)	XR	Displays information about the current job or all selected jobs, including the queue name, queue status, submit time, job size, job status, and printer control settings.
HJ (Hold Job)	XHJ	Places the current job or all selected jobs permanently on hold in the queue until you later release the job. This prevents the job from printing (or executing). This option is sometimes useful to hold back large print jobs until the printer is idle.
RJ (Release Job)	XRJ	Releases for printing (or execution) a job or all selected jobs previously placed on hold.
RQ (Requeue Job)	XRQ	Places a job or selected jobs back in the queue to be reprinted from the beginning page. This option is selected in the event of a printer jam. Select this option *before* clearing the printer jam.
RSJ (Restart Job)		Restarts a job that has stalled.
DLF (Delete Log File)	XDLF	Deletes the log file for the current batch job or all selected jobs.
PLF (Print Log File)	XPLF	Prints the log file for the current batch job or all selected jobs.
RLF (Read Log File)	XRLF	Displays the log file for the current batch job or all selected jobs.

ALL-IN-1 Utilities: User Setup, Interrupt Menu, and Scratch Pad

CHAPTER 5

This chapter describes three utilities that help you save time and work more efficiently in ALL-IN-1. In this chapter, you'll learn how to

- Customize your work environment in ALL-IN-1 by setting personal details and working conditions.
- Interrupt your current work in ALL-IN-1 to perform another task quickly such as reading a new mail message.
- Use the Scratch Pad to save a copy of information displayed on your screen.

5.1 CONTROLLING YOUR ENVIRONMENT WITH USER SETUP

Everyone's different! Most manufacturers of office equipment realize this and design their products to accommodate these differences. Your chair adjusts, and your terminal tilts. ALL-IN-1, too, can be modified to accommodate your needs.

Your site can modify ALL-IN-1's appearance and functionality to a great extent to better suit your organization's needs. Such changes are typically made by the ALL-IN-1 manager and are common to all users in a department or in the entire organization. You can further tailor ALL-IN-1 to suit your personal needs. The changes you're allowed to make are not quite as extensive, but you can, for example, choose your editor program or the format of the date that appears on menus.

In this section, you will learn how to make the following modifications:

- Change your VMS password and lock your keyboard for security reasons.
- Set the personal details, such as name, title, phone number, and address, that help identify you to other ALL-IN-1 users.
- Set such working conditions as editor type, the initial menu that ALL-IN-1 displays, and the format of the date that appears on menus.

5.1.1 Changing Your VMS Password

You should periodically change the password to your VMS account for security. Some sites set *password lifetimes* whereby the system periodically reminds you to change your password. If automatic password expiration is not in effect at your site, ask your system manager how often you should change your password.

You can change your password with the Change Password option on the User Setup menu, but you must first choose a new password. When choosing a password, remember these guidelines:

- Your password can be 1 to 31 characters in length; a minimum length of six characters is recommended and typically is enforced for security. Valid characters are *A* through *Z*, 0 through 9, $, and _ (underscore).
- The VMS operating system (version 5.4 or later) keeps track of old passwords and will not let you select a password that was used previously. In addition, VMS (version 5.4 or later) also checks your new password against a dictionary and will not let you choose a common word as a password. (Your system manager may have disabled these features.)
- Choose a password that you'll easily remember but that cannot be easily guessed by others. Do use several words or letters and numbers run together, such as IMANEXPERT, DONT_KNOW, and IM42NATE. Don't use any name or number associated with you. Don't use your middle name, maiden name, nickname, or the name of a close relative or pet. Don't use your birthdate, phone number, or license plate number.

Perform the following steps to change your VMS password:

US [RETURN]	a. From any menu, type "US" and press [RETURN] to display the User Setup menu.
CP [RETURN]	b. Type "CP" and press [RETURN].
Old password: {***old-password* [TAB]**}	c. Type your old password and press [TAB].
New password: {***new-password* [TAB]**}	d. Type your new password and press [TAB].
Verification: {***new-password* [RETURN]**}	e. Type your new password again for verification and press [RETURN]. For security reasons, passwords are not echoed as you type.

ALL-IN-1 displays the message "Password changed," then redisplays the User Setup menu.

5.1.2 Locking Your Keyboard for Security

The Lock Keyboard option allows you to lock your keyboard to prevent access to your account while you are temporarily away from your desk. This security feature comes in handy if you need to leave for a short while but intend to continue working in ALL-IN-1 when you return.

Keep the following points in mind when you lock your keyboard:

- Some sites run monitor programs to log out idle sessions automatically. You might be logged out by this type of program if you leave your terminal for a long period of time. Check with your system manager to see if you have such a program running, and if so, find out how much time it allows before logging out users.
- Although the Lock Keyboard option appears on the Interrupt menu, you cannot lock your keyboard while editing a document.
- You are allowed a limited number of tries[1] to enter your password when you return to your desk. If you exceed this limit, your session is automatically logged off the system.

Perform the following steps to lock your keyboard before you leave your desk:

LK [RETURN]	a. From any menu, type "LK" and press [RETURN].
Keyboard Lock Password: {*lock-password* **[TAB]**}	b. Type a lock password and press [TAB]. The password must be at least six characters in length and may consist of letters and numbers. This password can be something you think of when locking your keyboard. It does not have to be the same as your VMS password. For security reasons, your password is not echoed as you type.
Confirm Password: {*lock-password* **[RETURN]**}	c. Type the lock password again and press [RETURN]. Your screen is cleared, and the following text is displayed: `This keyboard is locked.`
Keyboard Lock Password: {*lock-password* **[RETURN]**}	d. When you return, type your lock password and press [RETURN]. The original screen is restored. *Note:* If you forget your password, press [RETURN] until you are logged out. (Usually, you must press [RETURN] about 10 times.) Then simply log back in and continue working.

5.1.3 Setting Personal Details

The ALL-IN-1 directory lists all users who have access to ALL-IN-1 on your system. Each directory entry contains a user's name, title, location, and address. You can access this information from the Directories menu to look up phone numbers and addresses. Some of this information is also included in mail messages. **(It is your responsibility to maintain your own personal details, and it's important that they be accurate because other people view this information.)**

1. By default, you are allowed 10 tries to log in before your session is terminated. However, your system manager can change this value.

```
                         Set Personal Details

Full Name:     Sarah Washington
Surname:       Washington
Given name:    Sarah                          Initials: SLW
Department:                                   Location:
Organization:  RBL Associates

You cannot change the above details

Internal Location:                  Generation:
Job title:            Information Systems Manager
Business number:
Internal number:
Postal address:       1234 Elm St. Suite 1140
                      Denver, CO

        Enter information and press RETURN,
        or press NEXT SCREEN for more fields                  (more...)
```

Figure 5.1 Set Personal Details form

The Set Personal Details option on the User Setup menu allows you to change your information in the ALL-IN-1 directory. You can change every detail except the fields of information shown at the top of Figure 5.1. Contact your system administrator if you find errors in information that you cannot access.

Perform the following steps to update your personal details:

US SPD [RETURN]

a. From any menu, type "US SPD" and press [RETURN] to display the Set Personal Details form shown in Figure 5.1.

b. Enter or change your personal details. See Section 3.2.1, "Completing a Data-Entry Form," for details on how to move around and enter information. Table 5.1 describes each field's purpose.

[NEXT SCREEN]

c. Press [NEXT SCREEN] (or [GOLD] [TAB]) to move to the second screen of information. Modify these details as necessary.

[RETURN]
[RETURN]

d. Press [RETURN] twice when you've finished modifying your personal details. This records your changes and returns you to the menu.

[EXIT]

Or press [EXIT] (F10 or Keypad-0) to exit this form without making any changes.

Table 5.1 Personal details

Personal Detail	*Description*
First Screen:	
Full Name[a]	Your first name and last name.
Surname[a]	Your last name.
Given Name[a]	Your first name or the name by which people refer to you, including your nickname and common misspellings for your first name.
Initials[a]	Your first, last, and middle initials.
Department[a]	Department, project, or work group name.
Location[a]	Name given to the location of your office, typically a building number, plant name, or city.
Organization[a]	Company name, division, or work group name.
Internal Location	The office, floor, or postal stop code within "Location" above.
Generation	The suffix added to your full name—for example, Jr., Sr., or II.
Job Title	Formal job title.
Business Number	Office phone number, including area code and extension.
Internal Number	The phone number that local employees dial to contact you, typically your extension.
Postal Address	Mailing address, complete except for the zip code.
Second Screen:	
Country	Country name used in a mailing address.
Zip Code	Postal code.
Given Name	Alternate first names by which you are known, including middle names and nicknames.
Surname	Alternate last names by which you are known, including family name and common misspellings of your last name.
Initials	Initials of alternate given and surnames by which you are known.
ALL-IN-1 Password	A password of six or more characters. You will be prompted for this password when you enter ALL-IN-1.

[a] You may not modify this information. Contact your system administrator to update this field if it is not accurate.

5.1.4 Setting Working Conditions

The Set Working Conditions option on the User Setup menu allows you to modify your ALL-IN-1 environment. These parameters affect the appearance or operation of many features in ALL-IN-1. For example, when you select the Delete option in Word and Document processing, you are asked to confirm whether you really want to delete the document. You can suppress this confirmation prompt by changing a parameter in Set Working Conditions.

```
                         Set Working Conditions

Status:
Main screen: MAIN                                Edit style: WPSPLUS
Mail menu:   EMC                           Mail destination: ALL-IN-1

Notification of:

  New mail:        Y    Print completion:  Y     Batch completion:     Y
  Display Tasks:   Y    Count Tasks:       Y     Send mail receipts:   Y

Initial TM form: TMMENU                      12 hour clock: Y

Working week:

  First day:   2    Start hour: 08:00am      Meal hour: Start: 12:00pm
  No. of days: 5    End hour:   05:00pm                   End: 01:00pm

  Advanced calendar day position: 2
  Calendar time increment (in minutes): 00015

Press RETURN to complete or press NEXT SCREEN for more details
                                                            (more...)
```

Figure 5.2 Set Working Conditions form

It is important to know how to set working conditions. You can save time and get the results you want by adjusting these parameters.

Perform the following steps to update your working conditions:

US SWC [RETURN]

a. From any menu, type "US SWC" and press [RETURN] to display the Set Working Conditions form shown in Figure 5.2.

b. Modify your working conditions. See Section 3.2.1, "Completing a Data-Entry Form," for details on how to move around and enter information. Table 5.2 describes the purpose of each field.

[NEXT SCREEN]

c. Press [NEXT SCREEN] (or [GOLD] [TAB]) to move to the second screen of the form. Modify these working conditions as necessary.

[RETURN]
[RETURN]

d. Press [RETURN] twice when you've finished modifying your working conditions. This records your changes and returns you to the menu.

[EXIT]

Or press [EXIT] (F10 or Keypad-0) to exit this form without making any changes.

Table 5.2 Working Conditions

Working Condition	*Description*
First Screen:	
Status	This message is immediately displayed when a co-worker addresses mail to you (but only if he or she has an account on the same system as yours). You can change this to "On vacation April 1 through 5," for example, to warn people that you won't be reading mail for a while.
Main Screen	If you consistently move to a particular menu whenever you get into ALL-IN-1, you can select that menu as your main screen. It then becomes the first screen you see whenever you invoke ALL-IN-1. This field is typically set to "MAIN." Other entries for this field include these: EMC — Electronic Messaging WP — Word and Document Processing TMMENU — Time Management
Edit Style[a]	The name of the editor you want to use for editing documents.
Mail Menu	The name of the menu form displayed for Electronic Messaging. Set this field to "EMC."
Mail Destination[a]	The destination of electronic messages sent to you. This is typically set as "ALL-IN-1," which causes your messages to be placed in your Inbox. Possible mail destinations include these: ALLIN1 — Places messages in your Inbox. ALL-IN-1 — Same as ALLIN1. NO MAIL — Indicates that you do not want to receive mail messages. PRINTER, PAPER-MAIL, HARD-COPY — Prints messages on the sender's printer when they are sent, presumably to be placed in an interoffice mail envelope and delivered manually. VMSMAIL, VAXMAIL — Places messages in the VMS Mail file to be read with the VMS Mail Utility.
Notification of:	Indicates that you want notification of certain events. Enter "Y" or "N" except where noted:
New Mail	Notifies you when you receive new mail.
Print Completion	Notifies you when your documents finish printing.
Batch Completion	Notifies you when your batch jobs are complete.
Display Tasks	Displays open tasks (Time Management subsystem) whenever you enter ALL-IN-1.
Count Tasks	Displays just a count of open tasks whenever you enter ALL-IN-1.

(continued)

Table 5.2 Working Conditions *(continued)*

Working Condition	*Description*
Send Mail Receipts	Enter "Y" if you want ALL-IN-1 to notify the sender when you read a message sent with a read receipt request. Enter "N" to suppress the return of a read receipt, or enter "A" if you want ALL-IN-1 to ask when you read a message whether to return a read receipt.
Initial TM Form[a]	Enter here the name of the form you want displayed when you enter the option "TM" to access Time Management. This is typically set as "TMMENU." See Section 19.1, "Customizing Time Management," for a table of form names.
12-Hour Clock	"Y" indicates that time should be displayed in 12-hour format (5:00 P.M., for example). "N" indicates that time should be displayed in 24-hour format (17:00, for example).
Working Week:	Identifies your standard working hours for the Time Management subsystem.
First Day	Enter a number between 1 and 7 to indicate the start of your workweek; 1 corresponds to Sunday, 2 corresponds to Monday, and so on.
No. of Days	The number of days in your workweek, typically 5.
Start Hour/End Hour	The start time and end time of your workday.
Meal Start/End	The start time and end time of your meal or break.
Advanced Calendar Day Position	Defines the line number (1 through 7) on which the current calendar day appears in the seven-day summary of the Events Plus index. Refer to Section 19.1, "Customizing Time Management," for further details.
Calendar Time Increment	The number of minutes contained in a single scheduling interval in your calendar. This value alters the amount of information displayed when you view or print your calendar.
Second Screen:	
Working Conditions When Reading:	Specifies defaults for display options when reading a document. Enter "Y" or "N" for the following:
Status Line Display	Displays a status line containing useful information, such as the document's title. You can set this to "N," then press [GOLD] Z to display the status when reading a document.
Read Screen Wide	If "Y," displays the document in 132-column format; if "N," displays it in 80-column format. You can set this to "N," then press [GOLD] E to expand the screen width only when reading a wide document.
Expired Message Warning	If "Y", displays a message when you attempt to read a message that has expired; if "N," ALL-IN-1 does not perform this check.
Allow System Deletion of Expired Messages in Your Inbox?	If "Y", the system deletes expired, unread messages from your Inbox; if "N", no expired messages are deleted from your Inbox.

Table 5.2 *(continued)*

Working Condition	*Description*
Display Distribution Lists on: Read (Y/N), Print (Y/N)	Specifies defaults for including the full distribution list of a message when you read or print a message. "Y" includes the distribution list; "N" suppresses it. "N" is recommended since you can override the default with [GOLD] V when reading or [GOLD] E when printing.
Confirmation Prompts:	Tells ALL-IN-1 to prompt for confirmation in certain instances. Enter a "Y" or "N" for the following:
GOLD GET Selection	Confirms whether the document you're retrieving is the correct one before including it in the document you're editing. A good option to turn on ("Y") if you work with large documents; otherwise, leave it off ("N").
New Folder	Confirms whether to create a new folder if you enter a folder name that does not exist. This confirmation avoids the creation of similarly named folders when you mistype a folder name.
Document Deletion	Confirms whether to delete the current document after you've selected the Delete option. Some people consider this confirmation prompt to be annoying because deleted documents are simply refiled in the Wastebasket folder and can be easily recovered.
Delete Job	Confirms whether to delete (stop) the current print or batch job when you select the Delete option in Job Services.
CDA Documents:	Specifies the handling of Compound Documents when you transfer them to your File Cabinet:
CDA Storage[a]	Indicates the method for storing CDA documents in your File Cabinet. Enter one of the following: P Packs the files in a CDA document together into a single document in Document Object Transport Syntax (DOTS) format. U Stores files unpacked in separate documents. Not all ALL-IN-1 systems can handle unpacked documents. A Asks whether you want packed or unpacked format each time you move a CDA document to your File Cabinet.
CDA Handling[a]	Indicates whether you want just the primary file transferred to your File Cabinet, or the primary file plus all files referenced in the primary file. Enter one of the following: N Transfers just the primary file. R Transfers the primary file and all files referenced in the primary file. A Asks each time you move a CDA document to your File Cabinet.
Forwarding Cover Note	Indicates whether you want to include a cover note when forwarding messages. Enter "Y" or "N". You can override this default when you forward a message.

(continued)

Table 5.2 Working Conditions *(continued)*

Working Condition	*Description*
Preferred Date Format[a]	Enter a number from 1 to 7 to indicate the format in which the date is displayed and the format in which the date must be entered. Typically, the value is 1, specifying the long format of dd-mmm-yyyy and the short format mm/dd/yy. Press [FIND] (or [GOLD] L) to list all of the various formats.
Keyboard Mapping[a]	Indicates the country code for your keyboard if you are not using a keyboard standard for the United States.
Language[a]	Indicates the language that appears on ALL-IN-1 menus and data-entry forms. Ask your ALL-IN-1 manager which languages are available on your system.

[a] ALL-IN-1's lookup feature can be used in this field. Press [ERASE LINE] (F13 or LF) to clear the field, then press [FIND] (or [GOLD] L) to display a list of possible entries. Refer to Section 3.2.2, "Using [FIND] to Complete a Field," for further information on the lookup feature.

5.1.5 Exercise: Setting Personal Details and Working Conditions

The following exercise shows you how to modify your personal details and working conditions with User Setup.

1. Display the Set Personal Details form.

US SPD [RETURN]	From any menu, type "US SPD" and press [RETURN] to display the Set Personal Details form.

2. Modify the Job Title field, and return to the menu.

[TAB] **[TAB]**	a. Press [TAB] twice to advance to the Job Title field.
Title: ***your-job-title***	b. Modify your job title. Capitalize the first letter of important words to ensure the proper appearance of your title.
[RETURN] **[RETURN]**	c. Press [RETURN] twice to return to the menu. Note that your new job title appears at the top of the User Setup menu.

3. Display the Set Working Conditions form.

SWC [RETURN]	Type "SWC" and press [RETURN].

4. Modify the Preferred Date Format field, and return to the menu.

[NEXT SCREEN] **[TAB]...**	a. Press [NEXT SCREEN (or [GOLD][TAB]) to advance to the second screen, then press [TAB] as

many times as necessary to advance to the Preferred Date Format field.

[LINE FEED] [FIND]

b. Press [LINE FEED] (F13) to clear the field, then press [FIND] (or [GOLD] L) to display the list of possible date formats.

line-number **[RETURN]**

c. ALL-IN-1 displays a list of choices. Type a line number and press [RETURN] to select a date format.

[RETURN]
[RETURN]

d. Press [RETURN] twice to return to the menu. Note that the date appears in the new format at the top of the User Setup menu.

5.2 THE INTERRUPT MENU

How often do you say to yourself, "If I have one more interruption today, I'll . . ."? Dealing with interruptions can be tiresome, but interruptions are unavoidable, especially if others rely on you for assistance. The Interrupt menu, shown in Figure 5.3, lets you deal quickly with interruptions and return to your work.

As an example, assume that you're editing a document in Word and Document Processing when notification of a mail message from your boss appears on your screen.

```
Sarah Washington        Information Systems Manager      Fri 11-Nov-1994
                        Interrupt Menu



TIME  Display time                       RN  Read new mail messages

DIR   Directories                        TM  Time management

DC    Desk calculator                    SP  Scratch pad

SMD   Search mail directory              JS  Job services

LK    Lock keyboard




Enter selection and press RETURN
```

Figure 5.3 ALL-IN-1's Interrupt menu

Just press [GOLD] I to display the Interrupt menu, read the message with the RN option, and press [RESUME] to return to your document.

There are some restrictions:

- If you access the Interrupt menu while editing a document, you cannot perform any operation that involves editing *another* document.
- You cannot lock your keyboard while editing a document.

5.2.1 Accessing the Interrupt Menu

Perform the following steps to access the Interrupt menu from anywhere in ALL-IN-1:

[GOLD] I	a. Press [GOLD] I (or F6).
***menu-option* [RETURN]**	b. Select the option you wish to perform and press [RETURN]. For example, type "RN" and press [RETURN] to read new mail.

Do the following to leave the Interrupt menu and return to your previous task:

[RESUME]	Press [RESUME] (F7), or press [EXIT].

5.3 THE SCRATCH PAD

A scratch pad is just as important as anything else on your desktop. You're probably used to jotting down notes on a piece of paper whenever you're faced with "brain overflow." ALL-IN-1 provides an electronic scratch pad for the same purpose.

You can save information on your screen by simply pressing [GOLD] P. ALL-IN-1 then copies the screen's contents to a Scratch Pad file. For the most part, information is permanently saved in the Scratch Pad until you erase it. Options on the Scratch Pad menu allow you to edit, display, and print the contents of your Scratch Pad.

Here are some good reasons to use the Scratch Pad:

- Index forms list items in a concise, efficient display. You can copy an index to the Scratch Pad and then print the Scratch Pad to get a hard-copy listing of items.
- You can display the function keypad layout, copy this display to the Scratch Pad, then print the Scratch Pad. A copy of this keypad layout is handy to have nearby while you're learning ALL-IN-1. The exercise at the end of this section shows you how to do this.
- You might want to include a copy of a menu, entry form, or index in a document you're preparing. (For example, many sites customize ALL-IN-1 and need to capture screen images when documenting the changes.) To do this, first copy the menu, entry form, or index to the Scratch Pad. Then create a document and retrieve the contents of the Scratch Pad with [GOLD] G.

- Whenever you see an error message that you don't understand on your screen, it is recommended that you send a copy of your screen to the ALL-IN-1 manager or support staff. Follow these steps:

  1. Press [GOLD] W. This displays additional information about the error.
  2. Press [GOLD] P to copy the error information to the Scratch Pad.
  3. Press [GOLD] * to display the Scratch Pad menu.
  4. Select Send to send a copy of your Scratch Pad to your ALL-IN-1 manager. Include a cover note explaining what you were doing when the error occurred.

5.3.1 Copying Your Screen to the Scratch Pad

Do the following to copy the information currently displayed on your terminal screen to the Scratch Pad:

[GOLD] P — Press [GOLD] P. ALL-IN-1 displays the following messages:

```
Copying screen to scratch pad...Screen
completed
```

Note the following:

- The screen's contents are appended to the end of the information currently in the Scratch Pad. You should periodically delete the Scratch Pad to erase its contents.
- Once you've copied the screen's contents to the Scratch Pad, you can edit, print, or file this information from the Scratch Pad menu.
- You cannot copy the screen's contents to the Scratch Pad while editing a document.

5.3.2 Accessing the Scratch Pad Menu

Perform these steps to access the Scratch Pad menu, shown in Figure 5.4, from anywhere in ALL-IN-1:

[GOLD] * — a. Press [GOLD] (PF1), then press "*" (asterisk).

***menu-option* [RETURN]** — b. Select an option from the Scratch Pad menu. (Table 5.3 describes these options.) For example, to display the contents of the Scratch Pad on your terminal, type "R" and press [RETURN].

[EXIT] — c. Press [EXIT] (F10 or Keypad-0) when you are finished with the Scratch Pad.

To access the Scratch Pad menu from any ALL-IN-1 menu, do the following:

SP [RETURN] — Type "SP" and press [RETURN].

```
                         Scratch Pad

      E  Edit              S  Send by mail
      P  Print             D  Delete contents
      R  Read              F  File contents


      Enter option and press RETURN
```

Figure 5.4 ALL-IN-1's Scratch Pad menu

Table 5.3 Scratch Pad menu options

Enter This Scratch Pad Menu Option	*To Perform the Following Action*
D (Delete)	Erase the Scratch Pad.
E (Edit)	Edit the Scratch Pad.
F (File contents)	Save a copy of the Scratch Pad as a document in your File Cabinet.
P (Print)	Print the Scratch Pad.
R (Read)	Display the Scratch Pad.
S (Send by mail)	Send a copy of the Scratch Pad to another user via Electronic Messaging.

5.3.3 Exercise: Using the Scratch Pad

The following exercise shows you how to use the Scratch Pad. In this exercise, you'll copy the first page of an index of your Read folder and the ALL-IN-1 keyboard layout to your Scratch Pad. You'll then print the Scratch Pad.

1. Erase the contents of your Scratch Pad.

[GOLD] *	a. Press [GOLD] (PF1) and type "*" to display the Scratch Pad menu.
D [RETURN]	b. Type "D" and press [RETURN]. ALL-IN-1 might display a confirmation prompt.
Y [RETURN]	c. If you see the prompt, type "Y" and press [RETURN] to confirm that you want to delete the Scratch Pad.
[EXIT]	d. Press [EXIT] (F10 or Keypad-0).

2. Create an index of your Read folder. Copy the first page of this index to your Scratch Pad (press [NEXT SCREEN], then [GOLD] P to copy additional pages).

EM IR [RETURN]	a. From any menu, type "EM IR" and press [RETURN] to display an index of your Read folder.
[GOLD] P	b. Press [GOLD] (PF1) and type "P" to copy the screen to your Scratch Pad.
[EXIT]	c. Press [EXIT] (F10 or Keypad-0) to return to the Electronic Messaging menu.

3. Display the keyboard layout, and copy this screen to your Scratch Pad. *Note:* In this case only, [GOLD] [SPACE] copies the screen to your Scratch Pad.

? [RETURN]	a. Type "?" and press [RETURN] to display the keyboard layout.
[GOLD] [SPACE]	b. Press [GOLD] (PF1) and then press [SPACE] to copy the screen to your Scratch Pad.
[SPACE]	c. Press [SPACE] to redisplay the Electronic Messaging menu.

4. Print a copy of your Scratch Pad.

[GOLD] *	a. Press [GOLD] (PF1) and type "*" to display the Scratch Pad menu.
P [RETURN]	b. Type "P" and press [RETURN]. ALL-IN-1 displays the Printing Document form.
[RETURN]	c. Press [RETURN] to print a copy of the Scratch Pad. Refer to Section 4.2, "Printing in ALL-IN-1," for further details. ALL-IN-1 redisplays the menu along with a notice that the document has been sent to the printer.
[EXIT]	d. Press [EXIT] (F10 or Keypad-0).

Electronic Messaging

PART II

Electronic Messaging allows you to communicate with other users by sending and receiving written memos. To a great extent, Electronic Messaging provides the same services as interoffice mail. So what's the advantage? The primary advantage is that Electronic Messaging is much faster than interoffice mail. In addition, because you're dealing with electronic documents instead of paper documents, all of the tedious work of copying, filing, and distributing messages is eliminated.

The following are among the features of Electronic Messaging:

- ALL-IN-1 automatically stores your messages in your personal File Cabinet and organizes incoming and outgoing messages into separate folders.
- Copies are made of all messages sent and forwarded to other employees. These copies are automatically stored in your File Cabinet. These outgoing messages as well as all incoming messages remain in your File Cabinet until you explicitly delete them.
- ALL-IN-1 allows you to defer the delivery of a message until a future date and time. For example, you can send reminders that individuals will get while you are out of the office.
- You can send messages with a Read Receipt Request. This instructs ALL-IN-1 to notify you when the addressee reads the message.
- Messages can be automatically forwarded to another user when you are out of the office for extended periods.
- You can prepare a "canned" response memo and instruct ALL-IN-1 to automatically return this memo to anyone who sends you mail. (This is good news for those who handle complaints!)
- You can create distribution lists to help address your messages to groups of individuals.
- You can define "nicknames" for individuals. Nicknames help simplify the process of addressing messages.
- You can manage co-workers' mail for them, including reading their messages and sending mail on their behalf.

Here's a summary of topics covered in the next three chapters on Electronic Messaging. Chapter 6, "Getting Started with Electronic Messaging," covers the basics. This chapter teaches you how to send, read, forward, reply to, delete, and refile messages. The simple exercises in this chapter take you through the steps of creating, sending, and reading mail.

Chapter 7, "Becoming More Proficient with Electronic Messaging," takes you one step farther. It covers features that help you work more efficiently with Electronic Messaging. This chapter describes in more detail the process of addressing a message, including how to create distribution lists and lists of nicknames. It also describes how to work from an index in Electronic Messaging and how to attach and route documents.

The final chapter in this part, "Advanced Electronic Messaging," discusses some options for the handling of your mail when you're unable to do it yourself. These options include automatic forwarding of messages, automatic replies to incoming messages, and Mail Surrogacy, which allows you to have someone else look after your mail.

MAIL FOLDERS

Electronic Messaging stores your messages in standard, predefined folders in the Main drawer of your File Cabinet. The names of these folders are Created, Outbox, Inbox, Read, and Wastebasket. Certain options on the Electronic Messaging menu move a message from one folder to another, automatically filing your messages (Figure II.1). However, you can refile your messages into any folder you wish.

Inbox	New incoming messages are placed in your Inbox folder. Messages remain in this folder until you read them.
Read	ALL-IN-1 refiles messages into your Read folder as you read them. Messages remain in this folder until you refile or delete them.
Wastebasket	ALL-IN-1 refiles messages from their current folders into the Wastebasket folder when you delete them. Messages remain in this folder until permanently removed from your File Cabinet by the Janitor or until you select the Empty Wastebasket option. The Janitor is a system program that runs periodically to empty everyone's Wastebasket folder.
Created	When you first create a new message, ALL-IN-1 stores it in your Created folder. The message remains in this folder until you send, refile, or delete it. You can make any number of changes to the message until you send it.
Outbox	When you send a message, ALL-IN-1 removes it from its original folder and sends it to one or more individuals. A copy of the message is placed in your Outbox folder. You can no longer edit a message once it has been sent.

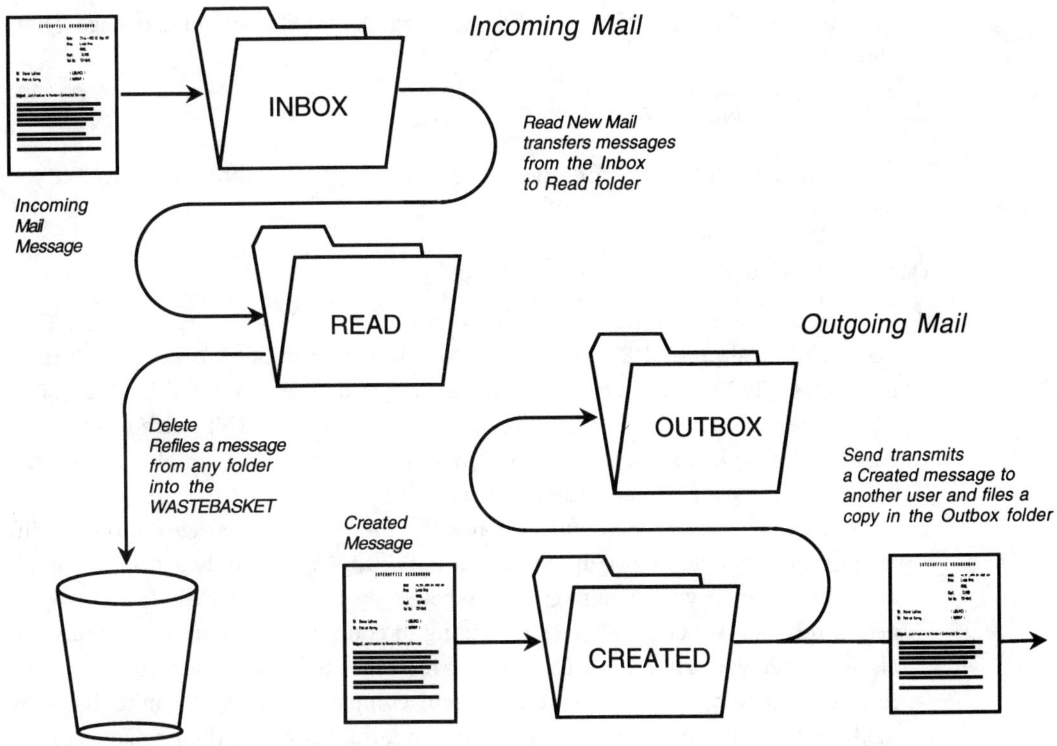

Figure II.1 Mail folders

ELECTRONIC MESSAGING Q&A

Following is a list of common questions about Electronic Messaging.

Q *How do I read new mail?*

A The number of new messages is displayed at the top of the menu as soon as you get into ALL-IN-1. If you have just a few new messages, it's easiest to type "EM RN" and press [RETURN]. This moves you to Electronic Messaging and displays the oldest message. Repeat the Read New (RN) option as necessary to read other new messages. If you have more than a few messages, it's more efficient to type "EM II ALL XR" and press [RETURN]. This series of selections moves you to the index of the Inbox in Electronic Messaging and selects and displays all of your new mail.

Q *Can I check for new mail without getting into ALL-IN-1?*

A Many users have access to the command level of VMS to run applications other than ALL-IN-1. When logging on to run other programs, these users find it inconvenient to start ALL-IN-1 simply to check for new messages. You can run ALL-IN-1 with a command qualifier to display the number of new mail messages without invoking ALL-IN-1. Simply enter the following Digital Command Language (DCL) command:

```
$ ALLIN1/CHECK=UNREAD
```

This program displays the message, "You have *x* new ALL-IN-1 messages," if you have new mail.

Q *I don't want to receive mail. Can I turn it off?*

A You can disable incoming mail with an option in Set Working Conditions. Type "US SWC" and press [RETURN]. ALL-IN-1 displays the Set Working Conditions form. Press [TAB] to move to the Mail Destination field. Press [ERASE LINE] (LF or F13) to clear this field, and type "NO MAIL." Press [RETURN] twice to save this change. Now, when someone addresses mail to you, ALL-IN-1 simply displays the message, "You cannot send messages to this user."

Some people disable incoming mail because they receive messages through a different e-mail system or at a different location. If this is your only access to e-mail, however, consider what you're giving up before disabling your mail delivery. Most people rely heavily on Electronic Messaging to communicate with other individuals. Although you will still be able to send messages to others, you will not be able to read their responses or receive important company notices. If you're disabling mail delivery simply to avoid receiving unimportant notices, then respond to the senders of these notices and ask them to remove you from their distribution lists instead.

Q *How do I send a message?*

A Sending mail requires two steps. You create a message, then send it—just like writing a letter, then mailing it. These steps are explained in detail in Section 6.2, "Creating and Sending a Message." Following is a brief overview of the steps involved.

Type "EM C" and press [RETURN] to move to the Electronic Messaging menu and create a message. ALL-IN-1 displays the Message Header. Type the usernames of people you want to send the message to, pressing [RETURN] after each name. Usually, you enter just the last names. You can also press [FIND] to display a list of names from which to select. Press [TAB] after entering all of the addressees, and type the names of those to whom you want to send a copy. Press [TAB], enter a subject, and press [RETURN] to complete the form. You can now enter the text of your message. When finished, press [GOLD] F to "seal" the message and return to the menu. Type "S" and press [RETURN] to send the message.

Q *How do I address a message?*

A You address a message by entering the addresses of individuals on the Message Header. This form is displayed immediately after you select the Create or Forward option. Typically, the "address" of an individual is the person's VMS username or starts with the person's last name. If you're not sure of someone's address, type the first few characters of either the person's username or last name, and press [FIND] ([GOLD] L). ALL-IN-1 displays matching entries from a directory of individuals who receive mail. In small to midsize companies, this directory usually lists all employees who receive mail. In large companies, this directory usually lists all employees at the same location. If you don't see the individual listed in the current directory, press [GOLD] M to display options for searching other directories.

To address a message to a group of individuals, you must enter the name of a distribution list or group. Distribution lists are entered with the format *@list-name* or *list-name:*. Groups are entered with the format **group-name*. If you're not sure which distribution lists or groups exist, type "@" or "*" and press [FIND].

You can send a message to anyone as long as you know the address and as long as there is a link between his or her mail system and yours. To make addressing easier, you can create your own directory with Nicknames and your own distribution lists. Chapter 7 discusses all of these addressing options in greater detail.

Q *I've noticed information displayed when I enter a name while addressing a message. Where does this come from?*

A Often, you see a message like, "In New York until September 15th," displayed at the bottom of your screen when you enter an address. This is the addressee's status message. It is intended to notify you that this person won't be reading your message for a while. You can enter the same sort of message for yourself with Set Working Conditions. Type "US SWC" and press [RETURN] to access this form. Enter a text message in the Status field (first field), and press [RETURN] twice. Remember to change or clear your status message when you return!

Q *I sent a message and then realized that I forgot to include someone in the list of addressees. How do I send the message to this person?*

A Simply select the message from your Outbox folder, then enter the Send (S) option. Enter the additional name on the Forwarding Message Header form, and then enter a subject. Press [RETURN] to complete this form. ALL-IN-1 asks if you want to add a cover note, but you can respond no to this prompt. The message is sent to the individual after you complete the Message Header and/or the cover note.

Q *How do I modify a message that I have already sent?*

A Sorry! You cannot edit or "take back" a message once it's been sent. The VMS file specification can be determined with the Show Header option, but accessing this file requires privileges as well as some knowledge of how ALL-IN-1 handles mail. In situations of extreme importance, contact your ALL-IN-1 system administrator for assistance—and act fast. Note that this task is further complicated if the message has attachments or has been sent to remote systems. It is often best to send a follow-up message with your corrections (and apologies).

Q *What's the difference between creating and sending memos from the Electronic Messaging menu versus the Word and Document Processing menu?*

A This question surprised me the first time I heard it. I'd never thought of creating and sending messages from Word and Document Processing. After I thought about it, though, I realized that you *can* create and send from this menu. Here's why you shouldn't use the Word and Document Processing menu for messages.

First, you must understand the difference between a message and a document. A message is a special type of document that contains information that you want to communicate quickly to others by electronic means. Messages have a predetermined format, consisting of the message (memo) header followed by free-form text. Messages are usually stored in the Inbox, Read, Created, or Outbox folders. A document, on the other hand, is simply a text file containing information that you want to communicate to others, typically by printing and distributing it manually. Documents have no predetermined format; the content is totally up to you. Documents are stored in whatever folder you want.

The Create (C) option on the Electronic Messaging menu creates a *message* and stores it in your Created folder. The Create option on the Word and Document Processing menu creates a *document* and stores it in any folder you specify. The Send (S) option on either menu sends the current message or document to another user. When you send a Created message, ALL-IN-1 transmits the message to the addressee and refiles the message in your Outbox. When you send a document, ALL-IN-1 creates and sends a new message and appends a copy of the document as an attachment. This is a handy method for passing the document to another user for further work, but then the document is filed in two places: in the original folder and as an attachment to the message in your Outbox folder.

In summary, create *messages* from the Electronic Messaging menu, and create *documents* from the Word and Document Processing menu. If you send a document, remember to delete the message with the attachment from your Outbox. This helps keep your File Cabinet clean!

Q *How can I skip reading a distribution list? How do I read a distribution list when it is not displayed with the message?*

A In Version 3.1 of ALL-IN-1, you can toggle the display of the distribution list on or off by pressing [GOLD] V while reading a memo. For example, if you see simply "12 addresses" next to the TO: label, press [GOLD] V to display all twelve names.

You can also change the default action with an option in Set Working Conditions. Type "US SWC" and press [RETURN]. ALL-IN-1 displays the Set Working Conditions form. Press [TAB] to move to the fields labeled "Display distribution lists on READ" or "Print" and enter "Y" to automatically display distribution lists or "N" to suppress the display.

Q *How do I send a message to everyone?*

A With proper authority, you can send a message to all users of the current system who receive ALL-IN-1 mail. Simply type "SUBSCRIBERS:" in the To: field. Addressing mail to subscribers requires authorization from your system administrator, however. This requirement prevents the distribution of some unnecessary mail.

Q *How do I create a distribution list?*

A Distribution lists are lists of addresses for groups of people to whom you frequently send mail. Type "DL C" and press [RETURN] to move to the Distribution List Management menu and create a new list. ALL-IN-1 asks you to enter a name for the new list. Type a name that begins with "@" or ends with ":" and press [RETURN]. Then enter the addresses of individuals you want on the distribution list. This is the same as entering names when addressing a memo. To file the list, press [RETURN] after the last name.

The next time you address a memo, simply type the name of your distribution list in either the To: or CC: field. Remember to include the "@" or ":"! Return to the Distribution List Management menu to add or remove names from the list. Refer to Section 7.3, "Creating and Maintaining Distribution Lists," for further details.

Q *How do I send a distribution list to another user?*

A You can send a distribution list to another user as easily as sending a document. From the Electronic Messaging or Word and Document Processing menu, type "SEL DISTRIBUTION LISTS" and press [RETURN]. This selects your most recent distribution list as the current document. Press [DOWN ARROW] to select the list you want to send. Type "S" and press [RETURN] to send the message and complete the Message Header form as usual. ALL-IN-1 sends the list as an attachment to your message.

The recipient must read the new message and enter "FA" to file the attached list. Make sure that the recipient files the list in the Distribution Lists folder. The recipient can then use the distribution list to address messages and can manage the list with Distribution List Management.

> *NOTE:* If a number of individuals use the same distribution list, ask your system administrator to create a system distribution list that everyone can access, and make sure that users delete their own personal copies. Then only the single system distribution list must be updated.

Q *How do I sort a distribution list?*

A Sorted distribution lists are easier to scan, especially when the list is very long. Some sites customize the Distribution List menu to add an option to sort the current list. If your site does not have this option, you can sort a distribution list if you have access to DCL.

Distribution lists are maintained in files stored in a subdirectory [.MSG]. You can sort names stored in these files with the VMS SORT utility. You first need to determine the distribution list file name. From the Distribution List menu, type "FULLDB" and press [RETURN] to display the file name of the current list. Exit ALL-IN-1 and set your default directory to [.MSG] (under your ALL-IN-1 subdirectory). Then sort the distribution list file with a command similar to the following:

```
$ SORT/KEY=(POSITION:40,SIZE:5) ZUHBHAFFT.DIS ZUHBHAFFT.DIS
```

The position and size specified here sort the distribution list based on the first five characters of the address. You might want to specify a different sort key.

CAUTION: Don't attempt to sort distribution lists unless you have access to DCL and are *very* familiar with DCL and the structure of files. You can accidentally corrupt or erase lists if you're not careful. Also, do not purge the original version of the distribution list file until you've had a chance to start ALL-IN-1 and review the new, sorted list from the Distribution List menu.

Q *What's the difference between Forward and Auto Forward?*

A The Forward option sends a copy of the current message to another individual. You therefore determine which messages are forwarded and when they are forwarded. By the way, before forwarding messages, display the list of recipients with the Show Header (SH) option to make sure you're not forwarding the message to one of the original addressees.

The Auto Forward option enables the automatic forwarding of your incoming mail to another individual. You cannot control which messages are forwarded or when. All messages are forwarded at the time of delivery. Auto-forwarding should be enabled for short periods of time only—for example, when you will be on vacation. Be sure to disable auto-forwarding when you return. Warn the people who send you mail—and especially the person who will receive your mail—before you enable auto-forwarding.

Q *Can I delete unopened (unread) mail?*

A Deleting unread mail requires authorization from your ALL-IN-1 system administrator. Without this authorization, you'll receive the message, "The current message is UNREAD—please read it first," when you attempt to delete a new message without reading it first.

Some individuals receive lots of mail and barely have time to review the titles let alone read all of the messages. With authorization, you can select and delete messages from your Inbox folder. A good way to do this is to type "EM II" and press [RETURN]. This displays the index of your Inbox folder. Type the line numbers of messages you want to delete separated by commas, press [SELECT], type "XD," and press [RETURN].

Q *How do I retrieve a message I accidentally deleted?*

A Recovering any deleted document or message is simply a case of refiling it from the Wastebasket folder back to its original folder. However, you must do so before the Janitor empties the Wastebasket. To recover a message, type "EM I WASTE-BASKET" and press [RETURN]. This moves you to the Electronic Messaging menu and displays an index of your Wastebasket folder. Locate the message you want to recover. (You might have to press [NEXT SCREEN] to display additional items.) Type the line number of the message and press [RETURN]. Type "RFD," followed by the message's original folder name ("CREATED," "OUTBOX," or "READ"). For example, if it were a message you received from someone else, you would type "RFD READ." This refiles the message from the Wastebasket to its original folder.

Q *How do I send a document to someone else? How do I attach a document?*

A The easiest way to send a document to another individual is to select the document and then enter "S" to send it. ALL-IN-1 displays the Message Header. Enter the address of the recipient and press [RETURN]. You can also indicate whether you want to include a cover note. ALL-IN-1 immediately sends the document as an attachment to the message. The recipient can read the document and select the File Attachment (FA) option to file the document for editing.

To send multiple documents, type "I," followed by the folder name, and press [RETURN]. This builds an index of documents in the folder. Type the line numbers of the documents you want to send separated by commas and press [SELECT]. Then type "XS" to send all selected documents as attachments to a single mail message.

If you've already created a message and want to attach a document, select the message and enter "ATT." ALL-IN-1 displays a form on which you can enter the folder and title of the document. Note that the message remains in your Created folder until you send it.

Q *Can I transfer external files with Electronic Messaging?*

A You can transfer binary files, program files, data files, and so on, with Electronic Messaging as easily as you transfer documents. You must first "import" the file to your File Cabinet. Type "DT" and press [RETURN] to display the Document Transfer menu. Select the Receive without Conversion (RVC) option. ALL-IN-1 asks for the VMS file name. (You can enter a VMS directory name and press the [FIND] key to display file names.) ALL-IN-1 asks you to specify a drawer, folder, and title for the document. It helps if you specify a unique folder name, such as Binary Transfer. Once the document has been imported to your File Cabinet, enter the Send option. The recipient must file the attachment, then export the document to VMS with the Send without Conversion (SVC) option on the Document Transfer menu.

Q *How do I read my VMS mail? How do I send mail to someone who doesn't have an ALL-IN-1 account?*

A If you log into the system and see the message, "You have *x* new Mail message(s)," this is an indication that someone has sent you mail using the VMS Mail Utility. ALL-IN-1 communicates with the VMS Mail Utility rather well. To read incoming mail sent to you via VMS Mail, simply select the VMSmail Import (V) option from the Electronic Messaging menu. This transfers mail from your VMS Mail NEWMAIL folder to your Inbox folder in ALL-IN-1. You can then select the Read New Mail (RN) option to read incoming messages.

Forwarding mail with the VMS Mail Set Forward command is another way to handle incoming VMS mail. Execute the following command within the VMS Mail Utility to forward your messages automatically to your ALL-IN-1 Inbox:

```
MAIL> SET FORWARD "MRGATE::""A1::your-username"""
```

You can also send messages via VMS Mail to someone without an ALL-IN-1 account. Simply address the message as described in Table 7.2 when completing the Message Header. For example, type JONEST@ASPEN@MRGATE to send a message to user JONEST on node ASPEN using the Message Router running on your system.

Q *How do I handle someone else's mail?*

A Electronic Messaging provides two methods for handling other people's mail. Both are described in Chapter 8.

You can use Auto Forward when you will be out of the office for a period of time and want to have incoming messages automatically forwarded to another individual. Select the Auto Forward (AF) option, and enter the address of the individual who will receive your mail. When you return, cancel auto-forwarding with the CF option. One drawback to Auto Forward is that it does not provide a record of the messages that were forwarded.

Mail Surrogacy lets you completely manage someone else's mail. This feature is used by people who handle their boss's mail. You can read, file, print, and delete messages sent to the other individual as well as create and send messages on his or her behalf. The other individual must first grant you this privilege by executing the Grant Mail Access (GMA) option. You must then execute the Set Mail User (SMU) option to change over to the other person's account before handling his or her mail.

ELECTRONIC MESSAGING DOs AND DON'Ts

Following are some suggestions for working efficiently with Electronic Messaging.

Do

- Log in regularly and read your mail! It's easy to keep up with your mail if you do this every day. It's not so easy if you let a week pass, and it's almost impossible if you wait longer than this. If you're going to be away for a long time, consider using the Auto Reply feature to notify others or the Auto Forward or Grant Mail Access option to allow someone else to handle your mail while you're gone.
- Delete or refile messages as you read them. This maintains your File Cabinet and makes it easier to locate messages down the road. You can enter both the Delete (D) and Refile Document (RFD) options while reading a message.

- Remember to use the [FIND] key when addressing a message. If you can't remember how to spell the addressee's name, enter the first character or two of the last name and press [FIND] (or [GOLD] L).
- Create nicknames and distribution lists to make addressing messages easier. The Create Nickname for Sender (CNS) and Create Distribution List from Message (DLM) options help with this task.
- Clean up your File Cabinet! Old, obsolete messages are the "cholesterol" of the mail system's arteries. Not only do obsolete messages take up storage space, but the task of locating a message is much harder when searching through 300 messages as opposed to 30. On a weekly or monthly basis, review your messages and get rid of those you no longer need. Concentrate on your Outbox and Read folders in particular, targeting messages such as forwarding cover notes, return receipts, and meeting notices. The Index (I) option provides an excellent way to search for and delete old or obsolete messages, as described in Section 6.7, "Deleting Messages."
- Ask your system administrator to create a system distribution list when there is a group of people who will use a particular list. This is more efficient than each person in the group creating and managing personal distribution lists with the same addresses.

Don't

- Don't type the entire name when entering an address in the Message Header. Simply enter enough characters to specify the address uniquely, and press [RETURN]. ALL-IN-1 fills in the rest of the address for you or displays a list of matching entries.
- Don't send messages Express unless you are sending an urgent memo to users on remote systems. Messages are always sent to local users immediately, and most systems transfer mail to remote users in a timely manner.
- Don't request Delivery receipts or Read receipts unnecessarily. Delivery receipts should only be used when sending important memos to remote users. Read receipts should only be used when you want to document the date and time that addressees read important memos. The overuse of Delivery and Read receipts results in your having more mail with which to deal.
- Don't send out low-priority notices and announcements to large groups of people with Electronic Messaging. Creating a "bulletin board" conference in Group Conferencing is a better alternative.

Getting Started with Electronic Messaging

CHAPTER 6

This chapter teaches you the basics of Electronic Messaging. The first three topics cover the most important tasks: accessing Electronic Messaging and sending and receiving mail. The remainder of the chapter covers tasks that most people perform regularly, including forwarding a message, responding to a message, and managing your File Cabinet by deleting and refiling messages. Although printing a message is also common, the procedure for printing a message is the same as for printing any other item. Refer to Chapter 4, "Reading and Printing in ALL-IN-1," for instructions on printing messages.

In this chapter, you'll learn how to perform the following tasks:

- Access Electronic Messaging.
- Create and send a message to another user.
- Read incoming messages.
- Select a message for subsequent editing, printing, and so on.
- Forward an incoming message to another user.
- Send a response to a message.
- Delete old messages to clean up your File Cabinet.
- Refile your messages.

6.1 ACCESSING ELECTRONIC MESSAGING

All of the features of Electronic Messaging are accessed from the Electronic Messaging menu. You can also select, read, print, delete, and index messages from the Word and Document Processing menu because ALL-IN-1 treats messages the same as documents as far as these options are concerned. However, you'll need to move to Electronic Messaging to work with other messaging options, such as replying to or forwarding a message.

Perform the following steps to access Electronic Messaging:

EM [RETURN]	a. From any menu, type "EM" and press [RETURN].
SDR MAIN [RETURN]	b. Before continuing, check the current drawer. Electronic Messaging works with messages only in the default drawer (typically Main). Type "SDR MAIN" and press [RETURN] if Main is not the current drawer. SDR is actually an option on the File Cabinet menu. All options on this menu can be selected from the Electronic Messaging menu.
[NEXT SCREEN]	c. Electronic Messaging has multiple screens of menu options. Press [NEXT SCREEN] (or [GOLD] A) to see additional options. If you know the option you want, you can enter it from any menu screen in Electronic Messaging, however.
***menu-option* [RETURN]**	d. Type an option and press [RETURN]. For example, to read new messages, type "RN" and press [RETURN]. Table 6.1 describes the common options. Table 6.2 describes advanced options, which are covered in upcoming chapters.

Table 6.1 Electronic Messaging menu options

Enter This Menu Option	*To Perform the Following Action*
A (Answer)	Create a reply to the current message. The reply is automatically addressed to the sender. The new message remains in your Created folder until you send it.
C (Create)	Create a new message that you will send later.
CAN (Cancel Deferred Delivery)	Cancel the delivery of a message sent with deferred delivery and refile the message in your Created folder. A message must have a status of "sent" for you to cancel delivery.
D (Delete)	Delete the current message and refile it in your Wastebasket folder.
DEF (Defer Delivery)	Send a message but defer delivery until a future date and/or time. If you delete a message sent with deferred delivery, you cannot cancel the delivery.
E (Edit)	Invoke the editor to make changes to the current created message. You can only change the text with the Edit option. Select the Modify Header (MH) option to change addressees, subject, or delivery details. Note that you cannot edit a message after it has been sent.
F (Forward)	Forward a copy of the current message to another individual.
FA (File Attachment as Document)	File a copy of an attachment to the current message as a separate document. This allows you to edit the attachment.

Table 6.1 *(continued)*

Enter This Menu Option	*To Perform the Following Action*
FAM (File Attachment as Message)	File a copy of the attachment to the current message as a message. This is useful if the attached document is a forwarded message.
FT (File Text)	File a copy of the text of the current message as a separate document. This allows you to edit the text.
I (Index)	Create an index of messages with which to work. You can also select one of the following options to build an index of a messaging folder quickly: IC Index of messages in your Created folder. II Index of incoming messages. IO Index of sent messages. IR Index of read messages.
IA (Index of Attachments)	Create an index listing all of the documents attached to the current message.
IDM (Index of Deferred Messages)	Create an index listing all messages that were sent with the Defer Delivery option, but not yet delivered.
MH (Modify Message Header)	Change the addressees, subject, or delivery information for the current created message.
P (Print)	Send a copy of the current message to the printer.
R (Read)	Display the current message on your terminal screen.
RN (Read New Mail)	Display the next message from your Inbox folder on the screen.
S (Send)	Send the current created message and file a copy of the message in your Outbox folder.
SEL (Select Message)	Select a message to work with (delete, print, etc.).
SH (Show Message Status)	Display information about the current message: title, sender's name, date, status, delivery options, and number of attachments.
TR (Training)	Start computer-based instruction for Electronic Messaging.
V (VMS Mail Import)	Import incoming mail messages from the VMS mail system to your Inbox and delete them from your VMS mail account.

Table 6.2 Advanced Electronic Messaging menu options

Enter This Menu Option	*To Perform the Following Action*
AF (Auto Forward)	Turn on the auto-forwarding of all of your incoming messages.
AR (Auto Reply)	Create a standard reply that will be returned to anyone who sends you mail.
ATT (Attach Document)	Attach a document to the current created message to send the document with the message.
CF (Cancel Auto Forward)	Turn off the auto-forwarding of all of your incoming messages.

(continued)

Table 6.2 Advanced Electronic Messaging menu options *(continued)*

Enter This Menu Option	*To Perform the Following Action*
CNS (Create Nickname for Sender)	Create a nickname for the sender of the current message (without having to type in the address of the sender). This is handy when you send and receive mail from someone with a long address, possibly someone on a different mail system.
CR (Cancel Auto Reply)	Disable the return of an Auto Reply message.
DET (Detach Document)	Detach the document previously attached to current message.
DL (Distribution List Management)	Move to the Distribution List Management menu.
DLM (Create Distribution List from Message)	Create a distribution list using the addressees on the current message. This is a quick way of creating a distribution list without having to enter all the names. (The sender already did this for you.)
DTO (DESKtop Options)	Display a menu of options to transfer mail between your workstation and the host system. This option requires an optional piece of software.
FC (File Cabinet Options)	Move to the File Cabinet Maintenance menu.
GMA (Grant Mail Access)	Grant access to your Main drawer to allow another individual to read and send your mail.
NI (Nickname Management)	Move to the Nickname Management menu.
O (Original Message)	Reselect the original incoming message to the current reply message (that is, a message created with the Answer option).
SMA (Set Mail Access)	"Place" yourself in the Main drawer of another individual so that you can read and send mail for him or her. The individual must first grant you this privilege by executing the GMA option.

6.2 CREATING AND SENDING A MESSAGE

Creating and sending an electronic message is much like writing and mailing a letter. You write your letter, place it in an envelope, and address the envelope. You then place the envelope in the outbox on your desk or in a mailbox. Unlike writing letters, however, in Electronic Messaging you address the message first, before writing the letter. You then select the Send option, which transmits the message, leaving a copy in your Outbox folder.

Perform the following steps to create a message:

C [RETURN]

a. From the Electronic Messaging menu or index, type "C" and press [RETURN]. ALL-IN-1 displays the Message Header form, shown in Figure 6.1.

TO: ***address* [RETURN]...**
TO: **[RETURN]**

b. Type the addresses of the people you want to send the message to, pressing [RETURN] after

```
                        Message Header

   Enter the name of one or more addressees:
TO:
TO:
TO:
TO:
TO:
TO:

   Enter names of people to receive copies:
CC:
CC:
CC:
CC:
CC:
CC:

Subject: ______________________________________________

Enter information and press RETURN, or GOLD M for menu,
or press GOLD E to expand address field                (more...)
```

Figure 6.1 Message Header form

each name. Enter as many addresses as you want. The addresses eventually scroll upward, allowing you to enter more. Press [RETURN] twice after the last address. The format of the address will vary, depending on how ALL-IN-1 is configured at your site. Typically, the address is either someone's username or last name.

Hint: ALL-IN-1's lookup feature is available when entering addresses. Press [FIND] (or [GOLD] L) to list all possible names, or even better, enter the first few characters of the name, then press [FIND]. Also, you don't need to spell out the address completely. Enter just enough characters to identify the addressee uniquely, and press [RETURN]. Refer to Section 7.1, "Addressing a Message," for details.

CC: *address* **[RETURN]...**
CC: **[RETURN]**

c. Type the addresses of individuals you want to "copy" and press [RETURN]. Press [RETURN] twice after the last address. If you do not want to send carbon copies to anyone, then simply press [RETURN] to move to the Subject field.

Subject: ***description***
[RETURN]

d. Type text that describes the content of the message in the Subject field, and press [RETURN]. To request special delivery options, press [NEXT SCREEN] and change the delivery options before pressing [RETURN].

e. Type the text of your message. You're now working with the same text editor that you use to create documents. All of the features of the text editor are available for preparing your message.

[EXIT]

f. Press [EXIT] (F10 or [GOLD] F) to exit the editor and file the message in your Created folder. (You can also press [GOLD] K or F8 to abort the creation of the message.) ALL-IN-1 redisplays the menu along with a note telling you to send the message when ready.

The message is now stored in your Created folder. You can modify the message with the options shown in Table 6.3 while it's in this folder, but you cannot modify the message after it has been sent.

When the message is complete, you might want to review it with the Read (R) option, then send the message with either Send (S) or Defer Delivery (DEF). Send delivers the message as soon as possible. Defer Delivery allows you to specify a future date and/or time for delivery. People sometimes use deferred delivery for reminders. For example, a supervisor might prepare a memo just before going on vacation and then defer delivery until several days later to remind employees of a deadline.

Do the following to send the message now:

S [RETURN]

Type "S" and press [RETURN]. ALL-IN-1 redisplays the menu, along with a note that the message has been sent. The message is now in your Outbox folder with a status of "sent."

Table 6.3 Menu options for modifying a created message

Enter This Menu Option	*To Perform the Following Action*
MH (Modify Header)	Change the list of addressees, the subject, or delivery information.
E (Edit)	Change the text of the message.
SC (Spell Check)	Perform a spell check on the text of the message. This feature is highly recommended for important messages.

To send the message at a future date and time, follow these steps:

DEF [RETURN]	a. Type "DEF" and press [RETURN]. ALL-IN-1 asks for the date and time you want to send the memo. The current date and time appear as the default.
Date and time: ***dd-mmm-yyyy hh:mm*** **[RETURN]**	b. Modify the date and time of delivery and press [RETURN]. You must specify a time in the future. ALL-IN-1 redisplays the menu, along with a note that the message has been deferred. The message is now in your Outbox folder with a status of "sent."

When sending deferred mail, keep the following in mind:

- Deferred mail is sent by a program called the Sender, which runs at regular intervals. Your message will be sent the first time this program runs after the time you specify. Therefore, there might be a short delay between the time you specify and when the message is actually sent.
- The message is stamped with the date and time it was created, not delivered. If you think this may confuse receipients to receive a message long after it was created, add something to your memo indicating it was sent with Defer Delivery.
- You can cancel the delivery of a deferred message up until the time it is actually sent. Select the message to make sure that it is current. Then enter the Cancel Delivery (CAN) option and press [RETURN]. The message will be placed back in your Created folder, and the status will be changed to "unsent."

6.2.1 Exercise: Creating and Sending a Message

The following exercise illustrates the steps for creating and sending a message. In this exercise, you'll send a message to yourself so that you can practice reading a message later.

1. Move to the Electronic Messaging menu.

EM [RETURN]	From any menu, type "EM" and press [RETURN] to move to Electronic Messaging.

2. Create the message.

C [RETURN]	a. Type "C" and press [RETURN]. ALL-IN-1 displays the Message Header, shown in Figure 6.1.
TO: **I [RETURN]** TO: **[RETURN]**	b. Type "I" and press [RETURN] twice. "I" is a pseudonym for yourself.

CC: **[RETURN]** c. Press [RETURN] to move to the Subject field.

Subject:**Test Memo [RETURN]** d. Enter "Test Memo" in the Subject field, and press [RETURN].

This is a test memo. e. Type the text, "This is a test memo."

[GOLD]F f. Press [GOLD] F to exit the editor and file the message in your Created folder. ALL-IN-1 redisplays the menu.

3. Send the message.

S [RETURN] Type "S" and press [RETURN]. ALL-IN-1 displays a confirmation that the message has been sent. You then receive notification that you have new mail (unless mail notification has been disabled with Set Working Conditions).

6.3 READING NEW MAIL

Often, the first task new users perform in ALL-IN-1 is to read new mail. We all experience a moment of joy in discovering that we have new mail messages, the same sort of feeling you have as you open the mailbox on Valentine's Day to find a card inside. (The feeling fades quickly, however, as we begin reading our messages, only to realize they're all from people who *want* something!)

ALL-IN-1 has two ways of notifying you of new messages. First, the number of new messages is always displayed at the top of a menu. Second, if you're working in ALL-IN-1 when someone sends you a message, you're immediately notified of its delivery (unless mail notification has been disabled with Set Working Conditions).

There are many ways to read incoming messages. Three common methods are described below. The first method is suitable for people who receive only a few messages daily. In this method, you read the messages in the order in which they were received. The second method is recommended for those who receive lots of mail messages. This method allows you to read messages in any order. In the third method, you temporarily interrupt your work to read a new message.

Method 1: Reading New Messages in the Order Received

ALL-IN-1 places incoming messages in your Inbox folder. Messages are organized in this folder in the order in which they were received, with the first (oldest) message at the top.

Perform the following steps to read new messages in the order received:

EM [RETURN] a. From any menu, type "EM" and press [RETURN] to move to the Electronic Messaging menu.

RN [RETURN]

b. Type "RN" and press [RETURN] to display the oldest message.

c. Read the message. Use any of the function keys described in Table 4.1 to move through the message text, or enter any of the menu options listed in Table 6.4.

Hint: This is a good time to select the Delete (D) option to get rid of the message if it's not really important. This reduces the time and effort you later spend cleaning up your File Cabinet.

[RETURN]

d. Press [RETURN] when you reach the bottom to clear the message and redisplay the menu.

Note: You can also press [CANCEL] (F8) to clear the message and return to the menu. However, the message is left in your Inbox with an Unread status. This is a handy way to keep track of messages you must reply to later.

e. Repeat steps b through d until ALL-IN-1 notifies you that there are no more new messages.

Method 2: Reading New Messages in Any Order

In this method, you first create an index of incoming messages, then read the messages in random order. This allows you to skip messages, targeting those that are most important.

Perform the following steps to read new messages in any order:

EM II [RETURN]

a. From any menu, type "EM II" and then press [RETURN] to move to Electronic Messaging and create an index of your incoming messages.

Hint: To quickly read all messages, add "ALL XR." This selects and displays all incoming messages as well. Press [EXIT] (F10 or Keypad-0) at any time to stop reading mail.

***line-number* R [RETURN]**

b. Type the line number of the message you want to read next, followed by a space and "R." Press [RETURN] to read the message. Use any of the function keys described in Table 4.1, or enter any of the menu options listed in Table 6.4 on page 119 (D, RFD, etc.).

[RETURN]

c. Press [RETURN] when you reach the bottom of the message. The index is redisplayed. Note that the folder name for the current message has been changed to "Read."

Note: You can also press [CANCEL] (F8) to clear the message. However, the message is left in your Inbox with an unread status.

d. Repeat steps b and c until you've read all of your messages.

Hint: This is a good time to select multiple messages and enter the Delete All Selected (XD) option to get rid of unimportant messages.

[EXIT]

e. Press [EXIT] (F10 or Keypad-0) to leave the index and return to the menu.

Method 3: Interrupting Your Work to Read a New Message

This method is useful when you are in the middle of a task and receive notification of new mail. Display the Interrupt menu, then select the Read New Mail (RN) option.

Perform the following steps to interrupt your current task and read new messages:

[GOLD] I

a. Press [GOLD] I to display the Interrupt menu.

RN [RETURN]

b. Type "RN" and press [RETURN] to read the incoming message.

c. Read the message. Press any of the function keys described in Table 4.1 to move through the message text.

[RETURN]

d. When you reach the bottom, press [RETURN] to redisplay the menu.

Note: You can also press [CANCEL] (F8) to clear the message. However, the message is left in your Inbox with an unread status.

e. Repeat steps b through d until ALL-IN-1 notifies you that there are no more new messages.

[RESUME]

f. Press [RESUME] (F7) to resume your previous work, or press [EXIT].

Table 4.1 lists the function keys that are active when you read a message. Note that when you press [RETURN] or [NEXT SCREEN] while reading a message, ALL-IN-1 scrolls forward a full screen of text and erases the line that you read last. This makes it hard to keep your place. Just press the [UP ARROW] after a [RETURN] to scroll back and display the last line from the previous page.

Table 6.4 Read menu options

Enter This Read Menu Option	*To Perform the Following Action*
A (Answer)	Create a response to the current message.
CNS (Create Nickname for Sender)	Create a nickname for the sender of the current message.
D (Delete)	Place the current message in the Wastebasket.
DLM (Create Distribution List from Message)	Create a distribution list from the list of addressees in the current message.
F (Forward)	Forward the current message to another user.
FA (File Attachment)	File the attachment to the current message as a separate document.
FAM (File Attachment as Message)	File an attachment to the current document as a message with a status of "read." This option is typically used when the attachment is a forwarded message.
FT (File Text)	File just the text of the current message as a separate document.
LU (Leave Message Unread)	Clear the message and leave it in the Inbox folder with an Unread status.
N (Read Next Selected Document)	Display the next selected message.
NA (Read from Next Attachment)	Display the next attachment.
NDL (View Message without Distribution List)	Redisplay message, suppress names of addressees.
PA (Read Previous Attachment)	Redisplay the previous attachment.
RFD (Refile Document)	Refile the current message in another folder.
S (Send)	Send the current message (when reading a created message).
SH (Show Status)	Display message status information, including the list of addressees.
VDL (View Message with Distribution List)	Redisplay message including all addressees.

Table 6.4 lists the menu options that you can enter when reading a message. These options apply to reading mail. A complete list is found in Section 4.1.1.2, "Read Menu Options."

6.3.1 Exercise: Reading a Message

The following exercise shows you how to read an incoming message. You should first perform the exercise in the previous section to create and send yourself a message.

1. Move to the Electronic Messaging menu.

EM [RETURN]	Type "EM" and press [RETURN] to move to Electronic Messaging.

2. Read a message from your Inbox folder.

RN [RETURN]	a. Type "RN" and press [RETURN]. ALL-IN-1 displays the message.
[GOLD] Z	b. Press [GOLD] Z to display message status information.
[GOLD] M	c. Press [GOLD] M to display the Read menu.
D [RETURN]	d. Type "D" and press [RETURN] to delete the message. *Caution:* Make sure that this is the message you created earlier as a test. Don't delete the message if it's important mail. ALL-IN-1 redisplays the menu with a note that the message has been placed in your Wastebasket.

6.4 SELECTING A MESSAGE

Many options on the Electronic Messaging menu perform actions on the *current* message. The current message is identified in the upper right-hand corner of the menu or by the current item pointer (>) in an index. If this message is not the one you want to work with, first select the message before entering options such as Delete, Print, Forward, and so on. Likewise, many options on the Electronic Messaging index perform actions on all selected messages. Before entering one of these options, you must first select one or more messages.

Sections 3.1.3, 3.3.5, and 3.3.6 describe these steps in great detail. Following is a brief summary.

Perform these steps to select a single message when working with a menu:

[SELECT]	a. Press [SELECT] (or type "SEL" and press [RETURN]). ALL-IN-1 displays a data-entry form. *Hint:* A quick method is to type "SEL" followed by a folder name (Created, Outbox, Inbox, or Read) and press [RETURN]. Then press [DOWN ARROW] to scroll down through messages in the folder. Remember that the most recent messages are at the top of the folder.
Folder: ***folder* [TAB]** Title: ***title* [RETURN]**	b. Enter the folder and title of the message that you want to work with, and press [RETURN]. The menu is redisplayed with the message shown in the current item block.

Hint: Press [FIND] (or [GOLD] L) here if you don't remember the titles.

To select a single message when working with an index, do the following:

***line-number* [RETURN]**	Type the line number of the message you want to work with, and press [RETURN]. The current item pointer (>) is positioned next to the message.

To select multiple messages when working with an index, do the following:

***line,line-line,...* [SELECT]**	Type the line numbers, or range of line numbers, of all of the messages you want to work with, and press [SELECT]. For example, type "1,3,5-7" to select messages 1, 3, 5, 6, and 7. An *x* appears next to each selected item. Press [NEXT SCREEN] (or [GOLD] A) if you need to display additional pages of messages.

6.5 FORWARDING A MESSAGE

The Forward (F) option on the Electronic Messaging menu forwards the current message to another person. The message is sent as an attachment to your cover memo. If the recipient wants to respond to the message you're forwarding, he or she must first file the attachment as a message with the File Attachment as Message (FAM) option and then send a response with the Answer (A) option.

You can select the Forward option while reading a message. You can also select and forward a message that you've previously read. Before forwarding any message, however, you might want to display the original list of recipients with the Show Header (SH) option. There's no need to forward the message to someone who's already received it!

Perform these steps to forward the current message or all selected messages to another individual:

F [RETURN] or **XF [RETURN]**	a. Type "F" and press [RETURN] to forward the current message, or type "XF" and press [RETURN] to forward all selected messages in the index. ALL-IN-1 displays the Forwarding Message Header.
TO: ***address(name)* [RETURN]...**	b. Enter the addresses of the individuals to whom you want to forward the message, then enter the subject. The steps to complete these fields are the same as for creating and sending a message (Section 6.2).

c. If you don't want a cover note, press [TAB] after completing the subject field and make sure that the cover note indicator is set to "N."

Note: The default response for a cover note can be changed by setting the Forwarding Cover Note flag with Set Working Conditions.

[RETURN]

d. Press [RETURN] when you've completed the forwarding information.

[GOLD] F

e. If you're adding a cover note, type the text of your cover note. Press [GOLD] F to exit the editor when finished. ALL-IN-1 redisplays the menu, along with a note telling you to send the message when ready. If you do not send the message, it remains in your Created folder.

S [RETURN]

f. If you're working from a menu, type "S" and press [RETURN] to forward the message.

Do you want to send this now [Y/N]?
Y [RETURN]

If you're working from an index, respond "Y" and press [RETURN] when asked if you want to send this message now. The message will be sent, and a copy will be placed in your Outbox folder with a status of "sent."

6.6 RESPONDING TO A MESSAGE

The Answer (A) option sends a reply to the current message. Electronic Messaging automatically addresses the message to the sender and completes the Subject field with the original subject text preceded by "Re:". If the original message was sent to other people as well, you're given the option of sending your reply to everyone or just to the sender.

You can enter this option while reading the message. This is handy if you want to respond to the message immediately. You can also select and respond to a message that you read previously. Simply select the message to answer before entering the Answer option.

GOLD Original Message is a handy feature for preparing your response. You can press [GOLD] O while preparing your response text. ALL-IN-1 displays a copy of the original memo (the memo to which you're responding). You can reread the text and can even select and cut a portion of this message to paste in as part of your response. Press [GOLD] F when you are ready to clear the original message and return to preparing your response.

Follow these steps to send a response to the current message:

A [RETURN]

a. Type "A" and press [RETURN].

Do you wish to reply
to all addressees [A]
or to the sender only [S]?
A or S [RETURN]

b. If the message was sent to other individuals, ALL-IN-1 asks if you want to send your response to everyone or just to the sender. Type "A" and press [RETURN] to send your response to the sender and all addressees. Type "S" and press [RETURN] to send your response only to the sender.

Note: You can add or remove addressees after creating your response with Modify Header (MH).

c. Type the text of your response. Press [GOLD] O if you want to display a copy of the original message (then press [GOLD] F to clear the original message and return to your response).

[GOLD] F

d. When the response is complete, press [GOLD] F to exit the editor and file the message in your Created folder. ALL-IN-1 redisplays the menu, along with a note telling you to send the message when ready. (You can also press [GOLD] K if you want to abort sending the reply.)

S [RETURN]

e. If you're working from a menu, type "S" and press [RETURN] to forward the message.

Do you want to send
this now [Y/N]?
Y [RETURN]

If you're working from an index, respond "Y" and press [RETURN] when asked if you want to send this message now. The message is sent, and a copy is placed in your Outbox folder with a status of "sent."

6.7 DELETING MESSAGES

As you work with Electronic Messaging, you'll find that messages tend to collect in your Read and Outbox folders over time. It helps to delete obsolete messages periodically to clean up your File Cabinet. This reduces the number of documents that you must work with to a more manageable size. Cleaning out your File Cabinet also improves the performance of any operation involving a document.

You probably want to retain important messages for a while, perhaps six months or so. Creating an index using date selection is a good method for searching for and deleting the older messages. Of course, the best time to delete a less important message is right after you've read or sent it. Remember that when you delete a message, it is simply placed in your Wastebasket folder and can be easily recovered before the Janitor runs.

You can delete a single message with the Delete (D) option. You can delete multiple messages with the Delete All Selected (XD) option when working from an index. Both methods are described below. Also explained is the procedure for recovering a message that was deleted unintentionally.

To delete the current message, perform these steps:

D [RETURN]

a. Type "D" and press [RETURN].

Y [RETURN]

b. If ALL-IN-1 asks you to confirm whether you want to delete the message, type "Y" and press [RETURN]. (This prompt can be suppressed with Set Working Conditions.) ALL-IN-1 displays a note advising you that the document has been deleted.

You can recover a message from your Wastebasket to prevent it from being removed by the Janitor. Simply select the message and refile it into the original folder—for example, the Read folder. The easiest way to do this is from an index of the Wastebasket.

Here is the procedure for recovering a message from the Wastebasket:

I WASTEBASKET [RETURN]

a. Type "I WASTEBASKET" and press [RETURN]. ALL-IN-1 displays an index of your Wastebasket folder.

***line-number* RFD *folder* [RETURN]**

b. Type the line number of the message you want to recover, followed by a space, "RFD", another space, and the original folder name—for example, "2 RFD READ." Then press [RETURN]. The folder of the current document is changed.

Perform the following steps to delete multiple messages:

I [RETURN]

a. From the Electronic Messaging menu, type "I" and press [RETURN] to create an index of messages. ALL-IN-1 displays a form for entering selection criteria.

Folder: ***folder* [TAB]...**

b. Enter information to build an index of messages. Include all information that pertains to the messages you wish to delete. Press [ERASE LINE] (F13 or LF) to clear the folder name and create an index of all messages and documents. When completing the fields, press [TAB] to move to the next field, or press [BACKSPACE] (F12) to move to the previous field.

Hint: To target very old messages and documents, clear the Folder field with [ERASE LINE] and press [TAB] to move to the Creation Date "To" field. Enter a date by typing "-6M," for example, to find messages and documents older than six months.

[RETURN] c. Press [RETURN] to create the index.

line,line-line,...
[SELECT] d. Type the line numbers, or range of line numbers, of all messages you want to delete. Then press [SELECT]. ALL-IN-1 places an *x* next to the selected messages.

Note: Press [NEXT PAGE] (or [GOLD] [TAB]) to display any additional pages of messages. Then enter line numbers and press [SELECT]. Repeat as necessary to select all desired messages.

To deselect messages, type the line numbers and press [GOLD] [SELECT] (or [GOLD] Keypad-Period).

Type "ALL" and press [RETURN] to select all messages, or type "CAS" and press [RETURN] to deselect messages.

XD [RETURN] e. Type "XD" and press [RETURN] to delete the selected messages.

Y [RETURN] f. If ALL-IN-1 asks you to confirm whether you want to delete these messages, type "Y" and press [RETURN]. ALL-IN-1 refiles the messages in the Wastebasket folder and displays a note indicating how many messages were deleted.

Note: If you accidentally deleted the wrong message, type the line number followed by "RFD" and the original folder name, then press [RETURN].

[EXIT] g. Press [EXIT] (F10 or Keypad-0) to redisplay the Electronic Messaging menu.

6.8 REFILING MESSAGES

ALL-IN-1 automatically refiles messages as you read, send, and delete. Reading moves the message from your Inbox to the Read folder. Sending moves the message from your Created folder to your Outbox. Deleting moves the message to your Wastebasket folder. You can refile messages at any time, placing them in any folder you wish. Table 6.5 describes several options for refiling messages or attached documents.

Table 6.5 Menu options for refiling messages

Enter This Menu Option	*To Perform the Following Action*
FA (File Attachment as Document)	File a copy of an attachment to a message you've received. The copy is filed as a separate document. You can then edit, print, and delete the copy without affecting the original message.
FAM (File Attachment as Message)	File a copy of an attachment as a separate message. FAM is typically used instead of FA when the attachment is a message—for example, a forwarded message. This option differs from FA in that you can perform messaging options on the filed attachment, such as reply to the sender.
FM (File Message)	Cross-file the current message into a second folder. This allows you to select the document from either folder.
FT (File Text)	File a copy of the text of the current message without the message header. The copy is filed as a separate document. You can then edit, print, and delete the copy without affecting the original message.
IA (Index of Attachments)	Create an index of the attachments to a message. This is very handy when two or more documents are attached to a message. Options that appear on the index menu include these: R — Read (attachment) XR — Read All Selected FA — File Attachment as Document XFA — File Selected Documents FAM — File Attachment as Message XFAM — File Selected Messages
RFD (Refile Document)	Move the current message to a new folder. This option also allows you to change the title.
U (Update Index)	Change the folder name, title, author, or handling of the current message.

Remember the following points when refiling messages or attachments:

- When someone sends you a document to work with, it's usually sent as an attachment to a message. Use the File Attachment (FA) option to move the attachment into your File Cabinet as a separate document. The Index of Attachments (IA) option makes it easy to work with multiple attachments. File Attachment files a *copy* of the document. The original remains as an attachment to the message. This is advantageous if you accidentally delete your copy or ruin it during editing. At some point, however, you should delete the original message to clean up your File Cabinet.
- Another way to copy and work with an attachment is to create a brand-new document, then press GOLD Get Document ([GOLD] G) to select and retrieve the attachment. You're already in the editor and can begin working. A word of caution: You'll lose any special print settings sent with the document.

- File Text (FT) is the option you want to choose when you need to modify the text of a message. This option places a copy of just the text of a message in a separate document. You might want to delete the original message to clean up your File Cabinet.
- A good habit when reading mail is to refile important messages after reading them to keep your Read folder to a manageable size. In addition, delete less important messages after you read them. Both Refile Document (RFD) and Delete (D) appear on the Read menu; therefore, you can enter them while reading the message.
- Refile Document (RFD) is preferable to File Message for refiling important messages because it moves the message out of the Read folder. File Message does not. Instead, the message ends up cross-filed in two folders.

Becoming More Proficient with Electronic Messaging

CHAPTER 7

This chapter describes some techniques for working more efficiently with Electronic Messaging. You'll be interested in all of the following topics if you're going to be using Electronic Messaging to any extent. They include methods to make addressing a message easier and techniques for routing documents by attaching them to messages.

This chapter teaches you how to perform the following tasks:

- Address a message.
- Create and manage nicknames to address messages.
- Create and manage distribution lists to address messages.
- Create and work with an index of messages.
- Attach documents to a message to send to another user.

7.1 ADDRESSING A MESSAGE

Addressing a letter sent through regular mail is fairly easy: You simply write the name, street address, city, state, and postal code on the envelope. The format of addresses throughout the United States is fairly consistent. However, addresses for large businesses can be more complex; they might include department names, mail stops, and/or internal post office boxes. As organizations grow larger, systems to handle the organization's mail grow larger and more complex.

Addressing electronic mail can sometimes be difficult because electronic mail systems within organizations can also be large and complex. A mail system in a large organization usually reaches across a network of computers from several manufacturers. As you know, not all computer manufacturers agree on how to do things.

ALL-IN-1 provides a number of tools to help with addressing. One of the most important tools is the *directory*. The Electronic Messaging directory is very much like a telephone directory. It lists the names and locations of individuals. Instead of searching this directory to find a telephone number, though, you search to find an electronic mail address. Directories are set up by the system manager and typically list everyone in the company. In very large organizations, it might not be possible to list everyone in the company in the directory—just everyone at your site or location. This does not mean, however, that you can't send mail to someone who is not listed in the directory; you just need to use a different method for addressing the message.

There are two ways to address a message in Electronic Messaging:

- Enter a name that appears in a mail directory. Typically, this is an individual's last name or ALL-IN-1 username. ALL-IN-1 then searches the directory to find the address for the individual. This first method is fairly easy and usually works when sending mail to individuals within your company or at your location.
- Enter the real or *physical* mail address for the individual. The format of the address varies, depending on the configuration of your mail network and that of the addressee. This method also requires some knowledge of the various mail systems in your organization. Depending on the ability of your system to communicate with other mail networks, it might be possible to send messages to individuals in companies located throughout the world.

Your system manager builds and maintains comprehensive directories for your use (Figure 7.1). There are two types of directories in ALL-IN-1, one of which is designated as the primary directory (the directory searched first).

ALL-IN-1 Directory	This directory lists the ALL-IN-1 usernames of individuals and gives their mail addresses.
Mail Directory	This directory lists the personal names of individuals plus their mail addresses. The Mail directory, also referred to as *Distributed Directory Services* (DDS), is typically imple-

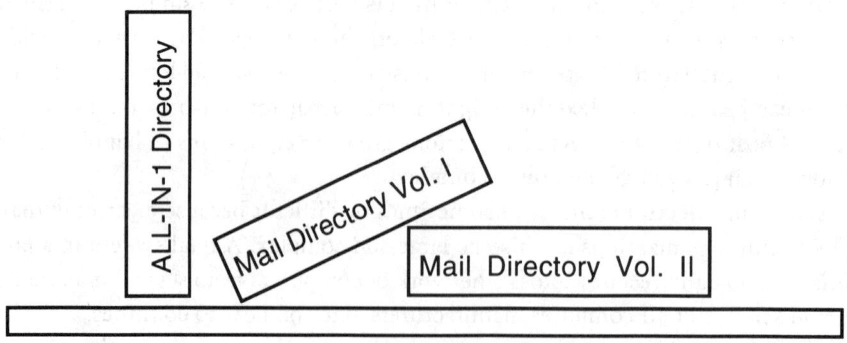

Figure 7.1 ALL-IN-1 directory and Mail directory

mented in a network environment in which mail is also sent to users of different mail systems.

If all of this sounds a little overwhelming, be aware that the following tools are provided to simplify addressing:

[FIND]	ALL-IN-1's lookup capability is available when addressing a message. To locate the address for an individual whose name begins with *C*, for example, type "C" and press [FIND]. ALL-IN-1 searches the primary directory and displays all names beginning with *C*.
Nicknames	You can create your own "nickname" for the address of an individual when you have trouble remembering the full address. This is extremely useful for writing to people who have very long addresses.
Distribution Lists	You can create a list containing addresses for everyone to whom you collectively send messages. Create the list once, then use it again and again to send messages.
Groups	Groups are similar to Distribution Lists; they are simply lists of individuals. Not everyone can create a group, but everyone does have access to the groups that have been created. You can enter group names as well as distribution list names when addressing a message.
Search Directories	ALL-IN-1 allows you to search a directory to find one or more addresses. You simply enter relevant details, such as a last name or department name. ALL-IN-1 then searches the directory and displays a list of everyone who matches these details.

7.1.1 The Message Header

The Create option in Electronic Messaging displays the Message Header form shown in Figure 7.2. You enter the addresses, the subject of the memo, and delivery details here. Table 7.1 describes the fields on this form.

Remember the following points when completing the Message Header form:

- You can enter delivery details on the second screen of this form. Press [NEXT SCREEN] (or [GOLD] A) and enter delivery details *before* pressing [RETURN].
- The Modify Header (MH) option on the Electronic Messaging menu allows you to change information in the message header once you've created the message. You must modify the header before sending the message, though, because you can't modify a message after it's been sent.

```
                         Message Header

    Enter the name of one or more addressees:
TO:
TO:
TO:
TO:
TO:
TO:

    Enter names of people to receive copies:
CC:
CC:
CC:
CC:
CC:
CC:

Subject: ______________________________________________

Enter information and press RETURN, or GOLD M for menu,
or press GOLD E to expand address field                 (more...)
```

Figure 7.2 Message Header form

Table 7.1 Message Header fields

Field	*Perform the Following Steps to Complete the Field*
First Screen:	
To:[a]	Enter the addresses of the people you want to send the message to, pressing [RETURN] after each entry. Enter as many addresses as you want. Your entries scroll up after you enter the sixth address, giving you room to enter more. You can enter any of the following items in this field: • A name that appears in the directory, typically the individual's ALL-IN-1 username or last name. • A nickname. • A distribution list name or group name. • A physical address. Press [TAB] to move to the CC: field after entering all of the addresses. Notes: • You don't have to enter the full address if it appears in a directory. Just enter enough characters to specify the name uniquely, and press [RETURN]. ALL-IN-1 searches the directory and fills in the full address. If you don't enter enough characters to specify a single name uniquely, ALL-IN-1 displays a selection list of names matching what you've entered.

Table 7.1 *(continued)*

Field	*Perform the Following Steps to Complete the Field*
	• If you don't know the address at all, press [GOLD] M to display the Message Header menu. Then select either the Search ALL-IN-1 Directory (SAD) option or the Search Mail Directory (SMD) option to scan either directory. • If you need to enter a long address, press [GOLD] E to expand the Address field. See Section 7.1.2, "Entering an Address," for further details.
CC:[a]	Enter the addresses of the individuals you want to receive a copy. All of the rules for entering an address in the "To:" field apply here. After completing this list, press [TAB] to move to the Subject field.
Subject	Enter a short description of the message's content. Put the important text at the beginning of this field. This is the text that appears when you list messages in an index.
Add a Cover Note?	This field appears only when forwarding a message. Enter "Y" if you want to include a cover note; otherwise, enter "N".
Second Screen:	
Priority[a]	To specify the method of delivery, enter one of the following: EXPRESS — Sends the message to local users immediately and across the network to remote users as soon as possible. Use Express only in urgent situations. FIRST_CLASS — Sends the message to local users immediately and to users on a remote system after the next mail "pickup." The frequency of mail pickups varies from one system to another, but it is usually between five and 15 minutes. First Class is suitable for almost any message. SECOND_CLASS — Sends the message to both local and remote users after the next mail pickup. If you're sending the message to local users, First Class is just as efficient as Express.
Delivery Receipt	Indicate here whether you want ALL-IN-1 to return a mail message notifying you that your message was delivered properly. Enter "Y" if you want a Delivery receipt returned; otherwise, enter "N". You should request a Delivery receipt if you're sending an important message across a communications line to another computer system or if you want to document the date and time that the addressee received the message. You will receive the Delivery receipt as a new incoming message.
Read Receipt	Indicate here whether you want ALL-IN-1 to send back notification when the recipient reads your message. Enter "Y" if you want a Read receipt; otherwise, enter "N". Request a Read receipt only if you are sending an important message and you want to document the date and time that the addressee read it. The recipient is notified that a

(continued)

Table 7.1 Message Header fields *(continued)*

Field	*Perform the Following Steps to Complete the Field*
	Read receipt has been returned *after* he or she has finished reading the message. You receive the receipt as a new incoming message. Note that you can control the automatic return of a Read receipt for messages sent to you by setting an option with Set Working Conditions.
Expiry Date	Optionally, enter a future date/time after which the content of the memo will no longer be relevant. Enter the date/time in the format dd-mmm-yy:hh:mm. If the recipient reads the memo after the specified date/time, he or she is notified that the message has expired.
Sensitivity[a]	Enter one of the following values to indicate the sensitivity of the message content: NOT SENSITIVE, PERSONAL, PRIVATE, COMPANY CONFIDENTIAL. If you change the default, the new value is displayed at the top of the message when read or printed.
Importance[a]	Enter one of the following values to indicate the importance of the message: LOW, NORMAL, HIGH. Messages tagged with HIGH importance are marked with an exclamation point (!) when listed in an index of messages.
BCC[a]	Enter the addresses of individuals you want to receive a Blind Carbon Copy. A copy of the message is forwarded to these individuals without the knowledge of the individuals listed in To: or CC:. All the rules for entering an address in the "To:" field apply here.

[a]ALL-IN-1's lookup feature can be used in this field. Press [ERASE LINE] (F13 or LF) to clear the field, then press [FIND] (or [GOLD] L) to display a list of possible entries. Refer to Section 3.2.2, "Using [FIND] to Complete a Field," for further information on the lookup feature.

7.1.2 Entering an Address

The following procedures show various methods for entering addresses in either the To:, CC:, or BCC: fields of the Message Header. To enter an address using the ALL-IN-1 directory:

TO: ***username* [RETURN]**	Type the individual's ALL-IN-1 username and press [RETURN]. *Note:* Press [FIND] (or [GOLD] L) to list all possible names, or even better, enter the first few characters of the name, then press [FIND]. You don't have to spell out the username completely. Enter just enough characters to specify the name uniquely, then press [RETURN].

To enter an address using the Mail directory (DDS):

TO: ***last-name* [RETURN]** TO: ***first-name last-name* [RETURN]** TO: ***first-initial last-name* [RETURN]**	Type the individual's name and press [RETURN]. There are several different formats for entering the name.

Note: Press [FIND] (or [GOLD] L) to list all possible names, or even better, enter the first few characters of the name, then press [FIND].

You don't have to spell out the name completely. Enter just enough characters to specify the name uniquely, then press [RETURN].

To enter an address when you're not sure what to enter:

TO: ***last-name*** **[RETURN]**

a. Try typing the individual's last name, and press [RETURN]. ALL-IN-1 will locate the proper address or display a list of all individuals with that last name.

TO: **C [FIND]**

If this doesn't work, type the first letter of the last name and press [FIND] (or [GOLD] L). ALL-IN-1 displays a list of all addresses beginning with the character you entered.

line-number **[RETURN]**

b. Type the line number next to the individual's name and press [RETURN]. If you don't see the name you want on the first page, press [RETURN] to see additional pages of names.

To enter a nickname:

TO: ***nickname*** **[RETURN]**

Type the nickname and press [RETURN].

Note: You must first create the nickname. Refer to Section 7.2, "Nickname Management," for details.

To address a message to everyone on a distribution list or everyone in a group:

TO: ***distribution-list*** **[RETURN]**

Type the name of the distribution list and press [RETURN]. Distribution list names either begin with the "at" symbol (@) or end with a colon (:).

TO: ****group-name*** **[RETURN]**

Type the group name and press [RETURN]. Group names begin with an asterisk (*).

Note: The distribution list or group must first be created. Refer to Section 7.3, "Creating and Maintaining Distribution Lists," and Chapter 14, "Group Services," for details.

If you don't remember a distribution list or group name, type "@" or "*" and press [FIND] to display a list.

After entering the distribution list or group name, press [GOLD] V to display the names of everyone included in the list or group.

To address a message to all users on the system who can receive ALL-IN-1 mail addressed to "subscribers":

TO: **SUBSCRIBERS: [RETURN]**	Type the name "SUBSCRIBERS:" and press [RETURN]. *Note:* You cannot address mail to "subscribers" unless the system administrator has granted PRVSUBSCR to your account. System administrators can disable an account from receiving messages sent to "Subscribers" by setting the RVC$SUB flag in the user's profile to "N." By default, users have this flag set to "Y."

To address a message to yourself (for training, perhaps):

TO: **I [RETURN]**	Type "I" or "ME" and press [RETURN].

To address a message to someone who has no access to e-mail:

TO: ***name* (PAPER MAIL) [RETURN]**	Type the name of the individual, followed by the words "(PAPER MAIL)" in parentheses. Then press [RETURN]. *Note:* When you send this message, ALL-IN-1 prints a hard copy of the message for you to send by mail. The message is sent to the default printer specified for your account. Your default printer setting can be modified by the system administrator or established with the following qualifier to the ALLIN1 command when you start ALL-IN-1: `$ ALLIN1 /PRINTER=print-queue`

To address a message to someone who uses a different mail system:

TO: ***full-address* [RETURN]**	Type the full address for the individual and press [RETURN]. Table 7.2 describes address formats for common mail systems.

Table 7.2 Address formats for common mail systems

Enter an Address With This Format	*To Send a Message to Someone Using*
username@A1@*node*	ALL-IN-1 on a remote system.
username@A1@*node*@*area*	ALL-IN-1 on a remote system in a different area.
username@AM@*node*	Digital Mailworks.
PRUSERNAME=*username*@PRLOCATION=*node*@MRP@*mrp-node*[a]	PROFS on an IBM system.
SNUSERNAME=*username*@SNLOCATION=*node*@MRS@*mrs-node*[a]	SNADS on an IBM system.
username@*node*@UMC@*umc-node*	ULTRIX mail.
_*nodename*::*username*	VMS Mail without MRGATE.
username@MRGATE@*node*	VMS Mail with MRGATE on their system.
username@*node*@MRGATE	VMS Mail with MRGATE on your system.
username@*node*@MRGATE@*mrgate-node*	VMS Mail with MRGATE on third system.
X400[a,b]	X.400

Notes:

- The term *node* refers to a name assigned to a computer system. When computer systems are linked together in a network, communications programs must be able to differentiate one system from another. Therefore, system managers assign a name to each computer in the network.
- A1, MRGATE, MRP, MRS, and UMC are names of *mailboxes*, a term with similar meaning here as in the office environment. Mail is dropped off by one mail system in a storage location called a mailbox, to be picked up later by another mail system. Each mail system is assigned a unique mailbox name. An address of SMITHR@ASPEN@MRGATE@DENVER, for example, is shorthand notation for "deliver this message to user SMITHR whose account is on node ASPEN by placing it in the MRGATE mailbox located on node DENVER."

[a]Details for your account must exist in the Mail Directory if you are to address a message to this mail system. These details are retrieved for outgoing mail. Ask your system manager to add you to the Mail Directory if you intend to send mail to someone using this mail system.

[b]Type "X400" and press [RETURN] to display a form that accepts information to build a full X.400 address. These addresses can be quite long, so it helps to create a Nickname for these individuals.

7.1.3 Searching for an Address

Directories are provided to help you locate an individual's address. If you're not sure of someone's name or address, you can search the directories for it. Just enter the information you're sure of, such as the department name. ALL-IN-1 then scans the directories to build a list of everyone who matches the information you've entered.

Perform the following steps to search a directory when entering an address:

[GOLD] M — a. When the Message Header form is displayed, press [GOLD] M. ALL-IN-1 displays the Message Header menu.

***menu-option* [RETURN]**	b. Type one of the following options and press [RETURN] to search a specific directory: SAD — Search the ALL-IN-1 directory. SMD — Search the Mail directory. SOM — Search other directories. ALL-IN-1 displays a form for entering selection criteria.
	c. Enter any information you know about the individual or group of individuals to whom you want to send the message.
[RETURN]	d. Press [RETURN] after entering selection criteria. ALL-IN-1 displays an index of matching addresses.[1]
***line-number,line-number,...* [SELECT]**	e. Type the line numbers of everyone to whom you want to send the message, then press [SELECT]. ALL-IN-1 places an *x* next to the names of selected individuals. *Note:* Press [NEXT SCREEN] (or [GOLD] A) to see additional pages of names. To deselect a name, type the line number and press [GOLD] [SELECT].
XADD [RETURN]	f. Type "XADD" and press [RETURN] to add the selected names to your message header.
[EXIT] **[EXIT]**	g. Press [EXIT] twice to leave the index and return to the Message Header. Note that the addresses you selected from the index have been added to the Message Header.

7.2 NICKNAME MANAGEMENT

Nicknames are pseudonyms for the addresses of individuals. For example, "BOB SMITH" might be a nickname for the address "SMITHR@A1@DENVER." To create a nickname, give ALL-IN-1 both the real address of the individual and the nickname

1. The search for matching addresses is automatically extended to the local Mail directory (if enabled) and then to other Mail directories. Depending on system configuration, you might be asked if you want to continue before the next directory is searched. These break points can be enabled for individual users, even when disabled systemwide, by setting the permanent symbols $EMDESCAL1 and $EMDESCAL2 to "1." Contact your system administrator for assistance in defining these symbols. Depending on system configuration, the list of matching addresses might or might not be sorted. Individual users can specify that the list be sorted, even when sorting is disabled systemwide, by setting the permanent symbol $EMMDSORT to "1."

you'll be entering to refer to the individual. You can then address a message by entering the nickname instead of by typing the real address. Nicknames offer these two advantages:

- You save typing by creating nicknames that are shorter than the real addresses of individuals. Some addresses, such as those for X.400, can be quite long.
- Nicknames are always easier to remember than real addresses.

7.2.1 Accessing Nickname Management

You create and maintain a list of nicknames with options on the Nickname Management menu. This list of nicknames has two columns: nicknames and real addresses. You add a line to this list by creating a nickname, change a line by editing a nickname, and so forth. ALL-IN-1 scans the list to find the real address for an individual whenever you enter a nickname.

Perform the following steps to access the Nickname Management menu:

NI [RETURN]

a. From any menu, type "NI" and then press [RETURN]. The Nickname Management menu is displayed.

***menu-option* [RETURN]**

b. Enter a menu option and press [RETURN]. Table 7.3 describes these options.

Note: You can also access the Nickname Management menu from the Interrupt menu. Press [GOLD] I to display the Interrupt menu, then enter "DIR NI" and press [RETURN].

Table 7.3 Nickname Management menu options

Enter the Menu Selection	*To Perform the Following Action*
C (Create)	Create a new nickname.
CO (Copy Nickname Address)	Copy the address for one nickname and create a new nickname.
D (Delete)	Delete the current nickname.
E (Edit)	Change the address for the current nickname.
I (Index)	Create an index of nicknames so that you can read, print, and delete names.
P (Print)	Print the entire list of nicknames.
R (Read)	Display the complete address for the current nickname.
SEL (Select)	Select a nickname with which to work.

7.2.2 Creating a Nickname

The Create option on the Nickname Management menu adds a new entry to your list of nicknames. You can also create a nickname for the sender of a message you've received with the Create Nickname for Sender option on the Electronic Messaging menu. Once a new nickname is added, you can enter the nickname to address new messages.

To create a new nickname with Nickname Management, do the following:

NI [RETURN]

a. From any menu, type "NI" and press [RETURN] to display the Nickname Management menu.

C [RETURN]

b. Type "C" and press [RETURN] to create a new nickname. ALL-IN-1 displays the form shown in Figure 7.3.

Nickname:
nickname **[RETURN]**

c. Type the new nickname and press [RETURN].

Mail address:
address **[RETURN]**

d. Type the full address for the individual and press [RETURN]. Enter the address exactly as you would if you were sending a message to this individual. There are a number of lines to handle long addresses for different mail systems. The lookup feature ([FIND] or [GOLD] L) is available here so you can search the directory.

Hint: If the address is remote, enter the following format: *first-name last-name (remote-address)*. For example:

```
Bob Smith (SMITHR@A1@DENVER)
```

ALL-IN-1 then substitutes the individual's name in the message header instead of the text "Remote Addressee."

Perform the steps on the next page to create a nickname for the sender of the current message you've received:

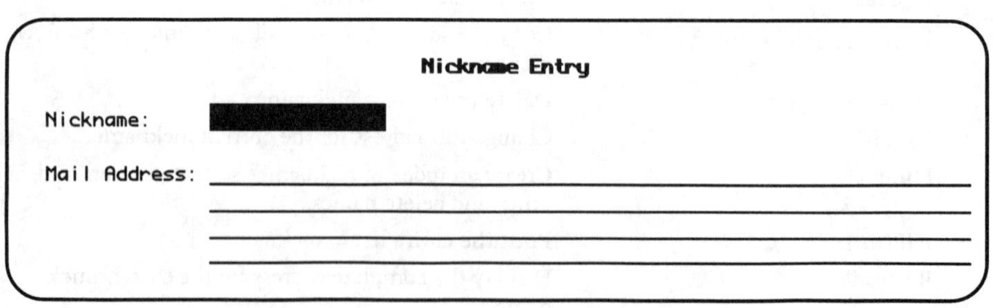
Nickname Entry

Nickname:

Mail Address:

Figure 7.3 Nickname Entry form

CNS [RETURN]

a. Type "CNS" and press [RETURN]. ALL-IN-1 displays the Create Nickname for Sender form with the sender's address appearing at the top.

Note: The CNS option also appears on the Read menu, so you can select this option while reading a message.

Nickname:
***nickname* [RETURN]**

b. Type the new nickname and press [RETURN]. ALL-IN-1 displays a message advising you that the new nickname has been created.

7.3 CREATING AND MAINTAINING DISTRIBUTION LISTS

Distribution lists allow you to address a message to a group of people quickly. A distribution list is simply a list of the addresses for individuals within a specific group or department. You save time addressing a message to a distribution list instead of entering all of the addresses appearing on the list.

There are two types of distribution lists:

- Personal distribution lists that you create and maintain for your private use. Everyone has the authority to create as many personal distribution lists as they choose.
- System distribution lists that are created and maintained for use by everyone on the system. Not everyone can create or modify a system distribution list, however. The system manager must authorize you to perform this function.

7.3.1 Accessing the Distribution List Menu

You create and maintain personal distribution lists with options on the Distribution List Management menu.

To access the Distribution List Management menu, do the following:

DL [RETURN]

a. From any menu, type "DL" and press [RETURN]. ALL-IN-1 displays the Distribution List Management menu.

***menu-option* [RETURN]**

b. Enter one of the options and press [RETURN]. Table 7.4 on the next page describes these options.

7.3.2 Creating a Distribution List

The Create option on the Distribution List Management menu creates a new list. You can also quickly create a distribution list with the Create Distribution List from Message option on the Electronic Messaging menu or with the Create Distribution List from Group option on the Group Services menu. Once you've created a new list, you can enter the distribution list name when addressing messages.

Table 7.4 Distribution List Management menu options

Enter This Menu Selection	*To Perform the Following Action*
C (Create)	Create a new distribution list.
CO (Copy)	Create a new distribution list by copying the names from an existing list.
D (Delete)	Delete the current distribution list.
E (Edit)	Add or remove names from the current distribution list.
I (Index of Personal Distribution Lists)	Create an index of personal distribution lists so that you can read, print, or delete multiple lists.
IS (Index of System Distribution Lists)	Create an index of system distribution lists so that you can read, print, or delete multiple lists.
P (Print)	Print the current distribution list.
R (Read)	Display the names appearing on the current distribution list.
SEL (Select)	Select a distribution list with which to work.

To create a personal distribution list from the Distribution List Management menu, follow these steps:

C [RETURN]

a. Type "C" and press [RETURN]. ALL-IN-1 asks you to enter a name for the new distribution list.

Name: ***@list-name*** **[RETURN]**
or
Name: ***list-name:*** **[RETURN]**

b. Type the name of the new distribution list and press [RETURN]. The distribution list name must begin with the "at" symbol (@) or end with a colon (:). This enables ALL-IN-1 to distinguish the list from a regular address when you enter the name on the Message Header. If your list name matches a system distribution list name, your list will be used instead of the system list when you address a message. ALL-IN-1 displays the Edit Distribution List form.

> ***address*** **[RETURN]...**
> **[RETURN]**

c. Enter the addresses of the individuals you want to include on this distribution list. Enter the addresses exactly as you would if addressing a message. Any type of address is valid, including nicknames, group names, and the names of other distribution lists. All of the features for addressing messages are available, including the lookup feature (press [FIND]) and the Message Header menu (press [GOLD] M). Press [RETURN] twice after the last name.

Hint: You might want to enter the names in alphabetical order. People find it easier to scan a distribution list sorted in alphabetical order.

Perform the following steps to create a distribution list from the list of addresses in the current message:

DLM [RETURN]

a. Type "DLM" and press [RETURN]. ALL-IN-1 asks for the name of the new distribution list.

Note: The DLM option also appears on the Read menu, so you can select this option while reading a message.

Distribution List Name:
@*list-name* [TAB]...

b. Type the new distribution list name and press [TAB]. Enter "Y" or "N" in the following three fields to indicate whether to include the names in the To:, CC:, and Sender fields in the distribution list.

[RETURN]

c. Press [RETURN] to complete the form. ALL-IN-1 displays a message indicating that the new list has been created.

Here's the procedure for creating a distribution list from a group:

GS [RETURN]

a. Type "GS" and press [RETURN] to move to Group Services.

SEL *group-name* [RETURN]

b. Select the group. If you don't know the group name, then type "SEL," press [RETURN], and press [FIND] to display group names.

CDG [RETURN]

c. Type "CDG" and press [RETURN]. ALL-IN-1 asks you to enter a name for the distribution list.

Name: **@*list-name* [RETURN]**

d. Type the new list name and press [RETURN]. ALL-IN-1 displays the Edit Distribution List form showing the individuals within the group. You can now add or remove names from the list as described in the following paragraph.

[EXIT]

e. Press [EXIT] (F10 or [GOLD] F) to exit and create your distribution list. ALL-IN-1 displays a message that the list has been created.

Once a list has been created, you can add or remove names with the Edit option. To remove a name, edit the list and move the cursor to the individual you want to remove, then press [ERASE LINE]. To add a name, move the cursor to a blank line and enter the new address.

7.3.3 Exercise: Creating a Distribution List

The following exercise shows you how to create a personal distribution list. It helps to have the following information before starting this exercise:

- Think of a group of individuals that you want to include in the distribution list—perhaps everyone in your department or work group. You might want to jot down their names before starting. If you know the addresses of these individuals (typically, their usernames), this is even better.
- Determine a name for the distribution list, possibly a department name.

1. Move to the System Distribution List Management menu.

DL [RETURN]	From any menu, type "DL" and press [RETURN]. ALL-IN-1 displays the Distribution List Management menu.

2. Create a system distribution list.

C [RETURN]	a. Type "C" and press [RETURN] to create a new distribution list. ALL-IN-1 asks you for the name of the new list.
Name: ***@list-name*** **[RETURN]**	b. Type the "@" followed by the name of the new distribution list, and press [RETURN]. To create a distribution list for the Accounting Department, for example, type: `@ACCOUNTING DEPT` ALL-IN-1 displays the Edit Distribution List form.
> ***address*** **[RETURN]...** > **[RETURN]**	c. Enter the addresses of everyone you want to appear on this distribution list. Enter these names exactly as you would if you were addressing a message. All of the features for addressing messages are available, including the lookup feature (press [FIND]) and the Message Header menu (press [GOLD] M). Press [RETURN] twice after the last name to return to the menu.

3. Display the distribution list.

R [RETURN]	a. Type "R" and press [RETURN] to display the new distribution list.
[RETURN]	b. Press [RETURN] to redisplay the menu.

4. Edit the distribution list.

E [RETURN] — a. Type "E" and press [RETURN] to edit the distribution list.

[DOWN ARROW] — b. Press [DOWN ARROW] to move to the second addressee.

[ERASE LINE] — c. Press [ERASE LINE] (F13 or LF) to remove the second addressee from the distribution list.

> *address* [RETURN] — d. Type a new address and press [RETURN] to add a name to the list.

[GOLD] F — e. Press [GOLD] F to save your change and return to the menu.

5. Try using the distribution list.

EM C [RETURN] — a. Type "EM C" and press [RETURN] to move to the Electronic Messaging menu and create a memo. ALL-IN-1 displays the Message Header form.

TO: *@list-name* [RETURN] — b. Type your new distribution list name and press [RETURN]. If the name is not accepted, check the spelling.

[UP ARROW] — c. Press [UP ARROW] to move back to the line where you entered the distribution list.

[GOLD] V — d. Press [GOLD] V to display the distribution list.

[RETURN] — e. Press [RETURN] to redisplay the Message Header.

[EXIT] — f. Press [EXIT] to quit and return to the menu (unless you want to continue and create a message).

7.4 WORKING WITH AN INDEX OF MESSAGES OR DOCUMENTS

Working with an index of messages (Figure 7.4) or documents provides many benefits compared with working from the menu. Selecting messages or documents and executing options are easier when working from an index. In addition, you can select and work with multiple messages or documents from an index.

Here are a few examples of when it's better to work from an index:

- Reading new incoming messages with the Index of Inbox (II) option is very efficient for people who receive a lot of mail. This index lists all of your messages so you can easily review your mail and read selected messages.

```
                              Index of Read Folder
(Selections: 0   ) (Drawer: MAIN                          ) (New messages:  1  )
--------------------------------------------------------------------------------
  No.  Folder     Title                               Sender          Received
--------------------------------------------------------------------------------
> 1    READ       Event -> 12-Dec-1994 08:00am JE Kenneth Jeffers 12-Nov-1994
  2    READ       Vacation Request                    Kenneth Jeffers 12-Nov-1994
! 3    READ       East Bay Utilities                  Kenneth Jeffers 12-Nov-1994
  4    READ       Administrator Privileges            ALL-IN-1 System 12-Nov-1994
  5    READ       Status of new accounts              ALL-IN-1 System 12-Nov-1994
  6    READ       New Accounts                        ALL-IN-1 System 07-Nov-1994

--------------------------------------------------------------------------------
Move to item, and enter option (press GOLD MENU to see options, or HELP for
more information)
```

Figure 7.4 Index of Messages

- The Index (I) option builds an index of messages and documents that match the selection criteria you enter, such as a folder, author, or phrase. This is an excellent tool for searching your File Cabinet to find a message or document.
- Creating an index using a range of dates as selection criteria is an excellent way to list old messages and documents. The ability to then select and delete multiple messages and documents makes it easy to clean up your File Cabinet.

Perform the following steps to work with an index of messages or documents:

I [RETURN]

a. From the Electronic Messaging or Word and Document Processing menu, type "I" and press [RETURN] to create an index. ALL-IN-1 displays the form for entering selection criteria, shown in Figure 7.5.

   Note: You can skip the selection process and quickly build an index for a specific folder by entering "I *folder-name*" or by entering one of the following options:

IC	Index of the Created folder.
IO	Index of the Outbox folder.
II	Index of the Inbox folder.
IR	Index of the Read folder.

```
Folder: ____________________
Title:  ________________________________________________
Author: ____________________                Status: _______
Number: ___  To: ___   Creation Date: __________ To: _______
Keywords: ______ ______ ______ ______       Match all keys?: N
Importance: ________        Sensitivity: ____________
Data type: __________          Handling: __________
Phrase: __________________________________________
```

Figure 7.5 Form for entering selection criteria

b. Enter information to build an index. Include all information that pertains to the messages or documents with which you want to work. Leave all fields blank to create an index of all messages and documents. Table 7.5 describes the fields on this form.

[RETURN]

c. Press [RETURN] when you've entered enough information to create an index. ALL-IN-1 displays an index of messages or documents.

***line-number* [RETURN]**

d. To work with a *single* item, type the line number and press [RETURN]. The current item pointer (>) moves to the specified message.

***line,line-line...* [SELECT]**

To work with *multiple* items, type the line numbers, or range of line numbers, and press [SELECT] (or Keypad-Period). For example, enter "2,5,7-9" [SELECT] to select items 2, 5, 7, 8, and 9. Press [NEXT SCREEN] (or [GOLD] A) to display any additional pages of items, then repeat the selection process. An *x* appears next to the selected items.

Note: To deselect an item, type the line number and press [GOLD] [SELECT].

***menu-option* [RETURN]**

e. Type a menu option and press [RETURN]. Tables 6.1 and 6.2 describe options that manage a single message. Table 9.1 describes options that manage a single document. Table 7.6 describes menu options that manage multiple messages or documents.

[EXIT]

f. Enter the information required for the selected menu option. Press [EXIT] (F10 or Keypad-0) when finished with the index to return to the menu.

Table 7.5 Document index selection criteria

Field	*Description*
Folder[a]	Folder name. It's recommended that you enter a folder name—for example, Created, Outbox, or Inbox—to reduce the number of documents listed to a manageable size. The index will include *all* messages and documents if you omit the folder name and all other criteria.
Title[a]	Subject of the message or title of the document. If you're searching for a document and remember only a word or phrase from the subject or title, enter it in this field.
Author[a]	Full name of the sender of the message or author of the document.
Status[a]	Status of the document: Read, Send, Unread, Unsent, Noted, Archived, Copied, or Reserved.
Number[a] To:[a]	Document number or range of document numbers.
Creation Date[a] To:[a]	Creation date of the message or document. You can specify a range of creation dates to list a group of documents. This is useful when searching for a document or when building an index of old documents during cleanup.
Keywords	Enter one or more keywords associated with the documents you're trying to list. The author must associate keywords with the message or document at the time of creation, or you must add keywords with the Update Index (U) option. Otherwise, searching by keywords doesn't list any documents.
Match All Keys?	Enter"Y" if you want the selected documents to match all the keywords entered. Enter "N" if you want to match any of the keywords.
Importance[a]	Importance of the message content: Low, Normal, or High.
Sensitivity[a]	Sensitivity of the message content: Not Sensitive, Personal, Private, Company Confidential.
Data Type[a]	The data type of the document. This specifies the way the information is stored and is set depending on the editor selected to prepare the text.
Handling[a]	Message handling. Handling tells certain options, such as Read and Print, how to process the text contained in the document.
Phrase	A phrase that appears in the text of selected documents. This field is very useful when you are trying to find a document and you remember only a word or phrase that appears in the text. Be forewarned: Searching by phrase takes a long time. Enter other selection criteria, such as a folder name or range of dates, to limit the search.

[a]ALL-IN-1's lookup feature can be used in this field. Press [ERASE LINE] (F13 or LF) to clear the field, then press [FIND] (or [GOLD] L) to display a list of possible entries. Refer to Section 3.2.2, "Using [FIND] to Complete a Field," for further information on the lookup feature.

Table 7.6 describes the options on the Index of Messages menu that manage multiple messages. These options appear also on the Index of Documents menu. Options on this menu for managing a single item are described in Tables 6.1, 6.2, and 9.1. In addition, options for maintaining your File Cabinet also appear on this menu and are described in Chapters 12 and 13.

Table 7.6 Index options for managing multiple messages and documents

Enter This Index Menu Selection	*To Perform the Following Action*
ALL (Select All)	Select all messages and documents appearing in the index.
CAS (Cancel All Selected)	Deselect all selected messages and documents.
XD (Delete All Selected)	Move selected messages and documents to the Wastebasket.
XDEF (Defer All Selected)	Send all selected messages in the Created folder at a future date or time.
XF (Forward All Selected)	Forward selected messages to another individual as attachments to a single mail message.
XFM (File Selected Messages)	Cross-file selected messages and documents in a new folder.
XFT (File Text of All Selected)	File copies of the text of all selected messages as separate documents.
XMCD (Make Copy of All Selected)	Make copies of the selected messages and documents.
XP (Print All Selected)	Print selected messages and documents.
XR (Read All Selected)	Display selected messages and documents.
XS (Send All Selected)	Send all the selected messages or documents.
XRFD (Refile All Selected)	Move selected messages and documents to a new folder.
XXFD (Cross-file All Selected)	Cross-file selected messages and documents in another folder without making additional copies.

7.5 ATTACHING DOCUMENTS TO MESSAGES

The Attach Document (ATT) option attaches a document to a Created message, just as if you stapled a document to a paper memo. You can attach any number of documents by simply repeating the option. When you send the message, the documents that are attached are sent along with the message. The recipient can then file the attached documents for editing, printing, and so forth.

You can also send files other than documents as attachments to messages. Import a binary file, such as a program file, with the Receive without Conversion (RVC) option on the Document Transfer menu, and select the Send option to transfer the file as an attachment. The addressee would then file the attachment and export the file to VMS with the Send without Conversion (SVC) option. This procedure is handy for transferring all sorts of data files, program files, procedures, and so on.

You can "tear off" the attachments to messages you receive and file them as separate documents in your File Cabinet with the File Attachment as Document (FA) option. This option is described in Section 6.8, "Refiling Messages." The Index of Attachments (IA) lists attached documents and provides a number of options for working with one or more attachments.

Print settings for attached documents "travel" with the document. If you receive, file, and print an attachment, the printing is controlled by settings established by the sender. This is helpful because the document prints the way the sender intended without your having to adjust the print settings.[2]

In addition to the Attach Document option, there are two alternatives for sending a document to another individual:

- Create a message that acts as the cover note. While in the editor, press [GOLD] G to display the Get Document menu, and select the document to include in your message. This differs from Attach Document because the document's contents become a part of the message text instead of an attachment. The addressee must use the File Text (FT) option to file a document sent in this fashion. This method does not retain the print settings of the document, however. Settings for the message apply to the entire document text.
- The easiest way to send a document is to select the document from either the Electronic Messaging menu or Word and Document Processing menu and select the Send (S) option. You then enter the address of the individual you want to send the document to, just as if you were forwarding a message. You can also include a cover note.

To attach a document to the current created message, perform these steps:

ATT [RETURN]

a. Type "ATT" and press [RETURN]. The Select a Document to Attach form, shown in Figure 7.6, is displayed.

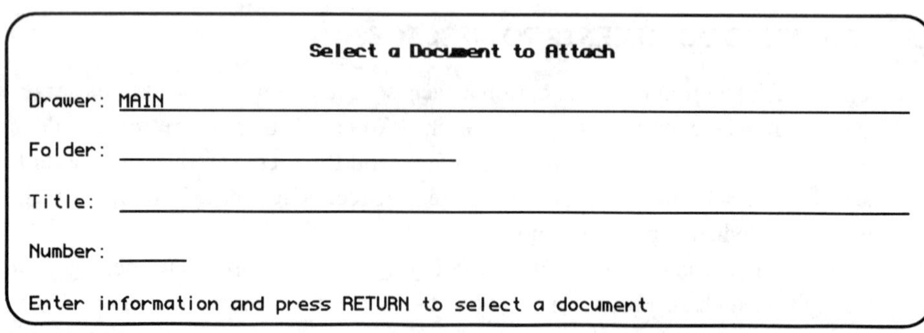

Select a Document to Attach

Drawer: MAIN

Folder:

Title:

Number:

Enter information and press RETURN to select a document

Figure 7.6 Select a Document to Attach form

2. A problem exists with printing attached documents with versions of ALL-IN-1 prior to version 3.0. If the sender selected a range of pages for printing, these settings are sent with the document. The result is that you see the entire document when editing, but only a portion of the document is printed. If this happens, simply reset the page range before printing.

Drawer: ***drawer* [TAB]**
Folder: ***folder* [TAB]**
Title: ***title***

b. Enter a drawer, folder, and title or a document number to select a document. Press [FIND] (or [GOLD] L) in any field to list possible entries.

[RETURN]

c. Press [RETURN] to attach the document. The menu is redisplayed with a note that the document has been attached.

Do the following to detach a document from the current message and prevent the document from being sent with the message:

DET [RETURN]

a. Type "DET" and press [RETURN].

***line-number* [RETURN]**

b. A list of attachments is displayed if there's more than one document attached to the message. Type the line number for the document you want to detach and press [RETURN]. A note is displayed verifying that the document has been detached from the message.

To send a group of documents, it's easiest to select the documents from an index, then enter the Forward All Selected (XF) option.

Advanced Electronic Messaging

CHAPTER 8

It sometimes isn't possible to handle your mail, either because you're out of the office or because you simply don't have the time. This chapter describes several features for handling these situations. The first two features, Auto Forwarding and Auto Reply, are helpful when you're away from the office for a while and won't be able to read your mail. The last feature, Mail Surrogacy, helps not only when you're away from the office, but also when you simply don't have the time to handle mail. Mail Surrogacy is perfect for executives who want their secretaries to handle their mail.

This chapter teaches you how to perform the following tasks:

- Enable or disable the automatic forwarding of your mail.
- Enable or disable the automatic return of a response memo to anyone who sends you mail.
- Give authority to someone to handle your mail.
- Handle someone else's mail.

8.1 AUTOMATIC FORWARDING OF MESSAGES

ALL-IN-1's Auto Forward feature allows you to forward incoming messages automatically to another person. This is helpful when you're away from the office for an extended period of time and want someone else to read your mail. You simply specify a forwarding address with the Auto Forward (AF) option. Incoming messages are then redirected to this individual until you cancel auto-forwarding.

Remember the following points when auto-forwarding your messages:

- Messages are *truly* redirected. You won't find copies of forwarded messages left in your Inbox. For this reason, you might want to grant mail access to your account instead (see Section 8.3, "Handling Someone Else's Mail").
- Return receipts and replies to incoming messages are returned to the sender from the user who actually read the message (the forwarding addressee). This sometimes confuses the sender because he or she didn't send the message to the "forwardee."

Therefore, warn those with whom you are in frequent contact that you'll be forwarding your mail. It helps to place a note in the Status field of Set Working Conditions.

- Messages are forwarded only once and are then delivered. This prevents mail from traveling around endlessly when too many people have auto-forward in effect.
- There are exceptions to auto-forwarding. Invitations to meetings sent by Time Management and messages sent to "subscribers" are not forwarded.

By the way, remember to first notify the person to whom you'll be forwarding your mail. A good method is to send a message asking if it's okay. This prepares the person to receive your mail and, more important, ensures that the forwarding address is valid.

Perform the following steps to forward your messages to another person:

AF [RETURN]

a. From the Electronic Messaging menu, type "AF" and press [RETURN]. ALL-IN-1 displays the Auto Forward Addressee form. If your messages are currently being forwarded, the present forwarding address appears at the top of this form.

New auto forward address: *forwarding-address*

b. Enter the address of the individual who will receive your mail. You can specify any valid individual address, including a nickname. Refer to Section 7.1, "Addressing a Message," for details.

Note: Make sure that the forwarding address is valid. Invalid forwarding addresses prevent the delivery of your mail.

[RETURN]

c. Press [RETURN] to complete the form. The menu is redisplayed with a note advising you that an auto-forward address has been selected.

To cancel automatic forwarding of your messages, do the following:

EM CF [RETURN]

From any menu, type "EM CF" and press [RETURN] to cancel auto-forwarding. ALL-IN-1 displays a note that auto-forwarding has been canceled.

8.2 AUTOMATIC REPLIES TO INCOMING MESSAGES

ALL-IN-1 automatically returns a standard response memo to anyone who sends you mail when you invoke the Auto Reply feature. This is also helpful when you're away from the office for an extended period. For example, you can create a memo that identifies the person who will be handling your work while you're gone.

To set up an Auto Reply, simply create or select a document that acts as your response memo. You'll continue to receive incoming messages while Auto Reply is in effect (unless messages are being auto-forwarded, of course). ALL-IN-1 files these messages in your Inbox and automatically returns a copy of the response memo to the sender of each message. In addition, ALL-IN-1 remembers who's received a copy of the response memo and only sends the memo to an individual once. When you're ready to disable the Auto Reply feature, simply select the Cancel Auto Reply option on the Electronic Messaging menu.

In addition to Auto Reply, the Status field in the Set Working Conditions screen in User Setup also notifies individuals of your status. This field accepts a single line of text—for example, "On vacation until June 14th. Contact B. Simpson." This status information is immediately displayed when someone enters your name while addressing a message. The advantage of this method is that the sender learns your status *before* sending the message. This feature has some limitations, however. Remote users will not see your status message, nor will anyone who uses a distribution list to send you mail.

To enable Auto Reply, do the following:

AR [RETURN]	a. From the Electronic Messaging menu, type "AR" and press [RETURN]. ALL-IN-1 asks if you want to create a new memo or select an existing document as your Auto Reply.
C [RETURN]	b. Type "C" and press [RETURN] to create a reply memo. The Creating New Document form is displayed.
SEL [RETURN]	Or type "SEL" and press [RETURN] to select an existing document in your default drawer (usually Main) as the reply.
Folder: ***folder* [TAB]** Title: ***title***	c. Enter the folder and title for the reply document. *Note:* If you're creating a new document, specify your Main drawer. You cannot use a document in any other drawer as your auto-reply.
[RETURN]	d. Press [RETURN] to complete the form. If you're creating a new document, the editor is invoked. If you're selecting an existing document, you're done. The menu is redisplayed with a note that an auto-reply has been set.
reply text	e. Type the text of your response memo.
[GOLD] F	f. When the auto-reply is complete, press [GOLD] F to exit the editor and file the document. ALL-IN-1

redisplays the menu with a note that an auto-reply message has been set.

To cancel Auto Reply, type "EM CR" from any menu and press [RETURN]. ALL-IN-1 displays a note that Auto Reply has been canceled. The response memo remains in your File Cabinet.

8.3 HANDLING SOMEONE ELSE'S MAIL

The Mail Surrogacy feature lets you handle someone else's mail. You can read, file, print, and delete messages sent to someone else as well as create and send mail from his or her account. This feature is ideal for a secretary who handles an executive's mail or for anyone handling the mail of someone on vacation.

For example, if Kenneth Jefferson has been given authority to handle Sarah Washington's mail, he can execute the Set Mail User option on the Electronic Messaging menu to change over to her account. Set Mail User effectively "closes" Kenneth's Main drawer and "opens" Sarah's. The username in the upper corner of the menu and the drawer name in the current item block are both altered to reflect this change. Any option then selected from the menu processes Sarah's messages. Kenneth must execute the Set Mail User option again to change back to his account before working with his own mail.

Keep the following points in mind when you execute Set Mail User to handle someone else's mail:

- All options on the Electronic Messaging menu work with messages or affect the account of the person whose mail you're managing. Distribution List menu options also manage the other person's lists, not yours. The exception is nicknames. Nickname Management works with your list of nicknames, and your list is searched when you enter a nickname on the Message Header.
- Your working conditions continue to control your environment. Notification of new mail, printing, and so on, is controlled by your working conditions, not those of the person whose mail you're managing. You cannot delete unread mail or address messages to "subscribers" unless you've been authorized to do so, regardless of the privileges granted to the other person.
- The notification of new mail means that you have a new message. Remember to Set Mail User back to your own account before attempting to read your mail.
- Set Mail User in Electronic Messaging is much like Set Owner in Time Management. If you read a meeting notice while Set Mail User is in effect, the meeting is correctly scheduled on the other person's calendar. If you move to Events in Time Management and create a meeting, it is also scheduled on the other person's calendar, and notices are sent from his or her account.
- This last point is rather important. When you set mail user to another person's account, you also have access to documents in his or her Main drawer. This is an ad-

vantage if you're also responsible for maintaining this person's documents. However, with privacy in mind, the following warning must be considered.

WARNING: Granting mail access to another individual also grants them access to every document in your Main drawer, regardless of the folder. Do not store in your Main drawer documents that you want to keep private. If you need to grant mail access *and* store private documents, create a second, private drawer and refile private documents to this drawer.

Two steps are needed to handle someone else's mail:

1. The person must give you the authority to handle his or her mail. This is done with Grant Mail Access (GMA). Three levels of authority can be granted:

   Process Mail — You can execute all options to create, edit, read, file, and print messages, but you cannot send mail from the other person's account.

   Send Mail — You can execute all options to process mail and can also send mail from the other person's account. When you send mail from someone else's account, the text "Sent by: *your-name*" is added to the message header. Figure 8.1 is a sample message sent from Sarah Washington's account by Kenneth Jefferson.

```
                    I N T E R O F F I C E   M E M O R A N D U M

                                          Date:     8-Aug-1992 07:17am GMT
                                          From:     Sarah Washington
                                                    WASHINGTON.SARAH
                                          Dept:
                                          Tel No:

                                          Sent By:  Kenneth Jefferson

TO: Karen Bennett                         ( BENNETT.KAREN )

Subject: Health Insurance Benefits

When you get a chance, could you please send me a copy of our health
insurance company's revised benefits.
```

Figure 8.1 Sample message

Control — You can execute all options to process and send mail. In addition, you can execute the Grant Mail Access option in the other person's account and change the list of people who can manage his or her mail.

2. Before working with someone else's mail, you must change over to his or her account. This is done with the Set Mail User (SMU) option.

The following pages describe both of these procedures in greater detail.

Perform the following steps to grant another individual authority to handle your mail:

GMA [RETURN] — a. From the Electronic Messaging menu, type "GMA" and press [RETURN]. ALL-IN-1 displays the Grant Mail Access form shown in Figure 8.2.

***username* [TAB]** — b. Type the username of the individual you want to handle your mail and press [TAB].

****group* [TAB]** — Or type the name of the group and press [TAB].

Note: Press [DOWN ARROW], if necessary, to first move to a blank line before entering a username or group.

Press [FIND] to display usernames, or type an asterisk (*) and press [FIND] to display group names.

Process Mail
Send Mail
Control — c. Type "Y" or enter a space in each of the following three fields to indicate the types of privileges you want to grant to this user or group. "Y"

```
                         Grant Mail Access
                         User: WASHINGTON.SARAH
--------------------------------------------------------------------------
                                      Permitted Access

                                   Process    Send
User or Group                        Mail     Mail    Control
--------------------------------------------------------------------------
__________________________            _        _        _
__________________________            _        _        _
__________________________            _        _        _
__________________________            _        _        _
__________________________            _        _        _
--------------------------------------------------------------------------
Enter information and press RETURN, or press GOLD F to complete the operation
```

Figure 8.2 Grant Mail Access form

grants authority; a space denies authority. Note that the cursor moves to the next field without your having to press [TAB].

d. Repeat steps b and c to grant access to other individuals or groups.

[RETURN] — e. Press [RETURN] (or [GOLD] F) to save your changes and redisplay the menu.

Perform the following steps to work with someone else's mail:

SMU [RETURN] — a. From the Electronic Messaging menu, type "SMU" and press [RETURN]. ALL-IN-1 displays the Set Mail User form that is shown in Figure 8.3 below.

***username* [RETURN]** — b. Type the username of the individual whose mail you want to manage, and press [RETURN]. ALL-IN-1 displays the following message:

```
Mail user is now username
```

The current drawer is changed to this user's Main drawer, and the username displayed in the upper right-hand corner is also changed.

Notes: An error message is displayed if the person has not given you authority to handle his or her mail. Ask this person to give you authority by executing Grant Mail Access.

You can leave this field blank and then press [FIND] to display the usernames of the people who have given you the authority to handle their mail.

```
                    Set Mail User

User:

Enter the user name and press RETURN
```

Figure 8.3 Set Mail User form

When ready to return to your own account and work with your mail, do the following:

SMU [RETURN]

a. From the Electronic Messaging menu, type "SMU" and press [RETURN]. ALL-IN-1 displays the Set Mail User form shown in Figure 8.3.

***your-username* [RETURN]**

b. Your username appears in the User field. Press [RETURN]. ALL-IN-1 displays a message that the mail user has been changed back to your account.

Word and Document Processing

PART III

Word and Document Processing is one of the most widely used subsystems in ALL-IN-1. From this menu, you create, modify, display, and print documents ranging from single-page letters to multipage reports and manuals. Often, you'll extract information from other subsystems to work with in Word and Document Processing, and vice versa. For example, you can prepare a travel itinerary in Time Management and import it into a document in Word and Document Processing, or you can create a report in Word and Document Processing and send it to other users with Electronic Messaging.

The features of Word and Document Processing include these:

- ALL-IN-1 provides a choice of editing programs for creating and modifying documents, each with unique features and capabilities. Digital's EDT and EVE editors and the WPS-PLUS word processor are included with ALL-IN-1. Other word-processing packages can be purchased separately and integrated with ALL-IN-1, including WordPerfect.
- Documents are automatically stored in your personal File Cabinet. File Cabinet Maintenance helps you manage your documents. Options on this menu allow you to refile, copy, and archive documents for organizing your File Cabinet. There are also a number of options for listing documents and folders when searching for a document.
- You can share documents with others by storing them in shared drawers. You have complete control over who has access to documents placed in one of your shared drawers.
- Spell checking is available for proofing all documents. Advanced writing aids, such as an on-line thesaurus, are available in WPS-PLUS and WordPerfect.
- Text style options, including font selection and text highlighting, are available for documents prepared with either WPS-PLUS or WordPerfect.
- PostScript images can be included in documents prepared with either WPS-PLUS or WordPerfect.
- Advanced information-processing capabilities are provided by WPS-PLUS and WordPerfect, including the ability to create tables of contents and indexes for large documents.

- Electronic messages can be accessed from the Word and Document Processing menu. Likewise, documents can be accessed from the Electronic Messaging menu.
- You can transfer documents between the VMS file system and your File Cabinet. You can send copies of documents to other users with Electronic Messaging.
- You can automate repetitive word-processing operations by creating User Defined Processes for WPS-PLUS or macros in WordPerfect.

This part of the manual teaches you how to create and edit documents with Word and Document Processing. There are three chapters: "Getting Started with Word and Document Processing," "Getting Started with an Editor," and "Advanced WPS-PLUS Features."

Chapter 9 describes the basics of working with documents, including how to create, read, and print documents and how to perform a spell check. This chapter is a must if you've never prepared documents in ALL-IN-1. In addition to these fundamentals, you'll also find a list of standard function keys for basic word-processing operations. Selecting an editor is one of the most important topics covered in this chapter. The editor you choose determines the word-processing features and function keys that are available when you prepare documents.

Chapter 10, "Getting Started with an Editor," contains more detailed instructions on how to work with a specific editor in ALL-IN-1. Topics include how to move around a document and how to perform basic editing operations, such as highlighting and moving text. The two most popular editors, WPS-PLUS and WordPerfect, are covered here. The EDT and EVE editors, which are standards for those who work with the VAX/VMS operating system, are also discussed.

The final chapter in this part, "Advanced WPS-PLUS Features," covers some of the abbreviations/library document, list processing, and paragraph numbering features of WPS-PLUS. These features can save you typing and should be read if you create many documents with WPS-PLUS. The first two features are important if you work with standard documents and blocks of text. Paragraph numbering is important if you prepare large documents or instruction manuals.

All of your documents are stored in your personal File Cabinet. Documents are organized in separate drawers and folders within the File Cabinet, just like in the real file cabinet shown in Figure III.1. You can select a document in any drawer you have access to, by specifying the drawer, folder name, and title of the document.

A brief description of the fields of information that identify a document follows.

Drawer	All documents in your File Cabinet are stored in drawers. Drawers separate documents that you want to keep private from documents that you want to share. Everyone is given one private drawer in which to store personal documents. You can create additional drawers in your own File Cabinet, and you can access drawers in other people's File Cabinets if you need to share documents. Your site might impose a restriction on the number of drawers you can

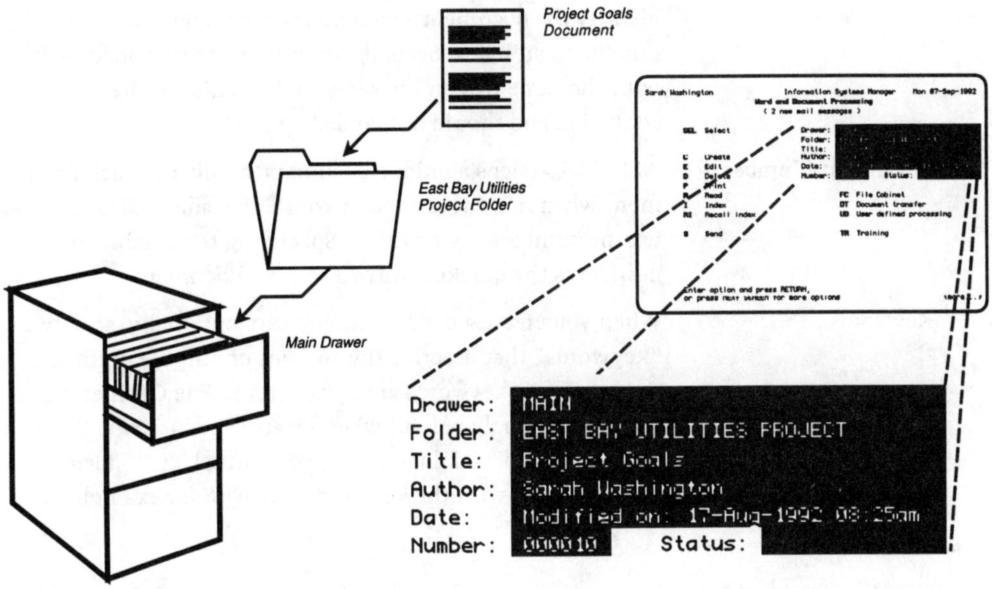

Figure III.1 ALL-IN-1 File Cabinet layout

create. This is sometimes done to reduce the amount of disk space consumed by the file structures required for additional drawers.

Folder

Documents with similar content or purpose are grouped together in folders. Some folders are created and managed by ALL-IN-1. These include the Created, Outbox, Inbox, and Read folders you work with in Electronic Messaging, as well as the Wastebasket folder. You can create as many additional folders as you like with whatever names you prefer. If you work with many documents, creating additional folders and carefully organizing documents within these folders helps tremendously when you try to locate and work with documents.

Title

When you create a document, you assign it a title to describe its content. Titles can be up to 71 characters in length, but only 30 characters are displayed in the index of documents. Therefore, make sure that the first few words of the title are unique and descriptive.

Two warnings on assigning titles to documents: First, you can create a document with a "missing" title. This is done by leaving the title field blank when creating the document. Try to avoid this because it makes it impossible to identify the document's contents when viewing a list of documents in an index. Second, you can create two documents with the same title in the same folder. This also leads to confusion and should be avoided.

Document Number — ALL-IN-1 assigns a unique document number to each document when it is first stored in your File Cabinet. These document numbers begin with 1. Specifying the document number is the quickest way to select a document.

Keywords — When you create a document, you can (optionally) specify "keywords" that describe the content or purpose of the document. These keywords are placed in the File Cabinet index and are extremely helpful when locating documents. When creating an index of documents, you can select all documents created with the keyword "budget," for example.

WORD AND DOCUMENT PROCESSING Q&A

Following is a list of common questions about Word and Document Processing. Refer also to the introduction to Part IV, "The File Cabinet," for additional questions about filing and searching for documents.

Q *How do I create and print a document?*

A From any ALL-IN-1 menu, type "WP" and press [RETURN] to move to the Word and Document Processing menu. You can create, edit, read, and print documents from this menu. Type "C" and press [RETURN] to create a document. Supply an appropriate drawer, folder name, and document title, and press [RETURN] to complete the Creating New Document form. Enter the text of your document, and press [GOLD] F to exit and file the document. The function keys and features that are available depend on your editor. Chapter 10 discusses basic editing operations for a few different editors.

To print the current document, type "P" and press [RETURN]. Enter the name of a printer in the Document Destination field, and press [RETURN] to complete the Printing Document form. Refer to Sections 9.3, "Creating a New Document," and 9.8, "Printing a Document," for more details.

Q *How do I bold text, center text, move text, and locate strings of text?*

A The steps to perform various word-processing operations vary according to the editor with which you're working. Chapter 10 describes the steps for performing basic editing operations in WPS-PLUS, WordPerfect, and EDT. If the operation you want to perform is not described in Chapter 10, refer to Appendix B. This appendix includes the steps for additional editing operations, listed alphabetically. The topics include highlighting, centering, moving, and searching for text.

Q *How do I select an editor? How do I change the editor?*

A You can prepare documents in ALL-IN-1 with any editor available on your system. The WPS-PLUS, EDT, and EVE editors are always available because they are included with ALL-IN-1. Other editors might be available, depending on your site's configuration.

You can select an editor as your "default" editor by modifying the Edit Style field on the Set Working Conditions form. From any menu, type "US SWC" and press [RETURN] to display this form. Press [TAB] to move to the Edit Style field. Press [ERASE LINE] (LF or F13) to clear this field, then press [FIND] (or [GOLD] L) to display the names of available editors. Select an editor by line number, and press [RETURN]. Press [RETURN] twice to complete the Set Working Conditions form. The editor you select will be invoked whenever you create a document or mail message.

You can select another editor when you create a new document. Before completing the Creating New Document form, press [NEXT SCREEN]. Move to the Handling field and press [FIND] to display and select from a list of available editors. Refer to Section 9.2, "Selecting an Editor," for more information.

Q *My keyboard is not a VT keyboard. Where are the function keys located on my keyboard?*

A A number of ALL-IN-1 users have non-DEC terminals and PCs. Your keyboard might thus be different from the standard DEC keyboard, making it difficult for you to locate function keys. If you're using a non-DEC terminal (as opposed to a PC), chances are that the key positions will resemble those of either a VT100 or LK201 keyboard, even though the keys are labeled differently. You'll have to rely on the positions of keys rather than the labels to identify important function keys. Keyboard overlays and decals can help to some extent.

If you're a PC user, the terminal-emulation program running on your PC defines the keyboard. Refer to the documentation for the program to see which PC keys represent standard VT keys. Typically, these programs define the F1 or NUM LOCK key as the [GOLD] key. Try pressing F1, then "\" ([GOLD] DATE/TIME). If the date and time are displayed, you've discovered the [GOLD] key. You will most likely have to contact the vendor of the terminal-emulation program if there is no documentation at your site.

Q *How do I change the folder name or title of a document?*

A Type "U" and press [RETURN] to change this information for the current document. The Update Index form is displayed, allowing you to change the folder or title. You can also use the Refile Document (RFD) option to change the drawer, folder, or title. Changing the drawer or folder essentially refiles the document.

Q *How do I number pages in my document?*

A Numbering pages is easy in both WPS-PLUS and WordPerfect. EDT and EVE do not support automatic page numbering.

In WPS-PLUS, you must edit the document and insert a control block to create a running header or footer. The TOP and BOTTOM control block commands create running headers and footers. Insert the control block in your document where you want page numbering to begin. The text that follows the TOP or BOTTOM command must include the string "\p." This tells WPS-PLUS to include the current page number in the header or footer when the document is printed. You can include other text before or after this string to embellish the page numbering. Including "Page \p" in a running footer inserts the text "Page 10" at the bottom of page 10, for example. An example is shown in Table B.2 in Appendix B under the topic "Pages, Number."

In WordPerfect, you select page numbering with the [FORMAT] function key. First move the cursor to the point in the document where you want page numbering to begin. Press [FORMAT] (PF1, F14), then press "2" (Page), "6" (Numbering), and "4" (Position). Type a number 1 through 8 to select the placement of the page number, and press [EXIT] to resume editing.

Note that you can reset the page number with a RESET control block command in WPS-PLUS or the [FORMAT] function in WordPerfect.

Q *How do I turn a page sideways?*

A You can turn a single page sideways to print in "landscape" mode, then print the remainder of the document in "portrait" mode in both WPS-PLUS and WordPerfect. This is useful when you have a wide chart or table of information. EDT and EVE do not allow you to print a specific page easily in landscape mode.

In WPS-PLUS, you must insert a New Page marker ([GOLD] N), followed by a control block that contains the command PRINTER FORMAT LANDSCAPE. Then type the text you want printed in landscape mode. Insert another New Page marker, followed by a control block that contains the command PRINTER FORMAT PORTRAIT to reset printing to portrait format. Refer to Section 10.1.6, "WPS-PLUS Control Blocks," for more information.

In WordPerfect, insert a page break with [HARD PAGE] (PF2 [RETURN]), then press [FORMAT] (PF1, F14). Type "2" (Page), type "7" (Paper Size), and press [DOWN ARROW] to highlight "Standard-Wide" format. Press [RETURN] to select this paper size and [EXIT] to resume editing. Type the text you want printed in landscape mode, and repeat these steps to reset printing to portrait mode; specify "Standard" as the paper size.

Q *How do I set up multiple columns (newspaper columns)?*

A Setting up newspaper columns is fairly easy in both WPS-PLUS and WordPerfect. EDT and EVE do not have the capability to create newspaper columns.

In WPS-PLUS, you invoke the multicolumn editor to create columns. Move the cursor to the point in your document where you want to begin multiple columns. Press [CHANGE EDITOR] ([GOLD]]). The expanded ruler appears so you can define the left and right margins for each column. Insert one pair of L/R markers for each column, and press [RETURN] to imbed the ruler. You can now enter the first column of text. When finished, press [GOLD] [TAB POS] [ADVANCE] ([GOLD], Keypad-8, Keypad-0) to move to the second column. Enter the second column of text, and press [CHANGE EDITOR] when finished to leave the multicolumn editor. Columns are rearranged to a stair-step format, but they will print properly. Refer to the topic "Multi-Columns, Create" in Table B.2 in Appendix B for more details.

In WordPerfect, you create newspaper columns with the [COLUMNS/TABLE] function key. Move the cursor to the point in the document where you want to begin newspaper columns. Press [COLUMNS/TABLE] (PF3, F13). Type "1" (Columns) and "3" (Define). You can now specify options that control the format of the columns or simply press [RETURN] to accept default values. Type "1" to turn columns on, and enter the text of your first column. Press [HARD PAGE] (PF2, [RETURN]), and type the text of your second column. To turn columns off, press [COLUMNS/TABLE], type "1," then type "2."

In either editor, you can change text in the columns by simply moving the cursor to the area you want to modify and adding or deleting characters as necessary. When working with WPS-PLUS, you can press the [CHANGE EDITOR] function key if you want to work with the columns side-by-side.

Q *How do I send my document to someone else?*

A Simply type "S" and press [RETURN] to send the current document to another user. ALL-IN-1 displays the message header so you can enter the recipient's address. Refer to Section 7.1, "Addressing a Message," for instructions on completing this form. The document is sent as an attachment to the memo.

The recipient must file the attachment as a separate document in order to work with it. To file the attachment, the recipient can type "FA," press [RETURN], then supply a folder name.

Q *How do I transfer a WordPerfect document from my PC to my File Cabinet in ALL-IN-1, and vice-versa?*

A This is typically a two-step process. You first transfer the file from the PC to the VMS file system. This is usually accomplished with KERMIT, XMODEM, or NFT. You can then create a document in ALL-IN-1 and use the [LIST FILES] (F11) function key to list and retrieve the file from VMS. Going in the reverse direction, you must transfer the document to VMS first, with Document Transfer. You can then use KERMIT, XMODEM, and so on, to transfer the file to your PC. Refer to Section 25.3, "Transferring Documents," for more detailed instructions.

Q *When I use the [LIST FILES] function key in WordPerfect, I see a list of file names instead of my document titles. How do I list documents in my File Cabinet in WordPerfect?*

A The WordPerfect [LIST FILES] function key displays a list of files stored in your VMS directory—*not* documents stored in your File Cabinet. Instead, use the [RETRIEVE] (PF1, F18) function key or [GOLD] G to list documents when editing a WordPerfect document. Select the File Cabinet Document option, and press

[RETURN]. When the Selecting Document to be Retrieved form is displayed, you can list folders and titles by moving to the appropriate field, clearing the field with [ERASE LINE] (F13), and pressing [FIND] (or [GOLD] L).

WORD AND DOCUMENT PROCESSING DOs AND DON'Ts

Here are some suggestions for preparing documents in Word and Document Processing:

Do

- Select Preview before Print (PV) to review the format of your document before printing. The document is formatted and displayed on your terminal.
- Use the [REVEAL CODES] function key in WordPerfect and the [GOLD] View function key in WPS-PLUS to examine areas of a document in which there is a formatting problem. Hidden control codes are often the cause. Remember that you can delete control codes just as you would delete characters.
- Spell-check and proofread your document after making changes. The Spell Check (SC) option on the Word and Document Processing menu checks a document prepared with WPS-PLUS, EDT, or EVE. The [SPELL] (PF2, F8) function key performs a spell check when editing a WordPerfect document.
- When imbedding a named ruler in a WPS-PLUS document, respond "Y" when asked if you want to make it a referring ruler. This will make it easier to update rulers globally in the document at a later date.
- Rely on widow/orphan control to prevent broken paragraphs as a result of automatic pagination. A *widow* is the first few lines of a broken paragraph where most of the paragraph is on the following page. An *orphan* is the last few lines of a broken paragraph where most of the paragraph is on the preceding page. Setting widow/orphan control to a value of "3" or more results in fewer broken or split paragraphs. See Section 10.1.10, "Paginating WPS-PLUS Documents," for details.
- Explore the Define Styles feature of WordPerfect if you prepare documents with a lot of specialized formatting. Define Styles lets you easily store and retrieve groups of formatting characteristics. This saves you the trouble of having to press all of the separate function keys to turn characteristics on and off throughout your document.

Don't

- Don't press [RETURN] to wrap to the next line as you approach the right-hand margin. All editors in ALL-IN-1 automatically wrap text when you approach the right-hand margin. Inserting a carriage return defeats the word processor's automatic wrapping and text justification features. Press [RETURN] only at the end of a paragraph or after a title.

- Don't indent the left margin of a paragraph by placing spaces or tabs at the beginning of each line. You won't be able to adjust the margins of the paragraph easily. Instead, adjust the left and right margins in the ruler before typing the paragraph, or indent the paragraph with the [GOLD] [INDENT TAB] ([GOLD] [TAB]) key in WPS-PLUS or the [>INDENT] (F10) function key in WordPerfect.
- Don't use spaces to align columns of numbers or to center strings of text. Text will not line up properly if you change to a proportional font. Align columns by setting tab stops and using the [TAB] key. Center strings with [GOLD] C in WPS-PLUS or [CENTER] (PF1, F12) in WordPerfect.

Getting Started with Word and Document Processing

CHAPTER 9

This chapter describes the basics of working with documents in Word and Document Processing, including how to create, read, and print. A large part of learning how to prepare documents is learning the editing techniques of a specific word processor. Chapter 10 and Appendix B teach you basic techniques for working with WPS-PLUS, WordPerfect, and EDT.

This chapter teaches you how to perform the following tasks:

- Access Word and Document Processing.
- Select an editor for creating and editing a document.
- Create a new document.
- Select a document for editing, reading, printing, and deleting.
- Edit an existing document.
- Check the spelling in an existing document.
- Read, print, or delete an existing document.

9.1 ACCESSING WORD AND DOCUMENT PROCESSING

You can edit, read, and print documents from either the Word and Document Processing menu or the Electronic Messaging menu. However, to access all of the options for document processing, you'll want to move to the Word and Document Processing menu or index.

Perform the following steps to access Word and Document Processing:

WP [RETURN]	a. From any menu, type "WP" and press [RETURN]. *Hint:* It saves time to include an option after "WP." For example, type "WP SEL *folder*" and

press [RETURN] to move to the Word and Document Processing menu and select the document at the top of the specified folder, or type "WP I *folder*" to work from an index of the specified folder.

[NEXT SCREEN]

b. Word and Document Processing has multiple screens of menu options. Press [NEXT SCREEN] (or [GOLD] A) to see additional options.

***menu-option* [RETURN]**

c. Type the desired menu option and then press [RETURN]. Table 9.1 describes menu options on the Word and Document Processing menu. Table 12.1 describes File Cabinet options that you can enter from the Word and Document Processing menu.

Table 9.1 Word and Document Processing Menu Options

Enter This Menu Option	*To Perform the Following Action*
C (Create)	Create a new document.
D (Delete)	Delete the current document, refiling it in your Wastebasket folder.
DIC (Dictionaries)	Move to the Dictionary Maintenance menu to create and maintain personal dictionaries containing personal names and unusual terms that are not found in the standard dictionary.
DP (DECpage Formatting)	Format the current document with DECpage for high-quality printing. DECpage must be installed on your system in order for you to select this option.
DT (Document Transfer)	Move to the Document Transfer menu to transfer documents from your DECmate and VMS directories to your ALL-IN-1 File Cabinet.
E (Edit)	Invoke the editor to make changes to the current document.
FC (File Cabinet)	Move to the File Cabinet Maintenance menu to manage documents in your File Cabinet.
FWP (Format to WPS-PLUS)	Create a formatted copy of the current WPS-PLUS document. The resulting output document need not be formatted before printing.
GC (Grammar Checker)	Check the current document for grammatical errors. The Grammar Checker must be installed on your system in order for you to select this option.
GCD (Grammar Checker Defaults)	Change parameters for the Grammar Checker.
I (Index)	Create an index of documents with which to work.

Table 9.1 *(continued)*

Enter This Menu Option	*To Perform the Following Action*
LP (List Processing)	Move to the List Processing menu to work with customer lists, vendor lists, and so forth. List Processing merges list names with the text of a template document to produce mailing labels and form letters.
P (Print)	Print the current document.
PT (Printer Tables)	Create and maintain printer control tables. This function is usually performed by your system manager.
PV (Preview before Printing)	Format the current document and display the result on your terminal to allow you to preview formatting (line wraps, pagination, page numbering, etc.) before printing.
PN (Paragraph Numbering)	Number all of the chapter, section, and subsection titles within the current document. Paragraph Numbering also creates a table of contents.
R (Read)	Display the current document on your terminal screen.
RI (Recall Index)	Redisplay the index created with the last Index operation.
S (Send)	Send the current document to another user via Electronic Messaging.
SEL (Select)	Select a document to work with (edit, delete, print, etc.).
SC (Spell Check)	Check the current document for spelling errors.
TR (Training)	Start computer-based instruction for Word and Document Processing.
UD (User-Defined Processing)	Move to the User Defined Process Maintenance menu to create and manage files containing stored keystrokes.

9.2 SELECTING AN EDITOR

An editor is a tool for creating, modifying, and formatting a document. There are a number of editing programs on the market. These programs vary in appearance, functionality, and performance. You might be familiar with the WPS-PLUS word processor or the EDT editing program from Digital, or perhaps you know WordPerfect from WordPerfect, the Novell Application Group.

You can use any of several different editors for preparing documents in ALL-IN-1. The editor you choose determines many important aspects of your edit session, including these:

- The format of the text as it appears on your terminal screen. The editors mentioned above, for example, each display information in a slightly different manner.
- The location of special function keys to perform word-processing operations, such as cutting, pasting, and searching for text. In WPS-PLUS, for example, [PF4] deletes a character; in EDT, the same key deletes an entire line.

- The availability of advanced word-processing capabilities, such as font selection, text highlighting, and on-line spell checking. You'll find that EDT has limited word-processing capabilities compared to WPS-PLUS and WordPerfect. However, EDT is easier to learn.

Digital Equipment Corporation supplies three different editors—WPS-PLUS, EDT, and EVE—as part of ALL-IN-1. You therefore always have your choice of these editors. Additional editors might have been purchased separately by your site and integrated with ALL-IN-1. WordPerfect is a popular alternative due to its widespread use on personal computers.

You can choose any editor you prefer as your "default" editor. The default editor is automatically invoked when you create a new document or message. You can override this default by selecting a different editor when you create a document. The editor selected to create the document is then automatically invoked whenever you edit the document.

Most people prefer to select an editor they feel comfortable with and to use this editor for everything—preparing messages as well as documents. Some people choose a simple editor, such as EDT, for preparing messages and most documents, then select a more advanced editor for specific documents. One problem encountered when using multiple editors is what I call "Keyboard Mania," having to make the mental switch from one editor's function key layout to another's. It might be worth the time to learn a more advanced editor and select it as your default.

The following procedures show you how to select a default editor and how to override the default when creating a new document. You can change your default editor with the following procedure. You can start working with the new editor immediately to prepare messages and documents without exiting ALL-IN-1 or logging out.

Perform the following steps to set your default editor:

US SWC [RETURN]	a. From any menu, type "US SWC" and press [RETURN] to move to the Set Working Conditions form.
[DOWN ARROW] [TAB]	b. Press [DOWN ARROW] and [TAB] to move to the Edit Style field.
[ERASE LINE]	c. Press [ERASE LINE] (LF or F13) to clear the contents of the field.
Edit style: ***editor*** **[RETURN]** **[RETURN]**	d. Type the name of the new default editor and press [RETURN] twice. The names of editors discussed in this manual are "WPSPLUS," "EDT," "EVE_WPS," "EVE_EDT," and "WPCORP." *Note:* Leave this field blank and press [FIND] (or [GOLD] L) to list the editors.
[EXIT]...	e. Continue to press [EXIT] (F10 or Keypad-0) to return to your original menu.

Perform the following steps to select an editor other than your default when creating a new document (refer to Section 9.3, "Creating a New Document," for more details):

[NEXT SCREEN]

a. *Before* pressing the [RETURN] to complete the Creating New Document form, press [NEXT SCREEN] (or [GOLD] A) to move to the second screen.

[TAB]

b. Press [TAB] to move to the Handling field.

[ERASE LINE]

c. Press [ERASE LINE] (LF or F13) to clear the contents of the field.

Handling: ***handling***

d. Enter the handling type for the document. Handling specifies the editor for the document and other handling attributes, such as the program called to format the document. Typical handling types are "WPSPLUS" to specify handling by the WPS-PLUS editor, "WPCORP" to specify handling by WordPerfect, "ASCII EDT" to specify handling by EDT, and either "ASCII EVE_WPS" or "ASCII EVE_EDT" for the EVE editor.

[RETURN]

e. Press [RETURN] to complete the form. The screen is cleared. You can now enter the text of your document.

9.3 CREATING A NEW DOCUMENT

The steps for creating a document are intuitive. You select the Create option and specify a drawer, folder, and title for the document. ALL-IN-1 invokes the editor, and you then enter the text of the document. After entering the text of the document, you exit the editor and file your document.

The next few sections show you how to begin and end the process of creating a document. These steps work the same way regardless of the editor you choose. The process of entering text is very different, though, depending on the editor you choose. Chapter 10 describes how to work with four of the common editors: WPS-PLUS, WordPerfect, EDT, and EVE.

In this section, you'll learn how to perform the following tasks:

- Invoke the editor to create a new document.
- Enter text in your new document, using standard function keys to perform basic editing functions.
- Exit the editor and save your changes.

9.3.1 Invoking the Editor to Create a New Document

To invoke an editor and create a new document, do the following:

C [RETURN]	a. From the Word and Document Processing menu or index, type "C" and press [RETURN]. ALL-IN-1 displays the Creating New Document form, shown in Figure 9.1.
	b. By default, ALL-IN-1 stores the document in the current drawer and folder. Proceed to step c if you want to store your document in this drawer and folder.
[BACKSPACE]... **[ERASE LINE]** Drawer: ***drawer*** **[TAB]** **[ERASE LINE]** Folder: ***folder*** **[TAB]**	To change either the drawer or the folder, [UP ARROW] to either field, press [ERASE LINE] (LF or F13) to clear the field, and enter the name of the new drawer or folder. *Notes:* Creating the first document in a new folder implicitly creates the new folder. ALL-IN-1 asks if you want to create this folder when you've set your New Folder confirmation prompt to "Y" in Set Working Conditions. This question is asked to keep you from accidentally creating two similarly named folders. ALL-IN-1's lookup feature is available in both fields. Press [FIND] (or [GOLD] L) to list drawer or folder names.
Title: ***title*** **[RETURN]**	c. Type the title of the document. If you don't want to specify keywords for indexing the document, press [RETURN] and proceed to step d.

```
                        Creating New Document

Drawer:   MAIN

Folder:   DOCUMENTS

Title:

Keywords:

        Enter information and press RETURN,
        or press NEXT SCREEN for more fields                  (more...)
```

Figure 9.1 Creating New Document form

[TAB]

Keywords: ***keyword keyword...***

To specify keywords, press [TAB] and enter the keywords, separated by spaces.

Note: You'll generally proceed to the next step to create a brand-new document with the default editor. If you want to select a different editor or a template document, press [NEXT SCREEN] and complete the additional fields for the Creating New Document form. Section 9.2, "Selecting an Editor," describes the Handling field on this form.

If you produce many similar documents, it's wise to create documents that serve as templates, or "shells." When you create a "production" document, you can complete the fields under Template Document to use a copy of the template document to get started.

[RETURN]

d. Press [RETURN] after completing the Creating New Document form. ALL-IN-1 invokes an editor, enabling you to enter the text of your document. All of the features of the text editor are available for preparing your document.

9.3.2 Entering the Text of Your Document

Even if you're unfamiliar with the editor, you can proceed to enter text. The following guidelines apply to all editors discussed in this book.

1. If you feel at all uncomfortable at a computer terminal, remember that the main keyboard works just like a typewriter. Numeric keys on the main keyboard, character keys, special punctuation keys, and the [TAB] and [SPACE] keys work the same regardless of the editor; they insert text and "white space."
2. The flashing cursor is the focus of activity. Characters are inserted at the current cursor position as you type; characters are removed in front of the cursor position when you press [DELETE].
3. Basic editing is accomplished by moving the cursor with your arrow keys, then typing characters to insert text or pressing [DELETE] to remove text. As you become more familiar with the editor, you'll want to use function keys to work more efficiently.
4. Function keys perform special operations, such as moving the cursor, selecting text, and inserting page breaks. Table 9.2 on page 179 lists the frequently used function keys that perform the same operation regardless of the editor. It is perhaps best to learn these keys first. The additional function keys available for each editor are described in Chapter 10.

CAUTION: Actions performed by other function keys vary greatly, depending on the editor. Refer to the table in Chapter 10 that describes the function keys for your editor before using them.

5. Advanced editors like WPS-PLUS and WordPerfect allow you to include characters in your document that specify the format of the printed document. These characters are referred to as "control codes." The best way to think of a control code as an instruction to the printer specifying how to format or highlight the text that follows. Think of your document being transferred to the printer character by character. When the printer receives text, it simply prints it on the page. When the printer receives a control code, it sees this as a new instruction on how to print upcoming text.[1]

   Following is an example of a control code (shown in bold) in WPS-PLUS. This particular control code is called a "ruler." It tells the printer what margins and tab stops to obey when spreading text across the page. The actual text of the document starts with "1."

```
L-W--T----T----T----T----T----T----T----R

1. The ruler in WPS-PLUS controls the format of text that follows. The
   "L" margin marker sets the left margin, "R" sets the right margin,
   and "W" defines the left margin after a word wrap.
```

   Following is an example of control codes (shown in bold) in WordPerfect. These codes cause the word "paired" to print in italics.

```
Some control codes in WordPerfect are [ITALICS] paired[italics]. That
is, two separate codes are required to specify an attribute: one to
enable the attribute and one to disable it.
```

   Keep the following points in mind when dealing with control codes:

   - Control codes can only be viewed when editing the document; they do *not* appear when you read or print the document. In WPS-PLUS, most control codes are always visible, such as the ruler. Others are only visible when you press [GOLD] [VIEW], such as the code to center text (†). In WordPerfect, control codes are invisible by default and can only be viewed when you press [REVEAL CODES] (F19).
   - The position of control codes within the text is crucial. Remember the following rule: Control codes specify the format of the text that *follows.* This means that it doesn't do any good to place a WPS-PLUS ruler or WordPerfect margin code at the bottom of your document. These codes must precede the text to affect the margins. Control codes placed in the wrong position within the document will not give you the results you want. The good news is that codes can be moved with cut and paste techniques. In WordPerfect, display codes with [REVEAL CODES] before attempting a move.

1. In reality, control codes are interpreted and processed during "formatting" of the document. Formatting occurs prior to printing, and it is the product of the formatting that is sent to the printer. Refer to Section 4.2.3, "Formatting a Document," for further details.

9.3.3 Standard Function Keys

Table 9.2 describes the function keys that perform the same operation regardless of the editor you choose. Additional function keys for specific editors are described in Chapter 10.

9.3.4 Exiting the Editor and Filing Your Document

Do the following when you've finished entering the text of your document:

[GOLD] F	Press [GOLD] F to exit the editor and file the document. (You can also press [GOLD] K to leave the editor without creating the document.) ALL-IN-1 redisplays the menu.

Table 9.2 Standard function keys

Function Key	*Keystrokes*[a]	*Description*
Bottom	[GOLD] B	Move to bottom of document.
Center	[GOLD] C	Center text.
Delete Character	[DELETE]	Delete the character before the cursor.
Down Arrow	[DOWN ARROW]	Move forward one line.
File	[GOLD] F	Exit editor and file document.
Get Document	[GOLD] G	Include another file or document.
Interrupt	[GOLD] I	Display the Interrupt menu.
Left Arrow	[LEFT ARROW]	Move back one character.
Menu	[GOLD] M	Display the editor menu.
Next Screen	[NEXT SCREEN]	Display next screen of text.
Page Break	[GOLD] P	Insert page break.
Previous Screen	[PREV SCREEN]	Display previous screen of text.
Quit	[GOLD] K	Exit the editor without saving changes.
Return	[RETURN]	Insert a new line (carriage return).
Right Arrow	[RIGHT ARROW]	Move forward one character.
Ruler	[GOLD] R	Display or change ruler (except EVE).
Top	[GOLD] T	Move to beginning of document.
UDP	[GOLD] U	Execute User Defined Procedure (macro).
Up Arrow	[UP ARROW]	Move back one line.

[a]All "GOLD" keys listed in this table require that you enter two separate keystrokes: Press the [GOLD] (PF1) key, followed by the second key indicated.

9.4 SELECTING A DOCUMENT

Many of the options on the Word and Document Processing menu perform actions on the "current" document, which is identified in the upper right-hand corner of the menu or by the current item pointer (>) in an index. If this document isn't the one you want to work with, select the desired document. You can then enter menu options to edit, read, or print the document. Several different methods for selecting a document are described below.

Perform the following steps to select a document with the Select option:

SEL [RETURN]

a. Type "SEL" and press [RETURN] (or simply press [SELECT]). The Selecting Current Document form shown in Figure 9.2 is displayed.

Hint: You can save time by including the name of the folder after the Select option. For example, "SEL READ" selects the document at the top of the specified folder without displaying a form. You can then press [DOWN ARROW] to select other documents in the folder.

Drawer: ***drawer* [TAB]**
Folder: ***folder* [TAB]**
Title: ***title***

b. Enter the drawer, folder, and title or the number for the document you wish to select. When completing these fields, press [TAB] to move to the next field or [BACKSPACE] (F12) to move to the previous field. Press [ERASE LINE] (LF or F13) and then [FIND] (or [GOLD] L) while cursor is in any field to list all possible entries.

Note: Press [GOLD] E in the Drawer field to select a drawer by system or user name. This field is described further in Chapter 13, "Accessing a Shared Drawer."

```
                    Selecting Current Document

Drawer: MAIN

Folder: DOCUMENTS

Title:

Number:

Enter information and press RETURN, or press GOLD E to expand drawer field
```

Figure 9.2 Selecting Current Document form

Table 9.3 Selecting documents with arrow keys

Press the Following Key(s)	*To Perform This Action*
[UP ARROW]	Select the first document in the current folder.
[DOWN ARROW]	Select the next document in the current folder.
[GOLD] [UP ARROW]	Select the first document in the first folder.
[GOLD] [DOWN ARROW]	Select the first document in the next folder.

[RETURN] c. Press [RETURN] once you've entered the necessary information. The Selecting Current Document form is cleared, and the selected document is shown in the current item block.

You can also select a document from the Word and Document Processing menu with any of the function keys listed in Table 9.3.

Perform the following steps to select a document from an index:

I [RETURN] a. Type "I" and press [RETURN] to create an index. *Hint:* You can add the name of a folder after the "I" to create an index quickly of all documents in the folder. For example, type "I SALES" to create an index of the Sales folder.

Folder: ***folder* [TAB]...** b. Enter information to build an index of documents. Include all information that pertains to the document you wish to select. If you are unsure of what to enter, press [ERASE LINE] (LF or F13) to clear the folder name and leave all other fields blank. This creates an index of all messages and documents. Press [FIND] (or [GOLD] L) while the cursor is in any field to list possible entries.

[RETURN] c. Press [RETURN] after you've entered enough information to create an index that includes the desired document. ALL-IN-1 displays an index of documents.

***line-number* [RETURN]** d. Type the line number of the document you want to select and press [RETURN]. You might want to press [NEXT SCREEN] first, however, to see additional pages of documents.

9.5 EDITING A DOCUMENT

You can make as many changes as you like to an existing document. Once you've created a document, it remains in your File Cabinet, and you can revise it whenever you wish. Remember, though, that only the latest revision of a document is retained. Earlier revisions are purged to conserve disk storage.

Perform the following steps to edit the current document:

E [RETURN]	a. Type "E" and press [RETURN]. The editor is invoked, and the contents of the document are displayed on your screen.
	b. Modify the document by moving the cursor to the proper location and inserting and removing text as necessary. Refer to Chapter 10 for instructions on how to use your particular editor.
[GOLD] F	c. Press [GOLD] F to exit the editor and file the document. (You can also press [GOLD] K to leave the editor without modifying the document.) ALL-IN-1 redisplays the menu.

9.6 CHECKING SPELLING WITHIN A DOCUMENT

Consider the following paragraphs extracted from a memo sent to an employee:

```
As senor partner of this firm, I would like to cammand you
on your continuing work on the Fall River project.
Such work grately increases our visibility in this market.
```

The above sentences contain three misspellings. As a result, the recipient will probably be confused about the intent of the memo. Is the boss applauding the employee's work, or is she taking charge of the project due to the employee's poor performance? These questions can be avoided if the boss simply checks the spelling of the memo before sending it.

ALL-IN-1 provides a spell checker utility that enables you to catch spelling errors before issuing a document. This utility is available in both Word and Document Processing and Electronic Messaging.

NOTE that if the document was created with WordPerfect, it is recommended that you use the spell checker included in WordPerfect. Edit the document and press the [SPELL] (PF2, F8) function key to spell-check a WordPerfect document. Refer to Appendix B for further information.

Perform the following steps to spell-check the current message or document:

SC [RETURN]	a. Type "SC" and press [RETURN]. ALL-IN-1 converts the document to WPS-PLUS if the document was prepared with another editor. The document is converted back to its original format when the spell check is finished. While this conversion has no adverse effect on documents

written in EDT and EVE, it can cause changes to the format of a WordPerfect document. For this reason, it is recommended that you use the [SPELL] function within WordPerfect to spell-check WordPerfect documents.

ALL-IN-1 then opens one or more dictionaries and initializes the Spell Checker. The document is displayed with the spell check window at the bottom of the screen (Figure 9.3).

[RETURN]

b. The first misspelled word is highlighted. Possible correct spellings for the word appear at the top of the spell check window. One of these words will typically be highlighted in reverse video as shown in Figure 9.3. You can replace the misspelled word with the highlighted word by simply pressing [RETURN].

If "[More...]" appears in the list of possible words, you can press [RIGHT ARROW] to see additional words. Continue pressing [RIGHT ARROW] until "[No More]" appears. Press [LEFT ARROW] to highlight a specific word, and press [RETURN] to replace the misspelled word.

If no words appear in the window, the Spell Checker couldn't come up with any possible

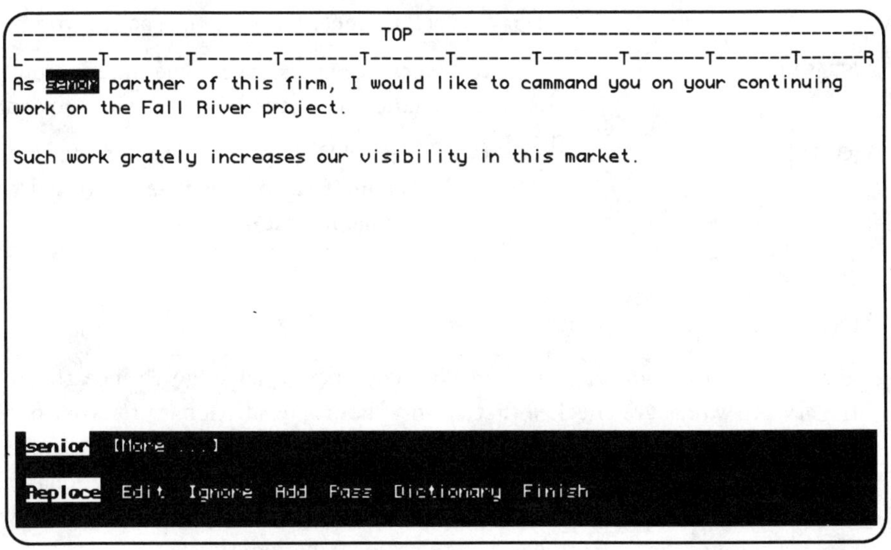

Figure 9.3 Document with Spell Check window

substitutions. In this case, you will have to edit the misspelled word.

***option* [RETURN]**

Alternatively, type the first character of one of the following options (or highlight the option by pressing [RIGHT ARROW] or [LEFT ARROW]) and press [RETURN].

Replace (R)	Replace the misspelled word with the selection.
Edit (E)	Allow editing of the misspelled word.
Ignore (I)	Ignore this word here and throughout the document.
Add (A)	Add the word to the personal dictionary and continue.
Pass (P)	Ignore this occurrence of the word.
Dictionary (D)	Select dictionary for Add option.
Finish (F)	Quit the spell check operation.

c. Enter any necessary information for the requested option and press [RETURN].

d. Repeat steps b and c as necessary whenever the Spell Checker locates a misspelled word.

[SPACE]

e. A message is displayed when the bottom of the document is reached. Press any key to continue.

[GOLD] F

f. Press [GOLD] F to exit the editor and return to the menu. The document is converted back to its original format if necessary.

9.6.1 Spell Check Dictionaries

The Spell Checker compares all words in a document against words appearing in a dictionary. All words are checked first against the master dictionary for your particular language. If the word is not found in the master dictionary, the Spell Checker then checks your personal dictionary. You can add words to your personal dictionary during a spell operation. The next time you spell-check a document, these words will be skipped because they are present in your personal dictionary.

You can create up to 10 additional dictionaries and have them open during a spell-check operation. This is helpful for checking the spelling of technical documents that contain uncommon words or business documents that contain a series of proper names.

The Dictionary Maintenance menu creates and maintains additional dictionaries. This menu also allows you to specify which dictionaries are to be open and referenced during a spell check operation.

To access Dictionary Maintenance, follow these steps:

WP DIC [RETURN]	a. From any menu, type "WP DIC" and press [RETURN].
***menu-option* [RETURN]**	b. Type the menu option and press [RETURN]. Menu options are described in Table 9.4.
	c. Enter the appropriate information for the selected option and press [RETURN].
[EXIT]	d. Press [EXIT] (F10 or Keypad-0) to return to the Word and Document Processing menu.

Table 9.4 Dictionary Maintenance menu options

Enter This Menu Option	*To Perform the Following Action*
C (Create)	Create a new dictionary. You must enter a folder and title for the dictionary. The editor is invoked so you can enter the words of the dictionary. Enter words separated by spaces. File the document with [GOLD] F when finished, then select the Format option.
E (Edit)	Edit the current dictionary to add, change, or remove words. Make sure that words are separated with spaces. File the document with [GOLD] F when finished, then select the Format option.
D (Delete)	Delete the current dictionary and refile it in your Wastebasket folder.
P (Print)	Print the current dictionary.
SEL (Select)	Select a dictionary with which to work.
R (Read)	Display the current dictionary.
LD (List Dictionaries)	Display a list of dictionaries.
F (Format)	Sort entries in the current dictionary and remove duplicates.
CMD (Choose Master Dictionary)	Select the master dictionary for subsequent spell checks.
LO (List Open Dictionaries)	Display a list of dictionaries open during a spell check.
OP (Open Current Dictionary)	Indicate that the current dictionary is to be open and searched during subsequent spell checks.
CL (Close Current Dictionary)	Indicate that the current dictionary is not to be opened for subsequent spell checks.
UL (Update Language)	Create a personal dictionary for the selected language.

9.7 READING A DOCUMENT

The Read (R) option in Word and Document Processing displays the current document on your terminal screen. This is perhaps the best way to review a document quickly before generating a hard copy. Running headers, footers, page numbering, and other special formatting are shown during a read operation. If this information is not displayed as expected, edit the document and check control information before you print. Special characters, graphics, and fonts cannot be displayed on most character cell terminals, however.

Perform the following steps to read the current document:

R [RETURN]	a. Type "R" and press [RETURN]. ALL-IN-1 clears the screen and displays the document.
function-key	b. Press any of the function keys listed in Table 4.1 to display the rest of the document.
***menu-option* [RETURN]**	Or enter any of the menu options listed in Table 4.2 to perform operations on the current document.
[EXIT]	c. Press [EXIT] (F10 or Keypad-0) to clear the screen and redisplay the menu when you've finished reviewing the document.

9.8 PRINTING A DOCUMENT

You can print a hard copy of a document with the Print (P) option on the Word and Document Processing menu. The following procedure shows you the minimum number of steps to print a document. Additional steps are described in Sections 4.2, "Printing in ALL-IN-1," and 10.1.9, "Printing WPS-PLUS Documents."

Perform the following steps to print a document:

P [RETURN]	a. Type "P" and press [RETURN] to print the current document. ALL-IN-1 displays the Printing Document form.
[RETURN]	b. Press [RETURN] to print the document if the information shown in the Printing Document form is correct. ALL-IN-1 redisplays the menu along with a note that the document has been submitted for printing. If this information is incorrect, enter the appropriate document destination, format style, or number of copies. Refer to Section 4.2, "Printing in ALL-IN-1," for details.

Hint: To preview the format of a document on your screen before printing, select the Preview before Printing (PV) option instead of Print (P). ALL-IN-1 sends the document to your terminal screen. This displays certain formatting not displayed during a Read operation—for example, side-by-side columns.

9.9 DELETING A DOCUMENT

You should periodically delete or archive obsolete documents. This reduces the number of documents that you have to manage and improves the performance of any operation involving the File Cabinet. This section describes how to delete documents. Archiving is described in Chapter 12.

Remember that when you delete a document, it is simply placed in your Wastebasket folder. It remains in your Wastebasket folder until the "Janitor" runs or until you select the Empty Wastebasket (EW) option. The Janitor is a system program that is run periodically to empty users' Wastebasket folders. This is equivalent to emptying your real wastebasket into the paper shredder. Once a document is removed by the Janitor, it cannot be recovered.

You can delete a single document with the Delete option on the Word and Document Processing menu. Perform the following steps to delete the current document:

D [RETURN] a. Type "D" and press [RETURN].

Y [RETURN] b. If ALL-IN-1 asks you to confirm whether or not you want to delete the document, type "Y" and press [RETURN]. (This prompt can be suppressed with Set Working Conditions.) ALL-IN-1 displays a note that the document has been deleted.

To delete multiple documents, it is more efficient to work with an index. Create an index of documents by following the steps outlined in Section 7.4, "Working with an Index of Messages or Documents." Then select documents and enter the Delete All Selected (XD) option. All selected documents are moved to the Wastebasket.

You can recover a document from your Wastebasket to prevent it from being removed by the Janitor. Simply select the document and refile it into the original folder. The easiest way to do this is from an index of the Wastebasket.

To recover a document from the Wastebasket, follow these steps:

I WASTEBASKET [RETURN] a. Type "I WASTEBASKET" and press [RETURN]. ALL-IN-1 displays an index of your Wastebasket folder.

line-number* RFD *folder
[RETURN]

b. Type the line number of the document you want to recover, followed by a space, "RFD", another space, and the original folder name—for example, "2 RFD BUDGET." Then press [RETURN]. The folder of the current document is changed.

Getting Started with an Editor

CHAPTER 10

A text editor is a tool for creating and modifying documents. Learning an editor is a large part of learning how to prepare documents: how to move around in the document, how to cut and paste text, how to highlight text, and so forth. The more you learn about the editor's features, the faster and easier it becomes to prepare documents.

This chapter describes four different editors: WPS-PLUS, WordPerfect, EDT, and EVE. The intent is to get you started working with a particular editor. Although you might want to review the capabilities of each editor, you really need to read only the section pertaining to the editor with which you've chosen to work.

Review the function key layout when reading, just to get a feel for the operations you can perform. It helps to make a copy of the function key layout and keep this next to your keyboard as you're learning the editor. There are short exercises contained in this chapter, but perhaps the best way to learn is to create a practice document and play! Try all of the basic operations, then refer to the additional editing procedures listed in Appendix B.

In addition to an overview of the editor's features and function keys, you'll learn how to perform the following tasks in this chapter:

- Move around in your document before inserting or deleting text.
- Perform basic editing operations, such as inserting, deleting, copying, highlighting, and searching for text.

10.1 GETTING STARTED WITH WPS-PLUS

WPS-PLUS is a full-function word processor available in ALL-IN-1 for the preparation of documents. WPS-PLUS is capable of producing documents ranging in size from single-page memos to large manuals. The advanced word-processing features of WPS-PLUS allow you to create publication-quality documents almost as easily as creating a simple letter.

The WPS-PLUS word processor includes the following features:

- A complete set of function keys that perform word-processing functions with one or two keystrokes.

- Advanced text highlighting capabilities that allow you to subscript, superscript, bold, underline, redline, or capitalize text. You can also select any character font that your printer supports.
- On-line writing aids, including a spell checker, thesaurus, and usage alert.
- Features for producing larger, more advanced documents, including automatic pagination, running headers and footers, footnoting, and multicolumn page formatting.
- The ability to include encapsulated PostScript images in your documents. A library of clip-art images from which you can select is supplied with WPS-PLUS.
- The ability to store keystrokes in a User Defined Process, then have WPS-PLUS automatically re-execute the keystrokes.
- WPS-PLUS Editor Math, which performs simple calculations on numbers included in your document. Editor Math has the ability to add, subtract, multiply, and divide values as well as compute subtotals, totals, and averages. Editor Math can also be performed automatically during List Processing, which is described below.
- The ability to save typing by entering the short abbreviation for a long string of text that appears in an abbreviation document. WPS-PLUS automatically retrieves and substitutes the expanded text.
- A Two Dimensional Editor (TDE) for drawing boxes around text and creating simple charts within your document.
- Paragraph Numbering, which automatically numbers your section titles and optionally produces a table of contents and index for your document.
- List Processing, which performs advanced operations on lists of items, such as generating form letters from a list of customers.
- Automatic keystroke journaling so that in the event of a system failure, most of your editing work can be recovered.

10.1.1 The WPS-PLUS Keyboard

Figure 10.1 shows the layout of the WPS-PLUS function keys that perform special word-processing operations. Function keys shown on the main keyboard require two separate keystrokes, the first being the [GOLD] key. For example, [GOLD] C centers a string of text. A tabular listing of function keys along with the specific keystrokes is contained in Appendix B.

10.1.2 Viewing Your Document in the Editor

Figure 10.2 shows an example of the screen layout in WPS-PLUS. The document being edited here is a simple business letter. The letter starts with the blank line that appears on the sixth line of the terminal screen, and it continues beyond the bottom of the

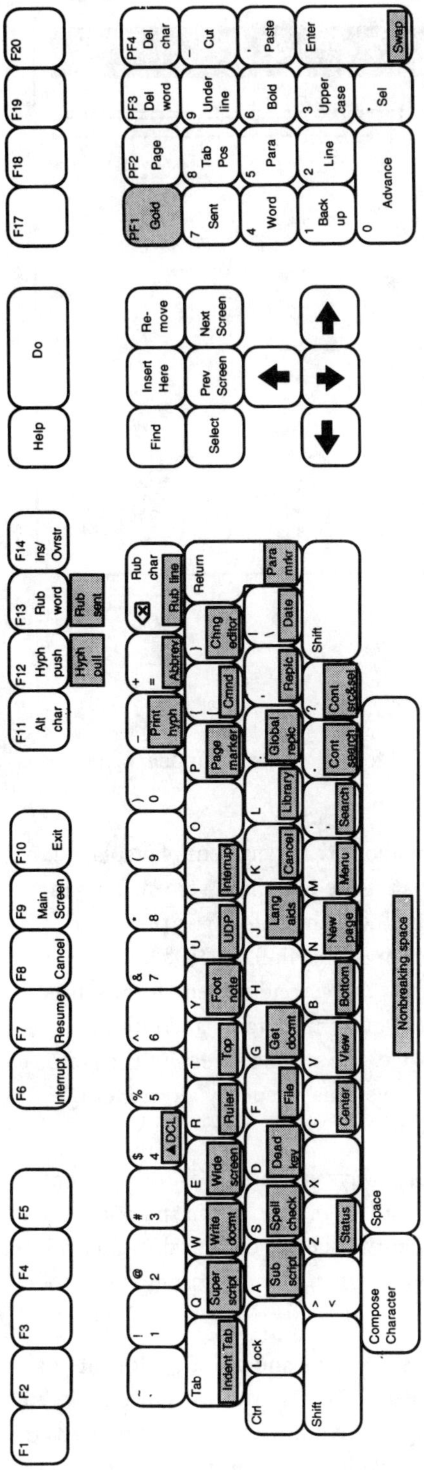

Figure 10.1 WPS-PLUS function key layout (LK201 keyboard)

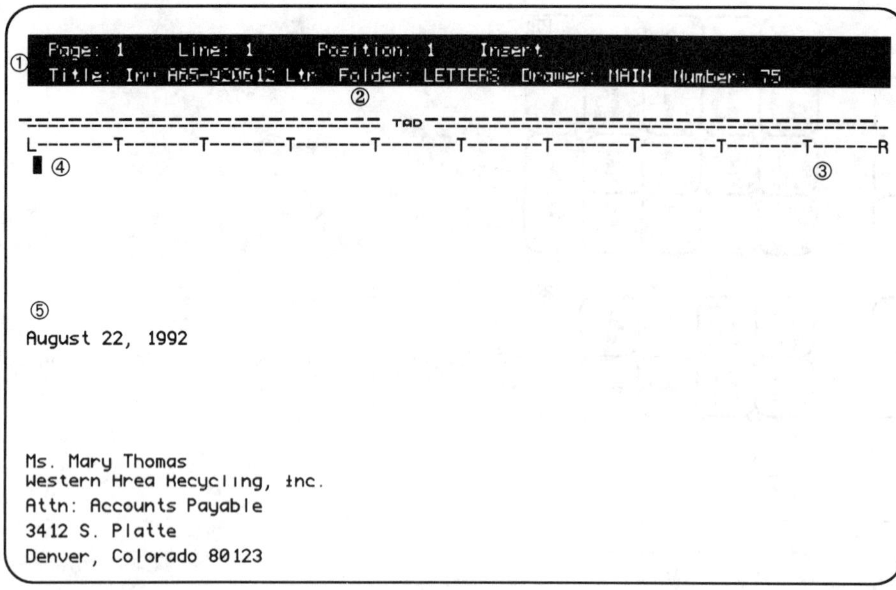

Figure 10.2 Viewing a document in the WPS-PLUS editor

screen. In addition to the text of the document, the following items appear when editing a WPS-PLUS document:

① Status Bar	Information about the document is displayed in the status bar at the top of the screen. This information includes the cursor position, edit mode (insert or overstrike), and the document identification. The second screen of the status bar shows the current margins and tab stops. You can display the second screen of the status bar or turn the status bar off by alternately pressing [GOLD] Z.
② Top of Document Marker	This marker always appears in your document before the first line of text. It appears only when editing to identify the top of your document; it does not appear when you read or print the document.
③ Ruler	The ruler sets margins and tab stops for the text that follows. The ruler shown in Figure 10.2 sets the left margin to column 0, the right margin to column 80, and tab stops every eighth position.

	Rulers appear only when editing; they do not appear when you read or print the document.
④ Cursor	The cursor is the flashing rectangle (or sometimes a flashing underscore).
⑤ Document Text	Following a number of blank lines, the first line of text is the date, which appears in the middle of the screen.

10.1.3 Moving Around in the Text

Only the top portion of the letter appears in Figure 10.2, although the letter continues beyond the bottom of the screen. Pressing [NEXT SCREEN] displays the salutation and the first paragraph of the body of the letter and moves the cursor forward in the document.

You must move the cursor to modify various portions of a document. Remember that the cursor is the focus of activity when you are editing. Characters are inserted at the cursor position as you type, and characters are deleted from the cursor position when you press [DELETE CHAR].

The following function keys move the cursor around in a document:

Function Key	*Keystrokes*	*Moves the Cursor*
[DOWN ARROW]		Forward one line.
[LEFT ARROW]		Back one character.
[RIGHT ARROW]		Forward one character.
[UP ARROW]		Back one line.
[BOTTOM]	[GOLD] B	To the bottom of the document.
[TOP]	[GOLD] T	To the top of the document.
[NEXT SCREEN]		Forward one screen.
[PREV SCREEN]		Back one screen.

The additional function keys listed later in this section also move the cursor around in a document. The [PARAGRAPH] (Keypad-5) key moves the cursor a single paragraph, for example. Movement with these keys is made in the current direction—forward or reverse. The following two keys set the current direction:

[ADVANCE]	Keypad-0	Sets the direction to forward and moves one character.
[BACKUP]	Keypad-1	Sets the direction to reverse and moves one character.

Therefore, to move one paragraph back, press [BACKUP] (Keypad-1) and then [PARAGRAPH]. Press [PARAGRAPH] again to move a second paragraph back. Press [ADVANCE] [PARAGRAPH] to move forward one paragraph.

By the way, you can highlight text as you move the cursor. Press [BOLD] (Keypad-6) or [UNDERLINE] (Keypad-9) before pressing any of the keys in the following table. Text is highlighted as the cursor moves. Press an arrow key or type any text to disable highlighting.

Function Key	*Keystrokes*	*Moves the Cursor in the Current Direction*
[LINE]	Keypad-2	To the beginning of the line.
[PAGE]	PF2	To the next page break.
[PARAGRAPH]	Keypad-5	One paragraph.
[PARA MARK]	[GOLD][RETURN]	To the paragraph indentation.
[SENTENCE]	Keypad-7	One sentence.
[TAB POS]	Keypad-8	One tab position.
[WORD]	Keypad-4	One word.

10.1.4 Basic Editing

Most people get by with just the basic editing operations described in this section. These include how to delete, highlight, search for, select, and cut and paste text. Procedures for performing more advanced operations are listed in Appendix B.

10.1.4.1 Deleting Text

Table 10.1 lists the function keys that delete text. To delete larger blocks of text, it's more efficient to select the block of text, then press [REMOVE] or [CUT].

10.1.4.2 Highlighting Text

To enable bolding, capitalizing, or underlining before typing the text, perform the following steps:

[SELECT] — a. Press [SELECT]. A select mark (◊) appears.

text — b. Type the text that you want highlighted.

function-key — c. Press one of the following function keys:

[UNDERLINE] (Keypad-9)

[BOLD] (Keypad-6)

[UPPERCASE] (Keypad-3)

To bold, capitalize, or underline existing text, do the following:

 — a. Move the cursor to the first character in the string you want to highlight.

[SELECT] — b. Press [SELECT] (or Keypad-Period).

Table 10.1 WPS-PLUS function keys to delete or restore text

Function Key	*Keystrokes*	*Description*
[DELETE]	⌫	Deletes the character in front of the cursor.
[DELETE CHAR]	PF4	Deletes the character at the cursor position.
[GOLD] [DEL CHAR]	[GOLD] PF4	Restores the last character deleted.
[ERASE LINE]	LF or F13	Deletes the word in front of the cursor.
[DELETE WORD]	PF3	Deletes the word at the cursor position.
[GOLD] [DEL WORD]	[GOLD] PF4	Restores the last word deleted.
[DELETE LINE]	[GOLD] ⌫	Deletes all characters from the beginning of the line to the cursor position.
[DELETE TO EOL]	[GOLD] F14	Deletes all characters from the cursor position to the end of the current line.
[DELETE SENT]	[GOLD] F12	Deletes all characters from the last period, question mark, or exclamation point to the cursor position.

←↕→ — c. Move the cursor beyond the last character in the string you want to highlight.

function-key — d. Press one of the function keys to highlight the text.

Perform the following steps to remove highlighting:

←↕→ — a. Move the cursor to the first highlighted character.

[SELECT] — b. Press [SELECT] (or Keypad-Period).

←↕→ — c. Move the cursor beyond the last highlighted character.

[GOLD] ***function-key*** — d. Press [GOLD] and then the function key that you pressed to highlight the text.

10.1.4.3 Searching for Text

Perform the following steps to search for a string of text in a document:

[FIND] — a. Press [FIND] (or [GOLD] Comma). The "Enter search string:" prompt is displayed at the bottom of your screen.

Enter search string:***string*** — b. Type the text you want to find. It will be stored in the "search" buffer.

[ADVANCE] or **[BACKUP]**

c. Press [ADVANCE] (Keypad-0) or [RETURN] to search forward for the first occurrence of the string, or press [BACKUP] (Keypad-1) to search in the reverse direction.

Note: To search for a control character (TAB, RETURN, etc.), turn on GOLD VIEW before step a.

Perform the following steps to search for the next occurrence of the string in the search buffer:

[CONT SEARCH]

Press [CONT SEARCH] ([GOLD] Period) to search for the string already stored in the search buffer. The search is performed in the direction currently in effect.

10.1.4.4 Selecting Text

To select a string of text for cutting, copying, highlighting, or spell checking, do the following:

a. Move the cursor to the first character in the string you want to select.

[SELECT]

b. Press [SELECT] (or Keypad-Period). WPS-PLUS "drops" the current line and displays a select mark (◊) before the first selected character.

c. Move the cursor beyond the last character in the string you want to select. Every character between the select mark (◊) and the cursor is part of the selected string. You can press [REMOVE], [BOLD], [SPELL CHECK], and so on, to manipulate the selected text.

Do the following to deselect a string of text and get rid of the select mark (◊):

[SELECT]

Press [SELECT] (or Keypad-Period) again to deselect text. The select mark (◊) is removed.

10.1.4.5 Cutting and Pasting Text

This is the procedure for selecting and cutting or copying a string of text:

a. Move the cursor to the first character in the string you want to cut or copy.

[SELECT]

b. Press [SELECT] (or Keypad-Period). WPS-PLUS "drops" the current line and displays a select mark (◊) before the first selected character.

c. Move the cursor beyond the last character in the string you want to cut or copy.

[CUT] or **[GOLD] [CUT]**

d. Press [CUT] ([REMOVE] or Keypad-Hyphen) to "cut" the selected text, or press [GOLD] [CUT] ([GOLD] [REMOVE] or [GOLD] Keypad-Hyphen) to copy the selected text.

Note: The selected text is stored in your paste buffer. You can now move the cursor and paste the text in another area of your document. See Appendix B for instructions on working with multiple paste buffers.

Perform the following steps to paste the string text that was last cut or copied:

a. Move the cursor to the point in your document where you want to paste the string of text.

[PASTE]

b. Press [PASTE] ([INSERT HERE] or Keypad-Comma) to paste the text.

[GOLD] [PASTE]

Or press [GOLD] [PASTE] ([GOLD] [INSERT HERE] or [GOLD] Keypad-Comma) to paste the text along with any rulers selected during the cut or copy operation.

Note: Text in the paste buffer is remembered even though you file the document and exit the editor. This allows you to cut or copy a string of text from one document and paste it in the next document you edit.

10.1.5 The WPS-Plus Ruler

If you look at any large, elaborate WPS-PLUS document while in the editor, you'll see lots of extra lines that don't appear in the printed document. What are these extra lines? They're formatting instructions that control the printing of the text. A ruler is the most common example of a formatting instruction.

The WPS-PLUS ruler defines margins, tab stops, paragraph indentation, and center points. A long document typically has several rulers, each resetting the margins and tab stops for the text that follows.

In the WPS-PLUS editor, a typical ruler looks like this:

```
L-------T-------T-------T-------T-------T-------T-------T-------T-------T------R
```

The letters *L*, *T*, and *R* act as "markers" to show the positions of the left margin, tab stops, and right margin, respectively. The text you enter after the ruler wraps between the left and right margins shown in the ruler. Following is a complete list of the marker characters that can appear in a ruler. Examples of these markers appear at the end of this section.

L	Left margin marker, sets single spacing.
D	Left margin marker, sets double spacing.
F	Left margin marker, sets half-line spacing.
N	Left margin marker, sets one and one-half spacing.
R	Right margin marker without justification.
J	Right margin marker with right margin justification (upon printing).
T	Tab marker with left justification.
>	Tab marker with right justification.
.	Tab marker with decimal point justification (for columns of numbers).
W	Indentation marker for the left margin after a word wrap.
P	Indentation marker after a new paragraph.
C	Center-point marker (for centering text independent of margins).
H	Typically precedes the right margin marker by about 8 to 10 spaces to create a hyphenation zone.

To understand rulers, it helps to imagine the system transferring your document to the printer line by line. When the system encounters a line of text, it sends it to the printer. When the system encounters a ruler, it doesn't send it to the printer but instead remembers this as the latest instruction on how to format the lines of text that follow.

Formatting documents with rulers provides great flexibility. You can insert as many rulers as you want to control the formatting of various sections of your document. You can later edit a ruler if you decide to change the format. In addition, you can save and recall ruler definitions. This helps you create documents with a consistent appearance.

Perform the following steps to create a new ruler:

[GOLD] R a. Press [GOLD] R. The expanded format of the ruler appears:

```
         10        20        30        40        50        60        70        80
....:....0....:....0....:....0....:....0....:....0....:....0....:....0....:....0
L        T        T         T        T         T         T        T        T     R
```

Note: Settings that appear in the expanded ruler are determined by the previous ruler. In a new document, the default settings are displayed. You can change the default ruler by changing the settings as described in step b, then "saving" the resulting ruler under number "0", as described in Section 10.1.5.2, "Storing and Recalling Ruler Settings."

[RIGHT ARROW]... or **[LEFT ARROW]...**

b. Move your cursor back and forth along the ruler with [RIGHT ARROW] and [LEFT ARROW]. You can move the cursor more quickly with [WORD] (Keypad-4) or [LINE] (Keypad-2).

Position the cursor in the column where you want a margin or tab stop, then press one of the valid marker characters listed earlier in this section. To clear a marker, position the cursor on the marker and press [SPACE].

[RETURN]

c. Press [RETURN] to insert the ruler and continue editing.

Note: If you want to save the ruler settings for use in other documents, press "S" and then type a number from 0 through 9 (or press [SHIFT], 0 through 9) *before* pressing [RETURN].

Perform the following steps to change an existing ruler:

a. Move the cursor to the line following the ruler, as follows:

```
L-------T-------T-------T-------T-------T-------T-------T-------T-------T------R
█
```

[GOLD] R

b. Press [GOLD] R. The ruler is expanded.

c. Follow steps b and c for creating a ruler.

Perform these steps to delete an existing ruler:

a. Move the cursor to the line following the ruler.

[GOLD] R

b. Press [GOLD] R. The ruler is expanded.

[DELETE WORD]

c. Press [DELETE WORD] (PF3).

[RETURN]

d. Press [RETURN]. Note that the ruler is removed from the document.

Note: You cannot eliminate the ruler at the top of the document. You need at least one ruler to control the formatting of document text.

10.1.5.1 *Examples*

Following are some examples of typical rulers showing the effect of various marker characters.

- The "T" marker character creates a left-justified tab position.

```
-L--------T-------T-------T-------------------T-------T---------------R-
  8/23/92  8:52am  #1245   Leave Denver        10:13am Arrive Los Angeles
  8/24/92  11:15am #1634   Leave Los Angeles   4:33pm  Arrive Houston
  8/26/92  5:22pm  #761    Leave Houston       6:57pm  Arrive Denver
```

- The "W" marker character sets the left margin after a word wrap. This is useful when setting up a list of numbered paragraphs.

```
-L----.-W-------------------------------------R-.
      1. You can cut and paste columns in
         WPS-PLUS.  To transpose the start time
         and flight number columns above, move
         the cursor to "8" in"8:52am" and press
         [SELECT].

      2. Move the cursor one character beyond
         "5:22pm" and press [GOLD] [TAB POS]
         [CUT]. The start time column is removed
         and remaining columns move left.

      3. Move the cursor under the second "T" in
         the ruler and press [GOLD] [TAB POS]
         [PASTE]. The start time column is
         inserted as the third column.
```

- The decimal point marker character aligns columns of decimal numbers.

```
-L--------------.---------.---------.---------.---------.--------------R-
              38.12    874.12   4895.12   2563.23    874.23
             874.45     88.23    674.16    652.82    764.65
             764.53     76.51    709.26    762.67    594.13
```

- The > marker character creates a right-justified tab position.

```
-L----T------T---------------------------->---------.---------.----R-
      C874   Cables                       5      5.00     25.00
      C654   Connectors                  10      3.45     34.50
      C234   Strip Outlets                3     14.95     44.85
```

10.1.5.2 *Storing and Recalling Ruler Settings*

The process of adjusting rulers can be time-consuming, especially if you're frequently changing the format of your document between paragraphs. To help make this easier, you can save a ruler setting after making adjustments. Then later in the document when you need to duplicate the same format, you can recall the saved ruler setting. Saved rulers are permanently stored so you can recall them when preparing other documents as well. This ensures a uniform format for all documents.

You can save ruler settings either by number or by name. Most people find that names are easier to remember than numbers, though you might find it easier to save and recall rulers by number.

You can store up to 10 numbered ruler settings with an assigned ruler number of 0 through 9. Ruler number 0 is your "default" ruler. In other words, whenever you create a new document, WPS-PLUS retrieves ruler number 0 and inserts it at the top of your document as the edit screen is displayed. Ruler number 9 is the default ruler for footnotes. You can change these default rulers or any numbered ruler with the following procedure.

Perform the following steps to save an existing ruler by number:

	a. Move the cursor to the left-most column of the line following the ruler.
[GOLD] R	b. Press [GOLD] R. The ruler is expanded.
S *ruler-number*	c. Press "S," then type a number 0 through 9 (or press [SHIFT], 0 through 9).
[RETURN]	d. Press [RETURN] to continue editing.

Perform the following steps to insert a numbered ruler in the current location of your document:

[GOLD] R	a. Press [GOLD] R.
ruler-number	b. Type the number (0 through 9) of the ruler you want to recall. Note that the ruler settings are quickly changed to those of the stored ruler. *Note:* If you don't remember the ruler number, just press numbers 0 through 9 until the ruler settings you want are displayed.
[RETURN]	c. Press [RETURN] to insert the ruler and continue editing.

10.1.5.3 Named Rulers

In addition to storing ruler settings by number, you can also store ruler settings by name. You can store as many named rulers as you like with the following procedure.

Perform the following steps to save an existing ruler by name:

	a. Move the cursor to the line following the ruler.
[GOLD] R	b. Press [GOLD] R. The ruler is expanded. At this point, you can make any final adjustments before saving the ruler.

[GOLD] W	c. Press [GOLD] W. WPS-PLUS asks for the name you want to assign to the ruler.
Enter name of ruler to store: ***ruler-name* [RETURN]**	d. Enter a meaningful name for the ruler and press [RETURN]. WPS-PLUS displays a message advising that the ruler has been stored.
[RETURN]	e. Press [RETURN] to resume editing.

To retrieve and insert a named ruler in the current location of your document, do the following:

[GOLD] R	a. Press [GOLD] R. The expanded ruler appears.
[GOLD] G	b. Press [GOLD] G. WPS-PLUS asks for the name of the ruler.
Enter name of ruler to get: ***ruler-name* [RETURN]**	c. Enter the name of the ruler and press [RETURN].
[FIND]	If you don't remember the name of the ruler, press [FIND] (or [GOLD] L) to display named rulers. A screen showing named rulers is displayed.
[DOWN ARROW]...	d. Press [DOWN ARROW] to move the current item pointer (>) to the ruler you want to retrieve. If necessary, press [NEXT SCREEN] to display any additional named rulers.
[SELECT]	e. Press [SELECT] to select the current ruler. WPS-PLUS asks if you want to make this a referring ruler (see next section).
[RETURN] or **Y [RETURN]**	f. Press [RETURN] if you don't want this to be a referring ruler, or type "Y" and press [RETURN] to create a referring ruler.
[RETURN]	g. Press [RETURN] to imbed the ruler and continue editing.

To modify a named ruler, do the following:

[GOLD] R...	a. Follow steps a through f for retrieving and inserting a ruler.
	b. Make the necessary modifications to the ruler.
[GOLD] W	c. Press [GOLD] W. WPS-PLUS asks for the name of the ruler.

Enter name of ruler to store: ***ruler-name* [RETURN]**	d. Enter the ruler name and press [RETURN]. WPS-PLUS displays a message that the ruler has been stored.
[RETURN]	e. Press [RETURN] to resume editing.

Follow this procedure to delete a named ruler:

[GOLD] R...	a. Follow steps a through d for retrieving and inserting a ruler.
[REMOVE]	b. Press [REMOVE] (or [DEL CHAR]) to delete the ruler.
[RETURN]	c. Press [RETURN] to resume editing.

10.1.5.4 Referring Rulers

When inserting a named ruler in your document, WPS-PLUS asks if you want to make it a "referring" ruler. The ruler is inserted in reverse video if you respond yes to this question. This is what a referring ruler looks like in a document:

```
----L---------------.---------------.---------------.---------------.----------R-----
```

A referring ruler is permanently "tied" to the named ruler. If you update the associated named ruler, you can then quickly update documents with references to the named ruler. Referring rulers therefore make it easy to make across-the-board modifications to the margins and tab settings in your documents.

As an example of how referring rulers help, suppose that you have a large instruction manual stored in a WPS-PLUS document. You've decided to change the binding method for the next printing of the manual, and the new binding requires that you indent both margins by five spaces. Normally, you would have to modify each and every ruler in the document to adjust the margins.[1] However, if you inserted referring rulers when creating the document, you could just edit the associated named rulers and update all references with a few simple keystrokes.

Perform these steps to insert a referring ruler in the current location in your document:

[GOLD] R	a. Press [GOLD] R. The expanded ruler appears.
[GOLD] G	b. Press [GOLD] G. WPS-PLUS asks for the name of the ruler.
Enter name of ruler to get: ***ruler-name* [RETURN]**	c. Enter the name of the ruler and press [RETURN]. (You can also press [FIND] to select from a list of

1. Refer to Chapter 26 if you're ever faced with such a task. User Defined Processes will save you a lot of time and effort.

named rulers.) WPS-PLUS asks if you want to make this a referring ruler.

Y [RETURN] d. Type "Y" and press [RETURN] to create a referring ruler.

[RETURN] e. Press [RETURN] to imbed the ruler and continue editing.

To delete a reference to a named ruler, do the following:

a. Move the cursor to the left-most column of the line following the referring ruler.

[GOLD] R b. Press [GOLD] R. The expanded ruler appears.

[DELETE WORD] c. Press [DELETE WORD] (PF3). WPS-PLUS displays a message that the reference to the ruler has been deleted.

The following procedure updates all references to named rulers in the current document:

[GOLD] R a. Press [GOLD] R. The expanded ruler appears.

[GOLD] B b. Press [GOLD] B. WPS-PLUS updates all references to named rulers with the current settings.

10.1.6 WPS-Plus Control Blocks

Today's laser printers offer a wide range of advanced formatting and highlighting capabilities. To take advantage of these capabilities, you must include formatting instructions in your documents. A ruler is one example of a short, simple formatting instruction telling ALL-IN-1 how to arrange text that follows the ruler. Control blocks are also formatting instructions.

Control blocks are lines of instructions inserted in your document to request specialized formatting for text that *follows*. These instructions or commands must be placed between the Start Control and End Control "markers" to distinguish them from the actual text of the document. Information in a control block is visible only when editing the document; you do not see it when displaying or printing the document.

Figure 10.3 shows an example of a control block that sets the font for the text that follows. As another example, the following control block numbers pages in the bottom margin. Pages are numbered using the format "- 1 -," "- 2 -," "- 3 -," and so forth.

```
----------------------- START CONTROL ----------------------
BOTTOM
                    - \p -
----------------------- END CONTROL -----------------------
```

```
---------------------------------- TOP -----------------------------------------
L-------T-------T-------T-------T-------T-------T-------T-------T-------T------R
---------------------------------- START CONTROL -------------------------------
PRINTER FONT 10_POINT_NEWCENTURYSCHLBK_ROMAN 0
---------------------------------- END   CONTROL -------------------------------




August 22, 1992




Ms. Mary Thomas
Western Hrea Hecycl ing, Inc.
Attn: Accounts Payable
3412 S. Platte
```

Figure 10.3 Document with WPS-PLUS control block to set font

The rest of this section shows you how to insert control blocks in your document and describes the various control block commands. Examples of some of the more common control block commands can be found in Appendix B.

Perform the following steps to insert a control block in your document:

a. First, move the cursor to the point in your document where you want to insert a control block. Remember, control blocks specify formatting for the text that *follows*.

[COMMAND]

b. Press [COMMAND] ([GOLD] [). The Start Control and End Control markers appear in your document.

***command* [RETURN]**

c. Type a control block command. Control block commands are listed in Table 10.2.

Note: The command should be on a line by itself immediately following the Start Control marker. Otherwise, unexpected results can occur.

Multiple commands can appear in the control block when separated with a bar (|), except for

TOP and BOTTOM (because these commands require additional lines of text).

d. Press [RETURN] and type any additional text if the control block command requires this. For example, the text of a header or footer is included in the control block after the TOP or BOTTOM command. This text can include any of the following characters:

Include These Two Characters	*To Perform the Following Function*
\a	Insert page letter.
\d	Insert the current date.
\p	Insert page number.
\s	Insert section number.

[DOWN ARROW]

e. Press [DOWN ARROW] to move below the End Control marker before you continue typing the text of the document.

Table 10.2 WPS-PLUS control block commands

Enter This Control Block Command	*To Perform the Following Function*
BOTTOM	Print the remaining text in the control block at the bottom of every page (running footer).
BOTTOM EVEN	Print the remaining text in the control block at the bottom of even-numbered pages (running footer).
BOTTOM ODD	Print the remaining text in the control block at the bottom of odd-numbered pages (running footer).
BOTTOM_MARGIN *lines*	Specify the number of lines reserved for the bottom margin of the page. This value can also be set with Pagination Settings when printing the document. The running footer prints in the bottom margin. Specify 3 plus the number of lines in the running footer; 1 to separate the last line of text from the first line of the footer and 2 blank lines below the last line of the footer.
COLUMN_MARGIN *number*	Specify the number of spaces between multiple columns. This setting is only valid when using multicolumns.
COMMENT	Include the remaining text in the control block as a comment that can only be seen when editing the document. Such comments are a way of passing information to anyone who might edit the document.

Table 10.2 *(continued)*

Enter This Control Block Command	*To Perform the Following Function*
EPS *file-spec dimensions position*	Include the specified encapsulated PostScript (EPS) graphic (picture) at this position in the document when printed. A number of standard images are included with WPS-PLUS. These files are stored in the directory WPS$LIB: and have the file type ".EPS". Dimensions of the picture can be specified after the file name with the format "*width* X *height* in" or "*width* X *height* cm"—for example, "2.5X2.5in". The position can be specified as LEFT, RIGHT, or CENTERED.
FOOTNOTE *number*	Set the number for the next footnote. The value *number* is optional. If omitted, the initial footnote number specified in Footnote Numbering is used.
HORIZONTAL_PITCH *pitch*	Specify the number of characters per inch on a line (0 to 20). This value can also be set with Pagination Settings when printing the document. A second value can be specified to set the ruler pitch.
JUSTIFY_ON	Enables right margin justification for the text that follows. All lines of text are justified between margins regardless of whether the R or J marker appears in the ruler, even lines ending with a carriage return.
JUSTIFY_OFF	Disables right margin justification for the text that follows.
LEFT_MARGIN *number*	Specify the number of spaces to the left of the print area.
MULTI *number-of-columns*	Print the text that follows in multiple columns. The number of columns is specified on the next line of the control block. This control block command is not necessary if you use the Multi-Column Editor to create columns.
NO_BREAK END_NO_BREAK	Prohibit the text between NO_BREAK and END_NO_BREAK from being printed on separate pages.
PAGE_SIZE *lines*	Specify the total number of lines per page (1 to 168), including top and bottom margins.
PRINTER FONT *font n*	Select a new character font where *font* is the name of the new font. Valid font names are listed in the document WPL$LIB:KEYWORDS.WPL. The second value *n* specifies the vertical spacing between lines in points and is optional. Include this parameter if you're using a font larger than 14 point; for best results, add 2 to the point size of the font.
PRINTER FOOTNOTE_FONT *font n*	Select a new character font for footnotes. The second parameter sets the vertical spacing between lines and is optional.

(continued)

Table 10.2 WPS-PLUS control block commands *(continued)*

Enter This Control Block Command	*To Perform the Following Function*
PRINTER FORMAT *format lines*	Select the page orientation for laser printers, where *format* is "PORTRAIT" or "LANDSCAPE." The second value specifies the number of lines per page and is optional.
PRINTER MODE *mode*	Select the print quality for appropriate printers, where *mode* is either "DRAFT" or "LETTER."
PRINTER SELECT *tray*	Select the appropriate paper tray, where *tray* is either "FRONT," "REAR," "LETTERHEAD," "ENVELOPE," "ALTERNATE," "NOTRAY," or a number from 0 to 10.
PRINTER TABLE *table-element*	Issue a specific control code from the table of elements associated with the printer. This table is usually established by the system manager to perform special print operations.
RESET *number*	Reset the page number. The value is optional. If omitted, the default is the number on first page specified with Pagination Settings.
SECTION *number*	Reset the section number to the specified value. The value is optional. If omitted, 1 is added to the last section number.
TOP	Print the remaining text in the control block at the top of every page (running header). It's recommended that you include an extra blank line after the last line of the header text to separate the header from the first line of text on the page.
TOP EVEN	Print the remaining text in the control block at the top of even-numbered pages (running header).
TOP ODD	Print the remaining text in the control block at the top of odd-numbered pages (running header).
TOP_MARGIN *lines*	Specify the number of lines reserved for the top margin of the page. This value can also be set with Pagination Settings when printing the document. The running header prints in the top margin. Specify at least as many lines as contained in the header.
VERTICAL_PITCH DOCUMENT *pitch*	Specify the number of vertical lines per inch (0 to 20). This value can also be set with Pagination Settings when printing the document.
VERTICAL_PITCH FOOTNOTE *pitch*	Specify the number of vertical lines per inch in footnotes (0 to 20).
WRAP_ON	Enable automatic text rewrapping for the text that follows. This feature is recommended when using proportional fonts. It can also be set with Pagination Settings when printing the document.
WRAP_OFF	Disable automatic text rewrapping for the text that follows.
WPSMATH	Perform calculations on specified values. For details, see the Digital manual *WPS-PLUS User's Reference.*

10.1.7 WPS-Plus Editor Menu

Options on the WPS-PLUS Editor menu set document format characteristics and editor attributes. You can access this menu whenever you're editing a document by performing the following steps:

[GOLD] M	a. Press [MENU] ([GOLD] M). The Editor menu is displayed.
***menu-option* [RETURN]**	b. Type the menu option and press [RETURN]. Menu options are described in Table 10.3.
	c. Enter any required information for the selected option and press [RETURN]. The Editor menu is redisplayed.
[EXIT]	d. Press [EXIT] (F10 or Keypad-0) to clear the Editor menu and return to editing your document.

Table 10.3 WPS-PLUS Editor menu options

Enter This Menu Option	*To Perform the Following Action*
AD (Specify Abbreviation)	Select a document that serves as a lookup table for abbreviations. See Section 11.1, "Abbreviations and Library Documents," for details.
LD (Specify Library)	Select a document that serves as a lookup table for standard phrases and sections of text. See Section 11.1, "Abbreviations and Library Documents," for details.
GS (Global Search and Replace)	Search for and replace all occurrences of a specific string of text.
PG (Automatic GOLD PAGE)	Automatically insert page markers throughout your document according to the page size. See Section 10.1.10, "Paginating WPS-PLUS Documents," for more information.
EA (Editor Attributes)	Set a series of editor and document characteristics, including display width, redline formatting, and page length. Also enable or disable Editor Math, the display of the status bar, the scrolling of documents retrieved with GET DOCUMENT, the ability to choose special symbols as words, and hyphenation checking.
SS (Save Editor Settings)	Save the Editor Attributes for later recall when editing other documents. You can save up to 10 groups of attributes under numbers 0 to 9.
RS (Restore Editor Settings)	Restore the Editor Attributes previously saved under numbers 0 through 9.
DA (Modify Date/Time Formats)	Specify the format of the date and time inserted when you press [GOLD] [DATE/TIME] or when you include a "\d" in a control block to insert the date in a running header or footer.

10.1.8 Editing Multiple Documents in WPS-PLUS

You have the ability to open more than one document in a single edit session. This makes it easy to cut and paste blocks of text between documents. This helps anyone who creates many documents that have similar content.

To edit multiple documents in a single session, you must invoke the editor with the Create (C) or Edit (E) option to create or edit the primary document. You can then follow the steps given in this section to open additional (secondary) documents once the editor is invoked. Secondary documents can be opened for full edit access or read-only access or can be created from scratch. Although you can view only one document at a time, you can easily "flip" back and forth between open documents. When you exit, changes made to any of the documents are saved (except for those opened for read-only access).

To open additional documents while editing, perform these steps:

[GOLD] [SENTENCE]

a. Press [GOLD] [SENTENCE] ([GOLD] Keypad-7). The following strip menu is displayed.

```
Show Open Documents  Edit Document  Create Document  Read Document
```

S, E, C, or R [RETURN]

b. Type the first letter of the option you want to select and press [RETURN].

c. Enter any information for the selected option.

To "flip" to the next open document, do the following:

[RESUME]

Press [RESUME] (F7). You can also press [GOLD] [RESUME] to "flip" back and forth between the two documents most recently viewed.

Editing multiple documents is a lot like juggling: The more documents you have open, the harder it is to keep track of them. Here are some recommendations for editing multiple documents:

- It's less confusing if you open only one document for *modification*. The primary document (edited or created from the menu) is always open for modification. Therefore, open additional documents with the Read Document option. Cut or copy text from the secondary documents and paste to the primary document. Opening up secondary documents for read-only access eliminates the possibility of your corrupting these documents by cutting text.
- If you do open more than one document for modification, close (F10 or [GOLD] F) secondary documents as soon as you finish working with them. Again, the fewer documents you have open, the easier it is to keep track of what you're doing.
- You can switch to any open document with the Show Open Documents option. It's faster to press [RESUME], however. Make sure that you have your status bar turned

on ([GOLD] Z) when flipping between open documents with the [RESUME] key. This helps you identify the current document.

10.1.9 Printing WPS-Plus Documents

There are a number of options, called *print settings*, for printing WPS-PLUS documents. Print settings control the final appearance of the document. For example, print settings control the horizontal and vertical placement of the text on the paper, the pagination of text, and the format of footnotes.

Changing print settings can greatly affect the appearance of your document. Increasing the left margin, for example, moves text to the right. If you specify too large a value, you can cause undesirable line wrapping.

Remember the following points when changing your print settings:

- Print settings work in conjunction with rulers and control blocks. For example, if you set your left margin in the ruler to column 10 and then set the print margin to 10, you will see 20 columns of space to the left of your text. Also, control block commands that dynamically set pitch, page size, and other attributes override values entered during printing.
- Some print settings override certain control information in the document. For example, if you set the Auto Paginate print setting to "Y," your document is repaginated during printing, even though you've manually placed "soft" Page Markers in your document with [GOLD] P. ("Hard" page markers inserted with [GOLD] N are always honored, however.)
- Print settings are "remembered." When you alter print settings and print a document, the settings are stored with the document. The next time you print or read the document, the same settings are used to format it. (This caused a problem in older versions. If you changed the first and last pages printed to 2 and 5, these were the only pages displayed or printed until you changed the values back to "1" and "0," respectively.)
- If you send a document to another individual, your print settings travel with the document. The document is received as an attachment and can be filed with the File Attachment (FA) menu option. This saves the recipient the trouble of having to adjust print settings to have the document print as you intended.
- You can modify a series of print settings for a particular document, then save the print settings for printing other documents of similar type. You can store up to 10 groups of print settings.

Perform the following steps to change the print settings while printing the current document:

P [RETURN]	a. Type "P" and press [RETURN]. ALL-IN-1 displays the Printing Document form.

Document destination: *document-destination* **[TAB]**
Format style: *format-style* **[TAB]**
Number of copies: *number*

b. Enter a document destination, format style, and number of copies. Refer to Section 4.2, "Printing in ALL-IN-1," for details. Do *not* press [RETURN] yet.

[NEXT SCREEN]

c. Press [NEXT SCREEN] (or [GOLD] A) to change print settings. ALL-IN-1 displays the Print Settings menu, shown in Figure 10.4.

Note: An error is displayed if the document is not a WPS-PLUS document.

menu-option **[RETURN]**

d. Type a Print Settings menu option and press [RETURN]. Table 10.4 describes the options on this menu.

...[RETURN]

e. The first six options display a data-entry form to accept the new print setting. Change the print setting and press [RETURN]. Tables 10.4 through 10.7 describe print settings.

f. Repeat steps d, e, and f if you need to change other print settings.

```
                 WPS-PLUS Formatter Print Settings Menu

PG   Change pagination settings
FS   Change footnote settings
FN   Change footnote numbering
DA   Change date/time format
CN   Change paragraph numbering styles
PA   Paragraph numbering output

SS   Save print and paragraph numbering settings:     # 0
RS   Restore print and paragraph numbering settings:  # 0
FR   First page printed:                                1
TO   Last page printed:                                 0
PT   Page range type (All, Physical, Single):           A

CS   Save current settings without printing
P    Print and save current settings



Enter option and press RETURN
```

Figure 10.4 WPS-PLUS Formatter Print Settings menu

P [RETURN] or **CS [RETURN]**

g. Type "P" and press [RETURN] to print the document on the destination printer, or type "CS" and press [RETURN] to simply save the new print settings with the document without printing.

Table 10.4 WPS-PLUS Print Settings menu options

Enter This Menu Option	*To Perform the Following Action*
PG (Change Paginations Settings)	Specify parameters that control the pagination of text and the placement of text on the paper (see Table 10.7).
FS (Change Footnote Settings)	Specify the placement of footnotes (see Table 10.5.)
FN (Change Footnote Numbering)	Specify the highlighting of footnotes and footnote markers (see Table 10.6).
DA (Modify Date/Time Formats)	Specify the format of the date and time inserted with [GOLD] [DATE/TIME] or a "\d" in a control block.
CN (Change Paragraph Numbering Styles)	Specify the numbering style used to number paragraphs during printing (see Section 11.3, "Paragraph Numbering").
PA (Paragraph Numbering Output)	Generate additional documents when paragraph numbering is performed during printing. These documents include the table of contents, table of authorities, and index (see Section 11.3, "Paragraph Numbering").
SS (Save Print Settings)	Assign a number from 0 to 9 to store the current print settings.
RS (Restore Print Settings)	Recall print settings previously stored by a number 0 to 9 with the Save Print Settings option.
FR (First Page Printed)	Specify the number of the first page to print when printing a range of pages. Set this to 1 when printing the entire document.
TO (Last Page Printed)	Specify the number of the last page to print when printing a range of pages. Set this to 0 when printing the entire document.
PT (Page Range Type)	Control the printing of duplicate ranges of pages. This setting applies only when selecting a page range with the FR/TO fields and the document contains duplicate ranges of pages due to the use of the RESET command in a control block to reset page numbers. Enter "A" to print all occurrences of the page range specified in FR/TO, enter "S" to print only the first occurrence, or enter "P" to ignore the RESET command and print the physical pages within the range.
CS (Save Current Settings without Printing)	Save all of the modifications to print settings without printing the document.
P (Print with Current Settings)	Print the current document with the current print settings.

Table 10.5 Footnote settings

Footnote Setting	*Description*
Footnotes or endnotes	Enter "F" to place footnote at the bottom of the page where it is referenced. Enter "E" to place all footnotes at the end of the document.
Minimum lines per page	Type a number from 1 to 168 to specify the minimum lines of text that must appear on a page. This value prevents footnotes from filling a page.
Continuation messages	Enter "Y" to request that a message be included whenever a footnote is continued to another page. Enter "N" to suppress this message. The continued footnote is properly identified regardless of this setting.
Separator character	The character or characters separating the last line of text from the first footnote. The default is the underscore character (_).
Separator length	The number of separator characters to print (0 to 256).
Separator position	The location of the separator characters: left, right, or centered.
Blank lines between last text line and separator line	Enter a number between 1 and 126.
Blank lines between separator line and first footnote	Enter a number between 1 and 126.
Blank lines between footnotes	Enter a number between 1 and 126.

Table 10.6 Footnote numbering

Footnote Numbering	*Description*
Numbering scheme	Enter "N" for a numeric numbering of footnotes (1, 2, 3, etc.), enter "A" or "a" for an alphabetic labeling of footnotes (A, B, C or a, b, c), enter "R" or "r" for Roman numerals (I, II, III or i, ii, iii), or enter "S" to label footnotes with the following special character.
Footnote number special character	Enter any other character such as "*" to label footnotes.
Initial footnote number	The number of the first footnote (1 to 9999).
Restart number on every page	Enter "Y" to renumber footnotes, starting with 1, on each page. Enter "N" to number footnotes consecutively throughout the document.
Highlighting of number in text	Defines how the footnote number is highlighted in the text. Enter "NORMAL," "SUPER" (superscript), "UNDER" (underline), "BOLD," "SUPER/UNDER," "SUPER/BOLD," "UNDER/BOLD," or "BOLD/UNDER/SUPER."
Extra character in text	Specifies which characters print next to the footnote number in the text. Enter "NONE," "PERIOD," "COMMA," "SLASH," "RIGHT_PARENTHESIS," or "LEFT/RIGHT_PARENTHESIS."

Table 10.6 *(continued)*

Footnote Numbering	*Description*
Highlighting of extra character in text	Defines how the extra character is highlighted in the text. Enter any of the values listed for highlighting the number in the text.
Highlighting of number in footnote	Defines how the footnote number is highlighted in the footnote section. Enter any of the values listed for highlighting the number in the text.
Extra character in footnote	Specifies which character prints next to the footnote number in the footnote. Enter any of the values listed for the extra character in text.
Highlighting of extra character in footnote	Defines how the extra character is highlighted in the footnote. Enter any of the values listed for highlighting the number in the text.

10.1.10 Paginating WPS-Plus Documents

Pagination is the process of breaking the text in a document into separate pages. Although you can manually paginate your document, it is less tedious to use automatic pagination.

Pagination can be performed in either of two cases:

- During an edit session when the Pagination Settings (PG) option on the editor menu is selected.
- During printing when the Auto Paginate flag on the Pagination Settings screen is set to "Y."

During pagination, "hard" page break markers ([GOLD] N) are honored, whereas the "soft" page break markers ([GOLD] P) are repositioned according to the specified number of lines per page, the top and the bottom margins, the location of NO_BREAK/END_NO_BREAK control blocks, and widow/orphan control.

Following is a recommended method for paginating documents:

1. When editing your document, insert hard page markers ([GOLD] N) in appropriate places, such as before the title of a new chapter or section. If there are blocks of text that you do not want separated by a page break, place a control block with a NO_BREAK command before the text and a control block with END_NO_BREAK after the text.
2. During printing, press [NEXT SCREEN] to move to the Print Settings menu, and select the Pagination Settings (PG) option. Review and adjust the following values:
   - Set the number of lines per page on the Pagination Settings screen to an appropriate value (look ahead to Table 10.7 on page 217). The number of lines per page depends on the vertical pitch. If you're using the standard six lines per inch, then a total of 66 lines will fit on an 11-inch piece of paper.

- Reserve enough space in the top and bottom margins for running headers and footers. Six lines each is usually sufficient.
- If you're using proportional fonts, set the Automatic Text Wrapping flag to "Y". Paragraphs are then rewrapped to fit as many characters as possible on each line. This usually means paragraphs end up having fewer lines than appear in the editor.
- Set the number of widow/orphan lines to an appropriate value, such as 2 or 3. This controls the breaking of paragraphs between pages. A *widow* is the first few lines of a broken paragraph where most of the paragraph is on the following page. An *orphan* is the last few lines of a broken paragraph where most of the paragraph is on the preceding page. When widow/orphan control is set to 3, a paragraph is not broken if fewer than three lines fall on a page alone. Instead, a page break is inserted, and the entire paragraph is printed on the following page. Setting widow/orphan lines to an even higher value of 4 or 5 prevents page breaking in the middle of most paragraphs, resulting in a little more "white space" but a document that is easier to read.
- Set the Auto Paginate flag on the Pagination Settings screen to "Y" to select pagination during printing.

The Pagination Settings option on the Print Settings menu displays the form shown in Figure 10.5. Table 10.7 describes each field on this form.

```
                              Pagination Settings

Vertical pitch:                          6    Number on first page:          1
Horizontal pitch:                       10    Widow/orphan lines:            0

Page size (lines):                      66    Auto paginate (Y/N):           Y
Top margin (lines):                      6    Shadow bolding (Y/N):          N
Bottom margin (lines):                   6    Extra dark (Y/N):              N
Column margin:                           0    Remove blank lines at
Left print margin:                       0      top of page (Y/N):           N

Print quality:                 DRAFT          Replacement character 1:       _
Sheet feeder tray:    NOTRAY                  Replacement character 2:       _

Hyphenation during formatting (Y/N):     N    Output leader (Y/N):           N
Maximum hyphenated lines in a row:       3    Leader character:              .
Language: AMERICAN                            Leader stop position:          5

Hanging punctuation (Y/N):               N    Hanging characters: .,-:;'"
Automatic text wrapping (Y/N):           N

Enter new settings and press RETURN
```

Figure 10.5 WPS-PLUS Pagination Settings form

Table 10.7 Pagination settings[a]

Setting	*Description*
Vertical pitch	The number of lines printed per vertical inch (0 to 20); 0 requests the default pitch for the specified printer table. The standard is 6 lines per inch. Increasing this value lets you fit more lines on a page, but the result might be harder to read.
Horizontal pitch	The number of characters printed per horizontal inch (0 to 20); 0 requests the default pitch for the specified printer table. Increasing this value lets you fit more characters on a line, but the result might be harder to read.
Page size (lines)	The total number of lines per page, including the lines within the top and bottom margin (1 to 168). This value is used to paginate during printing.
Top margin (lines)	The number of lines to skip before the first line of text (0 to 126). (*Note:* Header lines are printed in the top margin. Remember to reserve enough room to accommodate lines of text specified in the header control block.)
Bottom margin (lines)	The number of lines to skip after the last line of text (0 to 126). (*Note:* Footer lines are printed in the bottom margin.)
Column margin	The number of spaces between multiple columns of text (0 to 256). This setting is valid only when using control blocks to create multicolumn documents.
Left print margin	The number of spaces to the left of the print area (0 to 256). The print area might also include columns left blank due to the left margin ruler setting.
Print quality	Selects a print quality for certain models of printers. Enter "DRAFT" or "LETTER."
Sheet feeder tray	Selects a sheet feeder tray for the entire document. Enter "FRONT," "REAR," "ALTERNATE," "ENVELOPE," or "LETTERHEAD."
Hyphenation during formatting	Enter "Y" to request that text be rewrapped and hyphenated to fill lines during printing; enter "N" to request that text be printed as is.
Maximum hyphenated lines in a row	Sets a limit on the number of consecutive lines that can end in a hyphen (1 to 9). This value is ignored unless hyphenation during formatting is set to "Y."
Language	Specifies the dictionary that should be used when hyphenation during formatting is requested.
Automatic text wrapping	Enter "Y" to request that text be rewrapped to fill lines during printing; enter "N" to request that text be printed as is. All lines within paragraphs are rewrapped except those within WRAP_OFF/WRAP_ON control blocks. Set this value to "Y" when using proportional fonts.
Number on the first page	The number printed on the first page following a control block with either the TOP or BOTTOM command (0 to 4095).

(continued)

Table 10.7 Pagination settings[a] *(continued)*

Setting	*Description*
Widow/orphan control lines	The minimum number of lines left "straggling" at the bottom or top of a page when a paragraph is split between two pages (0 to 5). If the number of lines in a split paragraph is less than the value you enter, the entire paragraph is moved to the next page. A value of 2 or 3 is recommended.
Auto paginate	If set to "Y", the document will be paginated during printing according to the values specified for total lines, top margin, bottom margin, and widow/orphan control. If set to "N", the document is printed as is.
Shadow print	"Y" indicates that characters should be struck twice when printed but with a slight shift to produce a shadow effect. "N" indicates normal printing. This setting is valid only for certain printers.
Extra dark	Enter "Y" for bold print. This setting is valid only for certain printers.
Remove blank lines at top of page	Enter "Y" to request that blank lines of text appearing at the top of the page during pagination be skipped; enter "N" to request that blank lines always be printed. If you're leaving blank lines at the top of a letter to allow room for letterhead, set this to "N".
Replacement characters 1 and 2	Specifies one or two replacement characters that should be printed whenever specific characters are found in the text. Not valid for most printers.
Output leader	Enter "Y" to request that a leader character (typically a period) be inserted whenever text is tabbed over to the right margin. This is used primarily for producing a table of contents during paragraph numbering (see Section 11.3).
Leader character	Specifies the character to be inserted when Output Leader is set to "Y".
Leader stop position	The number of spaces between the last leader character and the page number when Output Leader is set to "Y" (0 to 50).
Hanging punctuation	Enter "Y" to request that any of the characters specified in the next field be printed when they appear at the end of a line justified to the right margin. "N" suppresses printing of these characters.
Hanging characters	Specifies the series of punctuation characters that can be omitted when they appear at the end of a justified line and when Hanging Punctuation is set to "N".

[a]The numbers in parentheses at the end of the first sentence of the description specify the valid range for the entry.

10.1.11 Exercise: Creating a Document

The following exercise takes you through the steps to create a simple document with WPS-PLUS. This exercise shows you how to highlight text, change the ruler, and move text.

Before continuing, make sure that you've selected WPS-PLUS as your default editor. Refer to Section 9.2, "Selecting an Editor," for instructions.

1. Select the Create option to create a new document.

WP C [RETURN]	a. From any menu or index, type "WP C" and press [RETURN]. ALL-IN-1 displays the Creating New Document form.
[UP ARROW] **[UP ARROW]** **[ERASE LINE]** Drawer: **MAIN [TAB]** **[ERASE LINE]** Folder: **TEST DOCUMENTS [TAB]** Title: **Bulletin [RETURN]**	b. Complete the Creating New Document form as shown in Figure 10.6, and press [RETURN]. ALL-IN-1 invokes WPS-PLUS for you to enter the text of the document.

2. When the WPS-PLUS top-of-document marker and ruler appear, start entering the text of the document.

[SELECT]	a. Press [SELECT] to select the title for bolding.
B U L L E T I N	b. Type "BULLETIN" in uppercase letters with spaces between the letters.
[BOLD]	c. Press [BOLD] (Keypad-6) to make the title bold.
[GOLD] C	d. Press [GOLD] C to center the title.
[RETURN]	e. Press [RETURN] to insert an extra blank line in the document.

```
                     Creating New Document

Drawer:   MAIN

Folder:   TEST DOCUMENTS

Title:    Bulletin

Keywords:

     Enter information and press RETURN,
     or press NEXT SCREEN for more fields              (more...)
```

Figure 10.6 Creating New Document form

f. Type the following text exactly as it appears in the box below. Do not press [RETURN] at the end of a line within a paragraph, only at the end of the first paragraph.

```
Human Resources, in conjunction with our health insurance carrier, American
Insurance Company is sponsoring a free blood pressure check for employees.
Report to the third floor conference room during the appropriate time speci-
fied below to take advantage of this service. Medical personnel will be
handing out information pamphlets and will answer any questions you have
about the procedure.

If you have any questions, please contact Connie at Extension 324.
```

Note that your text may wrap differently, depending on your ruler settings. Don't worry about this.

[RETURN]
[RETURN]

g. Press [RETURN] twice at the end of the last line to create a blank line.

3. Change the ruler settings to set up columns.

[GOLD] R

a. Press [GOLD] R. The expanded ruler appears.

[WORD] [SPACE]
[WORD] [SPACE]...

b. Clear all tab stops (T) by alternately pressing [WORD] (Keypad-4) and the space bar until you reach the right margin marker (R).

[BACKUP] [LINE]

c. Press [BACKUP] (Keypad-1) and [LINE] (Keypad-2) to move to the beginning of the ruler.

[RIGHT ARROW]...

d. Press [RIGHT ARROW] to move to column 10.

T

e. Type "T" to insert a tab marker.

f. Repeat steps d and e to place tab markers at columns 30, 50, and 60. The resulting ruler should look like this:

```
         10        20        30        40        50        60        70        80
....:....0....:....0....:....0....:....0....:....0....:....0....:....0....:....0
L        T                   T                   T         T                   R
```

[RETURN]

g. Press [RETURN] to imbed the new ruler in your document.

4. Type the titles for the columns of dates and times.

[TAB] [SELECT]

a. Press [TAB], then [SELECT] (or Keypad-Period) to select the titles for underlining.

LAST NAMES [TAB]
DATE [TAB]
TIME [TAB]

b. Type "LAST NAMES," press [TAB], type "DATE," press [TAB], and type "TIME" and press [TAB].

[UNDERLINE]

c. Press [UNDERLINE] (Keypad-9) to underline the column titles.

[RETURN]
[RETURN]

d. Press [RETURN] twice to create a blank line.

5. Type the columns of dates and times.

Type the following information. Type the text shown in the box, and press [TAB] where indicated.

```
[TAB] A - J [TAB] Mon, June 8th [TAB] 10:00am
[TAB] K - Q [TAB] Tues, June 9th [TAB] 10:00am
[TAB] R - Z [TAB] Wed, June 10th [TAB] 11:00am
```

6. Move the second paragraph of text to the bottom of the document.

a. Move the cursor to the "I" in "If you have any questions. . . ."

[SELECT]

b. Press [SELECT].

[DOWN ARROW]

c. Press [DOWN ARROW]. (If this paragraph is more than one line, press [DOWN ARROW] again.)

[CUT]

d. Press [CUT] (Keypad-Hyphen). The string of text is removed.

[GOLD] [DOWN ARROW]

e. Press [GOLD] [DOWN ARROW] to move to the bottom of the document.

[RETURN]
[RETURN]

f. Press [RETURN] twice to insert blank lines.

[PASTE]

g. Press [PASTE] (Keypad-Comma) to insert the text at the bottom of the document. Your document should look something like Figure 10.7.

7. File your document, then review the document with the Read option.

[GOLD] F

a. Press [GOLD] F to exit the editor and file the document.

R [RETURN]

b. Type "R" and press [RETURN] to read the document.

```
L-------T-------T-------T-------T-------T-------T-------T-------T-------T------R
                                 B U L L E T I N

Human Resources, in conjunction with our health insurance carrier, American
Insurance Company is sponsoring a free blood pressure check for employees.
Report to the third floor conference room during the appropriate time specified
below to take advantage of this service.  Medical personnel will be handing out
information pamphlets, and will answer any questions you have about the
procedure.


L--------T-------------------T-------------------T---------T-------------------R
         LAST NAMES          DATE                TIME

         A - J               Mon, June 8th       10:00am
         K - Q               Tue, June 9th       10:00am
         R - Z               Wed, June 10th      11:00am

If you have any questions, please contact Connie at Extension 324.
```

Figure 10.7 Sample document

[RETURN]
[RETURN]

c. Press [RETURN] twice to return to the menu.

10.2 GETTING STARTED WITH WORDPERFECT

WordPerfect is a full-function word processor that can be purchased separately, integrated into ALL-IN-1, and used to prepare documents. WordPerfect is perhaps the second most widely used word processor in ALL-IN-1 (WPS-PLUS being the first). This word-processing software is also popular for use with personal computers.

Like WPS-PLUS, WordPerfect is capable of producing documents ranging in size from single-page memos to large manuals. Its advanced word-processing features allow you to create publication-quality documents almost as easily as creating a simple letter.

The WordPerfect word processor has many features, including these:

- An extensive set of function keys for performing word-processing operations with just a few keystrokes.
- Advanced text highlighting capabilities to bold, underline, italicize, outline, shadow, and redline text.
- On-line writing aids, including a spell checker and thesaurus.

- Features for producing larger, more advanced documents, such as continuous automatic pagination, running headers and footers, footnoting, multicolumn page formatting, indexing, paragraph numbering, and generation of a table of contents.
- The Styles feature, which allows you to store and recall a group of print style settings easily.
- The Tables feature for quickly creating and entering tables of information for reports and manuals.
- The Sort feature for alphabetically sorting selected items to organize information in reports.
- Editor Math, which performs simple calculations on numbers included in your document.
- The Equation Editor, which lets you include scientific and mathematical equations in your document.
- The ability to store repetitively entered keystrokes as a "macro" and then enter a few simple keystrokes to repeat the keystrokes automatically.
- A line drawing capability for drawing boxes around text and creating simple charts in your document.
- The ability to include in your document images produced by a number of graphics packages. The standard clip-art images (pictures) shipped with WordPerfect can easily be included in your document to improve its appearance.
- Additional graphics capabilities, which let you create and label boxes, wrap text around figures, and rotate, enlarge, and reduce images.
- The ability to create compound documents with links to other documents and images.
- Periodic backup of keystrokes so that in the event of a system failure, most of your editing work is saved.

10.2.1 The WordPerfect Keyboard

Figures 10.8 and 10.9 show the layout of the function keys in WordPerfect that perform special word-processing operations. Figure 10.8 shows the layout of function keys in the numeric keypad. Keys PF1, PF2, and PF3 are important because they are used in combination with keys F6 through F20 to perform a wide range of functions, as shown in Figure 10.9. The next most important key is [HOME] (PF4). This key is used to move around the document. For example, [HOME] [DOWN ARROW] moves to the bottom of the screen, and [HOME] [HOME] [DOWN ARROW] moves to the bottom of the document. Keypad-0 toggles between insert and overstrike, and Keypad-Period deletes the current character. The remainder of the keys move the cursor.

Figure 10.9 shows the layout of the function keys in WordPerfect that perform most word-processing operations. These function keys are located in a single line at the top of

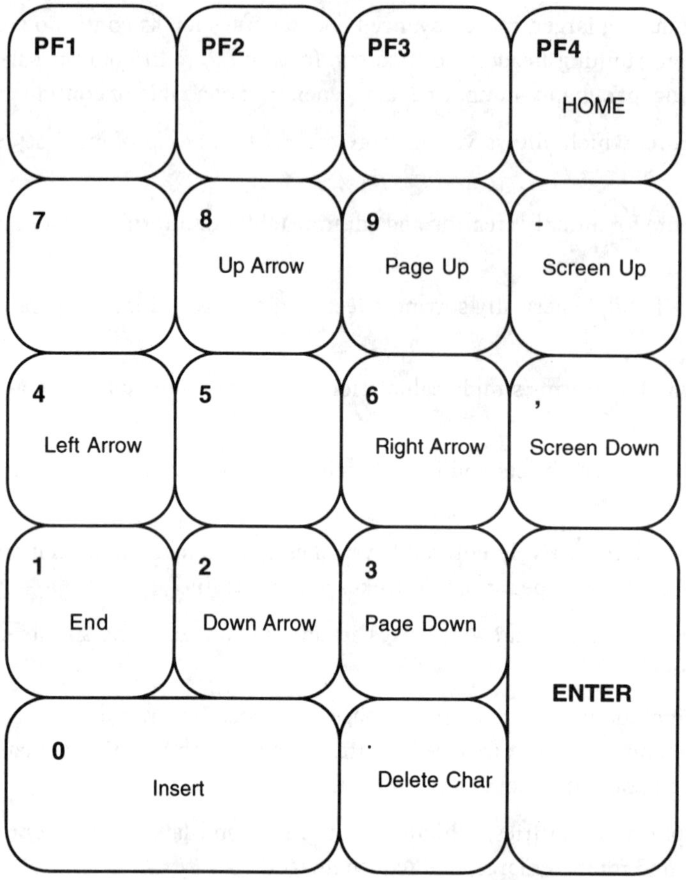

Figure 10.8 WordPerfect 5.1 numeric keypad layout

your VT keyboard. Note that most keys perform four separate functions. The function listed at the bottom of the strip menu is executed by simply pressing the function key. Other functions require that you press key PF1, PF2, or PF3 before pressing the function key. The legend to the left of the menu indicates which key to press first. For example, press F10 to indent a paragraph; press PF2, F10 to move the selected block of text.

10.2.2 Pull-down Menus

If you've reviewed the function keys in Figure 10.9, you've noticed that you can perform an overwhelming number of operations with these keys. Most people have difficulty remembering the location of all of these keys. There are three tools to help you with this:

- Keyboard templates. Novell Inc. provides plastic templates that can be placed on your keyboard to label function keys. Ask your system administrator for an extra keyboard template.

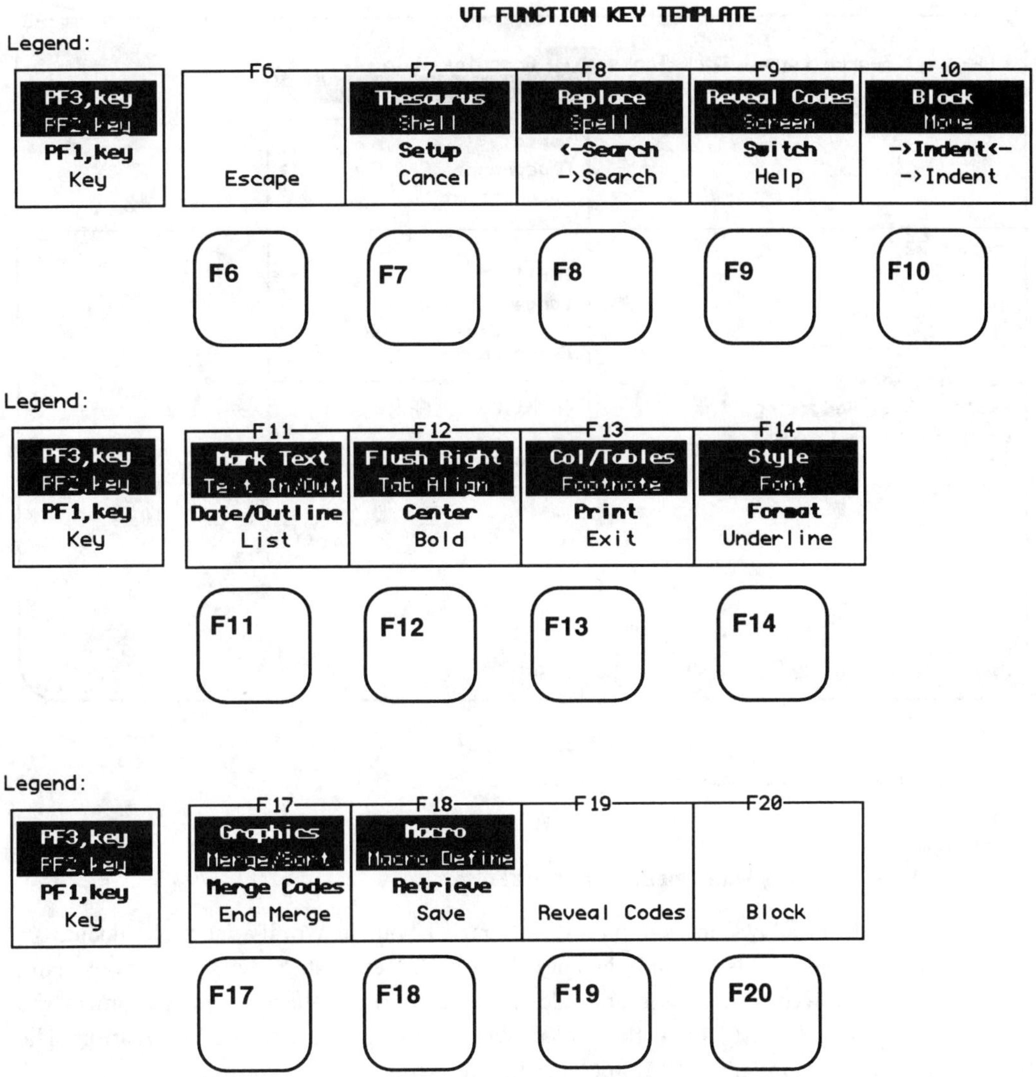

Figure 10.9 WordPerfect 5.1 function key layout (LK201 keyboard)

- [CONTROL] F. Press [CONTROL] F, then enter the first two characters of the function to invoke the function. For example, a new font can be selected by pressing [CONTROL] F and typing "FO."
- Pull-down menus. When you press [GOLD] [RIGHT ARROW], the strip menu shown at the top of Figure 10.10 is displayed. Press [DOWN ARROW] to display functions under the current category, then press [RIGHT ARROW] to slide across categories. Press your arrow keys to highlight the desired option, then press [RETURN]. If you want to erase the pull-down menu without selecting an option, just press [GOLD] [RIGHT ARROW].

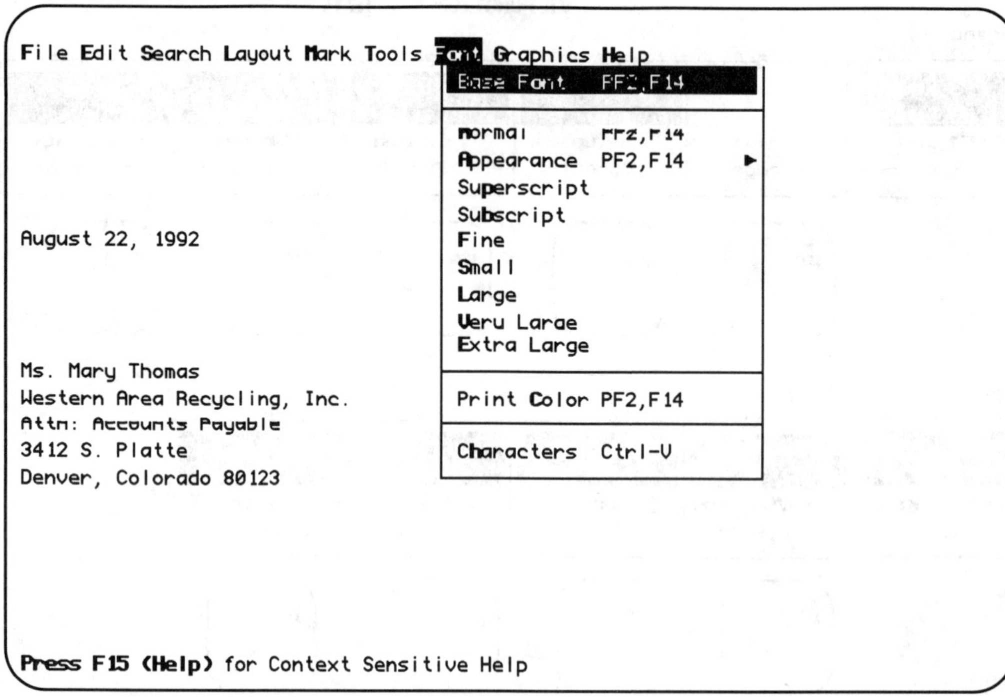

Figure 10.10 Pull-down menus in WordPerfect

10.2.3 Viewing Your Document in the Editor

Figure 10.11 shows an example of the screen layout in WordPerfect. The document being edited here is a simple business letter. The letter starts with a series of blank lines, followed by the date and addressee; it continues beyond the bottom of the screen. On the last line of the screen, WordPerfect displays status information. The screen shown in Figure 10.11 includes the following items:

① Cursor — The cursor is the flashing rectangle (or sometimes a flashing underscore).

② Document Text — Following a number of blank lines, the first line of text is the date.

③ Document Number — The document number is assigned by ALL-IN-1 when you create a document. It uniquely identifies a document within your File Cabinet.

④ Title — The title you specified when creating the document.

⑤ Relative Document Number (Doc) — You can edit more than one document during a WordPerfect edit session. This is useful when cutting and pasting text between documents. This number identifies

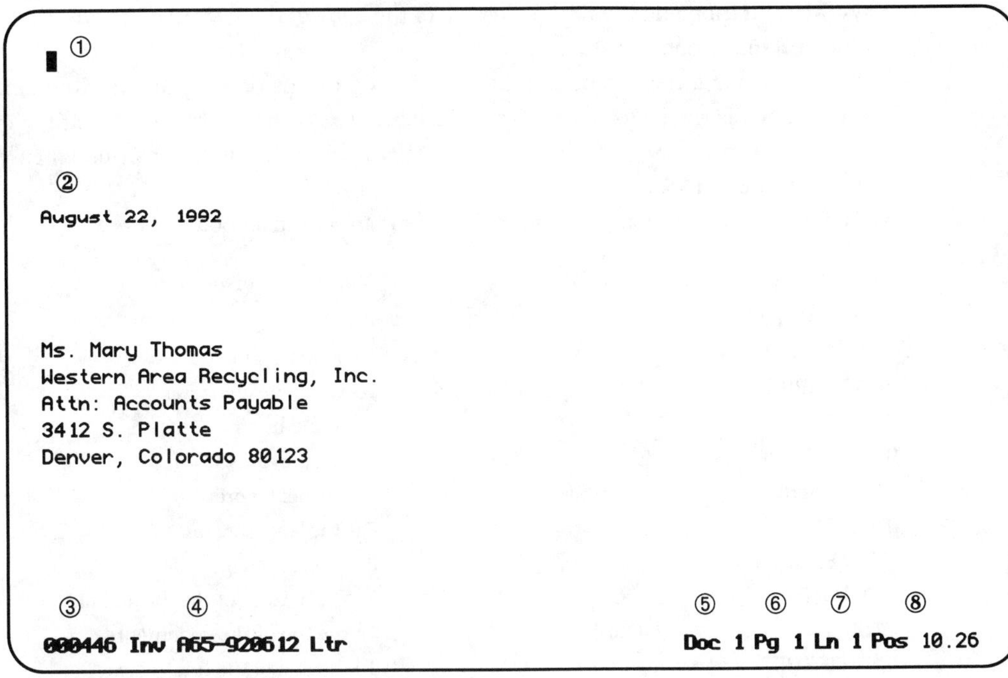

Figure 10.11 Viewing a document in WordPerfect

which document you're currently viewing; 1 for the first document you open, 2 for the second, and so on. For the most part, you will edit only one document at a time, so this number is usually set to "1."

⑥ Page Number (Pg) — The number of the page on which the cursor appears.

⑦ Line Number (Ln) — The line number of the cursor's position on the page.

⑧ Position (Pos) — The position of the cursor within the current line. The units of measurement are, by default, column positions. The position is a whole number when working with a nonproportional font; it is fractional when working with proportional fonts. You can change the units of measure to inches or points, if you prefer, with the [SETUP] function key.

10.2.4 Moving Around in the Text

Only the top portion of the letter appears in Figure 10.11, although the letter continues beyond the bottom of the screen. Pressing [DOWN ARROW] or [NEXT SCREEN] displays the salutation and the first paragraph of the body of the letter *and* moves the cursor forward in the document.

You must move the cursor to modify various portions of a document. Remember that the cursor is the focus of activity when editing. Characters are inserted at the cursor position as you type, and characters are deleted from the cursor position when you press [DELETE CHAR].

The following function keys move the cursor around in a document:

Function Key	*Keystrokes*	*Moves the Cursor*
[DOWN ARROW]		Forward one line.
[LEFT ARROW]		Back one character.
[RIGHT ARROW]		Forward one character.
[UP ARROW]		Back one line.
[PREV WORD]	PF2, [LEFT ARROW]	To the previous word.
[NEXT WORD]	PF2, [RIGHT ARROW]	To the next word.
[NEXT SCREEN]		Forward one screen.
[PREV SCREEN]		Back one screen.
[BOTTOM]	[GOLD] B	To the bottom of the document.
[TOP]	[GOLD] T	To the top of the document.
[END OF LINE]	Keypad-1	To the end of the line of text.
[GO TO]	PF2, PF4	To a specific character or page.
[PAGE UP]	Keypad-9	To the top of the previous page.
[PAGE DOWN]	Keypad-3	To the top of the next page.

Press the [HOME] (PF4) key and then the following key to move the cursor as indicated:

[LEFT ARROW]	To the beginning of the line.
[RIGHT ARROW]	To the end of the line.
[DOWN ARROW]	One screen forward.
[UP ARROW]	One screen back.

10.2.5 Basic Editing

Most people get by with the following basic procedures for deleting, highlighting, searching for, selecting, and cutting and pasting text. The procedures for performing more advanced operations are listed in Appendix B.

10.2.5.1 Deleting Text

Table 10.8 lists the function keys that delete text. To delete larger blocks of text, it's more efficient to select the block of text and then press [REMOVE].

Table 10.8 WordPerfect function keys to delete or restore text

Function Key	*Keystrokes*	*Description*
[DELETE]	⌫	Deletes the character in front of the cursor.
[DELETE CHAR]	Keypad-Period	Deletes the current character.
[DELETE WORD]	PF2, ⌫	Deletes the current word.
[DELETE TO EOL]	PF2, Keypad-1	Deletes all characters from the cursor position to the end of the line.
[DELETE PAGE]	PF2, Keypad-3	Deletes all text from the cursor position to the end of the page. (You are prompted to confirm this operation.)

To replace text deleted with any of the above function keys, do the following:

[CANCEL]

a. Press [CANCEL] (F7).

1

b. Type "1."

10.2.5.2 Highlighting Text

Perform the following steps to enable bolding or underlining before typing the text:

[BOLD] or **[UNDERLINE]**

a. Press one of the following function keys:

[BOLD] (F12)

[UNDERLINE] (F14)

text

b. Type the text. Note how it is highlighted.

[BOLD] or **[UNDERLINE]**

c. To disable highlighting, press the same function key as in step a, then continue typing.

Here is the procedure for highlighting existing text:

←↑↓→

a. Move the cursor to the first character in the string you want to highlight.

[SELECT]

b. Press [SELECT].

←↑↓→

c. Move the cursor beyond the last character in the string you want to highlight.

[FONT]

d. Press [FONT] (PF2, F14).

2

e. Type "2" to select font appearance.

number

f. Type a number from 1 to 9 to select highlighting.

To remove highlighting from existing text, delete the corresponding control code.

a. Move the cursor to the first character of the highlighted string.

[REVEAL CODES]

b. Press [REVEAL CODES] (F19) to display the control codes.

c. Move the cursor to highlight the control code in the bottom window.

[DELETE CHAR]

d. Press [DELETE CHAR] (Keypad-Period) to remove the highlighting.

[REVEAL CODES]

e. Press [REVEAL CODES] (F19) to resume editing.

To change the case (upper- or lowercase) of existing text, select the text and press [SWITCH] (PF1, F9).

10.2.5.3 Searching for Text

Perform the following steps to search for a string of text in a document:

[>SEARCH] or **[<SEARCH]**

a. Press [>SEARCH] (F8) to search in the forward direction, or press [<SEARCH] (PF1, F8) to search in the reverse direction.

Srch: ***string***

b. Enter the text you want to find. It will be stored in the "search" buffer.

c. Press [>SEARCH] (F8) or [<SEARCH] (PF1, F8).

To search for the next occurrence of the string, do the following:

[>SEARCH] [>SEARCH] or **[<SEARCH] [<SEARCH]**

Press [>SEARCH] (F8) twice, or press [<SEARCH] (PF1, F8) twice.

10.2.5.4 Selecting Text

Perform the following steps to select a block of text for cutting, copying, highlighting, and so on:

a. Move the cursor to the first character in the string you want to select.

[SELECT]

b. Press [SELECT] (or [BLOCK]).

c. Move the cursor beyond the last character of the string you want to select. Note that WordPerfect highlights text in reverse video as you move the cursor.

d. Press one of the following function keys:

Keystrokes	*Description*
[CENTER] (PF1, F12)	Centers text.
[DELETE]	Deletes text.
[FONT] (PF2, F14)	Changes text attributes.
[FLUSH RIGHT] (PF3, F12)	Right justifies text.
[MOVE] (PF2, F10)	Cuts or copies text.
[PRINT] (PF1, F13)	Prints text.
[SWITCH] (PF1, F9)	Converts case.

Do the following to deselect a block of text:

[SELECT]	Press [SELECT] (or [BLOCK]) again to deselect text. The reverse video highlighting is removed.

10.2.5.5 Cutting and Pasting Text

To select and cut or copy a block of text, perform these steps:

	a. Move the cursor beyond the first character of the string you want to cut or copy.
[SELECT]	b. Press [SELECT].
	c. Move the cursor to the last character in the string you want to cut or copy. Note the highlighting of the text as you select.
[MOVE]	d. Press [MOVE] (PF2, F10).
1	e. Type "1" (block).
1 or **2** or **4**	f. Type "1" to cut, "2" to copy, or "4" to append to paste buffer.
	g. Move the cursor to the position in the document where you want to insert the text stored in your paste buffer.
[RETURN]	h. Press [RETURN] to paste the text.

10.2.6 WordPerfect Control Codes

Section 9.3.2, "Entering the Text of Your Document," introduced you to the concept of control codes. Remember that control codes act as instructions to the printer on how to format the text that *follows*. WordPerfect suppresses the display of control codes by default to make it easier for you to view the text of your document. However, you can show this information with [REVEAL CODES] (F19). Figure 10.12 shows an example of the resulting display.

The top half of the screen displays the document as you're used to seeing it. The bottom half of the screen displays the same information *plus* the control codes. In this portion of the screen, you see a control code at the very beginning of the document to set the font to 10-point New Century Schoolbook. This tells the printer to print the letter with this font. The [HRt] control code also appears to show where carriage (hard) returns have been entered.

WordPerfect relies heavily on control codes to format documents properly. You'll probably spend a good deal of time working with control codes if you prepare many documents.

Keep in mind the following points when working with control codes:

1. Control codes are hidden so that you can view your document in the manner in which it prints. These codes are also hidden to improve performance when editing. You can display control codes at any time with [REVEAL CODES] (F19) and then

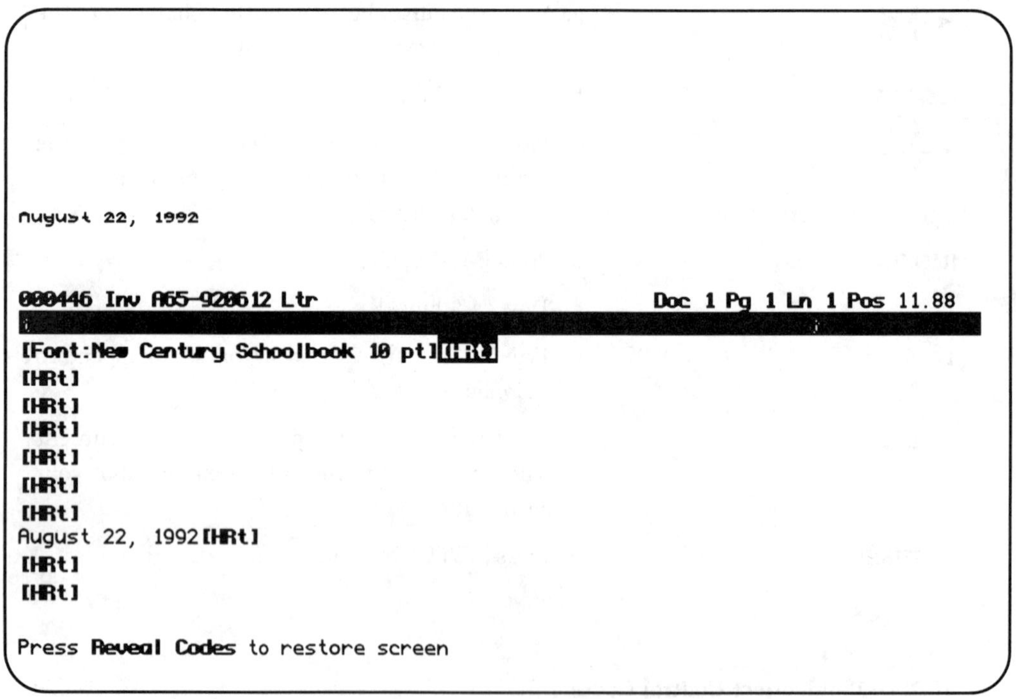

Figure 10.12 Displaying control codes with [REVEAL CODES]

clear this display by pressing [REVEAL CODES] again. It slows your edit session to leave control codes displayed constantly. For this reason, toggle the display of control codes on only when needed.

2. You'll notice that the cursor sometimes doesn't move when you press [RIGHT ARROW] or [LEFT ARROW]. This is because the cursor is actually moving through hidden control codes. An example is when you move the cursor into a string of bold text. You must press the [RIGHT ARROW] key twice to move into the first bold character because the cursor must first move through the [BOLD] control code. If you display the codes with [REVEAL CODES] and press an arrow key, you'll see this movement in the lower window.

3. It's often easier to reset an attribute by deleting a control code than by adding a new code with a function key. For example, to reset tab stops to the previous setting, it's easier to display the control codes and locate and delete the [Tab Set] code rather than go through the process of setting tabs with the [FORMAT] function.

4. The fact that codes are hidden sometimes causes confusion. For example, suppose you execute the [FORMAT] function at the beginning of the document to number pages. When you print the document, however, you notice that page numbering stops after the fifth page. When you edit, display the codes, and move through page 5, you will discover another control code that suppresses page numbering.

   To diagnose and correct this sort of problem, remember the following:

   - You can display codes with [REVEAL CODES] and then search for a particular control code. To search for a control code, press [>SEARCH]. When the "Srch:" prompt appears, press the function key or keys to create the code you want to find. When the control code appears next to the "Srch:" prompt, press [>SEARCH] again to start scanning the document for the code.

   - Control codes can be deleted or moved just like strings of characters. Display codes with [REVEAL CODES], and use [DELETE], [SELECT], and [MOVE] just as if you were working with text.

10.2.7 Editing Multiple Documents in WordPerfect

With WordPerfect, you have the ability to open more than one document in a single edit session. This makes it easy to move blocks of text back and forth between documents. This is helpful if you create many documents that have similar content.

To edit multiple documents in a single session, you must invoke the editor with the Create (C) or Edit (E) option to create or edit the primary document. Follow the steps below to open additional (secondary) documents once the editor is invoked. You can then "flip" back and forth between open documents. When you exit, changes made to any of the documents are saved.

Perform the following steps to open additional documents while editing:

[SWITCH]	a. Press [SWITCH] (PF1, F9). The second edit window is opened. Note the relative document number is now 2.
[GOLD] G	b. Press [GOLD] G.
1 [RETURN]	c. Type "1" and press [RETURN] to include a document from your File Cabinet in the second edit window. ALL-IN-1 displays the Selecting Document to be Retrieved form.
Drawer: ***drawer*** Folder: ***folder*** Title: ***title***	d. Enter a drawer, folder, and title to select the document for editing in the second window.
[RETURN]	e. Press [RETURN] to complete the form. The selected document is displayed in edit window 2.
[GOLD] F	f. When you've finished editing the additional document, press [GOLD] F to exit the document and save any changes.
[GOLD] K **Y**	Or press [GOLD] K and type "Y" to exit without saving changes.

To switch back and forth between open documents during the edit session, do the following:

[SWITCH]	Press [SWITCH] (PF1, F9).

Editing multiple documents is a lot like juggling: The more documents you have open, the harder it is to keep track of them. Here are some recommendations for editing multiple documents:

- It's less confusing if you modify only one document at a time. Modify the primary document (relative document number 1). Copy text from the secondary documents and paste to the primary document. Close secondary documents with [GOLD] K so that any changes made accidentally are not saved. Close the primary document with [GOLD] F to exit and save changes.
- If you're modifying more than one document in a single edit session, close secondary documents with [GOLD] F as soon as you finish working with them. Again, the fewer documents you have open, the easier it is to keep track of what you're doing.

10.2.8 Exercise: Creating a Document

The following exercise takes you through the steps for creating a simple document with WordPerfect. This exercise shows you how to highlight text, change tab settings, and move text.

Before continuing, make sure that you've selected WordPerfect as your default editor. Refer to Section 9.2, "Selecting an Editor," for instructions.

1. Select the Create option to create a new document.

WP C [RETURN]	a. From any menu or index, type "WP C" and press [RETURN]. ALL-IN-1 displays the Creating New Document form.
[UP ARROW] **[UP ARROW]** **[ERASE LINE]** Drawer: **MAIN [TAB]** **[ERASE LINE]** Folder: **TEST DOCUMENTS [TAB]** Title: **Bulletin [RETURN]**	b. Complete the Creating New Document form as shown in Figure 10.13 and press [RETURN]. ALL-IN-1 invokes WordPerfect so you can enter the text of the document.

2. When the screen is cleared after the WordPerfect banner is displayed, start entering the text of the document.

[CENTER]	a. Press [CENTER] (PF1, F12) to center the title.
[BOLD]	b. Press [BOLD] (F12) to bold the title.
B U L L E T I N	c. Type "BULLETIN" in uppercase letters with spaces between the letters.
[BOLD]	d. Press [BOLD] (F12) again to turn off bolding.
[RETURN] **[RETURN]**	e. Press [RETURN] twice to insert an extra blank line in the document.

```
                    Creating New Document

Drawer:   MAIN

Folder:   TEST DOCUMENTS

Title:    Bulletin

Keywords:

      Enter information and press RETURN,
      or press NEXT SCREEN for more fields              (more...)
```

Figure 10.13 Creating New Document form

f. Type the following text exactly as shown in the box below. Do not press [RETURN] at the end of a line within a paragraph, only at the end of the first paragraph.

```
Human Resources, in conjunction with our health insurance carrier,
American Insurance Company is sponsoring a free blood pressure
check for employees. Report to the third floor conference room
during the appropriate time specified below to take advantage of
this service. Medical personnel will be handing out information
pamphlets and will answer any questions you have about the
procedure.

If you have any questions, please contact Connie at Extension 324.
```

Note that your text may wrap differently, depending on your margin settings. Don't worry about this.

[RETURN]
[RETURN]

g. Press [RETURN] twice at the end of the last line to create a blank line.

3. Set tab stops to create columns.

[GOLD] R

a. Press [GOLD] R.

T

b. Type "T" to set tab stops. The expanded ruler appears:

```
L....L....L....L....L....L....L....L....L....L....L....L....L....L....L....L...
|    ^    |    ^    |    ^    |    ^    |    ^    |    ^    |    ^    |    ^
0        +10       +20       +30       +40       +50       +60       +70
Delete EOL (clear tabs); Enter Number (set tab); Del (clear tab);
Type; Left; Center; Right; Decimal; .= Dot Leader; Press Exit when done.
```

[DELETE EOL]

c. Press [DELETE EOL] (PF2, Keypad-1) to clear all tab stops.

[RIGHT ARROW]...

d. Press [RIGHT ARROW] to move to position 5 (0.5 inches).

L

e. Type "L" to set a tab stop.

f. Repeat steps d and e to set tab stops at positions 20 and 40.

[EXIT]
[EXIT]

g. Press [EXIT] (F13) twice to resume editing.

4. Type the titles for the columns of dates and times.

[TAB] [UNDERLINE]

a. Press [TAB] and then [UNDERLINE] (F14) to underline the titles.

LAST NAMES [TAB] **DATE [TAB]** **TIME**	b. Type "LAST NAMES," press [TAB], type "DATE," press [TAB], and type "TIME."
[UNDERLINE]	c. Press [UNDERLINE] (F14) again to turn off underlining.
[RETURN] **[RETURN]**	d. Press [RETURN] twice to create a blank line.

5. Type the columns of dates and times.

Type the following exactly as shown, and press [TAB] where indicated.

```
[TAB] A - J [TAB] Mon, June 8th [TAB] 10:00am
[TAB] K - Q [TAB] Tues, June 9th [TAB] 10:00am
[TAB] R - Z [TAB] Wed, June 10th [TAB] 11:00am
```

6. Move the second paragraph of text to the bottom of the document.

	a. Move the cursor to the "I" in "If you have any questions...."
[SELECT]	b. Press [SELECT].
[DOWN ARROW]	c. Press [DOWN ARROW]. (If this paragraph is more than one line, press [DOWN ARROW] again.)
[MOVE]	d. Press [MOVE] (PF2, F10).
1	e. Type "1" (Block).
1	f. Type "1" (Move).
[HOME] [HOME] **[DOWN ARROW]**	g. Press [HOME] (PF4) twice and then press [DOWN ARROW] to move to the bottom of the document.
[RETURN] **[RETURN]** **[RETURN]**	h. Press [RETURN] three times to paste the text and insert a blank line. Your document should look something like Figure 10.14.

7. View the control codes in your document.

[REVEAL CODES]	a. Press [REVEAL CODES] (F19) to display the control codes.
[REVEAL CODES]	b. Press [REVEAL CODES] (F19) again when finished viewing the control codes.

```
                         B U L L E T I N

Human Resources, in conjunction with our health insurance carrier,
American Insurance Company is sponsoring a free blood pressure
check for employees.  Report to the third floor conference room
during the appropriate time specified below to take advantage of
this service.  Medical personnel will be handing out information
pamphlets and will answer any questions you have about the
procedure.

If you have any questions, please contact Connie at Extension 324.

     LAST NAMES      DATE                TIME

     A - J           Mon, June 8th       10:00am
     K - Q           Tues, June 9th      10:00am
     R - Z           Wed, June 10th      11:00am




005484 Bulletin                             Doc 1 Pg 1 Ln 3.67" Pos 5.1"
```

Figure 10.14 Sample document

8. File your document, then review the document with the Read option.

[GOLD] F	a. Press [GOLD] F to exit the editor and file the document.
R [RETURN]	b. Type "R" and press [RETURN] to read the document.
[RETURN] **[RETURN]**	c. Press [RETURN] twice to return to the menu.

10.3 GETTING STARTED WITH EDT

The EDT editor is a standard text editor provided with VMS for preparing documents. If you have used EDT at the DCL command level of VMS, you'll have no problem using EDT in ALL-IN-1.

EDT is limited in capabilities compared to WPS-PLUS and WordPerfect. For this reason, however, you may find EDT easier to learn. If you prepare short, simple documents and require "nothing fancy" in terms of document formatting, you will be pleased with the EDT's capabilities.

Note that a document prepared in EDT can always be converted to WPS-PLUS or WordPerfect format to take advantage of the advanced word-processing capabilities of these programs. A word of caution, though: After converting a large document, you might have to do a certain amount of manual cleanup and reformatting.

The EDT editor includes these features:

- Support for both line mode and full-screen mode editing. In line mode, you locate a line of text and enter a command to modify the line. In full-screen mode, the lines of text are displayed on the terminal screen for you to move around and insert and remove text.
- A series of function keys that perform word-processing functions with a single keystroke. These functions include cursor movement, cutting and pasting text, and text removal.
- Automatic keystroke journaling so that in the event of a system failure, most of your editing work can be recovered.

The EDT editor also has some restrictions:

- EDT does not allow selection of font type or size. It is also very cumbersome to highlight text with bolding, underlining, or italics in EDT.
- EDT does not have on-line writing aids, such as a spell checker, usage alerts, or a thesaurus. You do have access to these tools, however, when you run a document prepared with EDT through the spell checker from the WP menu.
- EDT does not have such document formatting capabilities as footnoting, page numbering, and margin justification.

10.3.1 The EDT Keyboard

Figure 10.15 on the next page shows the location of the function keys in EDT that perform special editing operations. Appendix B contains a tabular listing of these EDT function keys.

10.3.2 Viewing Your Document in the Editor

Figure 10.16 on page 241 shows an example of the screen layout in EDT. The document being edited here is a simple business letter. The letter starts with a series of blank lines, followed by the date and addressee. The screen shown in the figure on the next page includes the following items:

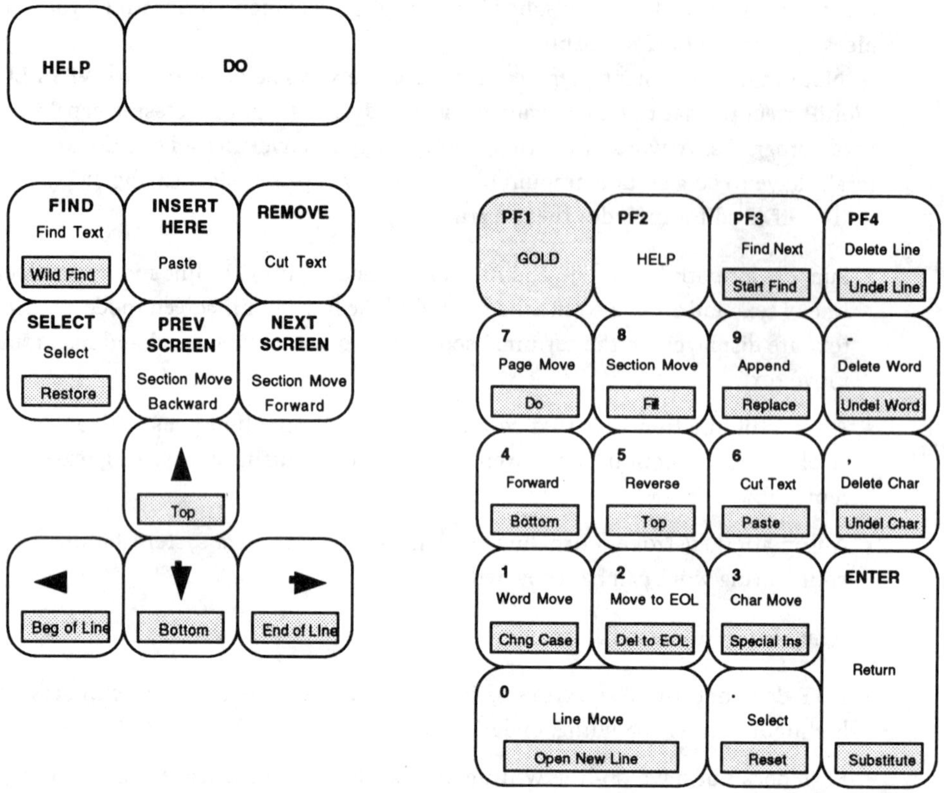

Figure 10.15 EDT function key layout (LK201 keyboard)

① Cursor — The cursor is the flashing rectangle (or sometimes a flashing underscore).

② Document Text — Following a number of blank lines, the first line of text is the date.

③ End of Buffer — The [EOB] marker indicates the bottom of text and always appears when you edit a document. However, this marker is not actually a part of the document and, of course, doesn't appear when the document is printed. Initially the [EOB] marker is all that appears on your screen when creating a new document. The marker moves down as you type text.

```
▮ ①




②
August 22, 1992




Ms. Mary Thomas
Western Area Recycling, Inc.
Attn: Accounts Payable
3412 S. Platte
Denver, Colorado 80123
[EOB] ③
```

Figure 10.16 Viewing a document in EDT

10.3.3 Moving Around in the Text

You must move the cursor to modify various portions of a document. Remember that the cursor is the focus of activity when editing. Characters are inserted at the cursor position as you type, and characters are deleted from the cursor position when you press [DELETE CHAR].

The following function keys move the cursor around in a document.

Function Key	*Keystrokes*	*Moves the Cursor*
[DOWN ARROW]		Forward one line.
[LEFT ARROW]		Back one character.
[RIGHT ARROW]		Forward one character.
[UP ARROW]		Back one line.
[BOTTOM]	[GOLD] Keypad-4	To the bottom of the document.
[TOP]	[GOLD] Keypad-5	To the top of the document.
[NEXT SCREEN]		Forward one screen.
[PREV SCREEN]		Back one screen.

Additional function keys for moving the cursor around in a document are listed at the end of this section. The [PAGE] (Keypad-7) key moves the cursor a single page, for example. Movement with these keys is made in the *current* direction: forward or reverse. The following two keys set the current direction.

[ADVANCE]	Keypad-4	Set direction to forward.
[BACKUP]	Keypad-5	Set direction to reverse.

Therefore, to move one page back you would press [BACKUP] (Keypad-5) and then [PAGE] (Keypad-7). Press [PAGE] again to move back a second page, and press [ADVANCE] (Keypad-4) [PAGE] to move forward one page.

Function Key	*Keystrokes*	*Moves the Cursor in the Current Direction*
[CHAR]	Keypad-3	One character.
[WORD]	Keypad-1	One word.
[END OF LINE]	Keypad-2	To the end of the line.
[LINE]	Keypad-0	To the beginning of the line.
[PAGE]	Keypad-7	To the next page break.
[SECTION]	Keypad-8	One screen.

10.3.4 Basic Editing

Most people get by with the following basic procedures for deleting, searching for, selecting, and cutting and pasting text. Procedures for more advanced operations are listed in Appendix B.

10.3.4.1 Deleting Text

Table 10.9 lists the function keys that delete text. To delete large blocks of text, it's more efficient to select the block of text and then press [REMOVE] or [CUT].

10.3.4.2 Searching for Text

Perform these steps to search for a string of text in the document:

[FIND]	a. Press [FIND] (or [GOLD] PF3). The "Search for:" prompt is displayed at the bottom of your screen.
Search for: ***string***	b. Type the text you want to find. It will be stored in the "search" buffer.
[FIND]	c. Press [FIND] (or PF3) to search for the string in the current direction. If necessary, first press [BACKUP] (Keypad-5) or [ADVANCE] (Keypad-4) to change direction.

Table 10.9 EDT function keys to delete or restore text

Function Key	*Keystrokes*	*Description*
[DELETE]	⌫	Deletes the character in front of the cursor.
[DELETE CHAR]	Keypad-Comma	Deletes the character at the cursor position.
[UNDELETE CHAR]	[GOLD] Keypad-Comma	Restores the last character deleted.
[LINE FEED]	[LINE FEED] (F13)	Deletes the word in front of the cursor.
[DELETE WORD]	Keypad-Hyphen	Deletes the current word.
[UNDELETE WORD]	[GOLD] Keypad-Hyphen	Restores the last word deleted.
[DELETE LINE]	PF4	Deletes the current line.
[DELETE TO EOL]	[GOLD] Keypad-2	Deletes text from the cursor to the end of the line.
[UNDELETE LINE]	[GOLD] PF4	Restores the last line deleted.

To search for the next occurrence of the string in the search buffer, do the following:

[FIND]

Press [FIND] (or PF3) to search for the string already stored in the search buffer. If necessary, first press [BACKUP] (Keypad-5) or [ADVANCE] (Keypad-4) to change direction.

10.3.4.3 Selecting Text

Perform these steps to select a string of text:

a. Move the cursor to the first character in the string you want to select.

[SELECT]

b. Press [SELECT] (or Keypad-Period).

c. Move the cursor beyond the last character of the string you want to select. Note that EDT highlights text in reverse video as you move the cursor.

Do the following to deselect a string of text:

[GOLD] Keypad-Period

Press [GOLD] Keypad-Period to deselect text. Note that the reverse video highlighting is removed.

10.3.4.4 Cutting and Pasting Text

To select and cut a block of text, follow these steps:

a. Move the cursor to the first character in the block you want to cut.

[SELECT]

b. Press [SELECT] (or Keypad-Period).

c. Move the cursor beyond the last character of the block you want to cut. Note the highlighting of the text as you select.

[REMOVE]

d. Press [REMOVE] (or Keypad-6) to cut the text. The text is now stored in your "paste buffer."

Note: If you want to leave the text here and make a copy elsewhere, immediately paste before moving the cursor.

To paste the block of text that was last cut or copied, do the following:

a. Move the cursor to the position in the document where you want to insert the text stored in your paste buffer.

[INSERT HERE]

b. Press [INSERT HERE] (or [GOLD] Keypad-6) to paste the text.

10.4 GETTING STARTED WITH EVE

The EVE editor is another standard text editor provided with VMS for preparing documents. This editor is popular with people who work at the DCL command level of VMS. If you are familiar with the VAX TPU/EVE editor from DCL, you'll have no problem using EVE in ALL-IN-1.

The EVE editor is similar to EDT. EVE is a full-screen editor with many of the same characteristics of EDT. In addition to these capabilities, EVE also supports a large number of editing commands for performing more advanced operations, such as setting margins, paginating a document, and creating multiple windows. Many people select EVE as an alternative to EDT for this reason. However, EVE is limited in terms of word-processing capabilities when compared to WPS-PLUS or WordPerfect.

Note that a document prepared in EVE can always be converted to WPS-PLUS or WordPerfect format to take advantage of the advanced word-processing capabilities of these programs. A word of caution, though: After converting a large document, you may have to do a certain amount of manual cleanup and reformatting.

The EVE editor includes the following features:

- A series of function keys that perform word-processing functions with a single keystroke. These functions include cursor movement, cutting and pasting text, and text removal. You can also select an EVE edit style that emulates the function key layout of either EDT or WPS-PLUS.

- Additional editing functions that can be performed by entering one of the many EVE editor commands.
- Automatic keystroke journaling so that in the event of a system failure, most of your editing work can be recovered.
- The ability to add new editing functions or to modify existing functions by writing or modifying programs written in a VAX Text Processing Utility (TPU). Many sites add or modify editor functions by developing TPU programs. The ability to extend or modify standard functions is another reason why many people prefer to use EVE rather than EDT. A discussion of developing TPU programs is beyond the scope of this manual. Refer to the VAX TPU manual in the VMS documentation set for additional information.

The EVE editor also has some restrictions:

- Although EVE emulates the function keys of WPS-PLUS, it does not support WPS-PLUS's advanced functions, such as formatting with rulers, on-line writing aids, and two-dimensional editing. Spell checking is available if DECspell is installed, however.
- EVE does not allow selection of font type or size. It is also very cumbersome to highlight text with bolding, underlining, or italics in EVE.
- EVE does not have document formatting capabilities, such as footnoting, page numbering, and margin justification.

10.4.1 Defining the Keyboard in EVE

Like all other editors discussed in this chapter, EVE allows you to perform special editing operations with function keys. EVE supports three different function key layouts: EDT, WPS-PLUS, and the default function key layout.

You select the function key layout when you select an editor. Section 9.2, "Selecting an Editor," shows you how to select any of the following edit styles, which will select EVE as the editor:

EVE_EDT	Selects the same function key layout as EDT. Refer to Figure 10.15 for the location of the EDT function keys.
EVE_WPS	Selects the same function key layout as WPS-PLUS. Refer to Figure 10.1 for the location of the WPS-PLUS function keys. Note that not all WPS-PLUS functions are available in EVE. The [BOLD] and [UNDERLINE] function keys are not active in EVE, for example, because EVE does not support text highlighting.

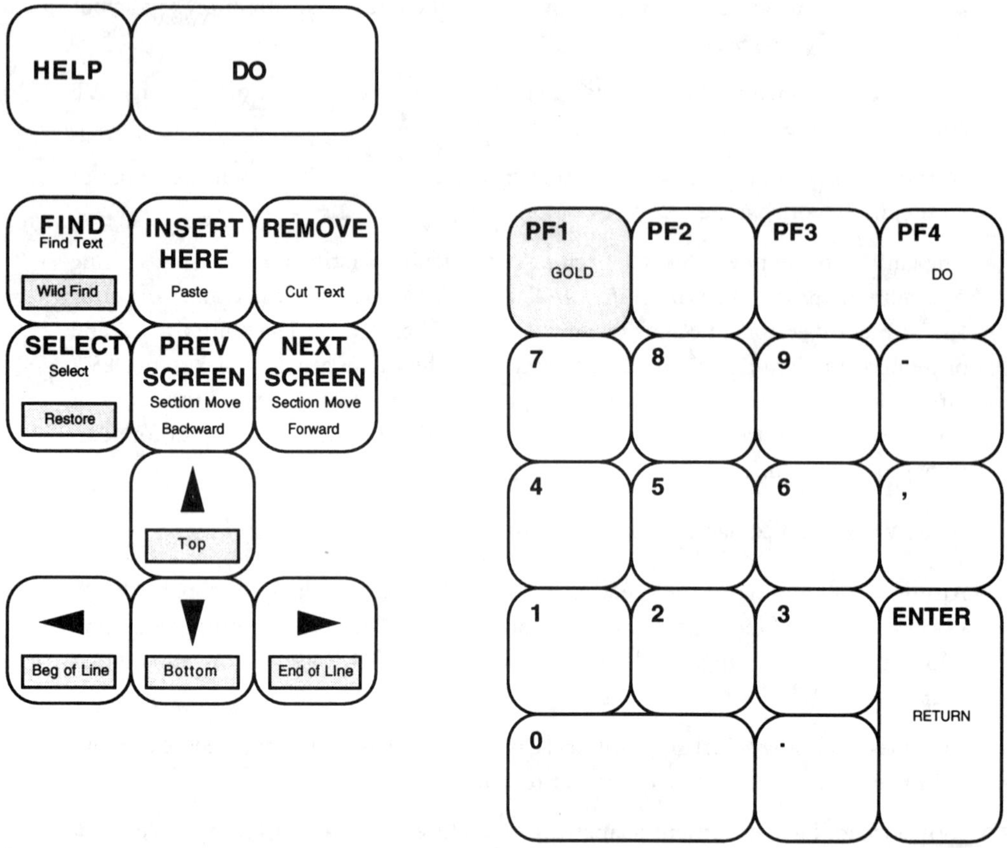

Figure 10.17 EVE function key layout (LK201 keyboard)

EVE Selects the default function key layout, shown in Figure 10.17. Note that this layout is rather limited compared to EDT or WPS-PLUS.

10.4.2 Viewing Your Document in the Editor

Figure 10.18 shows an example of the screen layout in EVE. The document being edited here is a simple business letter. The letter starts with a series of blank lines, followed by the date and addressee; the letter continues beyond the bottom of the screen. On the last line of the screen, EVE displays status information. The screen shown in Figure 10.18 includes the following items:

① Cursor — The cursor is the flashing rectangle (or sometimes a flashing underscore).

② Document Text — Following a number of blank lines, the first line of text is the date.

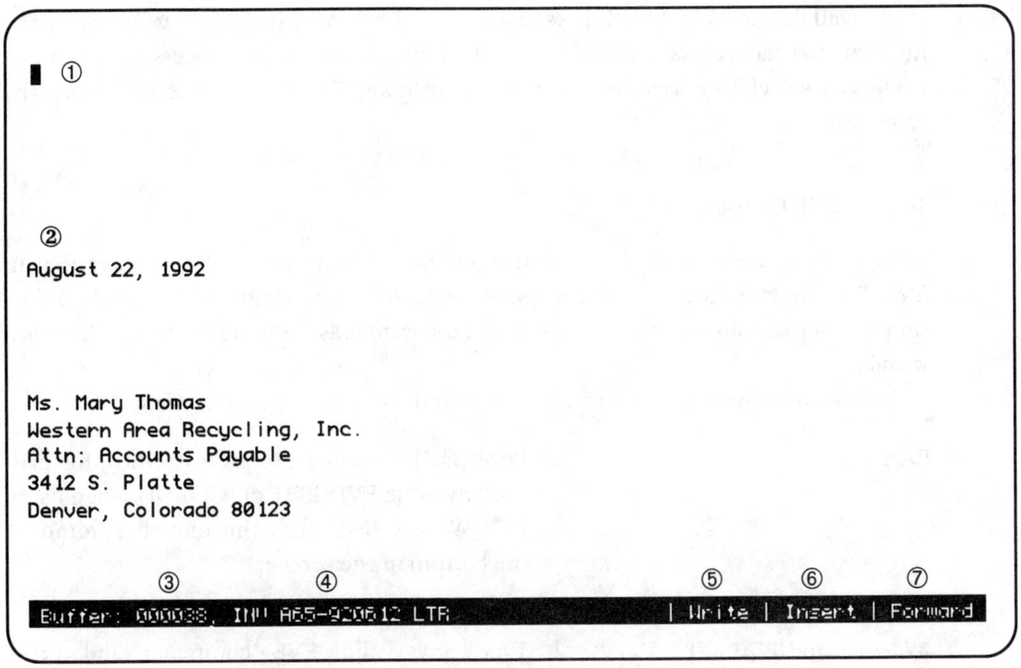

Figure 10.18 Viewing a document in EVE

③ Document Number	The document number is assigned by ALL-IN-1 when you create a document. It uniquely identifies a document in your File Cabinet.
④ Title	The title you specified when creating the document.
⑤ Read/Write Indicator	Indicates whether the document was opened to allow modifications (Write) or for read-only access (Read-only).
⑥ Edit Mode	The current edit mode: insert or overstrike. The edit mode is changed by pressing F14 or [CTRL] + A.
⑦ Current Direction	The current direction in which the cursor moves when certain function keys are pressed.

10.4.3 Basic Editing

The steps for performing basic editing operations vary, depending on which edit style you choose. Section 10.3.4, "Basic Editing," and Table B.6 in Appendix B describe basic editing procedures when you select EVE_EDT as your editor. Section 10.10.1.4, "Basic Editing," and Table B.2 in Appendix B describe basic editing procedures when you select EVE_WPS or EVE as your editor. Be aware, however, that not all editing operations available in WPS-PLUS are supported by EVE_WPS or EVE. For example, the numeric keypad enters numbers instead of performing word-processing functions when you select EVE as your editor, although many GOLD key functions work the same way.

10.4.4 EVE Commands

Table 10.10 describes some of the commands that perform special editing operations in EVE. You can enter these commands with the following procedure while editing a document. You can display the full list of EVE commands by entering the HELP command.

Follow these steps to enter an EVE command while editing a document:

[DO]	a. Press [DO]. (You can also press [GOLD], Keypad-7 when using EVE_EDT or [GOLD] [when using EVE_WPS.) EVE displays the following prompt at the bottom of the screen: `Command:`
***EVE-command* [RETURN]**	b. Type any valid EVE command and press [RETURN]. Some commands require you to enter additional information.

Table 10.10 EVE commands

Enter This Command	*To Perform the Following Action*
DEFINE KEY=*key-name EVE-command*	Define a function key to execute a specific EVE command when pressed. The following example programs the F18 key to center the current line. `DEFINE KEY=F18 CENTER LINE`
FILL PARAGRAPH	Rewrap words in the current paragraph to fill space between the left and right margins. This is useful after you've added text to the middle of a paragraph.
LEARN	Program a key to repeat a set of keystrokes when pressed. You are prompted to enter the keystrokes and must enter [CTRL] + R when finished. Then press the key you want to "program"—for example, F17 through F20.
REPLACE	Replace all occurrences of an old string with a new string. After entering this command, EVE prompts for the old string and new string. Enter these strings and press [RETURN]. EVE locates the first occurrence of the old string and asks if

Table 10.10 *(continued)*

Enter This Command	*To Perform the Following Action*
	you want to replace the string. Enter one of the following responses: Y (Yes) — Replace the current string and move to the next occurrence. N (No) — Do not replace the current string. Move to the next occurrence. A (All) — Replace the current string and all of the following occurrences of the string. L (Last) — Replace the current string and then exit from the Replace function. Q (Quit) — Exit the Replace function.
SET LEFT MARGIN *n*	Set the left margin to the specified column. This affects text centering and automatic wrapping.
SET RIGHT MARGIN *n*	Set the right margin to the specified column. This affects text centering and automatic wrapping.
SET WIDTH *n*	Set the width of the terminal screen to display 80 or 132 columns.
SET WRAP	Cause an automatic word wrap to the next line when the right margin is reached. The right margin is set with the Set Right Margin command.
WHAT LINE	Displays a message showing the cursor's line number, the total number of lines in the file, and what percentage of the file precedes the cursor position.

Advanced WPS-PLUS Features

CHAPTER 11

This chapter describes advanced features in Word and Document Processing when working with WPS-PLUS. The first two features discussed, Abbreviations and Library documents, can save typing if you frequently type standard phrases and blocks of text. List Processing is helpful if you need to produce a series of form letters, mailing labels, or lists of information. The last feature, Paragraph Numbering, saves you a lot of tedious work when preparing large documents or manuals by automatically generating a table of contents and index.

This chapter teaches you how to perform the following tasks:

- Store standard blocks of text in Abbreviations and Library documents and later retrieve them.
- Process lists of information to automatically print form letters and mailing labels, for example.
- Automatically number the titles of sections in your document and create a table of contents and index.

11.1 ABBREVIATIONS AND LIBRARY DOCUMENTS

Abbreviations and Library documents can save you a lot of typing. Create these documents to store all of the standard text that you frequently type when preparing documents. This includes short phrases, such as signature blocks, company names, and return addresses, and longer blocks of text from legal paragraphs to form letters.

Both documents contain short abbreviated names for standard blocks of text, followed by the full, expanded text. When preparing a document, you press a function key and then enter the abbreviation. WPS-PLUS retrieves the expanded text and copies it into the current document.

You can have one Abbreviations document and one Library document open for reference while editing. Abbreviations documents contain two-character Abbreviations followed by full words or phrases of text. Library documents typically contain longer abbreviations followed by larger blocks of text, such as a report header or form letter.

Perform the following steps to create an Abbreviations or Library document:

C [RETURN]

a. From the Word and Document Processing menu, type "C" and press [RETURN] to create a document.

Drawer: ***drawer*** **[TAB]**
Folder: ***folder*** **[TAB]**
Title: ***title*** **[RETURN]**

b. Complete the Creating New Document form with the appropriate information and press [RETURN] to enter the editor. Use a folder name like "LIBRARY TEXT" for storing Abbreviations and Library documents.

c. Enter the list of abbreviations followed by the full, expanded text.

For an Abbreviations document:

<<cs>>Stan Carter
Executive Vice President
<<da>>Anne Dutton
Executive Vice President...
<<th>>Thompson and Associates
2301 Oak Street, Suite 450
Denver, CO 80201
<<

Enter the two-character abbreviation (in double angle brackets), followed by the full word or phrase. You can include multiple lines in the full, expanded string of text.

Opening angle brackets (<<) for an abbreviation signal the end of the previous definition. Include a set of these brackets after the last abbreviation.

For a Library document:

<<appl_letter>>
L--------T--------T--------T--------T--------R
name
company
address
city, state zip
Dear name,
We have received your recent ...
<<accept_letter>>
:
:
<<

Enter a multicharacter abbreviation (one that includes no spaces and is enclosed in double angle brackets), followed by the full, expanded text starting on the next line. Note that you can include rulers and control blocks in the full, expanded text. Opening angle brackets (<<) for a library element signal the end of the previous definition. Include a set of open brackets after the last abbreviation.

[EXIT]

d. Press [EXIT] (F10 or [GOLD] F) to exit the editor and file your Abbreviations or Library document.

Perform the following steps to reference an Abbreviations or Library document while editing another document:

1. First specify the Abbreviations or Library document that you want to reference.

[GOLD] M

a. Press [MENU] ([GOLD] M) to display the Editor menu.

AD [RETURN] — b. Type "AD" and press [RETURN] to select an Abbreviations document.

LD [RETURN] — Or type "LD" and press [RETURN] to select a Library document.

Drawer: ***drawer* [TAB]**
Folder: ***folder* [TAB]**
Title: ***title* [RETURN]** — c. Enter the drawer, folder, and title for your Abbreviations or Library document and press [RETURN]. Refer to Section 9.4, "Selecting a Document," for details.

[EXIT] — d. Press [EXIT] (F10 or Keypad-0) to clear the Editor menu and return to editing your document.

Note: Once you've selected an Abbreviations or Library document, you don't need to do this again until you want to work with a different set of abbreviations or library text.

2. Press [ABBREVIATION] or [LIBRARY] whenever you want WPS-PLUS to look up an abbreviation and retrieve the full text.

[ABBREVIATION] — a. Press [ABBREVIATION] ([GOLD] =) to retrieve an abbreviation.

[LIBRARY] — Or press [LIBRARY] ([GOLD] L) to retrieve a library element.

ABBRV element: ***xx* [RETURN]** — b. Type the two-character abbreviation name and press [RETURN].

LIBRY element:
***libr-abbrv* [RETURN]** — Or type the library element name and press [RETURN]. WPS-PLUS inserts the full, expanded text in your document.

11.1.1 Exercise: Creating and Using an Abbreviations Document

In this exercise, you will create two documents. The first is an Abbreviations document in which you will enter two fictitious names and titles for use in signature blocks. When performing this exercise, feel free to substitute the names of people in your organization. You'll create the second document to test the Abbreviations document. While editing the second document, you'll fetch the information entered in the Abbreviations document.

Note that your editor style must be WPS-PLUS to perform this exercise. You can change your editor style to WPS-PLUS by following the steps in Section 9.2, "Selecting an Editor."

1. First move to the Word and Document Processing menu.

WP [RETURN] — From any menu, type "WP" and press [RETURN].

2. Create an Abbreviations document.

C [RETURN]

a. Type "C" and press [RETURN] to create the Abbreviations document.

b. Enter the folder name "LIBRARY TEXT" and the title "Abbreviations," as shown in Figure 11.1. Then press [RETURN].

Note: If ALL-IN-1 tells you that the folder does not exist, type "Y" and press [RETURN] to create it.

c. Type the following two abbreviations in your document. Type exactly what you see in the box below.

```
<<WN>>Mr. William Nelson

Vice President, Production
<<ST>>Ms. Susan Thorpe

Vice President, Sales and Marketing
<<
```

[EXIT]

d. When you've finished, press [EXIT] (F10 or [GOLD] F) to exit and file your document.

3. Create a test document.

C [RETURN]

a. Type "C" and press [RETURN] to create the test document.

```
                    Creating New Document

Drawer:   MAIN
Folder:   LIBRARY TEXT
Title:    Abbreviations
Keywords: 

      Enter information and press RETURN,
      or press NEXT SCREEN for more fields                (more...)
```

Figure 11.1 Creating New Document form for Abbreviations document

```
                    Creating New Document

Drawer:   MAIN

Folder:   TEST

Title:    Test for Abbreviations

Keywords: 

       Enter information and press RETURN,
       or press NEXT SCREEN for more fields              (more...)
```

Figure 11.2 Creating New Document form for test document

b. Enter the folder name "TEST" and the title "Test for Abbreviations," as shown in Figure 11.2. Then press [RETURN].

[MENU]

c. When the editor is invoked, press [MENU] ([GOLD] M) to display the Editor menu.

AD [RETURN]

d. Type "AD" and press [RETURN] to select an Abbreviations document.

[UP ARROW]
Folder: **LIBRARY TEXT [TAB]**
Title: **ABBREVIATIONS [RETURN]**

e. Enter the folder "LIBRARY TEXT" and the title "Abbreviations" and press [RETURN] to select your abbreviations document.

[EXIT]

f. Press [EXIT] (F10 or Keypad-0) to clear the Editor menu and return to editing your document.

4. Retrieve the text from your Abbreviations document.

[ABBREVIATION]

a. Press [ABBREVIATION] ([GOLD] =) to retrieve an abbreviation.

ABBRV element: **wn**

b. Type "wn." Note that William Nelson's name and title are inserted in your document.

[ABBREVIATION]

c. Press [ABBREVIATION] ([GOLD] =) to retrieve another abbreviation.

ABBRV element: **st**

d. Type "st." Note that Susan Thorpe's name and title are inserted in your document.

[EXIT]

e. Press [EXIT] (F10 or [GOLD] F) to exit the editor and file your test document.

11.2 LIST AND SORT PROCESSING

List Processing is an advanced feature of WPS-PLUS that is capable of processing lists of information. For example, List Processing can perform the following functions:

- Process a list of names and addresses to generate a batch of form letters or mailing labels automatically.
- Select and format records from the list to produce a directory.
- Perform mathematical operations on numbers that appear in the list to produce a report.

List Processing requires that you first prepare the documents shown in Figure 11.3.

① List Document

A List document contains a list of records. Each record of information contains various fields. A record consists of all pieces of information up to and including the next empty angle brackets "<>." Each record in Figure 11.3, for example, consists of a single client's title, name, address, and zip code. A list of customer names and addresses is a typical List document. The format of a List document is as follows:

```
<field1-name>field1-contents      <---- Record 1
<field2-name>field2-contents
              •
              •
<>
<field1-name>field1-contents      <---- Record 2
<field2-name>field2-contents
              •
              •
<>
              •
              •
```

② List Specification Document

The List Specification document selects records from the List document to format during list processing. Information in the record is tested against the selection rules in the List Specification document. For example, you might have a list of customers with addresses across the country, but you might only want to send a form letter to customers with certain zip codes. In the case of the first List document record shown in Figure 11.3, Acorn Printing's zip code *does* start with the three characters "606" and is therefore selected to create the first form letter. (The bracketed asterisk (<*>) in the List Specification document says that any number of

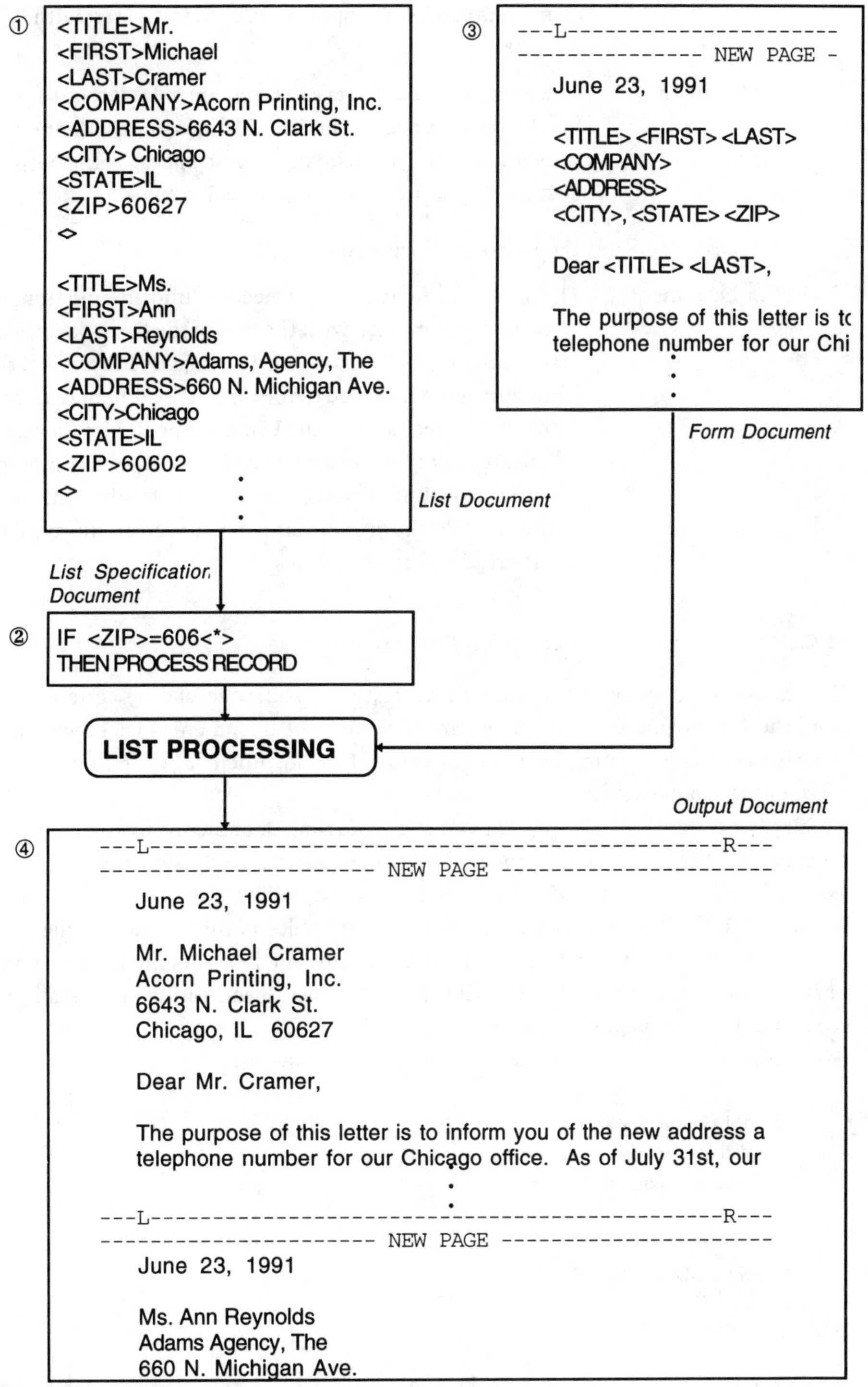

Figure 11.3 List Processing

characters can follow, but the zip code must start with "606.")

③ Form Document — The Form document acts as a template or boilerplate for the finished output document. The Form document contains the standard text strings that you want to appear in the output document, plus field names enclosed in angle brackets (<>).

List Processing creates the following document:

④ Output Document — The final document contains pieces of information from the List document merged with the text of the Form document to produce finished documents. During List Processing, the Form document is copied to the output document once for each record selected from the List document. List Processing substitutes information from the List document in appropriate locations in the copied Form document. While this is happening, List Processing displays on your screen the number of records read and processed.

11.2.1 Preparing a List Specification Document

One of List Processing's most useful features is its ability to choose certain records from the List document to become part of the output document. List Processing accomplishes this by testing each record of the List document against rules that you place in the List Specification document.

Simply create a new document from the Word and Document Processing menu to create a List Specification document. The List Specification document typically contains a sentence starting with the word "IF" and ending with the phrase "THEN PROCESS RECORD." This sentence should "test" fields of information in the record.

The simplest form of a List Specification document is a document that contains *only* the two words "PROCESS RECORD." This List Specification selects all of the records in the List document for processing.

Following is the format of a List Specification document:

```
IF <field-name>=value
 [additional-test]
 [additional-test]
       •
       •
THEN PROCESS RECORD
```

where:

field-name — is a bracketed field name that matches a field name in each record of your List document.

value — is a specific string of characters or numbers that you're searching for in the field. This string can also include the wild cards "<*>" or "<???...>" to perform pattern matching. Look ahead to Table 11.1 for examples of pattern matching.

additional-test — is additional test conditions for the specified field (or another field). The following formats are valid for additional test conditions. Note that these additional test conditions are optional.

```
OR=value2
OR LESS
OR MORE
THROUGH value2
AND <field-name2>=<value2>
BUT NOT IF <field-name2>=<value2>
```

When creating a List Specification document, keep the following points in mind:

- Type the field name exactly as you've entered it in the List document.
- Type the value directly after the equals sign.
- If you have additional test conditions, you can indent these lines for readability.
- Make sure that "THEN PROCESS RECORD" is on the last line by itself.

Table 11.1 shows examples of typical List Specification documents. Although fairly simple, these examples illustrate the most common tests included in a List Specification document. You can write much more elaborate sentences in a list specification to have greater control over record selection. Refer to the Digital manual *WPS-PLUS/VMS List and Sort Processing* for details on writing more advanced List Specification documents.

11.2.2 Sorting Records

Sort Processing allows you to copy and sort the List document. Sort Processing rearranges records based on the contents of a specific field. For example, suppose you've created your list of clients sorted alphabetically by the contents of the "COMPANY" field. You might want to sort this list numerically by zip code before creating mailing labels.

To sort output from List Processing, you must first sort your (input) List document with Sort Processing, then run List Processing against the new, sorted list.

Sort Processing requires that you first create a Sort Specification document describing how you want to sort your list. Then you run Sort Processing to make a copy of the original List document, sorting the records according to your instructions.

The Sort Specification document must contain either of the following sentences to sort a list based on the contents of a single field:

```
SORT ON <field-name> IN ASCENDING ORDER
```

Table 11.1 Examples of List Specifications

Example of List Specification	*Description*
PROCESS RECORD	No real test here. This list specification causes List Processing to select every record in the List document.
IF <STATE>=IL THEN PROCESS RECORD	Tests whether a field equals a specific string of characters. In this example, the contents of the field <STATE> must be "IL".
IF <ZIP>=606<*> THEN PROCESS RECORD	Tests whether a field begins with a specific string of characters. In this example, the zip code must begin with "606".
IF <ZIP>=606<??> THEN PROCESS RECORD	Tests the number of characters in a field. In this example, the zip code must be five digits, and the first three must be "606". (Any two digits can follow, as indicated by the two question marks.)
IF <:ZIP>=<60613> THRU <60626> THEN PROCESS RECORD	Makes a numeric test looking for value within a certain range. Note that the field name must have a preceding colon and the test values must be enclosed in brackets.
IF <:SALES>=<100000> OR MORE THEN PROCESS RECORD	Makes a numeric test looking for values exceeding some limit.
IF <:EMPL>=<10> OR LESS THEN PROCESS RECORD	Makes a numeric test looking for values less than some limit.
IF <CITY>=Los Angeles OR=LA THEN PROCESS RECORD	Tests if a field contains one of several different strings of characters.
IF <STATE>=NY AND <:EMPL> =<10> OR MORE THEN PROCESS RECORD	Tests more than one field in the record. In this example, the test is for all records for New York with 10 employees or more.
IF <STATE>=IL BUT NOT IF <CITY>=Chicago THEN PROCESS RECORD	Tests more than one field in the record. In this example, all records for Illinois are chosen except those for Chicago.

or

```
SORT ON <field-name> IN DESCENDING ORDER
```

where:

field-name is a bracketed field name that matches a field name within each record of your List document.

To sort on more than one field, add the word "AND" after "ORDER," and add another sort specification on the next line. For example, the following Sort Specification document would sort a list of clients first by zip code and then by company name:

```
SORT ON <ZIP> IN ASCENDING ORDER AND

SORT ON <COMPANY> IN ASCENDING ORDER
```

11.2.3 Running List Processing

Perform the following steps to run List Processing:

1. Create a List document, List Specification document, and Format document.
   - Create a List document with the Create (C) option on the Word and Document Processing menu. Refer to the beginning of this section for details on the format of a List document. It helps to add words like "List Doc," "List Spec," and "Format Doc" to the titles of all of the documents you create for List Processing, or keep them in different folders.

     To save time when creating a list, first create a "column" of the field names (without the data). When finished, go back and copy this column of field names with [GOLD] [CUT]. Before adding a new record, paste the field names, move the cursor to the first field, and press [ENTER]. The cursor moves to the end of the field. Type the data for the field and press [ENTER]. The cursor moves to the end of the next field. Continue to type data and press [ENTER] to complete the record.

     Don't group too many pieces of information in a single field. For example, if you include the PO box, street address, city, state, and zip all in a single field called "ADDRESS," you won't be able to select records by city and state.
   - Create a List Specification document with the Create (C) option on the Word and Document Processing menu. Refer to Section 11.2.1, "Preparing a List Specification Document," for details.
   - Create a Form document with the Create (C) option on the Word and Document Processing menu. Refer to the beginning of this section for an example.

     Place a page marker ([GOLD] N) at the *bottom* of the Form document if you want a page break between records. This is typical if you're creating a batch of form letters or mailing labels.
2. Run Sort Processing if you want information in the output document to be sorted differently from the List document.
   - Create a Sort Specification document with the Create (C) option on the Word and Document Processing menu. Refer to Section 11.2.2, "Sorting Records," for details.
   - Type "LP SR" and press [RETURN] to move to the List Processing Menu and run Sort Processing.
   - Enter the drawer, folder, and title for the List document you want to sort, and press [RETURN]. Enter the drawer, folder, and title for the Sort Specification document you just prepared, and press [RETURN]. ALL-IN-1 displays the Select Output Document option.
   - If an output document is displayed in the current item block, enter one of the following options, then press [RETURN]:

   O Overwrites the selected document with the new output.

B Adds the output to the bottom of the selected document.

T Inserts the output at the top of the selected document.

If no output document is selected, or if you want to create a new output document, type "COD" and press [RETURN]. Then specify the drawer, folder, title, and optional keywords for the new document and press [RETURN].

- When the Sort Processing Documents Selected screen is displayed, review the documents you specified. If everything is correct, press [RETURN] to start Sort Processing.

  If you need to change any of the documents, press [NEXT SCREEN] (or [GOLD] [TAB]) and reenter drawer, folder, and title names.

3. Run List Processing.

- From the List Processing menu, type "DOC" and press [RETURN] to select Document Processing. ALL-IN-1 asks you to select the List document, List Specification document, and Form document.

  Note: If you previously ran List Processing, the folders and titles are remembered and displayed here. If everything is OK, press [RETURN] and skip the next step. If you need to change any folder or title, press [NEXT SCREEN] (or [GOLD] A) and perform the next step.

- Enter the drawer, folder, and title for the List document, and press [RETURN]. Enter the drawer, folder, and title for the List Specification document and press [RETURN]. Enter the drawer, folder, and title or the document number for the Form document, and press [RETURN].

- If an output document is displayed in the current item block, enter one of the following options, then press [RETURN]:

O Overwrites the selected document with the new output.

B Adds the output to the bottom of the selected document.

T Inserts the output at the top of the selected document.

If no output document is selected, or if you want to create a new output document, type "COD"and press [RETURN]. Then specify the drawer, folder, title, and optional keywords for the new document, and press [RETURN].

- When the List Processing Documents Selected screen is displayed, review the documents. If everything is correct, press [RETURN]. If you need to change any of the documents, press [NEXT SCREEN] (or [GOLD] [TAB]) and reenter drawer, folder, and title names.

  At this point, you can also select a range of records to process, indicate whether you want to run List Processing in the background, and suppress output. Press [RETURN] to accept the defaults.

Notes: Background processing is recommended if you have a large List document.

When selected, ALL-IN-1 generates the output document in the background and you can continue using your terminal for other work. ALL-IN-1 notifies you when your work is complete so you can review the output document. A log of errors is produced and can be viewed with the RL option on the List Processing menu.

Suppress output if you have a large List document and are not running List Processing in the background. This tells ALL-IN-1 not to update the count of records being processed.

- When List Processing completes, your finished documents are in the output document, which becomes the selected document. Type "P" and press [RETURN] if you want to print the output document. (Enter "TERMINAL" as the Document Destination to preview the output documents. You can always edit the output document for a final "touch-up" with global search and replace.) Then follow the instructions given in Section 4.2, "Printing in ALL-IN-1."

11.2.4 Exercise: Generating Form Letters

In this exercise, you'll create a document containing two mailing addresses and a Form document containing the template of a form letter. You will then run List Processing to create the finished form letters.

Note that your editor style must be WPS-PLUS to perform this exercise. You can change your editor style to WPS-PLUS by following the steps in Section 9.2, "Selecting an Editor."

1. First move to the Word and Document Processing menu.

WP [RETURN]	From any menu, type "WP" and press [RETURN].

2. Create a List document.

C [RETURN]	a. Type "C" and press [RETURN] to create the List document.
	b. Enter the folder name "TEST LP" and the title "List Document," as shown in Figure 11.4. Then press [RETURN]. *Note:* If ALL-IN-1 tells you that the folder does not exist, type "Y" and press [RETURN] to create it.
	c. Type the following two "records" in your List document. Type exactly what you see in the box below. Press [RETURN] after each line to create a new line.

```
<TITLE>Mr.
<FIRST>Michael
<LAST>Cramer
<COMPANY>Acorn Printing, Inc.
<ADDRESS>6643 N. Clark St.
<CITY>Chicago
<STATE>IL
<ZIP>60627
<>
<TITLE>Ms.
<FIRST>Ann
<LAST>Reynolds
<COMPANY>Adams Agency, The
<ADDRESS>660 N. Michigan Ave.
<CITY>Chicago
<STATE>IL
<ZIP>60603
<>
```

[EXIT]

d. Press [EXIT] (F10 or [GOLD] F) to exit and file your document.

3. Create a List Specification document.

C [RETURN]

a. Type "C" and press [RETURN] to create the List Specification document.

b. Enter the folder name "TEST LP" and the title "List Specification Document," as shown in Figure 11.5. Then press [RETURN].

```
                    Creating New Document

Drawer:  MAIN

Folder:  TEST LP

Title:   List Document

Keywords:

      Enter information and press RETURN,
      or press NEXT SCREEN for more fields              (more...)
```

Figure 11.4 Creating New Document form for List document

c. Type the following line in your List Specification document. This specification tells List Processing to select all records for processing. Type exactly what you see displayed in the box below this item.

```
PROCESS RECORD
```

[EXIT]

d. When you've finished your List Specification document, press [EXIT] (F10 or [GOLD] F) to exit and file the document.

4. Create a Form document.

C [RETURN]

a. Type "C" and press [RETURN] to create the Form document.

b. Enter the folder name "LP TEST" and the title "Form Document," as shown in Figure 11.6 on the next page. Then press [RETURN].

c. Type the following letter in your Form document exactly as shown in the box at the top of page 266, but substitute your own name at the bottom. Let WPS-PLUS automatically wrap each line in a paragraph. Press [GOLD] N to insert a NEW PAGE marker at the bottom.

```
                        Creating New Document

Drawer:   MAIN

Folder:   TEST LP

Title:    List Specification Document

Keywords:


       Enter information and press RETURN,
       or press NEXT SCREEN for more fields                 (more...)
```

Figure 11.5 Creating New Document form for List Specification document

```
June 23, 1995
<TITLE> <FIRST> <LAST>
<COMPANY>
<ADDRESS>
<CITY>, <STATE> <ZIP>

Dear <TITLE> <LAST>,

The purpose of this letter is to inform you of the new address and
telephone number for our Chicago office. As of July 31st, our new
address and phone will be:

      1234 Michigan Ave.
      Suite 3112
      Chicago, IL     60603
      (312) 555-5555

We look forward to serving you from our new branch offices.

Sincerely,

your-name
------------NEW PAGE------------
```

[EXIT]

d. When you've finished your Form document, press [EXIT] (F10 or [GOLD] F) to exit and file your document.

5. Run List Processing.

LP [RETURN]

a. From the Word and Document Processing menu, type "LP" and press [RETURN].

DOC [RETURN]

b. Type "DOC" and press [RETURN] to select Document Processing. ALL-IN-1 asks you to specify

```
                          Creating New Document

Drawer:   MAIN

Folder:   TEST LP

Title:    Form Document

Keywords:


       Enter information and press RETURN,
       or press NEXT SCREEN for more fields                    (more...)
```

Figure 11.6 Creating New Document form for Form document

the titles of the List document, List Specification document, and Form document.

[NEXT SCREEN]

c. Document details are remembered when you run List Processing. You should now see the names of the documents selected during the last List Processing operation. If you see such a display (similar to that shown in Figure 11.7), press [NEXT SCREEN]. This allows you to specify the documents you just created.

[UP ARROW]
Folder: **TEST LP [TAB]**
Title: **LIST DOCUMENT**
[RETURN]

d. Enter the folder and title of the List document and press [RETURN].

[UP ARROW]
Folder: **TEST LP [TAB]**
Title: **LIST SPECIFICATION DOCUMENT**
[RETURN]

e. Enter the folder and title of the List Specification document and press [RETURN].

[UP ARROW]
Folder: **TEST LP [TAB]**
Title: **FORM DOCUMENT**
[RETURN]

f. Enter the folder and title of the Form document and press [RETURN].

COD [RETURN]

g. When the Output Document Options form is displayed, type "COD" and press [RETURN].

[UP ARROW]
Folder: **TEST LP [TAB]**
Title: **OUTPUT DOCUMENT**
[RETURN]

h. Specify a folder and title for the new document, and press [RETURN]. ALL-IN-1 displays the List Processing Documents Selected screen, shown in Figure 11.7.

[RETURN]

i. If everything is correct, press [RETURN].

Note: If you need to change any of the documents, press [NEXT SCREEN] (or [GOLD] [TAB]) and go back to step 5d.

[RETURN]

j. Press [RETURN] to create finished documents for all records in the List document.

P [RETURN]

k. Type "P" and press [RETURN] to print the output document when List Processing is completed.

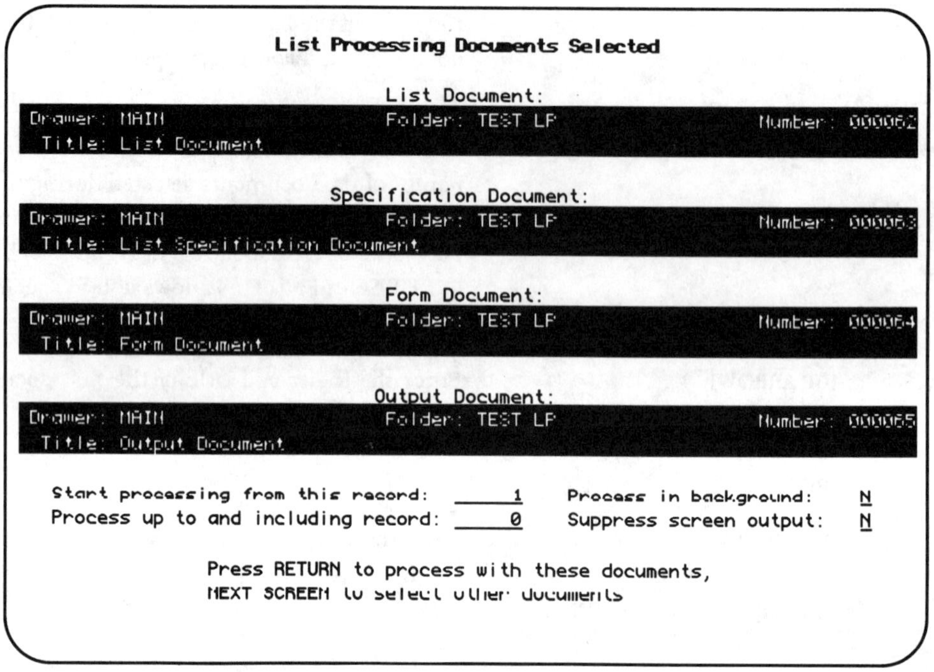

Figure 11.7 List Processing Documents Selected screen

Document destination:
TERMINAL [RETURN]

1. Type "TERMINAL" in the Document Destination field and press [RETURN] when the Printing Document form appears. ALL-IN-1 displays the finished form letters on your terminal.

11.3 PARAGRAPH NUMBERING

Paragraph Numbering is an advanced feature of WPS-PLUS that automatically numbers section titles to produce an outline format for your document. In addition, Paragraph Numbering also automatically produces a table of contents and an index for your document. In short, this feature can greatly enhance the appearance of a document while saving you time and effort.

Paragraph Numbering reads a source document and generates two output documents, as illustrated in Figure 11.8. You must first prepare the source document as input:

① Source Document

A source document contains the document's text plus:

- Section-level numbers enclosed in square brackets before each section title: "[1]" for the major section titles, "[2]" for minor section titles, "[3]" for subsections, and so forth.

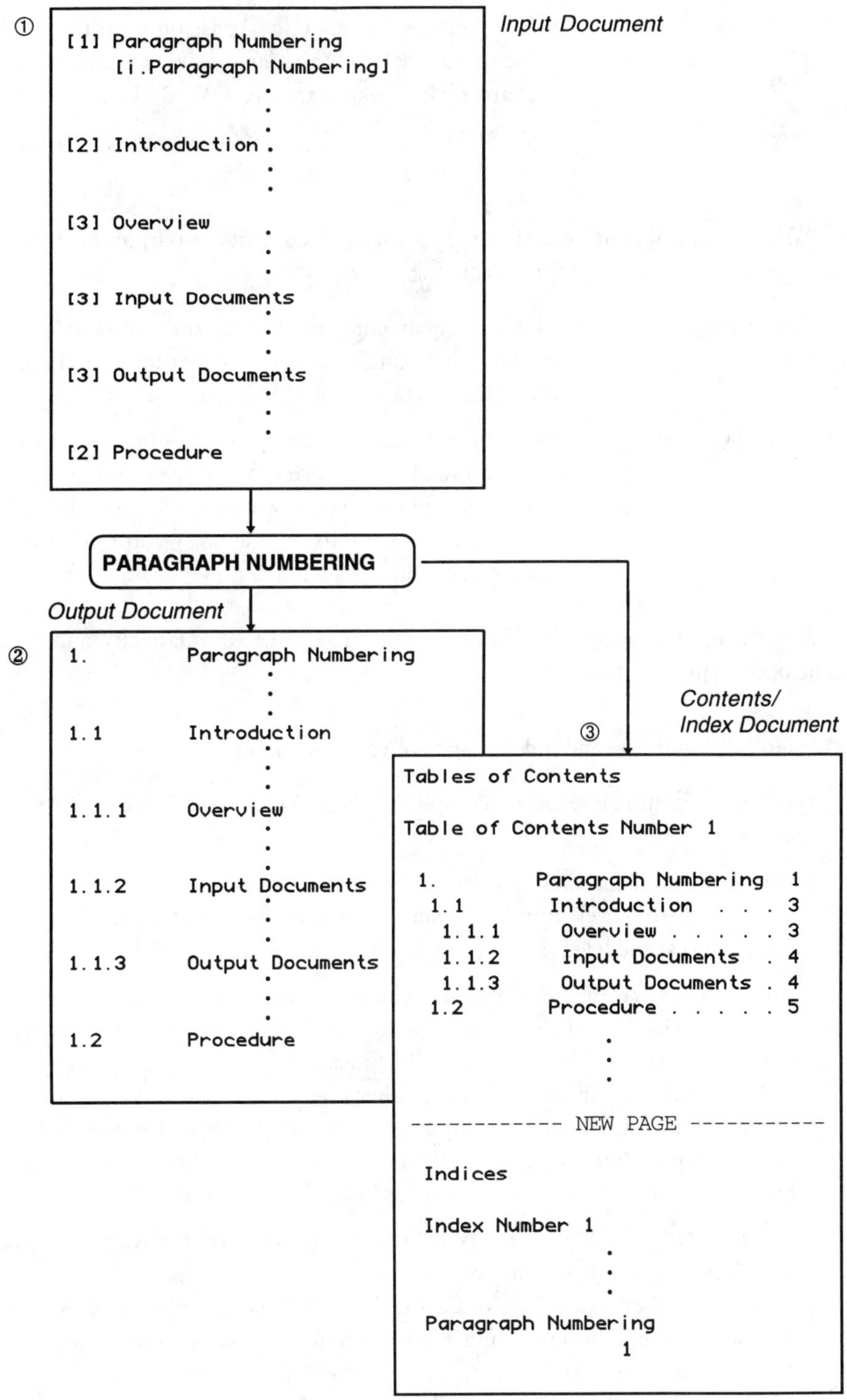

Figure 11.8 Paragraph Numbering

- Index entries that contain words you want to appear in the index; enclosed in square brackets preceded by the characters "i."—for example, [i.WPS-PLUS].
- WPS-PLUS rulers and control blocks to specify formatting of the text.

Paragraph Numbering generates the following documents as output. Each of these documents is stored in your File Cabinet.

② Output Document	The final document contains the numbered section titles, page numbers, and, of course, the text formatted according to the rulers and control blocks.
③ Table of Contents and Index	The table of contents contains a list of numbered section titles followed by the corresponding page number. Following the contents is a new page mark, then the index. The index contains a list of index keywords, followed by the corresponding page number.

Perform the following steps to number section titles automatically and create a table of contents and an index:

1. Insert level numbers and index entries in your document.

   - Edit your document with the Edit (E) option on the Word and Document Processing menu.
   - Place level numbers enclosed in brackets at the beginning of each line containing a section title. Level number [1] should be used for major topics, level [2] for minor topics, and level [3] for subtopics.
   - Add index keywords enclosed in brackets, preceded by "i."—for example, "[i.WPS-PLUS]." Enter the keyword in lowercase and place it as close as possible to the occurrence of the word in the document.

     Note that you can use characters other than square brackets to delimit level numbers and index entries as long as you indicate the characters used when you run Paragraph Numbering. If you're using brackets elsewhere in the document, enclose level numbers and index entries in braces ({}) instead.
   - Press [MENU] ([GOLD] M) to display the menu, and select the Automatic GOLD PAGE (PG) option to paginate your document.

     You should include a TOP or BOTTOM control block with the "\p" command to insert page numbers in running headers or footers. Refer to Appendix B for information on how to number pages in a WPS-PLUS document.
   - Press [EXIT] (F10 or [GOLD] F) to exit the editor and file your document.

2. Run Paragraph Numbering.[1]

   - Type "PN" and press [RETURN] to run Paragraph Numbering. ALL-IN-1 displays the Creating Output Document form.
   - Enter the drawer, folder, and title for the output document, and press [RETURN]. ALL-IN-1 displays the Paragraph Numbering Settings Menu. Table 11.2 describes options on this menu. In addition to the options described in this procedure, you should also execute the LD and RD options to specify the left and right delimiters if they are different from your source document.
   - Type "PA" and press [RETURN]. ALL-IN-1 displays the Paragraph Numbering form. Complete this form to specify the type of output you want, then press [RETURN]. If you want to generate a table of contents and an index, set both of these flags to "Y," and enter a drawer, folder, and title for the output document at the bottom of this form. Table 11.3 describes fields on this form.
   - Type "PN" and press [RETURN] to generate the output documents, table of contents, and index (if selected).

ALL-IN-1 runs Paragraph Numbering and creates the output documents. The menu is redisplayed, showing the output document as the current item. Review the output documents with the Read option before printing. If you find any problems, edit the source document and execute this procedure again.

1. Paragraph Numbering can also be performed when you print the source document. Press [NEXT SCREEN] when the Printing Document form appears. Select the PA option from the Print Settings menu, and set the appropriate parameters on the Paragraph Numbering Output form. Press [RETURN] and print as usual. The procedure described above creates the output documents without printing, allowing you to review the documents on your terminal.

Table 11.2 Paragraph Numbering Settings menu options

Enter This Menu Option	*To Perform the Following Action*
CN (Change Paragraph Numbering Styles)	Select the starting paragraph number, spacing, outline style, and numbering scheme for the output document, table of contents, and index.
PA (Paragraph Numbering Output)	Indicate whether you want to produce a table of contents, index, and/or table of authorities and specify the folder and title of the output document.
LD (Left Delimiter)	Specify the character used as the left delimiter for level numbers and index entries in your source document.
RD (Right Delimiter)	Specify the character used as the right delimiter for level numbers and index entries in your source document.
SS (Save Paragraph Numbering Settings)	Save all paragraph numbering settings on this and related forms by number. These settings can then be recalled to run paragraph numbering on other documents.
RS (Restore Paragraph Numbering Settings)	Recall settings previously saved by number to control paragraph numbering of the current source document.
CS (Save Current Settings without Paragraph Numbering)	Save all of the paragraph numbering settings with the current source document but do not run Paragraph Numbering at this time.
PN (Perform Paragraph Numbering)	Save all of the paragraph numbering settings with the current source document, run Paragraph Numbering, and generate the output document(s).

Table 11.3 Paragraph numbering settings

Paragraph Numbering Setting	*Description*
Output table of contents (Y/N)	Enter "Y" if you've included level numbers in your source document and want to create a table of contents.
Output table of authorities (Y/N)	Enter "Y" if you want to create a table of authorities.
Output index (Y/N)	Enter "Y" if you've included index entries in your source document and want to create an index.
Table of contents right margin	Enter a number from 30 to 256 to specify the right column position in the table of contents where the page numbers will appear.
Table of contents level indent	Enter a value from 0 to 50 to specify how many spaces you want each level indented in the table of contents.
Language	Specify the language used to create the source document.
Drawer, folder, title	If you entered "Y" in any of the first three fields, you must specify the drawer, folder, and title of the document that will be created when the table of contents, table of authorities, or index is generated.

The File Cabinet

PART IV

Many of the operations that manage documents in a real file cabinet can also be performed to manage documents in your ALL-IN-1 File Cabinet. The next three chapters describe how to manage your File Cabinet.

Chapter 12, "Managing Your File Cabinet," describes many of the housekeeping procedures for organizing and cleaning up your File Cabinet. The topics covered in this chapter are important to all users. You'll learn how to refile documents (including how to recover a document from the Wastebasket), copy documents, print an index of your File Cabinet, and archive documents to off-line storage.

As its title implies, Chapter 13 shows you how to work with shared documents. You'll learn how to access documents in a shared drawer, reserve shared documents for editing, create new drawers, and control access to shared drawers and documents.

The final chapter in this part, "Group Services," describes how to create and maintain group lists. A *group* is a list of users within an organization, department, or work group who need to share documents. Group lists simplify the task of controlling access to shared documents.

In the introduction to Part III, "Word and Document Processing," you learned that your ALL-IN-1 File Cabinet has the same organization as a real file cabinet. Documents with similar content are grouped together and stored in a folder, and multiple folders are stored in a single drawer. Up until now, the discussion of drawers has been limited to your Main drawer. In this part of the manual, you will see how to create additional drawers for storing shared documents. Figure IV.1 shows an example of a personal File Cabinet that contains an additional drawer for storing shared documents.

The following are important points to remember about the organization of your File Cabinet:

- Documents and messages are automatically stored in your File Cabinet when they are created or received. These documents and messages remain in your File Cabinet until you delete them.
- Only the latest revision of a document is stored in your File Cabinet. When you edit a document, the original version is purged to save disk space. If you need to save earlier versions, make a copy before editing. Be responsible, however. Most sites cannot permit unlimited use of disk space. In fact, some sites enforce document quotas to control the use of disk space.
- You should periodically clean out your File Cabinet. Some sites run procedures to purge older mail messages, but often this is the responsibility of individual users. Cleaning out your File Cabinet saves disk space and helps you access the remaining

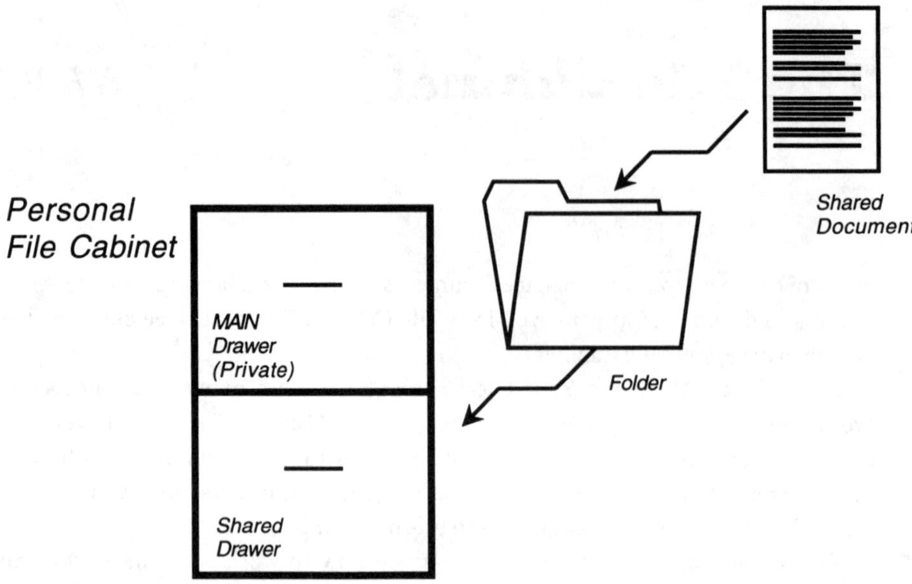

Figure IV.1 File Cabinet organization

documents more efficiently. Obsolete documents can be deleted or "archived" to off-line storage. Refer to Section 12.7, "Archiving Documents," for details.

- You have the ability to create a new, shared drawer in your File Cabinet. When you do, you can control who has access to this drawer and what operations they can perform. Your site might restrict the ability to create new drawers. Because shared drawers only need to be created once for each group that needs to share documents, it's possible that this function might be restricted to the system administrator. Whether or not you create or manage drawers, you will most likely be accessing existing drawers that contain shared documents. You'll find that accessing a document in another drawer is no more difficult that accessing a document in another folder. Refer to Chapter 13, "Sharing Documents," for further details.

FILE CABINET Q&A

Following are common questions about the File Cabinet.

Q *How do I refile a document?*

A You can move a document from one folder to another with the Refile Document (RFD) option. This option is executed from the Electronic Messaging, Word and Document Processing, and File Cabinet menus or index. Type "RFD," followed by a folder name, and press [RETURN] to move the current document—for example, "RFD CURRENT PROJECTS." If you don't remember the exact folder name, simply type "RFD" and press [RETURN]. When the Refiling Document form appears, clear the Folder Name field with [ERASE LINE], and press [FIND] to display folder names.

The Refile Folder (RFF) option moves all documents in the current folder to another folder. You can also create an index of documents, select specific documents, and move them to another folder with the Refile All Selected (XRFD) option.

Q *How do I find a document in my File Cabinet?*

A The best way to find a document or message is with the Index (I) option. Type "WP I" and press [RETURN]. ALL-IN-1 displays the Index of Documents. The form shown below in Figure IV.2 for entering selection criteria appears at the bottom of the screen. Enter as much information as possible to help ALL-IN-1 search for the document. The more information you enter, the faster ALL-IN-1 will locate the document. However, do not enter any information that you're not sure is correct. If you don't know the full, exact folder name, enter just the first few letters, or use [FIND] to determine the name.

Perhaps the most useful field on this form is at the bottom. Use the Phrase field to enter a word or phrase that you know appears in the text of the document. Be aware that a search by phrase alone will take some time. If possible, enter a folder, title, or author to limit the search.

Press [RETURN] to list all documents matching your selection criteria. You can then enter menu options to work with documents in the index. Note that the search is limited to the current drawer. To search multiple drawers, choose the Index option from the Drawer Management (DRM) menu, select the drawers you want to search, then enter the XI option.

Q *When I start ALL-IN-1, the Document Quota Exceeded menu is displayed. What do I do when I exceed my document quota?*

A The appearance of this menu indicates that you have more documents stored in your File Cabinet than permitted for your account. You must delete documents to take care of this problem. Perform the following steps:

1. Delete documents. The number of documents you must delete is indicated below the current item block. You can select and delete documents individually,

```
Folder:     ____________________
Title:      ____________________________________________________
Author:     ____________________                    Status: __________
Number:     ____  To: ____  Creation Date: __________  To: __________
Keywords:   ______  ______  ______  ______  Match all keys?: N
Importance: ______          Sensitivity: __________
Data type:  ______             Handling: ________
Phrase:     ____________________________________________
```

Figure IV.2 Form for entering selection criteria

but you might find it easier to select and delete documents collectively from an index. Refer to Section 9.9, "Deleting a Document," for specific instructions for both methods.

2. Type "EW" and press [RETURN] to empty the Wastebasket. Documents are simply filed into the Wastebasket folder when you delete them. Therefore, they remain in your File Cabinet. Emptying the Wastebasket erases the documents, thereby permanently removing them from your File Cabinet.
3. Type "RC" and press [RETURN] to recount your documents. If you still exceed your quota, you must perform the first two steps to delete additional documents.
4. Press [EXIT] (F10 or Keypad-0) to exit the Document Quota Exceeded menu when you no longer exceed your document quota. If you cannot delete enough documents to meet your quota, contact your system administrator to see if your document quota can be increased.

This problem is avoided if you periodically clean out your File Cabinet by deleting old, obsolete messages and documents.

Q *How can I get a list of folders?*

A An easy way to display a list of folders is with the [FIND] key. From the Electronic Messaging, Word and Document Processing, or File Cabinet menu, type "SEL" and press [RETURN]. ALL-IN-1 displays the Select Document form. Move to the Folder field, press [ERASE LINE] (F13 or LF) to clear the field, and press [FIND] (or [GOLD] L). ALL-IN-1 displays a list of folders.

There is also a valuable index option for listing folders. Type "FC IF" and press [RETURN]. ALL-IN-1 displays an Index of Folders (in the current drawer). Type "ALL XR" and press [RETURN] to display a summary showing the number of documents in each folder, or type "ALL XP" to print this summary.

Q *Can I get a printout of the titles and folders of my documents?*

A The Print Index option on the File Cabinet menu provides this capability. From the Electronic Messaging, Word and Document Processing, or File Cabinet menu, type "PI" and press [RETURN]. You can then select a drawer and/or folder for the listing. If you have a lot of documents, you might want to enter a folder name. After you enter selection criteria, press [RETURN], enter "B" to generate a brief listing (single line per document) or "F" to generate a full listing. Press [RETURN] and enter a document destination. ALL-IN-1 then prints information about selected documents, including the folder name, title, author, and creation date. Refer to Section 12.6, "Listing Folders and Documents," for an example.

Q *What do the reorganization options do? How often should I reorganize my File Cabinet?*

A File Cabinets have an associated file that describes each and every document in the cabinet. It is somewhat like the index card file that catalogs books at a library. Over time, the organization of this file worsens as documents are added, deleted, and so on. The File Cabinet Reorganization (FCO) and Drawer Reorganization (DRO) options reorganize the index file by cleaning out entries for deleted files and sorting the remaining entries for improved ordering. File Cabinet operations usually run faster after the File Cabinet has been reorganized.

You can reorganize your File Cabinet at any time, but avoid "overorganizing." Once a month should be sufficient for most users. Also, your File Cabinet drawers are typically reorganized by the Janitor when the Wastebasket is emptied. You might not have to reorganize your File Cabinet yourself if this is the case.

Q *How does the File Cabinet differ from my VMS directory?*

A Both the File Cabinet and your VMS directory are required to store and keep track of ALL-IN-1 documents. The ALL-IN-1 File Cabinet is actually a series of files and directories that resides one level below your "home" directory (your default directory upon logging into the system). The VMS directory name where ALL-IN-1 files reside is typically [*username*.ALLIN1] or [*username*.A1], but it can vary from site to site. Your system administrator knows for sure.

It is extremely important that you do not attempt to access or manipulate any file in your ALL-IN-1 subdirectory using DCL commands. This will most likely corrupt your File Cabinet.

Q *What happens to a document when it is archived?*

A When you archive a document, the actual contents of the document are moved to a different area—the current archive area. Therefore, you cannot edit, read, or print an archived document. Information about the document remains in your File Cabinet index, so you can recover the document from archive storage if the need arises.

You should archive old documents that are not referenced very often but that cannot be deleted because they contain important information. You can easily archive the current document with the Archive Document Now (ADN) option. You can restore a document from archive storage to your File Cabinet with the Recover Archive Document (RAC) option.

Q *How do I determine which drawers I can access?*

A The Index of Available Drawers is the easiest way to determine which drawers you can access. From any menu, type "FC DRM IAD" and press [RETURN] twice. ALL-IN-1 displays an index of the drawers you can access. At this point, you can press [GOLD] M to display the menu of options for managing these drawers, or you can press [EXIT] (F10 or Keypad-0) to clear the index. Chapter 13, "Sharing Documents," describes the menu options for managing drawers.

Q *Why would I need to create another drawer?*

A There are two basic reasons for creating another drawer, both of which involve sharing documents or messages. If neither of these situations applies to you, do not create additional drawers.

- You need to share documents with other users and none of the other users has already created a shared drawer in which to place these documents. If another user has already created a shared drawer, then simply add this drawer to your File Cabinet.

- You've granted mail access to someone who handles your mail. This implicitly gives this person access to documents in your Main drawer. In this situation, you might want to create a new *unshared* drawer in which to store private documents.

Refer to Section 13.6, "Creating a New Drawer," for information on how to create a drawer.

Q *What is the difference between creating a drawer and adding a drawer?*

A *Creating* a new drawer actually creates a new area in your File Cabinet for storing documents. When you create the drawer, you must indicate whether it is shared and who has access to it if it is shared. To share documents between members of a work group, a one member of the group needs to create a drawer—once! Other members of the work group can then select this drawer and create, read, edit, and print shared documents.

Any member of the group can *add* the existing shared drawer to his or her File Cabinet. This does not actually move or copy any documents. It simply adds information to your File Cabinet index that makes the drawer *appear* as if it were in your File Cabinet. It is easier to select a drawer that you've added to your File Cabinet, primarily because you can reference the name you assigned to the drawer. Refer to Section 13.4, "Adding an Existing Drawer to Your File Cabinet," for further information.

Q *What happens when I reserve a document? How do I reserve a document?*

A When documents are shared, it's possible that two people will want to work with the same document at the same time. This can cause problems that can be avoided if you reserve a shared document before making modifications. To reserve the current shared document, simply enter the Reserve Document (RSV) option. Other users will be able to read the document, but they cannot edit the document until you cancel your reservation with the Unreserve Document (URV) option. Additional menu options are available for reserving documents. Refer to Section 13.2, "Reserving Documents," for descriptions of these options.

Q *Why can't I find my Read folder? Where is my ??? folder?*

A If you access other drawers because you're sharing documents, it's easy to forget that you're working in another drawer. Check the drawer name that appears at the top of the index or menu. If it is not your Main drawer, this might explain why you cannot find familiar folders. Remember, most index listings are limited to the current drawer. To return to your Main drawer, simply type "SDR MAIN" and press [RETURN]. Then create an index for the folder.

Q *Why can't I create a group?*

A Groups are lists of users and are similar to distribution lists. These lists are helpful when granting access to a shared drawer. Instead of entering the usernames of everyone in the department, you can enter a group name instead. Groups are defined and updated with Group Services. You must be authorized by the system administrator to work with groups. There are two reasons why the privilege to maintain groups is restricted:

- Groups (lists) are shared by everyone on the system, just like the system distribution lists. Great care must be taken when adding members to or removing members from a group because everyone relies on these lists to be accurate.
- Modifications to group lists result in changes to important system files. These files are used systemwide for security purposes. (However, this does not imply that a group maintainer is given any special security clearance.)

FILE CABINET DOs AND DON'Ts

Here are some suggestions for working with the File Cabinet:

Do

- Spend time planning the organization of your File Cabinet before creating documents. Identify folder names you will need before you create documents. This avoids a lot of refiling. If you work with many documents, good naming conventions for folder names and titles will help you locate documents down the road. If you need to share documents, work with other users to create a shared drawer in someone's account and to adopt standards for the creation of folders and documents.
- Get in the habit of using keywords. Next to the folder name and title, keywords are the most important information you can specify to locate a document quickly. Note, however, that this method of searching for documents works only if you've assigned keywords to your documents.

  You can easily assign two or three keywords when creating a document. If you want to assign keywords to an existing document, select the document and execute the Update Index (U) option.
- When adding an existing drawer to your File Cabinet, change the name to the format *owner:drawer-name*. This makes it easier to identify the owner of a drawer in the following instances:
  - The drawer name is displayed in the current item block of the menu.
  - The drawer name is displayed at the top of the index of documents.
  - A list of drawer names is displayed when you press [FIND] while the cursor is in the Drawer field on the Select Document form.

Changing the drawer name to this format also helps you distinguish the drawers you created from the drawers you simply added to your File Cabinet.

Don't

- Don't create a new drawer in your File Cabinet just to organize documents. Instead, create new folders for this purpose. You should only create a new drawer if you need to share documents or messages and no shared drawer currently exists.

Managing Your File Cabinet

CHAPTER 12

This chapter describes utilities that help you organize and maintain your File Cabinet. You'll learn how to refile, cross-file, and copy documents and how to recover a deleted document from the Wastebasket. You'll also learn how to print hard-copy listings of the titles in your File Cabinet and how to archive documents that you don't use very often but nevertheless don't want to delete. These techniques are important for all users. Even if you only access ALL-IN-1 to send and receive mail, you'll be surprised at how fast the number of documents in your File Cabinet grows. Performing periodic maintenance and cleanup helps you locate and access documents more efficiently.

This chapter teaches you how to perform the following tasks:

- Access File Cabinet management.
- Recover a document from the Wastebasket and empty the Wastebasket to conserve storage space.
- Refile and cross-file documents to other folders to improve the organization of your File Cabinet.
- Make a copy of a document to preserve the original intact or to help you get started preparing a new, similar document.
- Make a copy of a document and convert its format so that you can use a different editor to work with it.
- Print hard-copy listings of folder and document details.
- Archive documents to off-line storage to conserve space.

12.1 ACCESSING FILE CABINET MANAGEMENT

The File Cabinet menu lists a number of options for organizing and maintaining your File Cabinet. As with any menu, the current document is identified in the upper right-hand corner, and many of the menu selections perform operations on the current document. You don't necessarily have to move to this menu to perform these operations. Most options on this menu can also be entered from the Electronic Messaging and Word and Document Processing menus.

Perform the following steps to access File Cabinet Management:

FC [RETURN]	a. From any menu, type "FC" and press [RETURN]. ALL-IN-1 displays the File Cabinet menu.
[NEXT SCREEN]	b. There are multiple screens of menu options in File Cabinet Management. To see additional options, press [NEXT SCREEN] (or [GOLD] A). If you know the option you want, you can enter it from any menu screen.
***menu-option* [RETURN]**	c. Type the menu option and press [RETURN]. Table 12.1 describes options on the File Cabinet menu.

Table 12.1 File Cabinet menu options

Enter This Menu Option	*To Perform the Following Action*
ADL (Archive Document Later)	Cross-file the current document in the Pending Archive folder and mark it for archiving during the next system archive operation.
ADN (Archive Document Now)	Archive the current document immediately.
AUA (Automatic Archiving)	Select documents for archiving by folder and modification date.
CD (Convert Document)	Copy the current document and convert the format to a new editor style.
CLA (Cancel Later Archiving)	Cancel the later archiving of the current document (cancel ADL).
DF (Delete Folder)	Delete all documents in the current folder, refiling them in the Wastebasket folder.
DRM (Drawer Management)	Display the Drawer Management menu to manage drawers in your File Cabinet.
DRO (Drawer Reorganization)	Sort and reorganize the index for a single drawer in your File Cabinet to improve access to documents.
DTF (Delete Temporary Files)	Delete the temporary files created in your account by batch and print operations. The log file created when you run List Processing in the background is an example. Deleting these files frees up disk space.
EW (Empty the Wastebasket)	Immediately erase all documents in the Wastebasket folder from the disk. When this operation is completed, the Wastebasket folder is eliminated until you delete another document.
FA (File Attachment as Document)	File a copy of an attachment to the current message as a separate document. This allows you to edit the attachment.

Table 12.1 *(continued)*

Enter This Menu Option	*To Perform the Following Action*
FAM (File Attachment as Message)	File a copy of the attachment to the current message as a message. This is useful if the attached document is a forwarded message.
FCO (File Cabinet Reorganization)	Sort and reorganize the index for your File Cabinet to improve access to documents.
FMD (Format Document)	Create a formatted copy of the current document. This creates a nonrevisable output document that is already formatted for printing. You can then do the following: • Print the formatted copy without having to wait for formatting to be completed. • Send the formatted copy to individuals who need to read or print the document but not revise it. • Send the document to someone for printing on a system without ALL-IN-1.
I (Index of Documents)	Create an index of documents with which to work.
IA (Index of Attachments)	Create an index listing all of the documents attached to the current message.
ID (Index of Drawers)	Create an index of drawers with which to work.
IDR (Index of Documents Awaiting Retrieval)	Display an index of documents that you want to be restored from off-line archive storage.
IF (Index of Folders)	Display the number of documents in selected folders.
IRD (Index of Reserved Documents)	Display an index of shared documents reserved for editing.
L (Locate Document)	Display a menu containing options for selecting a document.
MCD (Make Copy of Document)	Copy an existing document to create a new, additional document.
MCF (Make Copy of Folder)	Copy all documents in a specified folder.
MDO (Modify Document Access)	Change who has access to the current shared document and what privileges these individuals have to work with the document. See Section 13.7, "Working with Advanced Shared Drawers."
PDO (Print Document Access)	Print a listing of who has access to the current shared document and what types of access have been granted.
PI (Print Index)	Print a listing of documents showing the folder, title, document number, author, editor, file specification, keywords, and date.
RAD (Restore Archived Document)	Retrieve a previously archived document and move it back to your File Cabinet. This option sends a request to the system administrator to restore the document if it has been moved to off-line storage.
RFD (Refile Document)	Move a document to a different folder.
RFF (Refile Folder)	Move all documents in one folder to another folder.

(continued)

Table 12.1 File Cabinet menu options *(continued)*

Enter This Menu Option	*To Perform the Following Action*
RPC (Replace Document Copy)	Replace the working document previously reserved for editing with the updated copy. See Chapter 13, "Sharing Documents."
RSC (Reserve and Copy Document)	Make a copy of the current shared document and reserve the working document to prevent others from modifying it while you're editing the copy.
RSV (Reserve Document)	Reserve a shared document for editing. This prevents others from modifying it until you finish making revisions. See Chapter 13, "Sharing Documents."
SDR (Select Drawer)	Select a new drawer containing documents with which you want to work.
SEL (Select)	Select a document to work with (edit, delete, print, etc.).
SP (Scratch Pad)	Display the Scratch Pad menu.
TR (Training)	Start computer-based instruction for File Cabinet Maintenance.
U (Update Index Information)	Change the folder, title, author, handling, or keywords for the current document.
URV (Unreserve Document)	Cancel the reservation requested with the RSV or RSC options. This gives others access to the document. See Chapter 13, "Sharing Documents."
XFD (Cross-file Document)	Cross-file the current document in a separate folder without making an additional copy.
XFF (Cross-file Folder)	Cross-file all documents in the current folder to a new folder.

12.1.1 Exercise: Emptying the Wastebasket

The following exercise shows you how to empty the Wastebasket folder in your current drawer. (Note that each drawer has its own Wastebasket folder.) If document quotas are enforced on your system, you might need to perform these steps to reduce your current document count as you approach your quota. However, system managers frequently run the Janitor to empty all users' Wastebaskets, so you can always wait until the next Janitor run for your Wastebasket to be emptied.

It's recommended that before emptying the Wastebasket, you first review documents to make sure that nothing you need will be deleted. This exercise shows you how to review the Wastebasket and recover a document.

1. Move to the File Cabinet Maintenance menu.

FC [RETURN]	From any menu, type "FC" and press [RETURN].

2. List documents in the Wastebasket, review the list, and recover a document.

I WASTEBASKET [RETURN]

a. Type "I WASTEBASKET" and press [RETURN]. ALL-IN-1 displays the Index of Documents shown in Figure 12.1. A message indicating that no documents could be found is displayed if you have no documents in the Wastebasket folder.

1 RFD *folder* [RETURN]

b. Type "1 RFD" followed by a folder name to recover the first document from the Wastebasket folder. You can recover additional documents by typing the line number followed by "RFD" and a folder name.

3. Empty the Wastebasket.

NOTE: Once you empty the Wastebasket, all documents in this folder are removed from your File Cabinet and cannot be recovered. Emptying the Wastebasket is analogous to shredding documents.

Skip this step if you do not want to empty the Wastebasket at this time.

EW [RETURN]

a. Type "EW" and press [RETURN]. ALL-IN-1 asks you to confirm that you really want to delete the documents in your Wastebasket.

```
                              Index of Documents
(Selections: 0     ) (Drawer: MAIN                      ) (New messages: 2  )
------------------------------------------------------------------------------
  No.  Folder           Title                             Modified     Status
------------------------------------------------------------------------------
>  1   WASTEBASKET      PN TOC                            11-Sep-1992
   2   WASTEBASKET      Monthly Status report             30-Aug-1992 SENT
   3   WASTEBASKET      October Conference                30-Aug-1992 SENT
   4   WASTEBASKET      VMS Mail                          29-Aug-1992 READ
   5   WASTEBASKET      Event -> 01-Sep-1992 10:00am J 21-Aug-1992 SENT

------------------------------------------------------------------------------
Move to item, and enter option (press GOLD MENU to see options, or HELP for
more information)
```

Figure 12.1 Index of Documents

Y [RETURN]

b. Type "Y" and press [RETURN]. ALL-IN-1 empties the Wastebasket and redisplays the menu.

12.2 REFILING A DOCUMENT

You might occasionally need to move documents from one drawer or folder to another to improve the organization of your File Cabinet. The Refile Document (RFD) option on the File Cabinet menu moves a single document, and Refile Folder (RFF) moves all documents within a folder. Either of these operations can be performed from the Electronic Messaging, Word and Document Processing, and File Cabinet menus.

Perform the following steps to move the current document to another drawer or folder:

RFD [RETURN]

a. Type "RFD" and press [RETURN] to refile the current document. The Refiling Document form shown in Figure 12.2 is displayed.

Hint: You can type the new folder name after the menu option to save time—for example, "RFD SALES." The Refiling Document form is not displayed when you do this.

Drawer: ***drawer***
Folder: ***folder***
Title: ***title***

b. Type the new folder name. You can also move the document to another drawer or change the title with this form. Press [BACKSPACE] (F12) to move backward, press [TAB] to move forward, and press [ERASE LINE] (LF or F13) to clear a field.

Hint: Press [ERASE LINE] (LF or F13) and then [FIND] (or [GOLD] L) while the cursor is in either the Drawer or Folder field to list existing names.

```
                         Refiling Document

Drawer:  MAIN

Folder:

Title:   Health Insurance Packet

Enter the destination information for the new document and press RETURN
```

Figure 12.2 Refiling Document form

[RETURN] c. Press [RETURN] to complete the Refiling Document form. ALL-IN-1 redisplays the menu, showing the current document in the new folder.

Note: Specifying a new folder name implicitly creates the new folder. ALL-IN-1 might ask if you want to create this folder. This question keeps you from accidentally creating two similarly named folders. You can eliminate this prompt by setting the New Folder Confirmation prompt to "N" in Set Working Conditions.

12.3 CROSS-FILING A DOCUMENT

The content of certain documents might logically fall under two or more categories. When this is the case, you might want to file these documents in two or more folders by cross-filing the document. The Cross-file Document (XFD) option on the File Cabinet menu cross-files the current document, and the Cross-file Folder (XFF) option cross-files all documents in the current folder.

It's important to note that only a single copy of a cross-filed document exists, even though the document is listed in multiple folders. You can edit the document by selecting the document from any of the folders, but you must delete the document from every folder to move it to the Wastebasket. Note also that you cannot cross-file a document between drawers. This restriction is due to the method ALL-IN-1 uses to index documents within a drawer.

12.4 MAKING A COPY OF A DOCUMENT

Most people who create a lot of documents have many with similar content or format. If this is true for you, you'll find it handy to copy an existing document to get you started when preparing a new, similar document. You might also want to make a copy of an important document before making modifications that require approval. By default, ALL-IN-1 purges older revisions of a document whenever you complete an edit session. For this reason, editing the original might be risky.

The Make Copy of Document (MCD) option on the File Cabinet menu creates a copy of the current document. The copy of a document is treated as an entirely separate document. You can edit, delete, and refile the copy without affecting the original. The Make Copy of Folder (MCF) option copies an entire folder.

In addition to these options, you can also create a copy of an existing document when creating a new document with either of the following procedures:

- Before completing the Creating New Document form, press [NEXT SCREEN] (or [GOLD] A) and fill in the drawer, folder, and title of the existing document under the title "Template Document."

- Complete the Creating New Document form as usual, then press [GOLD] G when the editor is started. Complete the Get a Document form to retrieve the existing document. This method does *not* copy the print settings for the original document, however.

Be cautious when making copies of documents, particularly with the Make Copy of Folder option. You can quickly exceed your document quota or, at the least, use up disk space and expand your File Cabinet to an unmanageable size by making copies.

Perform the following steps to create a copy of the current document:

MCD [RETURN]	a. Type "MCD" and press [RETURN] to create a copy of the current document. The Making Copy of Document form is displayed.
Drawer: ***drawer*** Folder: ***folder*** Title: ***title***	b. Type the folder name and press [TAB]. To select a new title, press [LINE FEED] (F13) to clear the title and type a new title.
[RETURN]	c. Press [RETURN] to complete the form. ALL-IN-1 redisplays the menu or index.

12.5 CONVERTING THE FORMAT OF A DOCUMENT

The Convert Document (CD) option copies the document and converts the format from that of the original editor to the format recognized by a new editor. You can then use the new editor to work with the output document. Typically, you might convert a document for one of the following reasons:

- The document was originally prepared with a less sophisticated editor, and now you want to work on it with a more advanced editor.
- You want to send the document to someone who is unfamiliar with the editor used to create the document, and you need to convert the document to a format familiar to the other person.

During document conversion, control codes and special characters understood by the current editor are replaced with codes understood by the new editor. The resulting document usually requires some editing to correct problems caused by differences in the two editors. Keep the following points in mind when converting a document:

- Documents convert fairly well when converting from a less sophisticated editor to a more sophisticated editor. The output document generally requires no cleanup. This is not true when converting a document in the opposite direction. Features not supported by the target editor generally do not convert properly. For example, all bolding and underlining is removed when you convert a document from WPS-PLUS to ASCII EDT.

- Some cleanup might be required when converting a document between more advanced editors, such as WPS-PLUS and WordPerfect.

  When converting from WPS-PLUS to WordPerfect, most attributes convert correctly. Font selection can be a problem, however, and you might have to set the fonts in the output document with the [FONT] function. Also, page layout and pagination settings set during printing of the WPS-PLUS document might have to be set in the WordPerfect document with the [FORMAT] function.

  When converting from WordPerfect to WPS-PLUS, many of the common attributes convert correctly. You will have to rework parts of the document created with any WordPerfect function that is not available in WPS-PLUS. Tables, graphics, and some special characters are examples. "Tables" can be created in a WPS-PLUS document by setting up a new ruler with appropriate tab stops or by creating a number of multicolumn blocks. Line drawings can be converted to TDE pictures by selecting and cutting the drawing, opening a picture, and pasting the drawing in the TDE editor. Technical characters can be used to replace special characters that don't convert properly. Finally, if the output WPS-PLUS document contains too many rulers, they can be eliminated by selecting a block of text, pressing [CUT], and then pressing [PASTE] (to restore the text without the rulers).

To copy the current document and convert its format, type "CD" and press [RETURN]. ALL-IN-1 asks for the new data type. Enter a new data type or press [FIND] to list possible entries. Data types for editors discussed in this manual include ASCII EDT, ASCII EVE_EDT, ASCII EVE_WPS, WPSPLUS, and WPCORP. ALL-IN-1 then asks for a title for the new document. It's a good idea to include something in the title to distinguish the copy from the original. Include the data type in parenthesis after the title, for example. When you press [RETURN], ALL-IN-1 converts the document and redisplays the menu.

12.6 LISTING FOLDERS AND DOCUMENTS

You will find a hard-copy listing of the items in your File Cabinet to be helpful when cleaning up your File Cabinet or when trying to find a document. Two options on the File Cabinet menu provide an inventory of your File Cabinet:

Index of Folders (IF)	This option creates an index listing of all folders in your File Cabinet. The Read and Print options available on the Index menu list the total number of documents and messages in selected folders. (See Figure 12.3.)
Print Index (PI)	This option creates a hard-copy listing showing key pieces of information for selected documents. This information includes the folder, title, document number, author, edit style, and keywords. (Look ahead to Figure 12.5 on page 292.)

Directory Listing of File Cabinet Folders

Date: 24-Sep-1994 Page: 1

Folder Name	Documents	Messages	Archived	Total
CREATED	0	3	0	3
DEPT WORK SCHEDULES	1	0	0	1
DISTRIBUTION LISTS	6	0	0	6
EAST BAY UTILITIES PROJECT	1	0	0	1
ENGLISH DICTIONARIES	1	0	0	1
INBOX	0	2	0	2
	•			
	•			

Figure 12.3 Listing of folders produced with the Index of Folders

Perform the following steps to display or print a summary showing the number of documents per folder:

IF [RETURN]	a. Type "IF" and press [RETURN] to create an index of folders. ALL-IN-1 displays an index of folder names.
ALL [RETURN]	b. Type "ALL" and press [RETURN] to select all folders for the summary listing. (You can also type the line numbers for specific folders and press [SELECT] to list only these folders.)
XR [RETURN]	c. Type "XR" and press [RETURN] to display the summary.
XP [RETURN]	Or type "XP" and press [RETURN] to print the summary.
[RETURN]...	d. If you selected the Multiple Read option, press [RETURN] to review pages of the summary.
Document destination: *printer* **[RETURN]**	If you selected the Multiple Print option, complete the Printing Document form and press [RETURN]. ALL-IN-1 displays or prints a listing similar to the one shown in Figure 12.3.
[EXIT]	e. Press [EXIT] (F10 or Keypad-0) to exit the Index of Folders.

```
                     Print Index of a Folder

Drawer:  MAIN

Folder:

Enter information and press RETURN.
Leave FOLDER blank to print index of all folders.
```

Figure 12.4 Print Index of a Folder form

Perform the following steps to read or print a summary showing the number of documents per folder:

PI [RETURN]	a. Type "PI" and press [RETURN] to print an index of documents. ALL-IN-1 displays the form shown in Figure 12.4.
Folder: ***folder* [TAB]...**	b. Enter any information you want to select documents for the listing. Press [ERASE LINE] (LF or F13) to clear the Folder field to list all documents in the current drawer. *Note:* Leaving all fields blank to select all documents could result in a massive printout, depending on the number of documents you maintain.
[RETURN]	c. Press [RETURN] after entering selection criteria.
B[RETURN] or **F[RETURN]**	d. Type "B" and press [RETURN] to select a brief listing (one line per document), or type "F" and press [RETURN] to select a full listing.
Document destination: ***printer* [RETURN]**	e. Complete the Printing Document form and press [RETURN]. ALL-IN-1 prints a listing similar to the one shown in Figure 12.5 on the next page.

12.7 ARCHIVING DOCUMENTS

Archiving documents to off-line storage makes efficient use of storage media. Infrequently used documents are moved from expensive disk storage to less expensive magnetic tape storage. These documents are preserved on magnetic tape and can be reloaded into on-line disk storage when there is a need to modify, display, or print them.

```
Date: 26-Nov-1994   Directory Listing of File Cabinet Documents        Page: 1
                    ==========================================

Drawer: MAIN

------------------------------------------------------------------------------
Folder:         DOCUMENTS                            Document Number: 000002
Title:          ALL-IN-1 V3.1 New Features
Author:         Sarah Washington

Handling:                                 Document Type: DOCUMENT
Data Set Type: WPSPLUS
Keywords:
Created Date:   11-Nov-1994 02:55pm       Modified Date: 11-Nov-1994 02:55pm
Filename:       [.DOC2]ZVMILBBJR.WPL
File Size (blocks): 182
------------------------------------------------------------------------------
Folder:         INBOX                                Document Number: 000014
Title:          RE: Notes on Meeting with East Bay Utilities
Author:         Sarah Washington

Handling:                                 Document Type: MAIL
Data Set Type: WPSPLUS
Keywords:
Created Date:   20-Nov-1994 08:01pm       Modified Date: 20-Nov-1994 08:01pm
Filename:       OA$SHARA19:ZVMRSLO11.WPL
File Size (blocks): 3
------------------------------------------------------------------------------
Folder:         OUTBOX                               Document Number: 000013
Title:          Health Insurance Packet
Author:         Sarah Washington
```

Figure 12.5 Listing of documents produced with Print Index

Archiving in ALL-IN-1 is performed in stages. When you archive a document, it is not removed and written to tape immediately. Instead, the document is simply moved from your File Cabinet and placed in the current open archive area. The process is shown in Figure 12.6.

An *archive area* is storage area, much like your File Cabinet. Performing the Archive Document Now (ADN) operation moves the current document from your File Cabinet to the current open archive area, as seen in step 1 of Figure 12.6. You can move the document from the current archive area back to your File Cabinet with the Retrieve Archived Document (RAD) option. All users can archive documents to the open archive area and retrieve documents from this area, as seen in step 2.

Eventually, the open archive area fills up as users archive documents. In the next stage of archiving, the system administrator closes the old archive area and opens a new archive area. Archive Area B in Figure 12.6 is an example of a closed archive area. Users cannot move documents to a closed area, but they can retrieve them from this area with the RAD option, as seen in step 3.

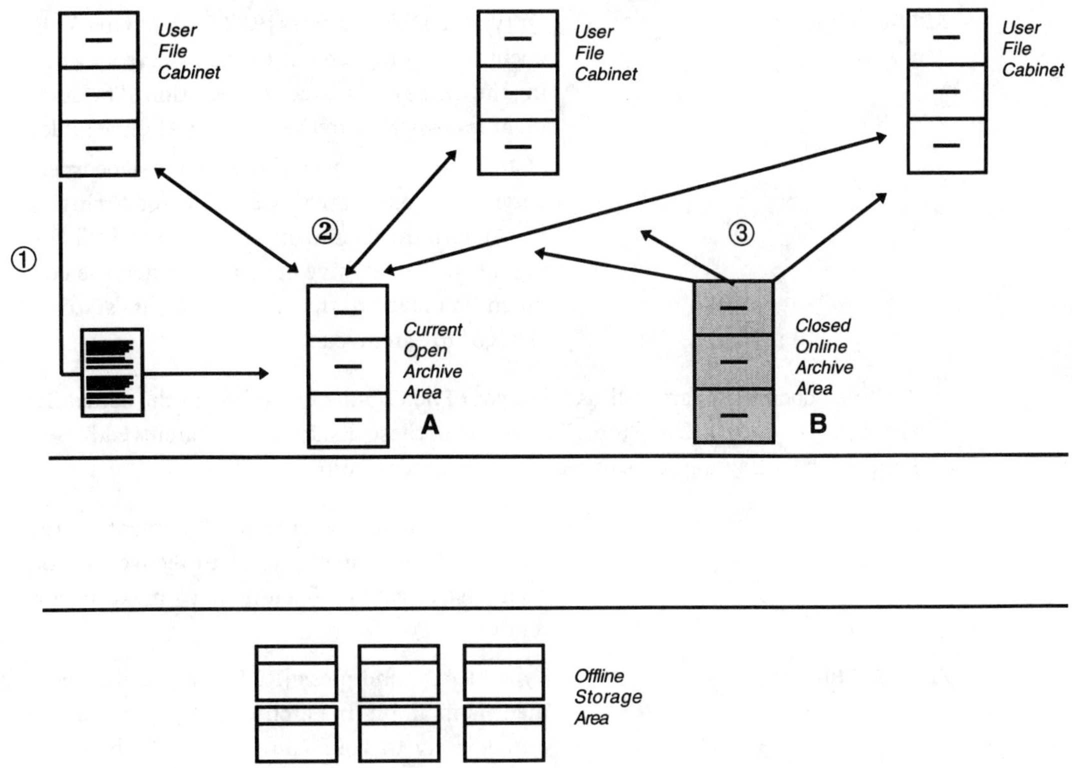

Figure 12.6 Archiving documents

In the final stage of archiving, the system administrator moves all documents in a closed area from on-line disk storage to off-line tape storage. This is analogous to moving all the documents in Archive Area B to a basement storage area. Once Archive Area B is emptied in this manner, it can be used as a new open archive area. By this time, Archive Area A might be full and might therefore be closed.

You can still retrieve a document from off-line storage with the RAD option. However, you'll have to wait for the system administrator to load the document back onto the disk. In the analogy shown in Figure 12.6, this is similar to waiting for someone to run to a basement storage area, locate the document, and return it to your file cabinet.

You'll find the process of archiving and recovering archived documents as easy as refiling. Following are the step-by-step procedures for archiving and recovering documents.

Perform the following steps to archive the current document:

ADN [RETURN]	a. Type "ADN" and press [RETURN] to immediately move the current document to the archive area. A message is displayed indicating that the document is being archived.

ADL [RETURN]

Or type "ADL" and press [RETURN] to mark the document for movement to the archive area during the next system archive operation. The document is cross-filed in the Pending Archive folder.

Note: You can cancel the Archive Document Later (ADL) option with Cancel Later Archiving (CLA) *until* the document is actually moved during the system archive operation. When the document is moved to the archive area, its status is changed to "archived."

Archived documents are still listed in your File Cabinet even though the actual file has been moved to an archive area. The status of these documents is "archived."

Perform the following steps to recover a document from an archive area:

a. Make sure that the current document is the archived document you want to recover. If not, then first select the document to make it current.

RAD [RETURN]

b. Type "RAD" and press [RETURN]. If the document is in an on-line archive area, it is restored immediately to your File Cabinet. If the document is off-line, you will receive an electronic message with the document attached as soon as the system administrator recovers the document from off-line storage.

The Automatic Archiving (AUA) option sets up your File Cabinet so that documents are automatically archived. This option allows you to select documents for automatic archiving based on modification date and folder name. Be cautious, however. Automatic archiving moves documents based solely on the modification date (date of last edit)—not the date the document was last read or printed.

Sharing Documents

CHAPTER 13

All organizations need to share information. Most organizations have a central files area for storing shared documents, for example. ALL-IN-1 allows you to share electronic documents with other users by placing the documents in shared File Cabinet drawers. A shared drawer is much like a real file cabinet drawer in a central files area; documents in the drawer are accessible to many individuals.

This chapter teaches you how to work with File Cabinet drawers to share documents. You'll learn how to perform the following tasks:

- Select a different drawer to work with a shared document.
- Reserve a shared document for modification. No one else can make changes to the document while you have reserved it.
- Access the Drawer Management menu to create and manage drawers.
- Add an existing shared drawer to your File Cabinet. This makes it easier to select and work with documents in the drawer.
- Create a new drawer in your File Cabinet.
- Control access to a shared drawer in your File Cabinet.

The key to learning how to share documents is understanding the concept of File Cabinet drawers. It helps to think of a real file cabinet like the one shown in Figure 13.1. The File Cabinet in the figure belongs to Sarah Washington. It contains two drawers: Main and Projects. Main is a private drawer.[1] Sarah alone has access to this drawer, which she uses to store mail messages and private documents. Projects, on the other hand, is a shared drawer. Sarah allows everyone in the Information Systems Department to access this drawer because it contains project documents. Two other individuals, Kenneth Jefferson and Carol Adams, have also been given access to the Projects drawer. Granting access to a shared drawer in ALL-IN-1 is much like handing someone a key to the drawer.

Creating a shared drawer and defining the access list is the first step in sharing documents. You or someone in your work group can create a shared drawer by following

1. Remember that your Main drawer is private by default unless you grant mail access, as described in Chapter 8, or modify the drawer's access. In the example shown in Figure 13.1, Sarah Washington has not granted any other individuals access to her Main drawer.

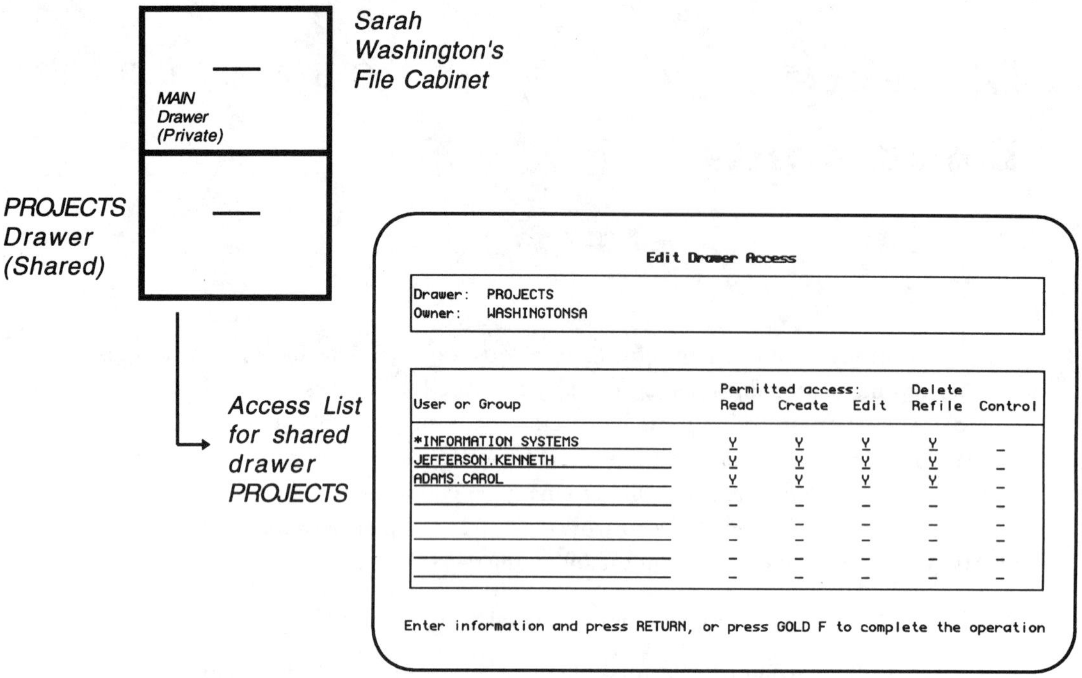

Figure 13.1 Shared drawer and its associated access list

the procedure outlined in Section 13.6, "Creating a New Drawer." The person who creates the shared drawer has complete control over who has access to it. Section 13.5, "Controlling Access to a Drawer," describes how to modify the access list.

The next step in sharing documents is to create documents in the shared drawer. Anyone with access to the drawer can select the drawer from the Word and Document Processing menu and choose options to create, read, edit, and print documents (assuming proper privileges).

Figure 13.2 shows one way to select and access a document in a shared drawer. Carol Adams occasionally needs to work with a document in the Projects drawer. She enters the Select option from the Word and Document Processing menu and completes the form shown in Figure 13.2. By selecting this new document, Carol effectively "closes" her Main drawer and "opens" the shared drawer belonging to Sarah Washington. Carol can now read, edit, and print the selected document, or she can easily select and work with other documents in this drawer. When finished, she will most likely follow the same procedure to select a document in her Main drawer, essentially closing the shared drawer and opening her private drawer.

Figure 13.3 shows another method for accessing a shared drawer. Kenneth Jefferson frequently works with documents in the shared drawer. He therefore chooses to add this drawer to his File Cabinet. This operation doesn't move or copy the drawer to his

```
                    Selecting Current Document

Drawer: [WASHINGTON]PROJECTS

Folder: PLANNING

Title:  E. Bay Utilities Implementation Plan

Number: 000001

Enter information and press RETURN, or press GOLD E to expand drawer field
```

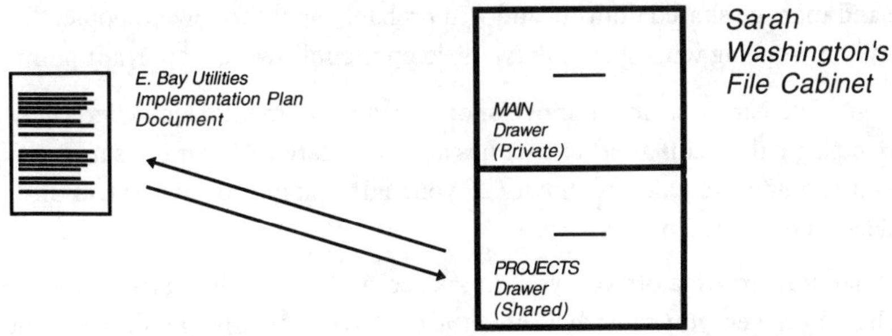

Figure 13.2 Selecting a document in a shared drawer

```
                    Add Drawer to File Cabinet

Owner:  WASHINGTON

Drawer: PROJECTS

Drawer name: WASHINGTON:PROJECTS

Description: Information Systems Projects Drawer

Enter a name for the drawer and press RETURN
```

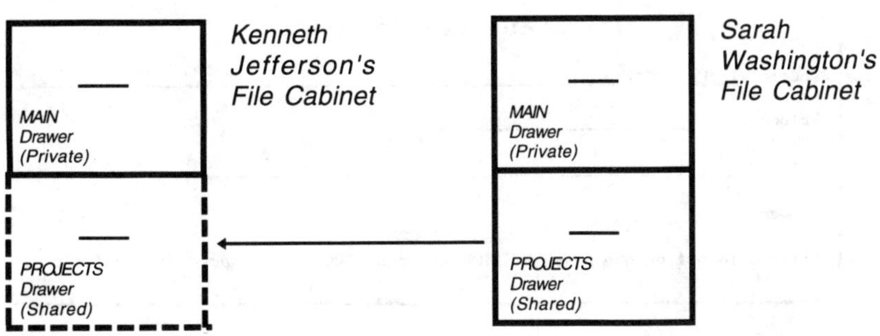

Figure 13.3 Adding a shared drawer to a File Cabinet

File Cabinet; it simply adds information to his File Cabinet to make the drawer *appear* as if it resides in his File Cabinet.

After adding the drawer, Kenneth can select and work with documents in it. The process of selecting a new drawer is somewhat simpler for Kenneth than for Carol because he has added the drawer to his File Cabinet. For example, when selecting a document, he can clear the Drawer field and list the drawers he has access to (see Figure 13.4).

The remainder of this chapter explains the details of working with shared drawers. The first two sections show you how to access documents in an existing shared drawer and how to reserve a shared document for editing. These instructions are important for anyone who needs to work with shared documents. Later sections explain how to create and manage shared drawers and will probably apply to fewer people.

When working with shared drawers, keep the following important points in mind:

- You can create additional drawers for sharing documents. However, there is no need to create a drawer if another user has already created one for the same group. Instead, you can add the existing drawer to your File Cabinet or just select and work with documents as the need arises.

- When you create a drawer, you must specify whether the drawer is shared. If it is a shared drawer, you must list which users have access to the drawer. You can enter either a list of ALL-IN-1 usernames or group names. Groups are lists of users, somewhat like distribution lists. Groups are defined from the Group Services menu and are discussed in the next chapter. In addition to listing who has access to the drawer, you can specify the level of access granted to each user or group, as described in Section 13.5, "Controlling Access to a Drawer." There are five levels of access: read, create, edit, delete/refile, and control.

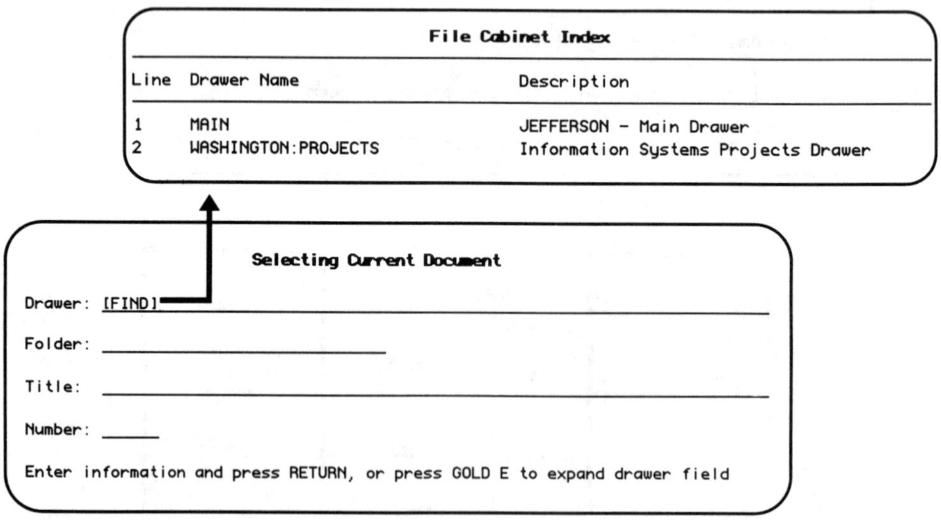

Figure 13.4 Displaying drawer names with [FIND]

- Storage space for all documents stored in a shared drawer is charged against the disk quota of the drawer's owner. If you place a large document in a shared drawer, you could inadvertently cause disk quota problems for the drawer's owner.
- The access list for a shared drawer can be changed at any time after the drawer has been created. The access list can be changed by the drawer owner, the system administrator, or anyone who has been given *control* access to the drawer.
- There are two types of shared drawers. You must specify one of the following when you create a shared drawer.

Regular shared	All documents in a regular shared drawer have the same access list. In other words, if you've been given access to a regular shared drawer, you have the same privileges to access any document in the drawer.
Advanced shared	Each document in an advanced shared drawer can have a different access list. Just because you can read and edit one document in an advanced shared drawer does not imply that you can read or edit another document. When you create an advanced shared drawer, you enter a default access list, which is automatically applied to new documents as they are created. The access list for an existing document can then be changed with the Modify Document Access (MDO) option.

- Shared documents can be accessed by a number of users. You can reserve a document to prevent anyone else from editing the document while you're making modifications. When you're finished updating the document, you can cancel your reservation to allow other users full access to the document.
- No account containing a shared drawer should be deleted if users continue to access documents in the drawer. Shared documents should first be refiled to another shared drawer before the account is deleted, or the drawer should be taken over by the system manager, as described in the *ALL-IN-1 System Management Guide*. You might consider having your system administrator set up a new ALL-IN-1 account for your department or work group. Then you can create shared drawers in this account rather than in specific user accounts.
- If the name of an account containing a shared drawer is changed, all users sharing the drawer must remove the drawer from their File Cabinet (option RDR), then add the drawer back (option ADR).

13.1 ACCESSING A SHARED DRAWER

Assuming that someone has created a shared drawer and has granted access to users in your work group, you can begin to share documents by selecting the drawer and creating, editing, reading, and printing documents.

It's fairly easy to select and work with documents in a shared drawer. There are two menu options for selecting a new drawer. These menu options are available on the Word and Document Processing, Electronic Messaging, and File Cabinet menus. Both options effectively close your current drawer and open a new drawer. You can then choose other menu options to work with any document in the shared drawer.

SEL (Select)	The standard Select option selects a new drawer, folder, and document.
SDR (Select Drawer)	The Select Drawer option selects a new drawer. You must then use the Select option, Index option, or arrow keys to select specific documents in the drawer.

Keep the following points in mind when you select a different drawer:

- The process of accessing a document in another drawer is no more complex than accessing a document in another folder. You simply select the drawer (folder and title), then choose menu options to work with the document. You must repeat the selection process to work with documents in another drawer.
- It's sometimes easy to forget that you're working in a shared drawer. Be careful when you delete or refile a document in a shared drawer. Other people might be looking for the document.
- Index (I) operations are limited to a single drawer. Check the drawer name if you can't seem to find a familiar document or folder, or use the Index of Selected Drawers (XI) option on the Index of Drawers to search multiple drawers.
- You're automatically returned to your default drawer (usually Main) when you select options to process messages, such as Read New Mail (RN). Electronic Messaging works with messages stored in your default drawer only.

Perform the following steps to access a different drawer:

1. Choose the Select (SEL) or Select Drawer (SDR) option.

[SELECT]	To select a different drawer and a specific document, press [SELECT] (or type "SEL" and press [RETURN]). ALL-IN-1 displays the Selecting Current Document form. Move to the Drawer field, and press [ERASE LINE] to clear the contents.
SDR [RETURN]	Or, to select a different drawer, type "SDR" and press [RETURN]. *Hint:* Type "SDR" followed by the drawer name and press [RETURN] to select a drawer quickly. For example, type "SDR MAIN" and press [RETURN] when you want to return to your Main drawer.

2. Enter the name of the drawer you want to access. Two different methods are described here. Follow the first method to select a drawer in your own File Cabinet, including a drawer that you've added to your File Cabinet. Use the second method to select a shared drawer that resides in another user's File Cabinet.

   To select a drawer in your own File Cabinet, do the following:

drawer-name **or [FIND]**	Type the drawer name, if you know it, or press [FIND] (or [GOLD] L) to display the names of the drawers in your File Cabinet. Then select a drawer by entering the line number.

   To select a drawer in another user's File Cabinet (assuming you have access to it), do the following:

[username] *drawer-name*	Type the username, enclosed in square brackets, followed by the drawer name, if you know both pieces of information.
[[FIND]	Or type "[" (open square bracket) and press [FIND] (or [GOLD] L) to display the names of the drawers to which you have access. Then select a drawer by entering a line number.
[GOLD] E	Or press [GOLD] E to expand the Drawer Name field. ALL-IN-1 displays the Selecting Full Drawer Name form, as shown in Figure 13.5. Complete this form by entering a username and drawer name. Press [FIND] in either field to list possible entries. *Note:* You can also specify a remote system name to access drawers on another system if the Distributed Sharing option to ALL-IN-1 is installed.

```
                    Selecting Full Drawer Name

System:      ________________________________________

User Name:   __________________

Drawer:      __________________

Enter information and press RETURN
```

Figure 13.5 Selecting Full Drawer Name form

3. After entering a drawer name, enter a folder and title if using the Select option, and press [RETURN] to select the specified drawer.

13.2 RESERVING DOCUMENTS

You can reserve a shared document to prevent other users from modifying the document while you're making changes. This solves problems that can surface when many people share documents. Obviously, you would not want several people making changes to the same document at once. ALL-IN-1 always locks a shared document while it is being edited to prevent anyone else from making changes. However, suppose you want to make a number of modifications to a document in several different edit sessions and don't want anyone to access the document between sessions. You can reserve the document, make your changes, and then "cancel" the reservation when you're through.

The following options on the File Cabinet menu allow you to reserve documents:

RSV (Reserve Document)	Reserves the current document. No one else can edit the document until you cancel the reservation with Unreserve Document (URV).
RSC (Reserve and Copy Document)	Makes a copy of the current document in a drawer that you specify and reserves the document. This option allows you to copy the document to a private drawer and make changes to the copy while other users read the original document. No one else can edit the original document until you replace the original with the modified copy or cancel the reservation.
RPL (Replace Document)	Replaces the original document with the modified copy and cancels the reservation.
URV (Unreserve Document)	Cancels a reservation that was made with either the Reserve Document (RSV) or Reserve and Copy Document (RSC) option.
IRD (Index of Reserved Documents)	Creates an index of documents that you have reserved. You can select documents from this index and enter the Replace Document (RPL) or Unreserve Document (URV) option.

The Reserve and Copy Document (RSC) option is the best way to prevent others from accessing a shared document that you're modifying. This option makes a copy of the shared document and reserves the original to prevent modification. You can work with the copy in private, making all the necessary changes during as many edit sessions as you require. When finished, the Replace Document (RPL) option replaces the original with your updated copy and cancels the reservation.

```
                 Reserving document, with copy

Drawer: ______________________________________________

Folder: ______________________

Title: _______________________________________________

Enter the destination information for the copied document and press RETURN
```

Figure 13.6 Reserving Document, with Copy form

Perform these steps to copy and reserve the current shared document for editing:

RSC [RETURN]

a. Type "RSC" and press [RETURN]. ALL-IN-1 displays the form shown in Figure 13.6.

Drawer: ***drawer* [TAB]...**

b. Enter a drawer, folder, and title for the copy. It makes sense to copy the document to an unshared drawer to work with it in private. Therefore, you might specify your Main drawer.

[RETURN]

c. Press [RETURN] to copy and reserve the document.

Perform the following steps to replace a reserved document with the updated copy:

IRD [RETURN]

a. Type "IRD" and press [RETURN]. ALL-IN-1 displays an index of reserved documents.

***line-number* RPC [RETURN]**

b. Type the line number of the document you want to replace followed by a space and the option "RPC." Then press [RETURN]. ALL-IN-1 replaces the copy and cancels the reservation.

13.3 ACCESSING DRAWER MANAGEMENT

The Drawer Management menu provides all of the tools you need for creating and managing drawers. Three options on this menu are important for everyone: Index of Drawers (I), Index of Available Drawers (IAD), and Add a Drawer (ADR). The remaining options are for users who create drawers or control access to shared drawers.

Perform the following steps to access the Drawer Management menu:

FC DRM [RETURN]

a. From any menu, type "FC DRM" and press [RETURN].

***menu-option* [RETURN]**

b. Type the menu option and press [RETURN]. Table 13.1 describes the options on this menu.

Table 13.1 Drawer Management menu options

Enter This Menu Option	*To Perform the Following Action*
SEL (Select)	Select a drawer to manage.
C (Create)	Create a new drawer in your File Cabinet.
E (Edit Drawer Access)	Modify the access list for the current drawer. This includes adding names to the list, removing names from the list, and changing the privileges granted to a user or group.
D (Delete Drawer and Contents)	Delete the current drawer and all documents in the drawer. Be cautious when you use this option. Documents cannot be recovered once the drawer has been deleted. Make sure that no one needs any of the documents stored in the drawer before deleting it.
P (Print)	Print details of the current drawer, including the description and access list.
R (Read)	Display details of the current drawer.
I (Index)	Display an index of drawers in your File Cabinet and enter options to manage drawers.
MDT (Modify Drawer Type)	Change the current drawer type to unshared, regular shared, or advanced shared.
RAS (Remove All Sharers)	Remove all names from the access list for the current drawer.
ASO (Advanced Sharing Options)	Display a menu to manage the access list for the current advanced shared drawer.
ADR (Add a Drawer)	Add information to your File Cabinet about a drawer that resides in another File Cabinet. This effectively adds the drawer to your File Cabinet.
UDR (Update Drawer Information)	Change the name or description of the current drawer.
RDR (Remove Drawer)	Remove information from your File Cabinet about a drawer that resides in another File Cabinet. You will still be able to access documents in the drawer.
IAD (Index of Available Drawers)	Display an index of all of the drawers to which you have access and enter options to manage these drawers.

13.4 ADDING AN EXISTING DRAWER TO YOUR FILE CABINET

The Add a Drawer (ADR) option on the Drawer Management menu "adds" an existing drawer to your File Cabinet. This option does not create a new drawer; it simply adds information to your File Cabinet about a drawer that exists in another File Cabinet. Adding an existing drawer to your File Cabinet makes it easier to select and work with documents in the drawer, almost as if the drawer were a part of your File Cabinet. When you add a drawer to your File Cabinet, you can select the drawer with a name that you choose.

Perform these steps to add an existing drawer to your File Cabinet:

IAD [RETURN]	a. From the Drawer Management menu, type "IAD" and press [RETURN]. ALL-IN-1 displays the Index of Available Drawers, which has a form at the bottom for entering selection criteria.
[RETURN]	b. Enter criteria if you want to list specific drawers, or press [RETURN] to create an index of all of the drawers to which you have access.
***line-number* R [RETURN]**	c. Review the list of drawers and locate the drawer you want to add to your File Cabinet. Type the line number for the drawer, followed by a space and "R" then press [RETURN]. ALL-IN-1 displays details of the drawer. Review these details and make sure that this is the drawer you want to add.
[RETURN]...	d. Continue to press [RETURN] until the index is redisplayed.
ADR [RETURN]	e. Type "ADR" and press [RETURN] to add the drawer to your File Cabinet. ALL-IN-1 displays the Add Drawer to File Cabinet form. Details of the drawer are already completed.
[ERASE LINE] Drawer name: ***name* [TAB]** Description: ***description***	f. The information entered on the Add Drawer form controls how the drawer is labeled in your File Cabinet only. You can change these details or press [RETURN] to accept the present drawer name and description. *Hint:* Change the drawer name to the format *owner:drawer-name.* This makes it easy to identify the drawer owner when the drawer name appears in a current item block or index. In the example that is shown in Figure 13.3, the drawer name would be changed to `WASHINGTON:PROJECTS.`
[RETURN]	g. Press [RETURN] to complete this form. ALL-IN-1 adds the drawer to your File Cabinet and redisplays the index.
[EXIT]	h. Press [EXIT] to return to the menu.

13.5 CONTROLLING ACCESS TO A DRAWER

You have complete control over who has access to any drawer you create. When you create a drawer, you must enter the names of the people who will have access to it. You can add names to or remove names from this access list later with the Edit Drawer Access (E) option on the Drawer Management menu.

You can grant access to a shared drawer to an individual user or to a group of users by entering the username or group name on the form shown in Figure 13.7. You must enter a valid ALL-IN-1 username or a group name defined with Group Services. In addition, you must specify which operations each individual or group can perform. Table 13.2 describes the privileges.

Perform the following steps to modify the current drawer's access list:

E [RETURN]

a. From the Drawer Management menu, type "E" and press [RETURN]. ALL-IN-1 displays an Edit Drawer Access form similar to the example shown in Figure 13.7.

[DOWN ARROW]...

b. Press [DOWN ARROW] to move to an existing name to delete or modify the privileges granted to the individual or group, or press [DOWN ARROW] to move to a blank line to add a new name to the access list.

Edit Drawer Access

Drawer: PROJECTS
Owner: WASHINGTON

User or Group	Permitted access: Read	Create	Edit	Delete Refile	Control
*INFORMATION SYSTEMS	Y	Y	Y	Y	_
JEFFERSON.KENNETH	Y	Y	Y	Y	_
ADAMS.CAROL	Y	Y	Y	Y	_
______	_	_	_	_	_
______	_	_	_	_	_
______	_	_	_	_	_
______	_	_	_	_	_
______	_	_	_	_	_

Enter information and press RETURN, or press GOLD F to complete the operation

Figure 13.7 Edit Drawer Access form

Table 13.2 Drawer access privileges

Privilege	*Allows the Group or User to Perform the Following Operations*
Read	Select, read, print, copy, and list documents.
Create	Perform all read operations and create new documents.
Edit	Perform all read and create operations and modify documents.
Delete/Refile	Perform all read, create, and edit operations and delete documents or refile documents to another folder or drawer.
Control	Perform all of the above operations and edit drawer access. This effectively gives someone the same privileges as the creator of the drawer.

[ERASE LINE]

c. To delete a name, press [ERASE LINE] (LF or F13).

[TAB]

To modify the privileges, press [TAB].

username **or** ****group*** **[TAB]**

To add a name, type the username or group name and press [TAB].

Read	Create	Edit	Delete Refile	Control
Y/SP	**Y/SP**	**Y/SP**	**Y/SP**	**Y/SP**

d. Type "Y" in any of the remaining five fields on the same line to grant a specific privilege. Press [SPACE] to deny the privilege.

Note: The cursor moves forward automatically without having to press [TAB].

e. Repeat steps b, c, and d to add or remove names and modify privileges. Refer to the notes that follow for additional information on completing lines on this form.

[GOLD] F

f. Press [GOLD] F to save updates to the access list when you're through making changes.

Here are some notes on editing drawer access:

- A name entered on the Edit Drawer Access form must be either a valid ALL-IN-1 username or a group name that has been defined with Group Services. Group names always begin with an asterisk (*). Refer to Chapter 14 for more information on groups.
- ALL-IN-1's lookup feature can help you enter usernames or group names. Press [FIND] (or [GOLD] L) in this field to display a list of usernames, or type an asterisk and press [FIND] to display group names. Even better, enter the first few characters of the username or an asterisk followed by the first few characters of the group name and press [FIND] to list matching entries.

- Privileges are "additive" as you move left to right on the form. For example, you cannot grant edit privilege without granting read privilege. You can save time by moving to the second through fifth column and entering a "Y" to fill in all preceding privileges with a "Y".

- The order in which you add names is important. ALL-IN-1 sorts the categories of names in the list, placing ALL-IN-1 usernames first, then VMS usernames, ALL-IN-1 groups, and finally special groups such as *LOCAL and *WORLD. Suppose, however, that user JONESR is a member of groups *ACCOUNTING and *SUPERVISORS, and you give access to these groups in the following order:

User or Group	Read	Create	Edit	Delete Refile	Control
*ACCOUNTING	Y				
*SUPERVISORS	Y	Y	Y	Y	

  This could present a problem: JONESR will *only* be allowed Read access. The reason is that this list is scanned from top to bottom when JONESR attempts to access the drawer. The first line that applies to JONESR is used to determine his access privileges. The remaining lines that apply to JONESR are not reviewed. If you want JONESR to have the authority to create, edit, and refile documents, reverse the order of these lines:

User or Group	Read	Create	Edit	Delete Refile	Control
*SUPERVISORS	Y	Y	Y	Y	
*ACCOUNTING	Y				

  To avoid problems caused by the order of names in the access list, place the most privileged users and groups at the top of the list.

- One final point that you should be aware of: Users with the system privilege SYSPRV have access to any drawer on the system. Because of this, you might want to review any account on your system that has SYSPRV privilege *and* access to ALL-IN-1. SYSPRV is usually granted only to system managers.

13.6 CREATING A NEW DRAWER

The Create (C) option on the Drawer Management menu creates a new drawer in your File Cabinet. There are two reasons you might want to create a drawer; both involve the sharing of documents or messages:

- You need to share documents with other users, and none of the other users has already created a shared drawer in which to place these documents. Note that if another user has already created a shared drawer, all you need to do is add this drawer to your File Cabinet (ADR option).

- You've granted mail access to someone else who handles your mail. This implicitly gives this person access to every document in your Main drawer. In this situation, you might want to create a new, private drawer in which to store private documents.

There is some overhead involved with creating a new drawer, including the creation of a number of files and directories in your account. For this reason, you should create drawers only when one of the above situations applies.

Perform the following steps to create a new drawer in your File Cabinet:

C [RETURN]	a. From the Drawer Management menu, type "C" and press [RETURN]. ALL-IN-1 displays the Create Drawer form shown in Figure 13.8.
Drawer name: ***drawer-name*** **[TAB]...**	b. Enter details for the new drawer. Table 13.3 on the next page describes the fields of information on this form. When entering drawer details, press [TAB] after completing a field to move to the next.
[RETURN]	c. Press [RETURN] after entering details for the new drawer. ALL-IN-1 creates the drawer. If you're creating a shared drawer, ALL-IN-1 displays the Edit Drawer Access form.
***name* [TAB]** ***access* [TAB]...**	d. Enter usernames or group names for those who need access to the drawer. Indicate the privileges you want to grant to each user or group. Refer to Section 13.5, "Controlling Access to a Drawer," for details on how to complete this form.

```
                          Create Drawer

Drawer name:  ____________________________

Description:  ______________________________________________________________

Shared (Y/N): N                  Drawer type: ___________________

Enter information and press RETURN
```

Figure 13.8 Create Drawer form

Table 13.3 Create Drawer details

Field	*Description*
Drawer Name	The name you want to assign to the drawer.
Description	A full description of the contents of the drawer.
Shared (Y/N)	"Y" creates a shared drawer; some or all of the documents stored in the drawer will be available to other users. "N" creates a private drawer. You might create a private drawer when you need to store sensitive information, and someone else has access to your Main drawer.
Drawer Type	Indicates the type of shared drawer. Two responses are allowed: Regular Shared or Advanced Shared. In a regular shared drawer, all documents have the same access list. In an advanced shared drawer, each document can have a different access list. This field can be accessed only if the Shared field is set to "Y."

[GOLD] F

e. Press [GOLD] F after completing the Edit Drawer Access form. If you're creating a regular shared drawer, the access list is updated, and the menu is redisplayed.

   Note: You can change the access list with the Edit Drawer Access (E) option after the drawer has been created.

f. If you're creating an advanced shared drawer, you are now asked to enter the default access list for any document created in the drawer. Remember that each document in an advanced shared drawer can have a different access list. It's best to be conservative and specify minimum privileges as the default. You can change the access list for specific documents later with Modify Document Access (MDO).

Table 13.3 describes the information entered when creating a new drawer.

13.7 WORKING WITH ADVANCED SHARED DRAWERS

Advanced shared drawers allow greater control over the access allowed to specific documents in the drawer. The drawer itself has an access list, and each document in the drawer has an access list. Thus, when you create an advanced shared drawer, you must specify two separate lists:

Drawer Access List — Controls access to the drawer itself. The privileges that can be granted at this level are read, create, delete, and control.

Default Document Access List	Controls access to specific documents. When a document is created in the drawer, the default document access list is assumed. The list can subsequently be updated with the Modify Document Access (MDO) option on the File Cabinet menu.

The drawer owner, system administrator, or any user with control privilege can change these access lists from the Advanced Sharing Options menu.

Perform the following steps to update the access lists for the current advanced shared drawer:

FC DRM ASO [RETURN]

a. From the Drawer Management menu, type "FC DRM ASO" and press [RETURN].

***menu-option* [RETURN]**

b. Type the menu option and press [RETURN]. Table 13.4 describes options on this menu.

c. Update the drawer or default access list as described in Section 13.5, "Controlling Access to a Drawer."

Table 13.4 Advanced sharing options

Enter This Menu Option	*To Perform the Following Action*
MDO (Modify Drawer Access)	Update the drawer access list for the current advanced shared drawer.
SDA (Set Default Access for New Documents)	Update the default access list applied to any new document created in the drawer.

Group Services

CHAPTER 14

In ALL-IN-1, *groups* refer to groups of people. Logically, a group is any collection of people who have something in common. Examples of groups are all employees in a certain department, all workers in a certain job class (supervisors, word processors, engineers, vice-presidents, etc.), and all users with specific expertise.

A group is actually not much more than a list of names, much like a distribution list. In fact, you can address a message to a group of individuals by entering either a group name or a distribution list name. The primary purpose of a group, however, is to make it easier to grant access to a shared drawer or document.

This chapter teaches you how to perform the following tasks to manage groups:

- Access Group Services to maintain group lists.
- Find out which groups you belong to.
- Create a new group.
- Add names to a group and remove names from a group.
- Give someone else the privilege to modify a group.

In Chapter 13, you found that giving other individuals access to a shared drawer is easy. Just enter usernames, followed by specific privileges. This procedure works well for many shared drawer owners. It provides great control over who can access the drawer and in what manner. If, over time, you realize that you're listing the same users when granting access to a shared drawer or folder, you'll probably benefit from working with groups instead of individual usernames.

There are two advantages to granting drawer access to a group instead of to a list of individuals:

- Entering a group name requires less typing than entering a list of usernames.
- More important, when a group is given access to a shared drawer or document, any individual added to or removed from the group is automatically granted or denied access to the drawer. You don't have to add or remove the individual from the list of users for each drawer shared by the group.

Group lists can contain any of the following entries. Each entry in a group list is called a *member*.

ALL-IN-1 Username — The most common entry in a group list. The ALL-IN-1 username is the same name that you enter when addressing mail to someone.

VMS Username	The username entered by an individual when logging into the system.
Group Name	The name of another group (subgroup). Subgroups allow you to create a hierarchy of group lists. This makes it easier to add and remove members. For example, the group *ALL DEPARTMENTS might consist solely of group names: *ACCOUNTING, *FINANCE, *SALES, and so on. Adding a new employee to the *SALES group automatically adds the employee to *ALL DEPARTMENTS.

Group lists are managed from the Group Services menu. Groups are created by defining a group name and entering the names of group members. The person who creates the group can designate other individuals as group *maintainers*—people who can add members to or remove members from the group. Once created, everyone on the system can refer to the group when granting access to a shared drawer or when addressing a message. Because group lists are shared by all users, the ability to create a group is restricted. Contact your system administrator if you require this privilege.

Two groups are established at all sites and can be referenced when granting access to a shared drawer:

*LOCAL	All users with hard-wired or LAT connections to the local system.
*WORLD	All users in the same network.

14.1 ACCESSING GROUP SERVICES

The Group Services menu provides the tools for managing groups. Keep in mind that certain options on this menu require privileges, as described in the footnotes to Table 14.1.

Perform the following steps to access the Group Services menu:

GS [RETURN]	a. From any menu, type "GS" and press [RETURN].
***menu-option* [RETURN]**	b. Type the menu option and press [RETURN]. Table 14.1 describes options on this menu.

14.2 DETERMINING GROUPS TO WHICH YOU BELONG

The Trace Group Membership (TG) option on the Group Services menu displays an index of the groups to which you belong. Trace Group Membership requires no special privileges.

Once the index is displayed, you can enter menu options described in Table 14.1. For example, the Read and Print options display and print more information about the groups. This information includes the names of group maintainers and other group members.

Table 14.1 Group Services menu options

Enter This Menu Option	*To Perform the Following Action*
AM (Add Members)	Add names to the current group.[a]
C (Create)	Create a new group and enter the list of group members.[b]
CO (Copy)	Copy an existing group list to create a new group.[b]
CDG (Create a Group from a Distribution List)	Create a new group from the list of names in a distribution list.[b]
CGD (Create a Distribution List from a Group)	Create a distribution list with the names in the current group.
CGM (Create a Group from a Mail Header)	Create a group from the list of names in a message header.[b]
D (Delete)	Delete the current group.[a]
E (Edit Group Description)	Modify the description of the current group.[a]
I (Index of Groups)	Display an index of groups with which to work.
IGM (Index of Group Members)	Display an index of members for the current group. Index menu options let you add and remove members.[a]
P (Print)	Print the list of members and maintainers for the current group.
R (Read)	Display the list of members and maintainers for the current group.
SEL (Select Group)	Select a new group with which to work.
TG (Trace Group Membership)	Display an index of groups to which you belong.
UML (Update Maintainers List)	Add or remove names of people who can maintain the current group.[a]

[a] Only the creator of the group, an authorized maintainer, or a privileged user can modify or delete a group.

[b] You must be given authority by the system administrator to create a group.

14.3 CREATING A GROUP

The Create option on the Group Services menu creates a new group. You create a group by defining the group name and description and entering the names of group members. Once a group has been created, all users on the system can reference the group name when granting access to a shared drawer or when addressing a message.

Keep in mind the following when creating a group:

- You must be given authority by the system administrator to create a group. This is because groups are "seen" by everyone on the system. Contact your system administrator if you receive a privilege violation when trying to create a group.

- When you create a group, you're given authority to maintain the group but are not automatically included as a member of the group. You must add your own username as a member to be included in the group. Maintainers show up when reading or printing the group list and should not be confused with the members of the group listed at the top of the report.

- ALL-IN-1 uses the VMS Access Control List mechanism to control access to shared drawers. (Refer to the *VMS Security Manual* for a full explanation of access control lists.) Creating a group adds a new "rights identifier" with the format OA$G_*xxx* to the system file RIGHTSLIST.DAT. Group members are granted this identifier upon login. An identifier is a "badge" of sorts, identifying the owner as a member of a group. The ability to modify this system file is another reason why the Create option is restricted.

Perform the following steps to create a new group:

C [RETURN]

a. From the Group Services menu, type "C" and press [RETURN] to create a group. The Create Group form shown in Figure 14.1 is displayed.

   Note: An error is displayed if you do not have authorization to create groups.

Name: ***group-name* [TAB]**
Description: ***description***
[RETURN]

b. Type a name for the group (without a preceding asterisk) and press [TAB]. Type a description for the group and press [RETURN]. The Add Group Member form shown in Figure 14.2 is displayed.

c. Enter the next group member:

***username* [RETURN]**

   - Type the username and press [RETURN].

***(VMS username)* [TAB]**
***mail-address* [RETURN]**

   - Or type the VMS username (enclosed in parentheses), press [TAB], type a mail address for the member, and press [RETURN].

****group* [RETURN]**

   - Or type an asterisk (*) and the name of another group and press [RETURN].

   ALL-IN-1 redisplays the Add Group Member form.

```
                         Create Group

Name:          ______________________

Description:   ______________________________________________

Enter information and press RETURN
```

Figure 14.1 Create Group form

```
                         Add Group Member

Name: ______________________________

Mail address:
______________________________________________________________

Enter information and press RETURN, or GOLD MENU for options
```

Figure 14.2 Add Group Member form

Note: Enter a partial username and press [FIND] (or [GOLD] L) to list matching names, or enter an asterisk (*) and press [FIND] to list groups. You can also press [GOLD] M to display a menu with options for selecting an ALL-IN-1 username, VMS username, or group name.

d. Repeat step c to add all members of the group.

[EXIT]

e. Press [EXIT] when you're finished entering member names. The new group is now the current group.

14.4 ADDING OR REMOVING MEMBERS

Once a group has been established, users can enter the group name when granting access to a drawer containing documents shared by the group. Members are typically added to and removed from a group over the course of its life as the need to share information changes. The creator of the group, an authorized maintainer, or the system administrator can add members to or remove members from a group.

The Add Group Member (AM) option adds new members to a group. This option can be executed from either the Group Services menu or the Index of Group Members. The Remove Member (RM) and Remove All Selected (XRM) options remove members and can be executed only from the Index of Group Members. Because a user is removed from all groups when his or her account is deleted, these options are typically used only when someone changes position within the organization.

Perform the following steps to add members to the current group:

AM [RETURN]

a. Type "AM" and press [RETURN]. The Add Group Member form is displayed.

***username* [RETURN]...**

b. Enter an ALL-IN-1 username, VMS username (surrounded by parentheses), or group name with a preceding asterisk, as described in Section 14.3, "Creating a Group."

Perform the following steps to remove members from the current group:

IGM [RETURN]	a. Type "IGM" and press [RETURN]. The Index of Group members is displayed.
***line-number* RM [RETURN]**	b. To remove a single member, type the line number next to the member's username, followed by a space and "RM". Then press [RETURN].
line,line-line,line **[SELECT]** **XRM [RETURN]**	To remove multiple members, type the line numbers or range of line numbers and press [SELECT]. Then type "XRM" and press [RETURN]. ALL-IN-1 asks you to confirm that you want to remove the member or members.
Y [RETURN]	c. Type "Y" and press [RETURN].

14.5 UPDATING GROUP MAINTAINERS

You have the authority to add members to or remove members from groups that you create. Sometimes, it helps to give someone else this authority to act as a backup. This person then becomes a maintainer for the group. If you don't designate any maintainers for the group, the system administrator can still act as a backup.

The Update Maintainer's List (UML) option on the Group Services menu adds or deletes names from the list of group maintainers. Each maintainer can be given the privileges listed in Table 14.2.

Table 14.2 Group Services maintainer privileges

Privilege	*Description*
Edit	Allows the maintainer to add members to the group, remove members from the group, and change the group's description.
Delete	Gives the maintainer all edit privileges plus the privilege to delete the group.
Control	Gives the maintainer all edit and delete privileges plus the privilege to update the list of maintainers.

Time Management PART V

Time Management helps you schedule your time more efficiently by maintaining a detailed calendar that shows appointments, meetings, and project schedules. You can display your calendar whenever you work with ALL-IN-1, and you can print a copy of your calendar for trips away from the office.

Time Management includes the following features:

- Time Management automatically sends electronic mail messages to attendees when you schedule a meeting, notifying them of the date, time, and purpose of the meeting.
- You receive an electronic message when you're invited to a meeting. As you read the message, you're asked whether you can attend. Your response is automatically sent back to the scheduler of the meeting, and the meeting is recorded in your calendar if you accept.
- Scan for Free Time searches calendars to locate open time slots for scheduling a meeting.
- Shared access to calendars enables you to review or schedule events in someone else's calendar. To ensure privacy, you have complete control over who has access to your calendar.
- You can display and print your calendar in a variety of formats.
- Open tasks recorded in your calendar can be automatically displayed whenever you enter ALL-IN-1 to remind you of pending work.

Time Management categorizes any item recorded in your calendar as either an event or a task.

Event	An event is an obligation to be somewhere at a specific date and time. Events include appointments with clients, department meetings, business trips, and personal appointments, such as a doctor's appointment or a lunch date. Figure V.1 shows how Time Management displays the day's events recorded in your calendar.
Task	A task is an obligation to perform some form of work. No time of day is associated with a task as with an event. However, you can specify start dates and completion dates for tasks. Figure V.2 shows how Time Management displays open tasks recorded in your calendar.

```
                 Events at a Glance: Friday        16-Sep-1994
(Selections: 0  )         (Meetings waiting: 0  )        (New messages: 1  )
Events for: WASHINGTON

   No. Type Start   End      Purpose

>  1     A  07:30am 09:46am 7:32am Continental Flight #1140 to Wash DC
   2     A  10:30am 11:30am Meeting with State Representative Taylor
   3     A  12:00pm 01:30pm Lunch at the Washington Hilton
   4     A  02:00pm 04:30pm Electronics Importers Trade Show - Wash. Hilton
   5     A  05:00pm 07:00pm 5:45pm Continental Flight #235 to Cleveland

Move to item and enter option (press GOLD MENU to see options,
or HELP for more information)
```

Figure V.1 Sample display of day's events

```
                 Tasks at a Glance: Wednesday     19-Oct-1994
(Selections: 0  )         (Meetings waiting: 0  )        (New messages: 1  )
Tasks for: WASHINGTON

  No. Category    Title       Due Date     Description

> 1   BUDGET      1.0 CURREN 31-Oct-1994 TRACK CURRENT YEAR EXPENSES
  2   BUDGET      1.1 MISC E 31-Oct-1994 Misc Exp Report from Beverly
  3   BUDGET      1.2 EXP RP 30-Oct-1994 Run Acctg expense report for cost cent
  4   TO DO ITEM  E. BAY UTI 30-Oct-1994 Prepare November Project Schedule
  5   TO DO ITEM  E. BAY UTI 23-Oct-1994 Prepare status report on E. Bay Utilit
  6   TO DO ITEM  REVIEW     04-Nov-1994 Complete Ken Jefferson's annual review

Move to item and enter option (press GOLD MENU to see options,
or HELP for more information)
```

Figure V.2 Sample display of open tasks

The chapters in this part discuss various aspects of Time Management. Chapter 15, "Getting Started with Time Management," shows you how to perform operations that are common to working with both events and tasks. This includes how to set the calendar date and select an event or task with which to work.

The next chapter, "Getting Started with Events," explains the basics of working with events. You'll learn how to schedule, reschedule, and cancel events in your calendar. Time Management's ability to schedule meetings is discussed, including how to set up a meeting and respond to a meeting notice.

Chapter 17 covers the basics of working with tasks. You'll learn how to record a task in your calendar, update a task, and close out a task. The exercise at the end of this chapter shows you a valuable method for tracking the progress of a project with tasks.

Chapter 18, "Displaying and Printing Your Calendar," shows you how to access the event and task information you've recorded. There are options for printing your calendar in a variety of formats. This chapter contains an example of each format, so you can choose the ones you like.

"Advanced Time Management," the final chapter in this part, discusses features that help you work more efficiently with Time Management. After learning the basics in the preceding chapters, you'll probably be interested in the first three topics: setting working conditions to control your environment in Time Management, working with index views of your calendar, and scheduling recurring events. The last topic explains how to share your calendar. You'll be interested in this information if you're responsible for managing someone else's calendar or if someone else handles *your* calendar.

TIME MANAGEMENT Q&A

Following is a list of common questions about Time Management.

Q *What is Time Management? How can it help me?*

A As explained in the introduction, Time Management helps you keep a record of the events and tasks scheduled in your calendar. The process is similar to recording this information on a paper calendar. However, with Time Management, you have all the advantages of maintaining this information on a computer: access from any terminal, easy updating and printing, and backup of information to prevent its loss.

The following Time Management features seem to benefit users the most:

- Time Management makes it easy to schedule meetings. Meeting notices are automatically sent through Electronic Messaging, and replies are automatically returned. This eliminates a lot of wasted time trying to phone attendees. The Scan for Free Time feature also makes it easy to find a block of time when all attendees are free. This also eliminates a lot of phone work.
- If other people need to review your calendar or schedule appointments for you, they can do so with the Set Owner feature. You must first authorize this activity, giving you complete control over who has access to your calendar.

- You can easily track projects with Time Management: adding tasks, modifying due dates, and closing out completed tasks. Reminders of open tasks are automatically displayed whenever you start ALL-IN-1.

Q *I find it easy to keep track of appointments with a pocket calendar. How would Time Management be better?*

A The advantage of a pocket calendar is obvious: Both paper and electronic pocket calendars are small and portable. It's easy to take your schedule with you on trips away from the office. But don't forget the advantages of Time Management:

- Your calendar cannot be lost or stolen, nor do you have to worry about losing the information if the batteries run down.
- Other people have access to your schedule when you're away from the office.
- Scheduling meetings with other ALL-IN-1 users is easier because of the integration of Electronic Messaging.

Combining the two resources works well for many people. Print your calendar before leaving on a trip. Schedule appointments in your pocket calendar when away from the office, and update your schedule in Time Management the next time you check in to read mail.

Q *How do I print my calendar?*

A There are a number of options on Time Management menus for printing your calendar. Sample printouts are shown in Chapter 18. Most print options require that you set the calendar date to the first date that you want to print. From the Events or Tasks menu, type "SD" and press [RETURN] to set the calendar date. Enter the start date and press [RETURN].

Once you've set the calendar date, select any option listed in Table 18.2 to print your calendar. The Print Events (PEG) and Print Events and Tasks (PET) options provide the most detail. Printouts generated with some of the other options are somewhat cryptic.

Another valuable method for printing your calendar is to display an index with either the Events at a Glance (EG) or the Tasks at a Glance (TG) option and copy the display to your Scratch Pad with [GOLD] P. Display the Scratch Pad menu with [GOLD] *, then select the Print (P) option. The resulting output is similar to the examples shown in Figures V.1 and V.2.

Q *What is the difference between an appointment and a meeting?*

A An appointment is an event scheduled only in your calendar. It does not involve other ALL-IN-1 users. You can schedule, change, and cancel appointments without notifying other users. A meeting is an event scheduled with other ALL-IN-1 users. When you schedule, change, or cancel a meeting, notices are automatically sent to those who were invited to the meeting.

If you want to schedule a meeting with other users and have ALL-IN-1 send out formal invitations, respond "Y" to the prompt "Invite Attendees?" when creating an event. Respond "N" to this prompt to schedule an appointment.

Q *How do I schedule a meeting?*

A Scheduling a meeting with Time Management is simple. Type "TM EV C" and press [RETURN] to move to the Events menu and create an event. Enter the date, start time, end time, purpose, and location of the meeting, and be sure to enter "Y" to indicate that you want to invite attendees. Press [RETURN] to complete the form, and ALL-IN-1 will ask for the names of attendees. Enter attendee names just as if you were addressing a message. You can invite any user you can send mail to—local or remote. Then indicate whether you want to add comments to the meeting invitation. If you respond "Y" to this prompt, type your comments and exit with [GOLD] F, as if completing a mail message.

ALL-IN-1 automatically addresses messages to the attendees with the information you've entered. The attendees read these messages and are asked whether they can attend. Responses are automatically returned to you as new mail messages.

ALL-IN-1's automatic handling of meeting invitations takes all of the phone work out of scheduling a meeting. Refer to Section 16.4, "Scheduling a Meeting," for more information.

Q *Is there any way to find out when people are available for a meeting before sending out meeting notices?*

A If you're inviting people with busy schedules, use the Scan for Free Time (SC) option to find a time slot for the meeting and to schedule the meeting, if desired. This option asks for the names of attendees, then prints a report organized to make it easy to find an open time slot. For this technique to work, however, the people you invite to the meeting must maintain their schedules in Time Management. The Scan for Free Time option is described further in Chapter 19.

Q *How do I invite someone to a meeting who does not have access to ALL-IN-1?*

A ALL-IN-1 sends meeting notices through Electronic Messaging. If an addressee does not have access to Electronic Messaging, you can still use Time Management to send a meeting notice. When you enter the person in the list of attendees, add the words "(PAPER MAIL)" enclosed in parentheses after the person's name. ALL-IN-1 will print a hard copy of the meeting notice for this individual, which can be sent through regular mail.

When the attendee responds, enter the response with the Reply for Attendee option (RFA). This updates information so that the next time you read the meeting, the person's name and response are properly displayed.

If you're scheduling a meeting and most attendees do not have access to ALL-IN-1, it makes more sense to schedule the meeting as an appointment (in your calendar only) rather than as a meeting.

Q *How do I specify a location for an appointment?*

A The Location field is only accessible if you invite attendees to the event (that is, when you create a meeting). When scheduling an appointment, you must include the location in the Purpose field.

Q *How do I schedule appointments on someone else's calendar?*

A To manage someone else's events, select the Set Owner (SO) option from the Events menu. Type "TM EV SO" and press [RETURN]. You will be asked to enter the name of the person whose calendar you want to access. Type the username and press [RETURN]. The name at the top of the menu is changed as a reminder that you're working in someone else's calendar. You can then select any option on the Events menu to manage the other person's calendar. Remember to switch back to your calendar before working with your own events.

There are two prerequisites for setting owner to someone else's calendar:

- The other person must give you permission with Calendar Access Management.
- The system administrator must authorize you to use the Set Owner option.

Set Owner is described in more detail in Chapter 19.

Q *How do I give someone the authority to schedule appointments on my calendar?*

A Options on the Calendar Access Management menu control access to your calendar. To authorize someone to schedule events for you, type "TM CAM A" and press [RETURN]. ALL-IN-1 displays the Add User form in Calendar Access Management. Type the username of the individual, press [TAB] twice, and enter a "Y" next to the prompt "Allow set owner?" Press [RETURN] to update access to your calendar.

You can also use Calendar Access Management to change or remove privileges granted to people with access to your calendar. Refer to Section 19.4.2, "Controlling Access to Your Calendar," for more information.

Q *How do I manage someone else's tasks?*

A Set Owner only allows you to work with someone else's events. You cannot access or manage someone else's tasks.

Q *How do I delete old events from my calendar?*

A The best way to get rid of old events and tasks is with the Delete All Selected (XD) option on the index. Type "TM EV I" and press [RETURN] to create an index of events. Fill in the Start Date—To field with a reasonably old date, three months or so. Then press [RETURN] to create an index of events older than this date. Type "ALL XD" and press [RETURN] to delete these events. Use the same procedure to delete old tasks, but type "TM T I" at the beginning to create an index of tasks.

TIME MANAGEMENT DOs AND DON'Ts

Here are some suggestions for working efficiently with Time Management:

Do

- Remember that you can print a copy of a display by writing the display to your Scratch Pad with [GOLD] P and then printing your Scratch Pad. Events at a Glance, Events Plus, and Tasks at a Glance provide valuable snapshots of your calendar and can be printed with this method. The exercise at the end of Chapter 17 shows you how to create and print an index of tasks.
- Keep your calendar up-to-date. Remember to record events in your ALL-IN-1 calendar that you've scheduled or changed when away from the office. This is particularly important if someone else accesses your calendar to view or schedule events.
- Tasks are organized in your calendar by category and title. When creating a task, use a project name for the category—for example, YEAR END CLOSE. Also, use a letter or number at the beginning of the title of a task. For example, start the titles of major tasks with 1.0, 2.0, 3.0, etc., and the titles of subtasks with 1.1, 1.2, 1.3, etc. Tasks are then properly sorted when viewed in an index like Tasks at a Glance. Refer to the exercise at the end of Chapter 17 to see how these naming conventions organize tasks in your calendar.
- Clean up your calendar by deleting old events and tasks. Your calendar is stored in a file and, of course, requires disk storage space. If you're a heavy user of Time Management, you should periodically delete old events and tasks to keep this file to a manageable size. The preceding Q&A section showed you an easy way to do this.

Don't

- Don't schedule a meeting with a large number of people to notify them of an event. It's better to notify people of an event by sending an electronic message or, even better, posting a notice in Group Conferencing. Scheduling a meeting with a large number of people results in a lot of acceptance/refusal memos that you probably don't have time to read.
- Don't use Calendar Access Management to give access to your calendar to someone who has a limited need to view your schedule. There are alternatives. The Scan for Free time feature described in Chapter 19 lets others see when you have appointments but does not let them see any details. If someone has a limited need to see the details of your calendar, print a copy of the Events at a Glance index to your Scratch Pad, and send the result. You can also print a portion of your calendar with Print Events (PEG); specify a document destination of "DOCUMENT," and send the resulting document.

Getting Started with Time Management

CHAPTER 15

In the introduction to Part V, you learned that Time Management classifies all calendar entries as either events or tasks. Menus and procedures vary depending on whether you're working with events or tasks. However, a few operations are the same in both environments.

This chapter describes the common procedures. You'll learn how to perform the following operations:

- Access the main Time Management menu.
- Set the calendar date to work with events and tasks for a specific day.
- Select an event or task with which to work.

15.1 ACCESSING TIME MANAGEMENT

Time Management contains a series of submenus and index forms with separate menus for maintaining events and tasks. You can reach these menus and index forms from the main Time Management menu.

Perform the following steps to access the main Time Management menu:

TM [RETURN]

a. From any menu, type "TM" and press [RETURN].

Note: It's common to also include the menu option to move directly to a submenu or index. For example, type "TM EV" and press [RETURN] to move directly to the Events menu.

You can set up your environment so that the global option TM displays a submenu or index instead of the main Time Management menu. When this is done, you must enter "TMMENU" and press [RETURN] to move to this menu. Refer to Section 19.1, "Customizing Time Management," for details.

Table 15.1 Main Time Management menu options

Enter This Menu Option	*To Perform the Following Action*
CAM (Calendar Access Management)	Display the Calendar Access Management menu to control who has access to your calendar.
EV (Events)	Display the Events menu to manage events in your calendar.
EG (Events at a Glance)	Display and work with an index of events for a single day. This index is the most popular method for working with events because it lists meetings and appointments for the day just like a desktop calendar.
EP (Events Plus)	Display and work with an index of events for a single day. This index also shows a weekly overview and monthly calendar.
ET (Events and Tasks)	Display and work with an index of events and tasks for a single day.
T (Tasks)	Display the Tasks menu to manage tasks recorded in your calendar.
TG (Tasks at a Glance)	Display and work with an index of open tasks.
TR (Training)	Start computer-based instruction for Time Management.

menu-option **[RETURN]**

b. Type an option and press [RETURN]. Table 15.1 lists the menu options on the Time Management menu.

Figure 15.1 shows the relationship between the main Time Management menu and the various submenus and index options listed on this menu. There's one menu for maintaining events and one for tasks. There are also a number of index forms for working with either events or tasks on a specific day. The Events and Tasks index is a combined index that lists both events and tasks for a specific day.

15.2 SETTING THE CALENDAR DATE

In a real appointment book, the calendar date is whatever date appears at the top of the current page. You must change this date by flipping pages before recording an appointment for a different date.

Similarly, the calendar date in Time Management appears at the top of the screen. You'll want to change this date for a number of reasons:

- Time Management automatically inserts the current calendar date in the form to create an event or task. You'll therefore find it more efficient to set the calendar date *before* creating a number of events or tasks for a specific day.
- Many of the options that display portions of your calendar begin with the current calendar date. You must change this date to view other portions of your calendar.

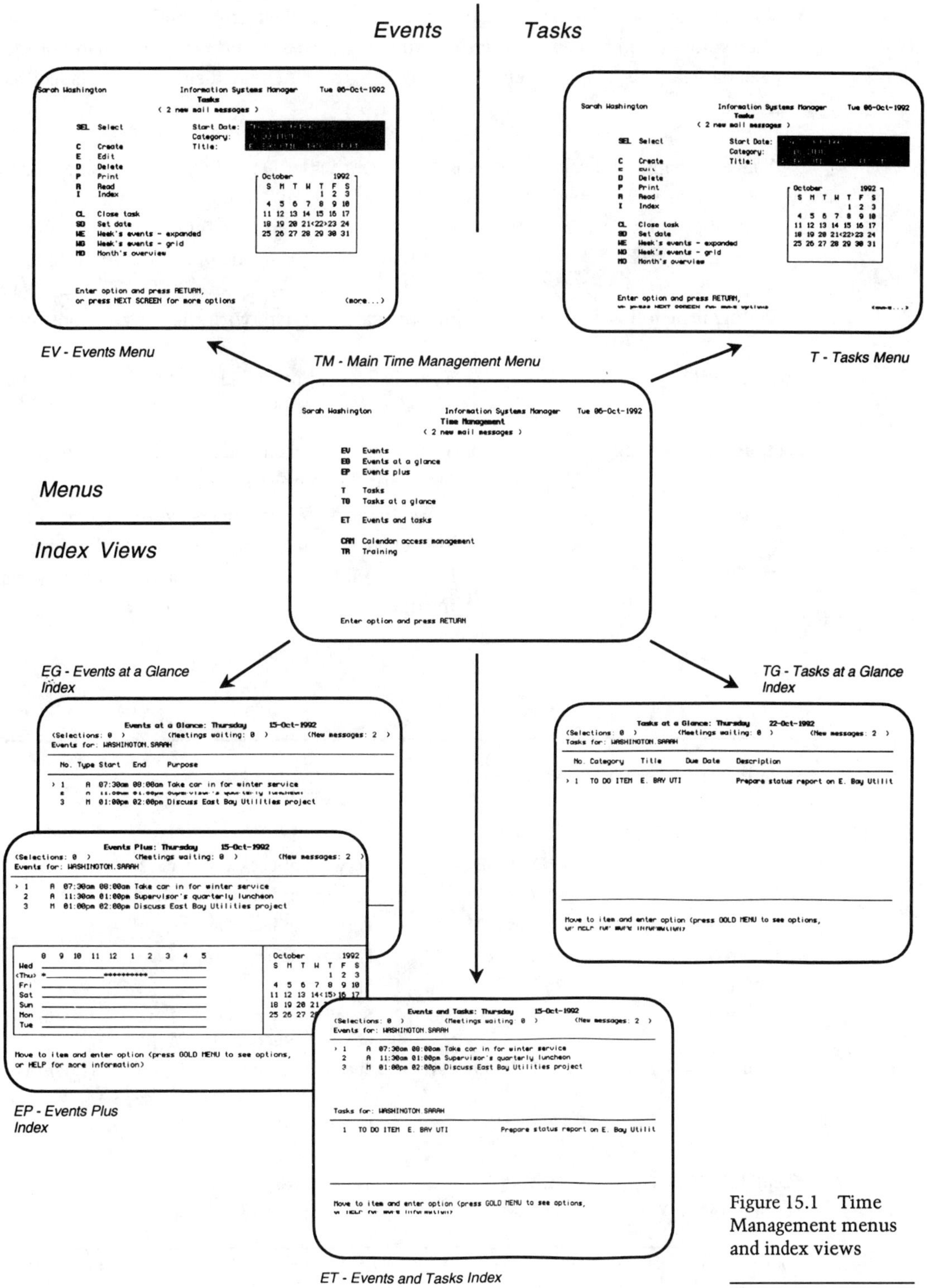

Figure 15.1 Time Management menus and index views

- The month's calendar for the current date is displayed on several menus in Time Management and is handy when you are trying to schedule events. Changing the calendar date to a new month also changes the calendar display to the specified month.

You can change the calendar date either with the Set Date (SD) option, as described below, or with your arrow keys, as described in Section 3.1.3, "Selecting an Item at a Menu." In either case, it's assumed that you're at an Events or Tasks menu or index. If not, first move to Events or Tasks by following the steps in the preceding section, "Accessing Time Management."

Perform the following steps to change the calendar date with the Set Date option:

SD [RETURN]	a. Type "SD" and press [RETURN]. ALL-IN-1 displays the Set Date form.
Set Date: ***date* [RETURN]**	b. Type over the current calendar date and enter the new date. Then press [RETURN]. *Note:* Instead of entering a specific date, you can also clear the field and enter any value that is listed in Table 15.2 to move forward or backward in time.

Table 15.2 Valid entries for Set Date

Entry Format	*Example*	*To Set the Calendar Date*
+*n*D or –*n*D	+2D or –3D	Forward or backward *n* days.
+*n*W or –*n*W	+1W or –2W	Forward or backward *n* weeks.
+*n*M or –*n*M	+1M or –1M	Forward or backward *n* months.
+*n*Y or –*n*Y	+Y or –Y	Forward or backward *n* years.
dd-mmm-yyyy[a]	31-DEC-1991	Specific date.
dd-mmm-yyyy +*nx*	1-JUN-1991 +1M	Specific date plus *n* days, weeks, months, or years, where *x* is D, W, M, or Y.
dd-mmm-yyyy –*nx*	2-AUG-1991 –1W	Specific date minus *n* days, weeks, months, or years, where *x* is D, W, M, or Y.
EOM	EOM	Last date of current month.
TODAY or TOD	TODAY	Current date.
TOMORROW or TOM	TOM	Tomorrow's date.
YESTERDAY or Y	Y	Yesterday's date.

[a] You can also enter dates numerically using a slash (/) or period (.) to separate month, day, and year—for example, "2/2/93" or "2.2.93."

15.3 SELECTING AN EVENT OR TASK

Many of the menu options in Time Management perform actions on the current event or task. The current item is identified in the upper right-hand corner of the menu or is shown by the current item pointer (>) in an index. You must select the desired event or task before editing, deleting, reading, or printing.

ALL-IN-1 automatically selects the first event or task for the day as the current item when you change the date of the calendar. It's easy to select another task or event for the day with either of the following procedures. Keep this in mind as a quick way to select an item.

Perform the following steps to select an event or task with the Select option at a menu:

SEL [RETURN]	a. Type "SEL" and press [RETURN] (or simply press [SELECT]). ALL-IN-1 displays a form for entering details for the event or task.
Date: ***date* [TAB]** Start Time: ***time***	b. To select an event, enter the date and time of the event.
Start Date: ***date* [TAB]** Category: ***category* [TAB]** Title: ***title***	To select a task, enter the start date, category, and title of the task you wish to select. *Hint:* ALL-IN-1's lookup feature is available when entering any of these items. Press [ERASE LINE] (LF or F13) and then [FIND] (or [GOLD] L) while the cursor is in any field to list existing events or tasks.
[RETURN]	c. Press [RETURN] once you've entered the necessary information. The form is cleared, and the selected event or task is shown in the upper right-hand corner of the menu.

Perform the following steps to select an event or task at an index:

***line-number* [RETURN]**	Type the line number of the event or task and press [RETURN]. The current item pointer (>) moves to the specified line. *Note:* You might first have to press [NEXT SCREEN] (or [GOLD] [TAB]) to move to additional pages of events or tasks. You can also select and manage multiple items as described in Section 19.2, "Working with an Index View of Your Calendar."

Getting Started with Events

CHAPTER 16

Most people use their calendar to keep a record of events. Events include appointments with clients, department meetings, business trips, and personal appointments like doctor's appointments and lunch dates. You might record an event in your calendar as a reminder to be somewhere at a specific time.

This chapter teaches you the basics of working with events in Time Management. You'll learn how to perform the following tasks:

- Schedule events in your calendar.
- Reschedule events when there is a change in the date, time, or location.
- Respond to meeting notices.

Events can be broken down into two categories: the events you attend on your own and the events to which you invite other attendees. In older versions of ALL-IN-1, these categories were known as *appointments* and *meetings*, respectively. These terms are still helpful in describing the difference between these types of events.

Appointments — An appointment is an event without attendees. It is scheduled only in your calendar and does not involve other ALL-IN-1 users. You can schedule, change, and cancel appointments without notifying other users.

Meetings — A meeting is an event scheduled with attendees. When you schedule, change, or cancel a meeting, notices are automatically sent to everyone invited to the meeting.

The following sections use the terms *appointment* and *meeting* in describing how to record events in your calendar. The procedures for handling the two are somewhat different, as you'll see.

16.1 ACCESSING THE EVENTS MENU

The Events menu contains options for scheduling, rescheduling, and canceling events in your calendar. This menu is a good place to start if you're used to working from a menu like the Electronic Messaging or Word and Document Processing menu. However, it is recommended that you explore working with one of the Events index menus as soon as possible. The index is particularly suited to working with Time Management because it resembles working with a desktop calendar. This will be apparent as you work through the exercises in upcoming chapters.

To access the Events menu, perform the following steps:

TM EV [RETURN]	a. From any menu, type "TM EV" and press [RETURN]. You can also enter the menu option from the Events menu. For example, type "TM EV C" and press [RETURN] to create an event.
***menu-option* [RETURN]**	b. Type the menu option and press [RETURN].

Table 16.1 describes the menu options on the Events menu. These options are also available on index menus: Events at a Glance (EV), Events Plus (EP), and Events and Tasks (ET).

Table 16.1 Events menu options

Enter This Menu Option	*To Perform the Following Action*
AA (Add Attendees)	Invite additional attendees to the current meeting.
AM (Answer Meeting Request)	Respond to a meeting notice.
C (Create)	Schedule a new event in your calendar.
CO (Conflicts)	Display a list of events that overlap during the current calendar day.
D (Delete)	Cancel the current event and remove it from your calendar.
E (Edit)	Reschedule the current event in your calendar or modify information about the event.
I (Index)	Display an index of events.
MA (Mail Message to Attendees)	Send additional information to attendees of the current meeting.
MO (Month's Overview)	Display a cryptic view of the current calendar month.
P (Print)	Print details of the current event.
PEG (Print Events)	Print events for the current calendar date and the days to follow.
PET (Print Events and Tasks)	Print events and open tasks for the current calendar date.
PMO (Print Monthly Overview)	Print a cryptic view of the current calendar month.
PWE (Print Week's Events—Expanded)	Print full details for events of the current calendar week in tabular format.
PWG (Print Week's Events—Grid)	Print brief information for events of the current calendar week in calendar format.
R (Read)	Display details of the current event.
RA (Remove Attendees)	"Un-invite" attendees to the current meeting and remove their names from the list of attendees.
RFA (Reply for Attendee)	Enter a response that was given to you verbally for an attendee of the current meeting.

Table 16.1 *(continued)*

Enter This Menu Option	*To Perform the Following Action*
SC (Scan for Free Time)	Find an available time slot for a meeting by searching the calendars of those whom you wish to invite to a meeting.
SD (Set Date)	Set the current calendar date.
SEL (Select)	Select an event with which to work.
SO (Set Owner)	Select the calendar with which you want to work.
SRE (Schedule Recurring Events)	Schedule an event that repeats at regular intervals, such as a weekly department meeting.
TC (Two Calendars)	View your calendar alongside that of another individual.
TR (Training)	Start computer-based instruction for events.
WE (Week's Events—Expanded)	Display full details for events of the current calendar week in tabular format.
WG (Week's Events—Grid)	Display brief information for events of the current calendar week in calendar format.

16.2 SCHEDULING AN APPOINTMENT

An appointment is an event that is scheduled only on your calendar and does not involve other ALL-IN-1 users. Meetings with clients, lunch dates with friends, doctor's appointments, and business trips are all examples of appointments.

You don't invite attendees when scheduling an appointment. Therefore, no notices are sent when you change or cancel an appointment. If you want to schedule an event with attendees, refer to Section 16.4, "Scheduling a Meeting."

Perform the following steps to schedule an appointment:

C [RETURN]

a. Type "C" and press [RETURN] to create an appointment. ALL-IN-1 displays the Create Event form.

Date: ***dd-mmm-yyyy* [TAB]**
Start Time: ***hh:mm* [TAB]**
End Time: ***hh:mm* [TAB]**
Purpose: ***description* [TAB]**
Confidential? (Y/N): **Y** or **N [TAB]**
Invite Attendees? (Y/N): **N**

b. Enter details of the appointment. When completing this form, press [TAB] to move to the next field, or press [BACKSPACE] (F12) to move to the previous field. Refer to Table 16.2 for descriptions of the fields on the Create Event form.

[RETURN]

c. Press [RETURN] when you complete the form to schedule the appointment in your calendar and return to the menu.

Note: If the time of the appointment overlaps an existing event, ALL-IN-1 displays a prompt at the bottom of the screen asking if you want to schedule the appointment anyway.

Table 16.2 Fields of information for an event

Field	*Description*
Date	The date of the appointment. The current calendar date already fills the Date field. To accept this date, simply press [TAB]. To change the date, simply type a new date. Note that all entries shown in Table 15.2 are also valid here. For example, you can enter "+1W" to specify a date one week from the current calendar date. When scheduling an event with attendees, you are not allowed to enter a date in the past!
Start Time	The beginning time of the appointment. Examples of valid time formats are "3:30pm," "3:30p," "3.30p," and "15:30." If you omit "am" or "pm," ALL-IN-1 makes an assumption based on how you've set your working hours in Set Working Conditions. If you've specified 8:00am to 5:00pm, for example, ALL-IN-1 assumes "pm" when you enter "3:00." If you receive the error, "Entry was not recognized," you probably entered an invalid time format.
End Time	The ending time of the appointment. This time must be later than the beginning time of the appointment. All the rules for entering the start time also apply here.
Purpose	A description of the appointment showing the purpose and possibly the location. Only the first 30 characters of the purpose are displayed for the current event on a menu. Therefore, you probably want the first 30 characters to be unique and descriptive.
Confidential?	Enter "N" if there is no need to keep the event confidential. Enter "Y" if you want this event to be hidden from the view of anyone who can view your calendar with the Two Calendars option.
Invite Attendees?	Enter "N" to schedule an appointment only in your calendar. Enter "Y" to schedule a meeting. If you invite attendees, you will be asked to enter their names so that meeting notices can be sent with Electronic Messaging.
Location	The location of the meeting. Identify the address, building number, room number, and so on, where the meeting will be held. You can reach this field only if you invite attendees.

16.3 RESCHEDULING AN APPOINTMENT

The Edit (E) option reschedules events in your calendar. You can change the date, start time, and end time, the purpose; and the confidentiality of the appointment with this option.

To edit the current appointment, do the following:

E [RETURN]	a. Type "E" and press [RETURN] to modify the appointment. ALL-IN-1 displays the Edit Event form.

Date: ***dd-mmm-yyyy* [TAB]...**
[RETURN]

b. Modify the details of the appointment and press [RETURN]. Refer to Table 16.2 for descriptions of the fields.

c. Press [RETURN] to reschedule the appointment in your calendar and return to the menu.

16.4 SCHEDULING A MEETING

A meeting is an event scheduled with other ALL-IN-1 users. Department meetings or meetings with your supervisor are examples.

When you schedule, change, or cancel a meeting, ALL-IN-1 sends notices to the attendees through Electronic Messaging.[1] Attendees read and respond to these notices, which are then returned to you. This automatic handling of meeting notices eliminates a lot of the "phone tag" that occurs when you try to schedule a meeting verbally.

Perform these steps to schedule a meeting:

C [RETURN]

a. Type "C" and press [RETURN]. ALL-IN-1 displays the Create Event form.

Date: ***dd-mmm-yyyy* [TAB]**
Start Time: ***hh:mm* [TAB]**
End Time: ***hh:mm* [TAB]**
Purpose: ***description* [TAB]**
Confidential? (Y/N): **Y** or **N [TAB]**
Invite Attendees? (Y/N): **Y [TAB]**
Location: ***location***

b. Enter the details of the meeting. When completing the form, press [TAB] to move to the next field, or press [BACKSPACE] (F12) to move to the previous field. Refer to Table 16.2 for descriptions of the fields on this form.

[RETURN]

c. Press [RETURN] when you've completed the Create Event form. ALL-IN-1 displays the Enter Attendees form.

Name: ***attendee-name***
[RETURN]...

d. Type the names of attendees, and press [RETURN] after each name. See the following notes for more information on completing this form.

[RETURN]

e. Press [RETURN] again after the last attendee. ALL-IN-1 asks whether you want to add comments.

Y [RETURN]

f. Type "Y" and press [RETURN] if you want to add comments for the meeting. These comments are added to the message sent to the attendees.

1. If most attendees don't have access to ALL-IN-1, you might want to schedule the event as an appointment.

ALL-IN-1 invokes the editor and displays details of the meeting. Enter your comments, and press [GOLD] F when you're finished.

N [RETURN] Type "N" and press [RETURN] if you do not want to add comments.

ALL-IN-1 redisplays the menu along with a message that the event has been scheduled and notices sent.

When scheduling a meeting, keep the following in mind:

- The attendee names are actually the Electronic Messaging addresses for individuals you want to invite to the meeting. (Addresses are required for ALL-IN-1 to send meeting notices.) Therefore, the format for entering an attendee's name is the same as an address: a username, last name, nickname, distribution list, remote address, and so forth. Refer to Section 7.1, "Addressing a Message," for details.
- To remove an attendee's name, move to the line containing the name, and press [ERASE LINE] (LF or F13) to clear the name.
- ALL-IN-1's lookup feature is available when entering attendees. Press [FIND] (or [GOLD] L) to list all possible names, or even better, enter the first few characters of the name, then press [FIND].
- If you know that an attendee does not have access to ALL-IN-1, enter his or her last name, followed by the words PAPER MAIL in parentheses. This tells ALL-IN-1 to print a hard copy of the meeting notice, which you can then send by interoffice mail.
- If the time of the appointment overlaps an existing event, ALL-IN-1 displays a prompt at the bottom of the screen asking if you want to schedule the event anyway. Respond by typing "Y" or "N," then press [RETURN].

16.5 RESCHEDULING A MEETING

Meetings that you've scheduled can be rescheduled with the Edit (E) option. You can change the date, start time, end time, purpose, and location of the meeting. ALL-IN-1 automatically sends notices to attendees to inform them of the changes when you edit a meeting.

If you edit a meeting that you were invited to, you're allowed to change only your response (whether or not you can attend) and your comments. ALL-IN-1 automatically sends this information back to the scheduler.

Here are some points to remember about rescheduling a meeting:

- The Scan for Free Time option can help you find a time when all of the attendees are available. Refer to Section 19.4.1.1, "Scan for Free Time," for details.

- The list of attendees is not changed with the Edit (E) option. Instead, you must use either the Add Attendees (AA) or Remove Attendees (RA) option.
- You can send notices to attendees of a meeting you've created with the Mail Message to Attendees (MA) option. Select this option when you want to provide additional information about the meeting.
- Many electronic mail messages are generated when you schedule and reschedule meetings. Deleting messages for old or rescheduled meetings is a quick way to clean up your Outbox and Read folders.

Perform the following steps to edit the current meeting:

E [RETURN]	a. Type "E" and press [RETURN] to edit the meeting. ALL-IN-1 displays the Edit Event form.
Date: ***dd-mmm-yyyy*** **[TAB]...**	b. Change the details of the meeting. To change any field of information, press [TAB] or [BACKSPACE] (F12) to move to the field, press [ERASE LINE] (LF or F13) to clear the field, and then enter the new information. Refer to Table 16.2 for descriptions of the fields on the Edit Events form.
[RETURN]	c. Press [RETURN] to reschedule the meeting in your calendar and return to the menu.

16.6 EXERCISE: SCHEDULING A MEETING

This exercise shows you how to schedule a meeting and add an attendee. This exercise requires you to send a meeting notice to two other individuals. You'll therefore have to pick two people and determine their addresses.

Perform the following steps to schedule this meeting:

1. Move to the Events menu in Time Management.

TM EV [RETURN]	From any menu, type "TM EV" and press [RETURN].

2. Set the calendar date to tomorrow's date.

SD [RETURN]	a. Type "SD" and press [RETURN] to set the calendar date.
Set Date: **TOMORROW [RETURN]**	b. Type "TOMORROW" and press [RETURN] to set the calendar date.

3. Create the meeting.

C [RETURN]	a. Type "C" and press [RETURN]. ALL-IN-1 displays the Create Event form.
	b. Enter details for the meeting. Press [TAB] to move to the next field. Make sure you enter "y" next to "Invite Attendees?" The result should look something like Figure 16.1.
[RETURN]	c. Press [RETURN] to complete the Create Event form. ALL-IN-1 displays the Enter Attendees form.
Name: ***attendee-name*** **[RETURN]**	d. Type the name of one person you would like to invite as an attendee, and press [RETURN]. If you don't know any valid names, press [FIND] (or [GOLD] L) to list all possible names and select a single name.
[RETURN]	e. Press [RETURN] again to complete the Enter Attendees form. ALL-IN-1 asks if you want to add comments.
Y [RETURN]	f. Type "Y" and press [RETURN].
This is a test meeting, please ignore.	g. When the editor displays meeting information on your screen, type a note indicating that this is a test meeting notice.
[GOLD] F	h. Press [FILE] ([GOLD] F) when you're finished entering the comment. ALL-IN-1 redisplays the menu with a message that the event has been scheduled and notices sent.

```
                              Create Event

Scheduler:   WASHINGTON

Date:        08-Oct-1994       Start Time: 08:00am     End Time: 09:00am
Purpose:     Review results of trip to Los Angeles
Confidential? (Y/N)      N
Invite Attendees? (Y/N)  Y
Location (if attendees): ____________________________

Enter information and press RETURN
```

Figure 16.1 Create Event form

4. Invite someone else to the meeting.

AA [RETURN]	a. Type "AA" and press [RETURN]. ALL-IN-1 displays the event.
[RETURN]	b. Press [RETURN] to add attendees. ALL-IN-1 displays the Enter Attendees form.
Name: *attendee-name* **[RETURN]**	c. Type the name of one other person you would like to invite to the meeting, and press [RETURN]. (Again, if you do not know any valid names, press [FIND] (or [GOLD] L) to list all possible names and select a single name.)
[RETURN]	d. Press [RETURN] again to complete the Enter Attendees form. ALL-IN-1 asks if you want to add comments.
Y [RETURN]	e. Type "Y" and press [RETURN].
This is a test meeting, please ignore.	f. When the editor displays meeting information on your screen, type the comment.
[GOLD] F	g. Press [FILE] ([GOLD] F) when you've finished entering the comment. ALL-IN-1 redisplays the menu with a message that the event has been scheduled and notices sent. You'll most likely receive replies back in the mail.

16.7 RESPONDING TO A MEETING NOTICE

ALL-IN-1 sends an electronic mail message notifying you when you've been invited to a meeting. This message is placed in your Inbox with all other incoming mail. You will therefore come across these invitations when reading new mail. When you finish reading a meeting notice, ALL-IN-1 asks whether you can attend the meeting. You are allowed to respond "YES" or "NO" and to add a comment. Your response is sent back to the scheduler of the meeting as an electronic message, and a copy is filed in your Outbox. ALL-IN-1 automatically schedules the event on your calendar if you accept the meeting.

You don't have to respond immediately to a meeting notice. ALL-IN-1 automatically checks your calendar for conflicts, but you might want to check the calendar yourself or perhaps check with other people before accepting a meeting. In this case, exit while reading the message. The message becomes an "unanswered" meeting request. ALL-IN-1 displays the number of unanswered meeting requests at the top of every menu. You can respond later with the Answer Meeting Request (AM) option.

You can also notify the scheduler verbally whether you can attend. ALL-IN-1 allows the scheduler of a meeting to record your response with the Reply for Attendee option. You'll still receive the meeting notice in your Inbox, however.

To read and respond to a meeting notice, do the following:

EM RN [RETURN]	a. From any menu, type "EM RN" and press [RETURN] when you receive notification of new mail.
[RETURN]...	b. Read the message. Meeting notices contain the phrase, "You are invited to the following meeting," followed by details of the meeting. Continue pressing [RETURN] until the Reply to Event form is displayed.
Can you attend? **Yes** or **No [TAB]** Comment: ***comment***	c. Type "NO" only if you cannot attend the meeting ("YES" is the default). If you want to add a comment, press [TAB] and type your comment. Comments are displayed next to attendees' names when the meeting is later read. *Note:* Press [EXIT] (F10 or Keypad-0) if you do not want to respond immediately to the meeting request. You can respond later with Answer Meeting Request (AM).
[RETURN]	d. Press [RETURN] after entering your response and a comment. If your response is "NO," ALL-IN-1 asks if you want to schedule the event in your calendar anyway. If so, type "Y" and press [RETURN]. ALL-IN-1 asks if you want to attach a memo to your reply.
Y [RETURN]	e. Type "Y" and press [RETURN] if you want to add a memo to your reply. Enter your memo and press [GOLD] F when finished.
N [RETURN]	Or, type "N" and press [RETURN] if you do not want to add a memo. ALL-IN-1 redisplays the menu along with a note that the message has been sent. This message is placed in your Outbox.

If you change your mind about attending a meeting, simply select and edit the event. Your new response is automatically sent to the scheduler of the meeting.

16.8 DISPLAYING AN EVENT

The Read (R) option on the Events menu and index displays full information for the current event. If the event is a meeting that you've scheduled, you'll see the list of attendees, along with their responses. This is therefore a quick way to determine who has responded to the meeting notices.

You can always select and read an event from the Events menu. However, you'll find it easier to select and read events from an index. The following procedure shows you how to read an event from the Events at a Glance index.

Perform these steps to display an event:

TM EG [RETURN]	a. From any menu, type "TM EG" and then press [RETURN] to move to the Events at a Glance index.
SD [RETURN]	b. Type "SD" and press [RETURN] to set the calendar date.
Set Date: ***date* [RETURN]**	c. Type the date of the event you want to display and press [RETURN]. ALL-IN-1 displays an index of all events for the specified date. *Hint:* If you don't remember the exact date, clear the date and press [FIND] (or [GOLD] L) to list events.
***line-number* R [RETURN]**	d. Type the line number of the event you want to view, followed by "R", and press [RETURN]. For example, type "3 R" and press [RETURN] to display the third event. ALL-IN-1 displays the event.
[EXIT]	e. Press [EXIT] (F10 or Keypad-0) to clear the event.
	f. Repeat steps d and e to display another event for the day. Repeat steps b through e to display events for another day.
[EXIT]	g. Press [EXIT] (F10 or Keypad-0) to clear the index and return to the menu.

16.9 CANCELING AN EVENT

The Delete (D) option on the Events menu cancels an event. This removes all information about the event from your calendar. If the event is a meeting that you scheduled, notices are automatically sent to the attendees to notify them that the meeting has been canceled. If the event is a meeting that someone else scheduled, no message is sent to the scheduler. You must first select the Edit (E) option and change your response to notify the scheduler that you will not be attending.

Deleting an event removes all information from your calendar; therefore, deleting old appointments and meetings obviously "cleans up" your calendar. This is recommended to keep your calendar down to a manageable size. An easy way to delete many old events is with the Multiple Delete (XD) option on the Events at a Glance menu.

To delete events, do the following:

TM EG [RETURN]	a. From any menu, type "TM EG" and press [RETURN] to move to the Events at a Glance index.
SD [RETURN]	b. Type "SD" and press [RETURN] to set the calendar date.
Set Date: ***date* [RETURN]**	c. Type the date of the event you want to delete, and press [RETURN]. ALL-IN-1 displays an index of all events for the specified date. If you don't remember the exact date, clear the date and press [FIND] (or [GOLD] L) to list events.
***line-number* [RETURN]**	d. To delete a single event, type the line number of the event you want to delete, and press [RETURN]. The current item pointer (>) is moved to the specified line.
line-line,line... **[SELECT]**	To delete multiple events, type the line numbers or range of line numbers of the event you want to delete, and press [SELECT] (or Keypad-Period). Selected events are marked with a small x.
D [RETURN]	e. To delete the current event, type "D" and press [RETURN].
XD [RETURN]	To delete all selected events, type "XD" and press [RETURN]. ALL-IN-1 asks you to confirm the deletion.
Y [RETURN]	f. Type "Y" and press [RETURN] to delete the event or events.
[EXIT]	g. Press [EXIT] (F10 or Keypad-0) to clear the index and return to the menu.

Getting Started with Tasks

CHAPTER 17

Tasks are obligations to perform work. Completing a report by a certain date, cleaning out your files, or simply running an errand are all examples of tasks. Time Management helps you keep track of tasks by recording information in your calendar. This information includes the project name, task title, description, start date, due date, and a status, indicating whether the task is "open" or "closed" (completed). ALL-IN-1 can be set up to display a list of open tasks whenever you start ALL-IN-1. This helps you keep on top of open projects.

This chapter teaches you the basics of working with tasks in Time Management. You'll learn how to perform the following tasks:

- Record tasks in your calendar.
- Modify due dates and close tasks as a project progresses.
- Display task information.
- Delete tasks after project completion.

17.1 ACCESSING THE TASKS MENU

The Tasks menu contains options for scheduling, updating, closing, and deleting tasks in your calendar.

Perform the following steps to access the Tasks menu:

TM T [RETURN]	a. From any menu, type "TM T" and then press [RETURN].
***menu-option* [RETURN]**	b. Type the menu option for the operation you want to perform, and press [RETURN].

Table 17.1 describes the options on the Tasks menu. Note that these options are also available on screens that display an index view of tasks: Tasks at a Glance (TG) and Events and Tasks (ET).

Table 17.1 Tasks menu options

Enter This Menu Option	*To Perform the Following Action*
C (Create)	Schedule a new task in your calendar.
CL (Close Task)	Close the current task.
D (Delete)	Delete all information for the current task from your calendar.
E (Edit)	Modify details for the current task in your calendar—change the due date, for example.
I (Index)	Display an index of tasks.
MO (Month's Overview)	Display a cryptic view of the current calendar month.
P (Print)	Print details of the current task.
PEG (Print Events)	Print events for the current calendar date and the days to follow.
PET (Print Events and Tasks)	Print events and open tasks for the current calendar date.
PMO (Print Month's Overview)	Print a cryptic view of the current calendar month.
PWE (Print Week's Events—Expanded)	Print full details for events of the current calendar week in tabular format.
PWG (Print Week's Events—Grid)	Print brief information for events of the current calendar week in calendar format.
R (Read)	Display details of the current task.
SD (Set Date)	Set the current calendar date.
SEL (Select)	Select a task with which to work.
WE (Week's Events—Expanded)	Display full details for events of the current calendar week in tabular format.
WG (Week's Events—Grid)	Display brief information for events of the current calendar week in calendar format.

17.2 RECORDING A TASK

The Create (C) option on the Tasks menu records information for a task in your calendar. This information includes a category name, title, start date, description, and due date. Review the description of these fields in Table 17.2 before entering this information in your calendar. It makes sense to choose an appropriate category name and title, and of course, the start and end dates must fit into your work schedule. Table 17.2 provides guidelines on choosing a category name and title.

Perform the following steps to schedule a task in your calendar:

C [RETURN]

a. From the Tasks menu or index, type "C" and press [RETURN] to create a task. ALL-IN-1 dis-

```
                              Create Task
Category:      TASK                 Title:   3
Start Date:    __________
Description:   ____________________________________________________
               ____________________________________________________

Due Date:      __________
Status:        _
```

Figure 17.1 Create Task form

plays the Create Task form that is shown in Figure 17.1.

Category: **category [TAB]**
Title: ***title***

b. Enter the category and title of the task. Note that both of these fields are already filled in. To accept the present category and title, press [RETURN]. To change the category and title, press [ERASE LINE] (LF or F13), type the new category, press [TAB] to move to the Title field, press [ERASE LINE] to clear the title, and type a new title. Refer to Table 17.2 for descriptions of the fields on this form.

[RETURN]

c. Press [RETURN] after entering the category and title. ALL-IN-1 checks to make sure that this task does not already exist.

Start Date: ***dd-mmm-yyyy* [TAB]**
Description: ***desc-line-1* [TAB]**
***desc-line-2* [TAB]**
Due Date: ***dd-mmm-yyyy***

d. Enter the remaining details of the task. When completing the form, press [TAB] to move to the next field, or press [BACKSPACE] (F12) to move to the previous field.

[RETURN]

e. Press [RETURN] to schedule the task in your calendar and return to the menu.

Table 17.2 **Fields of information for a task**

Field	*Description*
Category[a]	The group name for this task. This field is already filled in with the category "TASK." You can keep this category name or change it when creating a new task. However, once you complete the form, you cannot change the category. It is recommended that you change the contents of this field to something more meaningful when creating a new task; use a project name, for example. This allows you to list tasks by project in an index of tasks.
Title	A brief description of the task. This field is already filled in with a task number. You can keep this number as a title or change it when creating a new task. However, once you complete the form, you cannot change the title. It is important to remember that tasks are sorted by title within a category when listed on an index. Therefore, you may want to start your title with a letter or number to indicate the priority of the task within the category. If there are a number of tasks in a category, a decimal numbering scheme works well (1.0, 1.1, 1.1.1, 1.2, 1.3, 2.0, etc., at the beginning of each title). The exercise at the end of this chapter illustrates the value of numbering titles.
Start Date	The date on which work for this task begins. The current calendar date already fills the Start Date field when you create a new task. To accept this date, simply press [TAB]. To change the date, type a new date. Note that all entries shown in Table 15.2 are also valid here. For example, you can enter "+1W" to specify a date one week from the current calendar date.
Description	One or two lines of information describing work to be completed. This information is optional. If you feel the title is descriptive enough, omit the description. Note that only 10 characters of the title appear on an index of tasks, whereas 38 characters of the description are displayed.
Due Date	The target date for the work to be completed. This field does not have to be filled in when you create a task; you can fill in the due date later with the Edit option. All entries shown in Table 15.2 are valid for the due date.
Status	The status "O" indicates that the task is open. This value is entered automatically and cannot be changed when you create a task. The Close Task option allows you to change this value to "C," indicating that the work for the task has been completed. All open tasks with a start date earlier than the current date are displayed whenever you start ALL-IN-1. However, you can override this action with Set Working Conditions.

[a] ALL-IN-1's lookup feature helps complete this field. Press [ERASE LINE] (LF or F13) to clear the field, then press [FIND] (or [GOLD] L) to display a list of existing categories. Refer to Section 3.2.2, "Using [FIND] to Complete a Field," for further information on the lookup feature.

17.3 UPDATING AND CLOSING A TASK

As a project progresses, you might need to modify details of a task. You can change the task's start date, description, and due date with the Edit (E) option on the Tasks menu. Close the task when the work is finally completed or when circumstances prevent the task from being completed. ALL-IN-1 retains information in your calendar for the closed task but does not display the task when you start ALL-IN-1.

Do the following to edit the current task:

E [RETURN]	a. Type "E" and press [RETURN] to modify the task. ALL-IN-1 displays the Edit Task form.
Start Date: ***dd-mmm-yyyy...***	b. Modify the details of the task. To change information, press [TAB] or [BACKSPACE] (F12) to move to a particular field, press [ERASE LINE] (LF or F13) to clear the field, then enter the new information. Refer to Table 17.2 for descriptions of the fields on this form.
[RETURN]	c. Press [RETURN] to update the task in your calendar and return to the menu.

To close the current task, do the following:

CL [RETURN]	a. Type "CL" and press [RETURN] to close the task. ALL-IN-1 displays the Close Task form.
Closure Date: ***dd-mmm-yyyy*** **[TAB]**	b. The closure date is already filled in with today's date. Press [TAB] to accept this date, or enter a new date and press [TAB].
Closure Desc: ***desc-line-1*** **[TAB]** ***desc-line-2***	Type one or two lines of text to describe the final status of the task. This information is optional.
[RETURN] **[RETURN]**	c. Press [RETURN] twice to close the task and return to the menu.

Note that the Close All Selected (XCL) option on the index of tasks provides a quick way to close a number of tasks related to the same project.

17.4 DISPLAYING A TASK

The Read (R) option on the Tasks menu displays information for the current task. You might prefer the index view of tasks to display all tasks for a specific category or project.

Perform the following steps to display the current task:

R [RETURN]	a. Type "R" and press [RETURN]. ALL-IN-1 displays the task.
[EXIT]	b. Press [EXIT] (F10 or Keypad-0) when you're finished reviewing the task.

To display all tasks for a specific category (project), do the following:

TM T I [RETURN]	a. From any menu, type "TM T I" and press [RETURN] to display the index of tasks.
[DOWN ARROW] Category: ***category*** **[RETURN]**	b. Press [DOWN ARROW] to move the cursor to the Category field. Type a category name and press [RETURN]. ALL-IN-1's lookup feature is available for entering the category. Press [FIND] (or [GOLD] L) while the cursor is in this field to list existing categories. ALL-IN-1 displays an index of all tasks for the specified category.
line-number **R [RETURN]**	c. Type the line number of the task you want to display, followed by "R" and press [RETURN]. ALL-IN-1 displays the task.
[EXIT]	d. Press [EXIT] (F10 or Keypad-0) to clear the task.
	e. Repeat steps c and d to display any additional tasks. *Note:* You can also select multiple tasks and read them with the Read All Selected (XR) option.
[EXIT]	f. Press [EXIT] (F10 or Keypad-0) to clear the index and return to the menu.

17.5 DELETING A TASK

The Delete (D) option on the Tasks menu removes all information about a task from your calendar. You might typically delete a task long after completion. Deleting closed tasks cleans up your calendar and is recommended to keep your calendar down to a manageable size. The Multiple Delete (XD) option on the Tasks index provides an easy way to delete a number of tasks.

Perform these steps to delete the current task:

D [RETURN]	a. Type "D" and press [RETURN] to delete the task. ALL-IN-1 asks whether you want to delete the task.
Y [RETURN]	b. Type "Y" and press [RETURN] to confirm that you want the deletion. ALL-IN-1 clears the task from the menu.

To delete multiple tasks, do the following:

TM T I [RETURN]	a. From any menu, type "TM T I" and press [RETURN]. ALL-IN-1 displays an index of tasks with a form for entering selection criteria.

Task Status (O/C): ***status...***

b. Enter any information you want to select tasks for the index. When completing the form, press [TAB] to move to the next field, or press [BACKSPACE] (F12) to move to a previous field. Refer to Table 17.2 for descriptions of the fields on this form.

[RETURN]

c. Press [RETURN] to build an index of tasks. ALL-IN-1 displays an index of all tasks matching your selection criteria.

***line-line,line...* [SELECT]**

d. Type the line numbers or range of line numbers of all tasks you want to delete then press [SELECT].

Note: Press [NEXT PAGE] (or [GOLD] [TAB]) to display any additional pages of tasks. Repeat the selection process.

To deselect tasks, type the line number and press [GOLD] [SELECT] (or [GOLD] Keypad-Period).

To select all tasks, type "ALL" and press [RETURN]. Type "CAS" and press [RETURN] to deselect all tasks.

XD [RETURN]

e. Type "XD" and press [RETURN]. ALL-IN-1 asks whether you want to delete the selected tasks.

Y [RETURN]

f. Type "Y" and press [RETURN] to confirm the deletion. ALL-IN-1 clears the tasks from the index.

[EXIT]

g. Press [EXIT] (F10 or Keypad-0) to clear the index and return to the menu.

17.6 EXERCISE: TRACKING A PROJECT WITH TASKS

This exercise shows you how to organize a series of tasks and record them in your calendar with Time Management. The example on the next page lists eight of the tasks necessary to complete a project. You'll see how important it is to plan the project, even though the project itself is rather superficial: building a dog house.

This example illustrates the benefit of including a decimal numbering scheme in your title. Enter all of the major tasks (1.0, 2.0, 3.0) first, then enter all of the subtasks. You'll learn how to start a project by defining the major areas of work and then refine the work schedule by filling in detailed tasks as planning progresses.

SAMPLE PROJECT

Task	*Category*	*Title*	*Start Date*	*Due Date*	*Description*
1	DOG HOUSE	1.0	TODAY	TODAY	Plan construction.
2	DOG HOUSE	2.0	TODAY	TOMORROW	Purchase materials.
3	DOG HOUSE	3.0	TOMORROW	TOMORROW	Construction.
4	DOG HOUSE	1.1	TODAY	TODAY	Obtain book from library on dog house construction.
5	DOG HOUSE	1.2	TODAY	TODAY	Read book.
6	DOG HOUSE	2.1	TODAY	TODAY	Make a list of materials.
7	DOG HOUSE	2.2	TOMORROW	TOMORROW	Make a trip to lumber yard.
8	DOG HOUSE	3.1	TOMORROW	TOMORROW	Discuss various construction duties with kids: parents—supervisory, kids—labor.

Perform the following steps to schedule these tasks in your calendar:

1. Move to the Tasks menu in Time Management.

TM T [RETURN] — Type "TM T" and press [RETURN] to move to the Tasks menu.

2. Set the calendar date to today's date.

SD [RETURN] — a. Type "SD" and press [RETURN].

Set Date: **TODAY [RETURN]** — b. Enter "TODAY" (or "TOD") and press [RETURN] to set the calendar date to today.

3. Create the first task.

C [RETURN] — a. Type "C" and press [RETURN]. ALL-IN-1 displays the Create Task form.

Category: **[ERASE LINE] DOG HOUSE [TAB]**
Title: **[ERASE LINE] 1.0** — b. Enter the category "DOG HOUSE" and the title "1.0" for the first task. Press [ERASE LINE] (LF or F13) to clear each field before typing the new information. Press [TAB] to move to the Title field.

[RETURN] — c. Press [RETURN] after entering the category and title.

d. Enter the remaining details of the first task. Press [TAB] to move to the next field. The result should look like Figure 17.2.

[RETURN] — e. Press [RETURN] to schedule the task in your calendar and return to the menu.

```
                         Create Task
Category:      DOG HOUSE      Title: 1.0

Start Date:    02-Jan-1995

Description:   Plan Construction


Due Date:      02-Jan-1995
Status:        0
```

Figure 17.2 Sample Create Task form

4. Repeat the procedure in step 3 to add the other major tasks (tasks 2 and 3).
5. Display your tasks with the Tasks at a Glance index.

TG [RETURN]	Type "TG" and press [RETURN]. ALL-IN-1 displays a list of tasks like the one shown in Figure 17.3.

```
              Tasks at a Glance: Tuesday      03-Jan-1995
(Selections: 0  )        (Meetings waiting: 0  )        (New messages: 1  )
Tasks for: WASHINGTON

  No. Category     Title      Due Date     Description

> 1   DOG HOUSE    1.0        02-Jan-1995 Plan Construction
  2   DOG HOUSE    2.0        03-Jan-1995 Purchase Materials
  3   DOG HOUSE    3.0        03-Jan-1995 Construction


Move to item and enter option (press GOLD MENU to see options,
or HELP for more information)
```

Figure 17.3 Tasks at a Glance index

```
                  Tasks at a Glance: Tuesday        03-Jan-1995
(Selections: 0  )          (Meetings waiting: 0  )          (New messages: 1  )
Tasks for: WASHINGTON

  No. Category    Title      Due Date    Description

> 1   DOG HOUSE   1.0        02-Jan-1995 Plan Construction
  2   DOG HOUSE   1.1        02-Jan-1995 Obtain book from library on dog house
  3   DOG HOUSE   1.2        02-Jan-1995 Read book
  4   DOG HOUSE   2.0        03-Jan-1995 Purchase Materials
  5   DOG HOUSE   2.1        02-Jan-1995 Make list of materials
  6   DOG HOUSE   2.2        03-Jan-1995 Make a trip to lumbar yard
  7   DOG HOUSE   3.0        03-Jan-1995 Construction
  8   DOG HOUSE   3.1        03-Jan-1995 Discuss various construction duties wi

Move to item and enter option (press GOLD MENU to see options,
or HELP for more information)
```

Figure 17.4 Completed Tasks at a Glance index

6. Repeat the procedure in step 3 to add tasks 4 through 8. You can create tasks from the Tasks at a Glance menu. Note how your index changes as you add tasks. Subtasks are properly inserted under the major tasks because of the decimal numbering scheme used for the title. Finally, your index looks something like Figure 17.4

7. Assume that you've completed task 2, and close this task.

2 CL [RETURN]	a. Type "2 CL" and press [RETURN] to close the task. ALL-IN-1 displays the Close Task form.
Closure Date: **[TAB]** Closure Desc: **Task completed**	b. The closure date is already filled in with today's date. Press [TAB] to accept this date and move to the Closure Description field. Type a description.
[RETURN] **[RETURN]**	c. Press [RETURN] twice to close the task and return to the index. Note that the task is removed from the display.

8. Clear the index and return to the menu.

[EXIT]	When finished, press [EXIT] (F10 or Keypad-0) to erase the index and redisplay the menu.

Displaying and Printing Your Calendar

CHAPTER 18

This chapter describes additional methods for displaying and printing portions of your calendar. The figures in this chapter show the various formats available. You'll notice that some formats are more useful than others. When showing the week's events, for example, the expanded format shown in Figure 18.2 contains much more detail than the grid format shown in Figure 18.3.

The Events at a Glance and Tasks at a Glance index views described in Chapters 16 and 17 are also good methods for reviewing your calendar. If you want a hard copy of these displays, you can copy them to your Scratch Pad with [GOLD] P and print your Scratch Pad.

This chapter teaches you how to perform the following tasks:

- Display events that overlap in your calendar, causing a scheduling conflict.
- Display or print weekly and monthly overviews of events.
- Print events for a range of days.
- Print events and tasks.

18.1 DISPLAYING YOUR CALENDAR

Time Management provides a number of options for displaying your calendar in different formats. These options, listed in Table 18.1, are available on all events and tasks menus. Figures 18.1 through 18.4 show examples of several options.

The steps for displaying your calendar are listed below. An important step is to set the calendar date to the first day you want to review. Most of the options listed in Table 18.1 begin displaying your calendar with the current calendar date.

To display your calendar from any events or tasks menu, do the following:

SD [RETURN]	a. Type "SD" and press [RETURN] to set the calendar date to the specific day you want to display.
Set Date: ***date* [RETURN]**	b. Type the date and press [RETURN].

menu-option **[RETURN]**

c. Type a menu option to display your calendar and press [RETURN]. Table 18.1 lists menu options for displaying portions of your calendar. Enter any further information required, and press [RETURN]. ALL-IN-1 displays your calendar.

Table 18.1 Menu options for displaying the calendar

Enter This Menu Option	*To Perform the Following Action*
CO (Conflicts)	Display a list of events that overlap during the current calendar day. Figure 18.1 shows the display. Only overlapping events are listed in this display.
MO (Month's Overview)	Display a cryptic view of the current calendar month. Figure 18.4 shows the display. Although there is a lack of detail, this display is useful in identifying the busiest days of the month.
R (Read)	Display details of the current event.
TC (Two Calendars)	View your calendar alongside that of another person. To do this, you must enter the name of the other person and have access to view his or her calendar. The other person must first extend this privilege to you with Calendar Access Management.
WE (Week's Events—Expanded)	Display full details for the events of the current calendar week in tabular format. Figure 18.2 shows an example of the display.
WG (Week's Events—Grid)	Display brief information for events of the current calendar week in calendar format. Figure 18.3 shows the display. Time periods labeled with "*MULTIPLE*" identify conflicting events. (See the "Conflicts" entry in this table.)

```
             Schedule Conflicts for Friday   22-Jul-1994

WASHINGTON
 From       To        Description

 08:00am    05:00pm   East Bay Utilities project planning session
 09:00am    10:00am   Monthly supervisor's meeting
```

Figure 18.1 Conflicts (CO) display

```
Calendar Owner: WASHINGTON

             Schedule for the Week of 22-Jul-1994

                    Monday    18-Jul-1994

10:00am 11:00am        Weekly department meeting

11:30am 12:30pm        Lunch at The Seafood Diet

------------------------------------------------------------
                    Tuesday   19-Jul-1994

09:00am 09:30am        Meet with Digital to discuss Financial

01:00pm 05:00pm        Spreadsheet training - Alpha Computers

------------------------------------------------------------
                    Wednesday 20-Jul-1994


07:30am 08:00am        Take car in for service

01:00pm 01:30pm M YES Discuss East Bay Utilities project
                       My office

03:30pm 05:00pm M YES Discuss annual review - William Jefferson
                       My office
                            •
                            •
```

Figure 18.2 Week's Events—Expanded (WE and PWE) display

[RETURN]... d. Press [RETURN] to read additional pages of your calendar. Refer to Section 4.1.1, "Reading a Document," for details.

18.2 PRINTING YOUR CALENDAR

Time Management also provides a number of options for printing your calendar in different formats. These options are listed in Table 18.2. Some of these options print the calendar in the same format as the display options shown in Figures 18.1 through 18.4.

Perform the following steps to print your calendar from any events or tasks menu:

SD [RETURN] a. Type "SD" and press [RETURN] to set the calendar date to the specific day you want to print.

Set Date: ***date* [RETURN]** b. Type the date and press [RETURN].

Table 18.2 Menu options for printing the calendar

Enter This Menu Option	*To Perform the Following Action*
P (Print)	Print details of the current event.
PEG (Print Events)	Print events for the current calendar date and the days to follow. You will be asked to enter the number of days you wish to print. Figure 18.5 shows a sample printout. In this report, the Type field indicates whether the event is an appointment (A) or a meeting (M).
PET (Print Events and Tasks)	Print events and open tasks for the current calendar date. Figure 18.6 shows a sample printout.
PMO (Print Month's Overview)	Print a cryptic view of the current calendar month. The format is the same as the Month's Overview display shown in Figure 18.4.
PWE (Print Week's Events—Expanded)	Print full details for the events of the current calendar week in tabular format. The format is the same as the Week's Events—Expanded display shown in Figure 18.2.
PWG (Print Week's Events—Grid)	Print brief information for the events of the current calendar week in calendar format. The format is the same as the Week's Events—Grid display shown in Figure 18.3.

***menu-option* [RETURN]**

c. Type a menu option to print a portion of your calendar, and press [RETURN]. Table 18.2 lists menu options for displaying portions of your calendar. Some menu options require that you enter additional information before printing the calendar. Enter any further information required, and press [RETURN]. ALL-IN-1 displays the Printing Document form.

[RETURN]

d. Press [RETURN] to print the document if the information shown is correct. Refer to Section 4.2, "Printing in ALL-IN-1," for further details. ALL-IN-1 redisplays the menu with a note that the document has been submitted for printing.

```
                      Calendar Owner: WASHINGTON

                 Schedule for the Week of 22-Jul-1994

            Monday        Tuesday       Wednesday      Thursday       Friday
          18-Jul-1994   19-Jul-1994   20-Jul-1994   21-Jul-1994   22-Jul-1994

08:00am |             |             |             |             | East Bay U  |
08:15am |             |             |             |             | ***         |
08:30am |             |             |             |             | ***         |
08:45am |             |             |             |             | ***         |
09:00am |             | Meet with   |             |             | *MULTIPLE*  |
09:15am |             | ***         |             |             | *MULTIPLE*  |
09:30am |             |             |             |             | *MULTIPLE*  |
09:45am |             |             |             |             | *MULTIPLE*  |
10:00am | Weekly dep  |             |             |             | ***         |
10:15am | ***         |             |             |             | ***         |
10:30am | ***         |             |             |             | ***         |
10:45am | ***         |             |             |             | ***         |
10:45am | ***         |             |             |             | ***         |
11:00am |             |             |             |             | ***         |
11:15am |             |             |             |             | ***         |
11:30am | Lunch at T  |             |             |             | ***         |
11:45am | ***         |             |             |             | ***         |
12:00pm | ***         |             |             |             | ***         |
12:15pm | ***         |             |             |             | ***         |
12:30pm |             |             |             |             | ***         |
12:45pm |             |             |             |             | ***         |
01:00pm |             | Spreadshee  | #Discuss Ea |             | ***         |
01:15pm |             | ***         |  ***        |             | ***         |
01:30pm |             | ***         |             |             | ***         |
01:45pm |             | ***         |             |             | ***         |
02:00pm |             | ***         |             |             | ***         |
02:15pm |             | ***         |             |             | ***         |
02:30pm |             | ***         |             |             | ***         |
02:45pm |             | ***         |             |             | ***         |
03:00pm |             | ***         |             |             | ***         |
03:15pm |             | ***         |             |             | ***         |
03:30pm |             | ***         | #Discuss an |             | ***         |
03:45pm |             | ***         |  ***        |             | ***         |
04:00pm |             | ***         |  ***        |             | ***         |
                                        .
                                        .
```

Figure 18.3 Week's Events—Grid (WG and PWG) display

```
                        Sarah Washington
          Monthly Overview - As Of 22-Jul-1994 - for
                           July 1994

  Sunday  |  Monday  |  Tuesday |Wednesday | Thursday |  Friday  | Saturday
+---------+----------+----------+----------+----------+----------+----------+
|         |          |          |          |          | 1        | 2        |
|         |          |          |          |          |          |          |
|         |          |          |          |          |          |          |
|         |          |          |          |          |          |          |
|         |          |          |          |          |          |          |
+---------+----------+----------+----------+----------+----------+----------+
| 3       | 4        | 5        | 6        | 7        | 8        | 9        |
|         |          |          |          |          |          |          |
|         | 10:00am A| 08:00am A| 08:00am A| 08:00am A|          |          |
|         | Weekly de| Managemen| Managemen| Managemen|          |          |
|         |          |          |          |          |          |          |
|         |          |          |          |          |          |          |
+---------+----------+----------+----------+----------+----------+----------+
| 10      | 11       | 12       | 13       | 14       | 15       | 16       |
|         |          |          |          |          |          |          |
|         | 10:00am A| 11:30am A| 09:00am A| 03:00pm A| 08:00am A|          |
|         | Weekly de| Awards lu| Meet with| 4:10pm Un| Chicago -|          |
|         |          |          |          |          |          |          |
|         | 03:30pm A|          |          |          | 05:00pm A|          |
|         | Eye docto|          |          |          | 5:36pm Un|          |
|         |          |          |          |          |          |          |
+---------+----------+----------+----------+----------+----------+----------+
| 17      | 18       | 19       | 20       | 21       | 22       | 23       |
|         |          |          |          |          |          |          |
|         | 10:00am A| 09:00am A| 07:30am A|          | 08:00am A|          |
|         | Weekly de| Meet with| Take car |          | East Bay |          |
|         |          |          |          |          |          |          |
|         | 11:30am A| 01:00pm A| 01:00pm M|          | 09:00am A|          |
|         | Lunch at | Spreadshe| Discuss E|          | Monthly s|          |
|         |          |          |          |          |          |          |
|         |          |          | 03:30pm M|          |          |          |
|         |          |          | Discuss a|          |          |          |
|         |          |          |          |          |          |          |
+---------+----------+----------+----------+----------+----------+----------+
| 24      | 25       | 26       | 27       | 28       | 29       | 30       |
|         |          |          |          |          |          |          |
|         | 10:00am A|          |          |          |          |          |
|         | Weekly de|          |          |          |          |          |
|         |          |          |          |          |          |          |
                                     •
                                     •
```

Figure 18.4 Month's Overview (MO and PMO) display

```
Schedule for: WASHINGTON

                    Monday 18-Jul-1994

Start    End      Type  Answer  Location
-----    ---      ----  ------  --------
10:00am  11:00am  A
         Weekly department meeting

11:30am  12:30pm  A
         Lunch at The Seafood Diet

                    Tuesday 19-Jul-1994

Start    End      Type  Answer  Location
-----    ---      ----  ------  --------
09:00am  09:30am  A

09:00am  09:30am  A
         Meet with Digital to discuss Financial software

01:00pm  05:00pm  A
         Spreadsheet training - Alpha Computers
```

Figure 18.5 Print Events (PEG) sample printout

```
             Complete Schedule for WASHINGTON
                   Tuesday    19-Jul-1994

                          Events

09:00am 09:30am    Meet with Digital to discuss Financial

01:00pm 05:00pm    Spreadsheet training - Alpha Computers

-----------------------------------------------------------
                           Tasks

EAST BAY UTIL  1.0 IMPLEMENTATION PLAN    22-Jul-1994
Finalize implementation plan
```

Figure 18.6 Print Events and Tasks (PET) sample printout

Advanced Time Management

CHAPTER 19

The preceding chapters showed you the basics of working with Time Management. This chapter deals with more advanced topics. It teaches you how to perform the following tasks:

- Use Set Working Conditions to customize your Time Management environment.
- Work with an index view of events and tasks to manage your calendar.
- Schedule events so that they occur at regular intervals, such as a weekly department meeting.
- Access someone else's calendar and control access to your calendar.

19.1 CUSTOMIZING TIME MANAGEMENT

Set Working Conditions in User Setup allows you to modify many characteristics of your ALL-IN-1 environment. Many of these characteristics affect the display and handling of information in Time Management. For example, if the Calendar Time Increment field is set to 15 minutes, the Week's Events—Grid display shows 15-minute time intervals (8:00, 8:15, 8:30, etc.).

Table 19.1 describes all of the working conditions that affect Time Management. Following is a summary of how to change these working conditions. Refer to Section 5.1.4, "Setting Working Conditions," for further details.

Perform these steps to change the working conditions that affect Time Management:

US SWC [RETURN]

a. From any menu, type "US SWC" and press [RETURN] to display the Set Working Conditions form.

b. Modify your working conditions. The fields that control attributes of Time Management appear at the bottom of the first screen. Press [TAB] or [BACKSPACE] (F12) to move to any field. Press [ERASE LINE] to clear the field, then enter new information.

Table 19.1 Time Management working conditions

Working Condition	*Description*
Notification of:	
Display Tasks	"Y" displays a list of open tasks before displaying the initial menu when you enter ALL-IN-1. "N" suppresses this display and takes you right to your initial menu. You might want to set this parameter to "N" and Count Tasks to "Y".
Count Tasks	"Y" displays a count of open tasks at the bottom of the screen whenever you enter ALL-IN-1. "N" suppresses this information.
Initial TM Form[a]	The name of the form displayed when you enter the option "TM" to access Time Management. Typically, this is the main Time Management menu (TMMENU). However, if you frequently work from the Events Plus index, you can choose this form as your primary Time Management menu. Refer to Table 19.2 for a list of alternate entries for this field.
12 Hour Clock	"Y" causes the time to be displayed in 12-hour format—"6:00pm," for example. "N" causes the time to be displayed in 24-hour format—"18:00," for example.
Working Week:	Identifies your standard working hours to Time Management. This information is used to help schedule events.
First Day	A number 1 through 7 indicating the start of your workweek: 1 corresponds to Sunday, 2 corresponds to Monday, and so forth.
No. of Days	The number of days in your workweek, typically five.
Start Hour/ End Hour	The start time and end time of your workday. These values control how ALL-IN-1 recognizes start and end times that you enter. If you specify working hours of 8 A.M. to 5 P.M., for example, ALL-IN-1 displays an error message when you enter "6" in a time field. This error is displayed because 6 o'clock does not fall between 8 A.M. and 5 P.M., so ALL-IN-1 doesn't know if you mean 6 A.M. or 6 P.M. (Note that you would override this error by simply entering "6pm" or "18:00.")
Meal Start/End	The start time and end time of your meal or break.
Adv. Calendar Day Position	Defines the line number (1 through 7) on which the current calendar day appears in the seven-day summary of the Events Plus index. A value of 3 places the current calendar day summary in the middle of the display. You then see three days prior to the current day and three days following the current day.
Calendar Time Increment	The number of minutes contained in a single scheduling interval in your calendar. This is the increment in time between lines displayed in the Week's Events and Two Calendars reports. *CAUTION:* Specifying a small time interval increases the number of lines generated for certain menu options that print your calendar.

[a] ALL-IN-1's lookup feature can be used in this field. Press [ERASE LINE] (LF or F13) to clear the field, then press [FIND] (or [GOLD] L) to display a list of possible entries. Refer to Section 3.2.2, "Using [FIND] to Complete a Field," for further information on the lookup feature.

Table 19.2 Initial TM form entries

Initial TM Form	*Selects This Screen as Your Primary TM Menu*
TMMENU	Main Time Management menu
TMEG_MENU	Events at a Glance index
TMEP_MENU	Events Plus index
TMET_MENU	Events and Tasks index
TMS	Events menu
TMTG_MENU	Tasks at a Glance index
TMXT	Tasks menu

[RETURN]
[RETURN]

c. Press [RETURN] twice when you've finished updating your working conditions to save your changes and return to the menu.

19.1.1 Choosing an Initial TM Form

Time Management allows you to choose your primary Time Management form. The primary form is displayed when you enter the global option TM. Choose any menu or index listed in Table 19.2 as your primary form.

> *NOTE:* Instructions in the chapters in this part of the manual depend on your selecting TMMENU as the primary Time Management menu. Detailed instructions in this chapter won't work exactly as stated unless TMMENU is your primary menu. You might want to set your primary menu to TMMENU until you become familiar with Time Management.

19.2 WORKING WITH AN INDEX VIEW OF YOUR CALENDAR

Index forms in Time Management list events or open tasks for a specific day, just like a page of your paper calendar. In fact, working with an index view of your ALL-IN-1 calendar is very much like working with your paper calendar. Any new items scheduled or changed show up immediately in the index. You can easily "turn the page" forward by pressing [GOLD] [RIGHT ARROW] or backward by pressing [GOLD] [LEFT ARROW].

Figure 19.1 shows an example of the Events Plus index; one of the most valuable displays in Time Management. The top portion of the index shows the daily events. The bottom portion shows the weekly schedule. Time periods in which events are scheduled are marked with asterisks (*). A monthly calendar is displayed in the lower right-hand corner to help you plan activities for the month.

```
                    Events Plus: Monday          05-Dec-1994
(Selections: 0  )         (Meetings waiting: 0  )        (New messages: 1  )
Events for: WASHINGTON
--------------------------------------------------------------------------
> 1     A  07:30am 08:00am Take car in for winter service
  2     A  11:30am 01:00pm Supervisor's quarterly luncheon
  3     M  03:00pm 04:00pm Discuss December schedule

        8   9   10   11   12   1   2   3   4   5     December        1994
 Sun   ______________________________________        S  M  T  W  T  F  S
<Mon>  *_____________******_________****______                       1  2  3
 Tue   ______________________________________        4< 5> 6  7  8  9 10
 Wed   ______________________________________       11 12 13 14 15 16 17
 Thu   ____******************************____       18 19 20 21 22 23 24
 Fri   ______________________________________       25 26 27 28 29 30 31
 Sat   ______________________________________

Move to item and enter option (press GOLD MENU to see options,
or HELP for more information)
```

Figure 19.1 Events Plus index

You can schedule (create), read, print, and cancel (delete) events by entering menu options at the bottom of the screen. You can also select and work with multiple events as with any index.

This section briefly describes the various index views in Time Management and the procedure for working with an index. Refer to Chapter 3 for more information on working with index forms.

Perform the following steps to create and work with an index of events or tasks:

1. Display the index of events or tasks.

TM *index-option* [RETURN]	From any menu, type "TM" followed by an index option listed in Table 19.3, and press [RETURN]. *Note:* Your ALL-IN-1 account might be set up so that the global option TM does not display the main Time Management menu. In this case, enter "TMMENU" instead of "TM" and press [RETURN].

2. Set the calendar date.

SD [RETURN]	a. Type "SD" and press [RETURN].

Set Date: ***date*** **[RETURN]**

b. Type the date and press [RETURN]. All entries listed in Table 15.2 are valid here. ALL-IN-1 displays an index of events or open tasks for the specified date.

3. Select and manage events or tasks.

To select and manage a single event or task:

line menu-option**[RETURN]**

a. Type the line number followed by a space and the menu option, then press [RETURN]. For example, type "2 E" and press [RETURN] to edit the second item. Press [NEXT SCREEN] (or [GOLD] [TAB]), if necessary, to see any additional pages of items.

b. Enter whatever information is required for the menu option.

To enter a menu option that doesn't act on any particular item in the index:

menu-option **[RETURN]**

a. Type the menu option and press [RETURN]. For example, to create a new event or task, type "C" and press [RETURN].

b. Enter whatever information is required for the menu option.

To select and manage multiple events or tasks:

line,line-line,...**[SELECT]**

a. Type the line numbers or range of line numbers for the items and press [SELECT]. ALL-IN-1 places an *x* next to the selected items.

Note: Press [NEXT PAGE] (or [GOLD] [TAB]) to display any additional pages of items, then repeat the selection process.

To deselect items, type the line numbers and press [GOLD] [SELECT] (or [GOLD] Keypad-Period).

To select all items, type "ALL" and press [RETURN]. Type "CAS" and press [RETURN] to deselect all items.

menu-option **[RETURN]**

b. Enter a menu option and press [RETURN]. Menu options that manage multiple items are listed in Table 19.4.

c. Enter whatever information is required for the menu option.

The following options on the main Time Management menu display an index view of events or tasks. In addition to the options listed in Table 19.3, you can also create an index of events or tasks with just the Index (I) option on the Events or Tasks menu. Enter "TM EV I" to display an index of events, for example. You can then enter selection criteria to choose items for the index.

This allows you to select events or tasks scheduled over a range of days, weeks, or months. This is useful in deleting events and tasks to clean up your calendar.

Table 19.4 describes menu options that manage multiple events or tasks. These options appear on the index menus in Time Management.

Table 19.3 Time Management index views

Enter This Menu Option	*To Perform the Following Action*
EG (Events at a Glance)	Display an index view of events for a single day and manage events in your calendar.
EP (Events Plus)	Display an index view of events for a single day with a weekly overview and monthly calendar and manage events in your calendar. See Figure 19.1 for an example of an Events Plus index.
ET (Events and Tasks)	Display an index view of events and tasks for a single day and manage events and tasks.
TG (Tasks at a Glance)	Display an index view of open tasks and manage tasks in your calendar. Refer to Figure 17.4 for a sample Tasks at a Glance index.

Table 19.4 Index menu options for managing multiple items

Enter This Menu Option	*To Perform the Following Action*
ALL (Select All)	Select all events or tasks listed in the index.
CAS (Cancel All Selected)	Deselect all selected events or tasks.
XCL (Close All Selected)	Close all selected tasks—for example, when a project is complete.
XD (Delete All Selected)	Remove all information for the selected events and tasks from your calendar. Notices will be sent to the attendees of any meeting that is deleted (canceled). This option is recommended for deleting old events and tasks to clean up your calendar.
XP (Print All Selected)	Print full information about all selected events or tasks.
XR (Read All Selected)	Display full information for all selected events or tasks.

19.3 SCHEDULING RECURRING EVENTS

You undoubtedly attend events that repeat at regular intervals. Weekly or monthly department meetings are good examples. Schedule Recurring Events (SRE) makes it easy to schedule these types of events.

Schedule Recurring Events requires you to enter the same information as if scheduling a single event. You enter the date, start time, end time, purpose, and other information for the first event. Then you tell ALL-IN-1 how many times to reschedule the event and at what interval.

Here are some important points to remember when scheduling recurring events:

- Each event scheduled in your calendar is treated as a separate, unique event. For example, if you schedule three events with one SRE operation, you can then reschedule or cancel the first event without affecting the other two. Remember that multiple events are easily canceled with the Delete All Selected (XD) option on the Events index.
- Recurring events are automatically scheduled one by one in your calendar, starting with the first event. When a conflict arises, ALL-IN-1 stops scheduling and notifies you of the conflict. If you don't schedule the event due to the conflict, prior events are still scheduled, but the conflicting meeting and any meetings that follow are not. *Hint:* Continue scheduling all occurrences of the event *regardless* of conflicts, then go back and reschedule individual events that conflict.
- If you're invited to a meeting scheduled with Schedule Recurring Events, you receive only a single notice for all events. If you decline the meeting, none of the meetings are scheduled in your calendar. If you accept the meeting, an attempt is made to schedule all meetings in your calendar.

Perform the following steps to schedule a recurring event:

SRE [RETURN]	a. From an events menu or index, type "SRE" and press [RETURN]. ALL-IN-1 displays the Schedule Recurring Events form.
Date: ***dd-mmm-yyyy*** **[TAB]** Start Time: ***hh:mm*** **[TAB]** End Time: ***hh:mm*** **[TAB]** Purpose: ***description*** **[TAB]** Confidential? (Y/N): **Y** or **N [TAB]** Invite Attendees? (Y/N): **Y** or **N [TAB]** Location: ***location*** **[TAB]**	b. Enter the details of the first event. When completing the form, press [TAB] to move to the next field, or press [BACKSPACE] (F12) to move to the previous field. Refer to Table 16.2 for descriptions of the fields.
Include Weekends?: **Y** or **N [TAB]**	c. Enter "Y" to indicate that you do not want recurring events scheduled on a weekend. Enter "N" to schedule events on weekends. Then press [TAB].

style-number **[RETURN]**	d. Type a number (1, 2, 3, or 4) that corresponds to the scheduling style that best suits your needs. Then press [RETURN]. ALL-IN-1 displays the form for entering recurring event scheduling details. The form varies depending on the style you've selected. *Note:* Examples of the various styles appear on this form below the heading "Style Examples." When you select a style, you'll be asked to replace values that are underlined in the example with values of your own. See the notes that follow for recommendations on selecting a style.
On **MONDAY [TAB]** of every **1 [TAB]** rd week for the next **3** weeks	e. Enter the values for the style you selected. For example, if you selected style 4 to schedule a meeting on Monday morning for the next 3 weeks, enter the information shown.
[RETURN]	f. Press [RETURN] after entering the scheduling details. If you invited attendees, ALL-IN-1 asks you to enter their names and allows you to attach a memo to the meeting notice. See Section 16.4, "Scheduling a Meeting," for details. *Hint:* If you receive notice of a conflicting event, answer "Y" to continue scheduling. Then go back, and select and reschedule the conflicting event.

When selecting a scheduling style, keep the following in mind:

- Select style 1 if you want the same number of days to elapse between each event. Select style 4 if you want the same number of weeks between each event. Select styles 2 or 3 if you want the same number of months between each event.
- Select styles 3 or 4 to schedule the event consistently on the same day of the week. To schedule a meeting that recurs several days of the week—Monday, Wednesday, and Friday, for example—for several weeks in a row, execute the Schedule Recurring Events option three times, selecting style 4.
- If the start date doesn't fall on the day of the week that you selected with styles 3 and 4, ALL-IN-1 finds the first date that falls on the day of the week you selected *following* the specified start date.

19.4 CALENDAR SHARING

Time Management allows you to view other people's calendars. This helps when you're trying to coordinate schedules. Time Management also allows you to schedule and cancel events for someone else. This helps if you manage someone else's schedule. You cannot manage or review someone else's tasks, however. Calendar sharing applies only to events.

You control the degree to which others can view and modify your calendar. This ensures your privacy. You must grant access to your calendar before another user can review or schedule events for you.

19.4.1 Accessing Another User's Calendar

There are three options in Time Management for accessing someone else's calendar:

- Scan for Free Time (SC). Prints a summary of several users' calendars, showing available hours for scheduling a meeting. After printing the chart, ALL-IN-1 asks if you want to schedule a meeting. This option does not require any special privileges because no detailed information is included in this summary.
- Two Calendars (TC). Displays your calendar next to that of another user, listing all events for a single day. This display is organized so that you can easily find a free slot for a meeting. Two Calendars requires that you first be authorized by the other individual.
- Set Owner (SO). This option places you in someone else's calendar. Events menu options then act on the other user's calendar instead of on your own. You can schedule, reschedule, or cancel events as if you were the other user. This option helps those who are responsible for managing someone else's schedule. Set Owner requires that you first be authorized by the other individual.

19.4.1.1 Scan for Free Time

Scan for Free Time prints a summary of several users' calendars, showing which hours of the day are scheduled and which are free. The report is organized so that you can easily locate a time to schedule a meeting. After printing the chart, ALL-IN-1 asks if you want to schedule a meeting. Scan for Free Time requires no special privileges because no detailed information for any calendar is included in the report.

Follow these steps to print summaries of several users' calendars with the Scan for Free Time option:

SC [RETURN]

a. From an events menu or index, type "SC" and press [RETURN] to scan calendars for free time. ALL-IN-1 displays the Scan for Free Time form shown in Figure 19.2.

Date: ***date* [TAB]**
Number of days to Scan:
***number-of-days* [RETURN]**

b. Type the start date for the period you want to scan, press [TAB], type the number of days you want to scan, and press [RETURN]. Or you can simply press [RETURN] to accept the default values. ALL-IN-1 displays the Enter Attendees form.

```
                         Scan for Free Time

Scheduler:   WASHINGTON

Date:        19-Jul-1994        Number of days to Scan:  3
```

Figure 19.2 Scan for Free Time form

Name:*attendee-name* **[RETURN]...**

c. Type the names of the people whose calendars you want to scan. The format for entering names is the same as in Electronic Messaging: a username, last name, nickname, distribution list, remote address, etc. However, only ALL-IN-1 users can be specified. Addresses for different mail systems, such as VMS Mail, are not allowed. Refer to Section 7.1, "Addressing a Message," for details.

Note: Include your own name if you want your calendar to appear in the summary.

[RETURN]

d. Press [RETURN] again after the last name. ALL-IN-1 displays the Printing Document form.

[RETURN]

e. Press [RETURN] to accept the current document destination. ALL-IN-1 prints a summary similar to the one shown in Figure 19.3.

Hint: To display the summary, press [ERASE LINE] (LF or F13) to clear the document destination, type "TERMINAL," and press [RETURN].

Y or **N [RETURN]**

f. ALL-IN-1 asks if you want to schedule an event. Type "Y" and press [RETURN] to schedule a meeting. Follow the procedure listed under Section 16.4, "Scheduling a Meeting," to complete the Create Event and Enter Attendees forms.

Type "N" and press [RETURN] if you do not want to schedule a meeting at this time.

19.4.1.2 Two Calendars

Two Calendars displays your calendar alongside that of another user, listing all events for a single day. This display is organized so that you can easily find free time for a meeting. The other individual must first permit you to access his or her calendar, however. See Section 19.4.2, "Controlling Access to Your Calendar," for details.

```
                Available Schedules for 19-Jul-1994

               8   9   10  11  12  1   2   3   4   5

JEFFERSON      ------------------------**-----------
WASHINGTON     ----**--------------*****************

                Available Schedules for 20-Jul-1994

               8   9   10  11  12  1   2   3   4   5

JEFFERSON      ****************--------------*******
WASHINGTON     --------------------**--------*******

                Available Schedules for 21-Jul-1994

               8   9   10  11  12  1   2   3   4   5

JEFFERSON      -------------------------------------
WASHINGTON     -------------------------------------

Asterisks mean booked time, Dashes mean free time
All of the attendees' free time has been displayed
```

Figure 19.3 Scan for Free Time report

To display Two Calendars, perform these steps:

SD [RETURN]

a. From an events menu or index, type "SD" and press [RETURN] to set the calendar date.

Set Date: ***date* [RETURN]**

b. Type the date you want to display and press [RETURN].

TC [RETURN]

c. Type "TC" and press [RETURN]. ALL-IN-1 asks for the second user's name.

Enter the second user's name:
***name* [RETURN]**

d. Type the name of the other user and press [RETURN]. ALL-IN-1 displays the two calendars side by side, as shown in Figure 19.4, or a message appears advising you that no entries were found for the specific day.

Note: ALL-IN-1's lookup feature is available when entering the name of the other user. Press [FIND] (or [GOLD] L) to list names.

You will receive an error message if the owner of the calendar hasn't given you access to it.

```
JEFFERSON

         Schedule for Tuesday   19-Jul-1994

JEFFERSON                  WASHINGTON
 Time   Description         Time  Description

08:00am                    08:00am
08:30am                    08:30am
09:00am                    09:00am  Meet with Digital
09:30am                    09:30am
10:00am                    10:00am
10:30am                    10:30am
11:00am                    11:00am
11:30am                    11:30am
12:00pm                    12:00pm
12:30pm                    12:30pm
01:00pm                    01:00pm  Spreadsheet training
01:30pm                    01:30pm  ***
02:00pm  Conference call   02:00pm  ***
02:30pm                    02:30pm  ***
03:00pm                    03:00pm  ***
03:30pm                    03:30pm  ***
04:00pm                    04:00pm  ***
```

Figure 19.4 Two Calendars display

[RETURN]...

e. Press [RETURN] to read the additional pages. You can also press [NEXT SCREEN], [PREV SCREEN], or a number of other function keys to move between pages. Refer to Section 4.1.1, "Reading a Document," for details.

Note: Confidential entries for the second user are shown with a string of pound signs (###).

[EXIT]

f. Press [EXIT] (F10 or Keypad-0) to clear the display and return to the menu when finished reviewing the calendars.

19.4.1.3 Set Owner

Set Owner places you in another user's calendar, where you can review, schedule, reschedule, and cancel the other person's events. This option is useful if you're responsible for managing someone else's schedule.

Set Owner has some restrictions:

- This feature does not let you manage someone else's tasks.
- You must be authorized by the system administrator to use the Set Owner option.

- You must also be authorized by the owner of the calendar with which you want to work. See Section 19.4.2, "Controlling Access to Your Calendar."

Be careful when using Set Owner to access someone else's calendar. All changes are made to his or her calendar. The new name appearing at the top of menus is a reminder that you're working in someone else's calendar. Make sure that you switch back to your own calendar when you need to schedule your own events.

Perform the following steps to work in another user's calendar:

SO [RETURN]	a. From an events menu or index, type "SO" and press [RETURN] . ALL-IN-1 asks for the calendar owner's name.
Owner: ***name* [RETURN]**	b. Type the owner's name and press [RETURN]. ALL-IN-1 redisplays the menu. The name displayed in the Owner field is now changed. *Note:* ALL-IN-1's lookup feature is available for entering the calendar owner. Press [FIND] (or [GOLD] L) to list names. You will receive an error message if the system administrator has not authorized you to use Set Owner or if the calendar owner has not granted you access.
	c. You can now execute any option on the events menus. This includes creating, editing, displaying, printing, and deleting events.
SO [RETURN]...	d. When you've finished working in the other user's calendar, use Set Owner to switch back to your calendar, or simply exit ALL-IN-1. You'll notice that your name is automatically filled in as the calendar owner when you use Set Owner a second time. You need only press [RETURN] to switch back to your calendar.

19.4.2 Controlling Access to Your Calendar

You just learned how easy it is to access someone else's calendar. However, there's a security mechanism that controls your ability to view and modify other users' calendars. This ensures that everyone's calendar remains private.

Calendar Access Management lets you control access to your calendar. You can grant either of the privileges on the next page to specific individuals:[1]

1. Calendar Access Management applies only to events. You cannot authorize someone to access your tasks.

- The privilege to view events in your calendar with the Two Calendars option.
- The privilege to schedule, reschedule, display, and delete events in your calendar with the Set Owner option.

You can also list those who have access to your calendar and those whose calendars you can access. Options on the Calendar Access Management menu are described in Table 19.5.

Perform the following steps to grant another user access to your calendar:

TM CAM [RETURN]	a. From any menu, type "TM CAM" and press [RETURN].
A [RETURN]	b. Type "A" and press [RETURN] to give someone else authority to access your calendar. ALL-IN-1 displays the Add User form. *Note:* To modify or remove privileges previously given to another user, select the Edit (E) or Delete (D) option, as described in Table 19.5.
Access given to user: *name* **[RETURN]**	c. Type the name of the other user and press [RETURN]. ALL-IN-1's lookup feature is available. Press [FIND] (or [GOLD] L) to list names.
Allow two calendar? (Y/N): **Y** or **N [TAB]** Allow set owner? (Y/N): **Y** or **N**	d. Type "Y" or "N" in the remaining fields to grant the other user privilege to view your calendar with Two Calendars and/or to use Set Owner to modify your calendar.
[RETURN] **[RETURN]**	e. Press [RETURN] twice to add this user to your calendar access list. ALL-IN-1 redisplays the Calendar Access Menu.

Table 19.5 Calendar Access Management menu options

Enter This Menu Option	*To Perform the Following Task*
A (Add a User to Your Calendar Access List)	Grant someone privilege to access your calendar.
E (Edit a User's Access to Your Calendar)	Change the privileges previously granted to someone who has access to your calendar.
D (Delete a User's Access to Your Calendar)	Remove someone from your calendar access list.
LU (List Users with Access to Your Calendar)	List individuals who have access to your calendar.
LC (List Calendars to Which You Have Access)	List individuals whose calendars you can access.

Group Conferencing

PART VI

Group Conferencing allows people to exchange ideas about important topics. There are many similarities between Group Conferencing and a regular meeting. A moderator opens the discussion and announces the first topic. Participants state their views on the topic and, after sufficient discussion, move on to another topic. Eventually, participants leave the meeting when all topics have been sufficiently discussed.

Unlike a meeting, however, Group Conferencing does not require that participants be present in the same location at the same time. People who work different schedules in different locations can still hold a discussion with Group Conferencing. Participants attend the "electronic" conference at their convenience by preparing notes to state their views and reading notes prepared by others. Because the communication is written, minutes of the meeting are automatically recorded.

The following three chapters discuss Group Conferencing. As the title implies, Chapter 20, "Getting Started with Group Conferencing," covers the basics. This chapter shows you how to participate in a conference, including how to join a conference, read notes contributed by other participants, and add notes to state your own opinion. You'll want to cover these basics and perform the exercise at the end of the chapter if you're new to Group Conferencing. This chapter will take you through most of the fundamentals.

Chapter 21, "Becoming More Proficient with Group Conferencing," discusses features that help you work more efficiently with Group Conferencing. You'll learn how to set working conditions that control your Group Conferencing environment and how to work from an index view of notes in a conference. If you haven't worked much with an index, review Section 3.3.6, "Working with Multiple Items in an Index." Indexing is very important in Group Conferencing because it provides the best method for "attending" a conference.

The final chapter in this part, "Moderating a Conference," shows you how to create and moderate a new conference to discuss new topics of interest. This chapter is important for anyone who is interested in being a moderator. Even if you won't be moderating conferences, you might want to review this chapter to get a feel for the role of the moderator and the process of creating a new conference.

The remainder of this introduction explains important concepts and terminology to help you get started with Group Conferencing.

To understand how Group Conferencing works, consider the bulletin board shown in Figure VI.1. Let's assume that an employee is interested in learning how other peo-

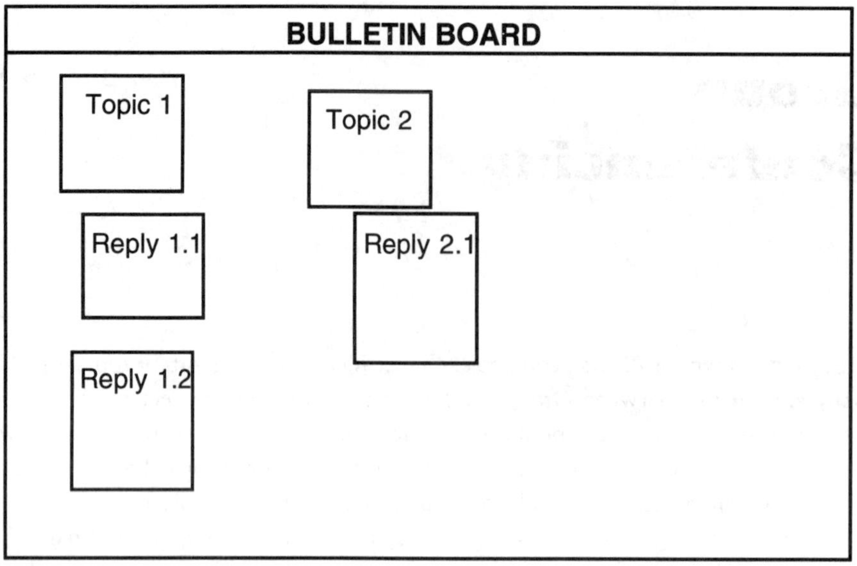

Figure VI.1 "Bulletin board" conferencing

ple feel about a particular subject, so she tacks a note on the bulletin board. The note starts out, "I would like to know your thoughts on . . ." A second employee sees the note, writes a reply, and posts it under the original note. A third employee reads both notes, writes a second reply, and posts it. The next day, the employee who wrote the original note returns and reads all of the replies. As the "discussion" continues, anyone who wishes to participate simply reads the previous notes and posts a reply.

NOTE: Group Conferencing uses the Digital software product VAX NOTES to implement this "bulletin board" method of communication. VAX NOTES and Group Conferencing must both be installed on your system before you can work with Group Conferencing.

Group Conferencing incorporates the following features:

- You can select the conferences and discussions in which you want to participate.
- Notes contributed to a conference are automatically numbered. The first topic is numbered "1.0," the first reply "1.1," the second reply "1.2," and so on. Remaining topics are numbered "2.0," "3.0," etc., and the replies are numbered "2.1," "2.2," etc. This decimal numbering scheme automatically organizes notes in the conference.
- Notes in a conference can be listed in an index. From the index it's easy to select and read notes of interest to you. In addition, you can select and work with multiple notes in an index.

- ALL-IN-1 keeps track of which notes you've already read so you don't waste time rereading notes in a discussion.
- Notes can easily be printed, copied to your File Cabinet, or sent to other individuals through Electronic Messaging. You can also include a document from your File Cabinet in a note you prepare.
- The moderator can restrict access to a conference, allowing only certain individuals to review and contribute notes. The moderator also has the authority to delete notes that don't pertain to the discussion.

You'll come across the following terms when working with Group Conferencing:

Notebook	You're allowed to choose the conferences you want to attend. Group Conferencing maintains information about conferences you've selected in what is called your personal *notebook*. To attend a new conference, you must first add information about the conference to this notebook.
Conference	A conference is a series of discussions on related topics of interest. Each conference is given a unique name that describes its content. You assign your own name to a conference when you first join. This helps you identify the conference in your notebook.
Class	Conferences can be grouped by class. You assign a class name to a conference when you first join. Class names help you organize conferences in much the same way that folders help you organize documents. For example, conferences named "1995 BUDGET," "1995 PROJECTS," and so forth, might be assigned the class name "1995 PLANNING." Class names help you index conferences.
Note	A note contains comments from a participant in a conference. You prepare a note using a text editor in the same way that you prepare a document. Typically, you read notes already posted for a conference before responding. (You want to be prepared!) As you read notes, ALL-IN-1 marks them as "seen." Then, whenever you return to the conference, you can catch up on the conversation by just reading the new, or "unseen," notes.
Discussion	A discussion is a stream or thread of notes containing comments on a specific topic of interest. A discussion consists of the topic note (the first note) and all reply notes.
Topic	The first note in a discussion is the topic. The topic usually poses a question or states the author's view on a particular subject.
Reply	All notes in a discussion other than the topic note are replies. Replies are posted under the topic note in the order in which they are received.

Keywords	Keywords are important words that appear in a note or that describe the content of a note. You can assign keywords when you create your note. This makes it easier for people to scan the conference quickly and find notes with a certain content.
Participant	Anyone who reviews or contributes notes to a conference is a participant.
Moderator	A moderator is the participant who opens a conference, keeps it on track, and closes it. Moderators have the authority to restrict conference participation to specific individuals and to control the content of discussions. By default, the moderator is the person who creates the conference. This person can appoint others to act as additional moderators.
Member	Members are participants in a restricted conference.

GROUP CONFERENCING Q&A

Following is a list of common questions about Group Conferencing.

Q *How does Group Conferencing compare with Electronic Messaging as far as communicating information? When should I use Group Conferencing rather than Electronic Messaging?*

A Electronic Messaging is a perfect way for two people to communicate, exchanging ideas on a variety of topics. This communication is direct and private. Tracking the exchange of messages on a particular topic is cumbersome, though, because all messages are collectively filed in the Read and Outbox folders.

Group Conferencing opens up communication to a larger group of people. Everyone "hears" the ongoing communication between participants. Tracking the exchange of ideas on a particular topic is easy because of the way Group Conferencing numbers and organizes notes.

You will probably want to use Group Conferencing in the following situations:

- You want to "publish" information, making it available to a large number of people. Group Conferencing is an excellent way to implement a bulletin board, help line, or panel discussion.
- You want the answer to a question or thoughts on a particular subject, and you want all of the participants to read the responses.
- You're answering mail messages and sending the reply to a large number of addressees, or you're receiving messages and replies with a large distribution.

Q *How do I access a group conference?*

A There are four basic steps for accessing a group conference:

1. Move to the Group Conferencing menu whenever you want to join or return to a conference. From any menu, type "GPC" and press [RETURN].
2. Add the conference to your notebook to join the conference. Type "AC" and press [RETURN]. Enter the name of the conference file and assign a class and conference name. Note that you only need to perform this step once for each conference you add to your notebook.
3. Select the conference. The Index of Conferences provides an easy way to select a conference in your notebook. Type "IC" and press [RETURN] twice. This displays the list of conferences in your notebook. Type the line number of the conference you want to "attend," and press [RETURN].
4. Create an index of notes for the conference. Type "I" and press [RETURN] twice to list all notes in the conference. You can then select and read specific notes for the conference, post replies, and create new topics.

Refer to Chapter 20 for more detailed instructions on attending a group conference.

Q *How do I read notes in a conference?*

A The Index of Notes option prepares you to read notes in a new conference. Type "I" and press [RETURN] to create an index of notes. Enter selection criteria to list specific notes, or simply press [RETURN] to list all notes. When the index is displayed, scan the list to find a title that interests you. If necessary, press [NEXT SCREEN] to list additional notes.

As you might expect, the Read (R) option displays notes in a conference. When you find a note that you want to read, type the line number followed by a space and "R." Press [RETURN] to display the note. You can then just keep hitting [RETURN] to advance through additional notes in the conference.

When you return to a conference, you might want to list notes with the Index of Unseen Notes (IU) option. This option lists only the notes you haven't read. From this index, you can select and read notes as described above.

Section 20.3, "Participating in a Conference," provides more details on selecting and reading notes in a conference.

Q *How do I find notes pertaining to a particular subject?*

A In a large conference, you'll often want to locate and list notes dealing with a particular subject. The Index of Notes option allows you to enter a wide range of selection criteria to find specific notes. Type "I" and press [RETURN] to create an index for the current conference. Press [DOWN ARROW] to move to the Phrase field, and type a word or phrase. Press [RETURN] to list all notes containing the word or phrase. You can then select and read specific notes, or you can type "ALL XR" and press [RETURN] to read through all of the notes listed in the index.

You can also locate notes by entering keywords when creating the index. However, for this method to work properly, all participants must religiously tag notes with keywords.

Q *How do I edit a note? How do I delete a note?*

A You cannot edit a note in a group conference. You'll notice that the Edit (E) option is not even listed on the Group Conferencing menu.

If you create a note and want to change its content, delete the note immediately. To do this, select the note and execute the Delete (D) option. The note is placed in your Wastebasket. Create a new reply or topic note. When the editor screen is displayed, press [GOLD] G and retrieve the original note from the Wastebasket folder. You can then make the necessary changes before exiting the editor.

Always take the time to reread your note before exiting the editor. Make sure it says exactly what you want it to say before you file it.

Q *How do I send a note to someone else? How do I file a note?*

A You can send a copy of a note to someone else with the Send (S) option. First select the note. This is easy to do with an index of notes. Type "I" and press [RETURN] twice to display a list of the notes in the current conference. Type the line number of the note you want to send, followed by a space and "S," and press [RETURN]. The Forwarding Message form is displayed. Enter one or more usernames and a subject for the message, and indicate whether you want a cover note. A copy of the note is sent when you complete this information.

However, remember that this is a *group* conference. The person you're sending the note to might want to participate in the conference and access other notes. If this is the case and the user has access to the conference file, help this person add the conference to his or her notebook.

To file a copy of a note as a document in your File Cabinet, follow the procedure for listing notes in a conference. Use the File Note (FN) option instead of Send, and enter a drawer, folder, and title for the new document. Notes are often filed so that they can be edited and perhaps included in other documents.

Q *Why use the Set Conference Seen option? How do I mark notes as "unseen"?*

A An established conference might have a large number of notes, many of which are outdated. When you join this type of conference, you might be interested in reading only current notes as they're added. The Set Conference Seen (SCS) option marks all existing notes in the current conference as "seen." You can then keep current by returning to the conference at any time and reading unseen notes with the Read Unseen (RU) or Index of Unseen Notes (IU) options.

If you mark notes as "seen" either by reading the notes or with the Set Conference Seen option, you can still select and reread notes with the Read (R) option. However, if you want to mark notes in the conference as "unseen," remove the conference from your notebook (option RC) and add the conference back (option AC).

GROUP CONFERENCING DOs AND DON'Ts

Here are some suggestions for working efficiently with Group Conferencing:

Do

- Write notes in a concise and informative manner, just as if you were writing a newspaper article. Remember that lots of people might read your notes. Here are some tips on good note-writing:
  - Try to get your point across in either the title or the first sentence of the note. Use the remainder of the note to explain your point. People tend to skip notes that don't have something meaningful in either the title or the first sentence.
  - Try to keep your note short and to the point. Most people don't have time to read lengthy notes in a conference. If possible, keep the length of your note to less than 18 lines of text (which will fit neatly on a single screen). Also, try to keep paragraphs to 8 lines or less. Short paragraphs are easier to comprehend than long ones.
  - Stick to the topic being discussed! Don't pose unrelated questions or discuss new topics in a reply. Create a new topic instead.
  - Use language that's easy to understand. Pretend that you're just talking to the reader. Tasteful humor, short stories, and analogies can make your note more enjoyable to read and more memorable.
  - Following are just a few of the "facial" expressions that you can include in the text of your note. The following elements are actually composed of typewritten characters: colon, hyphen, parenthesis, etc. *Hint:* Turn the book sideways!

    :-) Grinning face

    ;-) Wink

    :-(Unhappy face

    |-(Frown
  - When referring to a previous note in the current topic, provide a direct quote. Retrieve the previous note with the [GOLD] G function key, and extract a specific quote by cutting and pasting.
  - By all means, proof your note before you exit the editor. Return to the top of your note and reread the entire content. Make sure that your note says exactly what you want it to. Check your spelling, either with the on-line spell checker or manually.

    If you do add a note and then decide to make changes, delete the note immediately. The note is placed in your Wastebasket. Create a new note and use [GOLD] G to retrieve the original note from the Wastebasket folder. Edit and proofread the note before exiting the editor a second time.

- Adopt some convention for the format of a title. When titles are listed in an index of notes, it helps if you can easily distinguish topic notes from replies. Some options:
  - Use all uppercase letters for the titles of topic notes and mixed upper- and lowercase letters for the titles of replies.
  - Start the title of a topic note with one or two asterisks, or start the topic note with several spaces and use multiple hyphens (---) before and after the title.
  - Start the title of a reply note with a space, or a hyphen followed by a space. This creates a nice outline format in the index of notes.

Don't

- Don't use text highlighting or advanced formatting in your notes. Notes are converted to simple "no-frills" ASCII format before being stored in the note file. This allows notes to be displayed by a variety of front-end applications running on different systems. Text highlighting and advanced formatting are lost during the conversion.
- Don't use nonspecific titles like "For your information" for your notes. Instead, use meaningful titles like "ELVIS Spotted at Local Donut Shop." This helps participants identify the notes they want to read when viewing titles in an index.
- DON'T USE ALL UPPERCASE LETTERS IN THE TEXT OF YOUR NOTE EXCEPT WHEN YOU WANT TO SHOUT!
- Don't use foul language in your note, and don't disclose confidential information. Remember that a lot of people might read your note. If it contains objectionable or sensitive matter, the moderator will most likely delete it.
- Don't create a topic note when it makes more sense to create a reply to an existing note. This has a lot to do with improving the organization of notes in a conference. Notes are poorly organized when everyone contributes thoughts by creating a new topic. This makes it hard for people to follow the various streams of discussion when viewing notes in an index. Consider the following example:

Note	*Title*
1.0	1994 Happy Fun Ball Sales Figures
2.0	Negative Press for Baby Hurls-O-Lot Doll
3.0	1995 Sales Projections
4.0	Keep the Lid on Happy Fun Ball's Chemical Ingredients
5.0	TIMES Article on Baby Hurls-O-Lot Doll
6.0	Corporate Press Stance on Baby Hurls-O-Lot
7.0	Medical Problems -> Exposure to Ruptured Happy Fun Ball

Notes are more successfully organized when topic notes are general and replies are specific. The organization of the notes listed above could have been improved if the moderator had first created the topic notes "SALES INFORMATION" and "PRODUCT PUBLIC RELATIONS." Notice the use of all caps in the topic titles and the hyphen at the beginning of the reply titles.

Note	*Title*
1.0	SALES INFORMATION
1.1	- 1994 Happy Fun Ball Sales Figures
1.2	- 1995 Sales Projections
2.0	PRODUCT PUBLIC RELATIONS
2.1	- Negative Press for Baby Hurls-O-Lot Doll
2.2	- Keep the Lid on Happy Fun Ball's Chemical Ingredients
2.3	- TIMES Article on Baby Hurls-O-Lot Doll
2.4	- Corporate Press Stance on Baby Hurls-O-Lot
2.5	- Medical Problems -> Exposure to Ruptured Happy Fun Ball

Getting Started with Group Conferencing

CHAPTER 20

This chapter covers the basics of participating in a conference, describing techniques that are important to learn if you're new to Group Conferencing. You'll learn how to join and take part in a group conference, including how to

- Access the Group Conferencing menu.
- Join a conference by adding it to your notebook.
- Participate in a conference by reading the notes, posting replies, and creating new topics.

20.1 ACCESSING GROUP CONFERENCING

You can access Group Conferencing from the Information Management menu or by simply entering the global menu option GPC. The Group Conferencing menu contains all of the options for participating in and moderating a conference. This menu contains three screens. The first screen lists options for working with notes in the current conference. The second screen lists options for organizing conferences in your notebook. The third screen lists options for moderating a conference. Moderating a conference is discussed in Chapter 22.

Perform the following steps to access Group Conferencing:

GPC [RETURN]	a. From any of the menus, type "GPC" and press [RETURN].
***menu-option* [RETURN]**	b. Type the menu option and press [RETURN]. Tables 20.1 and 20.2 describe these options. Options for creating and moderating a conference are discussed in Chapter 22.

Table 20.1 Group Conferencing menu options for managing notes

Enter This Menu Option	*To Perform the Following Action*
CT (Create Topic)	Open a new topic for discussion in the current conference.
D (Delete)	Delete the current note and place a copy in the Wastebasket. You are allowed to delete only the notes you've created.
FN (File Note)	File a copy of the current note as a document in your File Cabinet.
FT (File Text)	File only the text of the current note as a document in your File Cabinet. This does not include the header information (topic, note title, etc.).
I (Index)	Display an index of notes for the current conference.
IU (Index Unseen Notes)	Display an index of unseen notes for the current conference. Unseen notes are notes that you have not previously read.
MN (Modify Note)	Edit details of the current note. You can only modify details of a note, not the text. In addition, it must be a note that you created.
P (Print)	Print the current note and mark the note as "seen."
PI (Print Index)	Print an index of notes for the current conference.
R (Read)	Display the current note on your terminal screen.
RE (Reply)	Post a reply note to the current topic for other participants to read.
RI (Recall Index)	Redisplay the last index of notes created with the Index option.
RU (Read Unseen Notes)	Display all unread notes for the current conference, starting with the earliest note.
S (Send)	Send a copy of the current note to another individual with Electronic Messaging.
SEL (Select)	Select a note or conference with which to work.

Table 20.2 Group Conferencing menu options for managing conferences

Enter This Menu Option	*To Perform the Following Action*
AC (Add Conference)	Add to your notebook a conference that you want to attend.
CP (Conference Profile)	Display information about the current conference.
DCF (Delete Conference File)	Delete the current conference. This option deletes the conference file, thereby deleting all notes in the conference. Only the conference moderator or someone with delete access to the conference file can delete a conference.
IC (Index of Conferences)	Display a list of the conferences in your notebook.
ICK (Index Conference Keywords)	Display an index of the keywords associated with notes for the current conference.

Table 20.2 *(continued)*

Enter This Menu Option	*To Perform the Following Action*
ICM (Index Conference Members)	Display an index of members participating in the current conference.
MC (Modify Conference Details)	Change the class or conference name that you assigned to the current conference.
RC (Remove Conference)	Remove a conference from your notebook when you no longer wish to participate.
SCS (Set Conference Seen)	Mark all existing notes in the current conference as "seen" even though you have not read them. This is sometimes done when joining a long-standing conference with a large number of notes. You can then keep up on current discussions with the Read Unseen Notes option.
SWC (Set Working Conditions)	Set parameters to customize your Group Conferencing working environment.

20.2 JOINING A CONFERENCE

Group Conferencing maintains a notebook that lists the conferences in which you participate. You must add the details of a conference to this notebook in order to join. The details include the conference file name, a class name, and a conference name. The moderator determines the conference file name when creating the conference. This file stores notes for the conference. You assign the class and conference names when you join. These names help you organize and identify conferences in your notebook. You can change both the class name and the conference name later if you decide to reorganize your notebook.

In this section, you'll learn how to perform the following tasks:

- Join a conference by adding it to your list of conferences.
- Modify the class and conference names assigned to a conference.
- Leave a conference by removing it from your list of conferences.

20.2.1 Adding a Conference

You must add a conference to your personal notebook before you can participate. Adding a conference enters the details of the conference into your notebook. You can then select the conference and read and add notes.

Follow these steps to add a conference to your notebook:

AC [RETURN]	a. Type "AC" and press [RETURN]. ALL-IN-1 displays the Add Conference form shown in Figure 20.1.

```
                         Add Conference

Conference filename: ________________________________________

Class:               MAIN______________________

Conference name:     ________________________________________

Enter conference details and press RETURN
```

Figure 20.1 Add Conference form

Conference: **[FIND]**

b. Press [FIND] (or [GOLD] L) while the cursor is in the Conference field. ALL-IN-1 displays a list of conferences.

   Note: Sometimes, other conferences exist than may be listed here. Conferences might not be included in this list in order to keep them private. If this is the case, obtain the conference file name from the moderator, and enter it in this field.

***line-number* [RETURN]**

c. Type the line number corresponding to the conference you want to access, and press [RETURN].

[TAB]
Class: ***class-name* [TAB]**
Conference Name: ***conf-name***

d. With the conference file name entered, press [TAB] and enter a class name and a conference name. Refer to Table 20.3 for descriptions of these items. When entering details, press [TAB] to move to the next field.

[RETURN]

e. Press [RETURN] after completing the Add Conference form. ALL-IN-1 redisplays the menu with a message that the conference has been added.

You can change the class or conference names later with Modify Conference Details (MC) if you decide to reclassify or rename the conference.

20.2.2 Removing a Conference

When you no longer want to participate in a conference, remove the conference from your notebook with the Remove Conference (RC) option. You can add a conference back to your notebook after removing it. However, the conference is added back to your notebook with all notes marked as "unseen."

Table 20.3 Add Conference details

Field	*Description*
Conference	The conference file name. A conference file is very much like a file cabinet. It stores notes for the conference in the same way that your File Cabinet stores documents. The file name identifies the location of the conference file. The format of a conference file name is as follows: *node::filespec* where *node* is the name for the VAX system where the conference file resides. "0::" can be substituted for the node if the file resides on the same system as your account. *filespec* is a VAX/VMS file specification for the conference file. This specification identifies the location and name of the file (disk drive, directory, file name, and type). A list of system conferences is maintained that includes the file name, making it easy to find the file name for a conference with [FIND]. If the conference is not included in this list, you must get the file name from the moderator.
Class	A category name. You can group conferences by class to improve the organization of your notebook. You assign a class name to a conference when you join. If you don't plan on participating in many conferences, simply use the class "MAIN."
Conference Name	A name for the conference. You assign this name when adding the conference to your notebook. Choose a name that best describes the content of the conference. For simplicity, the file name of the conference is often used as the conference name.

20.2.3 Selecting a Conference

You must select a conference before choosing options to read or write notes. Most options on the Group Conferencing menu act on the current conference.

There are several ways to select a conference, two of which follow. The first method selects a conference from the index of conferences in your notebook. This is convenient because you see the list of conferences while making a selection. The second method makes use of the Select option. This method might be preferable if you're in the habit of working from a menu.

To select a conference from the Index of Conferences in your notebook, do the following:

IC [RETURN]	a. Type "IC" and press [RETURN] to display the Index of Conferences.
[RETURN]	b. ALL-IN-1 allows you to enter a class name and conference name to list specific conferences. To list all conferences, leave both fields blank and press [RETURN].

***line-number* [RETURN]**	c. Type the line number of the conference you want to access, and press [RETURN]. The current item pointer (>) moves to the specified conference. *Note:* If necessary, display any additional conferences in the list by pressing [NEXT SCREEN] (or [GOLD] [TAB]).
I [RETURN] **[RETURN]**	d. Type "I" and press [RETURN] twice to work with an index of notes for the selected conference.
[GOLD] F	Or press [GOLD] F to select the current conference and return to working with the conference from the Group Conferencing menu.

Follow these steps to select a conference with the Select option:

SEL [RETURN]	a. Type "SEL" and press [RETURN]. ALL-IN-1 displays the Select Note form.
[UP ARROW] **[UP ARROW]**	b. Move the cursor back to the Class field by pressing [UP ARROW] twice.
Class: **[ERASE LINE] [TAB]** Conference: ***conf-name***	c. Press [ERASE LINE] (F13) to clear the class name, press [TAB], and type the conference name. ALL-IN-1's lookup feature is available for entering the conference name. Press [FIND] (or [GOLD] L) to display the names of the conferences in your notebook.
[RETURN]	d. Press [RETURN] when you complete the form. ALL-IN-1 redisplays the menu with the selected conference shown as current.

20.3 PARTICIPATING IN A CONFERENCE

Participating in a conference involves reading the comments of others and contributing comments of your own. After joining a conference, prepare to participate in the discussion by first reading the existing notes. You can then reply to notes in the discussion or create topics of your own.

In this section, you'll learn how to perform the following tasks:

- Read notes contributed by other participants in the conference.
- Add notes to a discussion.
- Select a note with which to work.
- Create new topics of discussion.

20.3.1 Reading New Notes in a Conference

Reading notes is how you "listen" to other participants in a Group Conference. Typically, you review notes immediately after joining a conference or returning to a conference. There are several options for reading notes in a conference:

- The Read (R) option, as you might have guessed, is the standard option for reading notes. One nice feature is that when you reach the end of a note and press [RETURN], the next note in the discussion is displayed. If you happen to be reading the last note in a topic, the next unseen note in the conference is displayed. An efficient way to read notes in a conference is to create an index of notes, find a topic that interests you, and read the first note. Then just keep pressing [RETURN] to read all of the replies.
- Read Unseen Notes (RU) is the best method for keeping on top of new notes added to a conference. This option displays all of the new notes for a conference, one by one. ALL-IN-1 marks a note as "seen" when you finish reading it. Read Unseen Notes skips over these notes the next time you read unseen notes for the conference.
- The Index of Unseen Notes (IU) lists new notes for the conference. As with all index screens, you can then select the items that you want to read. You might prefer this option to Read Unseen Notes when working with a large conference because it allows you to read just the unseen notes that interest you.

Figure 20.2 shows an example of a note displayed on your screen. A status block at the top of the screen contains information about the note, including the topic title, the note title (blank in this example), the number of lines of text in the note, the author's node and username, the note number, the creation date, and the number of reply notes.

Perform the following steps to read notes in the current conference:

1. Choose any of the following methods to start reading notes in the conference. The first method is suitable for most conferences. The second or third method is better for conferences with a large number of notes.

   To start reading notes from an index of notes or an index of unseen notes in the conference:

I [RETURN]	a. Type "I" and press [RETURN] to display an index of notes. ALL-IN-1 displays a form for entering selection criteria.
IU [RETURN]	Or type "IU" and press [RETURN] to display an index of unseen notes. Skip to step c.
[RETURN]	b. Enter information to select specific notes for the index, or simply leave all fields blank and press [RETURN] to list all notes. Refer to Chapter 21 for more information on completing this form.
***line-number* R [RETURN]**	c. Scan the list of titles to find a note you're interested in reading. Type the line number for the

```
Topic Title:  Welcome to Group Conferencing
Note Title:                                             Lines:   25
Author:       VAT69::ALLIN1
Number:       1.0   Created: 02-Nov-1989 12:20pm  Replies:  2
---------------------------- TOP ---------------------------
Group Conferencing is a computer-mediated conferencing
system that lets you conduct on-line conferences and
meetings.  Using Group Conferencing, you can communicate
                                  •
                                  •
```

Figure 20.2 Sample note

note, followed by a space and "R." Then press [RETURN]. If necessary, first press [NEXT SCREEN] to display additional pages of notes.

To start reading notes from unseen notes either from the menu or an index:

RU [RETURN]	Type "RU" and press [RETURN] to read unseen notes. ALL-IN-1 clears the screen and displays the oldest unseen note.

2. Continue reading notes in the conference.

[RETURN]...	a. In general, continue pressing [RETURN] to read notes. While reading a note, you can also do the following: • Press any of the function keys listed in Table 20.4 or Figure 20.3 to display other pages of the note or to move on to another note. • Enter any of the menu options listed in Table 20.5. Most of these menu options manage the current note. For example, type "P" and press [RETURN] to print a copy of the note.
[EXIT]	b. Press [EXIT] (F10 or Keypad-0) at any time to stop reading notes.

Table 20.4 and Figure 20.3 list function keys for reading notes. The numeric keypad provides a quick method for reading notes in a conference. Specific keys display the next note, previous note, next topic, or previous topic. Table 20.5 lists menu options that you can enter while reading notes. You can also use any function keys listed in Table 4.1 while reading notes.

Table 20.4 Function keys for reading notes

Press the Following Key(s)	*To Perform This Action While Reading a Note*
[RETURN] or [ENTER]	Display the next page of the note. If you are at the end of the note, display the next unseen note.
[DOWN ARROW]	Move one line down in text.
[UP ARROW]	Move one line up in text.
[EXIT] (F10 or Keypad-0)	Quit reading notes and return to the menu.
text [FIND]	Searches the current note to locate a specific string of text.
[GOLD] [DOWN ARROW]	Move to the top of the next page.
[GOLD] [UP ARROW]	Move to the top of the current page.
[GOLD] B	Move to the bottom of the document.
[GOLD] T	Move to the top of the document.
[GOLD] M	Display a menu of options that you can enter while reading a document. These options are listed in Table 20.5.
[NEXT SCREEN] (or [GOLD] A)	Display next page (screen) of document.
[PREV SCREEN] (or [GOLD] [BACKSPACE])	Display previous page (screen) of document.

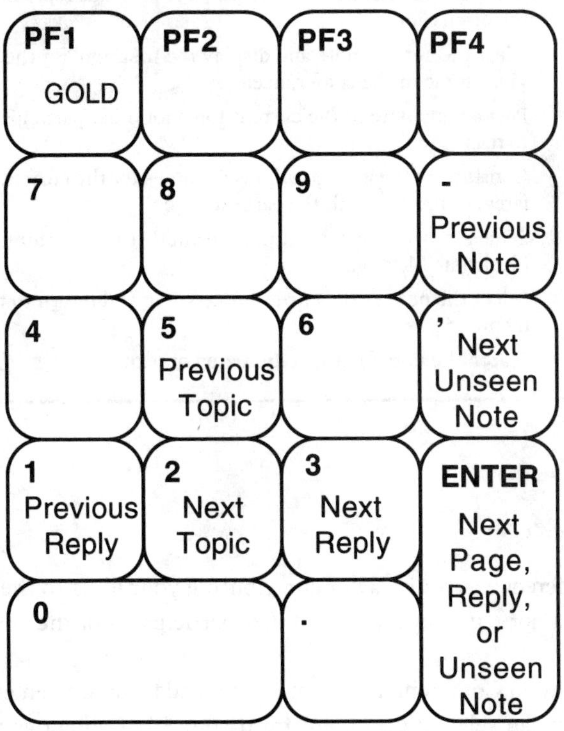

Figure 20.3 Keypad function keys for reading notes

Table 20.5 Read menu options

Enter This Read Menu Option	*To Perform the Following Action*
CT (Create Topic)	Open a new topic for discussion in the current conference.
D (Delete)	Delete the current note and place a copy in the Wastebasket. You are allowed to delete only the notes that you've created.
FN (File Note)	File a copy of the current note as a document in your File Cabinet.
FT (File Text)	File only the text of the current note as a document in your File Cabinet.
MN (Modify Note)	Edit details of the current note. You can only modify details of a note, not the text. In addition, it must be a note that you created.
N (Read Next Selected Note)	Clear the current note and display the next selected note (when working from an index in which multiple notes have been selected).
NR (Read Next Reply)	Clear the current note and display the next reply note in the discussion.
NT (Read Next Topic)	Clear the current note and display the first note for the next topic in the conference.
P (Print)	Print the current note.
PR (Read Previous Reply)	Clear the current note and display the previous reply note in the discussion.
PT (Read Previous Topic)	Clear the current note and display the first note for the previous topic in the conference.
RE (Reply)	Post a reply note to the current topic for other participants to read.
RU (Read Unseen Notes)	Continue the display of all unseen notes for the current conference, starting with the earliest note.
S (Send)	Send a copy of the current note to another person through Electronic Messaging.
SEL (Select)	Select the note as the current note when you return to the menu.
TS (Text Search in Note)	Search the note for a specific string of text.

20.3.2 Adding a Note to a Topic

Adding a note to a group conference is your way of contributing your ideas to the discussion. As soon as you add a note, it is available to other participants of the conference.

The Reply option on the Group Conferencing menu lets you add a note to an existing topic of conversation. You can select a document from your File Cabinet as your note, or you can prepare the note from scratch with your text editor. When you finish your note, Group Conferencing assigns a note number to it and adds the note to the topic of conversation.

You can enter the Reply option while reading notes for a conference. You can also add a reply to a discussion even though you're not currently reading notes. First select the relevant topic, then choose the Reply option to add a note. Select the topic by selecting *any* note in the topic.

This section describes the steps for adding a reply note to a conference. The Create Topic option lets you open an entirely new topic of conversation. This option is discussed later.

To add a reply note to the current topic of discussion, follow these steps:

RE [RETURN]	a. Type "RE" and press [RETURN]. ALL-IN-1 displays the Reply to Note form shown in Figure 20.4.
Note Title: ***note-title*** **[TAB]** Keywords: ***keyword,...*** **[TAB]** Note hidden: **Y** or **N**	b. Enter the details of your reply. Type a title for your note, enter keywords if desired, and indicate whether you want the note to be hidden. Table 20.6 describes these fields of information. ALL-IN-1's lookup feature is available for entering keywords. Press [FIND] (or [GOLD] L) while the cursor is in the Keywords field to list possible keywords.
[RETURN]	c. To create your note from scratch, press [RETURN] after completing the Reply to Note form, and skip to step d.
[NEXT SCREEN]	To select a document from your File Cabinet as your reply, press [NEXT SCREEN] (or [GOLD] A). ALL-IN-1 displays the Select Document form. Enter the drawer, folder, and title, and press

```
                              Reply to Note

Note Title:    ____________________________________________

Keywords:      ____________________________________________

Note hidden: N

Enter information and press RETURN,
or press NEXT SCREEN to submit a File Cabinet document          (more...)
```

Figure 20.4 Reply to Note form

Table 20.6 Note details

Field	*Description*
Note Title	A short description of the note that appears when you select a note or build an index of notes. When creating a note, choose a title that best summarizes the note's content. It's helpful to add characters at the beginning of the title to distinguish a reply from a topic when titles are listed in an index. For example, if you're creating a reply, begin the title with a hyphen and a space. This makes replies look like bulleted items listed under the topic note.
Keywords	One or more keywords that relate to the content of the note. Keywords are helpful when indexing notes for a conference. For example, you might want to create an index of specific notes in the BULLETIN BOARD conference by selecting those notes with the associated keyword "NEWS." When entering keywords, place a comma between words.
Personal Name	A name that identifies you as the author of the note. The personal name specified in Group Conferencing—Set Working Conditions is used when you create a note, but it can be changed with the Modify Note option.
Associated Conference	The name of another conference containing a discussion related to your note. This is an optional field that you can specify with Modify Note.
Note Hidden	Indicates whether the note is available to all participants or just to the moderators of the conference. If you specify "N," the note can be read by any conference participant. If you specify "Y," the note can be read only by you and the conference moderators. Hiding a note is an effective method for allowing the moderator to view the content of a note before opening the note to other participants. This field can then be changed with Modify Note.
Replies Allowed	"Y" indicates that other participants can reply to this topic note. "N" indicates that replies are not allowed. This field applies to a topic note only. For the most part, replies are allowed to all topic notes. Sometimes, however, a moderator creates one or two initial topic notes explaining the purpose of the conference. Replies are often not allowed for these topics.

[TAB]. Type "Y" or "N" to indicate whether you want to edit the document before adding it to the conference. If you respond "N," skip to step f. Press [RETURN] when you've completed the Select Document form.

d. Type the text of your reply. You're now working with the same text editor that you use to create documents. All of its features are available for preparing your note. However, avoid using video attributes like bolding and underlining because they will not appear when the note is posted.

Hint: When creating a reply, it's often valuable to include the portions of the note to which you are responding. For example, you might want to comment on a particular statement made in a prior note in the discussion. To retrieve an existing note, press [GOLD] G, enter "NOTE," and specify the note that you want to retrieve. Then extract portions of the note by cutting and pasting. It's common practice to delimit original text by placing angle brackets around it (>*text*<).

[GOLD] F

e. Press [GOLD] F when you've finished creating your note. ALL-IN-1 asks if you want to add this note to the conference.

Note: This prompt can be suppressed with Group Conferencing—Set Working Conditions (SWC).

Y [RETURN]

f. Type "Y" and press [RETURN] to add the note to the conference.

Table 20.6 describes note details. Some of this information is specified when adding a reply. Other information is specified when modifying the note or creating a topic.

20.3.3 Selecting a Note

Many options on the Group Conferencing menu apply to the current note. You must first select a note before choosing to read, edit, delete, or reply to a note.

Two methods for selecting a note are described below. It's easier to select a note if you're working from an index. You cannot use the [FIND] key to list possible entries when using the Select option from a menu.

Perform the following steps to select a note from an index:

***line-number* [RETURN]**

Type the line number of the note and press [RETURN]. The current item pointer (>) is moved to the specified line.

Notes: If necessary, display any additional pages of notes in the conference by pressing [NEXT SCREEN] (or [GOLD] [TAB]).

You can save time by entering an option after the line number. For example, type "3 P" and press [RETURN] to print the third note.

Perform the following steps to select a note from the menu:

SEL *note-number* [RETURN]

Type "SEL," followed by a space and the note number. Then press [RETURN]. If you don't know the note number, type "SEL 1.0" and press [RETURN] to select the first note. Then press [DOWN ARROW] to advance through the notes, and press [GOLD] [DOWN ARROW] to advance through the topics.

20.3.4 Deleting a Note

The Delete (D) option removes a note that you've added to a conference. As soon as you perform this function, the note is removed from the conference file and is no longer available to other participants. This option allows you to "take back" what you've said. However, exercising this option can be discourteous, especially if other participants have already replied to your note. Use this option sparingly.

You can only delete notes that you've contributed to the conference. You cannot delete other participants' notes unless you are the moderator. As moderator, you can delete any notes with the Moderator Delete Note option.

Deleting a note is similar to deleting a document. The deleted note is placed in your Wastebasket folder (unless you specify otherwise with Group Conferencing—Set Working Conditions). The note remains in your Wastebasket until it is removed by the Janitor.

Perform the following steps to delete the current note (one that you created):

D [RETURN]

a. Type "D" and press [RETURN] to delete the note. ALL-IN-1 will ask you if you want to delete the note.

Y [RETURN]

b. Type "Y" and then press [RETURN] to delete the note. ALL-IN-1 displays a message while the note is being copied to your Wastebasket folder, then displays the message that the note has been deleted.

20.3.5 Modifying Details of a Note

The Modify Note option lets you modify details of a note that you've created. This option allows you to change the title, keywords, and other information about the note.

Modify Note does *not* allow you to modify the content of the note. You must delete the note, then create a new reply to change the content. By the way, act fast if you add a note to a conference and then decide to change the content. Delete the note, placing it in your Wastebasket folder. Then create another reply. When the editor screen appears, use the [GOLD] G function to retrieve the note's contents from your Wastebasket. Edit the content, and file the note.

To modify the details of the current note (one that you created), follow these steps:

MN [RETURN] a. Type "MN" and press [RETURN] to modify the details of the current note. ALL-IN-1 displays the Modify Note form.

b. Modify the details of your note. Press [TAB] or [BACKSPACE] (F12) to move to a particular field, press [ERASE LINE] (LF or F13) to clear the field, and enter the new information. Refer to Table 20.6 for descriptions of the fields on this form.

[RETURN] c. Press [RETURN] when you've finished changing the details of the note.

20.3.6 Printing a Note

The Print option prints a hard copy of the current note. You can perform this function from the Group Conferencing menu, from an index, or while reading the note.

Perform the following steps to print the current note:

P [RETURN] a. Type "P" and press [RETURN] to print the note. ALL-IN-1 displays the Printing Document form.

[RETURN] b. Press [RETURN] to print the note if the information shown is correct. If the information is incorrect, enter the appropriate document destination, format style, or number of copies. Refer to Section 4.2, "Printing in ALL-IN-1," for further details. ALL-IN-1 displays a message that the note has been submitted for printing.

20.3.7 Creating a New Topic

In addition to participating in current discussions by reading notes and adding replies, you can create a new topic of conversation with the Create Topic (CT) option. This option lets you select a document from your File Cabinet as the topic note or prepare a new topic note in the editor.

To create a new topic of conversation in the current conference, use the following steps:

CT [RETURN] a. Type "CT" and press [RETURN] to create a new topic. ALL-IN-1 displays the Create Topic form shown in Figure 20.5.

```
                              Create Topic

Topic title: ____________________________________________

Keywords:    ____________________________________________

Note hidden: N      Replies allowed: Y

Enter information and press RETURN,
or press NEXT SCREEN to submit a File Cabinet document          (more...)
```

Figure 20.5 Create Topic form

Topic Title: ***title* [TAB]**
Keywords: ***keyword,...* [TAB]**
Note hidden: **Y** or **N**
Replies allowed: **Y** or **N**

b. Enter the details of your topic note. Table 20.6 describes these fields of information in detail. When entering details for the topic, press [TAB] to move to the next field.

[RETURN]

c. To create your topic note from scratch, press [RETURN] after completing the Create Topic form and skip to step d.

[NEXT SCREEN]

To select a document from your File Cabinet as your topic note and then press [NEXT SCREEN] (or [GOLD] A). ALL-IN-1 displays the Select Document form. Enter the drawer, folder, and title, and indicate whether you want to edit the document before adding it to the conference. If you respond "N", skip to step f. Press [RETURN] when you've completed the Select Document form.

d. Type the text of your topic note. You're working with the same text editor that you use to create documents. All of its features are available for preparing your note. However, avoid using video attributes like bolding and underlining because they will not appear when the note is posted.

[GOLD] F

e. Press [GOLD] F when you've finished editing your note. ALL-IN-1 asks if you want to add this note to the conference.

Y [RETURN]

f. Type "Y" and press [RETURN] to add the note to the conference.

20.3.8 Exercise: Participating in the Sample Conference

In this exercise, you'll perform all of the basic procedures for participating in a conference. You'll access the sample conference provided with ALL-IN-1, read unseen notes for the conference, add a topic, reply to a topic, and finally delete notes you've added.

This exercise accesses the sample conference placed on the system when Group Conferencing is installed. This conference might be in your notebook already. If you don't find the conference when listing the Index of Conferences in step 2, follow the procedure at the end of the exercise to add the conference to your notebook.

1. First move to the Group Conferencing menu.

GPC [RETURN]	From any menu, type "GPC" and then press [RETURN].

2. Select the sample conference.

IC [RETURN]	a. Type "IC" and press [RETURN]. ALL-IN-1 displays the Index of Conferences.
[RETURN]	b. Leave the selection criteria blank and press [RETURN] to display all conferences.
***line-number* [RETURN]**	c. Look for the conference with the name "Sample_Conference." Type the corresponding line number and press [RETURN]. ALL-IN-1 moves the current item pointer (>) to this conference. *Note:* The name of the conference might be different at your site. If you do not see a conference with a similar name, contact your system administrator for assistance.

3. Display the details of the conference with Conference Profile.

CP [RETURN]	a. Type "CP" and press [RETURN]. ALL-IN-1 displays the Conference Profile shown in Figure 20.6.
[RETURN]	b. Press [RETURN] to clear the Conference Profile and return to the index.

4. Change the details of the conference with Modify Conference details. Note that you can only change the class name and the conference name you assigned to the conference. These changes are made only to *your* list of conferences.

MC [RETURN]	a. Type "MC" and press [RETURN]. ALL-IN-1 displays the Modify Conference Details form.

```
                              Conference Profile

Conference:        Sample Conference
Class:             MAIN

Location:          OAN$SAMPLE_CONFERENCE
Last moderator:    VAT69::ALLIN1

Title:
Notice:            Welcome to Group Conferencing

Total notes:       4                  Unseen notes: 4
Total topics:      2

Membership restricted: N             Keyword creation restricted: Y
Notes may be written:  Y             Restricted to replies only:  N

Conference created: 02-Nov-1989      Last new note: 02-Nov-1989 12:30pm
```

Figure 20.6 Conference Profile

Class: **[ERASE LINE] EXAMPLES**	b. Make sure that the cursor is in the Class field. Press [ERASE LINE] (LF or F13) to clear this field. Type "EXAMPLES."
[RETURN]	c. Press [RETURN] to complete this form. ALL-IN-1 redisplays the index, showing the new class name.

5. Display an index of notes, and read all unseen notes for the conference.

I [RETURN]	a. Type "I" and press [RETURN] to create an index of notes, as shown in Figure 20.7.
[RETURN]	b. Leave all selection criteria blank and press [RETURN] again to list all notes.
RU [RETURN]	c. Type "RU" and press [RETURN]. ALL-IN-1 displays the first note of the "Welcome to Group Conferencing" topic.
[RETURN]...	d. Press [RETURN] until you reach the bottom of the note.
[RETURN]	e. Press [RETURN] again. ALL-IN-1 displays the next note in the topic. Note that the note number has changed.

```
                                Index of Notes
(Selected: 0 )      Conference: Sample Conference          (New messages: 1 )

 No.      Note     Title                        Replies Author           Date

> 1        1.0     Welcome to Group Conferen       2   VAT69::ALLIN1    02-Nov-1989
  2        1.1     Benefits and Applications       2   VAT69::ALLIN1    02-Nov-1989
  3        1.2     Some terms you should kno       2   VAT69::ALLIN1    02-Nov-1989
  4        2.0     Who Are You?                    0   VAT69::ALLIN1    02-Nov-1989

Move to item, and enter option (press GOLD MENU to see options, or HELP for
more information)
```

Figure 20.7 Index of Notes

f. Repeat steps d and e (keep pressing [RETURN]). ALL-IN-1 continues to display notes. Eventually, the first note for the second topic is displayed. Note that the topic number has changed to "2.0." If you continue pressing [RETURN], the index is redisplayed after the last note for the last topic has been displayed.

6. Create a new topic.

CT [RETURN]

a. Type "CT" and press [RETURN]. ALL-IN-1 displays the Create Topic form.

Topic Title: **Bill's Sample Topic [RETURN]**

b. Type a topic title and press [RETURN]. Use your name in the title, for example. ALL-IN-1 clears the screen and invokes the editor so you can enter your note.

This is a new topic note.

c. Type the text of your note.

[GOLD] F

d. Press [GOLD] F to exit the editor and create the topic. ALL-IN-1 asks if you want to add this note to the conference.

Y [RETURN]	e. Type "Y" and press [RETURN]. ALL-IN-1 redisplays the index. Your note does not appear on the index until you rebuild the index. *Note:* If you receive a privilege violation, this means that the sample conference is protected from updates. Contact your system administrator for assistance.
I [RETURN] **[RETURN]**	f. Type "I" and press [RETURN] twice to rebuild the index. Your new topic should now appear in the index.

7. Add a reply note to your topic.

***line-number* [RETURN]**	a. Type the line number of your new topic and press [RETURN]. ALL-IN-1 moves the current item pointer to your topic note.
RE [RETURN]	b. Type "RE" and press [RETURN]. ALL-IN-1 displays the Reply to Note form.
Note Title: **Bill's Second Note** **[RETURN]**	c. Type a note title and press [RETURN]. ALL-IN-1 clears the screen and invokes the editor so you can enter your note.
This is a test reply note.	d. Type the text of your note.
[GOLD] F	e. Press [GOLD] F to exit the editor and create the topic. ALL-IN-1 asks if you want to add this note to the conference.
Y [RETURN]	f. Type "Y" and press [RETURN].
I [RETURN] **[RETURN]**	g. Type "I" and press [RETURN] twice to rebuild the index. Your new reply should now appear in the index.

8. Delete both your topic note and your reply. (Remember, this is just practice!)

***line,line* [SELECT]**	a. Type the line numbers for your topic note and reply, and press [SELECT]. ALL-IN-1 marks the two notes with an *x*.
XD [RETURN]	b. Type "XD" and press [RETURN]. ALL-IN-1 asks if you want to delete the notes.
Y [RETURN]	c. Type "Y" and press [RETURN]. ALL-IN-1 displays a message that the notes have been deleted.

```
                         Add Conference

Conference:      ________________________________________

Class:           ______________________

Conference name: ________________________________________

Enter conference details and press RETURN
```

Figure 20.8 Add Conference form

NOTE: If you do not have the sample conference in your list of conferences, follow the steps listed below to add the conference to your notebook. Contact your system administrator if you have trouble accessing the sample conference.

AC [RETURN]	a. Type "AC" and press [RETURN]. ALL-IN-1 displays the Add Conference form shown in Figure 20.8.
	b. The cursor is in the field in which you enter the conference file. Press [FIND] (or [GOLD] L) to list the system conferences. *Note:* If there are a number of conferences, you might need to press [RETURN] to display additional conference names.
***line-number* [RETURN]**	c. Type the line number for the sample conference and press [RETURN]. ALL-IN-1 redisplays the Add Conference form with the name of the conference file.
Conference: **[TAB]** Class: **MAIN**	d. Press [TAB] to move to the class name and type "MAIN."
[RETURN]	e. Press [RETURN] to add the conference to your list of conferences. ALL-IN-1 redisplays the menu with a note that the conference has been added.

Becoming More Proficient with Group Conferencing

CHAPTER 21

This chapter describes features that help you work more efficiently with Group Conferencing. Topics include how to set up your Group Conferencing environment and how to work with the various index options. If you're new to Group Conferencing, you'll be interested in indexing. The ability to search for, list, and select items might be more important in Group Conferencing than in any other subsystem, perhaps because people tend to move around in the notes a lot, reading a whole group of notes at once for a given topic and jumping from one topic to the next.

This chapter shows you how to perform the following tasks:

- Customize your Group Conferencing working environment by setting working conditions.
- Work with the various index forms in Group Conferencing to manage a conference.

21.1 SET WORKING CONDITIONS

Set Working Conditions (SWC) lets you customize your Group Conferencing working environment. For example, if you decide that you like working from a index of conferences better than working from the menu, you can select this index as the form displayed whenever you enter the global option GPC. Table 21.1 describes Group Conferencing working conditions.

Perform the following steps to set working conditions in Group Conferencing:

SWC [RETURN]

a. Type "SWC" and press [RETURN]. ALL-IN-1 displays the GPC Set Working Conditions form.

b. Modify your Group Conferencing working conditions. Refer to Section 3.2.1, "Completing a Data-Entry Form," for details on completing this form.

[RETURN]

c. When you are finished making changes, press [RETURN] to update your working conditions.

Table 21.1 Group Conferencing working conditions

Working Condition	*Description*
Personal Name	The name that appears next to your username in the notes that you create. This defaults to your full name.
Initial GPC Display	The name of the first screen you see when entering Group Conferencing. If this field is blank, the Group Conferencing main menu is the first screen displayed. Possible entries include these: IC Index of conferences IU Index of unseen notes for the current conference
Editor[a]	The name of the editor that you want to use for preparing notes. The default is the same as the editor specified in your ALL-IN-1 working conditions.
Index Note Range From To	These two values serve as the default note numbers for the first and last notes to select when creating an index of notes. Refer to Table 21.2 on page 412 for examples.
Prompt to Confirm	"Y" indicates that you want to be asked to confirm the addition of the note you've just created to the conference. "N" suppresses this prompt. You might want to set this condition to "N" because you can always delete a note you've created to remove it from the conference.
Place Deleted Notes in Wastebasket	If you enter "N" in this field, deleted notes will not be placed in your Wastebasket and therefore cannot be recovered. You might want to set this to "Y" so that you can recover them.
Include Mail Header in Notes	"Y" indicates that you want to include the message header when you select a message from your File Cabinet as your note. This information is sometimes helpful to the reader of the note. "N" suppresses the header.
Page Break between Notes on Multiple Print	"Y" indicates you want a page break between each note when you select and print multiple notes from an index. "N" prints multiple notes without page breaks, therefore saving paper.

[a] ALL-IN-1's lookup feature can be used in this field. Press [ERASE LINE] (LF or F13) to clear the field, then press [FIND] (or [GOLD] L) to display a list of possible entries. Refer to Section 3.2.2, "Using [FIND] to Complete a Field," for further information.

21.2 WORKING WITH AN INDEX IN GROUP CONFERENCING

Group Conferencing provides several options for indexing notes. Similar to all other subsystems in ALL-IN-1, indexing gives you the ability to list, select, and work with a single item or to select and work with multiple items easily.

You can create the following lists in Group Conferencing:

- Notes in a conference.
- All unseen notes in a conference.
- Conferences in your list of conferences.
- Members for the current conference.
- Keywords for the current conference.

```
                              Index of Notes
(Selected: 0  )      Conference: Sample Conference          (New messages: 1  )
-------------------------------------------------------------------------------
 No.      Note     Title                       Replies Author           Date
-------------------------------------------------------------------------------
> 1        1.0     Welcome to Group Conferen         2  VAT69::ALLIN1    02-Nov-1989
  2        1.1     Benefits and Applications         2  VAT69::ALLIN1    02-Nov-1989
  3        1.2     Some terms you should kno         2  VAT69::ALLIN1    02-Nov-1989
  4        2.0     Who Are You?                      0  VAT69::ALLIN1    02-Nov-1989

-------------------------------------------------------------------------------
Move to item, and enter option (press GOLD MENU to see options, or HELP for
more information)
```

Figure 21.1 Index of Notes

Each of these indexes is described in greater detail in the following pages. The first three are valuable to all conference participants. An index of conferences is a valuable tool for selecting a conference with which to work. The Index of Members and the Index of Keywords are helpful to conference moderators. The Index of Notes (Figure 21.1) is given the most attention because you'll probably work from this index when participating in a conference. An overview of the information listed and the menu options is provided for the remaining indexes. Refer to Section 3.3.6, "Working with Multiple Items in an Index," for more information on working from an index.

21.2.1 Working with an Index of Notes

The Index (I) option on the Group Conferencing menu creates an index of notes for the current conference. You can list all notes for the conference or just specific notes by entering selection criteria. The list of notes shows the following information for each note:

- Note number
- Title
- Number of replies to the topic note
- Author's username
- Creation date of the note

Perform the following steps to create an index of notes for the current conference:

I [RETURN]	a. Type "I" and press [RETURN] to display an index of notes. ALL-IN-1 displays a form for entering selection criteria.
Note range from: *note* **[TAB]...**	b. Enter selection criteria if you want to list only certain notes in the conference. Table 21.2 describes the selection criteria. Leave all fields blank to list all notes in the conference.

Table 21.2 Selection criteria for the Index of Notes

Field	*Description*
Note Range From To	If you want to select notes for the index by note number, enter the first and last note numbers in these fields. The format of a note number is: *topic-number.reply-number* where *topic-number* is the number of the topic in the conference, 1 for the first topic, 2 for the second topic, and so on. *reply-number* is the number of the reply. The topic (first) note has a reply number of 0. The first reply has a reply number of 1, the second has a number of 2, and so on. You can substitute the asterisk (*) wild card character or the keywords "FIRST," "LAST," "ALL," or "TOPIC" for either the topic or the reply number to select ranges of notes. Keywords can also be abbreviated: F, L, A, T. Some examples follow:

From	*To*	*Selects the Following Notes*
1.*	LAST	All notes (1.0, 1.1, 1.2, 2.0, etc.)
ALL	–	All notes (1.0, 1.1, 1.2, 2.0, etc.)
LAST.LAST	1.0	All notes, listed in reverse order.
1	LAST	All topic notes (1.0, 2.0, etc.)
2.TOPIC	2.LAST	All notes for topic 2 (2.0, 2.1, etc.)
2.*	2.LAST	All notes for topic 2 (2.0, 2.1, etc.)

Field	*Description*
Title Containing	To select notes for the index that have specific text in the title, enter a character, word, or phrase in this field.
Author	To select notes for the index created by a particular author, enter all or part of the author's name.
Date Range From To	To select notes for the index that were created in a certain time interval, enter the "from" date and the "to" date in these fields. You can also enter any value that is valid for entering a date in Time Management—"TODAY" or "YESTERDAY," for example.
Created Date	To select notes for the index that were created on a specific date, enter the date in this field.

Table 21.2 *(continued)*

Field	*Description*
Seen Status	To select notes for the index by status, enter either "SEEN" or "UN-SEEN" in this field.
Keywords	To select notes for the index that were tagged with keywords when created, enter the keywords in this field. Separate multiple keywords with a comma. Press [FIND] (or [GOLD] L) to list possible keywords for the conference.
Phrase	To select notes for the index that contain a certain phrase, enter the word or phrase in this field.

[RETURN]

c. Press [RETURN] to create the index.

***line-number* [RETURN]**

d. To select a single note to work with, type the line number and press [RETURN].

***line,line-line,...*[SELECT]**

To select multiple notes to work with, type the line numbers or range of line numbers, separated by commas. Then press [SELECT]. ALL-IN-1 places an *x* next to the selected items.

Note: Press [NEXT SCREEN] (or [GOLD] [TAB]), if necessary, to display any additional pages of items.

***menu-option* [RETURN]**

e. Enter any of the menu options in Table 21.3. Type the menu option and press [RETURN]. To display the menu, press [GOLD] M.

f. Enter any information required for the menu option and press [RETURN].

[EXIT]

g. Perform steps d through f to manage other items in the index. Press [EXIT] (F10 or Keypad-0) to return to the menu when you're through.

The Index of Unseen Notes (IU) lists all notes that you have not yet read for the current conference. This is essentially the same as the Index of Notes, except that only unread notes are listed.

21.2.2 Working with an Index of Conferences

The Index of Conferences (IC) displays the list of conferences in your personal notebook. This is an excellent index for selecting a conference with which to work. You can list all of the conferences in your notebook or enter selection criteria to list specific

Table 21.3 Index of Notes menu options

Enter This Menu Option	*To Perform the Following Action*
ALL (Select All)	Select all notes in the index.
CAS (Cancel All Selected)	Deselect all notes in the index.
CP (Conference Profile)	Display information about the current conference.
CT (Create Topic)	Open a new topic for discussion in the current conference.
D (Delete)	Delete the current note and place a copy in the Wastebasket. You are allowed to delete only the notes you've created.
I (Index)	Create a new index of notes for the current conference.
ICK (Index Conference Keywords)	Display an index of the keywords associated with notes for the current conference.
ICM (Index Conference Members)	Display an index of members participating in the current conference.
IU (Index Unseen Notes)	Display an index of unseen notes for the current conference. Unseen notes are notes that you have not yet read.
MN (Modify Note)	Edit details of the current note. You can only modify details of a note, not the text. In addition, it must be a note that you created.
P (Print)	Print the current note and mark the note as "seen."
PI (Print Index)	Print an index of notes for the current conference.
R (Read)	Display the current note on your terminal screen.
RE (Reply)	Post a reply note to the current topic for other participants to read.
RU (Read Unseen Notes)	Display all unseen notes for the current conference, starting with the earliest note.
S (Send)	Send a copy of the current note to another individual with Electronic Messaging.
SS (Set Seen)	Mark the current note as "seen," even though you have not read it.
XD (Delete All Selected)	Delete all selected notes and place copies in the Wastebasket.
XP (Print All Selected)	Print all selected notes and mark them as "seen."
XR (Read All Selected)	Display all selected notes on your terminal screen.
XS (Send All Selected)	Send all selected notes to another individual with Electronic Messaging.
XSS (Set Seen All Selected)	Mark the selected notes as "seen," even though you have not read them.

conferences. Once you enter selection criteria, the list of conferences is displayed, showing the following information for each conference:

- Class
- Conference name
- Number of topics

- Number of unseen notes
- Creation date of the last note

You can enter any of the menu options listed in Table 21.4 to manage conferences in the index.

21.2.3 Working with an Index of Members

Some conferences have restricted access. The only people who can participate in the conference are those whom the conference moderator has designated as "members."

Table 21.4 Index of Conferences menu options

Enter This Menu Option	*To Perform the Following Action*
AC (Add Conference)	Add a conference to the list of conferences in which you participate.
ALL (Select All)	Select all conferences in the index.
CAS (Cancel All Selected)	Deselect all conferences in the index.
CP (Conference Profile)	Display information about the current conference.
CT (Create Topic)	Open a new topic for discussion in the current conference.
I (Index)	Create a new index of notes for the current conference.
ICK (Index Conference Keywords)	Display an index of the keywords associated with notes for the current conference.
ICM (Index Conference Members)	Display an index of members participating in the current conference.
IU (Index Unseen Notes)	Display an index of unseen notes for the current conference. Unseen notes are notes you have not previously read.
MC (Modify Conference Details)	Change the class name or conference name that you assigned to the current conference.
RC (Remove Conference)	Remove a conference from your list of conferences when you no longer wish to participate.
RU (Read Unseen Notes)	Display all unseen notes for the current conference, starting with the earliest note.
SCS (Set Conference Seen)	Mark the notes for the current conference as "seen," even though you have not read them.
UC (Update Conference)	Update information shown in the index for the current conference (number of topics, unseen notes, and last note creation date).
XRC (Remove Selected Conferences)	Remove all selected conferences from your list of conferences when you no longer wish to participate.
XUC (Update Selected Conferences)	Update information shown in the index (number of topics, unseen notes, and last note creation date).

The Index of Members lists either all members for a restricted conference or just the moderators for unrestricted conferences. This index helps a moderator review and update the membership list for the current conference. Section 22.2, "Controlling Access to a Conference," describes the procedures for maintaining a membership list in further detail.

The Index of Members shows the following information:

- Member's username
- Member's mailing address
- Whether the member is a moderator

You can manage the Index of Members with the menu options that are described in Table 21.5.

Table 21.5 Index of Members menu options

Enter This Menu Option	*To Perform the Following Action*
ALL (Select All)	Select all members in the index.
AM (Add Member)	Add a user to the list of members of the current conference.
CAS (Cancel All Selected)	Deselect all members in the index.
CP (Conference profile)	Display information about the current conference.
I (Index of Notes)	Display an index of notes for the current conference.
ICK (Index Conference Keywords)	Display an index of the keywords associated with notes for the current conference.
ICM (Index Conference Members)	Display an index of members participating in the current conference.
IU (Index Unseen Notes)	Display an index of unseen notes for the current conference. Unseen notes are notes that you have not previously read.
MM (Modify Member)	Modify details of a user's membership. These details include the user's mail address and whether the user can act as a moderator.
P (Print)	Print details for the current conference member.
R (Read)	Display details for the current conference member on your terminal screen.
RM (Remove Member)	Remove a user from the list of members of the current conference.
XP (Print All Selected)	Print details for all selected conference members.
XR (Read All Selected)	Display details for all selected conference members on your terminal screen.
XRM (Remove Member)	Remove all selected users from the list of members of the current conference.

21.2.4 Working with an Index of Keywords

The Index of Keywords (ICK) option creates an index of the keywords associated with notes in the current conference. It lists the keywords along with the numbers of the notes associated with each keyword. This index helps the moderator maintain keywords for the conference. Although it provides a method for searching the conference for notes pertaining to specific keywords, participants often prefer the Index of Notes for this purpose.

Table 21.6 describes the menu options that you can enter from the Index of Keywords to manage notes and keywords for the current conference.

Table 21.6 Index of Keywords menu options

Enter This Menu Option	*To Perform the Following Action*
ALL (Select All)	Select all keywords in the index.
CAS (Cancel All Selected)	Deselect all keywords in the index.
CK (Create Keyword)	Add a new word to the list of keywords associated with the current conference.
DK (Delete Keyword)	Delete a word from the list of keywords for the current conference.
MK (Modify Keyword)	Replace an existing keyword with a new word.
P (Print)	Print the current keyword and a list of associated notes.
R (Read)	Display the current keyword and a list of associated notes on your terminal screen.
XDK (Delete Keyword)	Delete all selected keywords from the list of keywords for the current conference.
XP (Print All Selected)	Print all selected keywords and a list of associated notes.
XR (Read All Selected)	Display all selected keywords and a list of associated notes on your terminal screen.

Moderating a Conference

CHAPTER 22

Group Conferencing allows you to create new conferences to exchange ideas on an entirely new list of topics. Creating a conference involves opening the conference file, notifying other participants of the existence of the conference, and moderating the conference.

By default, you act as the moderator for any conference that you create. If you like, you can appoint other conference participants as moderators. Moderators have certain responsibilities for the conference, and they are granted special privileges to carry out these responsibilities.

This chapter shows you how to perform the duties of a moderator, including how to do the following:

- Create a new conference and change the details of the conference.
- Add individuals' names to the list of conference members, remove names from this list, and change the privileges granted to a member.
- Add words to and delete words from the list of conference keywords.
- Close a conference when the discussion is complete.

The moderator's responsibilities include these:

- The moderator creates the conference. He or she should also create an introductory topic that outlines the purpose of the conference and states the guidelines for participation. The moderator might also create additional topic notes to begin specific discussions or pose questions to participants.
- If the conference is private, the moderator must identify participants by adding their usernames to the list of conference members. No one can participate in a private conference until his or her name has been added to this list.
- The moderator notifies participants when the conference is open and provides the name of the conference file.
- The moderator must periodically review the notes of the conference. If the conversation wanders away from the topic, the moderator should add a reply to keep the discussion on track. He or she also has the authority to delete notes that do not pertain to the discussion.

Table 22.1 Menu options for conference moderators

Enter This Menu Option	*To Perform the Following Action*
CC (Create Conference)	Create or open a new conference.
MCP (Modify Conference Profile)	Modify details of the current conference.
MDN (Moderator Delete Note)	Delete the current note from the conference.
MMN (Moderator Modify Note)	Modify details of the current note. These details include the title, keywords, author's name, and whether to allow replies.
AM (Add Member)	Add a user to the list of members for the current conference.
RM (Remove Member)	Remove a user from the list of members of the current conference.
MCM (Mail Conference Members)	Send an electronic message to all members of the current conference.
MM (Modify Member)	Modify details of a user's membership, including the user's mail address and whether the user can act as a moderator.
CK (Create Keyword)	Add a new word to the list of keywords associated with the current conference.
DK (Delete Keyword)	Delete a word from the list of keywords for the current conference.
MK (Modify Keyword)	Replace an existing keyword with a new word.

- The moderator can add words to and remove words from the list of keywords for the conference. Any participant can tag a note with one or more keywords to help other participants find notes with a particular subject matter.

Menu options for performing the duties of a moderator are listed on the third screen of the Group Conferencing menu and are described in Table 22.1.

22.1 CREATING A CONFERENCE

The Create Conference option creates and opens a new conference. If desired, you can create the first topic note to describe the purpose of the conference or to list topics of discussion.

Creating a conference creates a new conference file, which stores notes written by participants. You should have some knowledge of VMS files and file-naming conventions before continuing. If not, ask your system administrator for assistance.

Once you've created the conference, notify users of the new conference and create a membership list if the conference is private. There are several ways to notify other users of a new conference: send mail messages, add a notice to another conference, or have the system manager add information to the login notice.

Follow these steps to create a new conference:

CC [RETURN]	a. Type "CC" and press [RETURN]. ALL-IN-1 displays the Create Conference form.
VMS directory: ***directory*** **[TAB]...**	b. Enter the conference details described in Table 22.2. When entering conference details, press [TAB] after completing a field to move to the next one.
[RETURN]	c. Press [RETURN] after entering the conference details. ALL-IN-1 asks if you want to create an initial topic immediately.
Y or **N [RETURN]**	d. Type "Y" and press [RETURN] if you want to create an initial topic note. Enter the details of the new topic on the Create Topic form, press [RETURN], type the text of your topic note, and then press [GOLD] F. Refer to Section 20.3.7, "Creating a New Topic," for details. If you do not want to create an initial topic, type "N" and press [RETURN].

Table 22.2 Create Conference form details

Field	*Description*
VMS Directory	The name of the VMS directory in which the conference file resides. This name can be a main-level directory, a subdirectory, or the logical name for a directory. Typically, the logical directory NOTES$LIBRARY is established by system managers for public use. Contact your system administrator for assistance if you're not sure which directory name to specify.
Conference Name	The name of the file in which notes for the conference are stored. This name can be any valid VMS file name. You can include letters, numbers, and underscores in this name, but you cannot include a space. Use the underscore if you need to separate words in this name.
Class	The name under which you want this conference listed in *your* notebook.
Title	A title that indicates the purpose of the conference.
Notice	An optional text message that is displayed on the user's screen when the user opens the conference. In general, this should be a message welcoming the user to the conference or pointing to important information.
Restrict Membership	Enter "Y" to restrict membership to the conference, thereby creating a private conference. You must then specify (with the Add Member option) users who can access the conference. Enter "N" to create an open conference to which anyone can contribute comments.

(continued)

Table 22.2 Create Conference form details *(continued)*

Field	*Description*
Restrict Keyword Creation	Enter "Y" to prohibit participants (except for moderators) from creating new keywords for the conference. Enter "N" to allow any participant to create keywords.
Allow Notes to be Written	Enter "Y" to create a conference that permits users to contribute notes. Enter "N" to prohibit users from contributing notes. "N" creates a conference that participants can read only—sort of an "information booth." This field is also set to "N" with Modify Conference Profile when the moderator wants to close the conference.
Restrict to Replies Only	Enter "N" to allow other participants to create topics. Enter "Y" in this field to prohibit participants from creating new topics. Only moderators can create topics when this field is set to "Y".

Moderators can change details of the conference (Table 22.2) with the Modify Conference Profile option. To modify details of the current conference, do the following:

MCP [RETURN]

a. Type "MCP" and press [RETURN]. ALL-IN-1 displays the Modify Conference Profile form.

b. Modify the details of the conference. Press [TAB] or [BACKSPACE] (F12) to move to a particular field, press [ERASE LINE] (LF or F13) to clear the field, and enter the new information.

[RETURN]

c. Press [RETURN] when you've finished modifying conference details.

22.2 CONTROLLING ACCESS TO A CONFERENCE

In the preceding section, you learned how to create a private conference by restricting membership. Only those individuals added to the list of conference members can participate in a private conference.

Controlling access to a private conference is one of the responsibilities of the moderator. This involves adding names to the list of conference members, granting and modifying members' privileges, and removing names from the list of members.

A membership list is maintained for every conference. This list identifies the individuals who can participate in the conference if it is private. Regardless of whether the conference is restricted, the membership also identifies individuals who are granted special privileges, such as moderator privileges.

Perform the following steps to add a name to the list of members for the current conference:

AM [RETURN]

a. Type "AM" and press [RETURN]. ALL-IN-1 displays the Add Member form shown in Figure 22.1.

```
                              Add Member

Username:           ________________________

Mail address:       ________________________________________
Access nodes:       ______________________________________________________
                    ______________________________________________________

Privileges:         Moderator           N
                    Create keyword      N
                    Write regardless    N

Enter information and press RETURN
```

Figure 22.1 Add Member form

Username: ***username* [TAB]...**	b. Enter the details for the new member, as described in Table 22.3. When entering membership details, press [TAB] after completing a field to move to the next one.
[RETURN]	c. Press [RETURN] after entering the details.

Table 22.3 Conference member details

Field	*Description*
Username	The member's username.
Mail Address	The member's mail address. Any format acceptable for sending a message is valid in this field. Refer to Section 7.1, "Addressing a Message," for information on specifying mail addresses.
Access Nodes	The list of VMS system node names and accounts through which the member will access the conference.
Privileges:	
Moderator	Enter "Y" to allow the member to act as a conference moderator. Enter "N" if you do not want the member to act as a moderator.
Create Keyword	Enter "Y" to allow the member to create new keywords for the conference. Enter "N" to prohibit the member from creating new keywords. This field is relevant only if you restricted keyword creation when creating the conference.
Write Regardless	Enter "Y" to allow the member to add notes to the conference even after the conference has been closed. Enter "N" to prohibit the member from adding notes after the conference has been closed.

To modify details for a member of the current conference, follow these steps:

MM [RETURN]
a. Type "MM" and press [RETURN]. ALL-IN-1 displays the Modify Member form.

Username:
***username* [RETURN]**
b. Type the username of the member whose information you want to change, and press [RETURN].

Hint: Press [FIND] (or [GOLD] L) to list members.

...[RETURN]
c. Modify membership details, as described in Table 22.3, and press [RETURN] when finished. ALL-IN-1 displays a message that the member's details have been modified.

To remove a member from the current conference, do the following:

RM [RETURN]
a. Type "RM" and press [RETURN]. ALL-IN-1 displays the Remove Member form.

Username:
***username* [RETURN]**
b. Type the username of the member you want to remove, and press [RETURN]. ALL-IN-1 asks you to confirm whether you want to remove the member.

Hint: Press [FIND] (or [GOLD] L) to list members.

Y [RETURN]
c. Type "Y" and press [RETURN] to remove the member. ALL-IN-1 displays a message that the member has been removed.

22.3 MODERATING A CONFERENCE

It's the moderator's responsibility to keep the discussion flowing in a conference. As part of this responsibility, the moderator should frequently read the notes for the conference. If the conversation wanders away from the topic, the moderator can always add a reply to keep the discussion on track. In addition, the moderator has the authority to delete any notes that do not pertain to the subject matter being discussed.

The moderator also manages the list of keywords during the course of the conference. The moderator can add, delete, and rename words in the list of keywords.

22.3.1 Modifying Note Details

As a moderator, you have the authority to change the details of a note written by one of the participants. This option allows you to change the title, keywords, and other information about the note. However, Moderator Modify Note does *not* allow you to modify the content of the note.

Perform the following steps to modify the details of the current note:

MMN [RETURN]	a. Type "MMN" and press [RETURN]. (You can enter this option while reading the note.) ALL-IN-1 displays the Modify Note form.
...[RETURN]	b. Modify the details of the note and then press [RETURN] when finished. Refer to Table 20.6 for descriptions of the fields.

22.3.2 Deleting a Note

The moderator has the authority to remove a note written by a participant if the note does not pertain to the discussion. As soon as this function is performed, the note is removed from the conference file and is no longer available to participants.

Follow these steps to delete the current note:

MDN [RETURN]	a. Type "MDN" and press [RETURN] to delete the note. ALL-IN-1 asks if you want to delete the note.
Y [RETURN]	b. Type "Y" and press [RETURN] to delete the note. ALL-IN-1 displays a message while the note is being copied to *your* Wastebasket folder, then displays the message that the note has been deleted.

22.3.3 Maintaining Keywords

Participants can "tag" notes with certain keywords that relate to the content of the note. These keywords help other participants create an index of notes that pertain to specific subject matter. For example, when creating an index of notes for the BULLETIN BOARD conference, a participant could enter the keyword "SUGGESTIONS" as part of the selection criteria. The index then lists only the notes tagged with this keyword.

To tag a note with a keyword, the word must appear in the list of conference keywords. This list is created with the Add Keyword option on the Group Conferencing menu. The creator of the conference can restrict the ability to create keywords. In this case, only moderators can add or remove keywords.

Perform the following steps to create a new keyword for the current conference:

CK [RETURN]	a. Type "CK" and press [RETURN]. ALL-IN-1 displays the Create Keyword form.

Keyword: ***new-keyword***
[RETURN]

b. Type the new keyword and press [RETURN]. ALL-IN-1 displays a message indicating that the new keyword was created.

Note: ALL-IN-1 tells you if the keyword already exists in the list.

Do the following to replace an existing keyword with a new word for the current conference:

MK [RETURN]

a. Type "MK" and press [RETURN]. ALL-IN-1 displays the Modify Keyword form.

Keyword: ***old-keyword*** **[TAB]**
New Name: ***new-keyword***
[RETURN]

b. Type the old keyword, press [TAB], type the new keyword, and press [RETURN]. ALL-IN-1 displays a message indicating that the keyword was modified.

To remove a word from the list of conference keywords, follow these steps:

DK [RETURN]

a. Type "DK" and press [RETURN]. ALL-IN-1 displays the Delete Keyword form.

Keyword: ***keyword*** **[RETURN]**

b. Type the keyword and press [RETURN]. ALL-IN-1 asks if you want to delete the keyword.

Y [RETURN]

c. Type "Y" and press [RETURN] to delete the keyword. ALL-IN-1 displays a message indicating that the keyword was deleted.

22.4 CLOSING A CONFERENCE

When all topics in a conference have been discussed thoroughly, the meeting can be closed. The moderator can effectively close a conference by preventing participants from adding notes. This is accomplished by modifying the conference details. In addition, the moderator can change the notice for the meeting to indicate that the meeting has been closed. Before closing a conference, it's a good idea to notify the participants by including one last topic note stating that the meeting has been closed.

Perform the following steps to close a conference:

MCP [RETURN]

a. Type "MCP" and press [RETURN]. ALL-IN-1 displays the Modify Conference Profile form.

[TAB]
[TAB]

b. Press [TAB] twice to move the cursor to the Notice field.

Notice: ***closure-notice***
[TAB] [TAB]

c. Type a notice stating that the conference is now closed, then press [TAB] twice to move the cursor to the Allow Notes to Be Written field.

Allow notes to be written:
N [RETURN]

d. Type "N" and press [RETURN]. ALL-IN-1 redisplays the menu.

The conference is now closed. You might want to modify the privileges of any members who have the Write Notes Regardless privilege. See Section 22.2, "Controlling Access to a Conference," for details.

At some point in the future, you might want to delete the conference with the Delete Conference File option. Wait a while to do this, however. Allow enough time for participants to read the closure note and for the conference file to be saved during a system backup.

Desk Management and Communications

PART VII

Desk Management provides access to three features of ALL-IN-1: the Desk Calculator, Time Management, and Directories. The Communications subsystem lets you connect to remote computer systems, transfer documents between systems, and communicate interactively with other users.

Chapter 23 introduces you to the Desk Calculator, which performs the same functions as a pocket calculator: adding, subtracting, multiplying, dividing, and performing other mathematical functions on values entered from the keyboard. The Desk Calculator includes these features:

- You have immediate access to the calculator from any screen by pressing [GOLD] #. You can then perform calculations and return to your previous work with [GOLD] Q.
- You can access the Desk Calculator while preparing a document to calculate a value. The resulting value can then be easily inserted into your document.
- The Desk Calculator performs mathematical functions, including logarithmic and trigonometric functions.
- Three memory registers are available in addition to the display register for storing intermediate results.

Chapter 24 shows you how to maintain directories to keep track of names, addresses, and phone numbers of employees, business associates, customers, and vendors. ALL-IN-1 has three directories for storing this sort of information:

Corporate Phone directory

Personal Phone directory

ALL-IN-1 Phone directory

The Directories subsystem provides access to these directories as well as the Mail directory, Distribution Lists, and Nicknames, which are described in Chapter 7. The Directories subsystem includes these features:

- You can create, update, and access your own Personal Phone directory. Each entry in the directory includes an individual's name, title, business phone, home phone, company, department, and address.

- You have access to a shared Corporate Phone directory containing the names, addresses, and phone numbers of employees. In addition, you can add, change, and delete information in the Corporate Phone directory when authorized to do so by the system administrator.

Chapter 25 describes the basic utilities in the Communications subsystem: Terminal Phone and Document Transfer. Terminal Phone helps you communicate with other users. Document Transfer helps you transfer files back and forth between ALL-IN-1 and your DEC workstation or PC. This last topic is important if you'll be using your PC to work with documents or spreadsheets and then transferring these files to ALL-IN-1 to work with them or to send them to other users. Communications includes these features:

- Document Transfer exchanges documents between the ALL-IN-1 File Cabinet and your DEC workstation or between the File Cabinet and the VAX/VMS file system.
- Communications provides access to the VMS Terminal Phone utility. With Terminal Phone, you can communicate interactively with another user who is logged into the system.
- Communications Control lets you create and execute your own control files to connect your terminal to a remote system automatically.
- Your site can customize options on the Communications menu to establish a connection between your terminal and a remote computer system automatically.

DESK MANAGEMENT Q&A

Following is a list of common questions about Desk Management.

Q *How can I perform a calculation while editing a document?*

A You can access the short form of the Desk Calculator from anywhere in ALL-IN-1, even while you're editing a document. Press [GOLD] # to display the Desk Calculator. Enter your calculation just as if you were using a pocket calculator. Enter a value, press an operator key (+, –, *, or / for add, subtract, multiply, or divide), and enter the second value. Press [ENTER] or the equal sign to display the result. Press [GOLD] Q when you want to return to editing your document. To insert the final result of your calculations in the document, press [INSERT HERE] or [PASTE].

Q *Can I send my personal directory to another user? Can I copy directory entries from another user?*

A You cannot send all or part of your Personal Phone directory to another user—at least not in a form that can easily be added to the recipient's directory. If you like, you can create and send a document containing the entries. Create an index of entries by typing "DIR PER I" and pressing [RETURN] twice. Then select specific entries by line number, and enter the Multiple Print (XP) option. Select full output and specify "DOCUMENT" as the document destination. Create a new, revisable document. You can then select and send this document to someone else from the Electronic Messaging or Word and Document Processing menu. The recipient will have to enter the information manually, however.

Directory entries are stored in a file named PERPHONE.DAT in your VMS directory. Users with access to DCL and the proper privileges can copy this file or combine two similar files with SORT/MERGE. However, this requires knowledge of VMS file structures and utilities.

Q *Why can't I add or edit entries in the Corporate Phone directory?*

A You must be authorized by the system administrator before you can create, edit, or delete entries in the Corporate Phone directory. Contact your system administrator if you need to update this directory and do not have the necessary privilege.

Q *How do I look up a phone number in a directory?*

A The phone directory index provides an easy way to look up a phone number in a directory. From any menu, type "DIR PER I" to find a phone number in your Personal Phone directory or "DIR COR I" to find a number in the Corporate Phone directory, and press [RETURN]. Type the first letter of the name of the person or organization you want to locate, and press [RETURN] to list matching entries in the directory. The phone number is in the last column of the display.

Also, Chapter 26 contains a User Defined Procedure (UDP) for looking up a phone number in your Personal Phone directory from anywhere in ALL-IN-1. Refer to the instructions on creating a UDP and the examples that follow for details.

COMMUNICATIONS Q&A

Following is a list of common questions about Communications.

Q *How do I transfer a document between my PC and ALL-IN-1?*

A Transferring a document between your PC and the ALL-IN-1 File Cabinet is typically a two-step process. The first step is to transfer the document between the PC and your home directory on the VAX. This can be accomplished with KERMIT, XMODEM, or any similar utility you have on your PC. If your site is running PATHWORKS, you can transfer the file with Network File Transfer (NFT) or simply place the file on your personal file service drive. If you need help to accomplish the first step, ask your system administrator or refer to the documentation for the utility with which you've chosen to work.

The second step is to transfer the file between VMS and the ALL-IN-1 File Cabinet. If transferring the file from VMS to the File Cabinet, simply create a new document, then retrieve the file from VMS with the [GOLD] G function key. If transferring the file from the File Cabinet to VMS, move to the Document Transfer menu, select the document, and transfer it to VMS with the Send a Document to

VMS (SV) or Send a Document to VMS without Conversion (SVC) option. (See the following question for advice on which option to choose.)

When asked for the VMS file specification, enter a name using this format: "SYS$LOGIN:*filename.filetype*," where *filename* and *filetype* are names you assign to the file. The prefix "SYS$LOGIN:" ensures that the file is being copied to or from your home directory.

This process leaves an intermediate copy of the document in your home directory. Make sure that you delete this file at some point to conserve disk space. Refer to Section 25.3.3, "Transferring Documents to or from VMS," for more details.

Q *When should I use the Send Document without Conversion or Receive Document without Conversion options?*

A If you are transferring a WordPerfect document or spreadsheet between a PC and ALL-IN-1 and you will be using the same program on both systems to work with the file, transfer the file without conversion. If you are transferring a binary file or an indexed data file between VMS and ALL-IN-1 so that you can mail it to someone else, transfer the file without conversion. This includes graphics images. If you are transferring a document or spreadsheet between VMS and ALL-IN-1 so that you can use a different program to work with the file, transfer the file with conversion.

Q *Can I transfer a file to, or from, another DEC system in the network?*

A If you're sending a document to another system in the network that also has ALL-IN-1, simply send the document through Electronic Messaging. Select the document, and choose the Send (S) option. The document is sent as an attachment to the message.

If you're transferring the document between ALL-IN-1 and VMS, you can easily transfer the file to or from VMS on a remote system in the network. Move to Document Transfer, and select the Send a Document to VMS (SV) or Receive a Document from VMS (RV) option. When you enter the VMS file specification, include the name of a remote system in the file specification to transfer the file across the network. The full file specification format is:

```
node"username password"::disk:[directory]filename.filetype
```

In this file specification, *node* is the name for the remote system, *username* and *password* specify an account with access to the remote file or directory, and *disk*:[*directory*]*filename.filetype* is the path name or local file specification. Refer to Section 25.3, "Transferring Documents," for more information.

Q *How do I create a "conference" call with Terminal Phone?*

A You can create a conference call with Terminal Phone to communicate simultaneously with several users currently logged on the system. Place a call following the instructions in Section 25.2, "Communicating with Other Users." When the person responds, press the percent key (%) and type "DIAL," followed by a space and the name of the next person you want included in the conference call. When this person answers, your screen is split into three windows to show everyone's comments.

DESK MANAGEMENT AND COMMUNICATIONS DOs AND DON'Ts

Here are some suggestions for working with Desk Management and Communications.

Do

- When adding a business phone number to your personal directory, enter a person's last name followed by a comma and the first name in the Name field. Enter the company name in the Full Name field (and also in the Company field). The name, full name, and telephone number are displayed when viewing entries in an index.
- Provide the complete address and full telephone number, including area code and extension, when adding entries to the corporate directory. Other people rely on this information. It also helps if you use a consistent format for phone numbers and addresses. Include helpful information in the Comment field, such as the name and number of the person's secretary.
- Review your personal phone directory and the corporate phone directory at regular intervals. Create an index of entries, select all entries (or a range of entries), and enter the Multiple Print (XP) option to print the directory. Update outdated information, and delete obsolete entries. It's easier if you work from the index while updating the directory.
- If your company maintains a large corporate phone directory, you might include the following information in the Comment field for maintenance operations:
  - The name or initials of the person in your organization who requested the entry.
  - The date you added or updated the entry.
- If you transfer files between a PC and the ALL-IN-1 File Cabinet, remember to delete the intermediate files left in your VMS directory. These files tend to build up if you transfer a lot of documents, causing problems with disk storage quotas. You can place these files in your ALL-IN-1 temporary directory by entering a file specification of *OA$TEMP:filename.filetype* when transferring to VMS. These files can then be deleted periodically with the Delete Temporary Files (DTF) option on the File Cabinet (FC) menu. Note that when you transfer the file to or from a PC, you must specify the temporary directory by its full name, typically with the format [*username.ALL-IN-1_subdirectory*.OA$TEMP]. Ask your system administrator for assistance if you're unsure of the correct directory name.
- If you transfer documents back and forth between a PC and ALL-IN-1, you'll have versions of the document in two places. It helps if you make notes identifying which copy is the latest version. For example, if you transfer a document from the PC to ALL-IN-1, edit the PC version and place a note at the top of the document saying

something like "(Transferred to ALL-IN-1, 7/15/95)." When transferring the file to the PC, you can modify the title of the document in your File Cabinet and add the same sort of comment. Select the Update Index (U) option to modify the title. An alternative is to keep only one version of the document. In other words, delete the PC version after successfully transferring the document to ALL-IN-1, unless you want to keep the extra copy around for backup.

Don't

- If you're responsible for maintaining the corporate phone directory, don't add entries unless (1) you have complete information and (2) the entry is useful to more than one person. If a directory entry is useful to only one person, remind this user to add the entry to his or her personal phone directory.

Working with the Desk Calculator

CHAPTER 23

The Desk Calculator is just what its name implies. It can perform all of the functions of a pocket calculator, including adding, subtracting, multiplying, dividing, and other mathematical functions, on numbers entered from the keyboard.

This chapter shows you how to perform the following tasks with the Desk Calculator:

- Access both full and short forms of the Desk Calculator.
- Access the Desk Calculator while editing a document and paste the result of a calculation in the document.
- Perform basic calculations with the Desk Calculator.
- Enter a mathematical expression for evaluation.
- Use formula functions and trigonometric functions.

23.1 ACCESSING THE DESK CALCULATOR

There are two different display formats for the Desk Calculator: the full and short formats. You'll choose the format based on what you're currently doing in ALL-IN-1 and what calculations you need to perform.

23.1.1 Full Format

The full format covers the entire screen, as shown in Figure 23.1. It lists the calculator functions and keypad layout and displays memory contents and calculation results. Use the full format when you're working from a menu and need to perform a series of calculations.

Perform the following steps to access the full format of the Desk Calculator:

DC [RETURN]	a. From any menu, type "DC" and press [RETURN]. ALL-IN-1 displays the full format of the Desk Calculator, ready for calculations.
***calculation* [ENTER]**	b. In general, enter calculations as you would with a pocket calculator, and press [ENTER] to calculate the result. For example, to add the values

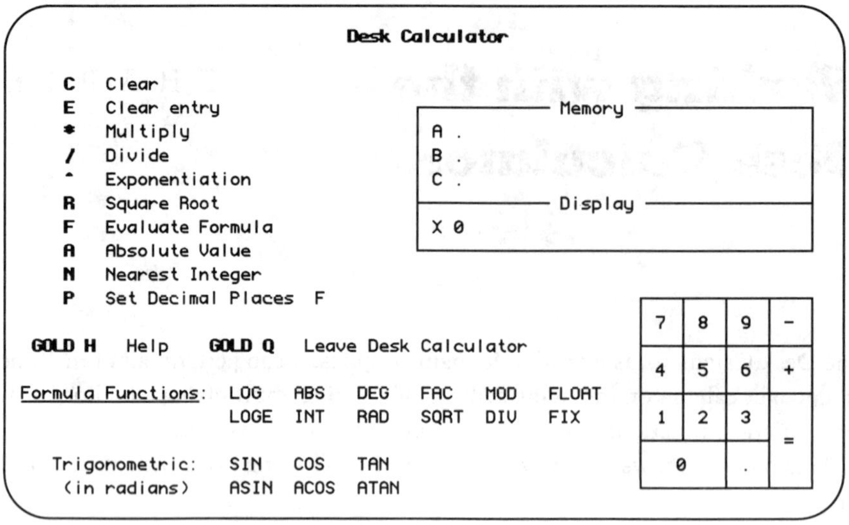

Figure 23.1 Full format of the Desk Calculator

382.4 and 588.3, type the following and press [ENTER]:

```
3 8 2 . 4 + 5 8 8 . 3 [ENTER]
```

The result is shown in the display register.

To leave the Desk Calculator when you've finished performing calculations, do the following:

[GOLD] Q Press [GOLD] Q to leave the Desk Calculator. ALL-IN-1 clears the Desk Calculator and redisplays the previous menu.

The Calculations (CA) menu also provides access to the full Desk Calculator and computer-based training for Calculations.

23.1.2 Short Format

The short format, shown in Figure 23.2, is overlaid on top of the menu or document with which you're working. The short format shows the result of your calculations and any formulas you enter. Use the short format if you're in the middle of performing another task in ALL-IN-1 and need to perform a calculation quickly.

Perform the following steps to access the short format of the Desk Calculator from anywhere in ALL-IN-1:

[GOLD] # a. Press [GOLD] (PF1), then press # to display the Desk Calculator. ALL-IN-1 displays the short

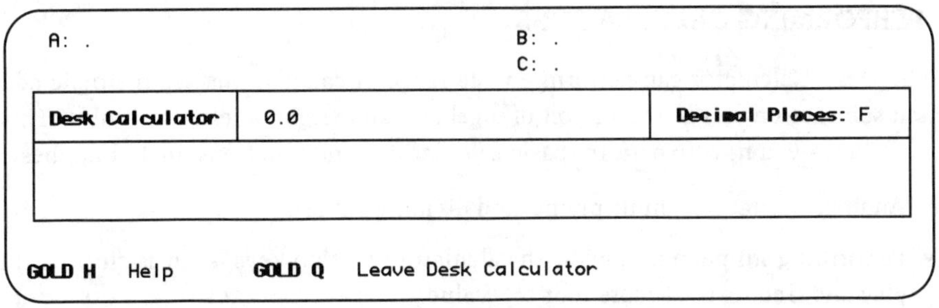

Figure 23.2 Short format of the Desk Calculator

format of the Desk Calculator at the bottom of the screen, ready for calculations.

***calculation* [ENTER]**

b. In general, enter calculations as you would with a pocket calculator, then press [ENTER] to calculate the result.

To leave the Desk Calculator when you've finished performing calculations, do the following:

[GOLD] Q

Press [GOLD] Q to leave the Desk Calculator. ALL-IN-1 clears the Desk Calculator and redisplays the previous screen.

You can easily access the short format of the Desk Calculator while editing a document. This allows you to perform quick calculations while working with a document and then include the result in your text.

Follow these steps to access the Desk Calculator while editing a document:

[GOLD] #

a. Press [GOLD] (PF1), then press #. The short format of the Desk Calculator is displayed, ready for you to enter calculations.

***calculation* [ENTER]**

b. In general, enter calculations as you would with a pocket calculator, then press [ENTER] to calculate the result.

[GOLD] Q

c. Press [GOLD] (PF1), then press Q to leave the Desk Calculator when finished. ALL-IN-1 clears the Desk Calculator and redisplays the document.

To insert the calculated value in the text of your document, do the following:

[PASTE]

Press [PASTE], (Keypad-Plus Sign) or [INSERT HERE]. The value is inserted at the current cursor location.

23.2 PERFORMING CALCULATIONS

The Desk Calculator can perform a wide range of calculations, from simple addition and subtraction to the evaluation of algebraic and trigonometric formulas. This section shows you how to perform basic calculations and functions, including these:

- Adding, subtracting, multiplying, and dividing values.
- Performing simple functions with calculator function keys, such as clearing the display and finding the square root of a value.
- Entering formulas for evaluation.

23.2.1 Basic Calculations

Enter basic calculations just as you would with a pocket calculator. For example, press the following eight keys to add the values 320 and 488:

```
3 2 0 + 4 8 8 =
```

Remember the following rules when working with the Desk Calculator:

- You can use either the main keyboard or the numeric keypad to enter numbers.
- Do not press [RETURN] or [TAB] after entering a value.
- The [ENTER] key, the [RETURN] key, and the equal sign (=) key all perform the same function: They calculate and display the result.
- Press "E" to clear the last value entered. Press "C" to clear the calculator and reset the display to 0.
- Large numbers are displayed with scientific notation. For example, "0.314 E + 18" represents the value 314,000,000,000,000,000.

23.2.2 Calculator Function Keys

The full format of the Desk Calculator displays a list of the calculator function keys that perform basic calculator functions. Table 23.1 describes these function keys.

23.2.3 Entering Formulas

The calculator function key [F] allows you to enter expressions and formulas for evaluation. For example, the entire expression "((29 * 18) / 9) * 27.5" can be entered all at once for evaluation. In addition to mathematical expressions, you can also perform algebraic, trigonometric, and other math functions when entering formulas.

Keep the following rules in mind when entering formulas:

- Expressions containing more than one arithmetic operator (+, –, /, *) are evaluated in the following order: multiplication and division first, then addition and subtraction. Include parentheses in your expressions to override this default. For example, the expression "3 + 10 / 2" produces a result of 8, whereas "(3 + 10) / 2" produces a result of 6.5.

Table 23.1 Desk Calculator function keys

Press This Key	*To Perform This Function*
C (Clear)	Clear the calculator and reset the display to 0.
E (Clear Entry)	Clear only the last value entered.
+ (Add)	Add two values.
– (Subtract)	Subtract the second value from the first value.
* (Multiply)	Multiply two values.
/ (Divide)	Divide the first value by the second value.
^ (Exponentiation)	Raise the first value to the power of the second value.
R (Square Root)	Find the square root of the displayed value.
F (Evaluate Formula)	Enter a formula.
A (Absolute Value)	Find the absolute value of the displayed value.
N (Nearest Integer)	Round the displayed value to the nearest whole number.
P (Set Decimal Places)	Set the number of decimal places shown in the display.

- A formula can contain any of the functions described in Table 23.2 on the next page.

Perform the following steps to enter a formula for evaluation:

F — a. Press [F].

formula — b. Type the formula.

[ENTER] — c. Press "=" (equal sign) or [ENTER] to evaluate the formula.

23.3 EXERCISE: BASIC CALCULATIONS

This exercise shows you how to perform basic calculations with the Desk Calculator. Let's assume that you need to purchase carpeting and want to estimate the cost. You've measured the room and found that it is 28 feet 7 inches long and 17 feet 3 inches wide. As a fudge factor, you decide to use 29 X 18 feet. The cost of the carpeting is $27.50 per square yard (installed).

Perform the following steps to calculate the cost of the carpet.

1. Move to the Desk Calculator.

   DC [RETURN] — From any menu, type "DC" and then press [RETURN].

2. Set the number of decimal places for the display to two.

   P 2 [ENTER] — Type "P 2" and press [ENTER].

Table 23.2 Summary of formula functions

Function	*Example*	*Result*	*Comment*
ABS (Absolute Value)	ABS(–783)	783	
ACOS (ARC Cosine)	ACOS(.866)	0.524	Radians
ASIN (ARC Sine)	DEG(ASIN(.5))	30.000	Degrees
ATAN (ARC Tangent)	ATAN(.5774)	0.524	Radians
COS (Cosine)	COS(RAD(60))	0.500	
DEG (Radians to Degrees)	DEG(.524)	30.023	Degrees
DIV (Integer Division)	(10)DIV(3)	3	FIX(10/3)
FAC (Factorial)	FAC(4)	24	1x2x3x4
FIX (Truncate to Integer)	FIX(5.875)	5	
FLOAT (Integer to Floating Point)	FLOAT(344)	344.000	
INT (Nearest Integer)	INT(5.875)	6.000	
LOG (Common Logarithm)	LOG(100)	2.000	
LOGE (Natural Logarithm)	LOGE(2.718)	1.000	
MOD (Remainder)	(11)MOD(3)	2	
RAD (Degrees to Radians)	RAD(30)	0.524	Radians
SQRT (Square Root)	SQRT(144)	12.000	
SIN (Sine)	SIN(RAD(30))	0.500	
TAN (Tangent)	TAN(RAD(30))	0.577	

3. Calculate the cost of the carpet. The formula is ((length × width) / 9 × the cost), or ((29 × 18) / 9) × 27.5. (The area is divided by 9 to compute square yards.)

29 * 18 [ENTER]

a. Type "29", press "*" (asterisk), type "18", and press [ENTER]. "522.00" appears in the display.

/ 9 [ENTER]

b. Press "/", type "9", and press [ENTER]. "58.00" appears in the display.

*** 27.5 [ENTER]**

c. Press "*", type "27.5", and press [ENTER]. "1595.00" appears in the display.

4. Exit the Desk Calculator.

[GOLD] Q

Press [GOLD] Q to exit the Desk Calculator. ALL-IN-1 displays the previous menu.

Working with Directories

CHAPTER 24

Directories are available in ALL-IN-1 for storing the phone numbers and addresses of employees, business associates, customers, and vendors. The Directories subsystem provides access to three different directories:

Corporate Phone directory

Personal Phone directory

ALL-IN-1 Phone directory

This chapter shows you how to access and maintain the Corporate, Personal, and ALL-IN-1 Phone directories. The Directories subsystem also provides access to the Mail directory, Nicknames, and Distribution Lists, which are discussed in Chapter 7, "Becoming More Proficient with Electronic Messaging."

This chapter teaches you how to perform the following tasks:

- Access the Directories menu.
- Create, edit, delete, display, and print directory entries.
- Work with an index to maintain a directory

24.1 ACCESSING DIRECTORIES

The Directories menu provides access to six different directories. The three directories described below help you communicate with others by phone or paper mail. The remaining three directories on this menu contain information to assist you in sending messages, as described in Chapter 7. This chapter discusses these three directories:

Corporate Phone directory — The Corporate Phone directory contains information about the employees of your company. This information might include the employee's name, title, business phone, home phone, department, and address. All employees can read this information, but not everyone has the authority to update it. Contact the person responsible for maintaining this information if you find details that are incorrect or missing.

Personal Phone directory	Your Personal Phone directory contains information about any individual or organization you choose to include: perhaps family members, business associates, customers, or vendors. Information in this directory can include the individual's name, title, business phone, home phone, company, department, and address. You alone have access to your Personal Phone directory, and you are responsible for maintaining all of the information in it.
ALL-IN-1 Phone directory	The ALL-IN-1 Phone directory contains information about other employees who have access to ALL-IN-1 on your computer system. This information includes username, full name, department, telephone number, and job title. All employees can read this information. You can change your own information either from the Directories subsystem or with the Set Personal Details option on the User Setup menu.

Perform the following steps to access the directories:

DIR [RETURN]	a. From any menu, type "DIR" and then press [RETURN].
***menu-option* [RETURN]**	b. Type the menu option and press [RETURN]. Table 24.1 describes the options on the Directories menu.

Table 24.1 Directories menu options

Enter This Menu Option	*To Perform the Following Action*
COR (Corporate)	Access the Corporate Phone directory.
PER (Personal)	Move to the Personal Phone Directory menu to access and maintain your personal phone list.
ALL (ALL-IN-1 Users)	Move to the ALL-IN-1 Directory menu to access the list of ALL-IN-1 users.
SMD (Search Mail Directory)	Scan the Mail directory to locate an address.
NI (Nicknames)	Move to the Nicknames Management menu to maintain nicknames.
DL (Distribution Lists)	Move to the Distribution List Management menu to maintain distribution lists.
TR (Training)	Start computer-based instruction for Directories.

24.2 MAINTAINING A DIRECTORY

This section describes how to access and maintain information in the Corporate, Personal, and ALL-IN-1 Phone directories. As you'll see, the steps are the same regardless of the directory with which you work.

In this section, you'll learn how to perform the following tasks:

- Create a new directory entry.
- Select an existing directory entry with which to work.
- Edit a directory entry.
- Delete a directory entry.
- Read or print a directory entry.

24.2.1 Creating an Entry

The Create (C) option adds a new directory entry, much like adding a new card to your Rolodex®. A directory entry might include full name, title, business phone number, home phone number, department, address, zip code, and comments. The comments can include any information you like.

You can always add entries to your Personal Phone directory. You can add entries to the Corporate Phone directory with prior authorization from the system administrator. You are not allowed to add entries to the ALL-IN-1 directory, however. Only the system administrator can add entries to this directory.

Perform the following steps to create a new directory entry:

DIR PER [RETURN]

a. From any menu, type "DIR PER" and press [RETURN] to add entries to your Personal directory.

DIR COR [RETURN]

Or type "DIR COR" and press [RETURN] to add entries to the Corporate directory. ALL-IN-1 displays the directory menu.

C [RETURN]

b. Type "C" and press [RETURN] to create a new entry. ALL-IN-1 displays the Phone Directory form shown in Figure 24.1.

Name: ***name* [RETURN]**

c. Enter a key name for this directory entry and press [RETURN]. This is typically a person's last name or a company name. Enter the name you typically use to refer to this individual or company. ALL-IN-1 moves the cursor to the next field and asks you to enter the data for the new entry.

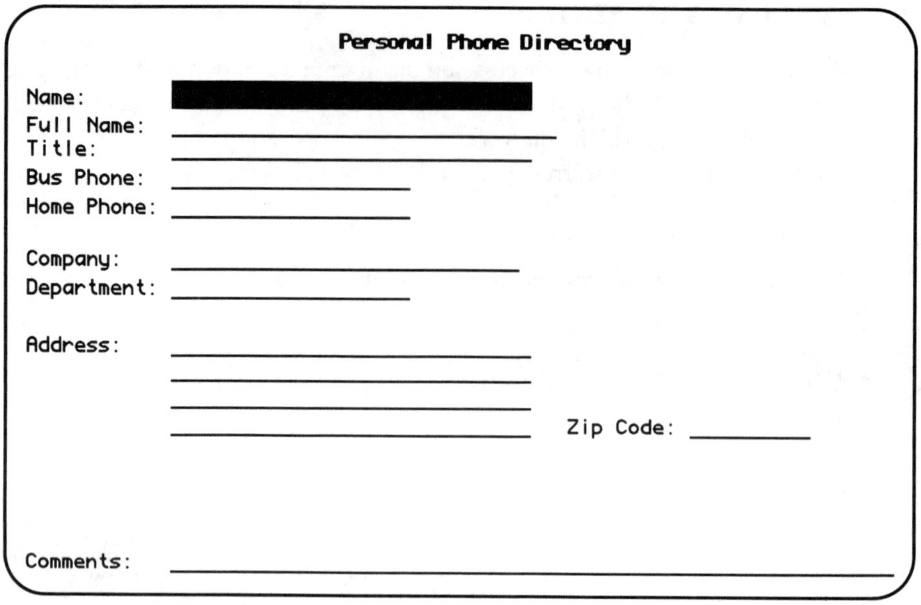
Personal Phone Directory

Name:
Full Name:
Title:
Bus Phone:
Home Phone:

Company:
Department:

Address:

Zip Code:

Comments:

Figure 24.1 Personal Phone Directory form

Full name: ***full-name***
[TAB]...

d. Enter all of the details for the new directory entry. When completing the form, press [TAB] to move to the next field, or press [BACKSPACE] (F12) to move to a previous field. Refer to Section 3.2.1, "Completing a Data-Entry Form," for details.

[RETURN]
[RETURN]

e. Press [RETURN] twice to complete the form and add the entry to the directory. The menu is redisplayed, and the new entry is shown as the current item.

24.2.2 Selecting an Entry

Many of the menu options manage the current directory entry, which is identified in the current item block of the menu or is indicated by the current item pointer (>) in an index. Select the entry you want to work with before choosing options to edit, delete, read, or print it.

To select a directory entry from a menu, follow these steps:

SEL [RETURN]

a. Type "SEL" and press [RETURN] (or press [SELECT]). ALL-IN-1 displays the Select Name form.

Name: ***name***

b. Press [ERASE LINE] (LF or F13) to clear the field. Type all or part of the name for the entry you want to edit, and press [RETURN]. You can leave the field blank and press [FIND] (or [GOLD] L) to list all possible entries.

[RETURN]

c. Press [RETURN] to select the specified entry.

To select a directory entry from an index, do the following:

***line-number* [RETURN]**

Type the line number of the entry you want to select, and press [RETURN]. ALL-IN-1 moves the current item pointer to this entry. If necessary, first press [NEXT SCREEN] (or [GOLD] [TAB]) to display additional entries.

24.2.3 Editing an Entry

The Edit (E) option updates a directory entry with new information. Select this option if you need to change the full name, address, or phone number for a directory entry. You can always update entries in your Personal Phone directory. However, you can edit entries in the Corporate Phone directory only when authorized to do so by the system administrator, and you can update only *your* entry in the ALL-IN-1 directory.

Perform these steps to edit the current directory entry:

E [RETURN]

a. Type "E" and press [RETURN] to edit the entry. ALL-IN-1 displays the full directory entry.

b. Modify details for the directory entry.

[RETURN]
[RETURN]

c. Press [RETURN] twice to update the directory entry when you've finished making changes.

24.2.4 Deleting an Entry

The Delete (D) option removes a directory entry, much like removing a card from your Rolodex®. All information for an entry is erased from the directory when deleted and cannot be recovered. You can always delete entries from your Personal Phone directory. However, you can delete entries from the Corporate Phone directory only when authorized to do so by the system administrator, and you cannot delete any entries from the ALL-IN-1 directory.

Perform the following steps to delete the current directory entry:

D [RETURN]

a. Type "D" and press [RETURN] to delete the entry. ALL-IN-1 displays the entry.

[RETURN] b. Press [RETURN] to delete the entry. (Press [EXIT] if you do not want to delete the entry.)

24.2.5 Reading or Printing an Entry

The Read (R) option displays the full directory entry. The Print (P) option sends a copy of the entry to the printer. When printing, you have the option of printing the full entry or just brief information for the entry. The brief format contains only the name and phone numbers. You can display or print entries from the Personal Phone directory, the Corporate Phone directory, or the ALL-IN-1 directory.

To display the current directory entry, follow these steps:

R [RETURN]	a. Type "R" and press [RETURN]. ALL-IN-1 displays the directory entry.
[RETURN]	b. Press [RETURN] to return to the menu or index when you've finished viewing the entry.

You use the Read option to look up a phone number in your phone directory. If you're just interested in finding the business phone number of someone in your personal phone directory, type "DIR PER I" from any menu and press [RETURN] twice. This displays an index of entries showing the business phone numbers. Even this can be a cumbersome way to look up a phone number, however. A better method is presented in Chapter 26. Among the sample User Defined Processes, you'll find one that allows you to look up phone numbers with the function key [GOLD] F20. Refer to Chapter 26 for more information on User Defined Processes.

Perform the following steps to print the current directory entry:

P [RETURN]	a. Type "P" and press [RETURN]. ALL-IN-1 asks if you want to print the full entry or just brief information.
B or **F [RETURN]**	b. Type "B" and press [RETURN] to print the name and phone numbers, or type "F" and press [RETURN] to print the full directory entry.
[RETURN]	c. When the Printing Document form is displayed, press [RETURN] again to send the printout to the current printer destination.

24.2.6 Exercise: Creating a Personal Phone Directory

This exercise shows you how to add entries to your Personal Phone directory and how to display an index of all entries. The steps for adding entries to the Corporate Phone directory are identical, except that you must move to the Corporate Phone menu instead of the Personal Phone menu. You must also be authorized by the system administrator to update the Corporate Phone directory.

1. Move to the Personal Phone Directory menu.

DIR PER [RETURN]	From any menu, type "DIR PER" and press [RETURN].

2. Create two entries in your Personal Phone directory.

C [RETURN]	a. Type "C" and press [RETURN] to create the first entry. ALL-IN-1 displays the Personal Phone Directory form.
Name: ***your-last-name*** **[RETURN]**	b. The first entry will contain information about you. Type your last name and press [RETURN].
Full Name: ***full-name*** **[TAB]...**	c. Enter the remaining details and press [RETURN].
[RETURN]	d. Press [RETURN] again to add this entry to your directory. The menu is redisplayed.
C [RETURN]	e. Type "C" and press [RETURN] to create the second entry.
Name: ***boss's-last-name*** **[RETURN]**	f. The second entry will contain information about your boss. Type your boss's last name and press [RETURN].
Full Name: ***full-name*** **[TAB]...**	g. Enter the remaining details and press [RETURN].
[RETURN]	h. Press [RETURN] again to add this entry to your directory. The menu is redisplayed.

3. Display an index of your Personal Phone directory.

I [RETURN]	a. Type "I" and press [RETURN] to create an index. ALL-IN-1 displays a blank index with a form for entering selection criteria.
[RETURN]	b. Leave the fields blank and press [RETURN]. This displays an index of all directory entries.
2 R [RETURN]	c. Type "2 R" and press [RETURN] to display the second entry.
[RETURN]	d. When finished viewing the entry, press [RETURN] again to redisplay the index.
[EXIT]	e. Press [EXIT] (F10 or Keypad-0) to return to the menu.

24.3 MANAGING A DIRECTORY FROM AN INDEX

The Index (I) option displays a list of directory entries. This index is handy when you're looking up a phone number. In addition, you can easily select and work with a single entry from the index, or you can select multiple entries and manage them by entering one of the options listed in Table 24.2. Figure 24.2 shows a sample Personal Phone Directory index.

Table 24.2 Index menu options for managing multiple items

Enter This Menu Option	*To Perform the Following Action*
ALL (Select All)	Select all entries listed in the index.
CAS (Cancel All Selected)	Deselect all selected entries.
XD (Delete All Selected)	Remove from the directory all information for the selected entries.
XP (Print All Selected)	Print full information about all selected entries.
XR (Read All Selected)	Display information for all selected entries.

```
                         Index of Personal Directory
 (Selections: 0    )                                      (New messages: 1  )
 ------------------------------------------------------------------------------
   No.   User                   Full name                    Phone no.
 ------------------------------------------------------------------------------
    1    AYAMA                  Ayama                        (303)443-9873
    2    CARDISH, JON           Jon Cardish                  (303)333-3142
    3    CONWAY, MARTIN         Martin Conway                (303)555-8132
    4    CRUMLY, MICHAEL        Michael Crumly               (301)555-1582
    5    DEC S/W SUPPORT        Digital Software Support     (800)555-8877
    6    DIXON, TIM             Tim Dixon                    (303)555-7588
    7    DUGAN, SEAN            Sean Dugan                   (213)555-8743
    8    LESSER, MARILYN        Marilyn Lesser               (719)555-4576
    9    MORITA, LARRY          Larry Morita                 (800)444-1994
   10    MURRAY, KEVIN          Kevin Murray                 (502)777-9876
   11    MURRAY, LISA & PAUL    Lisa and Paul Murray         (901)888-4172
   12    OTT, LEONARD           Leonard Ott                  (800)333-9745
 > 13    TRIPLETT, TIM          Tim Triplett                 (303)777-8984
   14    WONG, STOPHER          Stopher Wong                 (303)399-9988
 ------------------------------------------------------------------------------

 Move to item, and enter option (press GOLD MENU to see options, or HELP for
 more information)
```

Figure 24.2 Personal Phone Directory index and menu

Working with Communications

CHAPTER 25

This chapter teaches you the basics of working with Communications. Two topics are discussed: communicating with other users and transferring files. These are the most commonly used features in Communications.

In this section, you'll learn how to perform the following tasks:

- Access the Communications menu.
- Communicate interactively with another user who is currently logged into the system.
- Transfer documents between the ALL-IN-1 File Cabinet and your DEC workstation.
- Transfer documents between the File Cabinet and the VMS file system, which is usually the first step in transferring a file to or from a PC.

25.1 ACCESSING COMMUNICATIONS

Communications features are provided by the Communications menu, which your site can customize. In other words, some of the options you see on the Communications menu might have been added by your site. Therefore, they are not documented here or in any other ALL-IN-1 manual. Only standard Communications options are discussed in this chapter.

The menu contains three standard options: Communications Control (CC), Document Transfer (DT), and Terminal Phone (TP). This menu also contains at least one other option, Connect to System X (CS), which is often an inactive option. Systems personnel can customize this option to connect your terminal automatically to another computer system. In this case, the option is usually renamed, and "X" is replaced with the remote computer's name. Any other options appearing on this menu are custom options added to the menu by programmers at your site. Contact your system administrator for assistance with custom options.

Perform the following steps to access Communications:

COM [RETURN]	a. From any menu, type "COM" and then press [RETURN]. You can also enter the menu option. For example, type "COM TP" and press [RETURN] to access Terminal Phone.

Table 25.1 Communications menu options

Enter This Menu Option	*To Perform the Following Action*
CC (Communications Control)	Display the Communications Control menu to access other computer systems.
CS (Connect to System X)	This option is typically inactive. It must be activated at your site to connect to the other systems that your company accesses. You will receive the message "Custom option to specified by site" if this option has not been activated
DT (Document Transfer)	Display the Document Transfer menu to transfer documents between the ALL-IN-1 File Cabinet and your DEC workstation or between the File Cabinet and the VMS file system.
TP (Terminal Phone)	Start the Terminal Phone utility to communicate interactively with another user who is logged into the system.

***menu-option* [RETURN]**

b. Type the menu option and press [RETURN]. Table 25.1 describes standard menu options.

25.2 COMMUNICATING WITH OTHER USERS

The Terminal Phone is included with your VAX/VMS operating system software. This utility allows you to communicate with another user by typing messages. Your messages instantly appear on the other user's terminal screen. Any messages typed by the other person are, in turn, displayed on your screen.

Terminal Phone displays messages in dual "windows" on your terminal screen. One window displays messages that you type, and the other window displays messages that the user you're calling types. Figure 25.1 shows an example of Terminal Phone conversation. Note that both users see the same information.

Type "COM TP" and press [RETURN] to make a phone call with Terminal Phone. The menu is cleared, the Terminal Phone screen appears, and the cursor is placed directly after the % prompt. Type "DIRECTORY" and press [RETURN] to list users who are logged onto your system. You can't contact someone with the Terminal Phone unless he or she is currently logged on. Type "DIAL *username*" or simply *username* and press [RETURN] to make the call, where *username* is the name of the person you want to call. You receive a message that you are "ringing" the other user.

The person you're calling receives the message "*username* is phoning you on *node::*." At this point, he or she must type "COM TP" at a menu, press [RETURN], type "ANSWER" after the % prompt, and press [RETURN].

You receive a message when the person responds, and his or her username appears in the bottom window of the screen. Begin your conversation by typing a message.

```
                         VAX/VMS Phone Facility                  18-AUG-1991
%

--------------------------------------------------------------------------------
                              WASHINGTON
Sorry to bother you... I tried to reach you by telephone but there was no
answer at your extension.  So I called with Terminal Phone when I saw that
you were logged on.

I needed another copy of your report.


--------------------------------------------------------------------------------
                              JEFFERSON
Yes, I am in the training room instead of my office.  I will get another copy
to you by lunch.




--------------------------------------------------------------------------------
```

Figure 25.1 Sample Terminal Phone conversation

This message appears in your window. Wait for the other person to type a response. You'll see the response in the window below his or her username. When the other person has finished typing a response, type another message. You don't have to do anything special to move the cursor to your window except begin typing.

When you're through with your conversation, type a message like "BYE." Hang up and exit the Terminal Phone by pressing [CTRL]+C.

25.3 TRANSFERRING DOCUMENTS

The Document Transfer menu makes it easy for you to transfer documents between the ALL-IN-1 File Cabinet and your DEC workstation or between the File Cabinet and the VAX/VMS file system. The information is converted automatically as the document is transferred unless you request otherwise. You can thus work with the document immediately after the transfer is completed.

25.3.1 Accessing Document Transfer

You access Document Transfer from the Communications menu or by entering the global menu option DT. This menu contains several options for transferring documents between systems.

Table 25.2 Document Transfer menu options

Enter This Menu Option	*To Perform the Following Action*
SEL (Select)	Select a document to transfer.
RD (Receive a Document from DEC Workstation)	Transfer a document from the DEC workstation that you're currently using to the ALL-IN-1 File Cabinet.
SD (Send a Document to DEC Workstation)	Transfer a document from the ALL-IN-1 File Cabinet to the DEC workstation that you're currently using.
RV (Receive a Document from VMS)	Transfer a file from the VMS file system to your ALL-IN-1 File Cabinet.
RVC (Receive without Conversion)	Transfer a file from the VMS file system to your ALL-IN-1 File Cabinet without converting the format of the information in the file.
SV (Send a Document to VMS)	Transfer a document from your ALL-IN-1 File Cabinet to the VMS file system.
SVC (Send without Conversion)	Transfer a document from your ALL-IN-1 File Cabinet to the VMS file system without converting the format of the information in the file.

Follow these steps to access Document Transfer:

DT [RETURN]

a. From any menu, type "DT" and press [RETURN]. You can also enter the menu option. For example, type "DT SEL" and press [RETURN] to select a document for transfer.

***menu-option* [RETURN]**

b. Type the menu option and press [RETURN]. Table 25.2 lists menu options on the Document Transfer menu.

In addition to the options listed in Table 25.2, you can also enter any of the options that apppear on the File Cabinet maintenance menu from the Document Transfer menu.

25.3.2 Transferring Documents to or from a DEC Workstation

The Receive a Document from DEC Workstation (RD) and Send a Document to DEC Workstation (SD) options on the Communications menu transfer documents between the ALL-IN-1 File Cabinet and a DEC workstation. A DEC workstation is either a DECmate or a PC running WPS-PLUS/DOS version 2.0 or later and EASYCOM software. Note that you must be currently logged onto the ALL-IN-1 host system through your DEC workstation for these options to work properly.

There are a number of reasons for transferring documents between the File Cabinet and your DEC workstation. Transferring a document to your DEC workstation lets you work with the document even when the ALL-IN-1 host will not be available (down for maintenance, perhaps). On the other hand, information in a document transferred from the DEC workstation to the ALL-IN-1 File Cabinet can be processed by any application in ALL-IN-1. You can send the document to other users with the Send (S) option in Word and Document processing, for example, or check for grammatical errors with the Grammar Checker.

25.3.3 Transferring Documents to or from VMS

The Receive a Document from VMS (RV) and Send a Document to VMS (SV) options on the Communications menu transfer documents between the ALL-IN-1 File Cabinet and the VMS file system. These options convert the format of the document from WPS-PLUS (or WordPerfect) to the standard format acceptable to VMS, and vice versa.

The Receive without Conversion (RVC) and Send without Conversion (SVC) options transfer documents between the ALL-IN-1 File Cabinet and the VMS file system as well. However, these options do not convert the format of the file during a transfer.

There are many reasons for transferring documents from VMS to the ALL-IN-1 File Cabinet:

- Transferring a file from VMS to the File Cabinet is the second step in uploading a file from a PC. WordPerfect documents, Lotus spreadsheets, and other files are often transferred from a PC to ALL-IN-1 to work with the information on the host system. In addition, PC files are often transferred to ALL-IN-1 so that they can be sent to other users through Electronic Messaging.

  There are a number of ways to accomplish the first step of transferring the file from the PC to VMS. Here are two options:

  - Transfer the file to your home directory with KERMIT, XMODEM, or some other PC communications utility. *Note:* Transfer the file as a binary file when you intend to use the same program in ALL-IN-1 to work with the file. This includes WordPerfect and Lotus.
  - If you're a PATHWORKS user, you can copy the file to your home directory with NFT or simply place the file on your personal file service drive.

  After you complete the first step, move the file from VMS to your ALL-IN-1 File Cabinet with Document Transfer. If you're transferring the file to ALL-IN-1 to work with the same program as on the PC, use the RVC option. That is, if you're transferring a WordPerfect document from a PC to ALL-IN-1, transfer the document without conversion.
- Files produced by other applications running under VMS can be transferred to the File Cabinet where they can be modified with any ALL-IN-1 editor or sent to other users through Electronic Messaging. For example, you might want to send a monthly report produced by an accounting application to managers in the organization.

Similarly, there are many reasons for transferring documents from the ALL-IN-1 File Cabinet to VMS:

- Transferring a document from the File Cabinet to VMS is the first step in downloading the file to a PC. Users transfer documents to a PC to work with the document when the host system is not available or to work with the document in a PC Windows environment.

Once the file is sent to VMS, it can then be transferred to the PC with KERMIT, XMODEM, NFT, and so on. Transfer the file without conversion if it is a binary file or if you intend to use the same program on the PC to work with the file.

- Files created in ALL-IN-1 are sometimes transferred to VMS where they can be read by other applications that cannot access the ALL-IN-1 File Cabinet.

The procedure for transferring documents requires that you have some knowledge of VMS file-naming conventions. You'll be asked to supply a file name to complete the transfer. The full format of a VMS file name is as follows:

device:[directory]filename.filetype

where

device is the name of the disk drive.

directory is the name of the directory where the file is stored.

filename is the name assigned to the file.

filetype is the type of file.

An example is 1DUA1:[JONES]BUDGET.DAT. Contact your system administrator for assistance if you are unfamiliar with VMS file-naming conventions.

Follow these steps to transfer a document from the ALL-IN-1 File Cabinet to the VMS file system:

DT [RETURN]	a. From any menu, type "DT" and press [RETURN] to move to Document Transfer.
[SELECT]...	b. Make sure that the current document is the one you want to transfer. If it is not, select the correct document.
SV [RETURN]	c. Type "SV" and press [RETURN] to convert and transfer the document.
SVC [RETURN]	Or type "SVC" and press [RETURN] to transfer the document without conversion. Use this option if you're transferring a binary file or transferring a file to a PC and will use the same program on the PC to work with the file. ALL-IN-1 displays the Send a Document to VMS form.
VMS File Name: ***file-name*** **[RETURN]**	d. Type the full VMS file name and then press [RETURN]. ALL-IN-1 displays one message as the file is being copied and another upon completion.

Note: You will receive an error message if the file is empty.

If you intend to move the document to a PC or to another directory, it might be wise to transfer it to your home directory. Enter a file name in the format SYS$LOGIN:*filename.type*. For example, SYS$LOGIN:BUDGET.RPT.

Follow these steps to transfer a file from VMS to a document in your ALL-IN-1 File Cabinet:

DT RV [RETURN]

a. From any menu, type "DT RV" and press [RETURN] to transfer the document and convert the format.

DT RVC [RETURN]

Or type "DT RVC" and press [RETURN] to transfer the document without converting the format. Use this option if you're transferring a binary file or transferring a file from a PC and will use the same program in ALL-IN-1 to work with the file.

ALL-IN-1 displays the Receive a Document from VMS form.

VMS File Name: ***file-name*** **[RETURN]**

b. Type the full VMS file name and then press [RETURN]. ALL-IN-1 displays the Creating from VMS File form.

Hint: If you don't remember the exact file name, you can enter a file specification containing wild-card characters (*) and press [FIND] (or [GOLD] L) to list file names. For example, files ready for transfer are often stored in your home directory. Therefore, type SYS$LOGIN:*.* and press [FIND] to display file names in your home directory.

Drawer: ***drawer*** **[TAB]**
Folder: ***folder*** **[TAB]**
Title: ***title*** **[TAB]**

c. Enter a drawer, folder name, and title. To change the drawer or folder name, press [UP ARROW], type the new name, and press [TAB]. Type the title of the document, and enter keywords for the document if desired.

[RETURN]

d. Press [RETURN] after completing the form to initiate the transfer. ALL-IN-1 displays one message while the document is being transferred and another message on completion.

User Defined Processes

CHAPTER 26

User Defined Processes save you a great deal of time and effort! Anytime you find yourself repetitively performing the same task in ALL-IN-1, chances are you can automate this task by creating a User Defined Process (UDP).

So, what's a UDP? A UDP is a special document that contains "stored keystrokes." Whenever you repeatedly enter the same series of keystrokes (characters) in ALL-IN-1, you can store these keystrokes in a UDP document. Later, when you need to perform these keystrokes, you simply supply ALL-IN-1 with the name of your UDP. ALL-IN-1 then reads the keystrokes from the UDP and automatically enters them for you—just like a player piano.

User Defined Processes provide the following benefits:

- They save you the time it takes to enter keystrokes manually.
- They help you avoid making mistakes because the same keystrokes are always played back when you execute a UDP.
- They perform tasks more efficiently than you could manually. No matter how fast a typist you are, the system can read and enter keystrokes from a UDP faster than you could enter them.

This chapter teaches you how to work with User Defined Processes, including how to do the following:

- Design a UDP for a task that you frequently perform.
- Create a UDP to store keystrokes to perform the task automatically.
- Execute a UDP to play back the stored keystrokes and perform the work.
- Record keystrokes to create a UDP.

26.1 USER DEFINED PROCESSES Q&A

Following is a list of common questions about User Defined Processes.

Q *How do I create a UDP? How do I execute a UDP?*

A Creating a User Defined Process is essentially the same as creating a document. You select the Create (C) option, enter the text of your User Defined Process, and file the document with [GOLD] F when finished. There are two differences, however. First,

UDPs must be created from the User Defined Process Maintenance menu. Second, because you are attempting to store keystrokes that perform work, you cannot simply press the function keys you want stored in the UDP. If you want "[GOLD] M" stored in the UDP, for example, you have to type a representation of this key. This particular function key is represented by eight characters: **{GOLD M}**.

To execute a UDP, simply press [DO] (or [GOLD] U) and enter the name you assigned to the UDP when you created it. ALL-IN-1 reads the keystrokes entered in the UDP and automatically types them for you. If you assigned one of eight special names when creating the UDP—F17, F18, F19, F20, GOLDF17, GOLDF18, GOLDF19, GOLDF20—just press the corresponding function key to execute the UDP.

Refer to Sections 26.4, "Developing a User Defined Process," and 26.5, "Executing a User Defined Process," in this chapter for further details.

Q *Can I record keystrokes to create a UDP?*

A Yes. ALL-IN-1 Version 3.1 allows you to record keystrokes in a file with CTRL/UDP LEARN ([CTRL/L]). This makes it quite easy to create UDPs and eliminates the possibility of your making typing errors when creating the UDP by hand. Unfortunately, however, you cannot record keystrokes while editing a document. The exercise at the end of this chapter shows you how to record keystrokes to create a UDP.

Q *How do I stop a UDP?*

A If problems arise, you can stop the currently executing User Defined Process by pressing [CTRL/C] (press and hold [CTRL], then type "C"). ALL-IN-1 displays a message that the activity was aborted per your request.

Q *Do I have to use User Defined Processes to work with ALL-IN-1? Is it hard to learn how to create and use UDPs if you're not a programmer?*

A You don't have to create and maintain UDPs to work with ALL-IN-1, but they will save time if you perform repetitive tasks. If you think you have to be a programmer to develop UDPs, perhaps this chapter's exercises will change your mind. If you can type and keep a record of what you type, you can develop User Defined Processes.

Q *How do I change the name of a UDP?*

A You cannot rename a UDP unless you have access to DCL. However, you can change the name indirectly with the following procedure:

- Create a UDP with the new name. When the editor is displayed, press [GOLD] G, type "UDP," press [RETURN], and enter the (old) name of the UDP. This copies the UDP to the new name. Press [GOLD] F to exit the editor.
- Select and delete the old UDP.

Q *How do I send a UDP that I created to someone else?*

A You can send a UDP that you've created to another user with Electronic Messaging. Move to Electronic Messaging and create a message. Address the message to the person to whom you want to send the UDP. Press [GOLD] G when the editor screen appears, enter UDP, and specify the name of the UDP you want to transfer. This retrieves the UDP as the text of the message. File and send the message.

The recipient must read the message, move to the UDP Maintenance menu, and create a new UDP (with the same name as the original, which you should include in the comments!). When the editor screen appears, the recipient can retrieve the UDP with [GOLD] G, specifying the document in the Read folder. The recipient must delete the mail header from the UDP because this is actually a mail message. Once the UDP has been filed, it's ready to be executed.

Q *I can execute a UDP while in WPS-PLUS. Why can't I execute a UDP from WordPerfect or EDT?*

A Both of these editors use different techniques for storing and playing back keystrokes. The [MACRO DEFINE] and [MACRO] function keys store and play back keystrokes in WordPerfect. In EDT, press [CTRL/K] to program a key to execute a set of keystrokes; in EVE, press [DO] and type the command "LEARN."

26.2 USER DEFINED PROCESSES DOs AND DON'Ts

Here are some suggestions for working with User Defined Processes:

Do

- Start paying attention to your daily chores in ALL-IN-1. Are you repetitively performing the same operations in the same order? If so, think about writing a UDP to save yourself some time!
- Include comments with your UDPs. This is very important regardless of the length of the UDP. You can include comment lines in your UDP by beginning the line with an exclamation point (!). Your comments should include the name of the UDP, a description, your name, and the date you created the UDP. Comments are invaluable if you send the UDP to someone else. You'll also find them useful if you have to change the UDP a few months down the road!

Don't

- Don't write your UDP in a manner that requires you to be at a certain starting point to execute it. It's always better to begin the UDP with a global menu option (EM, WP, etc.). The UDP can then be executed from any menu.
- Don't write dangerous UDPs. It might be nice to have a UDP for a cleanup operation that selects and deletes all documents in the current index . You might know that you should first select only *old* documents for the index when using the UDP, but if you send the UDP to others, they might not understand this. Some tasks are better off done manually. Avoid UDPs that delete items. If you write this type of UDP, include comments that caution the user.

If you create or receive a "risky" UDP, you might want to insert the following two lines at the top of the UDP. These command lines send a prompt to the terminal and require an affirmative response before the rest of the UDP is executed. Include the lines exactly as stated, except change **xxxxxxxx** to a few words of text explaining exactly what the UDP does.

```
.FX YESNO_PROMPT "This UDP xxxxxxxx. Continue? (Y/N)"
.IF OA$PROMPT_TEXT:1 NES OA$Y THEN .EXIT
```

Details of these commands are contained in the *ALL-IN-1 Application Programming: Reference*, Volume 1.

26.3 ACCESSING THE USER DEFINED PROCESS MENU

The User Defined Process Maintenance menu contains options for creating and maintaining UDPs. Although there are similarities between creating documents and creating UDPs, you must maintain UDPs from the User Defined Process Maintenance menu, not from the Word and Document Processing menu. All of the options on the UDP Maintenance menu work the same as their counterparts on the Word and Document Processing menu. However, options on the UDP Maintenance menu store files in an area reserved for UDPs as opposed to the File Cabinet.

Perform the following steps to access User Defined Process Maintenance:

WP UD [RETURN]	a. From any menu, type "WP UD" and then press [RETURN].
***menu-option* [RETURN]**	b. Type the menu option and press [RETURN]. Table 26.1 describes these options.

26.4 DEVELOPING A USER DEFINED PROCESS

In general, creating a User Defined Process is just like creating a document. You select the Create (C) option to invoke the editor and enter the text of your UDP. You then enter [GOLD] F to close and file your UDP when finished.

There are two differences, however:

- User Defined Processes must be maintained (created, edited, deleted, etc.) with the User Defined Process Maintenance menu.
- The characters you enter are those that you want "played back" when the UDP is executed. This presents an interesting problem. If you want to store the keystroke [GOLD] M in your UDP, for example, you cannot simply press [GOLD] M while editing the document. This would display the editor menu while creating the UDP. Instead, you have to type the following eight characters in your UDP to represent this keystroke: {GOLD M}. That is, you must literally press the keys {, G, O, L, etc.

Table 26.1 User Defined Process Maintenance menu options

Enter This Menu Option	*To Perform the Following Action*
SEL (Select)	Select a User Defined Process with which to work.
C (Create)	Create a new User Defined Process.
E (Edit)	Modify the current User Defined Process.
D (Delete)	Delete the current User Defined Process.
P (Print)	Print a copy of the current User Defined Process.
R (Read)	Display the current User Defined Process.
I (Index)	Display and work from an index list of all User Defined Processes.
TR (Training)	Start computer-based training to learn the basics of User Defined Processes.

26.4.1 Designing the UDP

The process of designing a UDP is fairly easy. If you can keep track of what you type, you can develop a UDP. Here are the steps to follow when designing a UDP.

1. Pick some task that you frequently perform in ALL-IN-1 or WPS-PLUS. It should be a task that requires that you always enter the same series of keystrokes.
2. Perform the task manually. As you perform the task, write down each keystroke on a piece of paper. (Pretend that you are writing instructions for someone else to follow.) Write down function keys with whatever notation you want. For example, <RETURN>, <GOLD> <M>, etc. *Note:* Make sure that you record every keystroke in the same order that you enter it.
3. After writing down all of the keystrokes, go back and perform the task again. Press the keys you wrote down, in the exact sequence in which you recorded them. This is a good check to see if you left anything out.

   NOTE: In this step, you have the option of recording your keystrokes as you work. This automatically creates your UDP and allows you to skip steps 4 and 5. To record keystrokes, press [CTRL/L], enter a 1 to 9 character name for the UDP, and press [RETURN]. Then enter the keystrokes you wrote down. When finished, press [CTRL/L] again to stop recording and proceed to step 6.
4. When you're sure that your written procedure works properly, you're ready to convert your function keys to the proper format. Read back through your written procedure. Whenever you come across a function key, look up the proper UDP representation for the key in Tables 26.2 and 26.3. Cross out your representation for the function, and write in the proper UDP representation.
5. You're now ready to create the UDP. Guidelines and the step-by-step procedure for creating a UDP follow.

6. Try executing your UDP after you've finished creating it. If it doesn't work correctly, edit the UDP and try running it again.

Table 26.2 UDP representations for standard function keys

Function Key	*UDP Representation*	*Description*
F1...F20	{F1}...{F20}	Function keys.
Keypad-0...Keypad-9	{KEY 0}...{KEY 9}	Numeric keypad keys.
PF2, PF3, PF4	{PF2}, {PF3}, {PF4}	Function keys.
{	{LBRACE}	Left brace.
}	{RBRACE}	Right brace.
[BACKSPACE]	{F12}	Move back one field.
[DELETE]	{DELETE}	Delete character.
[DO]	{PC DO} or {GOLD U}	Execute a UDP.
[DOWN ARROW]	{DOWN}	Move forward one line.
[ENTER]	{ENTER}	Keypad [ENTER] key.
[ERASE LINE]	{F13} or {LF}	Erase a field.
[EXIT]	{PC EXIT}	Exit a form or menu.
[FIND]	{PC FIND} or {GOLD L}	List possible entries.
[HELP]	{HELP}	Display help.
[INSERT]	{F14}	Insert mode editing.
[INTERRUPT]	{PC INTERRUPT} or {GOLD I}	Display interrupt menu.
[LEFT ARROW]	{LEFT}	Move back one character.
[LINE FEED]	{F13}	Erase a field.
[MAIN SCREEN]	{PC MAIN SCREEN}	Display main menu.
[NEXT SCREEN]	{PC NEXT SCREEN}	Display next screen.
[OVERSTRIKE]	{PF3}	Overstrike mode editing.
[PREV FIELD]	{F12}	Move to previous field.
[PREV SCREEN]	{PC PREV SCREEN}	Display previous screen of text.
[RESUME]	{PC RESUME}	Resume processing.
[RETURN]	{RETURN} or {CR}	Execute or enter.
[RIGHT ARROW]	{RIGHT}	Move forward one character.
[SELECT]	{SELECT}	Select an item.
[TAB]	{TAB}	Move to next field.
[UP ARROW]	{UP}	Move back one line.
[GOLD]	{PF1}	Gold key.
[GOLD] #	{GOLD #}	Display Desk Calculator.
[GOLD] $	{GOLD $}	Access DCL.
[GOLD] *	{GOLD *}	Display Scratch Pad menu.
[GOLD] [SELECT]	{GOLD SELECT}	Deselect.
[GOLD] B	{GOLD B}	Bottom of form or document.

Table 26.2 *(continued)*

Function Key	*UDP Representation*	*Description*
[GOLD] C	{GOLD C}	Scroll output.
[GOLD] E	{GOLD E}	Wide screen.
[GOLD] F	{GOLD F} or {F10}	File.
[GOLD] I	{GOLD I} or {F6}	Display the Interrupt menu.
[GOLD] M	{GOLD M}	Display the menu.
[GOLD] P	{GOLD P}	Print screen to Scratch Pad.
[GOLD] S	{GOLD S}	Embedded search.
[GOLD] T	{GOLD T}	Beginning of form or document.
[GOLD] V	{GOLD V}	View item.
[GOLD] W	{GOLD W}	Display message.
[GOLD] X	{GOLD X}	Exit CBI lesson.
[GOLD] Z	{GOLD Z}	Display status.

Table 26.3 UDP representations for WPS-PLUS function keys

Function Key	*UDP Representation*	*Description*
ABBREVIATION	{GOLD =}	Retrieve expanded text.
ADVANCE	{ADV}	Set mode to forward.
ALT CHAR	{F11}	Enter a special character.
ALT CHAR MODE	{GOLD F11}	Toggle special character mode on/off.
BACKUP	{BACKUP}	Set mode to reverse.
BOLD	{BOLD}	Bold text.
BOTTOM	{GOLD B}	Move to bottom of document.
CANCEL	{PC CANCEL}	Exit editor without saving changes.
CENTER	{GOLD C}	Center preceding text.
CHANGE EDITOR	{GOLD]}	Invoke the TDE.
COMMAND	{GOLD [}	Start a format control block.
CONT SEARCH	{GOLD .}	Search again for text.
CONT SEARCH AND SEL	{GOLD /}	Search again for text and select.
COPY	{GOLD CUT}	Copy selected text.
CUT	{CUT}	Cut selected text.
DATE AND TIME	{GOLD \}	Insert present date and time.
DCL	{GOLD $}	Access DCL.
DEAD KEY	{GOLD D}	Overstrike last character.

(continued)

Table 26.3 UDP representations for WPS-PLUS function keys *(continued)*

Function Key	*UDP Representation*	*Description*
DELETE	{DELETE}	Delete previous character.
DELETE CHAR	{DELCHR}	Delete current character.
DELETE LINE	{RUBLIN}	Delete current line.
DELETE SENTENCE	{RUBSENT}	Delete current sentence.
DELETE WORD	{DELWRD}	Delete current word.
DO	{DO} or {GOLD U}	Execute a User Defined Process.
ENTER	{ENTER}	Move to next right bracket (>).
EXIT (MENU)	{ADV}	Exit menu and return to editing.
EXIT	{PC EXIT} or {F10}	Exit editor and save changes.
FIND	{PC FIND}	Search for a text string.
FOOTNOTE	{GOLD Y}	Create footnote.
GET DOCUMENT	{GOLD G}	Include document.
GLOBAL REPLACE	{GOLD ;}	Replace all occurrences of string.
GOLD DOWN ARROW	{GOLD DOWN}	Scroll to end of document.
GOLD LEFT ARROW	{GOLD LEFT}	Move to the beginning of current line.
GOLD RIGHT ARROW	{GOLD RIGHT}	Move to end of current line.
GOLD UP ARROW	{GOLD UP}	Scroll to beginning of document.
HYPHEN PUSH	{F12}	Force hyphen in nonbreaking word.
INDENT PARAGRAPH	{GOLD TAB}	Indent paragraph to next tab stop.
INSERT/OVERSTRIKE	{F14}	Toggle insert and overstrike.
LANGUAGE AIDS	{GOLD J}	Spelling, Thesaurus, Usage Alert
LIBRARY	{GOLD L}	Retrieve library text.
LINE	{LINE}	Move one line.
MENU	{GOLD M}	Display editor menu.
NEW PAGE	{GOLD N}	Insert page break.
PAGE	{PAGE}	Move to next page.
PAGE MARKER	{GOLD P}	Insert page marker.
PARAGRAPH	{PARA}	Move one paragraph.
PARAGRAPH MARK	{PARMRK}	Move to paragraph indentation.
PARAGRAPH REWRAP	{GOLD PARA}	Rewrap selected text to form a paragraph.
PASTE	{PASTE}	Paste selected text.
PASTE ALL	{GOLD PASTE}	Paste selected text, including rulers.
PRINT HYPHEN	{GOLD -}	Insert a breaking hyphen.
RETURN	{RETURN} or {CR}	Insert new line (carriage return).
RUB OUT CHAR	{RUBCHR}	Delete previous character.
RUB OUT WORD	{RUBWRD}	Delete previous word.
RULER	{GOLD R}	Create or update the ruler.

Table 26.3 *(continued)*

Function Key	*UDP Representation*	*Description*
SEARCH	{GOLD ,}	Search for a text string.
SEARCH AND SELECT	{GOLD /}	Search again and select string.
SELECT	{SEL}	Select text.
SENTENCE	{SENT}	Move one sentence.
SPACE	{SPACE}	Insert a space.
SPELL CHECK	{GOLD S}	Check spelling.
STATUS	{GOLD Z}	Display status information.
SUBSCRIPT	{GOLD A}	Subscript selected text.
SUPERSCRIPT	{GOLD Q}	Superscript selected text.
SWAP	{GOLD <>}	Transpose characters.
TAB POSITION	{TABPOS}	Move one tab position.
TOP	{GOLD T}	Move to top of document.
UDP	{PC DO} or {GOLD U}	Execute a User Defined Process.
UNDERLINE	{UNDER}	Underline text.
UPPERCASE	{UPPER}	Capitalize text.
VIEW	{GOLD V}	View mode.
WORD	{WORD}	Move one word.
WRITE DOC	{GOLD W}	Write document.

26.4.2 Guidelines for Writing a UDP

A good User Defined Process is one that works. A better User Defined Process is one that works and is easy to read and modify.

Here are some guidelines for writing better UDPs:

- Make sure that all function key names are enclosed in braces {}. Tables 26.2 and 26.3 list the proper representations for function keys in a UDP. Keystrokes other than function keys should not be enclosed in braces. For example, you would enter the following keystrokes to create a UDP for reading a new mail message:

```
EM RN{RETURN}
```

- You can place all keystrokes on the same line or on multiple lines. The UDP is easier to read and follow if you place keystrokes on multiple lines. The following two UDPs are equivalent, but the second is easier to follow:

```
EM II{RETURN}ALL XR{RETURN}
EM II{RETURN}

ALL XR{RETURN}
```

- Place comments in your UDP to describe the contents. Comment lines must begin with an exclamation point (!). It's a good idea to include the following information at the top of your UDP:
  - The name of the UDP.
  - A description of the UDP's purpose.
  - Your name.
  - The date you wrote the UDP.

  For example:

```
! UDP Name: NEWMAIL
!
! This UDP displays all new mail.
!
! Created by: S. Washington                Date: 6/12/94
!
! First build an index of the Inbox.
EM II{RETURN}
!
! Next select all messages and execute the Read
! All Selected option (XR).
!
ALL XR{RETURN}
```

26.4.3 Creating a UDP

The Create (C) option on the User Defined Process Maintenance menu creates a new User Defined Process. You can also create a UDP by recording keystrokes as shown in Section 26.8, "Exercise—Recording Keystrokes to Create a UDP." Once you create a UDP, you can select other options on this menu to edit, delete, print, read, and build an index of UDPs.

You must name a UDP when you create it. This name can include letters and numbers (no spaces) and can be up to nine characters in length. It's important to choose a name that is meaningful. This makes it easier to remember the name when you execute the UDP.

NOTE: If you assign one of these names to your UDP—F17, F18, F19, F20, GOLDF17, GOLDF18, GOLDF19, or GOLDF20—you can execute the UDP by simply pressing the corresponding function key. For example, you would press [GOLD] F20 to execute the UDP named "GOLDF20."

Perform the following steps to invoke an editor and create a new UDP:

C [RETURN]	a. From the UDP Maintenance menu, type "C" and press [RETURN] to create a UDP. ALL-IN-1 asks for the name of the UDP.

UDP name: ***udp-name***
[RETURN]

b. Type the name of the new UDP and press [RETURN]. ALL-IN-1 invokes the editor so you can enter your UDP.

c. Enter the contents of the UDP, following the instructions in Section 26.4.2, "Guidelines for Writing a UDP." You are now working with the same text editor that you use to create documents. All of the features of the text editor are available for preparing your UDP.

   Note: Refer to Tables 26.2 and 26.3 when you want to include a function key representation in your UDP. Do not include special formatting or control characters in your UDP. These characteristics either will be removed when the UDP is stored or will prevent the UDP from executing properly.

[GOLD] F

d. Press [GOLD] (PF1) and F when you've finished creating your UDP.

26.5 EXECUTING A USER DEFINED PROCESS

You can execute a User Defined Process when working from an ALL-IN-1 screen or when editing a document in WPS-PLUS. The [DO] key or [GOLD] U executes a UDP. Press [DO], enter the name of a UDP and, if desired, the number of times you want to repeat the UDP. ALL-IN-1 reads the keystrokes from the UDP and enters them for you, just as if you were typing them manually. If you enter a repeat count, the set of keystrokes is replayed the number of times you specify.

In addition to the [DO] key, there are eight function keys that trigger specially named UDPs. These function keys are F17 through F20 and [GOLD] F17 through [GOLD] F20. These keys trigger UDPs with the names F17, F18, F19, F20, GOLDF17, GOLDF18, GOLDF19, and GOLDF20, respectively. You'll want to assign these names to frequently used UDPs so that you can execute them with one or two keystrokes.

NOTE: Every User Defined Process plays back a *specific* sequence of keystrokes. The UDP might require that you be at a specific starting point (menu, data-entry form, etc.) before executing the UDP. Otherwise, it might not execute properly. If this is the case, this information should be included in the comments of the UDP.

Perform the following steps to execute (play back) a User Defined Process:

a. Make sure that you're in the proper place to start the UDP. Some UDPs require you to move to a certain menu, data-entry form, and so forth, before executing the UDP.

[F17]...
[GOLD] [F17]...

b. If the UDP is named F17, F18, F19, F20, GOLDF17, GOLDF18, GOLDF19, or GOLDF20, simply press the corresponding function key to execute the UDP. For example, press [GOLD] F17 to execute the UDP named GOLDF17.

[DO]

If the UDP does not have one of these names, press [DO] (or [GOLD] U) to execute it. ALL-IN-1 asks for the name of the UDP.

UDP name: ***udp-name***
[RETURN]

Type the name of the UDP and press [RETURN], or press [TAB] and enter the number of times you want to repeat the UDP, and then press [RETURN]. ALL-IN-1 starts the UDP.

Hint: If you don't remember the name, press [ERASE LINE] (LF or F13) to clear the Name field, and then press [FIND] (or [GOLD] L) to list all UDP names.

To stop a UDP while it is running, do the following:

[CTRL]+C

Press and hold [CTRL], then press C. ALL-IN-1 displays a message that activity was stopped at the user's request.

26.6 EXERCISE: CREATING AND EXECUTING A UDP

In this exercise, you'll create a User Defined Process for printing a copy of the current screen. This UDP is helpful if you ever want to print a copy of your working conditions, print settings, or an index of items (currently displayed).

WARNING: This UDP clears the Scratch Pad. You might want to print or file your Scratch Pad to preserve the contents before continuing.

Try entering all of the following keystrokes manually to get an understanding of the keystrokes in the sample UDP. Note that the third line might not be necessary if you've turned off the delete confirmation prompt with Set Working Conditions. If so, omit this line here and in the following procedure.

```
[GOLD] *

D [RETURN]

Y [RETURN]

[EXIT]

[GOLD] P

[GOLD] *
```

```
P [RETURN]

[RETURN]

[EXIT]
```

Perform the following steps to create and execute the sample UDP:

1. First move to the UDP menu.

WP UD [RETURN]	From any menu, type "WP UD" and then press [RETURN].

2. Create the UDP.

C [RETURN]	a. Type "C" and press [RETURN] to create a UDP. ALL-IN-1 displays the Create New UDP form.
UDP name: **GOLDF20 [RETURN]**	b. Type "GOLDF20" and press [RETURN]. ALL-IN-1 invokes the editor so you can enter your UDP.
	c. For the contents of the new UDP, type exactly what you see in Figure 26.1, except substitute your name and the current date where indicated.
[GOLD] F	d. Press [GOLD] F when you've finished creating the UDP. ALL-IN-1 redisplays the UDP Maintenance menu.

```
!
! UDP Name:  GOLDF20
!
! The following UDP prints a copy of the current screen.
! This is done by displaying the Scratch Pad menu, deleting
! the Scratch Pad, exiting and copying the screen to the
! Scratch Pad, then printing the Scratch Pad.
!
! Created by: your-name    Date: current date
!
{GOLD *}
D{RETURN}
Y{RETURN}
{PC EXIT}
{GOLD P}
{GOLD *}
P{RETURN}
{RETURN}
{PC EXIT}
```

Figure 26.1 UDP to copy the current screen to the Scratch Pad

3. Execute the UDP.

[GOLD] F20	Press [GOLD] (PF1), then press F20 to execute your UDP. The current screen is copied to the Scratch Pad and then printed.

You can now press [GOLD] F20 whenever you want a copy of the current menu, data-entry form, or index.

26.7 EXAMPLES OF USER DEFINED PROCESSES

Now that you've seen how User Defined Processes work, it's time to create some useful UDPs. Start in your own backyard. Pay attention to your work in ALL-IN-1, and see whether you perform any repetitive tasks. Do you go through the same steps to change or recall print settings when printing a document? Do you print your schedule on a daily or weekly basis? Do you follow the same steps to transfer a document? If so, you might want to develop UDPs to do this work for you.

Following are three User Defined Processes that you might find valuable. There are hundreds more. The best source of UDPs is probably other users in your organization. Storing UDPs in a group conference is a great way to share these procedures.

The second and third UDPs are somewhat advanced and contain instructions that are not discussed in this manual. These are the lines beginning with a period. Although a full explanation is beyond the scope of this manual, comments explain briefly what is happening in these lines. You can find complete details of these commands in the *ALL-IN-1 Applications Programming Reference,* Volume 1.

Be careful to enter these processes exactly as written to ensure that they work successfully.

26.7.1 UDP for Printing a Copy of an Error Message

The first UDP example, shown in Figure 26.2, is helpful when you receive an error message that you don't understand. This UDP is named GOLDF19, which means that you can press the [GOLD] key and then F19 to start the UDP. This UDP displays the full error text with [GOLD] W, copies the result to the Scratch Pad, and prints the Scratch Pad. You can take the printout to your system administrator or an experienced user for assistance.

There are no advanced commands in this example. If you like, you can try the keystrokes manually before creating the UDP.

26.7.2 UDP for Printing a Brief Listing of Documents

The second UDP example, shown in Figure 26.3, is named PI_BRIEF. This UDP creates a listing of all documents in your File Cabinet from the Index option on the Word and Document Processing menu. Each page of the index is then copied to your Scratch Pad for printing. The only unusual lines included in this example are those that stop the

```
!
! UDP Name: GOLDF20
!
! This UDP copies an error message to the Scratch Pad, then prints
! the Scratch Pad.
!
! Created by:  your-name      Date: current-date
!
! First display the full error message and copy to the Scratch Pad.
!
{GOLD W}
{GOLD P}
{RETURN}
!
! Now print the Scratch Pad.
!
{GOLD *}
P
{RETURN}
{RETURN}
{PC EXIT}
```

Figure 26.2 UDP to print a copy of an error message

```
!
! UDP Name: PI_BRIEF
!
! This UDP prints an index of the file cabinet to the Scratch Pad.
!
! Created by:  your-name      Date: current-date
!
! First create an index of all documents and copy the first
! page to the Scratch Pad.
!
WP I{RETURN}
{F13}{RETURN}
{GOLD P}
!
! Keep displaying the next page of documents and pasting the
! display to the Scratch Pad.  Stop when the last page of
! documents has been displayed.
!
.LABEL NEXT_SCREEN
{PC NEXT SCREEN}
.IF OA$MSG_ID EQS "SCLATLAST" THEN .EXIT
{GOLD P}
.GOTO NEXT_SCREEN
```

Figure 26.3 UDP to print a brief listing of your file cabinet

UDP from continuing when the last page of the index has been copied to the Scratch Pad.

After you create this UDP, press [DO] and type the name PI_BRIEF to copy the index of your documents to your Scratch Pad. Then read or print the Scratch Pad.

26.7.3 UDP for Looking Up a Phone Number

The last UDP example, shown in Figure 26.4, makes your personal phone directory more accessible. The name of this UDP is F20, which means that you can start this UDP by pressing the F20 function key. The UDP responds by asking you to enter a name that appears in your personal phone directory. When you enter a name and press [RETURN], the UDP displays the business and home phone numbers on line 24 of your screen. You can enter all or part of a name, and the UDP will find the first matching entry in your directory.

```
!
! UDP Name: F20
!
! This UDP prompts the user for a name that appears in his or
! her personal phone directory.  When the user enters a name,
! the business and home phone numbers are displayed at the
! bottom of the screen.
!
! Created by:  your-name     Date: current-date
!
! Prompt for the name and quit if no name is entered.
!
.FX PROMPT "Enter name: "
.IF OA$PROMPT_TEXT EQS "" THEN .EXIT
!
! Set the variable #FOUND to "Entry not found" just in case
! the name isn't in the directory.
!
.FX GET #FOUND = "Entry not found"
!
! Look for the name in the directory. Get the business and
! home phone numbers if found.
!
.FX FOR FIRST PHPENT WITH .USER CONTAINING OA$PROMPT_TEXT DO -
 GET #FOUND = .FULNAM " - Bus: " .PHONE "  Home: " .HOMEPH
!
! Display the phone numbers (if found).
!
.FX GET OA$DISPLAY = #FOUND \ FORCE
.EXIT
```

Figure 26.4 UDP to look up a phone number

This UDP contains mostly advanced commands. The intent here is not to make a programmer out of you, but to give you a useful tool for looking up a phone number. If you are interested in this type of UDP, refer to the *ALL-IN-1 Applications Programming Guide* for more information.

When entering this UDP, be careful to type exactly what you see in Figure 26.4. The line beginning with the text ".IF OA$PROMPT_TEXT..." has two double quotes. These quotes must be placed next to each other, with no intervening space. The line containing the text "GET #FOUND = .FULNAM" begins with a space and includes a space on either side of the double quote marks.

After you create this UDP, press F20 to look up a phone number in your personal directory.

NOTE: The following UDP references ALL-IN-1 *functions* (command verbs) and therefore requires your ALL-IN-1 account to have PRVUDPFNC privilege.

26.8 EXERCISE: RECORDING KEYSTROKES TO CREATE A UDP

In this exercise, you'll create a User Defined Process the easy way—by letting ALL-IN-1 record the keystrokes for you. This exercise allows ALL-IN-1's tracing feature to record the keystrokes for printing a daily schedule.

WARNINGS:

- This UDP clears the Scratch Pad. You might want to print or file your Scratch Pad to preserve the contents before continuing.
- You will start recording keystrokes in a file with the name you specify in step 1. If you do not complete this exercise properly and turn off recording in step 3, you will continue to record keystrokes. The UDP file could end up being very large if you do not turn off recording in step 3.

1. The first step is to turn on the recording of keystrokes.

[CTRL] + L	a. From any menu, press and hold [CTRL], then press "L". ALL-IN-1 prompts for the name of the new UDP.
Enter UDP name or press RETURN to use default: SCHED [RETURN]	b. Type "SCHED" and press [RETURN]. *Note:* UDP names must be 1 to 9 characters in length and cannot contain spaces.

NOTE: All keystrokes you enter are now being written to the UDP file. Now is *not* the time to quit this exercise. You must first perform step 3 to turn off recording if you want to quit.

2. Now execute the keystrokes you want included in your UDP. Remember: Your keystrokes are being recorded. You don't want to make mistakes. Take it slow, and be careful!

[GOLD] *	a. Press [GOLD] * to display the Scratch Pad menu.
D [RETURN]	b. Type "D" and press [RETURN] to delete the contents of the Scratch Pad.
Y [RETURN]	c. Type "Y" and press [RETURN] to confirm that you want to delete the Scratch Pad. *Note:* Omit this step if you've disabled this prompt with Set Working Conditions.
[EXIT]	d. Press [EXIT] (F10 or Keypad-0) to clear the Scratch Pad menu.
TM EP [RETURN]	e. Type "TM EP" and press [RETURN] to move to the Events Plus index.
[GOLD] P	f. Press [GOLD] P to copy the screen to your Scratch Pad. (Don't worry if the display is blank.)
[GOLD] *	g. Press [GOLD] * to display the Scratch Pad menu.
P [RETURN] **[RETURN]**	h. Type "P" and press [RETURN] to print the Scratch Pad to the current printer destination.
[EXIT]	i. Press [EXIT] to clear the Scratch Pad menu.

3. Now turn off the recording of keystrokes.

[CTRL] + L	a. Press [CTRL] + L. ALL-IN-1 stops recording keystrokes and displays a message that the UDP has been created.

4. You're ready to review the UDP and retrieve the recorded keystrokes.

WP UD [RETURN]	a. From any menu, type "WP UD" and then press [RETURN].
SEL SCHED [RETURN]	b. Type "SEL SCHED" and press [RETURN] to select the UDP.
E [RETURN]	c. Type "E" and press [RETURN]. ALL-IN-1 invokes the editor so you can edit your UDP. Your UDP should look like Figure 26.5.
[GOLD] F	d. Add comments to the top of your UDP preceded with an exclamation point (!), and press [GOLD] F when you've finished. ALL-IN-1 redisplays the UDP Maintenance menu.

5. Execute the UDP.

[DO]	a. Press [DO] (or [GOLD] U). ALL-IN-1 asks for the UDP name.

```
! Created using Learn Mode on 01-Jan-1994, at 12:23
{GOLD *}
D {CR}
Y {CR}
{KEY 0}
TM EP {CR}
{GOLD P}
{GOLD *}
P {CR}
{CR}
{KEY 0}
```

Figure 26.5 UDP to print the day's events

UDP Name: **SCHED**
[RETURN]

b. Type "SCHED" and press [RETURN]. Your UDP is executed.

You can now use this UDP any time you want to print your daily schedule.

Function Keys and Global Menu Selections

APPENDIX A

This appendix contains two valuable tables, which list function keys and menu selections that you'll frequently use when working with ALL-IN-1.

Table A.1 describes the function keys that are active in ALL-IN-1. They are listed by name and grouped according to use. The operations performed by many of these function keys are illustrated in the exercises in Chapter 3. This table does not describe the function keys that are active in the editor. Editor function keys are described in Appendix B.

Table A.2 lists the "global" menu options for ALL-IN-1. These are menu options that you can enter at any menu.

A.1 ALL-IN-1 FUNCTION KEYS (LISTED BY KEY NAME)

Table A.1 ALL-IN-1 function keys[a]

Press the Following Key(s)	*To Perform This Action*
General Purpose	
[BACKSPACE] (F12 or [CTRL]+H)	Move to the previous field on the form.
[CTRL/L]	Start/stop recording a UDP.
[CTRL/Q]	Restart terminal output.
[CTRL/S]	Suspend terminal output.
[CTRL/W]	Repaint the screen.
[DELETE]	Delete a character.
[DO]	Execute a User Defined Process.
[ERASE LINE] (LF, F13, or [CTRL]+J)	Clear the current field.
[EXIT] (F10 or Keypad-0)	Exit and return to the previous form.
[GOLD] #	Display the Desk Calculator.
[GOLD] $	Enter the DCL level temporarily.
[GOLD] *	Display the Scratch Pad menu.

(continued)

Table A.1 ALL-IN-1 function keys *(continued)*

Press the Following Key(s)	*To Perform This Action*
General Purpose	
[GOLD] \	Display the date and time.
[GOLD] H	Display Help information.
[GOLD] I	Display the Interrupt menu.
[GOLD] P	Copy the screen to the Scratch Pad.
[GOLD] Q	Quit and return to the previous form.
[GOLD] W	Display the full message.
[GOLD] Z	Toggle the document status display.
[GOLD] (PF1)	First character in a GOLD function key sequence.
[GOLD] [PF3]	Change to insert mode for the current field.
[HELP]	Display Help information.
[INSERT/OVERSTRIKE] (F14)	Toggle between insert and overstrike modes.
[INTERRUPT] (F6)	Display the Interrupt menu.
[MAIN SCREEN] (F9)	Return to the main menu setting.[b]
[NEXT SCREEN]	Display the next screen.
[PF3]	Change to overstrike mode for the current field.
[PREV FIELD] (BS, F12, or [CTRL]+H)	Move to the previous field on the form.
[PREV SCREEN]	Display the previous screen.
[RETURN]	Form complete, execute function.
[TAB]	Move to the next field on the form.
Menu Form	
[DOWN ARROW]	Select the next item.
[UP ARROW]	Select the first item or the previous item.
[EXIT] (F10 or Keypad-0)	Exit and return to the previous form.
[MAIN SCREEN] (F9)	Return to the main menu setting.
[NEXT SCREEN] (or [GOLD] A)	Display the next screen.
[PREV SCREEN] (or [GOLD] [BCKSP])	Display the previous screen.
[SELECT]	Select an item.
Data-Entry Form	
[DOWN ARROW]	Move to the next line.
[UP ARROW]	Move to the previous line.
[ERASE LINE] (F13, LF, or [CTRL]+J)	Erase the contents of the current field.
[EXIT] (F10 or Keypad-0)	Exit without saving changes.
[FIND]	Look up and list matching entries.
[GOLD] [PF3]	Change to insert mode for the current field.
[GOLD] B	Move to the last field on the current form.
[GOLD] S	Look up entries containing entered character(s).[c]
[GOLD] T	Move to the first field on the current form.
[GOLD] [DOWN ARROW]	Move to the last field on the current screen.
[GOLD] [UP ARROW]	Move to the first field on the current screen.

Table A.1 *(continued)*

Press the Following Key(s)	*To Perform This Action*
[INSERT/OVERSTRIKE] (F14)	Toggle between insert and overstrike modes.
[LEFT ARROW]	Move one character left.
[NEXT SCREEN] (or [GOLD] [TAB])	Display the next screen.
[PF3]	Change to overstrike mode for the current field.
[PREV FIELD] (F12 or [CTRL] H)	Move to the previous data field.
[PREV SCREEN] (or [GOLD] [BCKSP])	Display the previous screen.
[RETURN]	Complete the form.
[RIGHT ARROW]	Move one character right.
[TAB]	Move to the next data field.
Index Form	
[DOWN ARROW]	Move the current item pointer (>) down one line.
[UP ARROW]	Move the current item pointer (>) up one line.
[EXIT] (F10 or Keypad-0)	Exit the index.
[GOLD] [SELECT]	Deselect the current item.
[GOLD] B	Move to the last item in the index.
[GOLD] F	Select the current item and return to the menu.
[GOLD] M	Display the index menu.
[GOLD] T	Move to the first item in the index.
[GOLD] V	Display more information about the current item.
[NEXT SCREEN] (or [GOLD] [TAB])	Display the next screen of items.
[PREV SCREEN] (or [GOLD] [BKSP])	Display the previous screen of items.
[SELECT] (or Keypad-Period)	Select the current item.
Reading Documents	
[CANCEL] (F13 or [GOLD] K)	Quit reading the current message and leave status as unread.
[DOWN ARROW]	Move down one line in the text.
[UP ARROW]	Move up one line in the text.
[EXIT] (F10 or Keypad-0)	Quit reading the current document.
[GOLD] [DOWN ARROW]	Move forward one page.
[GOLD] [UP ARROW]	Move backward one page.
[GOLD] [LEFT ARROW]	Shift the text eight columns to the left.
[GOLD] [RIGHT ARROW]	Shift the text eight columns to the right.
[GOLD] [FIND] (or [GOLD] Period)	Locate the next occurrence of the string.
[GOLD] B	Move to the bottom of the document.
[GOLD] C	Start continuous forward scrolling of the document.
[GOLD] E	Toggle between 80 and 132 columns.
[GOLD] M	Display Read menu.
[GOLD] P	Copy the current screen to the Scratch Pad.

(continued)

Table A.1 ALL-IN-1 function keys *(continued)*

Press the Following Key(s)	*To Perform This Action*
Reading Documents	
[GOLD] T	Move to the top of the document.
[GOLD] V	Display or clear distribution list for the current message.
[GOLD] Z	Display or clear document status information.
[NEXT SCREEN] (or [GOLD] A)	Move forward one screen in the text.
[PREV SCREEN] (or [GOLD] [BKSP])	Move backward one screen in the text.
[RETURN]	Display the next screen or return to the menu.
text [FIND]	Locate the specified string of text.
Miscellaneous	
[CANCEL] (F8 or [GOLD] K)	Quit an edit session without saving changes.
[GOLD] F	File the current document.
[GOLD] P	Copy the current screen to the Scratch Pad.
[GOLD] Q	Leave the Desk Calculator.
[GOLD] X	Exit CBI.

[a] All [GOLD] keys listed in this table require that you enter two separate keystrokes: Press the [GOLD] (PF1) key, then press the second key indicated.

[b] The main menu is the initial menu form displayed when you start ALL-IN-1. You can select a form other than the standard main menu with User Setup in Set Working Conditions.

[c] [GOLD] S capability must be granted by your system administrator.

A.2 GLOBAL MENU SELECTIONS

Table A.2 Global menu selections

Enter This Selection at Any Menu	*To Access the Following*
AD or PD	Application Development
CA	Calculations
CM	Customization Management[a]
COM	Communications
DC	Desktop Calculator
DIR	Directories
DL	Distribution List Management
DM	Desk Management
DT	Document Transfer
EM	Electronic Messaging
EX	Exit Workstation
FC	File Cabinet Management
FD	Forms Development
GPC	Group Conferencing
GS	Group Services
IM	Information Management
JS	Job Services
MAIN	Main menu
NI	Nickname Management
PF	Programming Functions
PS	Profession Specific
SP	Scratch Pad
TM	Time Management
US	User Setup
WP	Word and Document Processing

[a] Requires privileges.

Editor Quick Reference Guides

APPENDIX B

This appendix provides step-by-step instructions for performing common word-processing operations in WPS-PLUS, WordPerfect, and EDT. (In general, you can follow the procedures for WPS-PLUS if you've selected EVE_WPS as your editor; follow the procedures for EDT if you've selected EVE_EDT as your editor.) Most common functions are included, but some of the more advanced, complex functions available in WPS-PLUS and WordPerfect have been omitted for brevity.

This appendix includes instructions for the following operations:

- Moving around in your document.
- Selecting, highlighting, and moving text.
- Searching for text.
- Deleting text.
- Setting margins and tab stops.
- Inserting page breaks and page numbers.
- Performing a spell check.
- Changing the font (WPS-PLUS and WordPerfect).
- Creating running headers and footers (WPS-PLUS and WordPerfect).

Keep the following points in mind when executing these procedures:

- The procedures are brief in nature, targeted toward readers with some editing experience. If you have no such experience, you might start by learning the basic editing procedures for your particular editor in Chapter 10.
- All [GOLD] keys listed in this appendix require that you enter two separate keystrokes: Press the [GOLD] (PF1) key, followed by the second key indicated.
- Many of the function key names enclosed in brackets [] do not represent actual key names printed on the keyboard. The actual keystrokes are therefore listed in parentheses following the function key. For example, the [MOVE] function key in WordPerfect copies selected text for movement to another area of the document. "(PF2, F10)" follows "[MOVE]" to indicate that you must press the PF2 key followed by the F10 key to start a move operation.

- Keystrokes refer to keys on the keyboard of a Digital VT terminal. If you're using a different terminal or a PC, review documentation for the terminal or PC (terminal-emulation program) to see how your keys map to those of a VT terminal.

B.1 WPS-PLUS QUICK REFERENCE GUIDE

Table B.1 lists the function keys active in WPS-PLUS for performing editing operations. This table also lists the individual keystrokes that must be entered on a VT-style terminal.

Table B.1 WPS-PLUS function keys

Function Key	*Keystrokes*[a,b]	*Description*
[ABBREVIATION]	[GOLD] =	Retrieve expanded text from the Abbreviations document.
[ADVANCE]	Keypad-0	Set mode to forward.
[ALT CHAR]	F11 (or [CTRL]+E)	Enter a special character.
[BACKUP]	Keypad-1	Set mode to backward.
[BOLD]	Keypad-6	Make the current character bold; set highlighting to bold.
[BOTTOM]	[GOLD] B	Move the cursor to the bottom of the document.
[CANCEL]	F8 (or [GOLD] K)	Exit the editor without saving changes.
[CENTER]	[GOLD] C	Center the preceding text.
[CHANGE EDITOR]	[GOLD]]	Invoke the Two Dimensional Editor for creating graphics or the Multi-Column Editor.
[COMMAND]	[GOLD] [	Start a format control block.
[COMPOSE CHAR]	[COMPOSE CHAR] (or [CTRL]+K)	Compose special character.
[CONT SEARCH]	[GOLD] [PERIOD]	Search again for text.
[CUT]	[REMOVE] (or Keypad-Hyphen)	Cut selected text.
[DATE & TIME]	[GOLD] \	Insert present date and time.
[DCL]	[GOLD] $	Access DCL.
[DEAD KEY]	[GOLD] D	Overstrike the last character.
[DELETE]	⌫	Delete the previous character.
[DELETE CHAR]	PF4	Delete the current character.
[DELETE LINE]	[GOLD] ⌫	Delete the current line.
[DELETE WORD]	PF3	Delete the current word.
[DELETE SENTENCE]	[GOLD] [BACKSPACE]	Delete the current sentence.
[DO]	[DO] (or [GOLD] U)	Execute a UDP.
[ENTER]	[ENTER]	Move to the next right angle bracket (>).
[EXIT]	F10 or [GOLD] F	Exit the editor and save changes.

Table B.1 *(continued)*

Function Key	*Keystrokes[a,b]*	*Description*
[EXIT] (MENU)	F10 (or Keypad-0)	Exit Editor menu or function and return to editing.
[FIND]	[FIND] (or [GOLD] Comma)	Search for a text string.
[FOOTNOTE]	[GOLD] Y	Create footnote.
[GET DOCUMENT]	[GOLD] G	Include document.
[GLOBAL REPLACE]	[GOLD] Semicolon	Replace all occurrences of a text string.
[HELP]	[HELP] (or [GOLD] H)	Display the keyboard diagram.
[HYPHEN PUSH]	F12 (or [BACKSPACE])	Force hyphen in a nonbreaking word.
[INSERT/OVRSTRK]	F14 (or [CTRL]+A)	Toggle between insert and overstrike modes.
[INTERRUPT]	F6 (or [GOLD] I)	Display Interrupt menu.
[LANGUAGE AIDS]	[GOLD] J	Spelling, Thesaurus, Usage Alert.
[LIBRARY]	[GOLD] L	Retrieve library text.
[LINE]	Keypad-2	Move the cursor one line.
[MENU]	F9 (or [GOLD] M)	Display Editor menu.
[NEW PAGE]	[GOLD] N	Insert hard page break.
[NONBR SPACE]	[GOLD] [SPACE]	Insert a nonbreaking space.
[PAGE MARKER]	[GOLD] P	Insert page marker.
[PAGE]	PF2	Move the cursor to the next page.
[PARAGRAPH]	Keypad-5	Move the cursor one paragraph.
[PARAGRAPH MARK]	[GOLD] [RETURN]	Move to paragraph indentation marker in ruler.
[PASTE]	[INSERT HERE] (Keypad-Comma)	Paste selected text.
[PRINT HYPHEN]	[GOLD] Hyphen	Insert a "breaking" hyphen.
[QUIT]	[GOLD] K	Exit editor without saving changes.
[REFRESH]	[CTRL]+W	Refresh screen.
[REPLACE]	[GOLD] ' (apostrophe)	Replace selected text with the paste buffer.
[RETURN]	[RETURN]	Insert new line (carriage return).
[RUBOUT CHAR]	⌫	Delete the character preceding the cursor.
[RUBOUT WORD]	F13 (or [ERASE LINE])	Delete the word preceding the cursor.
[RUBOUT SENTENCE]	[GOLD] F13 (or [GOLD] [ERASE LINE])	Delete sentence.
[RULER]	[GOLD] R	Create or update the ruler.
[SCRATCH PAD]	[GOLD] *	Display the Scratch Pad menu.
[SEARCH & SELECT]	[GOLD] /	Search again and select string.
[SEARCH]	[GOLD] Comma	Search for a text string.
[SELECT]	[SELECT] (or Keypad-Period)	Select text.
[SENTENCE]	Keypad-7	Move the cursor one sentence.

(continued)

Table B.1 WPS-PLUS function keys *(continued)*

Function Key	*Keystrokes*[a,b]	*Description*
[SPELL CHECK]	[GOLD] S	Check spelling of current word or selected text.
[STATUS]	[GOLD] Z	Display status information.
[SUBSCRIPT]	[GOLD] A	Change selected text to subscript.
[SUPERSCRIPT]	[GOLD] Q	Change selected text to superscript.
[SWAP]	[GOLD] [ENTER]	Transpose characters.
[TAB POSITION]	Keypad-8	Move the cursor one tab position.
[TOP]	[GOLD] T	Move the cursor to top of document.
[UDP]	[DO] (or [GOLD] U)	Execute a UDP.
[UDP17]...[UDP20]	[F17]...[F20]	Execute specific UDPs.
[GOLD UDP17]... [GOLD UDP20]	[GOLD] [F17]... [GOLD] [F20]	Execute specific UDPs.
[UNDERLINE]	Keypad-9	Underline current character; set highlighting to underline.
[UPPERCASE]	Keypad-3	Capitalize current character; set highlighting to uppercase.
[VIEW]	[GOLD] V	Toggle between viewing/not viewing special characters.
[WORD]	Keypad-4	Move the cursor one word.
[WRITE DOC]	[GOLD] W	Write selected text to a new document.

[a] In general, the keystrokes are the same for both the VT100 keyboard and the LK201 keyboard (VT200, VT300, VT400... series). VT100 keystrokes are listed in parentheses after the LK201 keystrokes when the keystrokes differ.

[b] All [GOLD] keys listed in this table require that you enter two separate keystrokes: Press the [GOLD] (PF1) key, followed by the second key indicated.

Table B.2 gives step-by-step instructions for basic editing procedures in WPS-PLUS version 4.1. Although this table does not list all of the functions that you can perform with the WPS-PLUS editor, it does list the most common ones. Refer to the *WPS-PLUS User's Reference* manual for additional editing procedures.

Table B.2 WPS-PLUS quick reference guide

To Perform This Function	*Follow These Steps*
Abbreviations	To retrieve and substitute the expanded text for an abbreviation: a. Press [ABBEVIATION] ([GOLD] =). b. Type the two-character abbreviation for the text that you want inserted in the document. *Note:* You must first select the Abbreviations Document with the Specify Abbreviation (AD) option on the Editor menu. Press [MENU] ([GOLD] M) to display this menu. See Section 11.1, "Abbreviations and Library Documents," for further details.
Alternate Characters, Insert	The ALT CHAR function allows you to insert special mathematical or technical symbols in your document, such as "π." a. Press [ALT CHAR] (F11 or [CTRL]+E). b. Press the key that corresponds to the special symbol. A short list of symbols and keys follows. Refer to the "Technical Character Set" table in the *WPS-PLUS User's Reference* manual for a complete list. *Symbol* — *Key* ~ (Approximate to) — N ∫ (Integral) — I *f* (Function) — f Σ (Sigma, sum) — S π (Pi) — { *Note:* If you need to insert a series of special characters, use [GOLD] F11 (or [GOLD] [CTRL]+E) to toggle special character mode on and off. If your terminal does not support the display of special characters, you might see a different character displayed on your screen. The special character should print properly, however. If the special character does not print, ask your system administrator which printer supports special characters.
Bold Text	(See **Highlight Text**.)
Bottom, Move to	Press [BOTTOM] ([GOLD] B).
Capitalize Text	(See **Highlight Text**.)
Center Text	To center text: a. Move the cursor to the character following the text that you want to center. b. Press [CENTER] ([GOLD] C). *Note:* Make sure that both left and right margins are set properly in your ruler. To remove centering: a. Move the cursor one character beyond the end of the centered text. b. Press [DELETE CHAR] (PF4).

Table B.2 WPS-PLUS quick reference guide *(continued)*

To Perform This Function	*Follow These Steps*
Characters, View Special	(See **View Mode**.)
Compose a Character	The [COMPOSE CHAR] key on the LK201 keyboard allows you to include a special symbol in your document, such as the copyright sign (©). If you do not have an LK201 keyboard, you can compose a character with the [DEAD KEY]. (See **Composite Character, Enter.**) a. Press [COMPOSE CHAR] (or [CTRL]+K). b. Type the two characters necessary to create the desired symbol. A short list of symbols and keys follows. Refer to the "Compose Character Sequence" table in the*WPS-PLUS User's Reference* manual for a complete list. *Symbol* — *Keystrokes* £ (British pound) — L = © (Copyright) — C 0 (zero) ¶ (Paragraph) — P ! *Note:* Composed characters are represented by a solid block on some terminals, but they will print correctly.
Composite Character, Enter	To insert a composite character—that is, to overstrike two or more characters during printing (÷, ≥, ≠): a. Type the first character (for example, ":"). b. Type the next character (for example "-"). c. Press [BACK UP] (Keypad-1). d. Press [DEAD KEY] ([GOLD] D). *Note:* Composite characters are represented by a solid block on some terminals, but they will print correctly. Repeat steps b through d to combine more than two characters. You can also use the [COMPOSE CHAR] key to create composite characters. (See **Compose a Character.**)

Contents, Table of	To generate a table of contents, you must place level numbers in brackets next to your section titles. For example,
	`[1] GETTING STARTED`
	`[2] The WPS-PLUS Keyboard`
	produces the following output:
	`1.0 GETTING STARTED`
	`1.1 The WPS-PLUS Keyboard`
	After placing level numbers in your document, exit the WPS-PLUS editor, and select the Paragraph Numbering option from the WP menu. Refer to Section 11.3, "Paragraph Numbering," for further details on creating a table of contents.

Control Block	To insert a control block in your document to request specialized formatting for the text that follows: a. Press [COMMAND] ([GOLD] [) to open the control block. The START CONTROL and END CONTROL markers appear.

Table B.2 *(continued)*

To Perform This Function	*Follow These Steps*
Control Block *(continued)*	b. Type a control block command and press [RETURN]. Control block commands are listed in Table 10.2. c. Type any text required for the control block command, and press [RETURN]. d. Press [DOWN ARROW] to move below the END CONTROL marker to continue editing. To edit a control block: a. Move the cursor to between the START CONTROL and END CONTROL markers. b. Add and delete characters as necessary. To remove a control block, treat the control block as characters in your document: a. Move the cursor to the START CONTROL marker. b. Press [DELETE CHAR] (PF4) to delete the START CONTROL marker and every character of the control block, including the END CONTROL marker. *Note:* It is more efficient to select and cut a control block, but this will update your paste buffer.
Cut and Paste Text **Cut or Copy Text**	a. Move the cursor to the first character in the string of text that you want to cut. b. Press [SELECT] (or Keypad-Period). Note the marker (◊) signaling the beginning of the selected text. c. Move the cursor beyond the last character in the string that you want to cut. d. Press [REMOVE] (or Keypad-Hyphen) to cut the text, or press [GOLD] [REMOVE] (or [GOLD] Keypad-Hyphen) to copy but not cut the text. The text is now stored in your paste buffer. *Note:* You can store up to 10 blocks of text in separate paste buffers. Precede [REMOVE] (or [GOLD] [REMOVE]) with [GOLD] *n*, where *n* is a number between 0 and 9, to indicate which of the 10 paste buffers to store. The following sequence copies the selected text to buffer 5, for example: [GOLD] 5 [GOLD] [REMOVE]
Paste Text	a. Move the cursor to the position in the document where you want to insert the text stored in your paste buffer. b. Press [INSERT HERE] (or Keypad-Comma) to paste the text, or press [GOLD] [INSERT HERE] to paste the text and any rulers in the paste buffer. *Note:* Precede [INSERT HERE] (or [GOLD] [INSERT HERE]) with [GOLD] *n* when pasting text from a buffer other than 0. Press [GOLD] Keypad-7 and then press [RETURN] to display a list showing the number of lines stored in each of the 10 paste buffers.

(continued)

Table B.2 WPS-PLUS quick reference guide *(continued)*

To Perform This Function	*Follow These Steps*
Delete Text	
Delete Character	Press [DELETE] to delete the previous character, or press [DELETE CHAR] (PF4) to delete the current character.
Undelete Character	Press [GOLD] [DELETE CHAR] ([GOLD] PF4) to replace the last character deleted.
Delete Word	Press [ERASE LINE] (LF or F13) to delete the previous word or press [DELETE WORD] (PF3) to delete the current word.
Undelete Word	Press [GOLD] [DELETE WORD] ([GOLD] PF3) to replace the last word deleted.
Delete Line	Press [DELETE LINE] ([GOLD] [DELETE]) to delete all characters from the beginning of the line to the cursor position.
Delete to EOL	Press [GOLD] F14 (or [GOLD] [CTRL]+D) to delete characters from the cursor position to the end of the line.
Delete Sentence	Press [DELETE SENTENCE] ([GOLD] [BACKSPACE]) to delete all characters from the last period, question mark, or exclamation point to the cursor position.
Draw Lines	(See **Two Dimensional Editor**.)
Exit	(See **File the Document** or **Quit**.)
File the Document	Press [FILE] (F10 or [GOLD] F) to exit the editor and save your changes. Press [QUIT] (F8 or [GOLD] K) to exit the editor without saving your changes.
Find Text	(See **Search for Text**.)
Finish	(See **File the Document** or **Quit**.)

Font, Select	To include special character fonts in your finished document (when sent to a printer that supports special fonts):
	a. Position the cursor before the first line of text to be printed in a special font.
	b. Press [COMMAND] ([GOLD] [) to start a control block.
	c. Type the words "PRINTER FONT" followed by a space and the name of the font you wish to select. The resulting control block should look something like this:
	`----------------START CONTROL---------------`
	`PRINTER FONT 12_POINT_HELVETICA`
	`----------------END CONTROL-----------------`
	d. Press [DOWN ARROW] to move below the END CONTROL marker, and type the text that you want to appear in the special font.
	e. After the last line of text, follow steps b and c and enter the command, "PRINTER FONT RESET." This resets the font to the default type for the remainder of the document.
	Note: Valid font names are listed in the WPS-PLUS document WPL$LIBRARY:KEYWORDS.WPL.

Table B.2 *(continued)*

To Perform This Function	*Follow These Steps*
Footer, Define a Page	Create a control block to include a running footer in your document: a. Position the cursor at the point in your document where you want to start a running footer (usually at the very beginning of a document or section). b. Press [COMMAND] ([GOLD] [). START and END control markers appear in the document. c. Type the word "BOTTOM" and press [RETURN]. d. Type the lines of text that will appear in your running footer. You can type "\p" in this text to tell WPS-PLUS to insert page numbers in the footer. (See **Pages, Number** for details.) e. Press [DOWN ARROW] to move beyond the END CONTROL marker before typing the text of your document. *Note:* Make sure that you leave enough room in the bottom margin in Pagination Settings before printing your document. You'll need three lines in the bottom margin plus the number of text lines in your footer. Six is usually sufficient.
Footnote	
Create Footnote	a. Press [FOOTNOTE] ([GOLD] Y) to create a footnote. b. Type the text of your footnote. Note that you can create a ruler to format your footnote before entering the text. c. Press [EXIT] ([GOLD] F) to complete the footnote and return to editing your document.
Edit Footnote	a. Place your cursor over the footnote mark "F" that you want to change. b. Press [FOOTNOTE] ([GOLD] Y) to edit the footnote. c. Edit the text of your footnote. d. Press [EXIT] ([GOLD] F) when finished editing the footnote.
Delete Footnote	a. Place your cursor over the footnote mark "F" that you want to delete. b. Press [SELECT] (Keypad-Period), then press [RIGHT ARROW] once to select the footnote. c. Press [REMOVE] (or Keypad-Hyphen) to delete the footnote.
Get a Document	To include the text from another file or document in the current document: a. Press [GET DOCUMENT] ([GOLD] G) to display the Get Document menu. b. Enter one of the following menu selections and press [RETURN]: DOC Document from the File Cabinet SP Contents of the Scratch Pad VMS VMS file UDP User Defined Process DEC Document from your DECmate NOTE Note from a group conference

(continued)

Table B.2 WPS-PLUS quick reference guide *(continued)*

To Perform This Function	*Follow These Steps*
Get a Document *(continued)*	c. Enter the requested information to specify the document that you want to retrieve, and press [RETURN]. *Note:* If you're retrieving a large document, press [GOLD] M, select the EA option, and set "GET DOCMT screen on" to "N." This prevents the scrolling of the entire document as it is retrieved.
Graphics	(See **PostScript Images, Include.**)
Header, Define a Page	Create a control block to include a running header in your document: a. Position the cursor at the point in your document where you want to start a running header (usually at the very beginning of a document or section). b. Press [COMMAND] ([GOLD] [). START and END control markers appear in the document. c. Type the word "TOP" and press [RETURN]. d. Type the lines of text that you want to appear in your running header. You will probably want to follow your header with at least one blank line. You can type "\p" in this text to tell WPS-PLUS to insert page numbers in the header. (See **Pages, Number** for details.) e. Press [DOWN ARROW] to move beyond the END CONTROL marker before typing the text of your document. *Note:* Make sure that you leave enough room in the top margin in Pagination Settings before printing your document. You'll need as many lines in the top margin as lines of text in your header. Six is usually sufficient.
Help, Access	Press [HELP] (or [GOLD] H).
Highlight Text	To enable bolding, capitalizing, or underlining, before typing the text: a. Press [SELECT]. b. Continue typing all of the text that you want highlighted. c. Press one of the following function keys: [BOLD] (Keypad-6) [UNDERLINE] (Keypad-9) [UPPERCASE] (Keypad-3) To bold, capitalize, or underline existing text: a. Move the cursor to the first character in the string that you want to highlight. b. Press [SELECT] (or Keypad-Period). c. Move the cursor beyond the last character in the string that you want to highlight. d. Press [BOLD], [UNDERLINE], or [UPPERCASE] to highlight text.

Table B.2 *(continued)*

To Perform This Function	*Follow These Steps*
Highlight Text *(continued)*	To remove highlighting: a. Move the cursor to the first highlighted character. b. Press [SELECT] (or Keypad-Period). c. Move the cursor beyond the last highlighted character. d. Press [GOLD] followed by the function key that was pressed to highlight the text (see list above).
Indent Paragraphs	Press [GOLD] [TAB] to indent the remainder of the paragraph to the next tab stop. This provides "hanging" indentation of the remainder of the paragraph.
Index, Create	To generate an index, you must place the words that you want to appear in the index within square brackets (or some other delimiter), preceded by "I."—for example: `. . . to display help,[I.help] press . . .` Place these entries in your document as close as possible to the text you want to index. After placing these entries in your document, you must exit the WPS-PLUS editor and select the Paragraph Numbering option from the WP menu. Refer to Section 11.3, "Paragraph Numbering," for details on creating an index.
Insert Mode, Edit	If the editor is currently set to overstrike mode, press F14 (or [CTRL]+A) to change to insert mode.
Insert Text	In general: a. Move the cursor to the position in the document where you want to insert the text. b. Start typing. To insert a new line: a. Move the cursor to the preceding line. b. Press [GOLD] [RIGHT ARROW] to move your cursor to the end of the line. c. Press [RETURN] to insert a new line.

Landscape Mode	To print the pages that follow in landscape mode (sideways):
	a. Position the cursor before the first line of text to be printed in landscape mode.
	b. Press [GOLD] N to insert a hard page break. (Skip this step if you're at the top of the document.)
	c. Press [COMMAND] ([GOLD] [) to start a control block. START and END control markers appear.
	d. Type the words "PRINTER FORMAT LANDSCAPE." The resulting control block should look something like this:
	`--------------START CONTROL--------------`
	`PRINTER FORMAT LANDSCAPE`
	`----------------END CONTROL--------------`

(continued)

Table B.2 WPS-PLUS quick reference guide *(continued)*

To Perform This Function	*Follow These Steps*
Landscape Mode *(continued)*	e. Press [DOWN ARROW] to move below the END CONTROL marker, and type the text that you want to appear in landscape format. f. To return to portrait format, repeat steps b through e, entering the command "PRINTER FORMAT PORTRAIT." This resets the format to portrait mode (letter style).
Macros	(See **User Defined Process.**)
Margins, Set	(See **Ruler, Set the.**)
Math, Editor	WPS-PLUS is capable of performing basic mathematical operations on numbers that appear in your document—for example, summing a column of numbers and inserting the total in your document. The procedure is too extensive to be easily summarized in this reference guide. For instructions on using Editor Math, refer to the Digital manual *WPS-PLUS User's Reference.*
Menu, Display Editor	
Display the Menu	Press [MENU] ([GOLD] M) to display the menu. You can then select an option from the menu.
Clear the Menu	Press [EXIT] (F10 or Keypad-0) to clear the menu and return to editing the document.
Move Around	

Keystroke(s)	*Moves the Cursor*
[DOWN ARROW]	Forward one line.
[LEFT ARROW]	Back one character.
[RIGHT ARROW]	Forward one character.
[UP ARROW]	Back one line.
[BOTTOM] ([GOLD] B)	To the bottom of the document.
[TOP] ([GOLD] T)	To the top of the document.
[NEXT SCREEN]	Forward one screen.
[PREV SCREEN]	Back one screen.

The following two keys set the current direction:

[ADVANCE] (Keypad-0)	Set direction to forward.
[BACKUP] (Keypad-1)	Set direction to reverse.

The following keys move the cursor in the current direction. Press [ADVANCE] or [BACKUP] if you want to change the direction before pressing one of the following keys.

Keystroke(s)	*Moves the Cursor*
[LINE] (Keypad-2)	To the beginning of the line.
[PAGE] (PF2)	To the next page break.
[PARAGRAPH] (Keypad-5)	One paragraph.
[PARA MARK] ([GOLD] [RET])	To paragraph indentation.
[SENTENCE] (Keypad-7)	One sentence.
[TAB POS] (Keypad-8)	One tab position.
[WORD] (Keypad-4)	One word.

Table B.2 *(continued)*

To Perform This Function	*Follow These Steps*
Move Text	(See **Cut and Paste Text.**)
Multi-Columns, Create	To create two or more (newspaper-style) columns: a. Press [CHANGE EDITOR] ([GOLD]]), type "M," and press [RETURN]. The expanded ruler appears. b. Press [RIGHT ARROW] and [LEFT ARROW] to move the cursor back and forth along the ruler. Insert one pair of left/right margin markers for each column. For example, type "L" (left margin marker) at positions 5 and 42, and type "R" (right margin marker) at positions 38 and 75. This creates two columns with four blank spaces between columns. c. Press [RETURN] to imbed the ruler. The cursor is placed at the top of the first column. d. Type the column of text. e. Press [GOLD] [TAB POS] [ADVANCE] (PF1, Keypad-8, Keypad-0) to move to the top of the next column. f. Repeat steps d and e for all columns. g. Press [CHANGE EDITOR] (GOLD]) to leave the Multi-Column Editor. Columns of text are rearranged to stair-step fashion but will print side by side. *Note:* Use the following keys to move around between columns while in the Multi-Column Editor: *Keystroke(s)* — *Moves the Cursor to* [GOLD] [TAB POS] [LEFT] — Next column, same row. [GOLD] [TAB POS] [RIGHT] — Previous column, same row. [GOLD] [TAB POS] [UP] — Top of current column. [GOLD] [TAB POS] [RIGHT] — Bottom of current column. [GOLD] [TAB POS] [ADV] — Top of next column. [GOLD] [TAB POS] [BACKUP] — Top of previous column. Create a new multicolumn block by repeating steps a through g in the following cases: • At the start of a new page. (Place a New Page marker between multicolumn blocks with [GOLD] N.) • When you want paragraphs to line up across the columns. To edit existing columns with the Multi-Column Editor, move the cursor into the columns and press [CHANGE EDITOR] ([GOLD]]). You can edit text within the columns without entering the Multi-Column Editor, however. When using a proportional font, text does not wrap according to the font size, but according to the number of character cells that fit in the current column on the terminal screen. Text wraps properly when printing, though, if you set Automatic Text Wrapping to "Y" in Pagination Settings. Using the standard monospaced font or setting Automatic Text Wrapping to "N" is easier for creating multiple columns because the document prints the way it is displayed in the editor.

(continued)

Table B.2 WPS-PLUS quick reference guide *(continued)*

To Perform This Function	*Follow These Steps*
Overstrike Mode, Edit	If the editor is currently set to insert mode, press F14 (or [CTRL]+A) to change to overstrike mode.
Page Break, Insert	Refer to Section 10.1.10, "Paginating WPS-PLUS Documents," for details on breaking your document into separate pages. To insert a hard page break at the current cursor position: Press [GOLD] N. WPS-PLUS inserts a NEW PAGE marker. To insert a soft, or floating, page break at the current cursor position: Press [GOLD] P. WPS-PLUS inserts a PAGE MARKER. To instruct WPS-PLUS to insert page breaks automatically during an edit session: a. Press [MENU] ([GOLD] M) to display the editor menu. b. Type "EA" and press [RETURN] to select the Editor Attributes option. c. Press [TAB] four times to move to the Lines per Page field, and type the desired number of lines per page. Then press [RETURN]. d. Type "PG" and press [RETURN] to insert page breaks and continue editing.

Pages, Number	Create a control block to include a running header or footer containing the page number in your document:
	a. Position the cursor to the point in your document where you want to start a running header or footer (usually at the beginning of a document or section).
	b. Press [COMMAND] ([GOLD] [). START and END control markers appear in the document.
	c. Type the word "TOP" to place page numbers at the top of the page, or type the word "BOTTOM" to place page numbers at the bottom. Then press [RETURN].
	d. Type the lines of text that will appear in your running header or footer, making sure that the text contains the characters "\p" (lowercase). For example, the following control block numbers pages at the bottom of the page with "Page 1," "Page 2," etc.:
	`--------------START CONTROL--------------`
	`BOTTOM`
	`Page \p`
	`--------------END CONTROL----------------`
	Hint: Press [GOLD] C to center page numbers. (See **Footer, Define a Page** and **Header, Define a Page** in this table. Also see Section 10.1.6, "WPS-PLUS Control Blocks," for more information.)

Paragraphs, Indent	(See **Ruler, Set the.**)

Table B.2 *(continued)*

To Perform This Function	*Follow These Steps*

PostScript Images, Include	Create a control block to include a PostScript clip art image (picture) in your document:
	a. Position the cursor at the point in your document where you want to include the picture.
	b. Press [COMMAND] ([GOLD] [). START and END control markers appear in the document.
	c. Type the following text in your control block:
	`EPS file widthXlength position`
	where file is the file specification for the picture, width is the number of inches wide, length is the number of inches long, and position is either "LEFT," "RIGHT," or "CENTERED." For example:
	`--------------START CONTROL------------`
	`EPS WPL$LIB:WORLD.EPS 2X2 RIGHT`
	`--------------END CONTROL--------------`
	Note: A number of PostScript clip art images are stored in the directory WPL$LIB: and have the file type ".EPS."

Print	To print your document, you must exit the editor and select the Print option from the WP menu. a. Press [FILE] (F10 or [GOLD] F) to exit the editor and save your changes. b. When the Word and Document Processing menu appears, type "P" and press [RETURN] to print the document.
Quit	a. Press [QUIT] (F8 or [GOLD] K) to exit the editor *without* saving your changes. b. Type "Y" and press [RETURN] when asked if you want to quit.
Ruler, Set the	A ruler controls the alignment of the text that follows. Refer to Section 10.1.5, "The WPS-PLUS Ruler," for further details on setting, storing, and recalling rulers.
Create a Ruler	a. Press [RULER] ([GOLD] R). The expanded ruler is displayed. b. Move the cursor with your right and left arrow keys to the point in the ruler where you want to insert a marker. c. Type the appropriate marker character to set a tab, indentation, or margin: C—center point, L—left margin, W—left margin after a word wrap, P—paragraph indentation, R—right margin, J—right margin (justified), T—left-hand tab stop, >—right-hand tab stop, . (period)—tab stop for decimal point. d. Press [RETURN] to imbed the ruler in your document.
Edit a Ruler	a. Move your cursor to the line directly below the ruler. b. Press [GOLD] R.

(continued)

Table B.2 WPS-PLUS quick reference guide *(continued)*

To Perform This Function	*Follow These Steps*
Edit a Ruler *(continued)*	c. Move the cursor with your right and left arrow keys to the point in the ruler where you want to insert or clear a marker. d. Type the appropriate marker character, or press [SPACE] to clear a marker. e. Press [RETURN] to store the ruler in your document.
Delete a Ruler	a. Move your cursor to the line directly below the ruler. b. Press [RULER] ([GOLD] R). c. Press [DELETE WORD] (PF3). d. Press [RETURN].
Search and Replace	
Replace Next	To search for a string of text and replace it: a. Type the new string anywhere in your document, then cut the string. (See **Cut and Paste Text**.) b. Press [FIND] (or [GOLD] Comma). c. Type the old string. d. Press [CONT SEARCH] ([GOLD] Period) to search for the string. e. Press [REPLACE] ([GOLD] ' —Apostrophe). Repeat steps d and e to search for and replace subsequent occurrences of the old string.
Replace All	To search for and replace all occurrences of a string of text: a. Press [TOP] ([GOLD] T) to move to the top of the document. b. Press [GLOBAL REPLACE] ([GOLD] Semicolon). c. Enter the old string and press [ENTER]. d. Enter the new string and press [ENTER]. *Note:* To replace special characters (TAB, RETURN, etc.), press [GOLD] V before step a.
Search for Text	
First Search	a. Press [FIND] (or [GOLD] Comma). The "Enter Search String:" prompt is displayed at the bottom of your screen. b. Type the text for which you want to search. It will be stored in the search buffer. c. Press [ADVANCE] (Keypad-0) or [RETURN] to search forward for the first occurrence of the string, or press [BACKUP] (Keypad-1) to search in the reverse direction. *Note:* To search for special characters (TAB, RETURN, etc.), press [GOLD] V before step a.
Search Again	Press [CONT SEARCH] ([GOLD] Period) to search for the string already stored in the search buffer. *Note:* The search will be performed in the direction currently in effect for moving the cursor. To change the direction, press [ADVANCE] (Keypad-0) or [BACKUP] (Keypad-1) before pressing [CONT SEARCH].

Table B.2 *(continued)*

To Perform This Function	*Follow These Steps*
Select Text	
Select Text	a. Move the cursor to the first character in the string of text that you want to select. b. Press [SELECT] (or Keypad-Period). WPS-PLUS "drops" the current line and displays a select mark (◊) before the first selected character. c. Move the cursor beyond the last character in the string that you want to select. d. You can now press [REMOVE], [BOLD], etc., to manipulate the selected text.
Deselect Text	Press [SELECT] (or Keypad-Period) to deselect text. The select mark (◊) is removed.
Spell Check	To spell-check a word in your document: a. Position the cursor on the word to be checked. b. Press [SPELL CHECK] ([GOLD] S). c. If the word is spelled correctly, no further action is necessary. d. If the word is spelled incorrectly, type one of the following characters to select an option, and press [RETURN]: R Replace word with correction E Edit the incorrect word I Ignore the incorrect word now and throughout this document A Add word to personal dictionary P Pass over this word, this time only F Quit the spell check To spell-check a section of your document: a. Position the cursor at the beginning of the section to be checked. (To check the entire document, press [GOLD] T.) b. Press [SELECT] (or Keypad-Period). c. Move the cursor to the end of the section to be checked. (To check the entire document, press [GOLD] B.) d. Press [SPELL CHECK] ([GOLD] S). e. WPS-PLUS locates the next misspelled word. f. Type one of the selections described above (R, E, I, A, P, F) and press [RETURN]. g. Repeat step f until you reach the end of the selected text.
Status, Display	Press [STATUS] ([GOLD] Z) to display, change, or clear status information.
Subscript, Enter **Superscript, Enter**	To change a character to a subscript or superscript: a. Position the cursor on the character.

(continued)

Table B.2 WPS-PLUS quick reference guide *(continued)*

To Perform This Function	*Follow These Steps*
Subscript, Enter **Superscript, Enter** *(continued)*	b. Press [SUBSCRIPT] ([GOLD] A) to make the character a subscript, or press [SUPERSCRIPT] ([GOLD] Q) to make the character a superscript. To change a string of text to subscript or superscript: a. Select the text. (See **Select Text.**) b. Press [SUBSCRIPT] ([GOLD] A) to change the string to subscript, or press [SUPERSCRIPT] ([GOLD] Q) to change the string to superscript. *Note:* Text will appear subscripted or superscripted only when printed. To remove superscript, follow the procedure for changing to subscript. To remove subscript, follow the procedure for changing to superscript.
Tabs, Set	(See **Ruler, Set the.**)
Thesaurus, Invoke	To search the on-line thesaurus for a synonym for the current word: a. Position the cursor on the word. b. Press [LANGUAGE AIDS] ([GOLD] J). c. Type "T" and press [RETURN]. Multiple definitions for the word will appear on your screen. d. With [DOWN ARROW], highlight the definition that describes how you're using the word in the sentence. The list of synonyms at the bottom of the screen changes. e. When you've selected the proper definition, move the cursor to the desired synonym with [RIGHT ARROW]. f. Press [RETURN] to replace the word with the selected synonym.
Top, Move to	Press [GOLD] T to move to the top of the document.
Two Dimensional Editor	You can draw lines and boxes in your document with the Two Dimensional Editor to create charts or simply outline text. To open a picture: Press [CHANGE EDITOR] ([GOLD]]), then press [RETURN] to open (create) a new picture, or position the cursor inside an existing picture and press [CHANGE EDITOR] ([GOLD]]) once. To close the current picture: Press [CHANGE EDITOR] ([GOLD]]). To turn the pen on and off: Press [ENTER] to toggle the pen on and off. The string "Pen =" at the bottom of the screen appears in bold type when the pen is on; it appears in plain type when the pen is off. To draw a line: a. Press your arrow keys to move the cursor to the start position of the line.

Table B.2 *(continued)*

To Perform This Function	*Follow These Steps*
Two Dimensional Editor *(continued)*	b. Press [ENTER] to turn the pen on. c. Press any arrow key to start drawing the line. d. Press [ENTER] to turn the pen off. To draw a box: a. Make sure that the pen is off. Press your arrow keys to move the cursor to the position of the upper left-hand corner of the box. b. Press [SELECT] (or Keypad-Period). c. Move the cursor to the lower right-hand corner of the box. d. Press Keypad-8 to draw the box. To include text in the picture: a. Make sure that the pen is off. Press your arrow keys to move the cursor to the start position of the text. b. Type the text. To erase: a. Press your arrow keys to move the cursor before the text or line that you want to erase. b. Press the [SPACE] bar to erase the text or line. *Note:* Press [HELP] (or [GOLD] H) to display the layout of the function keys that are active in the Two Dimensional Editor. A number of additional features of the Two Dimensional Editor are described in the *WPS-PLUS User's Reference* manual.
Underline Text	(See **Highlight Text**.)
Usage Alert, Invoke	You will occasionally need to check the spelling of a word based on its usage in a sentence. Unfortunately, the spell checker does not catch instances where you've substituted a homonym (similarly pronounced word) for the proper word in your sentence, whereas Usage Alert does—for example, "She *red* the book." To spell-check a word for a specific usage: a. Position the cursor on the word. b. Press [LANGUAGE AIDS] ([GOLD] J). c. Type "U" and press [RETURN]. A list of homonyms (if any exist) and their definitions appear on your screen along. d. With [DOWN ARROW], highlight the definition that best suits the usage of the word in your sentence. e. When you've selected the proper word, press [RETURN] to replace the current word with the selection.
User Defined Process	WPS-PLUS will automatically execute keystrokes stored in a file known as a User Defined Process. Refer to Chapter 26, "User Defined Processes," for complete details.
View Mode	Press [VIEW] ([GOLD] V) to enable or disable the display of special characters, such as tabs and carriage returns.

B.2 WORDPERFECT QUICK REFERENCE GUIDE

Table B.3 lists the function keys in WordPerfect that perform useful editing operations. Most function keys are actually composed of two separate keystrokes. This table also lists the individual keystrokes that must be entered on a VT-style terminal to perform the function.

Table B.3 WordPerfect function keys[a]

Function Key	*Keystrokes*	*Description*
[>INDENT<]	PF1, F10	Indent both margins.
[>INDENT]	F10	Indent left margin to next tab stop.
[<MARGIN RELEASE]	PF1, [TAB]	Move cursor beyond left margin.
[>SEARCH]	F8	Search for text (forward direction).
[<SEARCH]	PF1, F8	Search for text (reverse direction).
[BLOCK]	F20	Select a block of text.
[BLOCK]	PF3, F10	Select a block of text.
[BOLD]	F12	Make text bold.
[CANCEL]	F7	Cancel operation.
[CENTER]	PF1, F12	Center line(s) of text.
[COLUMNS/TABLES]	PF3, F13	Create multiple columns or tables.
[DATE/OUTLINE]	PF1, F11	Include date or paragraph number.
[DELETE]	⌫	Delete preceding character.
[DELETE CHAR]	Keypad-Period	Delete current character.
[DELETE WORD]	PF2, ⌫	Delete current word.
[END MERGE]	F17	End of input during a merge.
[END OF LINE]	Keypad-1	Move cursor to end of line.
[ESCAPE]	F6	Repeat keystroke.
[EXIT]	F13	Exit WordPerfect.
[FLUSH RIGHT]	PF3, F12	Justify selected line(s) on right.
[FONT]	PF2, F14	Change current font.
[FOOTNOTE]	PF2, F13	Create or edit footnote.
[FORMAT]	PF1, F14	Change document format.
[GOTO]	PF2, PF4	Move cursor to various locations.
[GRAPHICS]	PF3, F17	Include picture or graphics.
[HARD PAGE]	PF2, [RETURN]	Insert a (hard) page break.
[HELP]	F9	Display Help information.
[HOME]	PF4	First key of sequence to move cursor.
[LIST FILES]	F11	List files in a VMS directory.
[MACRO]	PF3, F18	Execute a macro.
[MACRO DEFINE]	PF2, F18	Record keystrokes in a macro.
[MARK TEXT]	PF3, F11	Mark text for index or table of contents.

Table B.3 *(continued)*

Function Key	*Keystrokes*	*Description*
[MERGE CODES]	PF1, F17	Insert merge codes.
[MERGE/SORT]	PF2, F17	Merge text with form letter or sort paragraphs.
[MOVE]	PF2, F10	Move, copy, or delete text.
[NUM LOCK]	PF1, PF1	Enable/disable mini-keypad for numeric entry.
[PRINT]	PF1, F13	Print document.
[REPLACE]	PF3, F8	Search for and replace text.
[RETRIEVE]	PF1, F18	Retrieve a document.
[REVEAL CODES]	F19	Display control codes.
[REVEAL CODES]	PF3, F9	Display control codes.
[SAVE]	F18	Exit and save changes.
[SCREEN]	PF2, F9	Create two windows or draw lines.
[SETUP]	PF1, F7	Change default settings.
[SHELL]	PF2, F7	Access DCL.
[SPELL]	PF2, F8	Perform a spell check.
[STYLE]	PF3, F14	Select a format style.
[SWITCH]	PF1, F9	Convert upper/lowercase or switch documents.
[TAB ALIGN]	PF2, F12	Align column of text to a tab stop.
[TEXT IN/OUT]	PF2, F11	Input/output text files.
[THESAURUS]	PF3, F7	List synonyms (thesaurus).
[UNDERLINE]	F14	Underline text.

[a] These are the keystrokes to enter on a VT200, VT300, VT400... series terminal with a LK201 keyboard.

The function keys listed in Table 9.2 are also active in WordPerfect. For example, you can file your document by pressing [GOLD] F. WordPerfect macros included with the ALL-IN-1 integration provide this capability.

Table B.4 lists step-by-step instructions for basic editing procedures for WordPerfect for VMS version 5.1. Although this chart does not list all of the functions that you can perform with the WordPerfect editor, it does list the most common ones. Refer to the *WordPerfect for VAX/VMS Reference* manual for further details.

Table B.4 WordPerfect quick reference guide

<table>
<tr><th>To Perform This Function</th><th>Follow These Steps</th></tr>
<tr><td>Block Operations</td><td>To select a block of text and perform an operation on the selected text:
a. Move the cursor to the first character in the string of text that you want to select.
b. Press [SELECT] or [BLOCK] (F20).
c. Move the cursor beyond the last character in the string that you want to select.
d. Press one of the following function keys:
<table>
<tr><th>Keystroke(s)</th><th>Description</th></tr>
<tr><td>[CENTER] (PF1, F12)</td><td>Centers text.</td></tr>
<tr><td>⌫</td><td>Deletes text.</td></tr>
<tr><td>[FONT] (PF2, F14)</td><td>Changes text attributes.</td></tr>
<tr><td>[FLUSH RIGHT] (PF3, F12)</td><td>Justifies text on the right.</td></tr>
<tr><td>[MOVE] (PF2, F10)</td><td>Cuts or copies text.</td></tr>
<tr><td>[PRINT] (PF1, F13)</td><td>Prints text.</td></tr>
<tr><td>[SWITCH] (PF1, F9)</td><td>Converts case.</td></tr>
</table></td></tr>
<tr><td>Bold Text</td><td>(See Highlight Text.)</td></tr>
<tr><td>Bottom, Move to</td><td>Press [HOME] (PF4) twice, then press [DOWN ARROW].</td></tr>
<tr><td>Center Text</td><td>a. Move the cursor in front of the text that you want to center, or select multiple lines.
b. Press [CENTER] (PF1, F12).</td></tr>
<tr><td>Characters, Insert Special</td><td>(See Compose.)</td></tr>
<tr><td>Columns, Create Multiple Text</td><td>To create newspaper-style columns:
a. Move the cursor to the location in your document where you want the columns to begin.
b. Press [COLUMNS/TABLE] (PF3, F13).
c. Type "1" (Columns).
d. Type "3" (Define).
e. Set the number of columns, the distance between columns, and the margins, if desired.
f. Press [RETURN].
g. Type "1" (On).
h. Type the first column of text.
i. Press [HARD PAGE] (PF2, [RETURN]).</td></tr>
</table>

Table B.4 *(continued)*

To Perform This Function	*Follow These Steps*
Columns, Create Multiple Text *(continued)*	j. Type the next column of text. k. Repeat steps i and j for all columns. l. Press [COLUMNS/TABLE] (PF3, F13). m. Type "1" (Column). n. Type "2" (Off) to turn off columns.
Columns of Numbers, Create	(See **Tables**.)
Commands	To perform functions when you don't know the location of the function keys: a. Press and hold [CTRL], then type "F." b. Enter the first two characters of the function—for example, "CE" for center or "FO" to set the font.
Compose	To insert special characters in your document: a. Press [COMPOSE] (hold [CTRL] and press 2). b. Type the two characters necessary to create the desired symbol. A short list of symbols and keys follows. Refer to the Appendix of the *WordPerfect for VAX/VMS* reference manual for a complete list. *Symbol* — *Keystrokes* £ (British pound) — L - © (Copyright) — c o ¶ (Paragraph) — P | • (Bullet) — * *
Contents, Table of	To mark text that you want to appear in the table of contents: a. Move the cursor to the beginning of the text that you want to appear in the table of contents. b. Press [SELECT]. c. Move the cursor to the end of the text. d. Press [MARK TEXT] (PF3, F11). e. Type "1" (ToC). f. Type a number from 1 to 5 and press [RETURN] to indicate the level. To create the table of contents: a. Press [HOME] (PF4) twice, then press [UP ARROW] to move to the beginning of the document. b. Press [RETURN] and [HARD PAGE] (PF2, [RETURN]) to insert a blank line and page break, then press [UP ARROW]. c. Type a heading for the table of contents. d. Press [MARK TEXT] (PF3, F11). e. Type "5" (Define).

(continued)

Table B.4 WordPerfect quick reference guide *(continued)*

To Perform This Function	*Follow These Steps*
Contents, Table of *(continued)*	f. Type "1" (Table of Contents). g. Type "1," enter the number of levels to include in the table, and press [RETURN]. h. Press [MARK TEXT] (PF3, F11). i. Type "6" (Generate). j. Type "5" (Generate). k. Press [RETURN].
Copy, Cut, and Paste Text	
Cut or Copy Text	a. Move the cursor to the first character in the string of text that you want to cut or copy. b. Press [SELECT]. c. Move the cursor beyond the last character in the string you want to cut or copy. Note the highlighting of the as you select. d. Press [MOVE] (PF2, F10). e. Type "1" (Block). f. Type "1" to cut, "2" to copy, or "4" to append to the paste buffer.
Paste Text	a. Move the cursor to the position in the document where you want to insert the text stored in your paste buffer. b. Press [RETURN] to paste the text.
Delete Text	
Delete Character	Press ⌫ to delete the previous character, or press [DELETE CHAR] (Keypad-Period) to delete the current character.
Delete Word	Press [DELETE WORD] (PF2, ⌫) to delete the current word.
Delete to EOL	Press PF2, Keypad-1 to delete all characters from the cursor to the end of the line.
Delete to End of Page	a. Press PF2, Keypad-3 to delete all characters from the cursor to the end of the page. b. Type "Y."
Undelete Text	To replace text deleted by any of the above procedures: a. Press [CANCEL] (F7). b. Type "1."
Draw Lines	To draw lines in your document to create forms or charts: a. Press [SCREEN] (PF2, F9). b. Perform one or more of the following procedures to draw, erase, or move the cursor. To draw a line: a. Type "2" (Line Draw). b. Move the cursor by pressing your arrow keys. Note the line being drawn.

Table B.4 *(continued)*

To Perform This Function	*Follow These Steps*
Draw Lines *(continued)*	To erase a line: a. Type "5" (Erase). b. Move the cursor by pressing your arrow keys. Note the line being erased. To move the cursor without drawing or erasing: a. Type "6" (Move). b. Move the cursor by pressing your arrow keys. To resume editing text: Press [CANCEL] (F7). *Note:* Select a monospaced font, such as Courier, before the line draw, especially if you're going to include text in the diagram. Type the text before drawing lines around it. Do not use tabs within the text; instead, use spaces.
Exit	a. Press [EXIT] (F13). b. Type "Y" to save the changes, or type "N" to exit without saving changes. (Press [CANCEL] (F7) to return to editing.) c. Type "Y" to exit WordPerfect.
File the Document	Press [GOLD] F to exit the editor and save your changes. Press [GOLD] K and type "Y" to exit the editor *without* saving your changes. (Press [CANCEL] (F7) to return to editing.)
Finish	(See **File the Document** or **Quit.**)
Font, Select	To select a new font for the text that follows: a. Move the cursor to before the text that you want printed in a special font. b. Press [FONT] (PF2, F14). c. Type "4" (Font). A list of available fonts is displayed. d. Type "N" followed by the first few characters of the font name—"HE", for example, to select Helvetica. e. Press [UP ARROW] or [DOWN ARROW] if necessary to highlight the exact font. f. Press [RETURN] twice to select the font. g. Type the desired point size and press [RETURN].
Font Size or Appearance, Select	To select the font size and appearance before typing the text: a. Press [FONT] (PF2, F14). b. Type "1" to select font size, "2" to select font appearance, or "3" to reset the font to normal. c. Type a number from 1 to 7 to select size, or type a number from 1 to 9 to select appearance. d. Start typing the text. e. Press [FONT] (PF2, F14), then type "3" to reset the font.

(continued)

Table B.4 WordPerfect quick reference guide *(continued)*

To Perform This Function	*Follow These Steps*
Font Size or Appearance, Select *(continued)*	To select font size or appearance for existing text: a. Move the cursor to the first character in the string of text. b. Press [SELECT]. c. Move the cursor to the last character in the string. d. Press [FONT] (PF2, F14). e. Type "1" to select font size, "2" to select font appearance, or "3" to reset the font to normal. f. Type a number from 1 to 7 to select size, or type a number from 1 to 9 to select appearance.
Footer, Define or Edit Page	a. Press [FORMAT] (PF1, F14). b. Type "2" (Page). c. Type "4" (Footers). d. Type "1" to select footer A, or type "2" to select footer B. (Footers A and B support even/odd page footers.) e. Type "1" to discontinue footers, type "2" to create a footer for every page, type "3" for odd pages, type "4" for even pages, or type "5" to edit the footer. f. Type or edit the text of your page footer. g. Press [EXIT] (F13) twice when finished entering your page footer. *Note:* You can also select a font or set margins within the footer.
Footnote	
Create Footnote	a. Move the cursor to the location where you want the footnote marker. b. Press [FOOTNOTE] (PF2, F13). c. Type "1" to create a footnote or "2" to create an endnote. d. Type "1" to create a new footnote. e. Type the text of your footnote. f. Press [EXIT] (F13) when you've finished typing the footnote.
Edit Footnote	a. Move the cursor to highlight the footnote mark (this is recommended). b. Press [FOOTNOTE] (PF2, F13). c. Type "1" to edit a footnote or "2" to edit an endnote. d. Type "2" to edit. e. Press [RETURN] if the footnote number is correct, or type the correct footnote number and press [RETURN]. f. Edit the text of your footnote. g. Press [EXIT] (F13) when you've finished typing the footnote.
Delete Footnote	a. Move the cursor to highlight the footnote number. b. Press [DELETE CHAR] (Keypad-Period) to delete the footnote marker. c. Type "Y" to delete the footnote.

Table B.4 *(continued)*

To Perform This Function	*Follow These Steps*
Get a Document	To include the text from another file or document in the current document: a. Press [RETRIEVE] (PF1, F18) to display the Retrieve Document menu. b. Type one of the following menu selections and press [RETURN]: 1 Get a document from the File Cabinet. 2 Get the contents of the Scratch Pad. 3 Get a VMS file. 4 Get a note from Group Conferencing. c. Enter details of the document, file, or note, and press [RETURN].
Go to Page	a. Press [GO TO] (PF2, PF4). b. Type the page number and press [RETURN].
Graphics	To include a picture or image in your document: a. Press [GRAPHICS] (PF3, F17). b. Type "1," "2," or "3" to select a box type. c. Type "1" (Create). d. Type "1," enter a filename, and press [RETURN]. The Appendix of the *WordPerfect for VAX/VMS* reference manual lists file names for standard clip art images included with WordPerfect. e. Type "3," enter a caption, and press [EXIT] (F13). f. Press [EXIT] (F13) to resume editing.
Header, Define or Edit Page	a. Press [FORMAT] (PF1, F14). b. Type "2" (Page). c. Type "3" (Headers). d. Type "1" to select header A, or type "2" to select header B. (Headers A and B support even/odd page headers.) e. Type "1" to discontinue headers, type "2" to create a header for every page, type "3" for odd pages, type "4" for even pages, or type "5" to edit the header. f. Type or edit the text of the page header. g. Press [EXIT] (F13) twice when finished entering the page header.
Help, Access	Press [HELP].
Highlight Text	To enable bolding or underlining before typing the text: a. Press one of the following function keys: [BOLD] (F12) [UNDERLINE] (F14)

(continued)

Table B.4 WordPerfect quick reference guide *(continued)*

To Perform This Function	*Follow These Steps*
Highlight Text *(continued)*	b. Continue typing text. Note the highlighting of the text. c. To disable highlighting, press the same function key, then continue typing. To highlight existing text: a. Move the cursor to the first character in the string that you want to highlight. b. Press [SELECT]. c. Move the cursor beyond the last character in the string that you want to highlight. d. Press [FONT] (PF2, F14). e. Type "2" to select font appearance. f. Type a number from 1 to 9 to select highlighting. To remove highlighting from existing text, delete the corresponding control code. a. Move the cursor to the first character of the highlighted string. b. Press [REVEAL CODES] (F19) to display control codes. c. Press your right or left arrow if necessary to highlight the control code that you want to remove. Highlight "[BOLD]," for example, to remove bolding. d. Press [DELETE CHAR] (Keypad-Period) to delete the highlighted control code. e. Press [REVEAL CODES] again to resume editing. To change the case (upper/lowercase) of existing text: a. Move the cursor to the first character of the string. b. Press [SELECT]. c. Move the cursor beyond the last character of the string. d. Press [SWITCH] (PF1, F9). e. Type "1" to change to uppercase or "2" to change to lowercase.
Indent Paragraphs	To indent the remainder of the paragraph to the next tab stop: Press [>INDENT] (F10) to indent the left margin only, or press [>INDENT<] (PF1, F10) to indent both left and right margins.
Index, Create	To mark words that you want to appear in the index: a. Move the cursor to the word that you want to appear in the index. b. Press [MARK TEXT] (PF3, F11). c. Type "3" (Index). d. Enter a heading and subheading (or just press [RETURN] twice). To create the index: a. Press [HOME] (PF4) twice, then press [DOWN ARROW] to move to the end of the document. b. Press [HARD PAGE] (PF2, [RETURN]) to insert a page break.

Table B.4 *(continued)*

To Perform This Function	*Follow These Steps*
Index, Create *(continued)*	c. Type a heading for the index. d. Press [MARK TEXT] (PF3, F11). e. Type "5" (Define). f. Type "3" (Index). g. Select a concordance file or press [RETURN]. (Refer to the *WordPerfect for VAX/VMS* reference for a description of the concordance file.) h. Enter a number 1 through 5 to select the index format (5 is recommended). i. Press [MARK TEXT] (PF3, F11). j. Type "6" (Generate). k. Type "5" (Generate). l. Type "Y" to confirm if you want the index updated.
Insert Mode, Edit	To toggle between insert and overstrike mode, press Keypad-0.
Insert Text	In general: a. Move the cursor to the position in the document where you want to insert the text. b. Start typing. To insert a new line: a. Move the cursor to the preceding line. b. Press [END OF LINE] (Keypad-1). c. Press [RETURN] to insert a new line.
Landscape Mode	To print the pages that follow in landscape mode (sideways): a. Position the cursor before the first line of text to be printed in landscape mode. b. Press [HARD PAGE] (PF2, RETURN) to insert a page break. (Skip this step if you're at the top of the document.) c. Press [FORMAT] (PF1, F14). d. Type "2" (Page). e. Type "7" (Paper Size). f. Press [DOWN ARROW] to highlight "Standard-Wide" paper size. g. Press [RETURN] to select this paper size. h. Press [EXIT] (F13) to resume editing. i. Type the text that you want to appear in landscape format. j. To return to portrait format, repeat steps b through h, highlighting "Standard" paper size in step f.
List	The [LIST] function key displays a list of files in your VMS directory. It does not list documents in your File Cabinet. To display a list of documents: a. Press [GOLD] G or [RETRIEVE] (PF1, F18). b. Press [RETURN] to display ALL-IN-1 documents.

(continued)

Table B.4 WordPerfect quick reference guide *(continued)*

To Perform This Function	*Follow These Steps*	
List *(continued)*	c. To list documents in the current folder, press [FIND] (or [GOLD] L). To list folders, press [UP ARROW], press [ERASE LINE] (LF or F13) to clear the Folder field, and press [FIND].	
	d. You can select a document and press [RETURN] to retrieve the document, or press [EXIT] (Keypad-0) to resume editing.	
Macros, Define and Execute		
Define a Macro	To start recording keystrokes as part of a macro:	
	a. Press [MACRO DEFINE] (PF2, F18).	
	b. Type a name for the new macro and press [RETURN].	
	c. Type a description for the new macro and press [RETURN].	
	d. Type any text and press any keys that you want recorded as part of the macro.	
	e. Press [MACRO DEFINE] (PF2, F18) to stop recording keystrokes.	
Execute a Macro	To automatically execute the keystrokes previously recorded as part of a macro:	
	a. Press [MACRO] (PF3, F18).	
	b. Type the name of the macro and press [RETURN].	
Margins, Set	a. Press [FORMAT] (PF1, F14).	
	b. Type "1" (Line).	
	c. Type "7" (Margins).	
	d. Type the number of inches in the left margin followed by a double quote (") and press [RETURN]. You can enter decimal values such as 1.5".	
	e. Type the number of inches in the right margin followed by a double quote (") and press [RETURN].	
	f. Press [EXIT] (F13) to resume editing.	
Menus, Pull-down	(See **Pull-down Menus.**)	
Move Around	*Keystroke(s)*	*Moves the Cursor*
	[DOWN ARROW]	Forward one line.
	[UP ARROW]	Back one line.
	[LEFT ARROW]	Back one character.
	[RIGHT ARROW]	Forward one character.
	[GOLD] B (PF1, B)	To the bottom of the document.
	[GOLD] T (PF1, T)	To the top of the document.
	[NEXT SCREEN]	One screen forward.
	[PREV SCREEN]	One screen back.
	[END OF LINE] (Keypad-1)	To the end of the line of text.
	[GO TO] (PF2, PF4)	To a specific character or page.
	[PAGE UP] (Keypad-9)	To the top of the previous page.
	[PAGE DOWN] (Keypad-3)	To the top of the next page.
	PF2, [LEFT ARROW]	To the previous word.
	PF2, [RIGHT ARROW]	To the next word.

Table B.4 *(continued)*

To Perform This Function	*Follow These Steps*
Move Around *(continued)*	Press the [HOME] (PF4) key, then the following key to move the cursor as indicated: [DOWN ARROW] — One screen forward. [UP ARROW] — One screen back. [LEFT ARROW] — To the beginning of the line. [RIGHT ARROW] — To the end of the line.
Move Text	(See **Copy, Cut, and Paste Text.**)
Overstrike Mode, Edit	To toggle between insert and overstrike mode, press Keypad-0.
Page Break, Insert	Press [HARD PAGE] (PF2, [RETURN]).
Pages, Number	a. Press [FORMAT] (PF1, F14). b. Type "2" (Page). c. Type "6" (Numbering). d. Type "4" (Position). e. Type a number 1 through 8 to select the placement of the page number. f. Press [EXIT] (F13) to resume editing.
Print	To print your document: a. Press [PRINT] (PF1, F13). b. Type "S" (Select Printer). c. Press [DOWN ARROW] or [UP ARROW] to highlight a printer. d. Press [RETURN] to select the printer. e. Type "1" to print the entire document, type "2" to print the current page, or type "5" to print a range of pages. *Note:* Press [CTRL/R] to erase print notification messages.
Pull-down Menus	To work with menus to select word-processing functions: a. Press PF1, [RIGHT ARROW] to display the main menu in the upper left-hand corner of the screen. b. Press [RIGHT ARROW] to move across the main menu to the desired option category. c. Press [DOWN ARROW] to move to the desired function. d. Press [RETURN] to select the function. To clear the pull-down menu without selecting an option: Press [CANCEL] (F7).
Quit	a. Press [EXIT] and type "N" to exit the editor *without* saving your changes. b. Type "Y" to exit Wordperfect and return to the menu.
Reveal Codes	To turn the display of control codes on or off, press [REVEAL CODES] (F19).

(continued)

Table B.4 WordPerfect quick reference guide *(continued)*

To Perform This Function	*Follow These Steps*
Search and Replace	a. Press [REPLACE] (PF3, F8). b. Type "Y" if you want to confirm each replacement, or type "N" to replace without intervention. c. Press [DOWN ARROW] to replace in the forward direction, or press [UP ARROW] to replace in the reverse direction. d. Type the old string you want to find, then press [SEARCH] (F8): `-> Srch:` ***`old-string`*** **`[F8]`** e. Type the new string to substitute for the old, and press [SEARCH] (F8): `Replace with:` ***`new-string`*** **`[F8]`**
Search for Text	
First Search	a. Press [SEARCH] (F8 or [FIND]). b. Enter the text you want to find. It will be stored in the search buffer. `-> Srch:` ***`string`*** c. Press [UP ARROW] if you want to search backward (the default is forward). d. Press [SEARCH] (F8).
Search Again	Press [SEARCH] (F8) twice.
Select Text	
Select Text	a. Move the cursor to the first character in the string that you want to select. b. Press [SELECT] or [BLOCK] (F20). c. Move the cursor beyond the last character in the string that you want to select. Note the highlighting of the text as you select.
Deselect Text	Press [SELECT] or [BLOCK] (F20) again to deselect the text. Note that the highlighting of the text is removed.
Spell Check	To spell-check your document: a. Press [SPELL] (PF2, F8). b. Type "1" to spell-check the current word, type "2" to spell-check the current page, or type "3" to spell-check the entire document. c. If a word is spelled incorrectly, a list of possible alternatives is displayed. Select one of the words from the list by letter, or type one of the following numbers to select an option: 1 Skip once. 2 Skip. 3 Add to your dictionary. 4 Edit the word.

Table B.4 *(continued)*

To Perform This Function	*Follow These Steps*
Spell Check *(continued)*	5 Look up additional words. 6 Ignore numbers. d. Repeat step c for all misspelled words.
Subscript Characters	(See **Highlight Text.**)
Superscript Characters	(See **Highlight Text.**)
Tables	To create a table to list rows and columns of information: a. Press [COLUMNS/TABLE] (PF3, F13). b. Type "2" (Tables). c. Type "1" (Create). d. Enter the number of columns and press [RETURN]. e. Enter the number of rows and press [RETURN]. f. Press [EXIT] (F13). To enter text in the table: a. Press [DOWN ARROW] or [UP ARROW] to move between rows, or press [TAB] to move across columns. b. Enter text in the current cell. If the text is wider than the column width, WordPerfect automatically wraps the text within the current cell. To modify a table by adding or removing rows and columns: a. Move the cursor inside the table to the cell where you want to add or remove rows or columns. b. Press [COLUMNS/TABLE] (PF3, F13). c. Press [INSERT HERE] to add columns or rows, or press [REMOVE] to remove columns or rows. d. Type "1" to add/remove rows, or type "2" to add/remove columns. e. Enter the number of rows or columns and press [RETURN]. f. Press [EXIT] (F13). To change the width of a column: a. Move the cursor inside the table to the specific column that you want to change. b. Press [COLUMNS/TABLE] (PF3, F13). c. Press PF2, [RIGHT ARROW] to increase the column width, or press PF2, [LEFT ARROW] to decrease the column width. d. Press [EXIT] (F13).
Tabs, Set	To set the tab stops in a document: a. Press [FORMAT] (PF1, F14). b. Type "1" (Line).

(continued)

Table B.4 WordPerfect quick reference guide *(continued)*

To Perform This Function	*Follow These Steps*
Tabs, Set	c. Type "8" (Tab Set). d. Move the cursor with your right and left arrow keys to the point in the ruler where you want to insert a marker. e. Type the appropriate marker character to set a tab stop: C—center, D—decimal, L—left justified, R—right justified. Press ⌫ to clear a tab stop. f. Press [EXIT] (F13) twice when finished.
Thesaurus	To find an alternative word (synonym): a. Move the cursor to the word that you want to replace. b. Press [THESAURUS] (PF3, F7). c. Press [DOWN ARROW] to see additional words if necessary. d. Type "1" (Replace Word). e. Type the letter for the word that you want to substitute for the current word.
Top, Move to	Press [HOME] (PF4) twice, then press [UP ARROW] to move to the top of the document.
Underline Text	(See **Highlight Text.**)

B.3 EDT QUICK REFERENCE GUIDE

Table B.5 lists the function keys in EDT that perform typical editing operations. Some of the function keys are actually composed of two separate keystrokes. The table also lists the individual keystrokes that must be entered on a VT-style terminal to perform the function.

Table B.5 EDT function keys

Function Key	*Keystrokes*[a,b]	*Description*
[ADVANCE]	Keypad-4	Set the current direction to forward.
[APPEND]	Keypad-9	Append the selected text to the paste buffer.
[BACKUP]	Keypad-5	Set the current direction to reverse.
[BEG OF LINE]	F12 (or [BACKSPACE])	Move the cursor to the beginning of the line.
[BOTTOM]	[GOLD] B	Move the cursor to the bottom of the document.
[BOTTOM]	[GOLD] Keypad-4	Move the cursor to the bottom of the document.
[CENTER]	[GOLD] C	Center the text.
[CHANGE CASE]	[GOLD] Keypad-1	Change the case of the selected text.
[CHAR]	Keypad-3	Move the cursor one character.
[COMMAND]	[GOLD] Keypad-7	Enter an editor command.
[CUT]	[REMOVE] (or Keypad-6)	Remove the selected text and place it in the paste buffer.
[DEFINE KEY]	[CTRL]+K	Define a macro.
[DELETE]	⌫	Delete the previous character.
[DELETE CHAR]	Keypad-Comma	Delete the current character.
[DELETE LINE]	PF4	Delete the line.
[DELETE TO EOL]	[GOLD] Keypad-2	Delete to the end of the line.
[DELETE WORD]	F13 (or [LINE FEED])	Delete the previous word.
[DELETE WORD]	Keypad-Hyphen	Delete the current word.
[DESELECT]	[GOLD] [SELECT] (or [GOLD] Keypad-Period)	Deselect the highlighted text.
[DOWN ARROW]	[DOWN ARROW]	Move the cursor forward one line.
[END OF LINE]	Keypad-2	Move the cursor to the end of the line.
[EXIT]	[GOLD] F	Exit editor and save changes.
[FILE]	[GOLD] F	Exit editor and file document.
[FILL]	[GOLD] Keypad-8	Rearrange the text to fill between the margins.
[FIND]	[FIND] (or [GOLD] PF3)	Search for text.
[FIND NEXT]	PF3	Search again.
[GET DOCUMENT]	[GOLD] G	Include another file or document.

(continued)

Table B.5 EDT function keys *(continued)*

Function Key	*Keystrokes*[a,b]	*Description*
[HELP]	[HELP] (or PF2)	Display Help information.
[INTERRUPT]	[GOLD] I	Display the Interrupt menu.
[LEFT ARROW]	[LEFT ARROW]	Move the cursor back one character.
[LINE]	Keypad-0	Move the cursor one line.
[LINE MODE]	[CTRL]+Z	Enter line-mode editing.
[MENU]	[GOLD] M	Display the Editor menu.
[NEXT SCREEN]	[NEXT SCREEN]	Move the cursor forward 16 lines.
[PAGE]	Keypad-7	Move the cursor to the next page break.
[PAGE BREAK]	[GOLD] P or [GOLD] N	Insert a page break.
[PASTE]	[INSERT HERE] (or [GOLD] Keypad-6)	Insert the text in the paste buffer.
[PREV SCREEN]	[PREV SCREEN]	Move the cursor back 16 lines.
[QUIT]	[GOLD] K	Exit the editor without saving changes.
[REFRESH]	[CTRL]+R or [CTRL]+W	Refresh the screen.
[REPLACE]	[GOLD] Keypad-9	Replace the selected text with the paste buffer.
[RETURN]	[RETURN]	Insert a new line (carriage return).
[RIGHT ARROW]	[RIGHT ARROW]	Move forward one character.
[RULER]	[GOLD] R	Display or change the ruler.
[SCRATCH PAD]	[GOLD] *	Display the Scratch Pad menu.
[SECTION]	Keypad-8	Move the cursor 16 lines.
[SELECT]	[SELECT] (or Keypad-Period)	Select text.
[SPECIAL INSERT]	[GOLD] Keypad-3	Insert a special character.
[SUBS]	[GOLD] [ENTER]	Substitute the search text with the paste buffer.
[SUBSTITUTE]	[GOLD] S	Substitute the old string with the new one.
[TOP]	[GOLD] Keypad-5	Move the cursor to the top of the document.
[TOP]	[GOLD] T	Move the cursor to the top of the document.
[UDP]	[GOLD] U	Execute a User Defined Process.
[UNDELETE CHAR]	[GOLD] Keypad-Comma	Replace the last deleted character.
[UNDELETE LINE]	[GOLD] PF4	Replace the last deleted line.
[UNDELETE WORD]	[GOLD] Keypad-Hyphen	Replace the last deleted word.
[UP ARROW]	[UP ARROW]	Move the cursor back one line.
[WORD]	Keypad-1	Move the cursor one word.

[a] In general, the keystrokes are the same for both the VT100 keyboard and the LK201 keyboard (VT200, VT300, VT400... series). VT100 keystrokes are listed in parentheses after the LK201 keystrokes when the keystrokes differ.

[b] All [GOLD] keys listed in this table require that you enter two separate keystrokes: Press the [GOLD] (PF1) key followed by the second key indicated.

Table B.6 lists step-by-step instructions for basic editing procedures in EVE or EVE_EDT. Although this table does not list all of the functions that you can perform with the EDT editor, it does list the most common ones. Refer to the *EDT Reference* manual in the VMS documentation set for further details.

Table B.6 EDT quick reference guide

To Perform This Function	*Follow These Steps*
Bottom, Move to	Press [BOTTOM] ([GOLD] B).
Center Text	a. Move the cursor to the character following the text that you want to center. b. Press [CENTER] ([GOLD] C).
Character, Insert Special	To insert a special ASCII character, such as an ESCAPE character: a. Press [GOLD]. b. Type the one- to three-digit numeric value for the ASCII character you want to insert in the document—for example, 13 for <CR>. c. Press [SPECIAL INSERT] ([GOLD] Keypad-3).
Columns, Create	(See **Ruler, Set the.**)
Compose a Character	The [COMPOSE] key on the LK201 keyboard allows you to include a special symbol in your document, such as the copyright symbol (©). a. Press [COMPOSE] (or [CTRL]+K). b. Type the two characters necessary to create the desired symbol. A short list of symbols and keys follows. Refer to the "Compose Character Sequence" table in a *WPS-PLUS User's Reference* manual for a complete list. *Symbol* — *Keystrokes* £ (British pound) — L = © (Copyright) — C 0 ¶ (Paragraph) — P !
Cut and Paste Text	
Cut Text	a. Move the cursor to the first character in the string of text that you want to cut. b. Press [SELECT] (or Keypad-Period). c. Move the cursor beyond the last character in the string that you want to cut. Note the highlighting of the text as you select. d. Press [REMOVE] (or Keypad-6) to cut the text. The text is now stored in your paste buffer.

(continued)

Table B.6 EDT quick reference guide *(continued)*

To Perform This Function	*Follow These Steps*
Paste Text	a. Move the cursor to the position in the document where you want to insert the text stored in your paste buffer. b. Press [INSERT HERE] (or [GOLD] Keypad-6) to paste the text.
Delete Text	
Delete Character	Press ⌫ to delete the previous character, or press [DELETE CHAR] (Keypad-Comma) to delete the current character.
Undelete Character	Press [UNDEL CHAR] ([GOLD] Keypad-Comma).
Delete Word	Press [LINE FEED] to delete the previous word, or press [DEL WORD] (Keypad-Hyphen) to delete the current word.
Undelete Word	Press [UNDEL WORD] ([GOLD] Keypad-Hyphen).
Delete Line	Press [DEL LINE] (PF4).
Delete to EOL	Press [DEL EOL] ([GOLD] Keypad-2) to delete all characters from the cursor to the end of the line.
Undelete Line	Press [UNDEL LINE] ([GOLD] PF4).
Exit	(See **File the Document** or **Quit**.)
File the Document	Press [FILE] ([GOLD] F) to exit the editor and save your changes. Press [QUIT] ([GOLD] K) to exit the editor *without* saving your changes.
Find Text	(See **Search for Text**.)
Finish	(See **File the Document** or **Quit**.)
Font, Select	Font selection is not available in EDT.
Footnote	Footnoting is not available in EDT.
Get a Document	To include the text from another file or document in the current document: a. Press [GET DOCUMENT] ([GOLD] G) to display the Get Document menu. b. Enter one of the following menu selections: SP Get the contents of the Scratch Pad. DOC Get a document from the File Cabinet. VMS Get a VMS file. UDP Get a User Defined Process. NOTE Get a note from a group conference. c. Enter the requested information to specify the document you want to retrieve, and press [RETURN].
Header, Define a Page	Automatic page headers are not available in EDT.
Help, Access	To display a diagram showing the layout of function keys, press [HELP] (or PF2).
Highlight Text	Bolding, underlining, and italics are not available in EDT.

Table B.6 *(continued)*

To Perform This Function	*Follow These Steps*
Highlight Text *(continued)*	To select text and convert the case from uppercase to lowercase, and vice versa: a. Move the cursor to the first character in the string that you want to capitalize. b. Press [SELECT] (or Keypad-Period). c. Move the cursor to the last character in the string that you want to capitalize. Note the highlighting of the text as you select. d. Press [CHG CASE] ([GOLD] Keypad-1) to change the case of the text.
Indent Paragraphs	Paragraph indentation must be performed manually in EDT.
Insert Mode, Edit	Insert mode editing is the default in EDT.
Insert Text	In general: a. Move the cursor to the position of the document where you want to insert the text. b. Start typing. To insert a new line: a. Move the cursor to the preceding line. b. Press [EOL] (Keypad-2). c. Press [RETURN] to insert a new line.
Macros, Define and Execute	
Define a Macro	a. Press [CTRL]+K. b. Press the key you will use to execute the macro. (Pressing Keypad-3 is recommended.) c. Press the function keys that you want executed as part of the macro. Press the keys in the order that you want them executed. *Note:* You cannot enter keys from the main keyboard as part of an EDT macro. d. Press [PERIOD], then press [ENTER] to finish defining the macro.
Execute a Macro	Press the key you previously defined in step b above. For example, press Keypad-3.
Margins, Set	(See **Ruler, Set the.**)
Menu, Display the Editor	
Display the Menu	Press [MENU] ([GOLD] M) to display the menu. You can then select an option from the menu.
Clear the Menu	Press [EXIT] (F10 or Keypad-0) to clear the menu and return to editing the document.

(continued)

Table B.6 EDT quick reference guide *(continued)*

To Perform This Function	*Follow These Steps*	
Move Around	Press one of the function keys listed in the table below to move the cursor.	
	Keystroke(s)	*Moves the Cursor*
	[DOWN ARROW]	Forward one line.
	[UP ARROW]	Back one line.
	[RIGHT ARROW]	Forward one character.
	[LEFT ARROW]	Back one character.
	[BOTTOM] ([GOLD] Keypad-4)	To the bottom of the document.
	[TOP] ([GOLD] Keypad-5)	To the top of the document.
	[NEXT SCREEN]	Forward one screen.
	[PREV SCREEN]	Back one screen.
	The following two keys set the current direction.	
	[ADVANCE] (Keypad-4)	Sets the direction to forward.
	[BACKUP] (Keypad-5)	Sets the direction to reverse.
	The following keys move the cursor in the current direction. Press [ADVANCE] or [BACKUP] if you want to change direction *before* pressing one of the following keys.	
	Keystroke(s)	*Moves the Cursor*
	[CHAR] (Keypad-3]	One character.
	[EOL] (Keypad-2)	To the end of the line.
	[LINE] (Keypad-0]	To the beginning of the line.
	[PAGE] (Keypad-7)	To the next page break.
	[SECTION] (Keypad-8)	One screen.
	[WORD] (Keypad-1)	One word.
Move Text	(See **Cut and Paste Text**.)	
Overstrike Mode, Edit	Overstrike editing is not available in EDT.	
Page Break, Insert	Press [PAGE BREAK] ([GOLD] N).	
Pages, Number	Automatic page numbering is not available in EDT.	
Print	To print your document, you must exit the editor and select the Print option from the WP menu. a. Press [FILE] ([GOLD] F) to exit the editor and save your changes. b. When the Word and Document Processing menu appears, type "P" and press [RETURN] to print the document.	
Quit	Press [QUIT] ([GOLD] K) to exit the editor without saving your changes.	
Ruler, Set the	To display the ruler and modify the right-hand margin: a. Press [RULER] ([GOLD] R). The expanded ruler is displayed. b. Move the cursor with your right arrow key to the point in the ruler where you want the right margin.	

Table B.6 *(continued)*

To Perform This Function	*Follow These Steps*
Ruler, Set the *(continued)*	c. Type "R" to set the right margin. d. Press [RETURN] to store the ruler in your document. *Note:* There is one ruler in EDT, and it applies to the entire document. If you change the ruler after entering text, however, the new margin will not cause reformatting of existing text. You must perform this task manually.
Search and Replace	To search for an old string of text and replace every occurrence with a new string: a. Press [GOLD] T to move to the top of the document. b. Press [SUBSTITUTE] ([GOLD] S) to display the "Change Every:" prompt. c. Type the old string of text that you want to replace, and press [ENTER]. The "To:" prompt is displayed. d. Type the new string of text and press [ENTER]. The number of substitutions is displayed.
Search for Text	
First Search	a. Press [FIND] (or [GOLD] PF3). The "Search for:" prompt is displayed at the bottom of your screen. b. Enter the text for which you want to search. It will be stored in the search buffer. c. Press [FIND] (or PF3) to search for the first occurrence of the string.
Search Again	Press [FIND] (or PF3) to search for the string already stored in the search buffer. *Note:* The search will be performed in the direction currently in effect for moving the cursor.
Select Text	
Select Text	a. Move the cursor to the first character in the string of text that you want to select. b. Press [SELECT] (or Keypad-Period). c. Move the cursor beyond the last character in the string that you want to select. Note the highlighting of the text as you select.
Deselect Text	Press [GOLD] Keypad-Period to deselect text. Note that the highlighting of the text is removed.
Spell Check	To spell-check your document, you must exit the editor and select the Spell Check option from the WP menu. a. Press [FILE] ([GOLD] F) to exit the editor and save your changes. b. When the Word and Document Processing Menu appears, type "SC" and press [RETURN] to spell-check the document. Refer to Section 9.6, "Checking Spelling within a Document," for further details.

(continued)

Table B.6 EDT quick reference guide *(continued)*

To Perform This Function	*Follow These Steps*
Subscript **Superscript**	Subscripted and superscripted characters are not available in EDT.
Tabs, Set	Tab stops can be set with the SET TAB command in EDT's line mode. However, this command only changes the display of text on your screen while editing. It does not format the text when printed.
Thesaurus, Invoke	The on-line thesaurus is not available in EDT.
Top, Move to	Press [TOP] ([GOLD] T) to move to the top of the document.
Usage Alert, Invoke	Usage alert is not available in EDT.
Word Wrap	Automatic word wrap at the right margin is the default. To turn this attribute off and on: a. Press [COMMAND] ([GOLD] Keypad-7). The "Command:" prompt appears. b. Type "SET NOWRAP" to turn off automatic word wrap. Type "SET WRAP column-number" to set an automatic word wrap at the specified column. c. Press [ENTER].

Glossary

account Authorization to use the computer system or ALL-IN-1. You must be authorized to use the computer system before logging in. You must be authorized to use ALL-IN-1 before you can start ALL-IN-1. When your account is established, you're provided with a private username/password for logging in and a directory structure for storing files.

ALL-IN-1 directory An area on a disk where your ALL-IN-1 files are stored, including your File Cabinet, calendar, and directories. *Important:* Do not attempt to access or modify any files in this directory with DCL commands or utilities.

append To add information to the bottom of existing information in a document.

ASCII An acronym for American Standard Code for Information Interchange. This code defines a format for storing numbers and text in files. Much of the information you enter in ALL-IN-1 is stored in ASCII format.

attachment A document that is attached to the end of an electronic message.

Auto Forward A feature that you can set in Electronic Messaging whereby any messages sent to you are automatically forwarded to another individual.

Auto Reply A feature that you can set in Electronic Messaging whereby a standard response memo is automatically sent back to anyone who sends you mail.

batch A method of performing work in which you place all of your instructions for the computer in a file and then submit the name of the file to the system to be run in the background.

batch queue A list of program files waiting to be executed in batch. VMS executes each entry in the batch queue in turn by opening the batch program file, reading the instructions, and executing them. When the end of the program file is reached, VMS moves on to the next entry in the queue.

carriage return A hidden character that causes the following text to begin on the next line. A carriage return is inserted in a document with the [RETURN] key.

CBI See **computer-based instruction.**

composite document A document containing multiple documents or attachments.

computer-based instruction (CBI) A method of learning in which the computer acts as your instructor. When you start computer-based instruction, the computer displays explanations of a program and examples.

conference A form of communication that takes place among a group of people. In ALL-IN-1, a conference is a collection of notes containing the comments of participants.

control document A document that contains special commands for controlling communications. Control documents typically contain commands that automatically establish a connection between your terminal and a remote computer system.

control file A file containing instructions to ALL-IN-1 for establishing a connection between your terminal and a remote computer system.

control key A combination of two keystrokes that performs a special function. You press and hold the [CTRL] key and then press the second key. For example, press and hold [CTRL], then press "W" to clear your screen.

Created folder A folder in your File Cabinet in which messages that you create are held until you send them.

current item The item (a document, message, or event) that is the object of an operation selected from a menu. The Print option on the Word and Document Processing menu prints the current document, for example.

cursor A flashing character, usually a block or an underscore, that shows you the position on the screen where characters that you type are inserted.

DDS An acronym for Distributed Directory Services, which provides a table of information that lists the names and addresses of everyone to whom you can send messages. The name refers to the fact that portions of the table reside on various systems throughout the network. DDS is typically used in a network environment where the network is very large or where users need to transfer messages through different mail systems.

data type The format in which information is stored. Different editors typically store documents using a different data type. When you edit a document with WPS-PLUS that was created with EDT, the document's data type is automatically converted before the editor screen appears. The document is converted back to the original format when you exit.

default The value assumed by ALL-IN-1 when you have not specified another value.

Delivery receipt A message that ALL-IN-1 automatically returns to you when a message you send is delivered to the addressee.

device A component of a computer system. Disk drives, terminals, communications lines, and printers are examples of computer system devices.

directory (1) A list of addresses and names to help you address a message. As with a phone directory, you can "look up" an individual's electronic mail address in a directory if you know his or her name. (2) A logical area on a disk drive where VMS files are stored, somewhat like a drawer in a File Cabinet.

disk A device for electronically storing information on a computer system. This information can consist of text documents and numerical data.

display register The location in a calculator used to store the result of calculations. The contents of this register are always displayed on the screen.

distribution list A list of the names of individuals who are related to one another in some way.

document Any type of text material, ranging in size from a single-page memo to a multi-page report.

document number A unique number assigned to a document in your File Cabinet. ALL-IN-1 assigns this number automatically when you create a new document.

document title A short summary of a document's content. You assign the title when you create a document.

drawer A subdivision of a File Cabinet. Drawers in ALL-IN-1 are used to store documents in the same manner as drawers in a real file cabinet. All users have a personal File Cabinet for storing documents. This File Cabinet has at least one drawer that can contain an unlimited number of folders, and each folder can contain an unlimited number of documents. Users can create additional drawers for organizing documents in the File Cabinet. However, it is only necessary to create an additional drawer if you need to share documents or messages.

editor A tool that you use to create or modify a document. The editor provides function keys for performing common word-processing functions, such as moving text. Several editors are provided with ALL-IN-1: EDT, EVE, and WPS-PLUS. In addition, your site can purchase and integrate other editors, such as WordPerfect or MASS-11.

EDT Digital's standard text editor, which you can use to prepare documents and messages.

[EXIT] Either the F10 key or the 0 key on the numeric keypad. [EXIT] clears the current form or files the current document.

field A location on a form for entering a single piece of information.

file An area for storing lines of related information, similar to a document. In fact, every document is stored in a separate file.

File Cabinet The area of a disk where your documents and messages are stored. Everyone has a personal File Cabinet for storing their own documents. In addition, your site might have one or more shared File Cabinets for storing shared documents.

FMS An acronym for Forms Management System, a layered software product that contains tools for building, maintaining, and using video forms in an application.

folder A place in your File Cabinet for storing documents that are similar in content. Folders help you organize documents in your File Cabinet.

footer One or more lines of text that appear at the bottom of every page in a document.

form A means of gathering information. Video forms are much like paper forms: They contain text labels that describe the information to enter, plus blank fields where you enter the information. ALL-IN-1 relies on video forms to gather information.

format The manner in which information is laid out or organized on your terminal screen or a piece of paper.

formatter A background program that formats a document in preparation for printing.

formula Symbolic notation describing a series of mathematical operations to be performed—for example, Average = Total / Number of Items.

function keys Keys on your keyboard that perform operations other than entering characters, such as moving the cursor and rubbing out text.

gateway Hardware and software that converts and transmits messages from one type of mail system to another. Gateways are necessary for sending mail to someone who uses a different mail system, such as VMSmail or IBM PROFS.

global menu selection A menu option that you can enter from any menu. EM (Electronic Messaging), WP (Word and Document Processing), and TM (Time Management) are examples of global menu selections. Refer to Appendix A for a more complete list.

[GOLD] key The key labeled "PF1" on your keyboard. This key is often the first key pressed in a sequence of keys that performs some special function.

group A list of users who have something in common—for example, all employees in a certain department, all workers in a certain job class (supervisors, word processors, engineers, vice-presidents, etc.), or all users with specific expertise. In ALL-IN-1, you can send mail to a group or share documents with a group.

handling type A characteristic of a document that describes the manner in which text is stored. This characteristic tells ALL-IN-1 which programs to invoke when the document is edited, printed, or transferred.

hard copy Any information printed on paper.

header One or more lines of text that appear at the top of every page in a document.

home directory An area on a disk where your personal files are stored. You have easy access to files in your home directory immediately after logging into the system.

Inbox folder A folder in your File Cabinet in which ALL-IN-1 places new, incoming messages sent to you by others.

index A list of key information about documents in your File Cabinet or items in your calendar. This list is displayed on an index form on which you can enter menu selections to manage items in the list.

insert A mode of editing information in which the characters you type are inserted between existing characters.

item A single document, message, event, or task that you create and manage.

Janitor A system program that runs at regular intervals, removing documents in each user's Wastebasket folder. A document removed by the Janitor cannot be recovered.

keypad The set of keys on your keyboard used primarily for entering numbers. Also known as the *numeric keypad*, *mini-keypad*, or *10-keypad.*

keyword An important word that appears in the text of a document. *Budget* is a keyword for a memo that deals with an organization's budget.

local node See **node.**

logging in The process of entering authorization information before being able to access information on a computer system. Also known as *signing on.*

logging off (logging out) The process of finishing your work session and securing your workstation.

mailbox A place where programs running on your system deposit information to pass on to other programs. Programs typically communicate by passing information back and forth through mailboxes.

Mail directory See DDS.

main keyboard The largest group of keys on your keyboard, used to enter characters, numbers, and punctuation marks. Sometimes referred to as the *typing keyboard.*

manager, ALL-IN-1 The person who manages your ALL-IN-1 system. The system manager has a number of responsibilities, including installing ALL-IN-1, upgrading the system to new versions, handling problems with the system, managing users, and scheduling housekeeping procedures (such as the Janitor).

memory register A location in a calculator where intermediate values are stored for later use in calculations.

menu A list of available options from which you can select. ALL-IN-1 is a "menu-driven" system. In other words, you select an option from a menu to indicate which task you want to perform next.

message A written form of communication with another individual sent using Electronic Messaging.

modem A device that enables the transmission of information between a terminal and a host computer across a telephone line.

MRGATE The name of the mailbox that ALL-IN-1 uses to pass messages to the VMS Mail system.

network A series of computer systems linked together by communications lines for the purpose of transferring information between systems.

nickname A pseudonym for an individual's Electronic Messaging address.

node A single computer system in a network of computers linked by communications lines. The *local node* is the system you're currently logged into. A *remote node* is any other system that is part of the computer network.

note A single document in a conference that contains the comments of a participant on a particular topic.

on-line The state in which a computer device is powered on and ready to send or receive information. Your terminal is on-line when powered on and ready for you to communicate with the computer system. A line printer is on-line when powered on and ready to receive text from the system.

option One of the items listed on a menu that you can enter to perform a specific task. For example, you enter "C" to select the Create option to create a new document or message.

orphan The last few lines of a broken paragraph where most of the paragraph is on the preceding page.

Outbox folder A folder in your File Cabinet in which copies of messages are placed after being sent to other users.

overstrike A mode of editing information in which characters you type replace existing characters.

overwrite The process of writing over—that is, replacing information in a document with new information.

pagination The process of breaking text in a document into pages by inserting page breaks. Properly paginated documents are easier to read.

password A private code that you enter to gain access to a computer system.

port printer A printer that receives information through a cable attached to a port on the back of your video terminal.

print job One or more documents sent to a queue for formatting and printing.

print queue A list of documents waiting to be sent to a specific printer. The name of each document waiting to be printed constitutes a separate *entry* in the queue. Entries in the queue are sent to the printer one at a time. This allows a large number of users to share a printer.

print settings A group of characteristics that tells ALL-IN-1 how to format and print text. Print settings control margins, line spacing, paper tray selection, etc.

privilege The authorization that the system administrator gives you to access certain features of ALL-IN-1 or the VMS operating system.

prompt A question that requires a response.

Read folder A folder in your File Cabinet in which incoming messages are placed after you read them.

Read receipt A message returned automatically by ALL-IN-1 when the person you sent mail to actually reads the message.

register A location in a calculator used to store a single number.

remote node See **node**.

[RETURN] The carriage return key on your main keyboard.

select The process of specifying the item with which you want to work. Typically, you type "SEL" and press [RETURN], or simply press the [SELECT] key, to start the selection process.

server queue A list of documents waiting in a queue to be formatted before printing. During formatting, the contents of the document file are copied to a temporary file, and all special code characters that signal bolding, underlining, and so forth, are converted to codes that the destination printer understands. Once formatting is complete, the resulting file is placed in a print queue.

subsystem A subset of the tools within ALL-IN-1 that manage similar types of information. The major subsystems in ALL-IN-1 are Word and Document Processing, Electronic Messaging, Time Management, Desk Management, Group Conferencing, and Communications.

system administrator A person who assists the ALL-IN-1 manager. The system administrator has a number of responsibilities, including authorizing users to access ALL-IN-1 and scheduling housekeeping procedures (such as the Janitor).

template document A utility document that defines the format of a finished document. List information is typically merged with the text appearing in a template to generate form letters and reports. Also referred to as *boilerplate documents* or *shell documents.*

terminal The device for entering and displaying information.

Terminal Phone A program included with the VMS operating system that allows two or more users to communicate interactively by typing messages.

terminal server A device that transmits information between the user's terminal and the host computer. Terminal servers simplify the wiring between terminals and the host computer. A number of terminals in an area can be wired to a nearby terminal server. Then a single wire runs from the terminal server to the host computer or the network of host computers. The user can then potentially access each host computer linked with the terminal server.

UDP See **User Defined Process.**

user An individual who is authorized to log onto a computer system and perform work.

User Defined Process (UDP) A file containing stored keystrokes. When you supply ALL-IN-1 with the name of a UDP, ALL-IN-1 automatically reads the file and enters the keystrokes for you.

username The name that the system manager assigns to you and that you enter when signing onto the computer system.

VAX The model name of the computer system (hardware) used for running ALL-IN-1. VAX stands for Virtual Address eXtension, referring to the fact that the VAX uses disk storage to virtually extend the size of memory storage.

video form See **form**.

VMS An acronym for Virtual Memory System (VMS), the name of the operating system software running on your VAX computer. The operating system manages all of the work in progress on a system. ALL-IN-1 runs under the supervision of the VMS operating system.

VMS Mail The mail system included with the VMS operating system. You can send messages to and receive messages from VMS users who might not have access to ALL-IN-1's mail system.

Wastebasket folder A folder in your File Cabinet in which messages and documents are placed after being deleted. The Wastebasket folder is emptied regularly by the Janitor.

widow The first few lines of a broken paragraph where most of the paragraph is on the following page.

window A portion of your terminal screen that acts as a "subscreen," displaying information without disturbing the rest of the screen. When you press [HELP] or [GOLD] H, for example, Help information is displayed in a window.

workstation A personal computer with processing capability and disk storage.

WPS-PLUS Digital's Word Processing System, an editor that you can use to prepare documents and messages.

X.400 A mail system that builds and transmits messages in accordance with X.400 recommendations, an internationally accepted set of recommendations for transferring messages. You can send mail to and receive mail from users on the X.400 mail network when the proper hardware and software are installed on your system.

Index